FIVE WORKS
by Octavio Paz

FIVE WORKS

• Alternating Current • Conjunctions and Disjunctions
• The Monkey Grammarian • Marcel Duchamp: Appearance
Stripped Bare • On Poets and Others

OCTAVIO PAZ

Arcade Publishing • New York

Arcade Publishing books may be purchased in bulk at special discounts for sales promotion, corporate gifts, fund-raising, or educational purposes. Special editions can also be created to specifications. For details, contact the Special Sales Department, Arcade Publishing, 307 West 36th Street, 11th Floor, New York, NY 10018 or arcade@skyhorsepublishing.com.

Arcade Publishing® is a registered trademark of Skyhorse Publishing, Inc.®, a Delaware corporation.

Acknowledgement is made to The Macmillan Company, M. B. Yeats, Macmillan of Bassingstoke & London, Macmillian Co. of Canada for material from *The Collected Poems of W. B. Yeats*, © Macmillan Company 1956.

Acknowledgment is made to New Directions Publishing Corp. and Faber and Faber Limited: "In a Station of the Metro" by Ezra Pound from *Personae* (New Directions) and *Collected Shorter Poems* (Faber and Faber), copyright © 1926 by Ezra Pound. Reprinted by permission of New Directions Publishing Corp. and Faber and Faber Limited.

Some of the material in this volume has appeared previously in the following publications:
In/Mediaciones, 1979, *Plural* 30, March 1974; *Plural* 51, December 1975; *El Pais*, 1980; *Alternating Current*, 1967; *Sur*, July 1943; *El Arcoyla Cira*, 1956; *Poetry Nation*, 1975.

Visit our website at www.arcadepub.com.

10 9 8 7 6 5 4 3 2 1

Library of Congress Cataloging-in-Publication Data is available on file.

ISBN: 978-1-61145-311-9

Printed in China

TABLE OF CONTENTS

Alternating Current   1

Conjunctions and Disjunctions   177

The Monkey Grammarian   285

Marcel Duchamp: Appearance Stipped Bare   377

On Poets and Others   537

ALTERNATING CURRENT

Translated from the Spanish
by Helen R. Lane

CONTENTS

1

Foreword 4
What Does Poetry Name? 5
Form and Meaning. 7
Homage to Aesop. 7
Language and Abstraction 8
A Peruvian Painter 9
Notes on *La realidad y el deseo*. 10
Landscape and the Novel in Mexico 14
Metamorphosis. 16
Invention, Underdevelopment, Modernity 16
The Seed. 21
Primitives and Barbarians. 24
Nature, Abstraction, Time 26
Figure and Presence 29
The New Acolytes 30
On Criticism 32

Mask and Transparency 36
Remedios Varo's Appearances and Disappearances 41
André Breton or the Quest of the Beginning. 42
The Verbal Pact and Correspondence 53
Recapitulations 58

2

Knowledge, Drugs, Inspiration 63
Henri Michaux 67
Grace, Asceticism, Merits 73
Paradises 77
The Metamorphoses of Stone. 80
The Symposium and the Hermit 82
Buñuel's Philosophical Cinema 90
Forms of Atheism. 95
Nihilism and Dialectics 101
Person and Principle 106
The Liberated Man and Liberators 114

3

Revolt, Revolution, Rebellion 119
The Verbal Round. 124
The City Mouse and the Country Mouse 128
The Channel and the Signs 132
Satiety and Nausea 138
The Two Forms of Reason 141
The Exception to the Rule 145
The Rules of the Exception 150
The End in the Beginning 154
A Form in Search of Itself 161
Revolt 166

FOREWORD

■ The majority of the texts in this book were first published in Hispano-American and French periodicals under the general title *Corriente Alterna*. They date from two periods: 1959 to 1961, and 1965 to March 1967. Rather than presenting these reflections on life in our time in the order in which they were written and published, I have decided to group them in three sections: the first deals with literature and art; the second with certain contemporary subjects (drugs, forms of atheism); the third with ethical and political problems. I hope that the contrapuntal unity of these pieces will be apparent despite their fragmentary nature. I believe the fragment to be the form that best reflects the ever-changing reality that we live and are. The fragment is not so much a seed as a stray atom that can be defined only by situating it relative to other atoms: it is nothing more nor less than a *relation*. This book is a tissue of relations.

—O. P.

1

What Does Poetry Name?

Poetry has been likened to mysticism and to eroticism. The similarities between them are obvious; the differences are no less apparent. The first and most important of these differences is the meaning, or rather the object of poetry: what the poet names. The mystical experience—including that of atheist sects such as primitive Buddhism and Tantrism—is a search for contact with a transcendent good. The object of poetic activity is essentially language: whatever his beliefs and convictions, the poet is more concerned with words than with what these words designate. This is not to say that the poetic universe lacks meaning or that its meaning is peripheral. I am simply saying that in poetry meaning is inseparable from words, whereas in ordinary discourse, and even in the discourse of the mystic, the meaning lies in what the words point to, in something *beyond* language. The experience of the poet is above all else a verbal experience; in poetry every experience immediately takes on a verbal quality. This has been true of all poets in every age, but since Romanticism this preoccupation with language has become what we may call a poetic *consciousness*, an attitude that played no part in the classical tradition. The poets of former times were as keenly aware of the value of words as modern poets; but they were less sensitive to meaning. Góngora's hermeticism does not imply a criticism of meaning, whereas that of Mallarmé or Joyce is primarily a criticism, and at times a destruction, of meaning. Modern poetry is inseparable from the criticism of language, which in turn is the most radical and the most virulent form of criticism of reality. Language now occupies the place once occupied by the gods or some other external entity or outward reality. The poem does not refer to anything outside itself; what a word refers to is another word. The meaning does not reside outside the poem but within it, not in what the words say, but in what *they say to each other*.

Góngora and Mallarmé, Donne and Rimbaud, cannot be read in the same way. The difficulties in Góngora are external; they are grammatical, linguistic, mythological. Góngora is not obscure: he is complicated. His syntax is unusual; there are veiled mythological and historical allusions; the meaning of each phrase and even each individual word is ambiguous. But, once these knotty problems and teasing enigmas have been solved, the meaning is clear. This is also true of Donne, a poet no less difficult than Góngora, who writes in a style that is even more dense. The difficulties presented by Donne's poetry are linguistic, intellectual, and theological. But once the reader has found the key, the poem opens like a tabernacle. Donne's best poems embody an erotic, intellectual, and religious paradox. In both these poets, the references are to something outside the poem: to nature, society, art, mythology, theology. The poet speaks of the eye of Polyphemus, the whiteness of Galatea, the horror of death, the presence of a young girl. In Rimbaud's major works, the attitude is completely different. In the first place, his *œuvre* is a criticism of reality and of the "values" that support it or justify it: Christianity, morality, beauty; in the second place, it is an attempt to lay the foundations of a new reality: a new fraternity, a new eroticism, a new man. All this is to be the mission of poetry, "the alchemy of the Word." Mallarmé is even more rigorous. His *œuvre*—if that is the proper word for a few signs left on a handful of pages, the traces of an unparalleled journey of exploration and a shipwreck—is something more than a criticism and a negation of reality: it is the obverse side of being. The word is the obverse side of reality: not nothingness but the Idea, the pure sign that no longer points to anything and is neither being nor nonbeing. The "theater of the spirit"—the Work or the Word—is not only the "double" of the universe: it is true reality. In Rimbaud and Mallarmé language turns back upon itself, it ceases to designate, it is neither a symbol of, nor does it refer to, external realities, whether physical or suprasensible objects. For Góngora a table is "squared pine," and for Donne the Christian Trinity is "bones to philosophy but milk to faith." Rimbaud does not address the world, but rather the Word on which that world rests:

Elle est retrouvée!
Quoi? L'éternité.
C'est la mer allée
Avec le soleil.

The difficulty of modern poetry does not stem from its complexity—Rimbaud is far simpler than Góngora or Donne—but rather from the fact that, like mysticism or love, it demands total surrender (and an equally total vigilance). If the word were not ambiguous, I would say that the nature of the difficulty is not intellectual but *moral*. It is an experience that implies a negation of the outer world, if only a provisional one, as in philosophical reflection. In short, modern poetry is an attempt to do away with all conventional meanings, because poetry itself becomes the ultimate meaning of life and of man; therefore, it is at once the destruction and the creation of language—the destruction of words and meanings, the realm of silence, but at the same time, words in search of the Word. Those who dismiss this quest as "utter madness" are legion. Nonetheless, for more than a century, a few solitary spirits, among them the noblest and most gifted human beings who have ever trod this earth, have unhesitatingly devoted their entire lives to this absurd undertaking.

Form and Meaning

The real ideas of a poem are not those that occur to the poet *before* he writes his poem, but rather those that appear in his work *afterward*, whether by design or by accident. Content stems from form, and not vice versa. Every form produces its own idea, its own vision of the world. Form has meaning; and, what is more, in the realm of art only form possesses meaning. The meaning of a poem does not lie in what the poet wanted to say, but in what the poem actually says. What we think we are saying and what we are really saying are two quite different things.

Homage to Aesop

Everything we name enters the circle of language, and therefore the circle of meaning. The world is a sphere of meanings, a language. But each word has its own particular meaning, which is different from and opposed to that of all other words. Within language, meanings battle among themselves, neutralize each other, annihilate each other. The statement: "Everything is meaningful because it is a part of language" can be reversed: "Nothing is meaningful because everything is language." The world is a sphere, etc. . .

Language and Abstraction

For many years now, it has been a commonplace that abstract painting has gone as far as it can go: it has reached its absolute limits. This seems to me to be a misstatement of the facts: what is most characteristic of the great movements in art is their radicalism, their continual surpassing of their own limits, their effort to approach the absolute, to go beyond the outermost boundaries of art. When that furthest limit has been reached, another painter arrives on the scene, makes the crucial leap, discovers yet another free space beyond, and once again is stopped short by a wall—a wall that he must leap over in order to reach the open spaces beyond. Retreat is impossible. Has abstraction become a new academism? It does not matter: all movements become formal schools and all styles mere recipes. What is deplorable is to end up being an academic painter; but making academism a steppingstone is not at all to be deplored. The great Baroque and Mannerist painters did not scorn the art of their predecessors; by exaggerating it, they went beyond it. The same thing is true of Symbolist poetry: Symbolist poets did not deny Romanticism; they made it aware of its real nature. After the classicism of the early abstractionists and the romanticism of "abstract expressionism," what we need is a Mannerism, a Baroque-abstract.

The real danger of sterility confronting abstract painting lies in its pretension that it is a language sufficient unto itself. By the very fact that it pretends to be totally subjective—since it is the individual painter and he alone who creates and uses this language—it lacks an element essential to all language: a system of signs and symbols with meanings shared by all those who use it. If each artist speaks in his own private language, the result is lack of communication, the death of language. A dialogue between schizophrenics. The best abstract painters arrived at a sort of universal language when they rediscovered certain archetypal forms that represent man's most ancient and most universal heritage. But was it really a language? It was, rather, a pre-language or a meta-language. Abstract painters waver between stammering and mystical illumination. Though they disdain communication, they occasionally contrive to express communion. The opposite is true of poetry: the only thing at a poet's disposal is words—each of which has a meaning that is the same for everyone—and it is out of these words that he must try to create a new language. The poet's words continue to be a language, but, at the same time, they are also something else: poetry, something *never before heard*, *never before expressed*, something that is language and at the same time something that denies language and goes beyond it. Abstract painting seeks to be a pure pictorial language, and thus attempts to escape the essential impurity of all languages: the recourse to signs or forms that have meanings shared by everyone. It either falls short of language or goes beyond it, resulting either in silence or in onomatopoeic interjection: Mondrian or Pollock. It is an attempt at expression that implicitly denies what it affirms. Therein perhaps lies its possibility of renewing itself: only that creative work which does not deny its own inner contradiction and brings it into the full light of day is capable of revealing its true nature, which is always twofold. If it were to take this contradiction as its point of departure and refuse to conjure it away, abstract painting might go beyond the limits imposed upon it and realize itself by affirming the very thing that denies it. That was the secret of Baroque art and poetry.

A Peruvian Painter

After many years, I have had the chance to see once again the works of Fernando de Szyszlo, for some of his latest paintings have recently been shown in Mexico City (1959). Szyszlo is Peru's best painter, or at any rate the Peruvian painter whose works are best known outside his own country. He was one of the first practitioners of abstract painting in Hispano-America, and he has not changed very much. I have a series of engravings entitled *Homage to César Vallejo*, dating from the years Szyszlo and I spent in Paris together, the period in his life when he managed to earn the praise of a severe judge, Hans Hartung. On comparing these works of Szyszlo's with his recent oil painting, I find that he is more the master of his craft, freer and more venturesome, though still the same; his style is still difficult and austere, at once violent and lyrical. It is painting that is not outgoing, that looks inward toward intimate truths, that disdains the complicity of the senses and demands a more ascetic contemplation on the part of the viewer. Among Mexican painters, Soriano would represent the opposite pole, all immediate impulse and effusion, a great fountain of dizzying colors and forms. I do not mean to say that Szyszlo's painting is only an intellectual construction. There is a visible struggle between rigorous discipline and spontaneity; he is not merely an intellectual painter: he has sensitivity. His taut, swooping forms can be aggressive and cruel; at other times, they are such dense concentrations of color that they give off sparks of boundless energy. A flight captured on canvas, an explosion, reserve. Many painters—spurred on by the example of Picasso—change style from one day to the next; but Szyszlo does not change: he matures. He explores more and more remote regions within himself.

Notes on *La realidad y el deseo**

In recent months (of the year 1958), a one-volume edition of Luis Cernuda's collected poems has been published. Cernuda has been faithful to himself all his life, and his book, which has grown slowly and steadily, as living things grow, has an internal consistency that is quite unusual in modern poetry. There are so many new poems in this latest edition, and they shed such revealing light on those published in the past, that for the first time we begin to catch a glimpse of the real significance of his *œuvre*. Like the voyager who sees the real outline of an unknown land gradually take shape before his eyes as he draws closer and closer to its coast, so in the space of the last twenty-five years our generation has witnessed the gradual revelation of a new poetic continent.

If we except Cernuda's critical essays and a number of his occasional fictional pieces—all written as an offshoot of his poetry—he is the author of a single book. It requires a great faith in one's own powers (or a proud despair) to thus gamble everything on a single card. Despair, faith, pride: contradictory words that nonetheless naturally go together. All of them

---

* *Reality and desire*

are related to yet another word that acts as a tenuous support for them: fate or necessity. Cernuda is one of the rare poets of our time marked with the brand of fate. He writes because he must write. To the poet fated to be a poet, self-expression is as natural and as involuntary as breathing is to us ordinary mortals. A demon, Cernuda's poetic conscience, refuses to lose its grip on him, demanding that he put into words what he has to say, come what may. Cernuda is fond of citing a phrase from Heraclitus: "Character is destiny."

Examples of different sorts of loyalty to the poetic demon: Eluard, the author of many books of poems, wrote only one poem all his life, and each of his books contains countless versions of this one poem; Cernuda, the author of a single book, is a poet of many poems.

I wrote: a poetic continent. Perhaps the expression is more applicable to Neruda, given the physical immensity, the natural massiveness, the awesome geographical monotony of that Chilean's poetry. Geography is of little concern to Cernuda, and in his poems, all of nature, from the sea and nameless rocky cliffs to the Castilian plateau, is steeped in history. Cernuda's *œuvre* is a spiritual biography, that is to say the precise opposite of a geography: a human world, a universe at whose center we find that half comic, half tragic creature, man. Lilting song and probing analysis, soliloquy and supplication, frenzy and irony, confession and circumspection, all governed by a consciousness seeking to transform lived experience into spiritual wisdom.

Critics have either said nothing about Cernuda's book, or they have heaped empty praise upon it—which is another way of saying nothing. As has happened with other great poets in the past, the critics' coolness toward Cernuda's poetry, their uneasiness and insecurity, are due to the unintentionally moral nature of his inspiration. His book does not point to a moral, to be sure; nonetheless, it puts before us a vision of reality that is a threat to the fragile edifice that goes by the name of Good and Evil. Blake said that every true poet, wittingly or unwittingly, is on the devil's side.

As a love-poet, Cernuda resembles Bécquer. As a poet of poetry, he is Baudelaire's descendant, having inherited his awareness of the loneliness of the poet, his vision of the modern city and its bestial powers, his split personality as lyric poet and critic. The two poets share the same desperate, mad yearning for happiness on earth and the same certainty that they have failed to attain it. The Christian note is missing in Cernuda: the consciousness of original sin, the nostalgia for paradise, a sense of the supernatural. At the same time, there is in Cernuda something almost without precedent in the history of Spanish poetry, which has always been profoundly Christian: a rebirth of the tragic consciousness, that is to say an acceptance of the human condition and the rejection of the possibility of any sort of afterlife, either in history or in eternity. Cernuda's pessimism is not a negation of life; it is, rather, a celebration of its powers: "Love does not die; it is only we who die . . ." But all this is merely a description of the surface of Cernuda's poetry. Perhaps all we need say about this poet is that he has written some of the most intense and most lucid poems in the history of the Spanish language. They cut into the flesh of reality like a knife.

Cernuda's book brings the Latin poets to mind. They have the reputation of being highly rhetorical and not very original. I believe that reputation to be undeserved; with the exception of Sappho, we would be hard put to name a Greek writer of love-poems as modern in feeling as those of Catullus and Propertius. These two poets were the first to reveal the ambivalent and destructive side of love. The idea of love is said to have been born in Provence. That is quite true, but Greece and Rome (not to mention the Arab world) give us glimpses of it much earlier. In Greece, love takes the form of homosexual passion; in Rome, it appears in the guise of unrequited passion. In the poetry of Catullus and Propertius, love is a sense of need rather than a fulfillment: a somber, raging, broodingly introspective passion. And on being subjected to psychological analysis, this passion proves to be humiliating for a twofold reason: because it is a desire for a despicable creature, and because satisfaction of this desire leaves an aftertaste of ashes. It is an emotion tinged with selfishness, with contempt for the object of one's desire and for oneself. Jealousy and sensuality, rapture and self-analysis, idolatry and hate: the whole endless dialectic of physical pleasure and humiliation that we find in the modern novel, from Benjamin Constant to F. Scott Fitzgerald. Love can only be born in the presence of a free being who graces us with her presence or deprives us of it. In antiquity, a woman might be an object of worship or desire, but never of love. A goddess or a slave, a sacred object or a household utensil, a mother or a courtesan, a daughter or a priestess, not even her body was her own: she was the ambiguous double of the cosmos, the repository of the beneficent or evil powers of the universe. Woman first begins the gradual reconquest of herself in Alexandria, and, even more importantly, in Rome. While denying her physical freedom, Christianity later gives her a soul and free will. This process of liberation, which is still far from ended today, began in Rome: that great city foreshadows the possibility of love, of the physical and spiritual dialogue between two free human beings. Is the freedom of the twentieth century true freedom or only a mask disguising a new form of slavery? I cannot say. In any event, love is not sexual freedom but the freedom to feel passion: not the right to perform a physiological act but the right to freely choose to be intoxicated.

La realidad y el deseo is not a book carefully planned in advance: it is poems allowed to grow naturally, finally becoming a book. If we separate any one part from the whole, we risk tearing a living thing apart, denaturing it. The level of intensity of Cernuda's poems varies, to be sure. Between 1929 and 1934, he discovers, simultaneously, Surrealism and erotic passion. Thanks to the moral influence of André Gide, he accepts his homosexuality. Far from hiding his nature, he uses it as a weapon against Spanish morality. It took great courage to do this in a society infected with machismo, as the Spain of those days was. His language later loses its tension and a rhetorical tone gradually creeps into his poems, drowning out his real poetic voice little by little: a poem becomes a dissertation and a condemnation of our time. The reader agrees with the moralist, but he cannot help wondering whether all this might not be better expressed in prose. The stiffness of written prose has won out, rather than the lively prose-rhythms of everyday spoken language, the fountainhead of modern poetry. Listening too intently to his own inner monologue, Cernuda failed to hear the voices of others. I wonder whether young people read Cernuda the way we did. I find it impossible to believe that they do not experience the same sensation—not amazement, but rather something much more rare and much more precious: the discovery of a spirit that knows itself and dares to confront itself, a rigorously disciplined, lucid passion, a freedom that is at once a rebellion against the world and the acceptance of one's own personal fate. No consolation, no preaching of comforting thoughts, no concessions. And above all else: a handful of poems in which the voice of the poet is the voice of poetry itself, timeless poems that will be forever fresh and young. Is that so little? I am inclined to think that it is quite enough. Sheer scope is not what counts: "More time is not more eternity," as Jiménez has reminded us.

Landscape and the Novel in Mexico*

I do not know whether literary nationalists have noticed that our novels present a rather sketchy and superficial image of the physical setting in Mexico. In a number of the best pages of two novelists writing in English, D. H. Lawrence and Malcolm Lowry, on the other hand, our mountains and our skies appear in all their somber, intoxicating grandeur, and in all their innocence and freshness as well. In *The Plumed Serpent* and various collections of short stories and critical pieces, Lawrence's prose reflects the extremely subtle, nearly imperceptible changes of light, the feeling of panic when torrential rains begin to fall, the terror of darkness descending on the altiplano, the shimmering vibrations of the sky at twilight in harmony with the respiratory rhythms of the great forests and the pulsing heartbeat of women. In *Under the Volcano*, the gardens of Cuernavaca, the flowers and plants, the distant volcanoes and the tangled green vines of the ravine—a true "gate of hell"—loom up before us bathed in the light of the first day of creation. The first day or the last? Perhaps both: the novel takes place on All Souls' Day in 1939, and during the twelve hours of this day the hero wanders about in a hallucinatory landscape that is also a labyrinth and a Purgatory, followed by a dog, the companion of the dead if we are to believe the Egyptians and the Aztecs.

---

* This note was written before the works of the new Mexican novelists had been published.

The real theme of *Under the Volcano* is the age-old story of the expulsion from Paradise; and that of *The Plumed Serpent* the construction of a magic space—that is to say, a nature that has regained its innocence—wherein the reconciliation of heaven and earth, of body and soul, of man and woman, is celebrated. For both these novelists, it is not the natural surroundings that give rise to the vision; on the contrary, it is the poetic vision that gives the landscape its concrete form. The spirit sustains the stone, rather than vice versa. The landscape does not function as the background or the physical setting of the narrative; it is something that is alive, something that takes on a thousand different forms; it is a symbol and something more than a symbol: a voice entering into the dialogue, and in the end the principal character in the story. A landscape is not the more or less accurate description of what our eyes see, but rather the revelation of what is behind visible appearances. A landscape never refers only to itself; it always points to something else, to something beyond itself. It is a metaphysic, a religion, an idea of man and the cosmos.

Whereas Malcolm Lowry's theme is the expulsion from Paradise, the theme of Juan Rulfo's novel *Pedro Paramo* is the return to Paradise. Hence the hero is a dead man: it is only after death that we can return to the Eden where we were born. But Rulfo's main character returns to a garden that has burned to a cinder, to a lunar landscape. The theme of return becomes that of an implacable judgment: Pedro Páramo's journey home is a new version of the wanderings of a soul in Purgatory. The title is a(n) (unconscious?) symbol: Pedro, Peter, the founder, the rock, the origin, the father, the guardian, and the keeper of the keys of Paradise, has died; Páramo (the Spanish word for *wasteland*) is his garden of long ago, now a desert plain, thirst and drought, the parched whispers of shadows and an eternal failure of communication. Our Lord's garden: Pedro's wasteland. Juan Rulfo is the only Mexican novelist to have provided us an image—rather than a mere description—of our physical surroundings. Like Lawrence and Lowry, what he has given us is not photographic documentation or an impressionist painting; he has incarnated his intuitions and his personal obsessions in stone, in dust, in desert sand. His vision of this world is really a vision of *another world*.

Metamorphosis

Apuleius recounts how Lucius was turned into an ass; Kafka tells us how Gregor Samsa was turned into a cockroach. We know what Lucius' sin was his interest in witchcraft and his concupiscence; we are not told what Samsa's fatal flaw was. Nor do we know who is punishing him: his judge is nameless and faceless. After he is turned into an ass, Lucius wanders all over Greece, and a thousand marvelous, terrible, or amusing things happen to him. He lives among bandits, assassins, slaves, vicious land-holders, and equally cruel peasants; he is made to transport on his back the altar of an Oriental goddess worshiped by sexually perverted priests, thieves, and devotees of flagellation; on a number of occasions his virility is endangered, though this does not prevent him from having amorous relations with a wealthy and passionate woman; he experiences both times of feast and times of famine . . . Nothing at all happens to Gregor Samsa: his horizon is bounded by the four dreary walls of a dreary house. Despite the beatings he suffers, the ass's health is never impaired; the cockroach is beyond both sickness and health: abjection is his permanent state. Lucius represents Mediterranean commonsense and truculence, gastronomy and a sensuality that has a faint tinge of sadism, Greco-Latin eloquence and Oriental mysticism—the Phallus and the Idea. All of which culminates in the glorious vision of Isis, the universal mother, one night on the seashore. The end for Gregor Samsa is a domestic serv-ant's broom sweeping out his room. Apuleius: the world seen and judged from the point of view of an ass. Kafka: the cockroach does not judge the world; he endures it.

Invention, Underdevelopment, Modernity

To us, the value of a work lies in its newness: the invention of new forms, or a novel combination of old forms, the discovery of unknown worlds or the exploration of unfamiliar areas in worlds already discovered—revelations, surprises. Dostoevsky digs down into the subsoil of the spirit; Whitman names realities that traditional poetry had disdained; Mallarmé subjects language to more rigorous experiments than those of Góngora and invents the critical poem; Joyce turns the spoken language into an epic and makes a hero of a linguistic happenstance (Tim Finnegan is the death and resurrection of English and every other language); Roussel makes a poem out of a charade . . . From the Romantic era onward, a work of art has had to be unique and inimitable. The history of art and literature has since assumed the form of a series of antagonistic movements, Romanticism, Realism, Naturalism, Symbolism. Tradition is no longer a continuity but a series of sharp breaks. The modern tradition is the tradition of revolt. The French Revolution is still our model today: history is violent change, and this change goes by the name of progress. I do not know whether these notions really apply to art. We may be convinced that driving a car is much better than riding horseback, but I fail to see how we can say that Egyptian sculpture is inferior to that of Henry Moore, or that Kafka is a greater writer than Cervantes. I believe in the tradition of a sharp break and in no way do I reject modern art: all I am saying is that we employ dubious standards in our attempt to understand it and judge it. Changes in our aesthetic tastes have no value or meaning in and of themselves; what has value and meaning is the idea of *change itself*. Or, better stated: not change in and of itself, but change as an agent or inspiration of modern creations. Imitation of nature and classical models—the idea of imitating, rather than the act of imitating—sustained the artists of the past; and for more than two centuries now, modernity—the notion of original and absolutely personal creation—has sustained us. Had such a notion not existed, the most perfect and most enduring works of our time would not have existed. The characteristic feature of modernity is criticism: what is new is set over and against what is old and it is this constant contrast that constitutes the *continuity* of tradition. In the past, continuity consisted in the prolongation or the persistence of certain archetypal forms or features in works of art; today, this continuity takes the form of negation or opposition. In classical art, novelty meant some sort of variation of the model; in Baroque art, an exaggeration; in modern art, a sharp break. In all three cases, tradition was a living relation, even when it was a polemical one, and the dialogue between generations was not broken off.

If imitation becomes mere repetition, the dialogue ceases and tradition petrifies; if modernity is not self-critical, if it is not a sharp break and simply considers itself a prolongation of "what is modern," tradition becomes paralyzed. This is what is taking place in a large sector of the so-called avant-garde. The reason for this is obvious: the idea of modernity is beginning to lose its vitality. It is losing it because modernity is no longer a critical attitude, but an accepted, codified convention. Rather than being a heresy, as in the nineteenth century and the first half of the twentieth century, it has become an article of faith that everyone subscribes to. The Institutional Revolutionary Party—that monumental logical and linguistic invention of Mexican politics—is a label that aptly describes a large part of contemporary art. For more than fifteen years now we have been greeted by a rather comical spectacle, in painting and sculpture in particular; although various "schools" follow one upon the other in rapid succession, all this raking of the coals can be reduced to a simple formula: repetition at an ever-accelerating rate. Never before has there been such frenzied, barefaced imitation masquerading as originality, invention, and innovation. For our forebears in the classical age, imitation was not only a legitimate practice but a duty; imitation did not stand in the way of the creation of new and truly original works. The artist is a living contradiction: he tries to imitate, and he invents; he tries to invent, and he copies. If contemporary artists sincerely seek to be original, unique, and new, they should begin by disregarding the notions of originality, individuality, and innovation: they are the clichés of our time.

A number of Mexican critics use the word "underdevelopment" to describe the present situation in Hispano-American arts and letters: our culture is "underdeveloped," the work of X or Y represents a breaking away from the "underdevelopment of the novel in our country," and so on and so forth. As I see it, the word refers to certain currents that are not to these critics' liking (or to mine): chauvinistic nationalism, academicism, traditionalism, and the like. But the word "underdevelopment" is a United Nations euphemism for backward nations. The notion of "underdevelopment" is an offshoot of the idea of social and economic progress. Aside from the fact that I am very much averse to reducing the plurality of cultures and the very destiny of man to a single model, industrial society, I have serious doubts as to whether the relationship between economic prosperity and artistic excellence is one of cause and effect. Cavafy, Borges, Unamuno, and Reyes cannot be labeled "underdeveloped" writers, despite the marginal economic status of Greece, Spain, and Latin America. Moreover, the rush to "develop" reminds me of nothing so much as a frantic race to arrive at the gates of Hell ahead of everyone else.

Many peoples and many cultures have taken their names from that of a god, a virtue, a destiny, a brotherhood: Islam, the Jews, the Japanese, the Tenochcas, the Aryans. Each one of these names is a sort of cornerstone, a covenant with permanence. Our age is the only one to have chosen a meaningless adjective to describe itself: modern. Since modern times will inevitably cease to be modern, this is tantamount to not having any name at all.

The idea of imitating the classics stems from a view of ongoing time as a falling away from a primordial time that is perfect. This is the exact opposite of the idea of progress: the present is insubstantial and imperfect by comparison with the past, and tomorrow will be the end of time. Implicit in this conception is the belief, first, that the past has restorative powers, and the belief, secondly, in an eternal repetition of the cycle of decadence, extinction, and a new beginning. Time consumes itself, and thereby re-engenders itself. The past is the model of the present: imitating the ancients and nature, the universal model within whose forms all times are contained, is a way of slowing up the process of decline. The idea of modernity is the product of rectilinear time: the present does not repeat the past, and each instant is unique, different, and self-sustaining. The aesthetic of modernity, as Baudelaire, one of the first to define it, was well aware, is not synonymous with the idea of progress: it is difficult—or even absurd—to believe that such a thing as progress exists in the realm of art. But modernity and progress resemble each other in that both are the products of a view of time as rectilinear. This view of time is dying today. We are witnessing a twofold phenomenon: a criticism of progress in the countries that are most highly developed, and a degeneration of the avant-garde in the realm of art and literature. What distinguishes modern art from the art of other ages is criticism—and the avant-garde is no longer critical. Its powers of negation are blunted when it enters the circuit of production and consumption of industrial society, either as an *object* or as *news*. In the first case, *price* becomes the one real criterion of the worth of a painting or a piece of sculpture; in the second case, what counts is not what the poem or novel says but what *is said* about them, pointless talk that degenerates into a mere flood of publicity.

Another art is dawning. The relation of art to the idea of rectilinear time is beginning to change, and this change will be even more radical than that of two centuries ago when the idea of modernity undermined the Christian notion of time as a finite process ending in motionless eternity. The future is losing its fascination as the idea of progress begins to decline. The end of our idea of time also means the end of "world centers of art." Today, we all speak, if not the same tongue, the same universal language. There is no one center, and time has lost its former coherence: East and West, yesterday and tomorrow exist as a confused jumble in each one of us. Different times and different spaces are combined in a here and now that is everywhere at once. A synchronic vision is replacing the former diachronic vision of art. This movement began when Apollinaire endeavored to juxtapose different spaces within a single poem; Pound and Eliot dealt with history in the same way, incorporating texts from other times and other languages in their works. These poets believed that, in so doing, they were being modern; their time was a *summa* of all times. But what they were really doing was taking the first step toward destroying modernity. The old frontiers are disappearing and others opening up; we are witnessing the end of the idea of art as aesthetic contemplation and returning to something that the West has long forgotten: the rebirth of art as collective action and representation, and the rebirth of their complementary opposite, solitary meditation. If the word had not lost its strict meaning, I would call the new art a *spiritual* art. A mental art, then, which will demand of the reader and the listener the sensitivity and the imagination of a performer who, like the musicians of India, is also a creator. The works of the new time that is aborning will not be based on the idea of linear succession, but on the idea of combination: the conjunction, the diffusion, the reunion of languages, spaces, and times. Fiesta and contemplation. *An art of confugation.*

The Seed

The art of the great historic civilizations, including those of pre-Columbian America, are capable of arousing our admiration and our enthusiasm, and may even enrapture us, but they never impress us as much as an Eskimo harpoon or a mask from the South Pacific. I use the word *impress* not only in the sense of causing us to feel strong emotion, but also in the etymological sense of "leaving a trace or mark by pressure." The contact is physical, and the feeling we experience is very much like acute anxiety. Inner or outer space, the world below or beyond, becomes a great weight pressing down upon us. Each work is a solid block of time, time standing still, time more massive than a mountain, despite the fact that it is as intangible as air or thought. Is it because these works are age-old, because the weight of thousands upon thousands of years has been compressed into a small chunk of matter? I do not believe so. The arts of so-called primitive peoples are not the most ancient arts we know of. Quite aside from the fact that many of these objects were created only yesterday, I would not venture to call the most ancient art we have any knowledge of, that of the Paleolithic era, a primitive art. What the animals painted on walls of caves in France, Spain, and elsewhere most resemble, if any comparison at all is possible, is the great figurative paintings decorating the walls of temples and palaces dating from the urban revolution. They not only have a similar form, but also a similar function. The theory that these figures were magic representations connected with hunting rites is giving way to the theory that they were a form of religious painting, at once naturalistic and symbolic. Specialists such as André Leroi-Gourhan believe these caves to be something like the cathedrals of Paleolithic man. No, the time of which the creations of primitive peoples are a living symbol is not antiquity; or rather, these works reveal another antiquity, a time previous to chronological time. A time before the idea of antiquity: the real original time, the time that is always *before*, no matter when it occurs. A Hopi doll or a Navajo painting are not *older* than the caves at Altamira or Lascaux: they are *before* them.

The handiwork of primitive peoples reveals the "time before time." What is this time like? It is almost impossible to describe it in words and concepts. I would call it "the original metaphor." The first seed within which everything that will later be the plant—roots, stem, leaves, fruit, and its final decay—has been quickened with a life that will unfold only in the future yet is also already present. To be more precise: it is the imminence of the unknown—not as a presence but as an expectation and a threat, as an emptiness. It is the breaking through of the *now* into the *here*, the present in all its instantaneous actuality and all its dizzying, hostile potentiality. What is this moment concealing? The present is both revealed and concealed in the handiwork of the primitive, as in the seed or the mask: it is both what it is and what it is not, the presence that both is and is not there before us. This present never occurs in historical or linear time, nor does it occur in religious or cyclical time. In profane and sacred time, the intermediaries—a god or a concept, a mythical date or the little hand of the clock—keep us from being battered by the great paw of the present. There is something or someone standing between us and brute time to defend us: the calendar clears a path through the dense thickets of time, makes its immense expanse navigable. The handiwork of the primitive cannot be dated, or rather, it is before any date on any calendar. It is the time previous to *before* and *after*.

The seed is the original metaphor: it falls on the ground, into a crack in the earth, and is nourished by the earth's substance. The idea of a Fall and that of spatial separation are implicit in our image of the seed. If we think of animal time as a seamless present with all of reality an endless *now*, human time will then appear to be a divided present. Separation, a sharp break: *now* falls into *before* and *after*. This fissure in time announces the advent of the kingdom of man. Its most perfect manifestation is the calendar, whose object is not so much to divide time up as to bridge the yawning gap between the precipice of yesterday and that of tomorrow. The calendar names time, and since it fails utterly to tame the present, it *distances* it. A date on the calendar masks the original instant: that moment when primitive man, suddenly aware that he is outside of natural or animal time, realizes that he is a stranger, a creature who has fallen into a literally fathomless *now*. As man's history unfolds, the fissure becomes broader and broader, deeper and deeper. Calendars, gods, and philosophies fall, one by one, into the great pit. Suspended over the abyss as we are today, our fall seems imminent. Our instruments can measure time, but our minds can no longer conceive it: it has become both too large and too small.

The handiwork of primitive peoples fascinates us because the situation that it reveals is somewhat analogous to the one in which we find ourselves today: time without intermediaries, the abyss of time that cannot be measured. Not so much a vacuum as the presence of the unknown, an immediate brute force. For thousands of years, the unknown had a name, many names: gods, signs, symbols, ideas, systems. Today, it has once again become the abyss that has no name, just as it was nameless before history began. The beginning and the end resemble each other. But primitive man is a creature who is less defenseless spiritually than we are. The moment the seed falls into a crack, it fills it and swells with life. Its fall is a resurrection; the gash is a scar; separation is reunion. All time lives in the seed.

A pygmy funeral hymn—to my mind, possessed of a taut, spare beauty far greater than that of many of our classic poems—expresses, better than any disquisition, this worldview in which fall and resurrection are simultaneous:

> An animal is born, passes this way, dies,
> And the great cold comes,
> The great cold of night, blackness.
>
> A bird passes this way, flies, dies,
> And the great cold comes,
> The great cold of night, blackness.
>
> A fish darts by, passes this way, dies,
> And the great cold comes,
> The great cold of night, blackness.
>
> A man is born, eats, sleeps,
> And the great cold comes,
> The great cold of night, blackness.

> The sky bursts into flame, its eyes go out,
> The morning star shines,
> The cold below, the light above.
>
> A man has passed this way, the prisoner is free,
> The shadow has melted away....

Primitives and Barbarians

The poem or sculpture of primitive man is the swollen seed, the superabundance of forms: a focal point of different times, the point of intersection of all spatial trajectories. I wonder whether the famous sculpture of Coatlicue in the Mexican National Museum, an enormous block of stone covered with signs and symbols, might not be described as primitive despite the fact that it belongs to a very definite historical period. On second thought: it is a barbarous work, like many others left to us by the Aztecs. It is barbarous because it does not possess the unity of the primitive artifact, which puts the contradictions of reality before us in the form of an instantaneous totality, as in the pygmy poem; and barbarous because it has no notion of the pause, of the empty space, of the transition between one state and another. What distinguishes classic art from primitive art is the intuition of time not as an instant but as succession, symbolized in the line that encloses a form without imprisoning it: Gupta or Renaissance painting, Egyptian or Huastec statuary, Greek or Teotihuacán architecture. Coatlicue is more an idea turned to stone than a palpable form. If we look on it as a discourse in stone, at once a hymn and a theology, its rigor may seem admirable. It strikes us as a cluster of meanings, its symbolic richness dazzles us, and its sheer geometrical proportions, which have a certain grandeur all their own, may awe us or horrify us—a basic function of a sacred presence. As a religious image, Coatlicue humbles us. But if we really study it, rather than simply thinking about it, we change our minds. It is not a creation; it is a construction. Its various elements and attributes never fuse into a form. This mass is the result of a process of superposition; more than a powerful accumulation of separate elements, it is a juxtaposition. Neither a seed nor a plant: neither primitive nor classical. And not Baroque either.

The Baroque is art reflecting itself, line that caresses itself or tears itself apart, a sort of narcissism of forms. A volute, a spiral, mirrors reflecting each other, the Baroque is a temporal art: sensuality and meditation, an art that feeds the illusions of the disillusioned. A dense jumble of forms, Coatlicue is the work of semicivilized barbarians: it attempts to say everything, and is not aware that the best way to express certain things is to say nothing about them. It scorns the expressive value of silence: the smile of archaic Greek art, the empty spaces of Teotihuacán. As rigid as a concept, it is totally unaware of ambiguity, allusion, indirect expression.

Coatlicue is a work of bloodthirsty theologians: pedantry and cruelty. In this sense, it is wholly modern. Today, too, we construct hybrid objects which, like Coatlicue, are mere juxtapositions of elements and forms. This trend, which has carried the day in New York and is now spreading all over the globe, has a twofold origin: the collage and the Dada object. But the collage was meant to be a fusion of heterogeneous materials and forms: a metaphor, a poetic image; and the Dada object was an attempt to destroy the idea of physical objects as useful tools and the idea of works of art as valuable things. By regarding the object as something that destroys itself, Dada made the useless the antivalue par excellence and thus attacked not only the object but the market. Today, the successors of Dada deify the object: their art is the consecration of the artifact. The art galleries and the museums of modern art are the chapels of the new cult, and their god goes by the name of the product: something that is bought, used, and thrown away. By the workings of the laws of the marketplace, justice is done, and artistic products suffer the same fate as other commercial objects: a wearing out that has no dignity whatsoever. Coatlicue does not wear out. It is not an object, but a concept in stone, an awesome idea of an awesome divinity. I realize that it is barbarous; but I also appreciate its power. Its richness strikes me as uneven and almost formless, but it is a genuine richness. It is a goddess, a great goddess.

Can we escape barbarism? There are two sorts of barbarians: the barbarian who knows he is one (a Vandal, an Aztec) and therefore seeks to borrow a civilized lifestyle; and the civilized man who knows that the "end of a world" is at hand and does his utmost to escape by plunging into the dark waters of savagery. The savage does not know that he is a savage; barbarism is a feeling of shame at being a savage or a nostalgia for a state of savagery. In both cases, its underlying cause is inauthenticity.

A truly modern art would be one that would reveal the hollowness rather than mask it. Not the object-that-is-a-mask, but the frankly truthful work, opening out like a fan. Was not the aim of Cubism and, more radically, the goal of Kandinsky the revelation of essence? For the primitive, the function of the mask is to reveal and conceal a terrible, contradictory reality: the seed that is life and death, fall and resurrection in a fathomless *now*. Today, the mask hides nothing. In our time, it may well be impossible for the artist to invoke presence. But another way, cleared for him by Mallarmé, is still open to him: manifesting absence, incarnating emptiness.

Nature, Abstraction, Time

"From the imitation of nature to its destruction": this might well be the title of a history of Western art. The most vital of modern artists, Picasso, may also have been the wisest: if we cannot escape nature, as a number of his successors and his contemporaries have vainly endeavored to do, we can at least disfigure it, destroy it. Basically, this is a new homage to nature. Nothing pleases nature more, Sade said, than the crimes whereby we attempt to violate her. In her eyes, creation and destruction are one and the same. Wrath, pleasure, sickness, or death wreak changes in the human being no less terrible (or comic) than the mutilations, the deformations, the furious stylizations that Picasso delights in.

Nature has no history, but its forms are the living embodiment of all the styles of the past, present, and future. I have seen the birth, the full flowering, and the decline of the Gothic style in rocks in the valley of Kabul. In a pond covered with green scum—full of little stones, aquatic plants, frogs, tiny monsters—I recognized both the temple sculpture of the Bayon at Angkor and one of the periods of Max Ernst. The form and plan of the buildings of Teotihuacán are a replica of the Valley of Mexico, but this landscape is also a prefiguration of Sung painting. The microscope reveals that the formula of the Tibetan *tankas* is already hidden in certain cells. The telescope shows me that Tamayo is not only a poet, but also an astronomer. White clouds are the quarries of the Greeks and the Arabs. I am bemused by *plata encantada*, obsidian covered with a vitreous, opalescent white substance: Monet and his followers. There is no escaping the fact: nature is better at abstract art than at figurative art.

Modern abstract painting has taken one of two forms: a search for essences (Kandinsky, Mondrian), or the naturalism of Anglo-American abstract expressionists.* The founders of the school wanted to get away from nature, to create a world of pure forms or reduce all forms to their essence. In this sense, the first abstract painters could be called *idealists*. Americans have not taken their inspiration from nature, but they have decided to work in the same way as nature. The act or the gesture of painting is more or less the ritual double of the natural phenomenon. Painting is *like* the action of sun, water, salt, fire, or time on things. To a certain degree, abstract painting and natural phenomena are an *accident*: the sudden, unforeseen intersection of two or more series of events. Many times, the result is striking: these paintings are fragments of living matter, chunks sliced out of the cosmos or heated to a seething boil. Nonetheless, it is an incomplete art, as can be seen in Pollock, one of the most powerful of these artists. His great canvases have no beginning or end; despite their huge dimensions and the energy with which they are painted, they seem to be giant chunks of matter rather than complete worlds. This kind of painting does not assuage our thirst for totality. Fragments and stammerings: a powerful urge to express, rather than a total expression.

Whether idealist or naturalist, abstract painting is a timeless art. Essence and nature lie outside the flow of human time: natural elements and the Idea have no date. I prefer the other current in modern art that endeavors to capture the meaning of change. Figuration, disfiguration, metamorphosis, a temporal art: Picasso at one end of the

---

* I don't like the term *expressionism* applied to abstract painting: there is a contradiction between expressionism and abstraction. The term "abstract painting" is no less misleading. As Benjamin Péret has pointed out, art is always concrete.

scale, Klee at the other, the great Surrealists in the middle. We owe to idealist abstract art some of the purest and most perfect creations of the first half of this century. The naturalist or expressionist tendency has left us great and intense works, tragic and, at times, hybrid art. It is the result of the contradiction between the natural phenomenon (pure objectivity) and human activity (subjectivity, intentionality). A mixture, a conflict, or a fusion of two different orders of reality: the living material of the painting (energy and inertia) and the romantic subjectivism of the painter. A heroic painting, but also a theatrical painting: part daring feat, part dramatic gesture. Temporal art, for its part, is a vision of the instant that envelops presence in its flame and consumes it: an art of presence even though it hacks it to pieces, as in Picasso's work. Presence is not only what we see: André Breton speaks of the "inner model," meaning that ghost that haunts our nights, that secret presence that is proof of the otherness of the world. Giacometti has said that the one thing he wants to do is to *really* paint or sculpture a face some day. Braque does not search for the essence of the object: he spreads it out over the transparent river of time. The empty hours of Chirico with not a single person in sight. Klee's lines, colors, arrows, circles: a poem of movement and metamorphosis. Presence is the cipher of the world, the cipher of being. It is also the scar, the trace of the temporal wound: it is the instant, instants. It is meaning pointing to the object designated, an object desired and never quite attained.

The search for meaning or its destruction (it makes no difference which: there is no way of escaping meaning) is central to both tendencies. The only meaningless art in our time is realism: and not only because its products are so mediocre, but also because it persists in reproducing a natural and social reality that has lost all meaning. Temporal art resolutely confronts this loss of meaning, and therefore it is an art of imagination par excellence. In this respect, the Dadaist movement was an example (and an inimitable one, despite its recent imitations in New York). Dada not only took the absence of meaning and absurdity as its province, but made lack of meaning its most effective instrument of intellectual demolition. Surrealism sought meaning in the magnetic excitement of the instant: love, inspiration. The key word was *encounter*. What is left of all this? A few canvases, a few poems: a branch of living time. That is enough. Meaning lies elsewhere: always just a few steps farther on.

Modern art oscillates between presence and its destruction, between meaning and the meaningless. But we thirst for a *complete art*. Are there any examples?

Figure and Presence

Dada torpedoed the speculative pretensions of Cubist painting, and the Surrealists countered the object-idea of Juan Gris, Villon, or Delaunay with an inner vision that destroyed its consistency as a *thing* and its coherence as a *system* of intellectual coordinates. Cubism had been an analysis of the object and an attempt to put it before us in its totality; both as analysis and as synthesis, it was a criticism of *appearance*. Surrealism transmuted the object, and suddenly a canvas became an *apparition*: a new figuration, a real transfiguration. This process is being repeated today. Abstract painting had rejected aesthetic reality along with every other reality—whether in the form of appearances or in the form of apparitions. Pop Art is the unexpected return of figurative art, a hostile and brutal reappearance of reality, such as we see it every day in our cities, before it is passed through the filter of analysis. Both Surrealism and Pop Art represent a reaction against the absolutism of pictorial speculation, in the form of a return to spontaneous, concrete vision. Fantasy, humor, provocation, hallucinatory realism. The differences between the two movements are as great as the similarities, however. We might even say that the resemblance is merely an outward one; it is not so much a fundamental similarity as a historical and formal coincidence: they are one extreme of the modern sensibility, which continually oscillates between love of the general and passion for the individual, between reflection and intuition. But Pop Art is not a total rebellion as Dada was, nor is it a movement of systematic subversion in the manner of Surrealism, with a program and an inner discipline. It is an individual attitude; a response to reality rather than a criticism of it. Its twin and its enemy, Op Art, is not even an attitude: it is literally a point of view, a procedure. It is really a more or less independent branch of the abstractionist tendency, as is clear in the works of one of the best representatives of the school: Vasarely.

The Pop artist accepts the world of things we live in and is accepted by the society that possesses and uses these things. Neither rejection nor separation: integration. Unlike Dada and Surrealism, Pop Art from the beginning was a tributary of the industrial current, a small stream feeding into the system of circulation of objects. Its products are not defiant challenges of the museum or rejections of the consumers' aesthetic that characterizes our time: they are consumer products. Far from being a criticism of the marketplace, this art is one of its manifestations. Its works are often ingenuous sublimations of the show windows and counter displays of the big department stores. Nonetheless, Pop Art is a healthy trend because it is a return to an immediate vision of reality, and, in its most intense expressions, a return to a vision of immediate reality. How can we fail to see the poetry of modern life, as defined by Apollinaire, in certain of Rauschenberg's works, for instance? The world of the streets, machines, lights, crowds—a world in which each color is an exclamation and each form a sign pointing to contrary meanings. Pop Art has reinvented the figure, and this figure is that of our cities and our obsessions. At times it has gone further and turned this mythology into a blank space and a question: the art of Jasper Johns is that of the object become a Saint Sebastian. A truly metaphysical art in the great tradition of Chirico, yet deeply American. But Johns is an exception—a more rigorous imagination beyond both the easy charms and the mindless brutality of most of Pop Art . . . What these artists have restored to us is a figure, not presence itself: a mannequin rather than a true apparition. The modern world is man, or his ghost, wandering among things and gadgets. In the work of these young people, I miss something that Pound saw in a Paris métro station and expressed in two lines:

> The apparition of these faces in the crowd;
> Petals on a wet, black bough.

The New Acolytes

Another similarity between yesterday's European avant-garde and today's American avant-garde: in both cases, poetry anticipated and paved the way for the new pictorial vision. Dada and Surrealism were above all else poetic movements in which poet-painters such as Arp and painter-poets such as Ernst and Miró participated. In the United States, the phenomenon is being repeated in a slightly different form. The change began in the 1950s, and the spark that set it off was the rebellion of poets against intellectual and academic poetry—a rebellion in which Pound and William Carlos Williams fulfilled the same exemplary (and ambiguous) function as Apollinaire and Reverdy within the Surrealist movement in France. A few years later, around 1960, American painters rebelled—independently but in much the same way—against abstract expressionism. It was more or less a repetition of what had happened in Europe, especially in France, between 1920 and 1925. Repetition, of course, is neither absolute similarity nor imitation. The resemblance stems from the fact that the circumstances are analogous, and may be regarded as an illustration of the rhythmic law that I have mentioned above: a swing of the pendulum between periods of reflection and periods of spontaneity.

The same cannot be said, however, of the Hispano-American imitators of the North Americans, at least in the realm of poetry (except for Brazil, where there is a genuine avant-garde in the strictest sense of the word: the concrete poets). Imitating Olson or Ginsberg in Lima, Caracas, Buenos Aires, Santiago, Mexico City, or Tegucigalpa is tantamount to ignoring—or, what is worse, forgetting—the fact that this poetic revolution has already taken place in the Spanish language. This movement began in our countries more than forty years ago; its founders were Macedonio Fernández, Huidobro, Tablada. It culminates in two moments that are true zeniths: the first represented primarily by the names Neruda and Vallejo; the second represented by a number of less widely known but equally important works by various poets of my generation: Lezama Lima, Nicanor Parra, Enrique Molina, Alberto Girri, Vitier, and a few others. It is a movement that has not yet come to an end, a living tradition.

The acolytes repeat and translate what has already been done: they are outsiders following a rite that they only half understand. Denying one's heritage has always seemed to me to be a tonic and a stimulant. Nonetheless, I believe that it is necessary to be acquainted first with what one is rejecting before it is possible to really reject it. Breton broke with Valéry's aesthetic only after many years of intimate contact with this poet's works; the Argentinian *ultras* rebelled against Lugones, but they

the creation of what we call a literature, which is not so much the sum of individual works as the system of relations between them: a field of affinities and oppositions.

Criticism and creation live in permanent symbiosis. Criticism feeds on poems and novels, but at the same time it is the water, bread, and air of creation. In the past, the "body of doctrine" was made up of closed systems: Dante was nourished by theology and Góngora by mythology. Modernity represents the rule of criticism: not a system, but the negation and the confrontation of all systems. Criticism has been the staple nourishment of all modern artists, from Baudelaire to Kafka, from Leopardi to the Russian Futurists. It has also become a form of creation: the work in the end becomes a celebration of negation (*Un coup de dés*) or a negation of the work itself (*Nadja*). In Spanish and Portuguese literature, there are very few examples of this sort of radicalism: there is Pessoa, and Jorge Luis Borges, both authors of a work built upon the dizzying theme of the absence of a work. Criticism as a method of creation, negation as a metaphysic and a rhetoric. Among those who have come after them—aside from Cortázar and Sarduy—I find no evidence of the will to construct a discourse based on the absence of discourse. *No* is a transparent obelisk, but our poets and novelists prefer geometric figures that are less disturbing; we have a number of extraordinary works based on a *yes*, at times a dense, compact affirmation, and at other times fissured with negations and ruptures.

If we turn from criticism as creation to criticism as intellectual sustenance, we encounter even greater poverty. The thinking of our time—ideas, theories, doubts, hypotheses—lies elsewhere, written in other languages. Except in rare moments bearing the names of Miguel de Unamuno and Ortega y Gasset, we are the parasites of Europe. If we turn, finally, to literary criticism per se, poverty becomes abject misery. The space that I have referred to, the space created by critical action, the place where works meet and confront each other, is a no man's land in our countries. The mission of criticism is not to invent works, but to establish relations between them: to order them, to lay bare their relative position within the whole on the basis of their biases and tendencies. In this sense, criticism has a creative function: it creates a literature (a perspective, an order) out of individual works. This is precisely what our criticism has failed to do. And that is why there is no Hispano-American literature, even though there exists a whole body of important works. And that is also why there is no point in attempting to solve the much-discussed question of the essential *nature* of Hispano-American literature. What is to the point is the need to ponder the *situation* of our literature: its frontiers, its form, its structure, its movements. To answer this question would be to relate individual works to each other, and show us that they are not isolated monoliths, not steles erected in a desert to commemorate a disaster, but a society: not a chorus but a dialogue of many contradictory voices.

There is little point in condemning sins of omission. But discussing sins of commission is not pointless. For a number of years now, our critics, those in particular who have immured themselves within the fortress of daily papers and periodicals, have had nothing but praise for "our great Latin-American literature." (Twenty or so years ago, it was fashionable to decry the poverty of our literature.) This recent, vociferous "critical" activity, which is almost indistinguishable from the more vacuous forms of publicity and consists largely of a string of name-dropping clichés, has now chosen as its warhorse the theme of "the success of our writers, especially novelists, in Europe and the US." The word "success" embarrasses me: it belongs not to the vocabulary of literature, but rather to that of business and sports. Moreover, the vogue for translations is a universal phenomenon, not restricted to Latin American works. It is a consequence of the increasing importance of publishing as a business enterprise, an epiphenomenon of the prosperity of industrial societies. Literary agents are now scouring the five continents, from the slums of Calcutta to the patios of Montevideo and the bazaars of Damascus, in search *of* manuscripts of novels. Literature is one thing and publishing quite another. The attitude of these critics is very much like that of the Latin American bourgeois twenty years ago who refused to drink anything but imported whisky or champagne. It would appear that, in order to receive any attention in Latin America, a work must first have the blessing of London, New York, or Paris. This situation might be amusing if it did not imply a dereliction of duty. The province of criticism is language, and giving up jurisdiction in that realm means giving up not only the right to render an opinion but also the use of words. This is abject surrender: the critic gives up the right to judge what is written in his own language.

I do not deny the need and even the necessity of criticism from abroad: I consider modern literatures to be a single literature. And how can we ignore the fact that often foreigners see what critics on the spot have failed to see? Caillois did not discover Borges, but he did something that those of us who admired him failed to do when he was a writer for a small audience: Caillois read him within a universal context. Instead of repeating what anonymous reviewers in Chicago or Milan say, our critics should read our authors as Caillois had read Borges: from the point of view of the modern tradition and as part of that tradition. Two complementary tasks: to show that Hispano-American works are a *single literature*, a field of antagonistic relations; and to describe the relationships of this literature to other literatures.

It is frequently said that the weakness of our criticism is due to the marginal, dependent status of our societies: it is regarded as one of the effects of "underdevelopment." This opinion is one of those half-truths that is more dangerous than an outright falsehood. This famous "underdevelopment" did not prevent Rodó from writing a fine critical essay on Darío. Literature admittedly has close ties to the society that produces it: though it is not simply a reflection of social relations, neither is it an entity that has no connection with history. Literature is a social relation, but at the same time it is a relation that is irreducible to others. To my mind, our lack of a solid body of criticism is more readily explainable as a result of our lack of communication. Latin America has no center comparable to Paris, New York, or London. In the past, Madrid more or less fulfilled that function (rather less than more). It was in Madrid that Darío, Reyes, Neruda, and a few others were first hailed as major writers. And, yet, we hypocritically refuse to forgive Spaniards for having ignored Huidobro and Vallejo (as though we ourselves had been models of generosity toward them: Vallejo died in exile, and one of Huidobro's last books is entitled, significantly enough, *El ciudadano del olvido* [*The Citizen of Oblivion*]). During the Spanish Civil War, Buenos Aires and Mexico City became the successors of Madrid. They had been literary capitals before the Civil War, but in the sense of being focuses of cosmopolitan and anti-Spanish rebellions such as modernism and avant-gardism. A literary center is a nervous system sensitive to any sort of stimulus: neither Buenos Aires nor Mexico City has been very responsive to the rest of Latin America. Argentinian Europeanism and Mexican nationalism are two different forms of the same infirmity: deafness. Things have admittedly changed somewhat in recent years. Other centers are coming into being: Havana, Caracas, Montevideo, Santiago, Lima. Periodicals and groups whose outlook is Latin American are appearing even in self-centered Bogotá and the Managua of Somoza the shark. Despite the fact that the media are almost always in the hands of dictators, government agencies, and large private corporations, communication is being established and gradually becoming a chaotic but vital reality.

Though literature is not communication—and may in fact be its very opposite, the *mise en question* of communication—it nonetheless is one of its products: *a contradictory product*. Criticism shares this ambiguous attitude toward communication: its mission lies not so much in transmitting information as in filtering, transmuting, and classifying it. The tools of criticism are selections and associations: it defines, it isolates, and then it relates. I will even go further: in our time, criticism is the cornerstone of literature. As literature comes to be a criticism of words and the world, a self-questioning, criticism comes to look upon literature as a world of words, as a verbal universe. Creation is criticism and criticism creation. Our literature lacks critical rigor, and our criticism lacks imagination.

Mask and Transparency

Carlos Fuentes's first book was a thin volume of short stories: *Los días enmascarados* [*Masked Days*] (1954). This title foreshadows the direction that his later work has taken. It refers to the last five days of the Aztec year, the *nemontani*: "five days masked/with maguey leaves" as the poet Tablada puts it. Five nameless days, empty days during which all activity was suspended—a fragile bridge between the end of one year and the beginning of another. In Fuentes' mind, doubtless, the expression also is more or less of a mocking question: "What is there behind these masks?" The vessel full of sacrificial blood in pre-Hispanic times, the taste of dust as a firing squad executes a prisoner at dawn, the black hole of sex, the hairy spiders of fear, the laughter of the basement and the privy. Since this strange book, Fuentes has published five novels, a *novella* that is both macabre and perfect (as the genre demands: geometry as the antechamber of horror), and another collection of short stories.* His first novel, *La región más transparente* (*Where the Air Is Clear*), would appear to be an answer to the short stories written in his youth: transparency versus the mask. The first modern vision of Mexico City as an urban complex, this book was a twofold revelation to Mexicans: it showed them the face of a city that was theirs but completely unknown to them, and it brought to their attention a young writer who would never cease to amaze them, disconcert them, and irritate them. The secret center of the novel is an enigmatic character, Ixca Cienfuegos; though he plays no part in the events of the book, he somehow precipitates them, and thus serves as a sort of consciousness of the city. He is the other half of Mexico City, the pre-Columbian past that is deeply buried, yet still alive. He is also a mask of Carlos Fuentes, just as Mexico City is a mask of Ixca. Literature as a mask of the author and the world. Yet the opposite is also true: Ixca is a critical conscience. Literature as a critique of the world and of the author himself. The novel centers on this duality: mask and consciousness, creative language and criticism, Ixca and modern Mexico City, Fuentes and Ixca.

The axis whose two poles are verbal invention and criticism of language is central to Fuentes' entire work, with the exception of *Las buenas conciencias,* an infelicitous attempt to return to traditional realism. Each one of his novels strikes the reader as a hieroglyph: and, at the same time, the invisible action underlying them is a passionate, persistent attempt to decipher this hieroglyph. Each sign leads to another sign: Mexico City leads to Ixca, Ixca to Artemio Cruz (an anti-Ixca, a man of action) and so on, from novel to novel and from character to character. Fuentes questions these signs, and these signs question him: the author is yet another sign. Writing is a ceaseless interrogation, an interminable task, and one

---

* The novels are *La región más transparente* (1958), *Las buenas conciencias* (1959), *La muerte de Artemio Cruz* (1962), *Zona sagrada* (1967), and *Cambio de piel* (1967). The novella is *Aura* (1962), and the book of short stories *Cantar de ciegos* (1964).

that the novelist is obliged to embark upon again and again: in order to decipher a hieroglyph, a writer's only recourse is signs (words) that immediately form another hieroglyph. Criticism bares the falsehoods of words by means of other words which congeal and become new masks the moment they are uttered. At the most obvious level, the duality takes the form of moral or political criticism and a nostalgia for a heroic age. The description of the contemporary social structure of Mexico is a cruel (and just) criticism of the world that our revolution created, but the very violence of this criticism immediately evokes another reality: the apocalyptic years of armed struggle. Criticism becomes the creation of a myth, and this myth, in turn, is constantly undermined by criticism.

The rise in society of the revolutionary and the moral degradation that results have been a persistent theme in the modern novel, ever since Balzac. *The Death of Artemio Cruz* is the story of a revolutionary who becomes corrupted. Cruz's fall gradually takes on a mythical tone. Fuentes is not so much consciously concerned with providing yet another example of the revolutionary origins of the conservative bourgeoisie as he is fascinated by the character he is attempting to portray, as he was in his earlier book by Ixca, the survivor of the pre-Hispanic era. If he can decipher the mystery of Cruz, he will be able to exorcise him. Cruz's death-throes are the deciphering of the mystery. The dying man relives his entire life: as a lover, as a guerrilla, as a political adventurer, as a businessman . . . Cruz as a young boy and Cruz as an adolescent spy upon his last moments, believing that his death will reveal what lies behind and beyond reality; as he breathes his last, the old man seeks in his past life the sign of what he really is, the pure moment that will allow him to gaze upon death face to face. These shifts in time do not occur one after the other, but simultaneously. Fuentes does away with *before* and *after*, a life-story as linear time: events do not follow one upon the other; all times and spaces coincide, conjoin in this final moment in which Artemio Cruz ponders his life. Cruz dies an undeciphered enigma. Or rather: his death traces another hieroglyph, the sum of everything Cruz the man was, and its negation. The whole process must be begun all over again.

The world is not presented as a reality to be described, but as a language to be decoded. Fuentes' motto might well be: *Tell me how you speak, and I will tell you who you are.* Individuals, social classes, historical periods, cities, deserts are languages: all the languages that go to make up the Hispano-Mexican language, and several other tongues as well. An enormous, joyous, painful, hallucinatory verbal material which may remind the reader of the Baroque style of José Lezama Lima's *Paradiso*—*if* the word Baroque is a proper description of two modern writers. But the vertigo we experience when we confront the constructions of the great Cuban poet is that caused by perfect, frozen immobility; his verbal world is that of the stalactite; Fuentes' reality, by contrast, is all movement, a continual explosion. Lezama Lima's universe is an accumulation, a petrification, an immense verbal geology; Fuentes' is a continual uprooting, an exodus of languages, tongues meeting and scattering to the four winds. The one solid earth, the other a great gale. Because of his cosmopolitanism, Fuentes may also appear to resemble Cortázar, paradoxically the writer furthest from and closest to his national roots: even when Cortázar writes in the dialect of Buenos Aires, there is an irony that separates the writer from the language he uses. The Hispano-American cosmopolitanism of Cortázar is the end product of a process of abstraction and purification, a crystallization, whereas Fuentes' cosmopolitanism consists of a juxtaposition and a combination of different idioms within the Spanish language and outside of it. Because it is turned in upon itself, Cortázar's language is a process of reflection that obliges the reader to venture out onto a thinner and thinner and sharper and sharper edge until he is confronted by an empty space: a destruction of language, a leap in the direction of silence. In Fuentes, on the other hand, there is verbal eroticism, violence and pleasure, an encounter and an explosion. A chemical retort and a fireworks display.

The body occupies a central place in Fuentes' universe. Cold, heat, thirst, the sexual urge, fatigue, the most immediate and direct sensations; and the most refined and complex sensations: combinations of desire and imagination, the derangements and the hallucinations of the senses, their errors and their divinations. Erotic passion has a privileged place, and therefore imagination, its implacable double, also is uniquely privileged. In two other important Hispano-American novelists, one belonging to his own generation and another belonging to the preceding generation,

Gabriel García Márquez and Adolfo Bioy Casares, love is also a sovereign passion. In García Márquez's world, love is the primordial power that reigns as an obscure, impersonal, and all-powerful presence: the world of the first day of creation, or, more precisely, the primordial night. Bioy Casares's theme is not cosmic, but metaphysical: the body is imaginary, and we bow to the tyranny of a phantom. Love is a privileged perception, the most complete and total perception, not only of the unreality of the world, but of our own unreality: not only do we traverse a realm of shadows; we ourselves are shadows.* Unlike García Márquez, Fuentes does not regard men and women as mere projections of desire: they are his accomplices and his enemies. Like Bioy Casares, he regards phantoms as no less real than physical bodies, except for the fact that these phantoms are incarnations: we can touch them, and they can touch us; they can rend our flesh. The body is a very real thing, and the revelation that it offers us, whether animal or divine, is inhuman: it tears us away from ourselves and projects us into another, more total, life or death.

Bodies are visible hieroglyphs. Every body is an erotic metaphor, and the meaning of all these metaphors is always the same: death. Love for Fuentes is a way of looking upon death, and through death he has a glimpse of that territory that was once called sacred or poetic, but lacks a name in our day. The modern world has not yet invented words to designate the other side of reality. Fuentes' obsession with the wrinkled, toothless countenance of a tyrannical, mad, passionate old woman should not surprise us. She is the age-old vampire, the witch, the white serpent of Chinese tales: the lady of dark passions, the outcast. Eroticism is inseparable from horror, and Fuentes is a past master of the horrible. In many passages in his novels and in almost every one of his short stories, he delights in displaying a sort of fierce joy. If what he is pleased to put before us is not the sacred, it is something no less violent: profanation. A humor in which three heritages—the American, Spanish, and Mexican

---

* Despite (or perhaps because of?) the fact that Bioy Casares has written two novels, *La invención de Morel* (*The Invention of Morel*) and *El sueño de los héroes* [*The Dream of Heroes*], which may be described, without exaggeration, as *perfect* novels, our critics have ignored them, or what is worse, have misinterpreted them by regarding them as two successful instances of fantastic literature.

traditions—are conjoined, a humor that is not intellectual but physical, sexual, visceral. A humor that goes beyond irony, the absurd, and satire, whose parodic exaggeration borders on the sublime—a humor that can only be described as bloodthirsty. A humor that is carnal, corporeal, and ritual, as incongruous as an Aztec sacrifice in Times Square.

A number of European critics have said that the second half of our century will be marked by the emergence of Latin American literature as its first half and the end of the nineteenth were marked by the rise of American and Russian literature. I do not place much faith in this sort of prophecy; what is more, I believe that these three literatures are intelligible only within the context of European literature. Moreover, contemporary literature tends to be world-wide in scope. We may deplore it, but it is a fact that the old historical oppositions between nation and nation, or between various cultures, are evaporating little by little. The new antagonisms are different in nature and are manifested *within* our societies: conflicts between industrial society and the Third World, the quarrel between generations and ethnic minorities within industrial society. Whether or not the prophecy concerning the future of literature in Latin America will come true does not worry me, but I am fascinated and excited by the works of a handful of Latin-American poets and novelists: they are not a promise, but a presence. Among these works are those of Carlos Fuentes. He is now at the peak of his powers and has not yet said all he has to say. I am certain that the mask will become a transparent one, not rock crystal but water.

Remedios Varo's Appearances and Disappearances*

With the invisible violence of wind scattering clouds, but with greater delicacy, as if she painted with her eyes rather than with her hands, Remedios sweeps the canvas clean and heaps up clarities on its transparent surface.

---

*Remedios Varo was a little-known Spanish Surrealist painter. The wife of the French poet Benjamin Péret, she went to Mexico during World War II and remained there until her death in the early 1960s.

In their struggle with reality, some painters violate it or cover it with signs, explode it or bury it, flay it. Remedios volatilizes it: it is not blood but light that flows through its body.

She slowly paints lightning-quick apparitions.

Appearances are the shadows of archetypes. Remedios does not invent: she remembers. Except that these appearances resemble nothing and no one.

Sea voyages within a precious stone.

A speculative painting, a mirror-image painting: not the world in reverse, but the reverse of the world.

The art of levitation: the loss of gravity, the loss of seriousness. Remedios laughs, but her laughter echoes in another world.

Space is not an expanse but a magnet attracting Appearances. A woman's hair—the strings of a harp—the sun's rays streaming down—the strings of a guitar. The world seen as music: listen to Remedios's lines.

The secret theme of her work: harmony—lost equality.

In Appearance she paints Disappearance.

Roots, fronds, rays, locks of hair, flowing beards, spirals of sound: threads of death, of life, of time. The weft is woven and unwoven: the unreality that we call life, the unreality that we call death—only the canvas is real. Remedios the anti-Moira.

She does not paint time, but the moments when time is resting. In her world of stopped clocks, we hear the flow of substances, the circulation of shadow and light: time ripening.

Forms seek their own form, form seeks its own dissolution.

André Breton or the Quest of the Beginning

It is impossible to write about André Breton in any other language than that of passion. To him, the powers of the word were no different from the powers of passion, and passion, in its highest and most intense form, was nothing less than language in its wildest, purest state: poetry. Breton: the language of passion—the passion of language. Perhaps even more than an exploration of unknown psychic territories, his lifelong quest represented the regaining of a lost kingdom: the original Word, man before men and civilizations. Surrealism was his order of chivalry and his entire life was a Quest of the Holy Grail. The surprising evolution of the Spanish word *querer* reflects very well the nature of this quest; *querer* comes from the Latin *quaerere* (to search, to inquire), but in Spanish, the meaning soon changed, and the word came to mean *to desire, to love*. *Querer*: a passionate, amorous quest. A quest whose goal lies neither in the future nor in the past, but at that point of convergence that is simultaneously the beginning and the end of all time: the day before the beginning and after the end.

Breton's indignation at the "infamous Christian idea of sin" is something more than a violent rejection of the traditional values of the West: it is an affirmation of the original innocence of man. This distinguishes him from almost all of his contemporaries and successors. For Georges Bataille, eroticism, death, and sin are interchangeable signs whose combinations repeat the same meaning again and again, with terrifying monotony: the nothingness of man, his irremediable abjection. For Sartre, too, man is an accursed creature, ontologically or historically, the victim of a malediction that may be labeled either anguish or working for a daily wage. Both are rebel sons of Christianity. Breton belongs to another tradition. His life and his work are proof that he was not so much the heir of Sade and Freud as of Rousseau and Meister Eckhart. He was not a philosopher, but a great poet, and, even more important, a man of honor in the old sense of the word. His stubborn refusal to entertain the idea of sin was a point of honor: the notion struck him as being in effect a *stain*, a blot not on man's life, but on man's dignity. Belief in sin was incompatible with his conception of man. This conviction, which made him a violent opponent of many modern philosophies and all religions, was itself basically religious: it was an act of faith. What is most amazing—or I should say most admirable—is that this faith never failed him. He denounced other people's weaknesses, their shortcomings, their betrayals, but he never believed that our guilt was congenital. He was a sectarian spirit, but one without the slightest trace of Manichaeism. For Breton, sinning and being born were not synonymous.

Man, even man debased by the neocapitalism and pseudosocialism of our time, is a marvelous being because he sometimes *speaks*. Language is the mark, the sign, not of his fall, but of his original innocence. Through the Word, we may regain the lost kingdom and recover powers we possessed in the far-distant past. These powers are not ours. The man inspired, the man who really speaks, does not say anything personal: language speaks through his mouth. Dreaming favors the explosion of the Word because it is an affective state: its passivity permits desire to be active. Dreaming is by nature passionate. Here, too, Breton's opposition to Christianity had religious roots: in order to express itself, language destroys the conscious self. Poetry does not redeem the poet's personal self: it dissolves it in the vaster, more powerful reality of language. The practice of poetry demands the surrender, the renunciation of the ego. It is regrettable that Buddhism did not interest him: that tradition also destroys the illusion of the self, though its aim is not to foster language but to foster silence. (I must add that this silence is one that for, more than two thousand years, has never ceased emitting meanings.) I mention Buddhism because I believe that "automatic writing" is something of a modern equivalent of Buddhist meditation; I do not think it is a method for writing poems, nor is it a rhetorical recipe: it is a psychic exercise, a convocation and an invocation meant to open the floodgates of the verbal stream. Poetic automatism, as Breton himself often emphasized, is very close to asceticism: a state of passivity must be reached, a very difficult task, for it requires the suspension of all criticism and self-criticism. It is a radical criticism of criticism, an interdiction of consciousness. In its way, it is a *via purgativa*, a method of negation aimed at calling forth the appearance of true reality: the primordial language.

The basis of "automatic writing" is the belief that speaking and thinking are one and the same thing. Man does not speak because he thinks; he thinks because he speaks. Or rather, speaking is no different from thinking: to speak is to think. Breton justifies this idea on the following grounds: "*Nous ne disposons spontanément pour nous exprimer que* *d'une* seule *structure verbale excluant de manière la plus catégorique toute autre structure apparemment chargée du même sens.*"* One immediate objection to this trenchant formula that we might raise is the fact that both in everyday speech and in written prose we come across phrases that might be expressed in different words or by the same words in a different order. Breton would rightly reply that, not only the syntactical structure, but also the idea itself would change from one version to another, even though the change might be imperceptible. Any change in the verbal structure results in a change of meaning. Strictly speaking, what we call synonyms are merely translations or equivalents within a language; and what we call translation is really only an approximation in another language or an interpretation. Words such as *nirvana, dharma, tao,* or *jen* are really untranslatable; the same is true of *physics, nature, democracy, revolution,* and other Western terms that have no exact equivalent in languages outside of our tradition. As the relation between the verbal structure and the meaning becomes more intimate—in mathematics and poetry, for instance, not to mention nonverbal languages such as music and painting—translation becomes more and more difficult. At either extreme of language—the exclamation and the equation—the two halves of the semantic sign become impossible to separate: the signifier and the signified are one and the same. Perhaps unwittingly, Breton thus opposes Saussure's view: language is not simply an arbitrary convention linking sound and meaning, as linguists are beginning to realize today.

There is a strong magical element in Breton's view of language. He not only made no distinction between magic and poetry; he also was convinced all his life that poetry was a force, a substance, an energy truly capable of changing reality. At the same time, his ideas were so precise and penetrating that I would not hesitate to call them scientific. On one hand, he saw language as an autonomous current possessed of a power all its own, a sort of universal magnetism; on the other hand, he conceived of this erotic substance as a system of signs governed by the twofold law

---

* "In spontaneous expression, we have at our disposal *only one* verbal structure, which categorically excludes any other structure supposedly possessing the same meaning."

of affinity and opposition, similarity and difference. This view is quite close to that held by modern linguists: words and their constituent elements are fields of energy, like atoms and their particles. The old notion of analogy is coming to the fore once again: nature is a language, and language in turn is a double of nature. To rediscover man's natural language is to return to nature, before the Fall and History: poetry is the proof of man's original innocence. *The Social Contract* becomes for Breton the verbal, poetic accord between man and nature, word and thought. Considered from this point of view, the oft-repeated statement that Surrealism is not a school of poetry, but a movement of liberation becomes more understandable. A way of rediscovering the language of innocence, a renewal of the primordial pact, poetry is the basic text, the foundation of the human order. Surrealism is revolutionary because it is a return to the beginning of all beginnings.

Breton's earliest poems bear the traces of a passionate reading of Mallarmé. Not even in his moments of greatest violence and verbal freedom did he ever abandon this predilection for words that are at once precise and precious. Words with iridescent colors, a language of echoing reverberations. He was a "Mannerist" poet, in the proper sense of the word: within the European tradition, he belongs to the family of poets descended from Góngora, Marino, Donne—poets I cannot be certain he read, poets whose poetic ethic I fear he would have disapproved of. Verbal splendor, and intellectual and emotional violence. A curious but not infrequent combination of prophecy and aestheticism that makes his best poems both objects of beauty and spiritual testaments. That is perhaps the reason why he worshiped Lautréamont, the poet who discovered the *form* in which to express psychic explosion. That may also be the reason for Breton's instinctive and openly avowed repugnance for the simplistic, brutal destructiveness of Dada, even though he considered it a "revolutionary necessity" that was both inevitable and healthy. There were different reasons underlying his reservations concerning other poets. His admiration for Apollinaire is somewhat hesitant because, to Breton, poetry was the creation of realities through the Word, and not simply verbal invention. Novelty and surprise in art pleased him, but the term *invention* was not to his liking; on the other hand, the word *revela-*

tion shines in many of his texts. Speaking is the noblest activity of all: revealing what is hidden, bringing the buried word back to life, calling forth our double, that Other which is us but which we never allow to exist—our suppressed half.

Revelation is resurrection, exposure, initiation. It is a word that calls for rites and ceremonies. Except as a means of provocation, of insulting the public, or rousing it to rebellion, Breton detested open-air spectacles: fiestas should be held in catacombs. Each of the Surrealist expositions revolved around two opposite poles: exhibitionism and secrecy, consecration and profanation. Consecration and conspiracy are consanguineous terms: revelation is also rebellion. The Other, our double, is a denial of the illusory solidity and security of our consciousness, that pillar of smoke on which we build our arrogant philosophical and religious constructs. The Others, proletarians and colonial slaves, women and poets, primitive myths and revolutionary utopias, are equally violent threats to the beliefs and institutions of the West. Breton reaches his hand out to all of them, to Fourier and the Papuan of New Guinea alike. Rebellion and revelation, language and passion are manifestations of a single reality. The true name of this reality is also a double one: innocence and marvels. Man is the creator of marvels; he is a poet because he is an innocent being. Children, women, lovers, the inspired, and even the insane are the incarnation of the marvelous. Everything they do is uncanny, and they do not realize it. They know not what they do: they are not responsible, they are innocents. Magnets, lightning rods, high-tension wires: their words and their acts are senseless, and yet they have a meaning. They are the scattered signs of a language in perpetual motion that opens out before our eyes a fan of contradictory meanings that in the end becomes a single, ultimate meaning. The universe speaks to us and to itself in and through them.

I have mentioned a number of Breton's words: revelation and rebellion, innocence and marvels, passion and language. There is another one: magnetism. He was one of the centers of gravity of our time. He not only believed that we humans are governed by laws of attraction and repulsion; he himself was the personal incarnation of these forces. I confess that, for a long time, the thought that I would say or do something that might provoke his reprobation kept me awake nights. I believe that many of his friends felt much the same way. A few years ago, Buñuel invited me to a private showing of one of his films. When it was over, he asked me: "Would Breton think it within the Surrealist tradition?" I mention Buñuel not only because he is a great artist, but also because he is a man possessed of great moral integrity and freedom of spirit. These feelings have nothing to do with fear or respect for a superior (although I believe that, if there is such a thing as superior men, Breton was one of them). I never considered him a leader, much less a Pope, to repeat the ignoble epithet popularized by certain swine. Despite the fact that we were personal friends, my activities within the Surrealist group were quite tangential. Nonetheless, his affection and generosity always amazed me, from the beginning of our relationship until the very end of his life. I have never known why he was so kind to me. Was it perhaps because I was from Mexico, a country he loved all his life? Apart from these personal reasons, I must confess that many times I write as though I were having a silent conversation with Breton: objections, answers, agreement, disagreement, homage, all these things at once. I am experiencing that sensation at this very moment.

In my adolescence, in a period of isolation and great elation, I happened to read a few pages which I found out later are Chapter V of *L'Amour fou*. In them, he tells of climbing the volcanic peak of Teide, on Tenerife, in the Canary Islands. This text, which I read at almost the same time as *The Marriage of Heaven and Hell*, opened the doors of modern poetry to me. It was an "art of loving," not in the trivial manner of Ovid's *Ars Amatoria*, but an initiation to something that my later life and the East have given me further proof of: the analogy, or, rather, the identity between woman and nature. Is water feminine, or is a woman a succession of waves, a river at night, a beach at dawn tattooed by the wind? If we are a metaphor of the universe, the human couple is the metaphor par excellence, the point of intersection of all forces and the seed of all forms. The couple is time recaptured, the return to the time before time. Against wind and tide, I have endeavored to be faithful to that revelation: the powers the word *love* has over me have remained intact. Or as Breton says: *"On n'en sera plus jamais quitte avec ces frondaisons de l'âge d'or."* *This

---

* "We will never again escape from these leafy fronds of the golden age."

stubborn belief in a paradisiac age, coupled with the vision of the primordial couple, can be seen in all his writings, from the first to the last. The woman is a bridge, a place where the natural world and the human are reconciled. She is language made palpable, revelation incarnate: *"La femme n'est plus qu'un calice débordant de voyelles."* *

Some years later, I met Benjamin Péret, Leonora Carrington, Wolfgang Paalen, Remedios Varo, and other Surrealists who had sought refuge in Mexico during World War II. Then the war ended, and I saw Benjamin again in Paris. He took me to the Café de la Place Blanche. I saw Breton frequently over a long period of time. Although spending a great deal of time together sometimes interferes with the interchange of ideas and feelings, I was often aware of that sort of free-flowing current that really unites two people talking together, even if their views are not identical. Among all these conversations, I shall never forget one we had in the summer of 1964, just before I returned to India. I remember it not because it was the last one we ever had, but because of the atmosphere surrounding it. This is not the proper place to tell about this meeting. (I have promised myself that someday I will write about it.) To me, it was an *encounter,* in Breton's meaning of the word: predestination and election. That night, as the two of us strolled through Les Halles together, the conversation turned to a subject that was worrying him: the future of the Surrealist movement. I remember what I told him, more or less: that, to me, Surrealism was the sacred malady of our world, like leprosy in the Middle Ages or the state of possession of the Spanish Illuminati in the sixteenth century; since it was a necessary negation in the West, it would remain alive as long as modern civilization remained alive, whatever political systems and ideologies might prevail in the future. My elation moved him, but he answered: "Negation is a function of affirmation and vice versa; I doubt very much whether the world that is now dawning can be defined in terms of affirmation or negation: we are entering a neutral zone, and the Surrealist rebellion will be obliged to express itself in forms that are neither negation nor affirmation. We have gone beyond approval or disapproval . . ." I would venture the guess that this was the idea behind the group's last exposition: total separation. This was

---

* "Woman is nothing more than a flower-cup overflowing with vowels."

not the first time that Breton had urged the Surrealists to "go underground," but he seldom had done so that frankly and openly. Perhaps he thought that the movement would become fertile again only if it proved capable of turning itself into a clandestine force. A return to the catacombs? I don't know. I wonder whether what Mallarmé called "limited action" *("l'action restreinte")* still makes sense in a society such as ours, a society in which the old contradictions have disappeared—not because they have been resolved in a higher synthesis, but because all values have so deteriorated that they cancel each other out. Is publishing still a form of action, or has it dissolved into an anonymous flood of publicity?

It is frequently said that the ambiguity of Surrealism stems from the fact that it is a movement of poets and painters who refuse to be judged on the basis of aesthetic criteria. Hasn't the same thing been true of all artistic schools in the past and all the works of the great poets and painters? "Art" is an invention of aesthetics, which in turn is an invention of philosophers. Nietzsche buried both and danced on their graves: what we call art is a game. The Surrealists' determination to abolish the boundaries separating art from life is nothing new; what is new are the terms Surrealists use to express themselves and the meaning of their activities. Neither "an artistic life" nor a "vital art": a return to the original source of language, to the moment when speaking is synonymous with creating. I have no idea what the future of the Surrealist group will be; I am certain, however, that the current that has flowed from German Romanticism and Blake to Surrealism will not disappear. It will live a life apart; it will be the *other* voice.

Surrealism is no longer in the vanguard, according to the critics. Quite apart from the fact that I thoroughly dislike that military term, I do not believe that novelty, that being in the vanguard of history, is the essential characteristic of Surrealism. Nor were the Dadaists as frantic worshipers of the new as the Futurists, for instance. Neither Dada nor Surrealism adored machines. Surrealism desecrated them: it built machines that produced nothing, "dust-raisers," melting watches. The machine as a method of criticism—of the cult of machines, of men who worship progress and their buffoonery. Is Duchamp the beginning or the end of painting? Through his *œuvre,* and even more importantly through his negation of "the work of art," Duchamp closes a period of Western art (that of painting properly speaking) and opens another which is no longer "artistic": the dissolving of art in life, of language in the circle of word games, of reason in its philosophical antidote, laughter. Duchamp undermines modernity with the same wave of the hand with which he dismisses tradition. In Breton's case, there is also his vision of time as an invisible, innocent present hidden beneath the flow of hours and days. The future fascinated him because it seemed to him to be the realm of the unexpected; not what *will be* according to the calculations of reason, but what *might be* according to the imagination. The destruction of today's world would permit the appearance of real time, not historical time but natural time, governed not by progress but by desire. This was what a Communist-libertarian society meant to him. In his eyes, there was no essential contradiction between myths and utopias, poetry and revolutionary programs. He read Fourier as we might read the Vedas or the Popul Vuh, and he regarded Eskimo poems as revolutionary prophecies. The dawn of history and the most remote future were naturally conjoined in his mind. His materialism was not a vulgar "scientism," and his irrationalism was not a hatred of reason.

The determination to embrace every sort of opposite—Sade and Rousseau, Novalis and Roussel, Juliette and Héloïse, Marx and Chateaubriand—is constantly in evidence, in his writings and in his acts. This attitude is at the furthest possible remove from the complacent tolerance of the skeptic. He detested eclecticism in the realm of thought and promiscuity in the realm of eroticism. His best pages, both in his prose works and in his poetry, are those inspired by the idea of free choice and its correlative, fidelity to what one has freely chosen, whether in art or in politics, in friendships or in love. This idea was the axis of his life and of his conception of love: a passion whose many facets have been polished by freedom. Our age has delivered love from the prison bars of the past century only to convert it into a pastime, one more consumer item in a society of busy consumers. Breton's vision is the exact opposite of almost everything that in our day passes for love and even for eroticism (another word in wide circulation, like a coin of very little value). I have the greatest difficulty understanding his boundless admiration for Sade's works. I can see why Sade's spirit of absolute negation moved him and excited him, but how can this total negation be reconciled with a belief in love as the radiant center of the golden age?

Sade denounces love: it is a hypocritical lie, or, worse still, an illusion. His system is hallucinatory, not incoherent: his negation is no less total than Saint Augustine's affirmation. Augustine and Sade are equally violent opponents of any sort of Manichaeism; for the Christian theologian, Evil has no ontological reality; for the atheist philosopher, what lacks reality is what we call Good: his version of *The Social Contract* is the statutes of the Society of the Friends of Crime. Bataille has endeavored to transform Sade's monologue into a dialogue, bringing absolute eroticism face to face with a no less absolute adversary: Christian divinity. The result is silence and laughter: "atheology." The unthinkable and the unnamable. Breton reintroduces love into eroticism, or, more exactly, consecrates eroticism through love. We find again, underlying his opposition to any and every religion, a passionate wish to consecrate. And even a passionate wish to reconcile. Commenting on a passage in the *New Justine*—the episode in which one of the characters mingles his sperm with the lava of Etna—Breton observes that the act is one of loving homage to nature, "*une façon, des plus folles, des plus indiscutables de l'aimer.*"* Breton's admiration for Sade was almost boundless, and all his life he believed that "*tant qu'on ne sera pas quitte avec l'idée de la transcendance d'un bien quelconque. . . la représentation exaltée du mal innégarderalaplus grande valeur révolutionnaire.*"† But, with this one reservation, in the dialogue between Sade and Rousseau, Breton is irresistibly inclined to side with the latter: with Rousseau the friend of primitive man, the lover of nature, as with Fourier the utopian. Love is not an illusion: it is the intermediary between man and nature, the place where terrestrial and spiritual magnetism intersect.

Each one of the facets of Breton's works reflects all the others. It is not the passive reflection of the mirror, however: it is not a repetition

---

* "One of the most insane, one of the most unquestionable ways of loving it."
† "So long as we have not freed ourselves of the idea of the transcendence of some sort of good . . . the impassioned representation of innate evil will continue to have the greatest revolutionary value."

but a reply. A play of contrary beams of light, a dialogue of glimmers. Magnetism, revelation, a thirst for innocence, and also disdain. Is there hauteur here? Yes, in the etymological sense of the word: Breton is a winged creature whose kingdom is the upper air, a bird whose realm is lofty heights. All the words of this family apply to him. He was a soaring spirit, a man exalted; his poetry uplifts us. Above all, he maintained that the body of the woman and the man are our only altars. And as for death? Every man is born several times and dies several times. This is not the first time that Breton has died. He knew, better than anyone, that we die more than once: each one of his central books is the story of a resurrection. I know that this time it is different, that we will never see him again. His latest death is not an illusion. Nonetheless, Breton lived certain instants, saw with his own eyes certain evidences that are the negation of time and what we call an everyday outlook on life. I call such moments poetic instants, even though they are experiences common to all men: the only difference is that the poet remembers them and endeavors to reincarnate them in words, sounds, colors. The man who has lived these instants and is capable of pondering their meaning knows that the self cannot be redeemed because it does not exist. He also knows that, as Breton repeatedly insisted, the boundaries between waking and dreaming, life and death, time and a timeless present are fluid and vague. We do not know what it is really like to die, except that it is the end of the individual self—the end of the prison. Breton broke out of this prison many times; he expanded time or denied it, and for a measureless instant coincided with the *other* time. This experience, the central core of his life and his thought, is invulnerable and untouchable: it is beyond time, beyond death—beyond us. Knowing that this is so reconciles me to his latest death and to all dying.

The Verbal Pact and Correspondence

The affinities between Rousseau and André Breton are both numerous and obvious. What is more, they are not only intellectual but also (and much more importantly) temperamental. Breton was aware of them, but, to my knowledge, critics have as yet written almost nothing about them. An excellent essay by the poet Ernesto Mejía Sánchez,* which I read shortly after writing the above pages in memory of Breton, has made the relationship between Rousseau and the founder of Surrealism even clearer. In this solid and scholarly work, Mejía Sánchez analyzes a little-known text of Rousseau's, the *Essai sur l'origine des langues (On the Origin of Languages)*, which may quite legitimately be regarded as a sort of anticipation of the Surrealist conception of language. I confess that I was not familiar with this work and have no idea whether Breton ever read it. I am inclined to believe he did not know it; if he had, he would have mentioned it in one or another of his writings. But whether due to sheer coincidence or a demonstrable influence, the similarity is immediately obvious. Breton, for example, believed that society is based on language, rather than vice versa; Mejía Sánchez points out that for Rousseau "there is a linguistic pact that antedates the social pact." I shall cite other striking similarities: the idea of language as a nonutilitarian mechanism aimed at satisfying our emotional needs *("On prétendque les homes inventèrent la parole pour exprimer leurs besoins; cette opinion me paraît insoutenable . . . [elle vient] des besoins moraux, des passions");*† metaphor as the primordial form of speech *("lepremier langage dut être figuré");*‡ and the connection between verbal image and passion *("l'image illusoire offerte par la passion se montrant la première, le langage qui lui répondait fut aussi le premier inventé; il devint ensuite métaphorique. . . . ").*§ Passion, primordial language, metaphor: Breton's ideas and pre-occupations were already implicit in the *Essai sur l'origine des langues.*

Despite these similarities, of all the writers of the eighteenth century it was not Rousseau but Sade whom Breton admired first and respected most. But did he love him, did he feel that he belonged to the same spir-

* "El pensamiento literario de Rousseau," in the volume *Presencia de Rousseau* (1962)

† "It is commonly said that men invented speech to express their needs; this opinion seems to me to be untenable . . . [language stems from] moral needs, from the passions."

‡ ". . . language in the beginning was no doubt figurative."

§ ". . . the illusory image offered by passion appearing first, the language that was its expression was also the first to be invented; it then became metaphorical."

itual family as Sade? I doubt it. I have already said that what fascinated Breton was Sade's thorough-going negation. A free spirit such as André Breton could not help but be moved by the persecution Sade suffered and the moral integrity with which he confronted his many tribulations, never once abjuring his ideas. Sade is an example of moral rectitude; Rousseau is not. Although Breton too was an incorruptible man of absolute integrity, his passions were not those of Sade but those of Rousseau, and the same holds true of his ideas. Both are centered upon a reality that Sade blindly and stubbornly refused to recognize: the human heart.

According to Rousseau, speech is born "of a mutual pact between men." But as Mejía Sánchez comments: "This unanimous and enduring pact is implicit in language itself, however. Speech does not exist in and for itself; it is speech with others. Rousseau failed to see, however, that a contradiction is involved here . . ." There is indeed a contradiction: language cannot antedate society because it implies the existence of social intercourse—it is *with and for others* by its very nature.

At the same time, it is not human society that creates language, but language that creates human society. Language lies outside of society because it is its foundation; but it also lies within society because that is the only place where it exists and the only place where it develops. Language lies on the border-line between nature and culture: it does not appear in the former and is the condition of the latter. How and when did men begin to speak? And above all, *why* did they speak? Whatever the cause or causes that led man to utter the first onomatopoeic syllables, the real mystery lies in the fact that of all living creatures man is the only one possessed of the faculty of speech. Since I do not believe that the riddle of the origin of language can be solved by historical methods, we are forced to rely on theology and philosophy or their modern successors, biology and anthropology. Among the hypotheses that have been advanced, two seem quite attractive to me. One of them is Rousseau's: the origin of speech is to be explained by the intervention of a nonhuman, *divine* power. The other is Lévi-Strauss's, even though he has never formulated it:[*] language is the result of the intervention of a

---

[*] I have deduced it from the ideas expressed in his writings.

nonhuman, *natural* power. By "nonhuman," I mean that language is not a product of society, but rather its condition or foundation; by "natural" I mean that the structure of human brain cells, which may be taken to be the ultimate source of the language faculty, can be described in terms of chemistry, and these in turn can be explained by physics. Animal language cannot explain human language: both are part of the system of relations constituting nature, but they are different answers to different problems of communication.

These two hypotheses are not as contradictory as they may initially appear to be. In both, there enters into play an element that is foreign to man and irreducible to human society: God or nature. This element is an agent that transcends the dichotomy between culture and nature and does away with the distinction between matter and thought. This latter fact is surprising. Thought, which science has expelled from its place at the top of the spiral of evolution, reappears at the bottom of it: the physical structure of atoms and their particles is a mathematical structure, a relation. What is equally extraordinary is that this structure can be reduced to a system of signs—and is therefore a language. The power of speech is a particular manifestation of natural communication; human language is one more dialect in the linguistic system of the universe. We might add: the cosmos is a language of languages. The new materialism is to nineteenth-century materialism what Marx and Darwin were to eighteenth-century materialism. Our materialism is not dialectical or biological but mathematical, linguistic, mental. Strictly speaking, it is neither idealism nor materialism. It is not idealism because it reduces the Idea to a combination of physicochemical stimuli and responses; it is not materialism because it regards matter as a system of communication: the phenomenon is a message or a relation between factors that continue to be called material only because of our lazy verbal habits. The basic structure of these factors is no different from that of mathematical and verbal symbols: it is a system of relations. Before our era a Providence or a Logos reigned, a matter or a history perpetually tending toward more perfect forms; now an unconscious thought, a mental mechanism guides us and thinks us. A mathematical structure determines us—*signifies* us.

The idea that language does not stem from physical necessity may seem strange, but it is not absurd. If we think about it, Rousseau was right. Whether it comes from God or from nature, language is not intended to satisfy biological needs, since animals survive as individuals and as species without articulate language. There is a gap between animal language and human language because the latter is intended to satisfy nonanimal necessities, the passions, and entities no less powerful and no less illusory than the passions: the tribe, the family, labor, the State, religion, myth, the awareness of death, rites, etc. These necessities are artificial ones since they are not found among animals, but the artifice that satisfies them is *natural:* a system of signs found in nature, from the stars to atomic particles. Rousseau's great merit was to have seen that the boundary lines between culture and nature are very tenuous. This is an idea that is equally repugnant to the Christian and the Marxist: both believe that man is historical, unique, singular. Returning to Rousseau is salutary: he is like one of those fountains we find at a cross roads at the entrance to a town. On drinking from it, we find the water delightfully cool and refreshing, and before losing ourselves in the dusty little streets of the town, we turn around one last time to listen to the wind in the trees. The wind may be saying the same thing as the water falling on the stone. For an instant, we glimpse the meaning of the word *reconciliation.*

Mejía Sánchez comments that Rousseau, "as though foreseeing the epidemic of *correspondences,* points out the false analogy between colors and sounds." Here I do not agree. If colors and sounds are languages (and they are), it is clear that there is a correspondence between them. It is not an explicit correspondence, because each language is in a different key: what colors say, for instance, must be transposed into the language of sounds or words. But we transpose the olfactory "key" into the verbal key and the verbal key into the auditory or tactile every day. This is what Lévi-Strauss has done in a most admirable way in *Le cru et le cuit (The Raw and the Cooked):* he has deciphered the mythological code of the Brazilian Indians and translated it into the terms of contemporary logic and science. We live our lives immersed in a language that is not only verbal, but also musical and visual, tactile and olfactory, sensory and mental. There are those who will maintain that these correspondences are illusory or subjective: the relation between the sign and what it signifies is arbitrary, the product of a convention. That is true—but only up to a certain point: this is a problem that has not been satisfactorily dealt with as yet. The objection carries little weight for another reason: if we accept Saussure's view that the connection between signifier and signified is an arbitrary one, we must also concede that, once the signs are constituted, we live in a universe of symbols governed by the correspondences between them. We enter the world of symbols the day we are born; once we are given a name, we are a symbol among other symbols, a word related to other words.

What in the past appeared to be fuzzy philosophizing by poets is today a scientifically recognized fact. A linguistic area is a system of symbols that vary from one subarea to another and even within the same language (Hispano-American linguistic symbolism, for example, is not the same throughout the continent). Each linguistic area in turn is related to all the others, and therefore there is a correspondence between the various symbolic systems that go to make up the whole of human societies. These systems are what we call civilizations, and all these systems, taken together, in turn form another universe of symbols. The verbal pact is both something more and something less than a historical fact: it is the symbol of symbols. It refers to the totality of facts, and each and every fact fulfills it, embodies it.

Recapitulations

The poem is unexplainable, not unintelligible.

A poem is rhythmic language—not language with a rhythm (song) or mere verbal rhythm (a property common to all language, including prose).

Rhythm is a relation of difference and similarity: this sound is *not* that one, this sound is *like* that one.

Rhythm is the original metaphor and encompasses all the others. It says: succession is repetition, time is nontime.

Whether lyric, epic, or dramatic, the poem is succession and repetition, a date on the calendar and a rite. The "happening" is also a poem (theater) and a rite (fiesta), but it lacks one essential element: rhythm, the reincarnation of the instant. We repeat Góngora's hendecasyllables and the final monosyllables of Huidobro's *Altazor* again and again; Swann listens to the Vinteuil sonata, Agamemnon sacrifices Iphigenia, Segismundo discovers he is dreaming with his eyes open, again and again. But the "happening" occurs only once.

The instant dissolves in the succession of other nameless instants. In order to *save it*, we must *convert it* into a rhythm. The "happening" opens up another possibility: the instant that is never repeated. By definition, this instant is the final one: the "happening"is an allegory of death.

The Roman circus is a "happening" *avant la lettre*—and its negation. If the participants in a "happening" were really faithful to their principles, all would die. Moreover, the true representation of the final instant would require the extermination of the human race. The one unrepeatable event: the end of the world. Somewhere between the Roman circus and the "happening": the bullfight. Risk, but also style.

A poem consisting of a single syllable is no less complex than the *Divine Comedy* or *Paradise Lost*. The Satasahasrika sutra sets forth the basic teachings in a hundred thousand strophes; the Eksaksari in one syllable: *a*. All language, all meaning, and at the same time the ultimate absence of meaning of language and the world, is condensed in the sound of this one vowel.

Understanding a poem means, first of all, *hearing it*.

Words enter through our ears, appear before our eyes, disappear in contemplation. Every reading of a poem tends to call forth silence.

To read a poem is to hear it with our eyes; to hear it is to see it with our ears.

In the United States, it has become the fashion for poets to read their poems in public. This is a dubious practice, because the ability to really listen to poetry is a lost art; what is more, modern poets are writers and therefore "poor actors of their own emotions." But poetry of the future will be oral. A collaboration between speaking machines, and an audience of poets, it will be the art of *listening to messages and combining them.* Isn't that what we do today every time we read a book of poems?

When we read a poem or listen to one, we do not smell, taste, or touch the words. All these sensations are mental images.

In order to experience a poem, we must understand it; in order to understand it, we must hear it, see it, contemplate it—convert it into an echo, a shadow, nothingness. Comprehension is a spiritual exercise.

Duchamp said: since a three-dimensional object casts a two-dimensional shadow, we should be able to imagine the unknown four-dimensional object whose shadow we are. I for my part am fascinated by the search for a one-dimensional object that casts no shadow at all.

Each reader is another poet; each poem another poem.

Though it perpetually changes, poetry does not advance.

In ordinary discourse one phrase lays the groundwork for the next; it is a chain with a beginning and an end. In a poem, the first phrase contains the last one and the last one evokes the first.

Poetry is our only recourse against rectilinear time—against progress.

The writer's morality does not lie in the subjects he deals with or the arguments he sets forth, but in his behavior toward language.

In poetry, technique is another name for morality: it is not a manipulation of words but a passion and an asceticism.

The false poet speaks of himself, almost invariably in the name of others. The true poet speaks with others when he talks to himself.

The difference between a "closed" work and an "open" work is not an absolute one. To be complete, the hermetic poem requires the intervention of a reader to decipher it. The open poem, in turn, implies at least a minimal structure: a starting point, or as the Buddhists put it, a "prop" for meditation. In the first case, the reader *opens* the poem; in the second, he completes it, he *closes* it.

The blank page or the page covered with nothing but punctuation marks is like a cage without a bird inside. The real openwork is the one that *closes* the door: the reader, on opening it, lets the bird, the poem, out.

Opening the poem in search of *this* and discovering *that*—always something different from what we expected.

Whether open or closed, the poem demands the demise of the poet who writes it and the birth of the poet who reads it.

Poetry is a perpetual struggle against meaning. Two extremes: the poem encompasses all meanings, it is the meaning of all meanings; or the poem denies language any sort of meaning. In the modern era, Mallarmé represents the attempt to write the first sort of poem; Dada the second. A language beyond language or the destruction of language by means of language.

Dada failed because it believed that the defeat of language would be the triumph of the poet. Surrealism proclaimed the supreme rule of language over the poet. It is up to young poets to abolish the distinction between creator and reader: to discover the meeting point between speaker and listener. This point is the heart of language.

Completing the work of Nietzsche, taking negation as far as it will go. At the end of the road, play awaits us: fiesta, the consummation of the work, its momentary incarnation and its dissolution.

Taking negation as far as it will go. Contemplation awaits us there: the disincarnation of language, transparency.

What Buddhism offers us is the end of relations, the abolition of dialectics—a silence that is not the dissolution but the *resolution* of language.

The poem must provoke the reader: force him to hear—to hear himself.

To hear oneself or to hie oneself: *oírse o irse.* To what place?

Poetic activity is born of desperation in the face of the impotence of the word and ends in the recognition of the omnipotence of silence.

No one is a poet unless he has felt the temptation to destroy language or create another one, unless he has experienced the fascination of non-meaning and the no less terrifying fascination of meaning that is inexpressible.

Between the cry and silence, between the meaning that is all meanings and the absence of meaning, the poem arises. What does this thin stream of words say? It says that it says nothing not already said by silence and shouting. And once this is said, the tumult and the silence cease. A precarious victory, ever threatened by words that say nothing, by the silence that says: nothing.

To believe in the immortality of a poem would be to believe in the immortality of language. We must bow to the evidence: languages are born and die; any meaning will one day cease to have meaning. And isn't this ceasing to have meaning the meaning of meaning? We must bow to the evidence . . .

Triumph of the Word: the poem is like those female nudes of German painting that symbolize the victory of death. Glorious living monuments of the corruption of the flesh.

Poetry and mathematics are the two extreme poles of language. Beyond them there is nothing—the realm of the inexpressible; between them the immense but finite realm of speech.

Enamored of silence, the poet's only recourse is to speak.

The Word has its roots in a silence *previous* to speech—a presentiment of language. Silence, *after* the Word, is based on a language—it is an encoded silence. The poem is the trajectory between these two silences—between the wish to speak and the silence that fuses the wishing and the speaking.

Beyond surprise and repetition: _____

2

Knowledge, Drugs, Inspiration

There is more than one similarity between modern poetry and science. Both are experiments, in the sense of "testing in a laboratory": an attempt is made to produce a certain phenomenon through the separation or combination of certain elements which the experimenter has either subjected to the pressure of some outward force or left to develop according to the laws of their own nature. This operation takes place in a closed space, in the most complete isolation possible. The poet deals with words as the scientist deals with cells, atoms, and other material particles: he extracts them from their natural medium, everyday language, isolates them in a sort of vacuum chamber, combines them or separates them; he observes and uses the properties of language as the scientific researcher observes and uses the properties of matter. The analogy might be carried further, but it is pointless to do so because the similarity lies not so much in the outward resemblances between verbal manipulations and laboratory testing as in the attitude toward the object.

As he writes, as he tests his ideas and his words, the poet does not know precisely what is going to happen. His attitude toward the poem is empirical. Unlike the religious believer, he is not attempting to confirm a revealed truth; unlike the mystic, he is not endeavoring to become one with a transcendent reality; unlike the ideologue, he is not trying to demonstrate a theory. The poet does not postulate or affirm anything a priori; he knows that what counts is not ideas but results, not intentions but works. Isn't this the same attitude as that of the scientist? Poetry and science do not imply a total rejection of prior conceptions and intuitions. But theories ("working hypotheses") are not what justify experiments; rather, the converse is true. Sometimes the "testing" produces results that are different from or entirely contrary to our expectations. The poet and the scientist do not find this difficult to accept; both are resigned to the fact that reality often acts quite independently of our philosophy. Poets and scientists are not doctrinaires; they do not offer us a priori systems but proven facts, results rather than hypotheses, works rather than ideas. The truths they seek are different, but they employ similar methods to ascertain them. The rigorous procedures they follow are accompanied by the strictest objectivity, that is to say, a respect for the autonomy of the phenomenon being investigated. A poem and a scientific truth are something more than a theory or a belief: they have withstood the acid of proof and the fire of criticism. Poems and scientific truths are something quite different from the ideas of poets and scientists. Artistic styles and the philosophy of science are transient things; works of art and the real truths of science are not.

Yet the similarities between science and poetry must not blind us to a crucial difference between them, one having to do with the subject of the experiment. The scientist is an observer, and plays no part, at least voluntarily, in the experiment. I say "voluntarily" because, at times, the observer inevitably becomes part of the phenomenon being observed. In the case of modern poetry, the subject of the experiment is the poet himself: he is both the observer and the phenomenon observed. His body and his psyche, his entire being, are the "field" in which all sorts of transformations take place. Modern poetry is an experimental process whereby the knowing subject is the object of knowledge. To see with our ears, to feel with our minds, to combine our powers and use them to the limit, to know a little more about ourselves and discover within us unknown realities: is that not the aim assigned poetry by spirits as different as Coleridge, Baudelaire, and Apollinaire? I mention only a few names because I believe that there is little doubt in anyone's mind that this is one of the cardinal directions that has consistently been taken by poets and poetry from the beginning of the nineteenth century to our own time. And I might even add that the real modernity of poetry lies in its having won its autonomy. Poetry has ceased to be the handmaiden of religion or philosophy; like science, it explores the universe on its own. And in this respect, also, there is a great similarity between certain poets and the scientists: they too have not hesitated to engage in dangerous experiments, at the risk of their lives or their spiritual wholeness, in order to explore forbidden zones. Poetry is a form of knowledge, of experimental knowledge.

Modern poetry claims to be a vision, that is to say, a knowledge of hidden, invisible realities. It is true that the poets of all times and all places have said as much. But Homer, Virgil, or Dante insist that their poetry has to do with a revelation that comes from outside themselves: a god or a demon speaks through their mouths. Even Góngora pretends to believe in this supernatural power: "*Cuántas me dictó versas dulce Musa.*"* The modern poet declares that he is speaking in his own name: he extracts his visions from within himself. The disturbing disappearance of divine powers has coincided with the appearance of drugs as the bestowers of the gift of poetic vision. The familiar demon, the muse, or the divine spirit have been supplanted by laudanum, opium, hashish, and, more recently, Mexican drugs: peyote (mescaline) and hallucinogenic mushrooms. Many drugs were known and used in the ancient world to further contemplation, revelation, and ecstasy. The original name of the Mexican sacred mushroom was *teononácatl*, which means "the flesh of of God, the divine mushroom." American Indians and many African and Eastern peoples still use drugs for religious purposes. I myself had the opportunity to try a variety of hashish called bhang during a religious festival in India; all those present, even the children, ate or drank it. But the difference is that, for believers, these practices constitute a rite; for a number of modern poets, they are an experiment.

Baudelaire is one of the first to have pondered "in a philosophic spirit," as he put it, the spiritual phenomena engendered by the use of drugs. It is quite true that many of his observations are borrowed from Thomas De Quincey and that Coleridge before him had confessed that the composition of one of his most celebrated poems stemmed from a vision produced by laudanum, during which "all the images rose up as things, with a parallel production of the correspondent expressions, without any sensation or consciousness of effort." But neither De Quincey nor Coleridge endeavored to extract an aesthetic and a philosophy from his experience. Baudelaire, on the other hand, stated that certain drugs intensify our sensations to such a degree and combine them in such a way that that they enable us to see life whole. Drugs provoke

---

* "How many verses the sweet Muse dictated to me."

the vision of the universal correspondence of all things, arouse the powers of analogy, set objects in motion, make the world a vast poem shaped by rhymes and rhythms. Drugs snatch us out of everyday reality, blur our perception, alter our sensations, and, in a word, put the entire universe in a state of suspension. This break with the outside world is only a preliminary phase; with the same implacable gentleness, drugs take us to the very heart of another reality: the world has not changed, but it is now seen to be governed by a secret harmony. Baudelaire's vision is a poet's vision. Hashish did not reveal to him the philosophy of universal correspondence or that of language as a living organism and a sort of archetype of reality: drugs served him as a way of reaching deeper levels within himself. Like other really crucial experiences, drugs turn everyday reality topsy-turvy and force us to contemplate our inner selves. They do not open the doors of another world nor do they free our fantasy: rather, they open the doors of *our world* and bring us face to face with *our phantoms*.

The temptation of drugs, Baudelaire said, is a sign of our love for the infinite. Drugs take us back to the center of the universe, the point of intersection of all the world's paths, and the place where all contradictions are reconciled. Man returns, so to speak, to his original state of innocence. Time stands still, though paradoxically it continues to flow, like a fountain whose waters continually circulate, so that ascent and fall become fused in a single movement. Space becomes a system of flashing signals, and the four cardinal points of the compass submit to our rule. All this is achieved by means of a chemical communion. A pharmaceutical compound, the poet pointed out, can open the gates of paradise to us. This idea shocks or irritates many people. It seems dangerous and antisocial: the use of drugs diverts man from his productive activities, it weakens his will, and makes him a parasite. Could we not say the same thing of mysticism and of all meditation in general? The condemnation of drugs on the grounds of their uselessness might be extended (and is in fact being extended) to mysticism, love, and art. All these activities are antisocial; since it is impossible to do away with them altogether, society continually attempts to limit them. Religious believers—and those who are upholders of conventional morality—are repelled by the idea of drugs as the key to divine vision, or at least to a certain spiritual peace. Those who react in this way may have failed to realize that drugs are not a substitute for the old supernatural powers. The disappearance of the idea of God in the modern world is not due to the appearance of drugs (for drugs have after all been known and used for thousands of years). We might, in fact, say the exact opposite: the use of drugs betrays the fact that man is not a *natural* being; he experiences not only thirst, hunger, dreams, and sexual pleasure, but also a nostalgia for the infinite. The supernatural—to use a convenient but inaccurate tenn—is part of his nature. Everything he does, including his simplest physical acts, is tinged with a yearning for the absolute. Imagination—the power to produce images and the temptation to incarnate these images—is part of his nature. Imagination: a faculty of our nature to change itself.

Henri Michaux

Henri Michaux has published three books in recent years dealing with his experience with mescaline.* He has also confronted us with a disturbing series of sketches—most of them in black and white, and a few in color—executed shortly after each of his experiences. His prose, his poems, and his sketches are intimately related, for each medium of expression reinforces and illuminates the others. The sketches are not simply illustrations of the texts. Michaux's painting has never been a mere adjunct to his poetry: the two are at once autonomous and complementary worlds. In the case of the "mescaline experience," lines and words form a whole almost impossible to break down into its component elements. Forms, ideas, and sensations intertwine as though they were a single, dizzyingly proliferating entity. In a certain sense the sketches, far from being *illustrations* of the written word, are a sort of *commentary*. The rhythm and the movement of the lines are mindful of a kind of curious musical notation, except that we are confronted not with a method of recording sounds but with vortexes, gashes, interweavings of being. Incisions in the bark

---

* *Misérable miracle* (1956); *L'infini turbulent* (1957); and *Paix dans les brisements* (1959). In *Les lettres nouvelles* (num. 35), there appeared a brief text of Michaux's on hallucinogenic mushrooms: "La Psilocybine (Expérience et autocritique)." See on this latter subject the book by Roger Heim and Gordon Wasson, *Les champignona hallucinogènes du Mexique* (1958).

of time, halfway between the ideograph and the magical sign, characters and forms "more palpable than legible," these sketches are a criticism of poetic and pictorial writing, that is to say, a step beyond the sign and the image, something transcending words and lines.

Painting and poetry are languages that Michaux has used to try to express something that is truly inexpressible. A poet first, he began to paint when he realized that this new medium might enable him to say what he had found it impossible to say in his poetry. But is it a question of expression? Perhaps Michaux has never tried to express anything. All his efforts have been directed at reaching that zone, by definition indescribable and incommunicable, in which meanings disappear. A center at once completely empty and completely full, a total vacuum and a total plenitude. The sign and the signified—the distance between the object and the conscience that contemplates it—melt away in the face of the overwhelming presence, the only thing that really exists. Michaux's *œuvre*—his poems, his real and imaginary travels, his painting—is an expedition winding its way toward some of our infinities—the most secret, the most fearful, and at times the most derisive ones—in a never-ending search for the *other* infinite.

Michaux travels via his languages: lines, words, colors, silences, rhythms. And he does not hesitate to break the back of a word, the way a horseman does not hesitate to wind his mount. In order to arrive: where? At that nowhere that is here, there, and everywhere. Language as a vehicle, but also language as a knife and a miner's lamp. Language as cautery and as bandage, language as fog and a siren amid the fog. A pick striking rock and a spark in the blackness. Words once again become tools, prolongations of the hand, of the eye, of thought. A nonartistic language. Slashing, cutting words, reduced to their most immediate and most forthright function: clearing a path. Their utility is paradoxical, however, since they are not employed to foster communication, but rather pressed into the service of the incommunicable. The extraordinary tension of Michaux's language stems from the fact that it is an undoubtedly effective tool, but its sole use is to bare something that is completely ineffective by its very nature: the state of nonknowledge that is beyond knowledge, the thought that no longer thinks because it has been united with itself, total transparency, a motionless whirlwind.

Misérable miracle opens with this phrase: "This is an exploration. Through the word, the sign, the sketch. Mescaline is what is explored." When I had read the last page, I asked myself whether the result of the experiment had not been precisely the opposite: the poet Michaux explored by mescaline. An exploration or an encounter? The latter, most probably. A physical encounter with the drug, with the earthquake, with the cataclysm of being, shaken to its very foundations by its inner enemy—an enemy that is one with our own intimate being, an enemy that is indistinguishable and inseparable from ourselves. An encounter with mescaline: an encounter with our own selves, with the known-unknown. The double that wears our own face as its mask. The face that is gradually obliterated and transformed into an immense mocking grimace. The devil. The clown. This thing that I am not. This thing that I am. A martyrisible apparition. And when my own face reappears, there is nobody there. I too have left myself. Space, space, pure vibration. A great gift of the gods, mescaline is a window through which we look out upon endless distances where nothing ever meets our eye but our own gaze. There is no *I*: there is space, vibration, perpetual animation. Battles, terrors, elation, panic, delight: is it Michaux or mescaline? It was all already there in Michaux, in his previous books. Mescaline was a *confirmation*. Mescaline: a testimony. The poet saw his inner space in outer space. The shift from the inside to the outside—an outside that is interiority itself, the heart of reality. A horrible, ineffable spectacle. Michaux can say: I left my life behind to catch a glimpse of life.

It all begins with a vibration. An imperceptible movement that accelerates minute by minute. Wind, a long screeching whistle, a lashing hurricane, a torrent of faces, forms, lines. Everything falling, rushing forward, ascending, disappearing, reappearing. A dizzying evaporation and condensation. Bubbles, more bubbles, pebbles, little stones. Rocky cliffs of gas. Lines that cross, rivers meeting, endless bifurcations, meanders, deltas, deserts that walk, deserts that fly. Disintegrations, agglutinations, fragmentations, reconstitutions. Shattered words, the copulation of syllables, the fornication of meanings. Destruction of language. Mescaline reigns through silence—and it screams, screams without a mouth, and we fall into its silence! A return to vibrations, a plunge into undulations. Repetitions: mescaline is an "infinity-machine." Heterogeneity, a continuous eruption of fragments, particles, pieces. Furious series. Nothing is fixed. Avalanches, the kingdom of uncountable numbers, accursed proliferation. Gangrenous space, cancerous time. Is there no center? Battered by the gale of mescaline, sucked up by the abstract whirlwind, the modern Westerner finds absolutely nothing to hold on to. He has forgotten the names, God is no longer called *God*. The Aztec or the Tarahumara had only to pronounce the name, and immediately the presence would descend, in all its infinite manifestations. Unity and plurality for the ancients. For us who lack gods: Pullulation and Time. We have lost the names. All we have left is "causes and effects, antecedents and consequences." Space teeming with trivialities. Heterogeneity is repetition, an amorphous mass. Miserable miracle.

Michaux's first encounter with mescaline ends with the discovery of an "infinity-machine." The endless production of colors, rhythms, and forms turns out in the end to be an awesome, absurd flood of cheap trinkets. We are millionaires with vast hoards of fairgrounds junk. The second series of experiments (*L'infini turbulent*) provoked unexpected reactions and visions. Subject to continuous physiological discharges and a pitiless psychic tension. Being split apart. The exploration of mescaline, like a great fire or an earthquake, was devastating; all that remained intact was the essential, that which, being infinitely weak, is infinitely strong. What name can we give this faculty? Is it in fact a faculty, a power, or is it an absence of power, the total helplessness of man? I am inclined to believe it is the latter. This helplessness is our strength. At the last moment, when there is nothing left in us—when self is lost, when identity is lost—a fusion takes place, a fusion with something alien to us that nonetheless is ours, the only thing that is truly ours. The empty pit, the hole that we are fills to overflowing, and becomes a wellspring once again. When the drought is most severe, water gushes forth. Perhaps there is a point where the being of man and the being of the universe meet. Apart from this, nothing positive: a hole, an abyss, a turbulent infinite. A forsakenness, alienation, but not insanity. Madmen are imprisoned within their madness, which is an ontological error, so to speak: taking the part for the whole. Equidistant from sanity and insanity, the vision Michaux describes is total: contemplation of the demoniacal and the divine—there is no way around these words—as an indivisible reality, as the ultimate reality. Of man or of the universe? I do not know. Perhaps of the man-universe. Man penetrated, conquered by the universe.

The demoniacal stage of the experiment was above all the revelation of a transhuman eroticism—and therefore infinitely perverted. A psychic rape, an insidious opening and extending and exhibiting of the most secret parts of being. Not at all sexual. An infinitely sensual universe, from which the human body and the human face had disappeared. Not the "triumph of matter" or that of the flesh, but the vision of the reverse side of the spirit. An abstract lasciviousness: "Dissolution—an apt word that I understood instantly. Delight in deliquescence." Temptation, in the literal sense of the word, as all the mystics (Christian, Buddhist, Arab) have reported. I nonetheless confess that I do not understand this passage at all. Perhaps the cause of Michaux's sense of repulsion was not so much the contact with Eros as the vision of the confusion of the cosmos, that is to say, the revelation of pure chaos. The visible entrails, the reverse side of presence, chaos is the primordial stuff, the original disorder, and also the universal womb. I felt a similar sensation, though a much less intense one, in the great summer of India, during my first visit in 1952. Once I had fallen into that panting maw, the universe seemed to me to be an immense, multiple fornication. I suddenly had a glimpse of the meaning of the architecture of Konarak and erotic asceticism. The vision of chaos is a sort of ritual bath, a regeneration through immersion in the original fountain, a return to the "life before." Primitive tribes, the early Greeks, the Chinese, Taoists, and other peoples have had no fear of this awesome contact. The Western attitude is unwholesome. It is moral. Morality, the great isolator, the great separator, divides man in half. To return to the unity of the vision is to reconcile body, soul, and the world. At the end of the experiment, Michaux recalls a fragment of a Tantric poem:

> Inaccessible to impregnations,
> Enjoying all joys,
> Touching everything like the wind,
> Everything penetrating it like ether,
> The ever-pure yogi

Bathes in the ever-flowing river.
He enjoys all joys and nothing defiles him.

The divine vision—inseparable from the demoniacal vision, since both are revelations of *unity*—began with "the appearance of the gods." Thousands, hundreds of thousands, one after the other, in an endless file, an infinity of august countenances, a horizon of beneficent presences. Amazement and gratitude. But before that: surges of whiteness. Whiteness everywhere, sonorous, resplendent. And light, seas of light. Afterward, the divine images disappeared though the tranquil, delightful cascade of being did not cease. Admiration: "I cling to the divine perfection of the continuation of Being through time, a continuation that is so beautiful—so beautiful that I lose consciousness—so beautiful that, as the Mahabharata says, the gods themselves grow jealous and come to admire it." Trust, faith (in what? simply faith), the sensation of being carried along by perfection that flows ceaselessly (and yet does not flow), ever identical with itself. An instant is born, ascends, opens out, disappears, just as another instant is born and ascends. One felicity after another. An inexpressible feeling of abandon and security. The vision of the gods is followed by nonvision: we are at the very heart of time. This journey is a return: a letting go, an unlearning, a traveling homeward to birth. On reading these pages of Michaux, I remembered a pre-Columbian object that the painter Paalen showed me some years ago: a block of quartz with the image of the old and wrinkled god Tlaloc engraved on it. He went over to a window and held it up to the light:

Touched by light
The quartz is suddenly a cascade.
The infant god floats on the waters.

Nonvision: outside of actuality, history, purposes, calculations, hate, love, "beyond resolution and want of resolution, *beyond preferences*," the poet journeys back to a perpetual birth and listens to "the endless poem, without rhymes, without music, without words, that the Universe ceaselessly recites." The experience is participation in an infinite that is measure and rhythm. The words *water, music, light, great open space,* echoing and re-echoing, inevitably come to our lips. The self disappears, but no other self appears to occupy the empty space it has left. No god but rather the divine. No faith but rather the primordial feeling that sustains all faith, all hope. No face but rather faceless being, the being that is all faces. Peace in the crater of the volcano, the reconciliation of man—what remains of man—with total presence.

On embarking on his experiment, Michaux wrote: "I propose to explore the mediocre human condition." The second part of this sentence—a sentence which applies, I might add, to Michaux's entire *œuvre* and to that of any great artist—turned out to be strikingly false. The exploration showed that man is not a mediocre creature. A part of oneself—a part walled in, obscured from the very beginning of the beginning—is open to the infinite. The so-called human condition is a point of intersection with other forces. Perhaps our condition is not merely human.

Grace, Asceticism, Merits *

Confronted by experiences such as those described by Michaux, we may again ask the question: is pharmacy a substitute for grace, is poetic vision a biochemical reaction? Coleridge attributed the composition of his extraordinary "Kubla Khan" to laudanum; Michaux believes that the combination of a state of physiological debility—a slight fever, tonsillitis—and an overdose is enough to unleash the torrent. There is unquestionably a relationship between physiological and psychic states. Fasting, breathing exercises, flagellation, prolonged immobility, solitary confinement in cells or caverns, exposure to the elements atop columns or mountains, songs, dances, perfumes, the repetition of a single word for hours at a time are practices that disturb our physical functions and provoke visions. What we call *mind* would appear to be a product of chemical and biological processes; and what we call *matter* has also

---

* Everything I have said above and am about to say in the following pages refers exclusively to hallucinogenic substances which have been recognized as being generally nonaddictive physiologically.

turned out to be energy, time, a hole, a fall, in short, something that is no longer "matter." Though the age-old quarrel between materialism and spiritualism scarcely concerns me, I find the fragility of our moral conceptions in the face of the onslaught of drugs disturbing. Among Michaux's many observations, there is one that has long preyed on my mind: the demoniacal vision came *after* the divine vision. This is a dualistic, moral conception, as I have suggested above: mescaline itself is singularly contemptuous of the ideas of good and evil. Or rather it is both contemptuous and generous, for it offers revelation without regard to the "merits" of the person who experiences it. Michaux speaks several times of an "undeserved infinite." It is worth our while to ponder this phrase that has echoed and re-echoed throughout man's history. Many mystics and visionaries have said precisely the same thing.

Radical physiological changes do not produce visions automatically; nor are all visions the same. To choose a convenient example, we need only compare the images that sacred Mexican mushrooms provoked in Wasson with those of the professors and students subjected to a similar experiment by Dr. Heim.* The role played by the individual psyche is crucial. Baudelaire had noted earlier, as had De Quincey before him, that the dreams induced by opium in a poet and in a butcher were quite different. Now, the most disturbing effect of drugs is their power in the sphere of morality: a murderer may have angelic visions, the upright man infernal dreams. The visions depend on a certain psychic sensibility that varies from individual to individual, independently of merit or personal conduct. Drugs are nihilistic: they undermine all values and radically overturn all our ideas about good and evil, what is just and what is unjust, what is permitted and what is forbidden. Their action is a mockery of our morality based on reward and punishment. I am both delighted and terrified by the realization that drugs introduce another brand of justice, based on chance or on circumstances that we are unable to determine. They carelessly offer anyone and everyone what has always been looked upon as the recompense of saints, wise men, and the just—the *summum bonum* that man can attain here on this earth: a vision, a glimpse of per-

---

* See Heim and Wasson, *Lea champignons hallucinogènes du Mexique.*

fect harmony. And, at the same time that they grant spiritual peace to the undeserving, they reward the innocent with the sufferings of Hell. If pharmacy has replaced God, we cannot help but feel that it is a perverse chemistry.

We might cease to be confused if, instead of thinking of a god that acts like a drug, we thought of a drug that acts like a god. What I mean is: if we use the notions of grace and freedom instead of those of chance and fatality. Drugs open the doors of "another world" to us. If this expression means anything at all, it means that we actually enter a kingdom ruled by different laws than those governing our world. Neither physical nor moral laws are the same in this kingdom. Isn't this precisely what happens in the mystical experience? All mystical texts stress the paradoxical nature of the vision. The total change in logical principles (*here* is *there, today* is *yesterday* or *tomorrow, movement* is *immobility*, etc.) is paralleled by a no less profound overturning of the customary moral laws: sinners are saved; those who are ignorant are the true wise men; innocence is not to be found among virgins but in bordellos; "the good thief" ascends with Christ to Paradise; the village idiot confounds the arrogant theologian; Che the highwayman is purer than the virtuous Confucius; Krishna incites Arjuna to murder . . . The Spanish theater, nourished by the Catholic doctrines of free will and grace, offers constant examples of this surprising dialectic in which evil is suddenly transformed into good, perdition into salvation, and the Fall into Assumption. How can these paradoxes be explained?

The mystical experience culminates in the vision of being or of nothingness, but in either case, whether it is in the end a plenitude or an emptiness, it begins as a criticism of this world and a negation of its values. The *other* reality requires the destruction of *this* reality. The vision is sustained not only by intellectual criticism but by a *bodily discipline* that rules one's entire being: mysticism of any sort implies an asceticism. Whatever his religion, the ascetic believes that there is a relation between the reality of the body and the reality of the psyche. The Christian humiliates his body, the yogi masters his; both believe implicitly in the connection between body and spirit. This is not surprising: ascetic practices are thousands of years old and antedate the appearance of the idea of the soul as an entity separate from the body. Like so many other techniques that we have inherited from prehistory, asceticism anticipates contemporary science. The analogy with drugs is striking: the action of the latter would be impossible if there were not in fact an intimate relation between physiological and psychological functions.

Ascetic practices and the use of hallucinogenic substances were undoubtedly part of the same ritual, as can be seen in the hymns of the Rig-Veda in praise of soma and the rites of the early Mexicans, still alive today among the Huichols and the Tarahumaras. There is a great deal of anthropological information on the subject. The drug user is admittedly unlike the ascetic in that he does not subject himself to any discipline. The absence of any ritual or discipline explains the destructive effects of drugs among their modern users. Though this is a crucial difference, it is not applicable to those who explore the universe of drugs with the aim of acquiring knowledge about it: scientists, poets. The similarity between drugs and asceticism extends to the sphere of morals and thought. The ascetic scorns worldly conventions, he takes no stock whatsoever in the ideas of progress and profit, he considers material gains to be losses, he looks upon the normality of the ordinary man as a real spiritual anomaly; in short, he wants nothing to do with either the duties or the pleasures of this world. The person who takes a drug implicitly doubts the solidity of reality—he is not sure that it is what it appears to be and what our instruments define it as being, or he suspects that another reality exists. Drugs and asceticism are alike in that both are a criticism and a negation of the world.

With this in mind, we may find it less difficult to understand the "injustice" of drugs. Aren't the infernal visions that Michaux describes the equivalent of the trials and temptations that all ascetics of all religions have undergone? If the drug brings on the appearance of horrifying images, might it not be because it is a mirror that reflects not what we pretend to be for others, but what we really are? The most immediate effect of the drug is to free us of the weight of external reality. It is therefore impossible to judge its action by the weights and measures of the everyday world. The drug does not bring us face to face with another world: Michaux's visions do not contradict his poems, they confirm them. Except that the "true self" that drugs confront us with—like the one we glimpse through poetry and eroticism—is a stranger, and its appearance is like the resurrection of someone whom we have long since buried. The person dead and buried is alive and his return terrifies us. Drugs transport us to an outside that is an inside: we inhabit a self that has no identity and no name, we live in a *there* that is a *here*, within something that we are and are not. Our acts have another consistency. another logic, and another gravity. The "merits" and the "faults" are different, and the balance in which they are weighed is different. A change of sign: more is less, cold is hot, exaltation is beatitude, rest and movement are the same. Moral values do not escape this metamorphosis. The notions of virtue, goodness, rectitude, and other similar concepts acquire a different and even a contrary meaning from the one they have in the pitiless world of human relations. The words *merit, reward, advantage, honor, profit, interest*, and others like them are mortally wounded; the blood drains from them and they literally become volatilized. A loss of gravity: true virtues weigh little and go by the name of *abandon, indifference, trust, surrender, nakedness*. What counts is not one's value but one's valor: the courage to explore the unknown. Being forsaken, forsaking. Lightness: disinterestedness, letting go. Once freed from "having to be," man may contemplate his true being. In this constellation, the central word is perhaps *innocence*: the "pureness of heart" of the early Christians, the "piece of unpolished wood" of the Taoists. A disappearance of one's ego and one's name, not a loss of being. The appearance of another reality, the reappearance of being. A moral lesson: the experience brings us face to face with the mystery that each of us is and reveals the vanity of our judgments. The world of judges is the world of injustice. Yes, a murderer may have angelic dreams. Each of us has the infinite he deserves. But this merit cannot be weighed with our scales.

Paradises

In Aldous Huxley's essays on mescaline, he emphasizes that one's personal visions almost always correspond to certain archetypes. The world described by Wasson in his book on Mexican hallucinogenic mushrooms immediately evokes the images of myths, poems, and paintings: great river landscapes, trees, thick green and russet foliage, amber-colored earth, all bathed in an otherworldly light. The sensation of movement—the great rivers, the wind, the earth's heartbeat-fuses with that of immobility and repose. Sometimes a woman appears on the bank of the sparkling river, lost in thought—an apparition reminiscent of early Greek sculpture and certain grave steles. A dawning age, a world of paradisiac meanings: how can we fail to be reminded of the images of Genesis, or Arab tales, of the myths of the South Pacific or Central Asia, of the Teotihuacán paradise of Tlaloc? But there is also another sort of vision: deserts, rocks, thirst, panting, the dagger-eye of the sun: the landscape of damnation, the "wasteland" of the Grail legend. Transparent infernos, a geometry of crystals; circular hells; hells of garish, clashing colors, a pullulation of forms and monsters, temptations of Saint Anthony, Goya's Sabbaths, Hindu copulations, Munch's frozen scream, Polynesian masks . . . Though the images are innumerable, all of them—whether blinding light or mineral blackness, solitude or promiscuity—reveal a universe with no way out. Weight, oppression, asphyxia: hells. We are trapped within ourselves; there is no way out; we cannot cease to be what we are; we cannot change. Hell: *petrification*. The image of heaven is a vision of freedom: *levitation, dissolution of the self.* Light versus stone.

The images of paradise can be reduced, Huxley tells us, to certain elements common to the "mescaline experience" and universal myth: earth and water, fertility, verdure. The idea of abundance (as opposed to the world of toil); the idea of an enchanted garden: "everything is palpable" and birds, beasts, and plants speak the same language. In the center: the couple. Huxley points out that the light in this paradise has a very special quality; it is a light that has no visible source, or to use an old expression, it is an *uncreated* light. And also a creative light (the landscape is born and grows in the rain of light) and a sheltering one (the garden, the visible, nestles within its invisible bosom). I would also mention another no less meaningful presence: water, the image of the return to the primeval age, the symbol of the woman and her powers. Water: calm. fertility, self-knowledge, but also loss, a fall into treacherous transparency. In a number of passages, Baudelaire ponders this vision: "Fugitive waters, frolicking waters, harmonious waterfalls, the immense azure sea, rocking itself, singing, falling asleep . . . The contemplation of this limpid abyss is perilous for a spirit enamored of space and crystal . . ." Water: Diana at her bath, the element that brings death to Actaeon and Siegfried.

Light is fixed, immaterial, central. At once fire and ice, it is the symbol of both objectivity and eternity. It is heaven's gaze itself. Clear and serene, it traces outlines, delimits, distributes space into symmetrical areas. It is justice, but it is also the Idea, the archetype engraved upon a cloudless sky. The sixteenth-century poet Herrera calls his beloved light his Idea. Light: the essence, the realm of the intemporal. Water is diffuse, elusive, formless. It evokes time, carnal love; it is the tide itself—death and resurrection—and the gateway to the elemental world. Everything is reflected in water, everything founders in it, everything is reborn in it. It is change, the ebb and flow of the universe. Light separates, water unites. Paradise would appear to be ruled by two warring sisters. In the center, the precious stone. Huxley reminds us that the gates of paradise are studded with diamonds, rubies, emeralds. As light passes through it, the humid landscape of the first day becomes an immense jewel: a golden sun, a silver moon, trees of jade. Light makes water a precious stone. It turns time into a mineral, makes it eternal. It congeals it into an impartial, uniform splendor and thus kills the life in it: it freezes its pulse. At the same time, light transmutes stone. Thanks to light, the opaque stone—a symbol of gravity: a heavy fallen weight—takes on the transparency and dancing swiftness of water. The stone sparkles, twinkles, quivers, like a drop of water or blood: it is alive. A moment later, mesmerized by the celestial flash of lightning, it becomes motionless: it is light now, time arrested, a fixed gaze.

The precious stone is an instant of equilibrium between water and light. Left to itself, in its natural state, it is opacity, inertia, brute existence. The dreamless slumber of stone. But the moment it becomes luminous and translucid, its moral nature changes. Its limpidity is as treacherously deceiving as that of water. The opal is an unlucky stone; there are emeralds that bring health; there are stones with a curse on them. This ambiguity should not surprise us. Life per se is neither good nor bad: it is sheer vitality, an appetite for being. In life at the most elementary level, we discover the *same unity* as in spiritual meditation. Diana and her bow,

Coatlicue and her skulls, goddesses covered with blood, are life itself, the perpetual rebirth and death of the seasons, time unfolding and turning back upon itself. The paradise of the Douanier Rousseau is a magic jungle, inhabited by wild beasts and ruled by a sorceress. The intruder is the *armed* man, who divides and separates: morality destroying the magic pact between nature and its creatures. The precious stone shares this indifference of life. A nexus of contrary meanings, it oscillates between water and light.

The Metamorphoses of Stone

André Pieyre de Mandiargues is one of the truly original writers to have appeared in France since World War II. His work is an apt, though unintentional, illustration of what we might call "the metamorphoses of stone." What he describes is a "Way of Perfection," fraught with arduous trials and sacrifices, which brute matter must follow if it is to become a precious stone, a solar stone. In one of Mandiargues's books, *Feu de braise*, there are three stories that describe the nature of stone, by turns baleful and beneficent. In the first story ("Les pierreuses"), a schoolteacher taking a walk on the outskirts of the city picks up a stone of the sort that geologists call geodes (rocks or stones, usually of a crystallized substance, with a hollow in the center). Impelled by curiosity—Pandora and her box reappear in many of this author's texts—the teacher opens the stone as though it were an oyster shell, and discovers three minuscule girls inside. The eldest tells him, in vulgar Latin, that she and her two sisters emerged naked from the womb of the Great Mother and will return to it naked. They have been cast into the geode by a "black sun." Their being set free presages their death and that of their liberator, because, she adds, "the emanations of stone are deadly." There would be no point in pondering the meaning of each individual element of this fantasy: all the details fit the conception of stone as a crystallization of water and its awesome powers.

In "Le diamant," Sara, the daughter of a Jewish jeweler, faints after having long contemplated a perfect diamond, an "ice palace." When she comes to her senses again, she finds herself inside the stone. The coldness of the jewel threatens to freeze her instantly, but the morning sun pours through the window and lights on the diamond, transforming it into a fiery furnace. "Like a fish in water," Sara has no difficulty withstanding the great heat. A moment later, she gives herself to a ruddy-faced man with a leonine head. Strange nuptials uniting a Jewish virgin and a solar deity: the fecundation of water by light. The beam of sunlight moves away, it turns freezing cold inside the diamond once again, the young girl loses consciousness a second time, and on coming to her senses realizes that she has left the nuptial stone "as mysteriously, as naturally as she had entered it." Sara examines the diamond and notices that a tiny reddish flaw mars its perfection, the only trace of her marvelous encounter. A material "defect" that is also a mystic stigma.

In "Le diamant," the metamorphosis is the opposite of that in "Les pierreuses." The "ice palace" is opened like the geode; the teacher finds three naked girls inside the stone and Sara too is naked inside the diamond. Water—a naked woman—inhabits stone like an unpredictable substance that may impart either life or death. The geode is a mineral womb; when a ray of light falls upon it, it becomes a tomb; the diamond, on being subjected to a similar influence, is turned into an alchemical furnace. Fire and water symbolize transmutation. (There is a Nahuatl expression that has the same meaning: "burning water.") Sara's metamorphoses are a parallel of the transformations of the diamond, a stone for sale that becomes a jewel representing mystic union. In "Les pierreuses," the schoolteacher's idle curiosity is rewarded only by the revelation of death; in "Le diamant," trust in the unknown—a spirit of true disinterestedness—leads to union with the solar principle. The schoolteacher is a man of reason and a skeptic who is not at all surprised to discover three lovely little creatures inside the geode. (The one thought that crosses his mind is that his grasp of vulgar Latin is faulty.) Sara "trusts in the power of the absurd," calmly accepts the mystery, and allows herself to be guided by the unexpected. There is nothing at all arbitrary about the professor's death or Sara's marvelous fecundation. But it is a matter of spiritual rather than logical consistency.

"L'enfantillage" deals with the experience we might call "the capital vision," to use Mandiargues's own language. A man goes to bed with a strange woman. While one part of himself anticipates the moment of physical discharge, the other part of himself regresses to his earliest childhood memory: a cart full of Italian peasants plunging over a cliff and his nursemaid's gnarled hand covering his eyes. This frightful image fuses with his rapt contemplation of a gilded knob of the bedstead, gleaming in the light of the noonday sun in the warm shadow. The wanderings of his mind become a delirium: held by the hand by the old woman, he draws closer and closer to the abyss, until the gilded sphere and the old woman's face become one. For a truly glorious instant, the double vision is transformed into a single literally blinding insight: "Is this finally love? Father Sun . . ." Matter has pursued the path of initiation to its end. and now gleams like a naked star. The brass knob is a central sun. "Purity regained," Mandiargues says of this revelation. Is it death or life? The stone, by turns opacity and transparency, water and light, finally becomes incandescent, a state of fusion, the disappearance of contraries.

In the foreword to a book published shortly after World War II,[*] Mandiargues says that "the hour of total emptiness is also the hour of idiocy, the two ultimate faces of what is sometimes called mysticism . . ." This phrase is proof that those poets who yield to delirium with the greatest abandon are also the poets who are most lucid. The school-teacher of "Les pierreuses" is doomed because his knowledge is nothing but a series of "known facts;" Sara is saved because she has no "fund of knowledge," only a trust in life. In both cases the vision is dualist. The "capital vision" evokes that instant in which the blood of the victim spurts from his body with amazing energy and abundance, a symbol of both life and death. "L'enfantillage" is not the vision of the triumph of life over intellect, nor of the coexistence of contradictory forces, but that of their mutual destruction in the fire of a blinding truth. The hour, the instant, of he emptying out of self: the reconquest of nonknowledge.

The Symposium and the Hermit

My commentaries on the experiences of Huxley and Michaux were written and published many years before the use of hallucinogenic drugs had become a popular subject and the occasion of public debate. A rite

[*] *Le musée noir* (1946)

or a mystery from antiquity till only yesterday, the use of drugs is now a more or less widespread practice and a subject of discussion in the press and on television and radio. Speaking of certain things only at certain moments was a sign of wisdom as well as politeness among the ancients: words had weight, they were something real. By diminishing the value of silence, publicity has also diminished that of language. The two are inseparable: knowing how to speak has always meant knowing how to keep silent, knowing that there are times when one should say nothing. In the case of drugs, everybody talks about them, but there are few people who listen to those who really have something to say: scientists and poets. The number of young people who have taken LSD and other drugs has admittedly reached such proportions, especially in the United States, that the public's excitement and the authorities' alarm are readily understandable. It is equally obvious that legal measures and police enforcement are neither a solution nor a step toward understanding the problem. On the contrary, they aggravate it and make it an even more inflammatory issue.

We do not have to be sociologists or anthropologists to realize that drug addiction is merely one of the results of the changes industrial society has undergone since World War II. Nor is it surprising that this development is most serious and most widespread in the country where these changes have been greatest: the United States. It would be absurd to maintain that drugs have the power to subvert and undermine American society: youngsters have not ceased to believe in "the American way of life" because they take drugs—they take drugs because they have ceased to believe in these ideas and are fumblingly searching for new ones. The attitude of young people is intelligible only within the general context of rebellion against the society of abundance and its moral and political presuppositions. The increasingly widespread use of drugs is yet another indication of a change in contemporary sensibilities. This change may well be more profound than the material transformations and the ideological struggles of the first half of the century.

It has not been proved that hallucinogenic substances are more harmful than alcohol. Although the reaction in both cases depends on the individual's constitution, it is a well-known fact that alcohol brings our aggressive tendencies to the fore, whereas hallucinogenic substances foster introversion. Sahagún reports that at the end of the sacred-mushroom ceremony a number of the celebrants went off alone and were silent for a long time; others talked to themselves or laughed and wept in a corner. Travelers and anthropologists who have lived with the Huichol Indians confirm Sahagún's observation: peyote may lead in rare instances to suicide, but never to murder. Alcohol draws us out: hallucinogens make us retreat within ourselves. Many psychiatrists share Huxley's belief: these substances are less dangerous than alcohol. We need not necessarily agree entirely with this opinion—though it seems to me that it is not very far from the truth—and still grant that the reasons that the authorities prohibit these substances have more to do with public morality than with public health. They are a threat to the ideas of enterprise, usefulness, progress, work, and other notions that justify our daily comings and goings.

Alcoholism is an infraction of social rules; everyone tolerates this breaking of the rules because it is a violation that confirms them. Prostitution is a similar case: neither the drunk nor the whore and her client question the rules that they break. Their acts are a disturbance of law and order, a departure from the rules of Society, not a criticism of them. The recourse to hallucinogens implies a negation of social values, and it is an attempt—though doubtless an illusory one—to escape from this world and drop out from Society. We are now in a position to understand the real reason for the condemnation of hallucinogens and why their use is punished: the authorities do not behave as though they were trying to stamp out a harmful practice or a vice, but as though they were attempting to stamp out dissidence. Since this is a form of dissidence that is becoming more widespread, the prohibition takes on the proportions of a campaign against a spiritual contagion, against an *opinion*. What the authorities are displaying is *ideological* zeal: they are punishing a heresy, not a crime. They are thus taking the same attitude as that taken in other centuries toward leprosy and insanity, which were not regarded as diseases but as incarnations of evil. There is even the same superstitious, ambivalent awe involved: like the leper in the Middle Ages, the drug-taker is the victim of a sacred evil; like the utterances of a madman, his words are revelations of another world. Those who hound the users of hallucinatory drugs are no less credulous than those who worship these drugs. There is little use reminding both sides that all the experiments and studies on the subject agree on at least one point: no known substance can make a genius of someone who is not one.

Alcohol and the hallucinogenic drugs are opposites. The drunk is loquacious and expansive; the drug-taker silent and withdrawn. When a person starts drinking, he first gets very sociable and wants everybody to be his pal, drapes his arm around people, and tells them his secrets. Then gradually he gets more and more boisterous, bursting into song or loud laughter, and finally the whole scene ends in angry shouts and racking sobs or some hostile act of violence. In each of these stages of inebriation, there is one common note: the desire to speak and interact with others, to address them as an audience or fight them as opponents. The solitary drinker has always been regarded as a peculiar creature, worse off than a cripple or an onanist. He is lacking something: another person, other people. In Mexico, conversation becomes more of a pleasure if people are drinking, and there is a saying that aptly describes our attitude toward alcohol: "letting the cup have its say." Heavy drinking in the Protestant countries is a way of leaping over the wall that separates one person from another. Protestant society is a community of introverts in which each person mutters a secret monologue under his breath: the morality of personal responsibility is an invisible gag. Alcohol loosens people's tongues, their senses, and their consciences. Drunkenness in other parts of the world is orgiastic. Among the Russians and the Poles it takes the form of an explosion, public confession, and a universal embrace: we are all one, and each one is all.

Alcoholism has been a social problem in two periods of modern history: in Europe during the first industrial revolution, and in the United States in the years immediately following World War I. Dickens and Zola have left us terrifying descriptions of the life of the working class in the large cities; among other terrible consequences the sudden transition from rural life to urban life was responsible for a traumatic rupture of traditional ties, and therefore a breakdown of communication. Zola's novels show that alcoholism was the result. In the United States. the phenomenon may have had different causes but its meaning was the same: it was a reaction to the alienation and the tensions and conflicts engendered when strangers, peoples belonging to different ethnic groups, with different traditions and languages, were forced to live together. In both cases—peasants from the countryside lost in the industrial suburbs and immigrants uprooted from a continent boiling over—alcoholism was a substitute for the old social bonds that had been broken or had disappeared, a desperate attempt to establish communication. Alcoholism is a search for a common language, or at least, it is a compensation for a language that has been lost. The use of drugs does not imply the overestimation of the value of language but of silence. Drunkenness exaggerates communication; drugs destroy it. Young people's preference for drugs reveals a change in the contemporary attitude toward language and communication.

The first to see the differences between drugs and wine was Baudelaire: "Wine exalts the will; hashish destroys it. Wine is a physical stimulant; hashish a suicide weapon. Wine mellows us and makes us sociable; hashish isolates us." Wine is social, drugs solitary; the one inflames the senses, the other rouses the imagination. It is unfortunate that Baudelaire did not venture to draw the conclusions that logically follow from his distinction. He might have added that it is not the merits or the defects of alcohol and drugs that are most important, but their relation to communication. Drinking stimulates communication at first, and then turns it into stammering and fuzzy-headedness. The toper drinks to drown his sorrows and ends up drowning himself. Drunkenness is contradictory: it overvalues communication and destroys it. It is a failure of communication: it first exaggerates it and then degrades it. A caricature of communication, it is a parody of two forms of intercourse that our civilization, from its very beginning, has venerated above all others: religious communion and philosophical dialogue. It is not mere happenstance that distilled alcohol has replaced grape wine in the modern world; this change parallels the gradual disfavor into which conversation, banquets, and religious rites have fallen.

Wine always occupied a central place in the rites, festivals, and ceremonies of pagan antiquity and the Christian West. Without wine, no meal is worth eating. When we say that "wine flowed abundantly" or that a banquet was *washed down* by choice vintages, we are referring to a magic quality of wine: a homologue of water, semen, and the "spiritual fluid" of the ancients, it is fertility, resurrection, and the animation of matter. A circulation of the vital essence, its effect on men is similar to that of irrigation in agriculture. It is the agent that transmits fellow feeling: it exalts us, binds us together, reunites us. It is brotherhood. Communication is also communion: in Christian worship, wine is the godhead incarnate. The eucharist is a mystery that is present in all our rituals, whether religious or erotic. The two most beautiful and meaningful images that tradition has passed down to us are the Platonic symposium and Christ's Last Supper. In both, wine is a cardinal symbol whereby our civilization defines its dual vocation; it is the archetype of communication—with others and with the Other.

Isolation and seclusion play a certain role in antiquity and Christianity, but the hermit is not a central figure in our mythology. The philosopher, the wise man, and the savior live among other men; they break the bread of truth together. Wisdom and illumination are common property, like language. To us the anchorite is a venerable figure, not a model or an example. The Oriental attitude is precisely the opposite. India has worshiped the hermit as the supreme figure since the very beginning. To Western peoples, the *summum bonum* is synonymous with communion; to Eastern peoples the key word is liberation. The superior life involves a double liberation: first from social bonds, whether those of caste, family, or community, and second from the chain of transmigration. This is the opposite of the etymological meaning of the word *religion*; it is not a reuniting, a reforging of bonds, but a loosening, a letting go, an escape. Both in Brahmanism and in Buddhism, the image of the saint and the wise man shown us in iconography, art, and poetry is the figure of the hermit in his cave or beneath a tree. Nothing could be further from the banquet table or the open communion of Christians.

India creates extremes: the caste system exaggerates the social bond; asceticism exalts the isolation of the individual. The Hindu continually oscillates between these two poles. There is no meeting point, no point of convergence: there is no symposium, no communion. A large part of the Buddhist canon is in the form of dialogues of the Illuminated with his disciples, but the object of these conversations is not communion: they are sermons extolling solitary meditation. The Platonic philosopher's goal is the contemplation of the Idea; the Buddhist's goal the dissolution of the Idea in emptiness (sunyata). The great Christian mystery is that of divine incarnation; the aim of all the religions and doctrines of India is liberation, disincarnation (moksha, nirvana). In the hymns of the Rig-Veda and the Atharva-Veda, there are many references to a mysterious substance, soma, which many modern Orientalists are convinced was a form of hashish. It is quite likely soma is the same thing as bhang, a drug commonly used in modern India, especially among the sadhus and sannyasis. According to the Vedic hymns, soma brings illumination and knowledge: it is the food of seers and poets, the rishis. Wine, dialogue, communion, incarnation; drugs, introspection, liberation, disincarnation. The Word and the Silence.

All this gives us good reason to believe that the popularity of hallucinogenic substances is a symptom of a shift in modern sensibilities. Does this shift represent a change of goals or an absence of goals? Both things. The traditional symbols have lost their meaning. They are empty signs. In a world ruled by the communications media no one has anything to say or anything to hear. If words have lost their meaning, why not look for meaning in silence? The popular interest in Buddhism and other Oriental religions and doctrines betrays the same sense of deprivation and the same appetite. It would be a mistake to believe that we are looking to Buddhism for a truth that is foreign to our tradition: what we are seeking is a confirmation of a truth we already know. The new attitude is not a result of a new knowledge of Eastern doctrines, but a result of our own history. No one ever learns a truth from outside: each person must think it through and experience it for himself. It would not be difficult to prove that three contemporary thinkers—Wittgenstein, Heidegger, and Lévi-Strauss—give evidence in their works of a surprising unconscious affinity with Buddhism. Their philosophies have not been influenced in any way by Eastern thought, and their respective philosophical positions are so different that they would appear to be irreconcilable. Yet the preoccupation with language is central in all three, and each of them has been led to a similar conclusion: all speech ends in silence. I might mention other examples in the sphere of literature and art, but there are so many of them and they are so well known that I prefer not to do so. I shall merely limit myself to pointing out once again that, if any poet of the recent past is our precursor, our master, and our contemporary, it is Mallarmé. And the fact is that all his poetry is an attempt to realize what may well be an impossible ambition, one mindful of the paradoxes of the Prajnaparamita sutras: incarnating absence, naming emptiness, speaking of silence. Modern art is a destruction of meaning—or of communication—but it is also a search for meaning. Perhaps this exploration will result in the discovery that nonmeaning is identical with meaning.

Now that we have examined the general context in which this change has occurred, we can better understand the meaning of the more and more widespread use of hallucinogenic substances. Like alcoholism, it is a revolt; like alcoholism, it is a revolt that is self-defeating: drugs can give us blissful or terrifying visions, but they cannot give us either silence or wisdom. Unlike alcoholism, drugs are not an exaggeration of a traditional value (communication) but of something foreign to our tradition. Alcoholism is a caricature of the Platonic symposium and of communion; drugs are its negation.

Drugs have always been used in conjunction with a ritual of some sort. Since antiquity, they have been an adjunct either of ascetic practices or of initiation ceremonies and other rites. Each year, the Huichol Indians go on an arduous expedition in search of peyote, and, during the entire time, they forgo bathing, abstain from any sort of sexual contact, and undergo endless privations. When they find the cactus, they do not consume it immediately; they wait until a ceremony can be held, in the course of which, among other rites, public confession takes place. Once purified, they eat the peyote. According to the Huichol Indians, horrible visions are a sort of punishment visited upon those who have lied during the confession or committed other deceitful and mendacious acts. The entire rite and all of its attendant sufferings center around the ideas of trust, unselfishness, pureness of heart, generosity. The beliefs of the Huichols confirm what I have pointed out above with regard to the "morality" of hallucinogenic drugs and their surprising justice. There is little point in listing other examples: in all periods of history and in all cultures the use of drugs is associated with a ritual and some form of asceticism.*

The same is true of sexual practices and ritual meals within the tradition of Tantrism. It is not surprising, therefore, that in the United States, many semireligious and semiartistic groups are attempting to surround the use of drugs with a sort of ritual. It is the only way of taking advantage of the unquestionable power of drugs as hallucinatory agents and instruments of self-knowledge. But such experiments are doomed to failure. Rites cannot be invented: they develop little by little, through the creation of myths, beliefs, and religious practices. Modern society has emptied traditional rites of all their content and has not yet succeeded in creating others to take their place. The prime ritual gathering of the century—political meetings—served for a time as a replacement for traditional rites. But, today, they have turned into dull official ceremonies and have preserved their vitality only in China and other underdeveloped countries. The reason for this is obvious: rites are based on the idea of time as repetition: they are a date that recurs again and again, representing a present that is also a past and a future.

Modern, historical time is linear and inevitably proves fatal to the rite; the past is irreversible and will never return. The ultimate meaning of the use of drugs in our time is thus clearer now: it is a criticism of linear time and a nostalgia for (or a presentiment of) another sort of time. These remarks on drugs lead to a subject that I shall discuss in the third part of this book: the end of linear time.

Buñuel's Philosophical Cinema

Some years ago, I wrote a few pages about Buñuel. This is what I said: "Even though the common and ultimate aim of all the arts, including those that are most abstract, is the expression and re-creation of man and his conflicts, each one of them has its own particular means for casting its spell over us, and thus each is a separate domain. Music is one thing,

---

* The brahmin who engages in the soma sacrifice "must abstain from all contact with men of impure castes and with women; he must not answer anyone who asks him a question, and no one must touch him." Louis Renou, *L'Inde classique*.

poetry another, cinema yet another. But, occasionally, an artist succeeds in going beyond the limits of his art; we then come face to face with a work whose equivalents lie outside its own world. A number of Buñuel's films—*L'Age d'or*, *Los olvidados*—belong to the realm of cinema but at the same time they bring us closer to other regions of the human spirit: certain of Goya's engravings, poems by Quevedo or Péret, a passage by Sade, one or another of Valle Inclán's *esperpentos*, a page by Gómez de la Serna . . . These films can be enjoyed and judged as cinema and at the same time as something belonging to the wider and freer universe of these works of surpassing value whose object is both to reveal human reality to us and to show us a way to go beyond it. Despite the obstacles which our contemporary world places in the way of such endeavors, Buñuel's work continues to pass through the double arch of beauty and rebellion.

"In *Nazarín*, in a style that rejects any sort of suspect lyricism, Buñuel tells us the story of a priest akin to Don Quixote, whose conception of Christianity soon earns him the enmity of the Church, society, and the police. Like so many of Pérez Galdós's characters, Nazarín belongs to the great tradition of Spanish madmen. His madness consists of taking Christianity seriously and attempting to live according to its gospel. He is a madman who refuses to admit that what we call reality is *really* reality and not just a horrible caricature of true reality. Like Don Quixote, who saw his Dulcinea in a farm girl, Nazarín can make out the image of fallen man in the monstrous features of the prostitute, Andra, and the hunchback, Ujo, and recognize the face of divine love in the erotic delirium of a hysterical woman, Beatriz. In the course of the film—in which there are many scenes where Buñuel is at his greatest and most awesome, for here his fury is more concentrated than ever and thus more explosive—we are witness to the attempt to 'cure' the madman. He is rejected by one and all: by those who are powerful because they look on him as a nuisance and ultimately a dangerous troublemaker; by the insulted and injured because they need another, more effective kind of consolation. He is not only persecuted by the authorities; he is constantly a victim of misunderstandings. If he seeks alms, he is accused of being a social parasite; if he seeks work, he is accused of taking the bread from the mouths of other laborers. Even his women disciples, reincarnations of Mary Magdalene, have ambivalent feelings about him in the end. Thrown into jail as a result of his good works, the ultimate revelation comes to him there behind bars: his own 'goodness' and the 'evil' of one of his fellow prisoners, a murderer and a robber of churches, are equally useless in a world that worships efficiency as the supreme value.

"Faithful to the tradition of the Spanish madman, from Cervantes to Pérez Galdós, Buñuel's film recounts a loss of illusions. For Don Quixote the illusion was the spirit of chivalry, for Nazarín Christianity. But there is something else besides. As the image of Christ pales in Nazarín's consciousness, another image begins to take its place: that of man. By putting before us a series of exemplary episodes, in the true sense of the word, Buñuel makes us witnesses of a twofold process: the gradual fading away of the illusion of divinity and the discovery of the reality of man. The supernatural yields its place to the marvelous: human nature and its powers. This revelation is embodied in two unforgettable moments: the scene where Nazarín offers the consolations of the beyond to the dying woman in love, who clutches the photograph of her lover and answers: '*Heaven no, Juan yes*;' and the scene at the end when Nazarín first refuses the alms of a poor woman and then accepts them after a moment's hesitation—not as a charitable offering but as a sign of fraternity. Nazarín the solitary man is no longer alone: he has lost God but he has found men."

This short text appeared in the printed program given out at the showing of *Nazarín* at the Cannes Film Festival. It was feared—and doubtless for good reason—that the meaning of the film might be misunderstood. The risk of confusion that threatens every work of art was even greater in this case because of the nature of the novel that inspired the film. Pérez Galdós's theme is the age-old conflict between evangelical Christianity and its ecclesiastical and historical deformations. The hero of his book is a rebellious *illuminato*, a true protestant: he leaves the church but keeps his faith in God. Buñuel's film is meant to demonstrate the exact opposite: the disappearance of the figure of Christ in the conscience of a sincere and pure-hearted believer. In the scene with the dying girl, which is a transposition of Sade's *Dialogue Between a Priest and a Dying Man*, the woman's words are an affirmation of the irreplaceable value of terrestrial love: if there is a heaven, it is here and now, at the moment of carnal embrace, not in a beyond where there is no time, where there are no bodies. In the prison scene, the sacrilegious thief is shown to be a creature no less absurd than the priest. The crimes of the thief are as illusory as the sanctity of Nazarín: if there is no God, there is also no sacrilege and no salvation.

Nazarín is not Buñuel's best film, but it is typical of the duality that governs his entire work. On one hand, ferocity and lyricism, a world of dreams and blood that immediately calls to mind two other great Spaniards, Quevedo and Goya. On the other hand, a bare, spare style that is not at all Baroque and results in a sort of exaggerated sobriety. The straight line, not the Surrealist arabesque. The rigor of rational thought: each one of his films, from *L'Age d'or* to *Viridiana*, unfolds like a *logical proof.* The most violent and most freely soaring imagination in the service of a syllogism as sharp as a knife, as irrefutable as a boulder: Buñuel's logic is the implacable reason of the Marquis de Sade. This name sheds light on the relation between Buñuel and Surrealism: without this movement, Buñuel would still have been a poet and a rebel, but thanks to it, he was able to hone his weapons to a keener edge. Surrealism, which revealed Sade's thought to him, was not a school where he learned the uses of delirium, but rather the uses of reason: without ceasing to be poetry, his cinematic poems became criticism. Within the closed arena of criticism, delirium spread its wings and clawed its own chest with its sharp talons. A Surrealism of the bull ring, but also a critical Surrealism: the bullfight as philosophical argument.

In a major text of modern letters, *De la littérature considérée comme une tauromachie* [*Literature as Tauromachy*], Michel Leiris says that he was fascinated by the bullfight because it is a perfect blend of danger and style: the *diestro* (one of the Spanish words for the bullfighter, meaning "the man of skill") must meet the bull's attack without losing his composure. This is true: when we die and when we kill, impeccable manners are absolutely necessary, at least if one believes, as I do, that these two biological acts are also rites, ceremonies. In the bullfight, danger takes on the dignity of form and form the truthfulness of death. The bullfighter strictly complies with a form at the risk of his life. It is what we call *temple* in Spanish: a cool boldness, a well-tempered musical harmony, stubborn courage and flexibility. The bullfighter, like the photographer, must calculate his exposures, and Buñuel's style, by deliberate aesthetic and philosophical choice, is one of exposure. Exposing oneself, taking risks. To expose is also to exhibit, to bare, to demonstrate. Buñuel's films are a process of exposure: they reveal human realities by subjecting them to the light of criticism, as though they were photographic plates. Buñuel's bullfighting is a philosophical discourse, and his films are the modern equivalent of the philosophical novels of the Marquis de Sade. But Sade, while an original philosopher, was only an average artist: he failed to realize that art, which takes rhythm and litany to its bosom, refuses to tolerate mechanical repetition and reiteration. Buñuel is an artist, and if his films are open to criticism, it is on philosophical rather than aesthetic grounds.

The argument underlying Sade's entire *œuvre* can be reduced to a single idea: man is his instincts, and the real name of what we call God is fear and frustrated desire. Our morality is a codification of aggression and humiliation: reason itself is only an instinct that knows it is an instinct and therefore fears itself. Sade did not endeavor to demonstrate that God does not exist: he took it for granted. He tried to show what human relations would be like in a truly atheist society. This is what constitutes his real originality, and what explains the absolute consistency of all his writings. The archetypes of a republic of truly free men is the "Society of the Friends of Crime;" and the archetype of the true philosopher is this libertine ascetic who managed to reach a state of perfect insensibility, moved neither to laughter nor to tears. Sade's logic is unassailable and circular: it destroys God but it does not respect man. His system is open to criticism on many grounds, but we cannot possibly accuse him of inconsistency. His negation embraces everything: if he affirms anything at all, it is the right to destroy and be destroyed. Buñuel's criticism has a limit: man. All our crimes are the crimes of a ghost: God. Buñuel's theme is not man's guilt but God's. This idea, present in all his films, is most explicit and most frankly expressed in *L'Age d'or* and *Viridiana*, which, with *Los olvidados*, seem to me to be his most fully developed and most perfect creations. If Buñuel's *œuvre* is a criticism of the illusion of God, that deforming mirror which does not allow us to see man as he is, what are men *really* like, and what meaning will the words love and brotherhood have in a *truly* atheist society?

Sade's answer doubtless does not satisfy Buñuel. Nor do I believe that he is content at this point with the descriptions to be found in philosophical and political utopias. Apart from the fact that these prophecies cannot be proved to be either true or false, at least for the present, it is obvious that they are not consonant with what we know about man, his history, and his nature. To believe in an atheist society governed by natural harmony—a dream we have all had—would today be tantamount to repeating Pascal's wager, though this time the bet would be precisely the opposite. It would be more of an act of desperation than a paradox: it would earn our admiration, but not our approval. I do not know how Buñuel would answer such questions. Surrealism, which denied so many things, was propelled along by a great gust of generosity and faith. Among its ancestors we find not only Sade and Lautréamont, but also Fourier and Rousseau. And at least for André Breton, it was perhaps the two latter who were the real source of the movement: the celebration of man's passions, the limitless trust in man's natural powers. I do not know whether Buñuel feels more of an affinity with Sade or with Rousseau; most probably the two of them are at war within him. Whatever his beliefs in this regard, it is certain that we will not find a reply to either Sade or Rousseau in his films. Whether due to reticence, timidity, or disdain, his silence is disturbing, not only because he is one of the great artists of our time, but also because it is the silence of all the art of the first half of this century. Since Sade, no one to my knowledge has dared describe an atheist society. Something is missing in the works of our contemporaries: not God but men without God.

Forms of Atheism

It is almost impossible to write about the *death of God*. It is not a suitable subject for a dissertation, even though for more than a half century it has occasioned hymns of rejoicing and hallelujahs. This vast and sometimes unreadable literature does not exhaust the subject: everything we say and do today bears the mark of this event. Whether implicit or explicit, atheism is universal. But we must make a distinction between various brands of atheists: those who believe they believe in a living God and who really think and live as though he had never existed: these are the real atheists, and most of our fellow citizens are of this persuasion; the pseudoatheists, for whom God has not died because he never existed, though they nonetheless believe in one or another of his successors (reason, progress, history); and finally those who accept his death and try to live their lives within this unprecedented perspective. These latter are a minority that can be divided in turn into two groups: those who do not resign themselves, and like Nietzsche's Madman, intone their *Requiem aeternam deo* in empty churches; and those for whom atheism is an *act of faith*. Both groups live the death of God religiously, lightheartedly, and gravely. Lightheartedly, because they live as though a great weight had been removed from their shoulders; gravely, because with the disappearance of the divine power, the support of all creation, the very ground beneath their feet is shaky. Without God, the world has become lighter and man heavier.

The death of God is a chapter in the history of the world's religions, like the death of the Great Pan or the sudden disappearance of Quetzalcoatl. It is also a phase of the modern consciousness. This phase is a religious one. It is religious in a very special way, however, and living through this particular moment calls for a frame of mind that is a combination, in varying proportions, of rigorous thought and passionate faith. Like any other moment, it is transitory; like every religious moment, it is crucial. Bathed in the light of the divine, the religious moment shines brightly and says: forever. It is human time suspended from eternity by a thread, the thread of supernatural presence; if this thread breaks, man falls. The moment that the atheist lives is crucial for the opposite reason: his horizon is the total absence of supernatural presence. As in the religious moment, in the moment of the atheist, too, human time is accepted as fragility and contingency in the face of an extratemporal dimension: the absence of God, like His presence, is eternal. The positive religious moment is the end of profane time and the beginning of sacred time: this end is a resurrection. The negative religious moment is the end of eternity and the beginning of profane time: this beginning is a fall. There is no resurrection because the beginning is an end: the atheist falls into an eternity of successive time in which each minute repeats some other minute. What he has been condemned to is not the pains of hell but repetition. The positive religious moment is a conversion; the negative moment is a reversion. For the believer, this moment is an appeal and a response; for the atheist, a silence without appeal.

The atheist's reaction to the silence that results from the death of God is incredulous surprise. Suddenly, literally beside himself, dumped into the world outside himself, he shouts: "I am trying to find God!" A cry that makes no sense because he knows that "we all killed him together: you killed him, and I killed him. We are all his murderers." The Madman knows that God is dead because he killed him. Perhaps that is why he cannot resign himself to his death and literally cannot believe what he says. So he shouts and sings, tortures himself and rejoices. He is beside himself. The death of God has exiled him from his own being and made him deny his human essence. The Madman wants to be a god because he is searching for God. The other sort of atheist faces up to what has happened in an equally religious and no less contradictory frame of mind: he knows that the death of God is not a fact but a belief. And he believes. But what can he base his belief on, how can he manifest his faith, in what form can he embody it? It is an empty belief. Both cases involve something that scarcely satisfies the demands of human reason. The incredulity of the Madman is a fit of delirium that cannot answer one major argument: if God is still alive, it means that the moment of his death was also that of his resurrection. The credulity of the other sort of atheist also defies logical proof: if it is a belief, who and what is there to prove that it is true? There is no one who can testify to it or confirm it. It is an anonymous truth, since no one embodies it or accepts it save the atheist, and he embodies it as a negation. The atheist's certainty is a very odd sort of thing: he is a believer only if he believes in nothing.

Nietzsche saw the difficulties of atheism with blinding clarity. They seemed to him to be insuperable, at least so long as man continued to be merely man. For that reason, in order to really fulfill itself, to "surpass itself," his "nihilism" required the advent of the superman. Only the superman can be an atheist because only he knows how to play the game.

In the famous passage in *The Gay Science,* the Madman, after having announced the murder of God in public squares and marketplaces, says that this is an act that is *excessive* by human standards: "Never has a more magnificent act been committed, and because of it those who are born after us will be part of a more illustrious history than any other . . ." Though the magnitude of this crime over whelms us, has another breed of men capable of bearing this terrible burden already been born? And if not, are there signs that such a breed will appear in the future? Nietzsche announced the death of God in 1882; it is not presuming too much to say that the superman has not yet been born . . . The Madman knows that, once God is dead, man must live like a god: man must go beyond the limits of his own being, leave his own nature behind and assume the burden, the risk, and the pleasure of divinity. The death of God forces him to change his nature, to stake his own life in the gamble for divine life. From now on, man must look on all of life, his own life and that of the cosmos, from the viewpoint of a god: as a game. All of creation is a game, a representation. Nietzsche says again and again: in our time, what counts is art, not truth. Man works and learns; the gods play and create. Whole worlds rested in the hand of God; now it is man who must support them. They weigh no more than they did yesterday, nor is it their weight that flings man into the precipice of time without end. Our abyss is not the cosmic infinite but death. Man bears the mark of contingency—and knows it. He thus cannot play like a god. Gravity, his original ponderousness, rivets him to the earth. He does not dance on the heights; he dances over a bottomless pit. Man remembers his fall and his dance is a dance of terror.

Nietzsche's subject is not the death of God but his murder. Even though the philosophical name of the murderers is *will to power,* the real guilty parties are each and every one of us. The death of God can be viewed as a historical fact, that is to say, we may believe that he died a natural death, from old age or some illness. In this case, we must look not to philosophy or theology for a diagnosis, but to the history of the ideas and beliefs of the West. It is a familiar one. The idea of a single god may have appeared first in Egypt. This solar divinity of a great empire then underwent a series of metamorphoses: a tribal god who supplants a volcanic deity, the lord of a chosen people, the redeemer of mankind, the creator and king of this world and the other world. Although the Greeks and Romans had philosophized about Being and conceived of the Idea and the Unmoved Mover, the notion of a single Creator was foreign to them. There is an insuperable contradiction between the Judeo-Christian God and the Being of pagan metaphysics: the attributes of Being are not applicable to a personal god who is a creator and a savior. Being is not God. And, what is more: Being is incompatible with any sort of monotheism. Being is necessarily either atheistic or polytheistic. God, our God, was a victim of philosophical infection: the Logos was the virus, the cause of death. Thus the history of philosophy purges us of guilt for the death of God: we were not the murderers; it was time and its accidents. Perhaps this explanation is merely a subterfuge. On close examination, this argument does not hold water: God died within a Christian society, and died precisely because that society was not Christian enough. Our conversion from paganism was so far from total that we Christians have used pagan philosophy to kill our god. Philosophy was the weapon, but the hand that wielded it was our hand. We are obliged to go back to Nietzsche's idea: within the perspective of the death of God, atheism can only be experienced as a personal act—even though this thought is unbearable and intolerable. Only Christians call really kill God.

I am barely acquainted with the world's other great monotheism. But I suspect that Islam has experienced difficulties similar to those Christianity has undergone. Finding it impossible to discover any rational or philosophical ground for belief in a single God, Abu Hamid Chazali writes his *Incoherence of Philosophy*; a century later, Averroes answers with his *Incoherence of Incoherence.** For Muslims, too, the battle between God and philosophy was a fight to the death. In this instance God won, and a Muslim Nietzsche might have written: "Philosophy is dead; we all killed it together; you killed it, and I killed it." In India, there is no one divinity that has created the world and will destroy it—these functions are the

---

* Henri Corbin prefers to translate the titles of these two works as *The Self-Destruction of the Philosophers* and *The Self-Destruction of Self-Destruction*, respectively (*Histoire de la philosophie islamique*, 1964).

responsibility of specialized gods. Indians saved God from the twofold imperfection of creating and of creating imperfect worlds and creatures. In reality they did away with God: if God is not a creator, what kind of god is He? (And if he is a creator . . .) The Hindu divinity is immersed in an abstract, infinite self-contemplation. It is not interested in human events, nor does it intervene in the march of time: it knows that everything is illusion. Its inactivity does not affect believers: myriad minor gods look after their everyday needs. Not satisfied with the existence of many heavens and many hells, each one populated by innumerable gods and demons, the Buddhists conceived the idea of Bodhisattvas, beings (or rather nonbeings) who share both the impassible perfection of the Buddha and the active compassion of the minor divinities: they are not gods but metaphysical entities endowed with redeeming passion. India could dispense with the idea of a Creator because it had already critically examined the notion of time. If true reality is motionless Being—or its contrary, the equally motionless Nothingness of Buddhism—time is unreal and illusory. There would have been no point in inventing a God who is the creator of an illusion.

The difficulties of atheism in the West stem from the notion of time: if time is real, the God who creates it must exist before time. He is its origin and its support. Nietzsche attempted to resolve this mind-boggling puzzle by means of the Eternal Return: the death of God is a moment in circular time, an end that is a beginning. But this cyclical time results in another contradiction: the time of the death of God will be followed by that of his resurrection. As Nerval put it: *"Ils reviendront, ces Dieux que tu pleures toujours!"* The Eternal Return converts God into a manifestation of time, but it does not abolish him. In order to be done with God, time must be done away with: this is the lesson of Buddhism. If we were to venture to formulate a criticism of time as radical as that of Buddhism, it would have to be on entirely different grounds. Whereas the Buddha confronted a time that was cyclical, our time is linear, successive, and unrepeatable. For us, God is not in time but *before* time . . . Perhaps atheism is a problem of *position:* not our

---

* "Those Gods whose deaths you still mourn will return!"

position vis-à-vis God but of God vis-à-vis time. A problem of conceiving of God *after* time. Of thinking of time as having an end—and a purpose: not the creation of a superman but the creation of a real God. Such a God could be thought of without anguish and inner conflict, because he would be not the Creator, but the Creature. Not a child of ours, but the Child of time who is born when time dies. A problem of conceiving of time not as succession and an infinite fall, but as a finite creative principle: a God developing in the once-empty womb of the instant. If the atheist could conceive of a God that awaits him at the end of time, would this resolve the contradiction and put an end to his rage and remorse? God has not died and no one has killed him: he has not been born yet. This notion is no less terrifying than Nietzsche's, since it leads to a conclusion that the West has rejected with horror from the very beginning of its history: the end of time. Will those of us who have killed God dare to kill time?

Nihilism and Dialectics

God and philosophy could not live together peacefully: can philosophy survive without God? Once its adversary has disappeared, metaphysics ceases to be the science of sciences and becomes logic, psychology, anthropology, history, economics, linguistics. What was once the great realm of philosophy has today become the ever-shrinking territory not yet explored by the experimental sciences. If we are to believe the logicians, all that remains of metaphysics is no more than the nonscientific residuum of thought—a few errors of language. Perhaps tomorrow's metaphysics, should man feel a need to think metaphysically, will begin as a critique of science, just as in classical antiquity it began as a critique of the gods. This metaphysics would ask itself the same questions as classical philosophy, but the starting point of the interrogation would not be the traditional one *before* all science, but one *after* the sciences. It is difficult to imagine man returning to metaphysics. Having been so deeply disappointed by science and technology, he will seek a poetics. Not the secret of immortality or the key to eternal life: the source of movement and change itself, the stream that fuses life and death in a single image.

The death of God implies the disappearance of metaphysics, even if we do not accept Heidegger's interpretation of Nietzsche's phrase. In his remarkable study—perhaps the best ever written on the subject-Heidegger tells us that the word God designates not only the Christian God, but the suprasensible world in general: "God is the name Nietzsche gives to the sphere of Ideas and Ideals." If this were true, the death of God would be merely one episode in a vaster drama: a chapter, the last one, in the history of metaphysics. I do not believe this to be the case. Nietzsche's Madman does not say that God has died a natural or historical death; he says that we have murdered him. This is a personal act, and we may understand the grandeur of our era only if we think of it as a crime committed by each and all of us. But even if God is regarded as having died a natural or philosophical death, his disappearance will inevitably lead to the death of metaphysics: thought has now lost its object, its *obstacle*. The philosophy of the West fed on God's flesh; once divinity has disappeared, thought perishes. Without sacred food, there is no metaphysics.

Once having devoured the pagan gods, classical metaphysics erected its beautiful systems. When all its enemies had been annihilated, it disintegrated into sects and schools (Stoicism, Epicureanism) or dwindled away in the attempt to found religions (Neoplatonism). This last undertaking proved to be fruitless: metaphysics receives its sustenance from religion but it is not a creator of religions. Philosophical schools, on the other hand, gave the ancients something that our modem philosophies have failed to give us: *wisdom*. None of our philosophies has produced a Hadrian or a Marcus Aurelius. Or even a Seneca. Our Marxist philosophers prefer "self-criticism" to hemlock. Modern philosophy has admittedly given us a politics, and our revered philosophers go by the names of Lenin, Trotsky, Stalin, and Mao Tse-tung. The descent from these first two names to the last two is a dizzying one. In less than fifty years, Marxism, which Marx defined as a critical system of thought, has turned into a scholastic philosophy of executioners (Stalinism) and the elementary catechism of seven hundred million human beings (Maoism). The source of modem "wisdom" is not philosophy but art. And it is not "wisdom" but madness, a poetics. In the last century, it went by the name of Romanticism, and in the first half of our century, by the name of Surrealism. Neither philosophy nor religion nor politics has been able to withstand the attack of science and technology. But art has borne up under the onslaught. Dadaists—above all Duchamp and Picabia—exploited technology to make a mockery of it: they turned it into something *useless*. Modem art is a passion, a critique, and a cult. It is also a game and a form of wisdom—the wisdom of madness.

Pagan philosophy created no religion of its own, but it killed the new religion. Christianity brought Plato and Aristotle back to life, and from that point on, God and Being, the One and the Only, were locked in mortal embrace. Reason absorbed God and crowned itself queen: if it was no longer possible to adore a rational God, divine reason at least might be worshiped. Kant dethroned reason. Undermined by his criticism as it had itself undermined the idea of God, reason became dialectics. The transition from the dialectics of spirit to dialectical materialism was the last chapter. The relation between Marx and philosophy is analogous to that between Nietzsche and Christianity. In both cases, the crucial factor is a personal act that lays claim to being a universal method; there is no such thing as a history of philosophy: there are philosophers within history. Nietzsche destroyed the principles or the foundations of metaphysics by turning them upside down, a process that resulted in the subversion of all values. Marx's method was similar. As he himself says, his one aim was to put dialectics back in its *natural* position: feet down and head up. The sensible, the material world, was the foundation of the universe, and the old foundation, the idea, was its expression. To Marx, the word *natural* means something beyond the usual meaning of the word. It is more than a return to the old materialism. Marx's nature is historical. His great originality lies in his humanization of matter: human action, praxis, makes the opaque natural world intelligible. He attempted thereby to escape the contradiction of traditional materialism, but in so doing he created another pair of opposites that none of his followers has been able to reconcile: the nature/spirit dichotomy reappears as a nature/history duality. If nature is dialectical, history is part of nature and the entire theory of praxis—human action that converts matter into history—turns out to be superfluous; the distinction between dialectical materialism and the old materialism of the eighteenth century turns out to be illusory: Marxism is not a historicism but a naturalism. The other possibility is equally contradictory: if nature is *not* dialectical, a dichotomy appears and there is again a dualism.

According to Heidegger, the method of "total nihilism" involves not so much the change of values or their devaluation as the reversal of the value of values. Denying that the suprasensible—the Idea, God, the Categorical Imperative, Progress—is the supreme value does not necessarily imply the total destruction of values, but rather the appearance of a new principle as the source and basis of all values. This principle is life. And life in its most direct and aggressive form: the will to power. The essence of life is will, and will expresses itself as power. I am not at all certain that the essence of life is the will to power. In any event, it does not seem to me to be the source or the origin of value, its underlying cause; nor do I believe that it is its foundation. The essence of the will to power can be summed up in the word *more*. It is an appetite: not more being, but being more. Not *being*, but a passionate *wish to be*. This passionate wish to be is the wound through which the will to power is drained of its blood. Just as movement cannot be the cause or the principle of movement (*who* moves it, *what* supports it?), the will to power is not being but an urge to be and therefore incapable of becoming its own foundation or the foundation of values. It is by nature a going-beyond-itself; in order to discover its reason for being, its prime cause, its *principle*, its impetus must be totally expended, it must go on to the very end: a return to the beginning. Implicit within the Eternal Return of the Same is a new subversion of values: the restoration of the Idea, of the suprasensible, as the foundation of value. Neither the will to power nor the Idea are principles: they are only moments of the Eternal Return, recurring phases of the Same.

Reason encounters similar difficulties when it confronts dialectical materialism. Dialectics is the manner of being, the form in which matter, the only true reality, manifests itself; matter in motion is the foundation of all values. But there is a contradiction between matter and dialectics: the so-called laws of dialectics are not observable in the processes and transformations of matter. If they were, matter would cease to be matter: it would be history, thought, or Idea. On the other hand, dialectics cannot be its own foundation because, by its very nature, it denies itself the moment it affirms itself. It is perpetual rebirth and perpetual death. If the will to power is continually threatened by the return of the Same, dialectics is similarly threatened by its own movement: every time it affirms itself, it denies itself. In order not to cancel itself out, it needs some sort of ground, some principle *prior* to movement. If Marxism rejects Spirit or the Idea as its foundation, and if matter also cannot be its foundation, the Marxist is trapped in a vicious circle. In the case of both the will to power and the dialectics of matter, the sensible is "an implicit denial of its essence." This essence is precisely what both Nietzsche's doctrine of the will to power and Marxist dialectics do away with: the suprasensible as the foundation of reality, the original principle and the reality of all realities. Both tendencies lead in the end to nihilism. Nietzsche's nihilism is aware of its own nature, and therefore is "total": it looks forward to nothing but the return of the Same and at this particular point in history it is in essence a game: a tragedy being staged, art. Marx's nihilism is not aware of its own nature. Although it is Promethean, critical, and philanthropic in spirit, it is nonetheless nihilistic.

Dialectical materialism and the Nietzschean doctrine of the will to power succeeded in bringing about a subversion of values that both lightened our burden and tempered our souls. But they have now lost their power of contagion.* Both tendencies are essentially a drive for *more*, but as this awesome energy accelerates, its force decreases. Today, the best expression of this drive for *more* is not thought (art or politics) but technology. The inversion of values wrought by technology leads to a devaluation of all values, not excluding those of Marxism and those of Nietzsche. Life ceases to be an art or a game and becomes "a technique for living." The same thing happens in the realm of politics: the technician and the expert replace the revolutionary. Socialism no longer means the transformation of human relations but economic development, the raising of the standard of living, and the utilization of the labor force as a lever in the struggle for power and world supremacy. Socialism has become an ideology, and in those countries where it has won the day, it is a new

---

* Marxism has lost this power as a philosophy, but not as a revolutionary "ideology" of the "underdeveloped" countries.

form of alienation. The superman has not yet been born, even though men today have a power that a Caesar or an Alexander never dreamed of. Technological man is a combination of Prometheus and Sancho Panza. The American: a titan enamored of progress, a fanatical giant who worships "getting things done" but never asks himself what he is doing nor why he is doing it. His activity is not creative play but mindless sport: he drops bombs in Vietnam and sends messages home on Mother's Day; he believes in sentimental love, and his sadism goes by the name of mental hygiene; he razes cities and visits his psychiatrist. He is still tied by his umbilical cord even though he is the explorer of outer space. Progress, solidarity, good intentions, and despicable acts. He does not suffer from hubris; he is simply lawless, perpetually repentant and perpetually self-satisfied . . . These reflections are not a complaint. Our world is no worse than yesterday's, nor will the world of tomorrow be any better. Moreover, there is no possible way of returning to the past. Marx's and Nietzsche's criticism of our values was so radical that nothing remains of these constructs. Their criticism is our starting point, our only way of clearing a path that will lead us—where? Perhaps this *where* is not located in any future time or in any place further ahead, but there in *this* space and *this* time that is our very own present. Is there anything left? Art is what remains of religion: the dance above the yawning abyss. Criticism is what remains of dialectics: starting all over again.

Person and Principle

A remarkable recent study of the Hindu caste system by Louis Dumont (*Homo hierarchicus*, Paris, 1966) is surprising confirmation, for me at least, of the remarks I have ventured with regard to the difficulties of being atheistic in the West and monotheistic in India. This French Orientalist points out that castes are not units or elements in the same sense as the proletariat, the bureaucracy, the Army, or the Church: that is, corporations, social bodies, each different from all others. Castes cannot be described as substances; they are not *classes*, but a system of relations. Each caste, naturally, has it own distinguishing characteristics: its own territory, occupation, function, diet, marriage customs, ceremonies, rituals, and so on. But these features are not what go to make up a caste: they define its relation to other castes. They are indicative of its position within the whole, characteristics distinguishing it rather than constituting it. What constitutes a caste is the over-all system; what defines it is its position within the system. This conception is the exact opposite of ours: to our way of thinking, the individual is the basis of society, and both the individual and society are self-sufficient units. In the West, society is either a collection of individuals or a totality, something resembling a collective individual. When politicians call upon the people to "march forward as one," they are not merely mouthing a cliché: they are saying that the group is an individual, what the English tradition calls "the body politic." To us, the nation is a projection of the individual; in India, the individual is a projection of society. Our public law is embodied in a *constitution*, a word that derives from the Latin word *stare*: to stand firmly and immovably in one spot. It denotes the collective will to stand together as a single entity, as an individual. There is nothing similar in India. Every political and moral concept in that country—from the idea of monarchical rule to the hierarchical system that extends from the varnas to dharma—have nothing whatsoever to do with the idea of society as the common will. In the languages of India, there is no word to designate the reality that we call a *nation*.

The basic unit of Western thought is an indivisible entity, whether metaphysical (being), psychological (the self), or social (nation, class, political bodies). This model, however, does not correspond to reality, and reality continually destroys it: dialectics, poetry, eroticism, mysticism, and in the realm of history, war and internal conflicts are the violent, spontaneous forms whereby Otherness reminds the One of its existence. The great discovery of modem thought in many different disciplines—from physics and chemistry to linguistics, anthropology and psychology—has in fact been the discovery of relationship; a totality of unstable, evanescent particles has taken the place of an ultimate irreducible element. The basic unit is now multiple, contradictory, insubstantial, ever-changing; hence contemporary thought has failed to corroborate the suppositions underlying the central traditions of the West. The archetype, the basic intellectual framework of India, by contrast, is plurality, flux, relation; just as elements are combinations, the individual is a society. The notions of interdependence and hierarchy are a natural consequence of the basic idea of relation. We look upon the system as an individual; the Hindus look upon the individual as a system. Our notion of the community of nations is that of an assembly of equals, at least potentially if not in actual fact; underlying the caste system is the concept of a hierarchical interdependence. In the West, individualism, equality, rivalry; in India, relation, interdependence, hierarchy. The idea of substance underlies our concepts; the caste system lacks substance: it is a chain of relations. To say that the world of castes is a world of relations is a world of relations is tantamount to saying that

> *la caste particuliére, l'homme particulier, n'ont pas de substance; ils existent empiriquement, ils n'ont pas d'être . . . L'individu n'est pas. C'est pourquoi, pour les hindous eux-mêmes, dès qu'iis prennent un point de vue substantialiste, tout, y compris les dieux, est irréel: l'illusionisme est ici en germe, sa popularité et celle du monisme ne sauraient étonner.*[*]

But before taking a look at how philosophical thought dissolves the gods, let us see how the popular imagination conceives of them.

Time and again, my Hindu friends have tried to explain polytheism to me by means of a simple, and essentially European, formula: the gods are manifestations of the divine. But this explanation does not tell us why the gods of India change name from region to region and from caste to caste. To call this phenomenon an instance of syncretism is to offer a handy label for it rather than an interpretation of it; this syncretism would require explanation in turn. What is more, the position of the gods in the hierarchy and their meaning also change: in one place they are creators and in another destroyers. These changes are related to the calendar: there is a rotation of divinities, a divine revolution similar to that of the

---

[*] " . . . any one caste, any one man has no real existence; they exist empirically, but they have no true essence . . . There is no such thing as an individual. That is why everything, including the gods, is unreal to the Hindus themselves the moment they adopt a substantialist point of view: this is an embryonic form of illusionism, and the popularity of this concept and that of monism should not surprise us."

planets. The explanation offered by modem Hindus—that the names change but the god remains—is only a partial one, and, moreover, it too is European: it endows the divinities with substance, turns them into individuals. The truth would seem to be precisely the opposite: the gods are interchangeable because they are nonsubstantial. They are at once the same and different because they have no autonomous existence; their being is not really being; it is the embodiment of a momentary conjuncture of relations. The god is merely a cluster of attributes—propitious, harmful, and indifferent—being actualized within a given context. The meaning of the god—the actualization of this set of attributes or that—depends on his position within the over-all system. Since the system perpetually rotates, the position of the gods continually shifts.

There is one other peculiar feature: the god is almost always accompanied by consorts. Duality, a basic feature of Tantrism, permeates all of Hindu religious life: male and female, pure and impure, left and right. Lastly, the god is the possessor of a "vehicle"—Siva's bull, Ganesha's rat, Durga's lion—and is surrounded by a multitude of familiars and parasites. Each couple rules over a great throng of minor divinities. Gods who continually change; a couple; a multitude: not individuals but relations. The Hindu pantheon is a hierarchy of crowds, a system of systems. It thus more or less mirrors the caste system. Nonetheless, it would be an error to consider it a mere reflection of the social structure, as proponents of an elementary sort of Marxism might maintain, for the caste system depends in turn on the distinction between the pure and the impure. Hindu Society is religious and Hindu religion social. Everything fits together. The divine is not the godhead; nor is it an impersonal substance, a fluid. The divine is a society: a tissue of relations, a magnetic field, a phrase. The gods are something like the atoms, the cells, or the phonemes of the divine.

I would like to offer a criticism of Dumont's theory here. It seems to me that something essential is missing in his book on Hinduism: the description of what distinguishes human society from divine society. Some distinctive feature, note, or sign must separate the sacred from the profane, the pure from the impure, the castes from the divine multitudes. Dumont tells us how the system functions and describes its structure, but he fails to tell us *what it is*. His definition is not inaccurate: rather, it is formal, and therefore disregards the content of the phenomenon being studied. I will not discuss this point further, because my purpose here is not to examine the phenomenology of Hinduism but to outline the solution to this very same problem that has been arrived at by the Brahmins and Indian philosophy.

The question may be stated, rather roughly, as follows: what is the divine? The answer, one as old as the Upanishads, is simple and clear-cut: there is an impersonal being, forever identical with itself, a being impermeable to change that simply *is*, in which all the gods, all realities, times, and beings are dissolved and reabsorbed: Brahma. This notion reduces the heavenly and the earthly world, time and space, to a phantasmagorical unreality. Later on, a complementary notion appears: the being of man, Atman, is identical with the being of the world. Hence, the subject is entirely eliminated. This absolute monism requires a no less absolute denial of reality and time. What is more, this unalterable and indestructible being can be defined only in negative terms. It is not this or that or the other: *neti, neti*. It is neither the whole nor its parts; it is neither transcendence nor immanence; it is nowhere and yet it is always everywhere. Negation opened the door to Samkhya pluralism and Buddhism: the one step required was to apply the criticism of change and reality to the idea of Brahma and its correlative, Atman. Buddhism followed the road to its very end: there is neither being nor individual selves; everything is causal relation. Samkhya pluralism postulated a godless nature (prakriti) and individual souls (purusha). The fan of Hindu thought unfolds between these two extremes: an absolute monism and an equally absolute pluralism. However profound the differences between these many positions may appear to be, they are all dissolved or reconciled in the final phase of philosophical meditation: moksha, nirvana. The annihilation, the reabsorption, or the liberation of the individual ego is tantamount to the disappearance of one of the terms. Change, duality, time, the illusory reality of the self are done away with. Bhakti itself—amorous union of the worshiper with his deity—is no exception: however individual and substantialized Krishna may appear to us to be, he is merely an avatar of Vishnu, a manifestation of impersonal being, as the well-known and impressive passage in the Bhagavad-Gita tells us.

The enormous effort of speculative thought to endow the divine system with substance, to convert a relationship into distinct and self-sufficient being, culminates either in an explicit monism (the Vedanta) or an implicit monism (Madhyamika Buddhism). In all cases, the One wins out. This description would appear to be an oversimplification, but in fact it is not too far from the truth: for all these pluralisms, first, lead to the idea of moksha or nirvana, which cancel out the differences between them; and secondly, the opposition between Hinduism and Buddhism—in their most extreme forms: the monism of Shankara and the relativism of Nagarjuna—is a complementary one. The white and the black version of a single line of thought: two parallel arguments, pursued with equal rigor, the one proving the unreality of everything that is not Being, the other the unreality of everything that is not Change. The affirmation of Being is arrived at through a series of absolute negations: neither this nor that. The affirmation of Change is also negative and absolute: "In primitive Buddhism all elements are interdependent and real; in the new Buddhism, they are unreal because they are interdependent."* Being and sunyata (absolute emptiness) are identical: there is no way to speak of them except uttering the syllable *no*. In Sanskrit *zero* may be spoken of as either *sunya* (empty) or *purna* (full).

We now have a clearer idea of what the shift from relation to unity entails. Relation disappears in one of two ways: it is either absorbed in Being or dissolved in Non-Being. It disappears but it is not transformed into a substance. Neither of these two concepts with which it fuses—Being or Emptiness—bears any resemblance to what might appear to be parallel concepts in Western thought: the principle of sufficient reason, the prime cause, the ground. Neither the Being of the Vedanta nor the Emptiness of Buddhism is the ground or source of phenomenal reality: rather, they dissolve it. Man does not begin with them; he ends with them. They are the final truth. They are not at the *beginning*, like being, energy, spirit, or the Christian God; they are *beyond*, in a region that only

---

* T. Scherbatsky, *Buddhist Logic* (1962).

negation can describe. They are liberation, the unconditioned; neither death nor life, but freedom from the chain of birth and death. In fact, they are not ontological concepts at all, at least not in the Western sense. Translating Brahma as *Being* and sunyata as *Emptiness* is something worse than a misuse of language: it is a spiritual infidelity.

One of the results of this way of thinking is that the problems of time and creation are relegated to the background. The notion of a time that is irreversible and the correlative notion of a god who is the creator of this time are ideas that, strictly speaking, play no part in the logic of the system. They are superfluous ideas, concepts that are the products of illusion or sectarian curiosities. The idea of a personal god admittedly plays a very important role in Hindu religious life, but, as I have already noted, this god always appears as a manifestation or an avatar of another divinity who in turn is only a relation in the whole tissue of relations going to make up the divine system. Within Hindu speculation as a whole, deism is a secondary phenomenon. It is so in two respects: in the first place, as Hajime Nakamura points out, "the ultimate Absolute presumed by the Indian is not a personal god but an impersonal Principle";* and, second, such a deity is a creator by error or inadvertence, a god misled by the power of illusion (maya). Or, as Nakamura puts it: "There is no maya in God himself but when he created the world . . . maya attaches itself to him. God is an illusory state." God has no Being.

The Hindu Brahma does not correspond to our idea of Being: it is an empty, impersonal, substanceless concept—the other pole and the complement of the notion of relation. What I mean is this: the contrary of Being is Non-Being, and Greek and European metaphysics are built on this pair; the contrary of relation is the absence of relation, nullity, zero (sunya). The Hindu Absolute, Brahma, has no relations; the Buddhist Absolute, sunyata, knows nothing but unreal relations. Both are defined by absence, and both eliminate or absorb the contrary term: they cancel out relation. In the West, what is basic is affirmation: we view Non-Being from the point of view of Being. In India what is basic is negation: they see relation—the human world and the divine world—from the point

* Hajime Nakamura, *Ways of Thinking of Eastern Peoples* (1964).

of view of an Absolute that is defined negatively or *is* negation itself. The Non-Being of the West is subordinate to Being; it is *lack* of reality. Hindu relation, the vital flux, is subordinate to zero; it is an unreal *excess*. In the first case, the unity of Being is positive; in the second it is negative. Hence, in essence, Brahma is identical with sunyata: both are the No that is the answer of the Absolute both to relation—the world, time, gods—and to discursive thought. We have a tendency to exaggerate the opposition between Brahma and sunyata, between the theory of Atman (Being) and that of Anatta (Non-Being), because we conceive of this opposition in terms of Western metaphysics. Thus Raymundo Panikar regrets that "Between the Parmenides of India and its Heraclitus, no Aristotle has as yet appeared . . . to prove how the being that moves, changes, and is not *Brahma*, at the same time is not an unreal nothingness."* But I repeat: mediation is impossible because the opposition is not between Being and Non-Being, nor between Being and Change, but between two concepts that have their roots in something entirely foreign to the Greek and European tradition. The thought of the West is based on the idea of substance, thing, element, being; that of India on relation, interpenetration, interaction, flux. It therefore defines the Absolute as the cessation of Change, that is to say, as negation of relation and action. India does not deny Being: it ignores it. It denies Change: it is maya, illusion. European thought does not deny relation: it ignores it. It affirms Change: Change is Being unfolding or manifesting itself.

Negation and the idea of static balance or immobility are two constant features of Indian thought, both in Hinduism and in Buddhism. Nakamura points out how fond Indians are of negative expressions; they abound both in Sanskrit and Pali and in the modern languages of India. While the European speaks of "Victory or defeat," an Indian speaks of "victory or nonvictory." He does not speak of peace, but of "nonviolence" and what we would call "diligence" he calls "nonlaziness." Change is "impermanence," and the person who has attained illumination or liberation "goes to a nonencounter with the King of the dead." The negative abstracts, impersonalizes, sucks the substance from ideas, names, acts.

---

* Raymundo Panikar, *Maya e Apocalisse* (1966).

Nagarjuna summed up his entire doctrine in Eight Negatives. If the real is negation, change is unreal. For us, the real is positive and, therefore, change is not a synonym of unreality. Change may be an imperfect mode of being *in relation to* essence, but it is not an illusion. For the Hindu, change is an illusion because it *lacks any relation* with the Absolute.

The most notable—and the most basic—feature of Indian thought is the identification of reality with negation. Its conception of change is also a prominent feature. The Greek says: everything is in flux; the Hindu says: everything is impermanent. It is hard for a Westerner to conceive of Nothingness, and Heidegger has shown that it is literally unthinkable: it is the fathomless abyss above which metaphysical thought flaps its wings. In India it is Being that is difficult to conceive. Essence, the reality of all realities, is formless and nameless. For Plato, the essence is the *Idea:* a form, an archetype. The Greeks invented geometry; Hindus the zero. To us, Hindu religion is atheistic. A Hindu might well reply that even our science and our atheism are steeped in monotheism. Time and change are real to us because they are modes of being—a being that emerges from chaos or nothingness and unfolds like an apparition. The divinities of the West are presences that radiate energy. Otto's notion of the numinous reflects our instinctive conviction that the godhead is a magnetic presence: the divine is the "fluid" of deity, its emanation, its product. In India, the god is the product of the divine. For us, the divine is concentrated in a Person; for Hindus, it dissolves in the Impersonal.

The Liberated Man and Liberators

Nagarjuna's dialectic is a system of universal negation: the road to emptiness; in Hegel's dialectic, negation is a creative moment within the process and negativity the road to Being. In the Hegelian dialectic, contradiction "does not result in absolute nullity or Nothingness: it is essentially a negation of its own content:"* Western philosophy has not been blind to the negativity inherent in the concept, but it has always viewed it as an aspect of the idea, being, or reality rather than an abso-

---

* T. Scherbatsky, *Buddhist Logic* (in the chapter on dialectics: "European parallels: Kant and Hegel").

lute, and certainly never as the Absolute. Hence, the West has invented creative negation, revolutionary criticism, the contradiction that affirms the very thing it denies. India has invented liberation by way of negation and made it the nameless mother of all living creatures. These two contrary visions have in turn engendered two types of wisdom, two models of spiritual life: the liberator and the liberated man. For the latter, criticism is a means of letting go: his goal is not self-creation but self-abandonment; for the former, criticism is a means of creation: his goal is reunion with himself and with the world. The Hindu practices negation as an inner method: his goal is not to save the world but to destroy the world within himself; the European practices it as a penetration of reality, as a way of appropriating the world: through negation, the concept changes the world and makes him its master. The liberated man approaches criticism as an apprenticeship in silence; the liberator uses it to subject headstrong language to the rule of reason. The Hindu maintains that once language has reached a certain level, it lacks meaning; the Westerner has decided that anything that lacks meaning also lacks reality. In European thought, criticism determines the causes and structures of things and is such a delicate instrument of mediation that it has made indetermination itself a principle of physics. Indian negation, which is no less subtle than that of the West though it is applied to other phenomena, is intended to foster indetermination: its role is to open the door to the unconditioned . . . But perhaps it would be better to attempt to draw the parallel from the point of view of anthropology. I shall return to Dumont's book, an incomparable guide.

As a way of comparing modern Western society with Hindu society, the French anthropologist, like his mentor Lévi-Strauss, draws up a table of bipolar oppositions. The substantive in India is the religious pair pure-impure, a distinction that serves as the foundation of the social structure: a hierarchical society (interdependence and separation of castes). In the West, the substantive is an a religious one, the individual, which serves as the basis of an egalitarian Society and the idea of nationhood. In India, the social structure is religious; in Europe, it is economic and political. Thus, the adjective in the Hindu world is the economico-political; in the West, the adjective is religious (a private matter). The contradictions, which are also adjectival, are: in India sects, and in the West totalitarianisms, racisms, classes, and social hierarchy (holdovers of an aristocracy, the Army, the Church, etc.). All these oppositions can be summed up in two principal ones: man as a society (hierarchical man), and society as an individual (egalitarian man). Hierarchical society is total but not totalitarian, and thus it has invented a way of escape for the individual man: the free life of the sannyasi, the sadhu, and the Buddhist and Jainist monks. Freedom is attained through renouncing the world: that is to say the duties and advantages of one's caste. Dumont finds no equivalent in the Western tradition. The classical ideal of the sage, in fact, was so closely linked to the idea of the "polis" that there is little need to stress the fact that Greco-Roman wisdom was deeply social in nature. During the heyday of Christianity, the saints and the religious orders were active in this world, even though they were serving a divine cause and a divine truth. In India, on the other hand, the sannyasi lives outside of society: he escapes its rules and his activities are aimed neither at reforming the world nor at saving souls.* Is there anything in the modern Western world comparable to the institution of the sannyasi? Dumont does not think so. I believe there is: the rebel artist and the professional revolutionary.

Both the vagabond seeking liberation and those who aspire to free mankind are outsiders in their respective societies. Thus, we must first compare their relations to their worlds. The sannyasi does not fight the world: he denies it; the artist assumes a pose on the sidelines, jeering

---

* It is quite true that those of us living in New Delhi in 1966 were witness to a popular demonstration headed by several hundred sadhus; a furious pitched battle with the police took place at the entrance to the Indian Parliament. It was a demonstration against the slaughter of cows, and therefore a religious act. I do not deny that in this case, as in others, those involved have been influenced by Western methods, if not Western ideas. Egalitarian ideology has not destroyed the caste system, but it threatens to turn it into something very dangerous: in a number of places the castes are now behaving like individuals and have become closed political corporations. Egalitarianism has undermined the notions of hierarchy and interdependence and has made the castes aggressive entities. Egalitarianism is contradictory: it is an attempt to found social harmony on equality and, at the same time, it opens the door to competition and rivalry. Its real name is envy. The same phenomenon can be observed in the "communalist" struggles, as the struggles among Hindus, Muslims, and Sikhs are called.

and scoffing at it; and the revolutionary actively opposes it: his goal is to destroy it and build a better one. The relationship of the sannyasi to his world is a religious one and one of indifference; that of the artist and revolutionary is secular, active, and antagonistic. The reaction of society is also different. The Hindu adopts an attitude of reverence and extreme benevolence toward the sannyasi. He may practice the most extravagant, cruel, or repulsive rites, uphold the most unconventional opinions, wander about either clothed or naked, as he pleases: such behavior in no way lessens his prestige or compromises his respectability. He is an *untouchable*, and, at the same time, his touch does not defile: it illuminates, it purifies. He is the holy exception, the sanctioned violation, the permissible transgression—fiesta incarnated in an individual. He is free of all relations, undefinable in terms of the caste system, a pure soul, wandering where he pleases. The artist is the man misunderstood, the eccentric; he lives in a closed group and even the section of town he lives in with his fellow artists is a dubious sort of place; the bourgeois, the proletarian, and the professor look upon him with suspicion. The revolutionary is the man hounded by the police of every country, the man with no passport and a thousand names, denounced by the press, and sought by the examining magistrate: any step taken to neutralize him is considered legitimate. Another surprising contradiction: once the artist is recognized, he returns to the world, he is a millionaire or a national glory, and if he is Mexican, he is buried in the Pantheon of Illustrious Men when he dies; once the revolutionary has taken over, he immediately sets up a Committee of Public Safety and persecutes dissidents even more cruelly than the former tyrant. The sannyasi, on the other hand, cannot return to the world, for if he does so he risks becoming an untouchable, a real one this time, one of those whose shadow defiles even the sacred waters of the Ganges.

The Hindu ascetic aspires to liberation: ending the cycle of death and birth, destroying the self, dissolving himself in the unlimited and unconditioned, doing away with *this* and *that*, subject and object—entering the dark night of Negation with his eyes wide open. The artist seeks to realize himself or realize a work, rescue beauty or change the language, dynamite men's consciousness or free their passions, do battle with death,

3

Revolt, Revolution, Rebellion

The word *revuelta* is not often used in Spanish. Most people prefer to use the words *revolución* and *rebelión*. On first reflection, the contrary would seem more natural: the word *revuelta* is more popular and more expressive. In the year 1611, Covarrubias defines this latter concept as follows: "*Rebolver es ir con chismerías de una parte a otra y causar enemistades y quistiones: y a éste llamamos rebolvedor y rebeltoso, rebuelta la cuestión.*" The meanings of the Spanish word *revuelta* are numerous, ranging from *return* to *confusion* to a *mixture* of one thing with another; all these meanings have to do with the idea of a recurrence of something accompanied by disorder and irregularity. None of these meanings is a positive one; none of them suggests that *revuelta* is a good thing. In a society such as that of seventeenth-century Spain, *revuelta* was regarded as the root of many evils: the confusion of classes, the return to primordial chaos, agitation, and disorder that threatens the very fabric of society. *Revuelta* was something that reduced distinctions to a formless mass. For Bernardo de Balbuena (the sixteenth-century Spanish poet), the foundation of civilization is the establishment of hierarchies, thus creating a necessary inequality between individuals; barbarism is a return to the state of nature, to equality. It is no easy task to determine when the word *revuelta* came to be used with the meaning of a spontaneous uprising of the people. The word *révolte* appears in French around 1500, in the sense of "a change of party," and does not take on the connotation of *rebellion* until a century later. Although the Littré dictionary indicates that *révolte* comes from the Italian *rivoltare* (to turn inside out or upside down), Corominas believes that it may come from the Catalan *revolt*,

---

* Joan Corominas: *Diccionario crítico-etimológico de la lengua castellana.* "*Rebolver* is to go about spreading gossip and causing enmity and quarrels: and we call such a person a *rebolvedor* and a *rebeltoso*, and the action, *rebuelta*."

temps de revolt. Whatever its origin, most Spanish-speaking people now use the word *revolución*, both in conversation and in writing, to refer to public disturbances and uprisings. The word *revuelta* is reserved for riots or agitation with no clearly defined purpose. It is a plebeian word.

There are marked differences in Spanish between the *revoltoso*, the *rebelde*, and the *revolucionario*. The first is a dissatisfied individual who is fond of intrigue and sows confusion; the second is someone who refuses to submit to authority, a disobedient or unruly person; the third is a person who seeks to change institutions through the use of violence. (I use the definitions in our dictionaries even though they seem to be inspired by Police Headquarters.) Despite these differences, the three words are intimately related. This relationship is a hierarchical one: *revuelta* lives in the subsoil of the language; *rebelión* is individualist; *revolución* is an intellectual word and refers more to the uprisings of entire peoples and the laws of history than to the deeds of a rebellious hero. *Rebelión* is a military term; it comes from the Latin *bellum* and evokes the image of civil war. Minorities are rebels; majorities, revolutionaries. Although the origin of *revolución* is the same as that of *revuelta* (as is that of the two English words *revolution* and *revolt*, i.e., Latin *volvere*, to revolve, to turn around, to unroll), and although both words connote a *return* or a *recurrence*, the origin of *revolución* is philosophical and astronomical: the return of the stars and the planets to their earlier position, rotation around an axis, the cycle of the seasons and historical eras. The connotations of *return* and *movement* in the word *revolución* suggest an underlying order; these same connotations in the word *revuelta* suggest disorder. Thus, *revuelta* does not imply any cosmic or historical vision; it is the chaotic or tumultuous present. In order for revolt to cease to be a mere passing disturbance and take its place in history, it must be transformed into a revolution. The same is true of rebellion: the acts of the rebel, however daring they may be, are fruitless gestures if they are not based on a revolutionary doctrine. Ever since the end of the eighteenth century, the cardinal word of this triad has been revolution. Bathed in the light of the Idea, it is philosophy in action, criticism that has become an act, violence with a clear purpose. As popular as revolt and as generous as rebellion, it encompasses them and guides them. Revolt is the violence of an entire people; rebellion the unruliness of an individual or an uprising by a minority; both are spontaneous and blind. Revolution is both planned and spontaneous, a science and an art.

The discredit into which the word *revuelta* has fallen is due to a precise historical fact. It is a word that aptly expresses the unrest and the discontent of a people still under the sway of the idea that authority is sacred, even though it may rise up in arms against one specific injustice or another. Although it is egalitarian, revolt respects the divine right of the monarch: *de rey abajo, ninguno.* Its violence is the breaking of the ocean wave against the rocky cliff; the wave bathes the cliff in foam and retreats. The modern meaning of *revolución* in Spain and Hispano-America was an importation by intellectuals. *Revuelta*, a popular, spontaneous word but one that pointed in no particular direction, was replaced by one that had philosophical prestige. The fact that the new word became a very fashionable one is indicative not so much of a historical revolt, a popular uprising, as of the appearance of a new power: philosophy. From the eighteenth century on, reason becomes a subversive political principle. The revolutionary is a philosopher, or at least an intellectual: a man of ideas. The word *revolution* calls up many names and many meanings: Kant, the Encyclopedia, the Jacobin Terror, and, most vividly of all, the destruction of the order of privileges and exceptions and the founding of an order based not on authority but on the free exercise of reason. The old virtues went by the names of faith, fealty, honor. All of them strengthened the social bond and each of them was related to a universally recognized value: faith in the Church as the incarnation of revealed truth; fealty to the sacred authority of the monarch; honor to the tradition based on blood ties. These virtues had their counter-part in the charity of the Church, the magnanimity of the king, and the loyalty of feudal subjects, whether villeins or great lords. Revolution is a word for the new virtue: justice. All the other new virtues—liberty, fraternity, equality—are based on it. It is a virtue that does not depend on revelation, power, or blood. As universal as reason, it admits of no exceptions and is equally far removed from arbitrariness and compassion. Revolution: a word belonging to the vocabulary of the just and the dealers of justice. A little later another word suddenly appears, one previously looked upon with horror: rebellion. From the very outset it was a romantic, bellicose, aristocratic word referring to outlaws. The rebel: the accursed hero, the solitary poet, lovers who trample social conventions underfoot, the plebe of genius who defies one and all, the dandy, the pirate. Rebellion also has religious connotations. It refers not to Heaven but to Hell: the towering pride of the prince of darkness, the blasphemy of the titan in chains. Rebellion: melancholy and irony. Art and love were rebels; politics and philosophy revolutionaries.

In the second half of the nineteenth century, another word appears: *reformista*. This word came not from France but from the English-speaking countries. The word was not a new one; what was new was its meaning and the aura surrounding it. An optimistic word and an austere one, an unusual combination of Protestantism and Positivism. This alliance of the old heresy and the new, of Lutheranism and science, aroused the enmity of both the purists and the conservatives. There were good reasons for their hatred; the word concealed revolutionary contraband beneath its respectable outward trappings. It was a "decent" word. The place where it was heard most often was not in the haunts of the *revoltosos* or in the catacombs of the rebels, but in academic lecture halls and among the editorial staff of periodicals. The revolutionary appealed to philosophy; the reformist to the sciences, commerce, and industry: he was a fanatical admirer of Spencer and the railroads. Ortega y Gasset very cleverly, though perhaps not accurately, points out a basic difference between the revolutionary and the reformist: the former tries to change customary uses; the latter, to correct abuses. If this were true, the reformist would be a rebel who had come to his senses, a Satan who is eager to collaborate with the powers that be. I say this because the rebel, unlike the revolutionary, does not attempt to undermine the social order as a whole. The rebel attacks the tyrant; the revolutionary attacks tyranny. I grant that there are rebels who regard all governments as tyrannical; nonetheless, it is abuses that they condemn, not power itself. Revolutionaries, on the other hand, are convinced that the evil does not lie in the excesses of the constituted order but in order itself. The difference, it seems to me, is considerable. As I see it, the similarities between the revolutionary and the reformist are greater than the differences that separate them. Both are intellectuals, both believe in progress, both reject myths: their faith in reason is unswerving. The reformist is a revolutionary who has chosen the path of evolution rather than violence. His methods are different, but not his goals: the reformist also wants to change institutions. The revolutionary is an advocate of a sudden great leap forward; the reformist of one step at a time. Both believe in history as a linear process and as progress. Both are the offspring of the bourgeoisie, both are modern.

Revolution is a word that implies the notion of cyclical time and therefore that of regular and recurrent change. But the modern meaning of the word does not refer to an eternal return, the circular movement of worlds and stars, but rather to a sudden and *definitive* change in direction of public affairs. Cyclical time is brought to an end and a new rectilinear time begins. The new meaning destroys the old: the past will not return, and the archetype of events is not what has been but what will be. In its original meaning, revolution is a word that affirms the primacy of the past: anything new is a return. The second meaning implies the primacy of the future: the gravitational field of the word shifts from the yesterday that is known to the tomorrow that is yet to be discovered. It is a cluster of new meanings: the pre-eminence of the future, the belief in continuous progress and the perfectibility of the species, rationalism, the discredit of tradition and authority, humanism. All these ideas fuse in that of rectilinear time: history conceived as an onward march. This new cluster of meanings marks the sudden appearance of profane time. Christian time was finite: it began with the Fall and ended in Eternity, the day after the Last Judgment. Modern time, whether revolutionary or reformist, rectilinear or spiral, is infinite.

The change in meaning of the word *revolution* also affects the word *revolt*. Guided by philosophy, it becomes a prerevolutionary activity: it enters the realm of history and the future. The martial word *rebellion*, in turn, absorbs the old meanings of the words *revolt* and *revolution*. Like revolt, it is a spontaneous protest against power; like revolution, it represents cyclical time that ceaselessly reverses top and bottom. The rebel, a fallen angel or a titan in disgrace, is the eternal nonconformist. His action is not engraved upon the rectilinear time of history, the realm of the revolutionary and the reformist, but on the circular time of myth: Jupiter will be dethroned, Quetzalcoatl will reappear, Lucifer will return to heaven. During all of the nineteenth century, the rebel lives on the margin of society. Revolutionaries and reformists look upon him with the same mistrust as Plato passing judgment on poets, and for the same reason: the rebel prolongs the fascination of myth.

The Verbal Round

The meanings of the three words revolt, rebellion, and revolution remained intact, but their position changed. It was a threefold change: these three words that were viewed with suspicion and disapproval ascend to the verbal heaven and replace three other venerable words: king, tradition, God. Within the triangle, revolution becomes the central word; and within each word the secondary meanings become the most important: revolt is not so much confusion as a popular uprising; rebellion ceases to be headstrong disobedience and becomes generous protest; revolution is not a return to origins but the creation of the future. As with the position of chromosomes in hereditary cells, these shifts were the cause of others in our system of beliefs and values. The words and the meanings were the same, but, like choreographic figures in a ballet or the rotation of the stars in the sky, the shift in position of these words revealed a different orientation of society. This change also produced a change in our vital rhythms. Rectilinear time, modern time, now comes to occupy the center of the verbal constellation, and circular time, the image of eternal perfection for Plato and Aristotle, abandons the sphere of reason and degenerates into a more or less unconscious belief. The idea of perfection becomes at once boundless and available to everyone: it is continuous progress, not by the individual but by mankind as a whole. The human species recovers its original innocence, since it is perfectible through its works rather than through divine grace; the individual man loses the possibility of perfection, since it is not he himself, but all of humanity that is the subject of this endless progress. The species goes on although the individual is doomed. Original sin disappears and at the same time Heaven is depopulated. This change in orientation of men's thoughts and actions is accompanied by a corresponding change of rhythm: rectilinear time is accelerated time. The old time was governed by the past: tradition was the archetype of the present and the future. Modern time considers the past mere ballast, and throws it overboard. Technology has not been the creator of speed: it was the beginning of modern time that made the speed of technology possible. This is the meaning underlying the common phrase, "we live at a faster pace today." The feeling that everything has speeded up stems from the fact that we live face to face with the future, in a horizontal time and in a straight line.

For a protagonist of modern history, this shift in position of these three words is a revolution in the political sense: a radical and crucial change. For a spectator standing outside the historical whirlwind this change would also be a revolution—in the astronomical sense: a particular phase in the world's rotation. The second point of view is not absurd. A new shift is occurring within the present pattern of meanings: as we draw further and further away from the nineteenth century and its philosophies, the figure of the revolutionary is losing its bright glow and that of the rebel is ascending on the horizon. This is a phenomenon that is affecting half of contemporary society: the industrial or "developed" countries. The change is noticeable in all the arts, from those that are the most abstract, music and poetry, to those that are the most popular, the novel and films. The change is also evident in public life and in the imagination of the masses. Our heroes and heroines, as always, are exceptional creatures, but unlike those of the past, they not only defy social laws but also make a mockery of them. Our vision of time has changed once more: meaning lies neither in the past nor in the future but in the instant. One by one the old barriers have fallen in the name of the instant; the forbidden, an immense territory a century ago, is today a public square which any youngster in the neighborhood has the right to enter.

Fashion, popular songs, dances, erotic customs, publicity, and entertainment all are bathed in the ambiguous light of subversion. Because our rebellion is ambiguous. A figure halfway between the revolutionary and the tyrant, the modern rebel embodies the dreams and the terrors of a society that for the first time in history is simultaneously experiencing collective abundance and psychological insecurity. A world of mechanical objects obeys our bidding and yet we have never had less confidence in traditional values and utopian values, in religious faith, and in reason. People in industrial societies are not believers: they are credulous. On the one hand, they worship progress and science; on the other, they have ceased to trust in reason. Though they are fascinated by anything new and are antitraditionalists, they have nonetheless completely abandoned the idea of revolution. The disappearance of the values of the past and the future explains why our contemporaries embrace the instant so frantically. They are not aware that they are embracing a phantom; in this respect they are different from both the Epicureans and the Romantics. In the past, worship of the instant was a form of "wisdom" or an act of despair. In Greco-Roman antiquity, it was a philosophy enabling man to confront death; in the Romantic era, it is the passion that transforms the instant into a unique act. The instant represented not only the transitory but the exceptional, what happened to us only once and forevermore: the "fatal instant," that of death or love, the moment of truth. It was not only exceptional and fateful; it was also a *personal* experience. The new rebellion turns the instant into an everyday occurrence and thus robs it of its greatest attraction: surprise. It is no longer something that will happen to us the day we least expect it; it is what happens all the time. It is a promiscuous cult: it encompasses all classes, ages, and sexes. For our forebears, the instant was a synonym of separation, a line drawn between *before* and *after*; today it designates the indiscriminate mixture of one thing with another. Not fusion: confusion. The notion of a group, something apart from and opposed to society, is giving way to that of a "wave" that comes to the surface and then immediately disappears again in the liquid mass.

The indifference of the public to present-day leaders is understandable: no head of government in the developed countries has the power to proclaim universal subversion. The love or the terror inspired by Lenin and Trotsky, Stalin and Hitler seem to us today to have been collective aberrations. Now that the breed of great revolutionaries and great despots has died out, the new heads of government are not leaders or guides but administrators. When a charismatic personality suddenly appears, the politicians and the masses cannot conceal their anxiety. Americans mourned Kennedy's death and then breathed freely again: they could once more live complacent lives. Kennedy's assassination reflects the state of mind of American society. In the beginning, it was thought that the young President had been the victim of a conspiracy, either of the right or the left: another "ideological" crime. But the Warren investigation has apparently proved that it was the individual act of a confused loner. In Lope de Vega's play, the judge asks: "Who killed the Comendador?" and the people answer in chorus: "We all did, as one!" Everyone killed Kennedy. This "everyone" has no face: he is the universal nobody. It is not surprising that General de Gaulle is an exceptional figure in this world of dull functionaries: he is a holdover from the heroic age. Far from being a revolutionary, he is the very incarnation of tradition, and, at the same time in his own inimitable way, he represents rebellion: a head of government with style is something unprecedented in a world of undistinguished leaders. Khrushchev spoke in proverbs, like Sancho Panza; Eisenhower could barely repeat the clichés he borrowed from the *Reader's Digest*; Johnson expresses himself in a hybrid dialect, a mixture of the rhetoric of the New Deal and the crude speech of a Texas sheriff; others mouth the impersonal and bastard jargon of the U.N. "experts." But the moment we turn to the Third World, we see something quite different: Mao Tse-tung or Nasser are something more than heads of government: they are at once leaders and symbols. Their names are talismans that open the doors of history, symbols of the destiny of their people. Such figures enjoy both the traditional prestige of the hero and the more modern prestige of the revolutionary. They are power and philosophy, Aristotle and Alexander rolled into one. To find anyone like them in the "developed" countries, we would have to look to the real popular heroes: singers, dancers, actresses, space explorers.

The decline of iron-fisted leaders and revolutionaries with programs as rigid as geometries might appear to be a sign of a renaissance of libertarian and anarchist movements. But this is not what this decline represents: we are the witnesses of the decadence of systems and the twilight of tyrants, not of the appearance of a new brand of critical thought. Nonconformists and rebels abound, but their rebellion is sentimental and emotional, stemming from an instinctive and perhaps legitimate distrust of ideas; it is not a judgment passed on society, but a negation; it is not sustained action, but a series of sporadic outbursts followed by a return to a passive position on the sidelines. Today's rebels come from minority groups; it is not workers or the popular masses, but intellectuals and students who demonstrate against the Vietnam war in the United States. Rebellion is the privilege of groups who enjoy something that industrial society has not yet been able (or willing) to give everyone: leisure and education. The new rebellion is neither proletarian nor popular, and thus yet another indication of the progressive decline in value of two words that accompanied the word revolution in its upward climb and its gradual slide downhill: *people* and *class*. The word *people* summed up a Romantic notion associated with the French Revolution which inflamed people's spirits in the nineteenth century. Marxism replaced this word with a concept that seemed more accurate: classes. But, today, these latter are tending to become sectors: the public and private, the industrial and the agricultural. In place of a dynamic image of society as a contradictory totality, sociologists and economists now offer us a classification of human beings according to their occupations.

The City Mouse and the Country Mouse

Marxism taught us that modern society is defined by the contradiction between capital and labor, the bourgeoisie and the proletariat. Though François Perroux does not deny that society is contradictory, he has established a classification that seems to him to correspond more closely to reality in the industrial era: he divides people into masters and servants of machines. The category of masters does not apply only to the owners of these machines; it also includes administrators, technicians, managers, and experts. This classification offers the advantage of accounting for forms of noncapitalist exploitation that Marx had not foreseen—those of the Soviet regime, for instance. At the same time, it does away with the Marxist vision of history as a conflict bearing a certain resemblance to classical tragedy, with a proletarian Prometheus overthrowing the authority of the gods and inaugurating the reign of freedom over necessity. Instead of classes, Perroux deals with functions; he views history not as nemesis but as *social dialogue*, which, in his words, "obeys a logic all its own, which is different from that of violent struggle." Raymond Aron has evolved another concept that has become widely accepted: the definition of the developed countries, whatever their politico-economic form, as industrial societies. Aron is not blind to the profound differences separating the societies of the West and those of Eastern Europe nor does he minimize their importance, but he rightly maintains that in both the determining factor is not so much the political system as the relation of science and technology to the means of production. Hence, Aron proposes that we call this totality of nations and peoples "industrial civilization."

All these conceptions have one feature in common: they replace the old dichotomies—classes, philosophies, civilizations—with an image of society as a sum of equations. For the ancients, human society was a sort of metaphor of the body, a superior animal (the *body politic* of English political philosophy); Michelet looked on history as epic poetry; to Marx and Nietzsche it was a theatrical performance, or, more exactly, that region where theater ceases to be representation and becomes a living embodiment of the life and death of men and societies. The archetypes today are neither biology nor theater, but communications theory. Inspired by mathematics and symbolic logic, our vision is a formal one: we are not interested in knowing *what* messages say or *who* formulates them, but *how* they are expressed, the form in which they are transmitted and received. Aron writes:

> There would be no point in trying to discover what the mental outlook of the manager of an Anglo-American company and the director of a Soviet trust have in common . . . but as economies become industrialized, both must calculate expenses and income, make *long-term plans*—the production schedule—and translate all these data into comparable *quantitative* terms.

The unique nature of the phenomenon, the meaning of the message, is being supplanted by a formal, quantitative conception. Industrial society uses the instruments provided by science, and its methods are no different from those of the laboratory. What counts, therefore, are the means, and not the ends or the goals of each society. History as passion is disappearing.

The concept of class has fared no better within regimes claiming to be Marxist. The idea of the proletariat as a universal class is central to Marxism; without it the entire theory collapses: if there is no universal class, there is no world revolution and no international Socialist society. The idea has been undermined in two ways by Marx's heirs. The first revision took place in Yugoslavia, and has now become quasiofficial Communist doctrine. The proponents of this revised theory maintain that each nation must arrive at Socialism by its own path and its own means. Marx had emphasized that proletarian internationalism was not a philosophical idea resembling the cosmopolitanism of the Stoics, but rather the consequence of a social reality: the relation between the worker and the means of production. The proletarian, unlike the artisan, not only is not the master of his work and the owner of his work tools; he also sees his existence as a person reduced to the category of an "abstract work force." He, therefore, is subject to the same process of sheer quantification as the other means of production. Like electricity, coal, or petroleum, the worker knows no nationality and has no local color. Being uprooted is his natural condition and his only tradition is the struggle that links him to others who are uprooted, his fellow proletarians. The new interpretation is a radical inversion of Marx's idea: the nebulous idea of the *nation* becomes predominant, and nationalism becomes the way to Socialism. Marx hoped that the proletariat would destroy the boundaries between countries; his heirs have made nationalism respectable again.

The other modification is not an attempt to subordinate the internationalism of the proletariat to nationalism; it aims, rather, at extending this internationalism to other classes. This is the Chinese thesis: exacerbating the conflict between the countryside and the city is the proper strategy for world revolution, the form that the class struggle has taken in the second half of our century. Marx was convinced that it would be the urban proletariat that would resolve the conflict between the countryside and the city once it had seized power; Mao Tse-tung believes that it will be the peasants. Whether correct or not, this idea is anti-Marxist and would have shocked both Lenin and Rosa Luxemburg, both Trotsky and Stalin. The universality of the urban working class is not quantitative (it was not the largest class in Marx's day and never has been); rather, it is the result of its historical position: it is the most advanced class. The daughter of industry and science, it is the most recent human social product, the class that has inherited all the achievements of the bourgeoisie and the other classes that were the masters before it. Therefore it represents the common, general interest: "The revolutionary class . . . does not present itself as a class but as the representative of the whole of society; it appears as the total mass of society confronting the dominant class."* Just as the bourgeoisie destroyed the narrow particularism of feudalism and built the national State, so the proletariat destroys bourgeois nationalism and establishes an international society. Peasants and workers are natural allies because they are the classes that are most oppressed and largest in number, but this identity of interests does not cancel out their differences: peasants are the oldest class, workers the most recent; the former are a holdover from the preindustrial era and the latter the founders of a new age. Marx never set any store in a Communist revolution by peasants. Late in life, in 1870, he wrote in a letter to Kugelmann: "Only England can serve as a fulcrum for a genuine economic revolution. It is the one country where there are no longer any peasants." He had previously stated: "A Communist movement can never begin in the countryside" (*The German Ideology*). According to Marx, the relation of each class with industry, that is to say with the most advanced and perfect form of the system of production of our age, determines its historical function. The function of the peasant is a passive one: he is a victim of the action of machines as consumers of raw material and natural products, and thus his opposition has no effect. Tied to the land, the farm laborer may rebel, but his rebellion is local, or, at most, national. Though industry is world-wide in scope, the bourgeoisie's relation to it is contradictory: industry is international and the bourgeoisie national; the former is social and the latter private. The proletariat resolves this contradiction because, like industry, it is international and socializes manufactured products.

All this is common knowledge. I have mentioned it not because I believe that every line that Marx wrote is true, but because it is instructive to put his words side by side with those who claim to be his disciples

* Karl Marx and Friedrich Engels, *The German Ideology* (1845).

and are doing their utmost to destroy their opponents by labeling them "revisionists." It is obvious that the proletariat has not performed the international revolutionary role assigned it by Marx. Nonetheless, all of Marxist theory is based on this central idea, and therefore none of its proponents ever questioned it. Lenin believed that the struggle for national independence of colonial and semicolonial countries, especially those in Asia, would aggravate the situation of the imperialist countries and dissipate "the entirely false aura of social peace" that reigned in them, thanks to the concessions granted the oppressed masses "at the expense of the conquered countries and the colonial peoples" by the bourgeoisie that had emerged the victor of World War I. This struggle "would culminate in a total crisis of world capitalism." Thus, for Lenin, the principal axis was still the working class, and revolution was inseparable from a crisis of capitalism. Trotsky was even more explicit, and said in 1939 that World War II would bring on

> . . . a proletarian revolution in the advanced countries that will inevitably spread to the Soviet Union, destroy the bureaucracy, and bring about the regeneration of the October Revolution . . . Nonetheless, if the war does not result in a proletarian revolution—or if the working class takes power, is incapable of retaining it, and hands it over to a bureaucracy—we would be forced to recognize that the trust and hope that Marxism has placed in the proletariat have proved false.

Rosa Luxemburg, who was one of the first to point out the importance of the "underdeveloped" world in the evolution of contemporary history, never doubted that the industrial working class would be the central revolutionary force.

The Channel and the Signs

Marx reduced ideas to reflections of the mode of production and the class struggle; for Nietzsche they were masks that the will to power tears off; Freud described them as sublimations of the unconscious. Now Marshall McLuhan wishes to persuade us that they are products of the communications media. McLuhan is a talented writer, and I am not attempting to use the stupid argument of the authority of these predecessors to demolish him when I cite his name after those of Marx, Nietzsche, and Freud. I mention him because his thoughts on the matter are an example of the fate that these three precursors and critics of modern civilization have suffered. McLuhan is a very popular author, as Spengler was forty years ago. I must add that unlike Spengler, he is not a reactionary; at the same time, he lacks the somber genius of that German author. McLuhan has borrowed Spengler's concept of technology as an extension of the human body; but whereas for Spengler a man's hand is a claw, for McLuhan it is a sign: the former was a prophet of Armageddon and the latter of Madison Avenue. McLuhan's writings abound in paradoxes (usually ingenious ones) and stimulating statements (often quite perceptive ones). We may be disturbed by his emphatic tone, his inordinate fondness for quotations, and the logical inconsistencies of his arguments, but these rhetorical vices are characteristic of his country and our era: McLuhan is a writer typical of his time and his milieu. Hence it is symptomatic, or rather, significant, that the central theme of his writings is *meaning*.

McLuhan's views are an exaggeration and a simplification of what Peirce, Wittgenstein, Heidegger, and Lévi-Strauss, among others, have said. I hasten to add that these authors in no way resemble each other, except for one thing: all four conceive of reality as a tissue of meanings, and all of them are persuaded that there is no such thing as an ultimate meaning to this totality of meanings, or if there is, it is inexpressible. For two of them there is something beyond language which only silence can point to (Wittgenstein), or perhaps poetry (Heidegger); for the other two either are trapped in a net of language that is both transparent and inescapable (Peirce: "The meaning of a symbol is another symbol") or are at best only a link in this unbreakable chain, a sign, a single phrase in the message that nature murmurs to itself (Lévi-Strauss: "Myths communicate with each other through men without their being aware of this fact"). McLuhan reduces these ideas to the level of the advertising industry: the message depends on the medium of communication, and if this medium changes, the meanings also change or disappear.

There is no question that there are crucial differences between participating in a Platonic dialogue and reading the *Symposium* aloud before an audience, between reading the *Critique of Pure Reason* all by oneself and watching a group of professors discussing Kant's critique on television. The differences are not merely formal ones: the change in the medium of communication alters the message. The shift from dialogue to exposition alters the very meaning of the word philosophy. None of this is new, and Max Weber, among others, has given us brilliant descriptions of the interrelation between ideas and social forms. Nor is the idea that technology is the origin of the Logos a radically new one: Engels blithely assigned industry the philosophical role of doing away with Kant's "thing in itself." What is new, however, is making one branch of technology—the communications media—the "motor" of history. Radio and television take the place of Providence and Economics, of the Genius of the world's peoples and the Unconscious. Now, if the changes in the means of communication determine and explain other social changes, who and what is responsible for the changes in the means of communication? McLuhan neither asks this question nor tries to answer it.

Saussure's distinction between the signifier and the signified, a twofold characteristic of all signs, may help to clarify matters. McLuhan begins by identifying the message with the medium of communication, thereby converting the latter into a sign. For McLuhan, the media are signifiers, but what they signify can be reduced to the following tautology: the communications media signify communications media. An example may make my point clearer. In one of the first pages of *Understanding Media*, McLuhan states: ". . . the 'content' of any medium is always another medium. The content of writing is speech, just as the written word is the content of print, and print is the content of the telegraph."* Quite apart from the fact that this is a parody of the sentence of Peirce's that I cited above, it confuses the issue in several ways. McLuhan's application of the concept of form and content to phenomena in the field of communications is misleading. It is obvious that a jar may contain water, wine, or some other liquid. A jar, however, is not *defined* by

* *Understanding Media* (1964).

its content but by its function or by its meaning: a jar is an object used to contain substances, generally liquid ones. The same is true of the media of communication: writing "contains" words, but it may also "contain" numbers, musical notes, and so on. Strictly speaking, writing does not *contain*: it *signifies*. It is a visual sign that points to another sign: the spoken word. To be absolutely precise, we would have to say that the communications media—radio and television for example—in fact have no content at all; they are always empty: they are simply conduits, channels through which signs flow. These signs, in turn, are like capsules containing meanings. The signifier—musical notes, letters, or any other mark—"discharges" its meaning if someone sets the "firing mechanism" in motion: reading, for instance, in the case of the written word.

The notion of content can be applied more accurately to signs than to the channels that transmit them. However, since the old metaphor of form and content introduces dangerous confusions, no one uses it nowadays. The terms *signifier* and *signified* are not identical with *form* and *content*. A jar may contain water, oil, or wine; the linguistic element *Tuesday*, however, refers to the day that comes immediately after Monday and to no other day. The signifier/signified duality also occurs at the level of the sentence, the paragraph, the text, and speech as a whole. Writing does not *contain language*: it *is* language. The same thing is true of the printed text, the Morse code, and the spoken word.

When McLuhan claims that the medium is the message, he is saying that the message is not what we say but what the media say, despite us or without our knowledge. The media become signifiers and produce meaning inevitably and automatically. This idea presupposes a natural or immanent relation between the signifier and what is signified, an idea that goes back as far as Plato. But the truth is precisely the opposite: the relation between the signifier and the signified is conventional. I would say that it is one of the products of the social contract. The sound *pan* in Spanish designates bread, but in Urdu and Hindustani it means betel. To us, the sign of the cross is the symbol of Christianity; to a Mayan of the fifth century, this sign may well have stood for fertility or some other idea, or may have been simply decorative. The meaning of signs is the product of convention. If the communications media are signs, as

McLuhan asserts, their meaning too is necessarily the result of a convention, either an explicit one or a tacit one. The key of meaning therefore does not lie in the communications media, but in the structure of the society that has created these media and made them signifiers. Media are not what signify; society is what signifies, and what it signifies is *us*, in and through these media.

McLuhan is quite right when he asserts that the communications media also signify, that they are also messages. It is obvious that any medium can become a sign. But there are many different sorts of media, many different sorts of signs. The spoken word is one medium of communication and radio another. In the case of the spoken word, sign and medium are inseparable: so long as the sound *pan* is not pronounced, the meaning *bread* is not forthcoming. The sound is the signifier by means of which the signified appears. Radio waves, on the other hand, are means by which all sorts of signs appear—including nonverbal signs: music, natural or artificial sounds, and so on. The relation between signifier and signified is an initmate, fundamental one in the case of the spoken word: the former depends on the latter and vice versa. In the case of radio, there is no such relation between signifier and signified. Or, more precisely, this relation is obviously of very little importance. When McLuhan says that the medium is the message, what he is really saying is that the medium— radio, television, and so on—has become a linguistic sign; but if we break down the radio sign into its two components, the signifier and the signified, we find that the one is *radio* and the other is also *radio*. Having arrived at this point, I shall recall what Roman Jakobson has said about linguistic functions. Among these functions, language may take the form of a message whose object is "to establish, prolong, or interrupt communication, to test whether the circuit is functioning." This is a function that is frequently fulfilled in conversation on the telephone: "Hello!" "Can you hear me?" In everyday life it is a ritual: "How are you?" "How nice to see you!" "What's that?" "Er, hmmm, hey there," etc. Among primitive peoples, what Malinowski calls the "phatic function" of language is of prime importance, being both magical and ceremonial. Jakobson points out that it also appears among myna birds, parrots, and other species that "talk." This is the only linguistic function these creatures have in common with us. It is also the first to appear among children when they learn to talk. If we are to believe McLuhan, the era of planetary and interplanetary communications media is that of the return to the tautology of animal language. Like that of talking birds, the object of our communication is to communicate communication.

The spontaneity of history and the universality of reason were conjoined in the word revolution: it was the Logos in action and incarnated among men. Now technology absorbs all these meanings and becomes the active agent of history. Marx had great faith in industry, but he believed that in and of themselves, machines lacked meaning; the function of machines seemed intelligible to him only within the social context: who are their owners and who controls them? It is man who gives his tools meaning. Lévi-Strauss has shown that the invention of writing coincides with the birth of the great empires in Mesopotamia and Egypt: writing was the monopoly of the priestly bureaucracy and an instrument of oppression for centuries thereafter. In the hands of the bourgeoisie, printing broke the clerical monopoly on knowledge and forever ended the status of writing as something *sacred* because it was *secret*. Thus the meaning of writing and printing depended on the social context: it was society that gave them meaning, and not vice versa. In the first half of our century, many writers of every political persuasion published books on the technique of revolution; today, books and articles on the revolution of technique are published every day. It would be absurd to deny that technology changes us; but it would be equally absurd to disregard the fact that all techniques are the product of a given society and of concrete individuals. There is no point in stressing the undeniable importance of technology in the modern world. What I denounce is our superstitious worship of the *idea* of technology. This notion is as powerful a myth as that of reason or revolution, though it differs from them in one important respect: it is a nihilist myth, neither pointing to nor preaching nor denying a set of values. The systems of the past, from Christianity to Marxism, were at once a criticism of reality and an image of another reality. They were a vision of the world. Technology is not an image of the world but a way of operating on reality. The nihilism of technology lies not only in the fact that it is the most perfect expression of the will to power, as Heidegger believes, but also in the fact that it lacks meaning. *Why?* and *To what purpose?* are questions that technology does not ask itself. What is more, it is not technology, but we ourselves, who should be asking these questions.

Satiety and Nausea

The worship of the idea of technology involves a decline in value of all other ideas. This phenomenon is particularly striking in the realm of art. The new avant-garde makes no attempt to justify itself either rationally or philosophically. Dada claimed to be a metaphysical rebellion. The theoretical literature of Italian Futurism was the most significant feature of that movement. The critical and utopian thought of the Surrealists was as important as the creations of its poets and painters. Today, however, the majority of artists prefer the act to the program, the gesture to the work of art. Mayakovsky extolled technology and Lawrence denounced it; the new artists neither praise nor condemn: they manipulate modern apparatuses and artifacts. Rebellion yesterday was a passionate cry or a deadly silence; today it is a shrug of the shoulders: "why not?" as a reason for being. The aim of poetry, from the Romantics to the Surrealists, was the fusion of contraries, the transformation of an object into its contrary. Creation and destruction were the two poles of one and the same vital energy and the tension between the two sustained modern art. The basis of the new aesthetic is indifference. Not metaphor: juxtaposition, a sort of neutrality between the elements of the painting or poem. Not art or antiart: nonart. The privative *a* reigns supreme over man and his language.

The shift of emphasis in the verbal triangle—from revolt to revolution and from revolution to rebellion—would seem to point to a change in orientation: a shift from utopia to myth, the end of rectilinear time and the beginning of cyclical time. This is not the case. In the West, an interregnum has ensued: nothing has yet taken the place of the old principles of faith or reason. The fact that this is the heyday of the rebel, and the fact that his rebellion is ambiguous, indicate that there is something missing. Whatever society he comes from, the rebel is an outsider: if he ceases to be one, he ceases to be a rebel. Hence he cannot be either a source of change or a guide. He is the lonely combatant, the dissident, an isolated fact, and an exception. Industrial society has lost its center, rectilinear time has cut it off from its source and literally uprooted it: it has lost its foundation, that *anterior* principle, that "time immemorial" which is the justification of the present and the future, the reason for being of any and every community. Cut off from the past and continually hurtling toward some vague future at such a dizzy pace that it cannot take root, it merely survives from one day to the next: it is unable to return to its beginnings and thus recover its powers of renewal. Its material abundance and intellectual riches cannot conceal its essential poverty: it is the master of the superfluous but lacks the essential. Being has drained out of it through a bottomless hole, time, which has lost its age-old consistency. This vacuum is experienced as disorientation, and disorientation in turn is experienced as ceaseless movement. And because this movement is completely aimless, it is equivalent to a frantic marking time in one place.

When there are no rules, the exception becomes the rule: the rebel is crowned king in an effort to make the eccentric the center. But the moment the exception becomes the rule, there is a cry for a new exception to take its place. The rule of fashion is extended to ideas, morality, art, and social customs. The restless need to seize upon each new exception that comes along—in order to assimilate it, castrate it, and cast it aside—explains why the powers that be, especially in the United States, are so tolerant of the new rebellion. The ambiguous nihilism of rebel artists is the mirror-image of the complacent, self-satisfied nihilism of those in power. The destiny of the rebel in the past was defeat or submission. Defeat is almost impossible today: the authorities tolerate any sort of rebellion, once they have clipped its nails and claws. I do not regard rebellion as the basic value of art, but it saddens me to see one of man's most generous impulses being simulated or cleverly exploited. It is hard to resign oneself to the corruption of the word *no*, which today has become merely the key or the jimmy to force the doors of fame and fortune. Making the rebel an object of worship is a way of domesticating him. In the past, the rebel was part of an immutable cycle. As the cosmos revolved, glory and punishment were the two faces of his destiny, the recto and the verso: Prometheus and Lucifer, generosity and consciousness. The modern rebel is the offshoot of a society expanding horizon-

in the Neolithic period: the change from hunting to agriculture radically altered man's relation to nature, and the emancipation of women will wreak equally profound changes in human sexual relations, the family, and individual feelings. Rimbaud said that we would have to "reinvent love": perhaps this is the mission of women in our time. The movement of young people is an epiphenomenon, because it is a rebellion that depends on the system against which it is rebelling. It is a protest against the powers that be rather than an attempt to create a new order. The youth movement and the struggles of the ethnic minorities are not really revolutionary. They are rebellions. In our time, we must make a distinction between *rebellion* from within and *revolt* from without. Rebellion from within is a sign of health; a society that examines itself, denies itself, and absorbs its negations is a functioning society. Revolt from without represents a contradiction that thus far has proved insuperable. It is Contradiction itself, the other face of reality. Though it has lessened the tensions between classes, industrial society has failed to do away with the contradiction that has typified it from the beginning. It has merely exteriorized it. The contradiction today is not *within* industrial society but in its relations to the world *outside* it: not the proletariat but the "underdeveloped" countries. And it is not a revolution—it is a revolt.

The Two Forms of Reason

Some forty years ago, Ortega y Gasset wrote a critique of geometrical reason and the revolutionary spirit; Sartre has written an equally penetrating critique of rebellion. Their two points of view represent a sort of symmetrical contradiction; this fact seems to me to merit discussion, for I am not certain that anyone has pointed out the similarities between the French and the Spanish philosopher. Ortega y Gasset's name is seldom mentioned these days, whereas Sartre is famous the world over. This may be because Ortega was a conservative, while Sartre is a revolutionary. Although the views of both have their origin in German phenomenology, this common source is not the only reason for the similarities between them. What makes these two philosophers resemble each other is not so much the ideas they share as their style of attacking them, making them their own, and sharing them with the reader. Though the two of them struck out in opposite directions, each of them in his own way turned modern German thought into a moral and historical meditation. Despite the fact that neither of them cultivates a spoken style, we *hear* them thinking: the tone of their writings is at once passionate and peremptory—a magisterial tone, in both the good and the bad senses of the world. They excite us and irritate us, and thus force us to participate in their demonstrations. Ortega once said that he was only a journalist, and Heidegger has said the same of Sartre. This is quite true: they are not the philosophers of our time, but philosophy in our time.

The French writer is more systematic, and his *œuvre* is more broad in scope and more varied than that of the Spaniard. His public acts have also been more generous and more daring. Sartre has set out to do something that is doomed to failure: to reconcile concrete life and historical life, existentialism and Marxism. His originality as a philosopher does not lie, however, in this immense and disjointed effort to elaborate a synthesis, but rather in the flashes of insight that at times enrich his reflection. Though he may have failed to construct an ethical system, he has reminded us that thinking and writing are not ceremonies but acts. Writing is not simply a chance activity; it is a deliberate choice; beauty creates an atmosphere of responsibility that neither the writer nor the reader can escape with impunity. Ortega's virtues are quite different. A Mediterranean with a Catholic background, while Sartre is Nordic and Protestant, his prose is clear and sensuous. It is not clouded by the "sublimeness" of his German masters, nor is it affected by that underlying religious tension that exacerbates Sartre's prose, betraying his perpetual rebellion against the Protestantism of his childhood. Sartre has banished God from his system, but not Christianity. Ortega's pessimism is more radical and his recognition of vital human values does not imply the recognition of any sort of transcendence, not even one that has assumed the mask of history. Ortega is a pagan, Sartre an apostate from Christianity. Ortega had a more penetrating understanding of history, and many of his predictions have come true. The same cannot be said of Sartre. This is not the first time that a reactionary philosopher has proved to have strange gifts of prophecy. I have always marveled at the brilliant foresight of Chateaubriand, Tocqueville, Donoso Cortés, Henry Adams. They were clairvoyant despite the fact that their values were those of the past—or perhaps because of that very fact: for them, the old notion of time as cyclical was still a vital concept.

According to Ortega, the bankruptcy of geometrical reason was a portent of the decline of the revolutionary spirit, the child of European rationalism. Reason, the source of utopias and revolutionary projects, had come down to earth and become historical reason: it was no longer a timeless construct but something that unfolds in time. I think he was quite right, and his acuity amazes me: it required an extraordinary perspicacity to foresee the present situation in Europe in the heyday of Bolshevik utopianism. But his critique was superficial, and the new principle that he proclaimed, historical reason, strikes me as no more than a slightly updated version of German vitalism and historicism. As Ortega saw it, our era is one marked by an absence of fundamental principles; but its new principle lies precisely in this absence: its underlying vital or historical cause is simply change itself. The Spanish philosopher neither explains the reason behind this change nor describes the forms that it is taking.

Sartre has encountered a similar obstacle: finding a foundation for dialectics. An heir of reason (whether pure, geometrical, or analytical), dialectics is true historical reason: it is the only method that accounts for society, its changes, and its internal relations (classes) or its relations with nature and other non-historical, primitive, or marginal societies. But dialectical reason fails to account for man's concrete existence: there is a part of a man's self, Sartre maintains, that is irreducible to the determinations of history and historical classes. What is more: dialectics cannot explain itself, it is not self-constitutive: the moment it constitutes itself, it is self-divisive. Lévi-Strauss's critique of Sartre is very much to the point: if there is a fundamental opposition between dialectical reason and analytical reason, one of the two must be "less rational;" since the latter is the foundation of the exact sciences, what kind of reason can dialectical reason be? The other alternative is equally contradictory: if dialectics is reason, its only possible foundation is analytical reason. In Lévi-Strauss's view, the difference between these two sorts of reason belongs to the category of complementary opposition: dialectical reason is nothing other than analytical reason, and at the same time it is what enables the latter to understand society and its changes, its institutions and its representations. Lévi-Strauss's critique is half correct: it reveals the contradiction at the heart of Sartre's philosophy, but it neither resolves it nor transcends it. What is the foundation of the new element that appears in analytical reason when it becomes dialectical reason? Vital reason and dialectical reason are philosophical approaches continually searching for a principle of *sufficient* reason.

Ortega studies the reformist as the figure who is the precise opposite of the revolutionary; Sartre the rebel. In his essay on Baudelaire, the French writer takes an idea not very different from Ortega's as his point of departure: the revolutionary seeks to destroy the ruling order and institute another, more just one; the rebel fights against the excesses of power. Ortega had said: the revolutionary wishes to change customary uses; the reformist to correct abuses. Though their points of departure are similar, the conclusions they reach are not: Ortega foresees the decline of revolutions; Sartre unmasks the rebel in order to proclaim the primacy of the revolutionary. I have discussed Ortega's ideas elsewhere; what I would like to do here is follow Sartre's line of argument.

The figure of the rebel quite naturally fascinates and irritates Sartre: for one thing, the rebel was the model that caused him to break with his world in his youth; for another thing, it is an exception that belies the revolutionary rule. To reveal that Baudelaire's refusal to conform in no way undermined the order that he pretended to attack, and that his rebellion was a paradoxical homage to power, is tantamount to demonstrating that the revolutionary rule is universal and that the revolt of artists, from Baudelaire to Surrealism, has been a private quarrel among the bourgeoisie. The rebel is a pillar of power: if that power should crumble, he would be crushed to death. What is more, he is also its parasite. The rebel feeds on power: the iniquity of those above him justifies his blasphemies. His *raison d'être* has its roots in the injustice of his social status; once this injustice ceases, his reason for existing also ceases. Satan does not want God to disappear: if the godhead were to disappear, he, too, would disappear. Diabolism can survive only as an exception, and it therefore confirms the rule. To rebel is to resign oneself to being a prisoner of the rules of power; if the rebel really wanted to be free, he would not challenge the power of the rules but the rules of power; he would not attack the tyrant but power itself. The rebel cannot claim that his reason for being is any sort of special or exceptional status—including that of being a poet, a black, or a proletarian—without contradicting himself, and without being in bad faith in the moral sphere.

Real rebellion must be based on a project that includes others and, therefore, it must be universal. The black does not seek recognition of his blackness but of his humanity: he fights to make blackness a fundamental, recognized component of the human species, and thus his rebellion becomes part of a universal undertaking: the liberation of mankind as a whole. Rebellion is a pattern of behavior that inevitably leads either to revolution or to self-betrayal. Baudelaire's rebellion was a sort of circular simulation; his protest did not become a cause and the misfortune of others played no part in it. An exaltation of his feelings of humiliation as an individual, it was the counterpart of a tyrannical God. The rebellion of the poet was a comedy in which his ego played a game with power without ever having the courage to destroy it. Baudelaire neither wanted nor tried to be free: if he had really dared to be a free man, he would have ceased to regard himself as an object and ceased to be a *thing*, viewed respectively with scorn and tenderness by the cruel Stepfather and the perfidious Mother. His rebellion was a part of his *dandyism*. The poet wished to be seen. Or rather, he wished to watch others watching him: the gaze of others made him aware of himself and at the same time it turned him to stone. His secret and ambivalent desire was fulfilled in two ways: he became both a heart-rending spectacle for others and an imperturbable statue in his own eyes. His *dandyism* consisted of making himself at once invulnerable and the object of the gaze of others. His rebellion was a nostalgia for childhood and a homage to power: consciousness of separation and a yearning to return to the "green paradise." A paradise he did not believe in. His rebellion condemned him to perpetually peering into a mirror: what he saw in it was not other people but his own gaze gazing back at him.

The Exception to the Rule

Sartre wants Baudelaire to have ceased being what he was and become: who and what? He does not say, though he compares him unfavorably to Victor Hugo. Or rather, to the *idea* of Victor Hugo, for I suspect that deep down Sartre really prefers Baudelaire's poems. More than once, Sartre indulges in what he criticizes most severely: abstractions. In the realm of politics, it was the *idea* of revolution, more than the actual situation in the Soviet Union, that led him around 1950 to defend the entire Soviet regime, including Stalin and his concentration camps. Not because he approved of them, but because in his eyes they did not deny the (ideal) reality: the camps were a blot but they nonetheless did not destroy the Socialist structure of the regime. The arguments put forth in Sartre's review, *Les Temps Modernes*, were similar to those previously employed by Trotsky at the time of the Soviet-German pact and the invasion of Finland: the latter's notion of a "degenerated workers' State" which nonetheless preserved intact the bases of state ownership of property, was not very different from that of a "stalled revolution" put before the readers of *Les Temps Modernes* by Sartre and Merleau-Ponty. There are other, more grievous examples. For instance, during the Hungarian revolution Sartre made a number of very curious statements:

> The most serious error has doubtless been Khrushchev's report, his solemn and public denunciation, the detailed exposure of all the crimes of a sacred person [Stalin], who has long been the symbol of the regime; this is madness when such frankness has not been preceded by any appreciable rise in the standard of living of the population . . . The masses were not prepared for this sort of revelation of the truth. . . .

To make the masses' ability to understand the truth dependent on their standard of living is to give proof of a quite unrevolutionary conception of the proletariat and a quite unphilosophical conception of truth . . . Nonetheless, how can we forget Sartre's attitude during the Algerian conflict, and his present position against the war of extermination that Americans are waging in Vietnam?

Sartre's essay on Genet gives us an even clearer picture of his ideas concerning rebellion. I mention this book, perhaps one of his best, not as a model of literary criticism or of psychological analysis but rather as an exposition of some of his ideas on the subject. In Genet's case the rebel has managed to transcend his initial attitude: his absolute negation has been transformed through writing into an affirmation. By embracing his fate as a social outcast, as an ejaculation of society, Genet performs an act of self-projection, of self-ejection—he transfigures himself and thus frees himself. In Sartre's book, the poet Genet becomes a conceptual entity. While concepts are manipulable entities, human beings are irreducible realities: after reading this essay we are much better acquainted with Sartre's thought, but Genet, the real man in the flesh, has evaporated, having been reduced to an example illustrating an argument. Genet chooses "evil" and becomes a "saint;" Saint Teresa chooses "good" and becomes a "whore." I do not know what Genet would think of this statement; I am certain that the Spanish nun would have roared with laughter at it. I suspect that Genet does not believe in the ontological reality of evil, even though the entire line of Sartre's argument is intended to prove that evil is the very basis of Genet's "existential project;" on the other hand, the one reality for Saint Teresa was unquestionably God, who for her was not an ideal reality but a palpable spiritual one. Why is Genet's negation "good" and Saint Teresa's affirmation, which is no less total than Genet's denial, "evil"? Perhaps Sartre is attempting to prove that abjection and sanctity have the same roots and that at a certain point the two fuse. There is some truth in this idea, but examining it here would lead me too far astray. What prevents me from accepting Sartre's judgment of Genet is his conception of the latter's "existential project": if Genet has chosen evil, why does he write and why does he write so well?

The tendency to explain one level of reality by another older, unconscious one—the social order or a person's instinctive life—is something we have inherited from Marx, Nietzsche, and Freud. This way of thinking has changed our view of the world and been responsible for numerous discoveries. But, at the same time, how can we fail to see its limitations? I will mention Polanyi's criticism here: a watch is made up of molecules and atoms governed by the physical laws of matter; if these laws were to momentarily cease functioning, the watch would stop. But this would not be the case if the situation were reversed: if the watch is smashed to bits, the fragments will continue to obey the same laws . . . Two different levels of meaning are involved here. For Sartre the "project" is a mediation between two realities: the self and its world. In his latest philosophical work the same idea reappears: "*L'homme est médié par les choses dans la mesure même où les choses sont médiées par l'homme.*"* Since man is not a simple being, mediation implies at least three levels: instinctive or unconscious reality, consciousness, and the world (things and other people). I do not believe that Sartre's method can explain creative works: although they are part of a person's "existential project," their meaning transcends that of this project. There is a gap between a man's works and his biography. This relation between the two is the same as that between the molecules and the watch in Polanyi's analogy. Sartre criticizes our belief in the eternity of creative works because he regards them as historical signs, hieroglyphs of temporality. But even though works may not be eternal—what possible meaning can this word have?—they nonetheless have a longer life span than individuals. They endure for two reasons: they are independent of their authors and their readers; and, since they have a life of their own, their meanings change for each generation and even for each reader. Works are mechanisms for creating multiple meanings, which cannot be reduced to the "project" of the person who writes them.

Sartre condemns literature as an illusion: we write because we cannot live as we would like to. Literature is the expression of a feeling of deprivation, a recourse against a sense of something missing. But the contrary is also true: language is what makes us human. It is a recourse against the meaningless noise and silence of nature and history. Living implies speaking, and without speech man cannot have a full life. Poetry, which is the perfection of speech—language speaking to itself—is an invitation to enjoy the whole of life. Sartre's contempt for language betrays his nostalgia, not for the fullness of human life but for the plenitude of Being: the gods do not speak because they are self-sufficient realities. In his atheism there is a sort of religious frenzy that is absent in the sages and in other atheist philosophers. Though the central word in his phi-

---

* "Man is mediated by things to the very same degree that things are mediated by man."

losophy is *freedom*, it must also be said that it is a freedom whose source is a *curse*. For the French writer we are doomed to be free, and that is why we speak, write, and each day begin anew to carve our statue of ourselves out of smoke: an absurd rebellion against our death and an image of our destruction. Sartre's vision of man is that of the Fall: we are flawed, guilty, empty. The "project" is an attempt to fill the yawning hole, the lack of Being. But his conception of the "project" tells us nothing about a reality that reveals our plenitude in the very heart of emptiness: works of art. Thanks to those works, we may enter another world of meanings and see our own intimate self in another light: we escape the prison walls of the self. Genet and Saint Teresa are both authors of an *œuvre*. Genet is an original writer; Saint Teresa is something more, something infinitely more precious: a visionary spirit coupled with an extraordinary critical awareness. (Compare Sartre's autobiographical *Les mots* [*The Words*] with what the Spanish nun tells us of her life.) These works take on a life independent of their authors and are intelligible to us even though the life of their creators may not be.

Baudelaire's answer to Sartre's criticism is his poems. Where does the truth lie: in his letters and other private documents or in his published work? Born of bad faith and the masochistic narcissism of a voyeur, for whom the nakedness of a woman is a mirror that reduces him to a mere reflection and thus preserves him from the gaze of others, does this poetry free us or enslave us, does it lie to us or does it tell us something essential about man and his language? Every great work of art forces us to ask ourselves what language is. This question places the meanings, the world of convictions that sustain the historical man, between parentheses, in order that the *other* may appear. Although Sartre has asked himself this question, he does not believe that it is the task of poetry to pose it and answer it: he is persuaded that the poet turns words into things. But once they are touched by the hand of man, things become suffused with meaning; they become a question or an answer. All human works are languages. The poet does not transform the word into an object: he gives the sign back its multiple meaning as a signifier and obliges the reader to complete his work. A poem is a continual recreation. Sartre's purpose was not to judge poetry but to unmask the poet, to destroy the myth of the poet. He failed. For one thing, the analysis of Baudelaire's "existential project" sheds no lights on the real meaning of his work; for another, Baudelaire's life is unintelligible without his poems. I do not say that his work explains his life; what I mean to say is that it is an integral part of his life: without his poems Baudelaire would not be Baudelaire. The paradoxical nature of the relations between a life and an *œuvre* stem from the fact that they are complementary realities in only one sense: we can read Baudelaire's poems without knowing a single detail of his biography; but we cannot study his life if we ignore the fact that he was the author of *Les fleurs du mal*.

The Rules of the Exception

Sartre's critique of Baudelaire has a more general interest since in this essay he outlines a distinction between rebels and revolutionaries that seems to me to be central to his political thought. His starting point is not so much the contrast between uses and abuses as between an unjust order and the injustices of order: the uses of the bourgeois regime are genuine abuses, while the abuses of the Socialist regimes are transitory historical evils. The reason for this relativism is not difficult to grasp. Bourgeois society can give us freedoms, but its real structures are essentially a denial of freedom; evil is inherent in its very nature: it stems from the private ownership of the means of production. The morality and the laws of bourgeois society hide its reality: the exploitation of man by man.

Though a Communist regime deprives its subjects of certain rights and freedoms for a more or less extended period of time, its ultimate goal is freedom: it is based on the principle of collective ownership and the cornerstone of its ethic is the universal liberation of mankind. The first question we might ask ourselves is whether the actual situation in China or the Soviet Union bears any real relation to this idea. At this point in history, it would seem absurd to maintain that there is such a relationship between the idea and the reality: the claim that human exploitation has disappeared in these countries, or that it is well on its way to disappearing, belongs more to the realm of belief than to the realm of experience and reason. But let us grant the fact that the dichotomy is real. If so, what attitude should Chinese, Russian, or Yugoslavian citizens take with regard to the abuses of their governments? Some will say that the import of their rebellion is different: in a bourgeois regime, customary uses are abuses; in a Socialist regime uses and abuses are two quite different things, and, as a consequence, rebellion is legitimate: it is not merely an instance of bad faith. I shall note that this line of argument justifies the rebellion of citizens in these countries but not the conduct of revolutionary governments. I grant that a revolutionary government may stray from the straight and narrow path from time to time. Nonetheless, the universal rule splits down the middle: there are two types of abuses and two types of rebels, the good and the bad, theirs and ours. The citizen of a Socialist country may be a rebel but not a revolutionary; the citizen of a bourgeois nation must be a revolutionary rather than a rebel. This is the subject of several of Sartre's plays, and it gives rise to another question: what is the proper attitude of a revolutionary in the West toward the rebels of the Socialist countries? Should he condemn them in the name of the universal undertaking that socialism represents, or should he help them by any means at his disposal? The first attitude would be a return to Stalinism, and the second . . .

I am well aware that the actual circumstances are much more complicated and that a number of positions are possible between the two extremes that I have pointed out; what I would like to emphasize is the shakiness of a distinction that at first glance may appear to apply universally. In theory, Sartre is quite right: his moral relativism is not all that relative since it is based on a valid rule that applies to everyone in this period of history. This rule is not an ironclad law: it is based on a universal goal, the liberation of all mankind, which is both a consequence of modern history and a matter of free choice. This goal or "project" is the mediation between us and the world we live in. Moral distinctions depend on this project, and this project, in turn, depends on the real situation of the society one belongs to: doing away with the abuses of a bourgeois regime is not enough, because its injustice is radical and built into the system. Nonetheless, the issue becomes clouded the moment we compare the rule to the reality: the dichotomy cannot withstand scrutiny and vanishes in thin air.

In our day, a new element has entered the picture, the revolt of the Third World: does the distinction between revolutionaries and rebels apply to us too? It obviously does not, and Sartre has supported movements of rebellion in the European colonies and in Latin America. Hardly any of these movements are Socialist, in the strict sense of the word, and all of them are ardently nationalist. Many of them are a paradoxical combination of both tendencies: Nasser's version of Arab Socialism or that of the Algerians is not an attempt to fuse the pan-Arab movement with Socialism but rather to Arabize the latter. Their rebellion is that of a particularism, precisely the contrary of what Sartre claims to be the case: the dissolution of the exception in the universal rule. The same thing is happening in other nations of Asia and Africa. And in countries where the leaders proclaim themselves disciples of Marx and Lenin, as in Cuba, they nonetheless continue to stress the fact that their national revolutions are original and independent movements. Thus there is a third class of rebels, to which Sartre's distinction is not applicable: their rebellion is an affirmation of their uniqueness.

The dissension among the already well-established powers is equally palpable. The quarrel between the Russians and the Chinese is the most serious one dividing the Socialist states but not the only one. Although these differences take the form of ideological quarrels, their real roots lie in the national particularisms and the conflicting political and economic interests of the members of the "Socialist" group. There are also splits within the other bloc and it too threatens to fall apart. The tendencies represented by General de Gaulle are not merely a transitory phenomenon, as the Americans would have us believe, but a sign of the political resurrection of Western Europe. In the not too distant future, the nations of Europe, by forming a community or by concluding bilateral pacts, will establish an independent policy that will soon cause conflicts of interest with both the Americans and the Russians. Japan will shortly follow the same path. The gradual breaking up of the "free world" alliance is the counterpart in reverse of that taking place in the other bloc: in the West, political and economic differences are the first to make themselves felt, then national ones, and finally ideological ones. And it is significant that the divisions within these two former solid blocs are not the reflection of any sort of transformation of social and economic structures or of a change in political philosophy: one bloc continues to call itself Socialist and the other democratic.

The contradiction in our time is not the one Marxism made us aware of—that between capital and labor—but another one that neither the founders of the doctrine nor their disciples foresaw. This conflict is that between the "developed" and the "underdeveloped" countries. The irreducible and increasingly severe antagonism between the bourgeoisie and the proletariat that Marx predicted has proven to be more strictly applicable to the relations between these two groups: the rich nations are becoming richer and the poor nations poorer every day. But the categories of Marxism do not fit the present situation nor do they explain the new contradiction. The revolt of the Third World is a pluralist movement, and the creation of a universal society is not one of its goals. The political and social forms that it adopts, from State Socialism to a private economy, are not ends in themselves but means to speed up its historical evolution and become modern. Hence, they are not a universal model. The Third World lacks a general revolutionary theory and a program; it has no philosophy nor does it aspire to construct the city of the future according to the dictates of reason or the logic of history; nor is it a doctrine of salvation or liberation as Buddhism, Christianity, the French Revolution, and revolutionary Marxism were in their time. In short, it is a world-wide revolt but it is not ecumenical; it is an affirmation of a particularism through a universalism—and not vice versa. I do not mean to say thereby that it is illegitimate. On the contrary, it not only seems right to me, but I also believe that it is the last chance we Latin Americans have of becoming historical subjects after the great failure of our struggle for independence. It is the only way that we will cease to be objects, to use Sartre's vocabulary, and begin to be our own masters. This is what our revolt is. But it is not a universal project, and as a consequence we cannot deduce any universal rule from it. The distinction between rebels and revolutionaries vanishes because no single goal is discernible in contemporary history. To deny that such a goal exists does not mean that we have regressed to a crude empiricism. If a change in the nature of human time is taking place, as I firmly believe, the phenomenon is affecting our beliefs and systems of thought. What is happening is that rectilinear time is ending and another time is beginning.

The End in the Beginning

The use of the word *revolution* in the sense of a violent and crucial change of society belongs to a period that conceived of history as an endless process. Whether rectilinear, evolutionary, or dialectical, history had a more or less predictable direction. It was of little moment that this process appeared to have the form of a curve or a spiral or a zigzag when examined in detail; in the final analysis it was a straight line: history was a continuous forward march. This idea could not have come to the fore during the reign of the cyclical conception of time, and of the Christian idea of eternity. The destruction of both ideas was the work of reason. But this destruction was possible only because a change in the status of reason had already occurred. Metaphysics regarded reason as the foundation of the order of the universe, the sufficient principle of everything that exists; reason was the guarantee of the coherency of the universe, that is to say its *cohesion*, and thus it was the origin and the center of movement itself. There was a pact, so to speak, between Christian time and Greek geometry: the rectilinear and finite time of mankind ruled on earth; the circular and eternal time of the stars and the angels ruled in the heavens. After the critique of the gods, reason criticized itself and ceased to occupy the center of the cosmos. But it did not lose its privileges thereby: it became the revolutionary principle par excellence. An agent capable of modifying the course of events, reason became active and libertarian. Active: it was movement, an ever-changing, ever-ascending principle; libertarian: it was men's instrument to change the world and change themselves. Human society became the field of operation of reason, and history the unfolding of an idea: a discourse that man had been delivering since the beginning. The first words of history were a stammer; they soon became a march of syllogisms. The progress of society was also that of reason: the story of the feats of technology possessed the clarity and the perfect consistency of a logical demonstration.

Marxism has been the most coherent and most convincing expression of this way of thinking. It combines the prestige of science and that of morality; at the same time it is a total system of thought, like the religions and philosophies of the past. If history is the convergent march of society and reason, revolutionary action will consist in suppressing the contradictions between them at higher and higher levels. Reason must march along with its feet on the ground, and simultaneously society and nature must be humanized: that is, their action must promote freedom and take on the logical necessity of a rational operation. In the bourgeois era the basic contradiction is the divergence between the system of ownership and the system of production: the second is "more rational" than the first. Industrial production tends toward universality, it is energy tamed by man which in turn can tame nature forever; private property stifles the social force of production, the proletariat, and stands in the way of the universal availability of products by withdrawing them from circulation, either through accumulation or through waste. The industrial system creates abundance, but capitalism prevents the masses, either the proletariat or the huge numbers of colonial slaves, from sharing it. The meaning of Communist theory is twofold: Communism frees the forces of production and universalizes the distribution of products. Abundance makes equality possible and the two together bring about authentic, concrete freedom. As the revolutionary process is completed, classes and nations disappear; civil and economic society become one; the contradictions between economics and politics fade away: the State, its morality and its police, wither away. Finally, in its most advanced stage Communism dissolves the fundamental contradiction of what Marx called human "pre-history": the economic system becomes totally social, that is to say rational and universal; and reason becomes socialized. At that moment other contradictions, which are not specified in Communist doctrine, arise . . . As we all know, the contradictions that actually developed were different, and appeared before the revolutionary process that corresponds to this era was completed. There is no point in drawing up a list of them: the universal class, the proletariat, remained under the sway of reformism and nationalism; no revolutions took place in the developed countries; Nazism triumphed in Germany; in Russia, Stalinism liquidated Lenin's comrades; and in the Third World, the central protagonists of revolt today are the peasants, the petty bourgeoisie, and

reveals that this time is not the only kind of time there is. And we might perhaps add: if dialectics has proven incapable of discovering its constitutive principle it is because, like all modern philosophies, it is built over an abyss. This abyss is the great yawning gap left when the old cyclical time split apart. Our time is that of the search for a foundation, or as Hegel said, that of the consciousness of a split. Marxism has been an attempt to unite what was separated. Its central concern was society: it discovered that the basic cell is a complex organism, a tissue of relations determined by the social process of economic production; it also revealed the interdependence of interests and ideas; and, finally, it demonstrated that societies are not formless amalgams but totalities of unconscious and semiconscious forces (economics, superstructures, and ideologies constantly interacting) which obey certain laws that are independent of our will. But, today, many of its theories, from the concept of culture as a reflection of the social relations of production to the idea of the universal revolutionary mission of the proletariat, strike us as quite dubious. We have a different view at present of the correspondences and interrelations between the systems of production, philosophies, institutions, and artistic styles of each historical period.

Marx was the founder of the science of social relations. He failed, however, to deal with the morphology of societies and civilizations, with what separates them and distinguishes them above and beyond their economic production. There are many things that have no place within the Marxist schema, from works of art to human passions: everything that is *unique*, either within an individual person or within civilizations. Marx was insensitive to something that was to be one of Nietzsche's discoveries: the physiognomy of cultures, the particular form and the unique mission of each of them. He did not see that the so-called superstructures, far from being mere reflections of the systems of production, are also symbolic expressions and that history, which is a language, is above all else a metaphor. This metaphor is many metaphors: human societies, civilizations. And it is also a single metaphor: the dialogue between man and the world. Marx was unable to account for the "miracle" of Greek art: it did not correspond to the social system of Greece. What would he have said if he had been intimately acquainted with the arts of primitive peoples or those of the Orient and pre-Columbian America? Yet, the nature of these arts is no different from that of the arts of modern times or those of the Renaissance: they are metaphors of man as he confronts the world, metaphors of the world within man. Marxism, finally, has been one of the agents of the historical change of our century, but its explanation of these changes has been inadequate and above all its pronouncements as to its meaning and its predictions as to its direction have proven false. From this point of view, the truth of the matter is precisely the contrary of what Sartre believes: Marxism is not a *body of knowledge* or a *method of investigation* but an *ideology*. It is so on two counts: in the Communist countries, it hides social realities beneath a veil of concepts and thus serves as a coverup for basically unjust social relations; and in the non-Communist countries, as Sartre himself admits, it has turned into a "dogmatic metaphysics."

Although Marxism has become an ideology, it was a critical philosophy in the beginning. The secret of its vitality today, and the seeds of its future fertility lie in its critical powers. When I speak of the vitality of critical Marxism today, I am not thinking of Sartre's disquisitions on dialectics or Althusser's ingenious and scholarly variations on Marxist themes, but in the resurrection of the critical spirit in Poland, Czechoslovakia, and other nations of Eastern Europe—if the books and essays by Kolakowski and others are any indication. Sartre is attempting to reconcile Marxism and existentialism; Althusser Marxism and structuralism. Both have made contributions to Marxism as an "ideology": by that I mean that even when they criticize the vulgar versions of Marxism or those considered to be such (the dialectic of nature, "economism," etc.), these authors carefully refrain from criticizing it as "ideology," thereby enhancing its status as a sacred body of writing. Sartre regards Marxism as a historical dialectic and thus distorts it and transforms it into a "method of investigation"—a philosophy with no foundation outside of itself that is continually forced to constitute and reconstitute itself. Althusser attempts to restore the dignity of Marxism as a science and a theory: structure over against history. This interpretation also distorts Marxism, not by transforming it into a "total philosophy" but into a science of sciences. The historical element disappears from Marxism, just as Sartre had previously undermined it as a structure. As François Furet puts it:

> Structural analysis is an attempt to extend the methods of the natural sciences to the human sciences, but Althusser and his friends are subtly forcing it in the direction of Marxist dogmatism, which they claim to be an *a priori* of reflection—since from the very beginning they have regarded this latter as an equivalent of the mathematical model.

Althusser's source is Marx's *General Introduction to the Critique of Political Economy* (1857), in whose pages the latter outlines a program for the methodology of this science in terms that to a certain degree anticipate structuralism. (This is not surprising; I have said above that Marx's model was the cell: "merchandise is the cellular economic form," he states in the preface of *Das Kapital*.) But in this same *Introduction* Marx relentlessly hammers home the point that social science is historical: "When we speak of production, it is always a question of production in a specific state of social evolution." Althusser grants that Marx produced new knowledge without being entirely aware that he had done so. This idea is a hundred-percent Marxist: science and work *produce* knowledge, they make matter human and intelligible. And precisely because it is a product, this knowledge is historical—it is not a mathematical structure. Sartre regards Marxism as a history and an ethic; Althusser regards it as a science. Both claim that their aim is to make it invulnerable to any sort of criticism. In actual fact, they do not criticize it at all: they set it up as an untouchable model, either of the historical process or of the structures of science.

If the essence of Marxism is criticism, it can be revised only by an act of self-criticism. Criticism of Marxism as an *ideology* is indispensable if there is to be a rebirth of revolutionary thought. The program for this critical revision was outlined by Marx himself, and as Kostas

Papaioannou points out[*] we need only substitute the words *ideological Marxism* for *religion* in the following passage to see how perfectly it applies to our time:

> Criticism of religion is the necessary condition of all criticism . . . the foundation of unreligious criticism is this: man makes religion, not religion man . . . But man is the world of man, the State, society. This State and this society produce religion: an absurd awareness of the world, because they themselves constitute an absurd world. Religion is the general theory of this world, its encyclopedic compendium, its logic in popular form . . . its moral sanction, its general principle of justification and consolation . . . the fight against religion is thus automatically a fight against this world . . . the criticism of religion is inherently that of this vale of tears . . . the criticism of heaven becomes the criticism of earth, the criticism of religion that of law, the criticism of theology that of politics . . .

I would gladly exchange all the speculations of modern Marxists with regard to dialectics, language, structure, or praxis among Lacandonians for a concrete analysis of the social relations of production in the Soviet Union or China. But the criticism of earth is impossible without the criticism of heaven. No, Marxism is neither a complete philosophy nor an ideology, even though those who govern (and speak) in its name have made it into a "general theory of the world" and an "encyclopedic compendium." In the prologue to his *Critique of Political Economy* (1859), Marx relates how he and Engels decided in 1845 to make their "examination of philosophical conscience." The result was *The German Ideology*. Perhaps someone in our generation will have the courage and the genius to undertake an equally rigorous examination. Until that day, our philosophers, sages, and poets, not content with putting before us the apology of the ideological heaven, will continue to put before us that of the earth and its tyrants.

---

[*] *L'Idéologie froide* (1967).

A Form in Search of Itself

The destiny of the revolutionary, as a hero or an archetype of rectilinear time, has been parallel to that of the theories that have simultaneously expressed and shaped our era, from Machiavelli to Trotsky. When man is confronted with a state of affairs that is unjust he rebels. This rebellion begins as a naysaying and gradually becomes a consciousness: it becomes a critique of the existing order and a determination to bring about a new just, rational, universal order. Criticism is followed by action: waging revolution demands the invention of a technique and an ethic. Revolutionary technique views violence as an instrument and power as a lever. It transforms human relations into physical objects, mechanisms, or forces. Reactionary violence is passionate: it takes the form of punishment, humiliation, vengeance, sacrifice; revolutionary violence is rational and abstract: not a passion but a technique. If violence becomes a technique, a new ethic is needed to justify or reconcile the contradiction between force and reason, freedom and power. Traditional ethics distinguished between means and ends—a theoretical distinction that rarely prevented crime and abuses but a distinction nonetheless. The revolutionary, as Trotsky explains with a sort of icy passion in *Their Morals and Ours*, cannot allow himself the luxury of making such a distinction. Ends and means are not good or bad in themselves: they simply further revolution or they do not. The ethics of the categorical imperative, or any other similar ethic, is viable only in a society that has forever destroyed the sources of coercion and violence: private property and the State. Two extremes: Gandhi and Trotsky. The first was persuaded that the only thing that counts are means: if they are good, the ends will also be good. Trotsky refuses to make a distinction between means and ends: both depend on specific historical situations. Means are ends and ends are means: what counts is the historical context, the class struggle.

Trotsky's ideas may alarm us, but we cannot label them immoral without proving ourselves hypocrites or falling into Manichaeism. Everything changes, however, once the revolutionary seizes power. The contradiction between reason and violence, power and freedom, which has been veiled during revolutionary struggle, now becomes blindingly apparent: on assuming authority, the revolutionary is no longer the instrument of the violence of the slave but of the injustice of power. I grant that it is not impossible to justify terror: if the revolutionary State must ward off attacks from its enemies, both within and without, violence is legitimate. But who is to judge whether terror is legitimate: its victims or the theologians in power? This point could be debated endlessly. Whatever our views on the matter, there is one thing that seems to be beyond question: terror is an exceptional means. Its continued use betrays the fact that the revolutionary State has degenerated into a Caesarism. Moreover, when the revolutionary seizes power, he is faced with another problem: the new state of affairs never quite coincides with revolutionary ideas and programs. It would be surprising if it did: these programs are applied not to physical objects but to human societies which by their very nature are unpredictable. In the face of the opacity of the new situation, two paths are open to the revolutionary: rebellion or power, the scaffold or administration. The revolutionary ends up exactly where he began: he must either submit or rebel. Whichever solution he chooses, he ceases to be a revolutionary. The cycle comes to an end and another begins. It is the end of rectilinear time: history is not a continuous march forward.

The end of rectilinear time can be interpreted in two ways. It may be thought of as the absolute end of human history: an atomic holocaust, for instance, might destroy all mankind. This apocalyptic vision, full of disturbing Christian overtones, is the very basis of the Soviet Union's policy of peaceful coexistence. Not without reason, the Chinese find this scandalous and have denounced it as a betrayal of Marxist doctrine. The claim that history may well end in a great burst of fire involves a number of minor heresies and one major one: history ceases to be a dialectical process and the march of reality toward rationality ends in an irrational act, one that is meaningless by definition: a physical explosion. The second way of conceiving of the end of rectilinear time is a much more modest one: we may simply note that the orientation of modern history has changed, and that times literally are changing: a real *revuelta*. To say that rectilinear time is drawing to a close is not an intellectual heresy nor does it betray a nostalgia for myth and its bloody and fateful cycles. Time is changing form and with it our vision of the world, our intellectual concepts, our art, and our politics. Perhaps it is premature to try to say what form time is assuming; but we may nonetheless single out, here and there, a few signs pointing to such a change.

Since 1905, the universe has changed shape and the straight line has lost its pre-eminence. "Einstein's space is no longer the stage on which the drama of physics was played out; space today is one of the actors because gravitation is entirely controlled by curvature, a geometrical property of space," Whittaker says. We need hardly mention the modern conception of the structure of the atom: the elementary particles are not really elements but zones of interaction, fields of relations. A similar change can be noted in the other sciences: the biology of microevolution, linguistics, information theory, and Lévi-Strauss's structural anthropology are abandoning linear explanations; all of them view reality as a system of synchronic relations. The cell, the word, the sign, the social group: each of these units is a totality of particles, like those that go to make up the atom; rather than an isolated unit, each of these particles is a relation.

Linguistic analysis, according to Roman Jakobson, distinguishes two levels within language: the semantic level, from the morpheme to the word, the phrase, and the text; and the phonological level: phonemes and distinctive particles. The first level is governed by meaning; the second is a structure that might be called "presignificative," though without it there would be no meaning. The phonemes are "systems of symbolic atoms," each one of which is composed of differentiating particles: although the phonemes and their particles have no meaning in and of themselves, they participate in the process of signification because they serve to distinguish one phonological unit from another. They are units of differentiation: *this* is not *that*. At its simplest level language is a system of relationships of opposition or association, and all the immense wealth of linguistic forms and meanings is based on this binary structure. If we go from the phonemic level to the level of words, we again see that language is a sort of transformation mechanism: the different combinations of words—that is to say, their position within the phrase—produce meaning. This phenomenon is repeated again on the level of the text: the meaning varies according to the position of the sentences. These relations are not "historical," or diachronic: language is a permanent structure. I. A. Richards has recently pointed out that the same combinatory process operates in microbiology: "The molecular, chromosomatic and cellular levels are the counterparts of the morpheme, the phrase and the text in the linguistic hierarchy." The analogy can be extended to anthropology, to communications theory, and to other fields, not excluding artistic and poetic creation.

In a recent book by Stephen Toulmin and June Goodfield (*The Architecture of Matter*), I read: "The distinction between living and non-living things can no longer be drawn in *material* terms. What marks them off from one another is not the stuff of which they are made: the contrast is rather one between systems where organization and activities differ in complexity." An organization, a structure: a circuit of relations. All these conceptions reduce rectilinear time to a variable in the system of relations. Chronology, the order in which one thing follows upon another, is a relation but it is not the only one or the most important one. The modern sciences—physics, linguistics, genetics, anthropology—study synchronic rather than diachronic relations. The model of science is not history. Strictly speaking, *before* and *after* are ways of referring to phenomena: symbolic expressions or metaphors, linguistic devices.

In *The Idea of Progress*, the English historian J. B. Bury describes the efforts of Sociologists and historians of the past century to discover the law of motion of civilization. Despite Immanuel Kant's hopes, no Kepler or Newton has yet discovered this historical law. For a time the theory of evolution, rather than physics or astronomy, seemed to offer a solid foundation. Darwin ended his *Origin of Species* with these words:

> As all the living forms of life are the lineal descendants of these which lived before the Silurian epoch, we may feel certain that the ordinary succession by generation has never once broken, and that no cataclysm has desolated the whole world . . . And as natural selection works solely by and for the good of each being, all corporeal and mental environments will tend towards perfection.

But contemporary physics and astronomy, first of all, lean toward the view that the universe has been, and still remains, the theater of continuous explosions and cataclysms; and second, even if it were true that natural selection operates as a Providence "by and for the good of each being"—it is a biological law that is not applicable to human history. On the other hand, by discovering the plurality of societies and civilizations, history and ethnology have shown that the idea of progress, not as a law but as an ideological agent of social change, has had very little influence on mankind, save in the Western world and in modern times. Our civilization has not been (and will not be) the only civilization, and the idea of progress has likewise not been (and will not be) the only one to inspire men. The notion of progress, Bury says, implies "the illusion of deliberate purpose." At the same time it, destroys it. If everything is change, the idea of progress is condemned to death by this process itself: "another star, unnoticed now or invisible, will climb up the intellectual heaven, and human emotions will react to its influence, human plans respond to its guidance."

The artistic forms of the past, both classical and Baroque, were closed forms. Intended to present reality, they always had an over-all pattern enclosed within definite boundaries. Since Symbolism, artists have isolated the elements, broken the form, and split the presence. The aim of Symbolism was not so much to convoke reality as to evoke it. Poetry became a liturgy of absence, and later a verbal explosion. The other arts followed in poetry's footsteps. The breaking of closed form was followed by the attack on language; the destruction of meaning by the destruction of the sign; the destruction of the image by that of the painted representation. In extreme forms, as in "concrete poetry," the poem is a typographical composition halfway between the sign and the signified; and painting has ceased to be painting in the strict sense of the word: it is the triumph of the object over representation (Pop Art) and of technique over expression (Op Art). But the history of modern art is not merely the history of the breaking up of closed form. At the end of the last century, shortly before his death, Mallarmé published *Un coup de dés*. In 1965, in *Los signos en rótación* [*Signs in Rotation*], I discussed this text. I shall repeat here that Mallarmé's work represented more than the birth of a style or a movement: it was the appearance of an open form, the purpose of which was to escape linear writing. A form that destroys itself and starts all over: it is reborn only to fall to pieces again and reconstruct itself again. The page also ceases to be mere background: it is a space that participates in the meaning, not because it possesses meaning in and of itself but because it enters into alternate relations of opposition and conjunction with the writing that by turn covers it and leaves it bare. The poem changes meaning as the position of its elements changes: words, phrases, and blanks. The page is writing; the writing space. In constant rotation, in perpetual quest of its ultimate meaning without ever reaching it, the poem is a transformation mechanism, like cells and atoms. These latter are transformers of energy and life; the poem, of symbolic representations. Both are apparatuses for producing metaphors . . . Any work that really counts as our century goes on, whether in literature, music, or painting, is governed by a similar principle. Neither a circle traced around a fixed center nor a straight line: a wandering duality that expands and contracts, one and a thousand, yet always twofold, an eternal pair in conjunction or opposition, a relation that leads neither to unity nor to separation, meaning destroying itself and being reborn in its contrary. A form in search of itself.

Revolt

A civilization is a system of communicating vessels. There is therefore a certain justification for my translating what I have said above regarding the tendencies of modern thought into historical and political terms. My first observation is this: if history does not march in a straight line, neither is it a circular process. Space moves along with us: it has ceased to be the stage and become one of the actors. The space in which the drama of history has been performed in recent centuries goes by the name of Latin America, Asia, and Africa. In Europe, the various peoples of that continent were, to a certain degree, the agents of history; in our countries they have been the objects of history. It is no exaggeration to say that we have been treated as a landscape, as things, or as inert space. Today this space has come alive and is participating in the drama. This brings me to my second point: if space is an actor, it is also an author. With its continual changes of cast and plot, history is no longer a play written by a philosopher, a party, or a powerful State; there is no such thing as "manifest destiny": no nation or class has a monopoly on the future. History is a daily invention, a permanent creation: a hypothesis, a game, a wager against the unpredictable. Not a science, but a form of wisdom; not a technique, but an art.

The end of rectilinear time is also the end of revolution, in the modern meaning of the word: a crucial change in a neutral space. But in the other, older sense, the end of the straight line confirms the fact that we are participating in a revolution: the wheeling of the stars, the rotation of civilizations and peoples. The shift in position of the words in our verbal universe can help us understand the meaning of what is happening. The word *revolt* was supplanted by the word *revolution*; faithful to its etymology, this latter word is today returning to its old meaning, to its origin: we are living the beginning of a new time. The insurrection of the peoples of the Third World is not a rebellion: whereas rebellions are eccentric, marginal, minority movements, this movement encompasses the greater part of humanity, and even though it began on the periphery of the industrial societies, it has become the focal point of our concerns today. The insurrection of the Third World is not a revolution either. We are witnesses of a pluralistic movement that does not fit our ideas of what a revolution is or ought to be. What it really represents is a popular and spontaneous revolt that is still in search of its ultimate meaning. It is being torn between extremes, and at the same time nourished by them: universal ideas are being used to justify its particularism; the originality of its age-old religions, arts, and philosophies is being used to justify its right to universality. A motley collection of peoples in rags and civilizations in tatters, the heterogeneity of the Third World is becoming a unity as it aligns itself against the West: it is the *other* by definition, its caricature and its conscience, the other face of its inventions, its justice, its charity, its worship of the individual person, and its systems of social security. A reflection of a past that antedates Christ and machines, it is also a determination to be modern; as a traditionalist movement, the prisoner of rites and customs that go back thousands of years, it is unaware of the value and the meaning of its tradition; as a modernist movement it wavers between Buddha and Marx, Siva and Darwin, Allah and cybernetics. It feels a fascination and a horror, a love and an envy of its former masters: it wants to be both like the "developed nations" and unlike them. The Third World has no idea what it is above and beyond a will to being.

The industrial societies enjoy a prosperity that no other civilization in the past has ever attained. This abundance is not a synonym of health: never in history has nihilism been so widespread and so total. I shall not indulge in fateful prophecies of its imminent collapse. I do not feel that such a collapse is close at hand. Though I do not believe that the end of industrial societies is in store, neither do I refuse to see what is all too obvious: these societies are moving ahead rapidly, but they no longer have any idea of where they are going or why. In the last twenty years we have seen the universalist pretensions of the Soviet Union crumble. I place great hopes in Russian poets, sages, and artists. I hope, above all, that the Russian people will awaken: I would like to hear that deep rumbling voice like a great clap of thunder that we sometimes hear when we read that country's poets and novelists. I believe in the spirit of the Russian people, but fortunately for them and for us, Moscow is not Rome. As for the United States, even though it is the most powerful country on earth, it lacks a philosophy worthy of its great strength. The political thought of Americans has been borrowed from the English. It suited their needs in the era of Yankee expansion in Latin America; but today as a global ideology, it is as antiquated as the doctrine of "free enterprise," the steamboat, and other relics of the nineteenth century. The United States is a unique case in history: an imperialism in search of universality. Might the secret of the Vitality of "isolationist" tendencies in America not lie in that nation's dim awareness that there is a profound contradiction between its power and the political philosophy on which that power is based? I must confess that my belief in the critical and democratic tradition of the United States is greater still than my belief in the religious spirit of the Russians. It is a political and intellectual tradition and, at the same time, a poetic and prophetic tradition. Its roots are in the Reformation, and thus it is a religious tradition and a tradition of criticism of institutionalized religion. It has produced one of the great literatures of the modern era, from Thoreau and Melville to our days. The United States is the world center of economic and political power but it is also the world center of rebellion and self-criticism. This is what Latin Americans seldom see . . . The United States can no longer aspire to global hegemony, not only because of the existence of the Soviet Union—whose role as a rival has been diminished though not eliminated—but also because of the birth of China and the rebirth of Europe and Japan. The key to the future of the industrial societies, and to a great extent that of the revolt of the Third World, lies in Eastern and Western Europe. Great changes will occur there. An independent European policy would alter the relations between the superpowers and have a decisive effect on history in Africa, Asia, and Latin America. The industrial societies thus might begin a new sort of dialogue between themselves and the rest of the world.

I do know what fate is in store for the revolt of the Third World. Economic and social development is an obsession with the leaders of these nations and their "intelligentsia." almost all of whom have been educated in the former metropolises. Some of them look on the more or less bureaucratic versions of "Socialism" as the most rapid way of reaching the industrial level; others place their trust in a "mixed economy," technology, foreign loans, education, and so on. At this point in history it is no longer possible to have the same confidence in bureaucratic "Socialism" as twenty years ago. Its defects have become obvious. The other solution is equally dubious. Foreign loans, which are always too small and always have strings attached, are frequently counterproductive; they increase the rate of inflation rather than speeding up development, and since it is necessary to administer them, they spawn new armies of bureaucrats and "experts." These latter are the modern form of the plague; while in the past smallpox and malaria decimated the population, this new plague from abroad paralyzes people's minds and imaginations. As for technology: it is not only a method of development, but first and foremost a state of mind, an attitude toward nature and society. The majority of the peoples of Asia and Africa look on technology as a miracle, a form of magic rather than an operation in which a quantitative approach to the world plays the central role.

Modern education has thus far been the dubious privilege of a minority. Its most immediate and most obvious result has been to erect a wall between an elite who have had a Western-style education and the masses who have a traditional culture. Minorities without a people and a people without minorities. What is more, the victims of Western-style education suffer the illness called a "split personality," or in moral terms, "inauthenticity." Hence the most urgent task confronting the Third World is to regain its own being and face up to the realities of its situation. This requires pitiless self-criticism, and an equally rigorous examination of the true nature of its relations to modern ideas. These ideas in many cases have been mere superficial borrowings: they have not been instruments of liberation but masks. Like all masks, their function is to shield us from the gaze of others, and, by a circular process that has often been described, to shield us from our own gaze. By hiding us from others, the mask also hides us from ourselves. For all these reasons, the Third World needs not so much political leaders, a common species, as something far more rare and precious: critics. We need many Swifts, Voltaires, Zamyatins, Orwells. And since in these countries, once the homelands of dionysiac orgies and erotic wisdom, a hypocritical and pedantic puritanism reigns today, we also need a Rabelais and a Restif de la Bretonne.

The great problem that the industrial societies will confront in the next few decades is leisure. Leisure has been both the blessing and the curse of a privileged minority. It will now be that of the masses. This is a problem that will not be resolved without the intervention of poetic imagination, in the strict sense of the words poetry and imagination. In the precapitalist era, people were poorer, but they worked fewer hours and there were more holidays. Time never hung heavy on their hands, thanks to the many ceremonies, festivals, pilgrimages, and religious rites they took part in. Leisure is an art we have forgotten, as we have lost that of meditation and solitary contemplation. The West must rediscover the secret of the incarnation of poetry in collective life: the fiesta. The descent of the Word among men and the sharing of it: Pentecost and Passion. The other alternative is the debased leisures of the great empires, the Roman circus and the Byzantine hippodrome. Although the problems of the "underdeveloped" societies are exactly the contrary, they likewise require the exercise of imagination, both political and poetic. We have to invent models of development that are less costly than those constructed by Western "experts." More viable ones, and above all, ones more in keeping with each country's national character and its history. I mentioned above the need for an Indonesian Swift or an Arab Voltaire; the presence of an active imagination, rooted in native mental soil, is also indispensable: dreaming and working in terms of one's own reality. These peoples were the creators of architectonic complexes that were also centers of human community, points of convergence of imagination and practical action, human passions and contemplation, pleasure and politics, peoples who made the garden a mirror of geometry. the temple a great piece of sculpture palpitating with symbols, the sound of water falling on stone a language rivaling that of the birds—how is it possible that they have denied their history and their destiny so radically? The leaders of these countries, despite their nationalism—or perhaps *because* of this very nationalism, which is yet another European mask—prefer the abstract language that they have learned in schools of economics in London, Paris, or Amsterdam.

In a moment of understandable exasperation, the only Hindu Zamyatin that I know of, Nirad C. Chaudhuri, has written that the first thing that must be done is to expel all foreign experts from India; to reject all foreign aid, which is niggardly, humiliating, and corrupting; to liquidate the handful of elite leaders, whether rightist or leftist, who worship Her Britannic Majesty or the Russian Communist Party, the Pentagon or Chairman Mao . . . and begin all over again, as the Aryan tribes did four thousand years ago. But the Third World is *condemned* to modernity and the task confronting us is not so much to escape this fate as to discover a less inhuman form of conversion. A form that does not bring duplicity and split personalities in its wake, as is the case today. A form that does not bring on the ultimate alienation: the death of the soul. Hence the need for self-criticism and imagination. Self-criticism puts its finger on the wound: falsehood; imagination projects models of development that are models of coexistence: the "standard of living" is an abstract category, whereas real life is concrete and particular . . . The revolt of the Third World has not discovered its proper form and therefore it has degenerated into different varieties of frenzied Caesarism or languishes beneath the stranglehold of bureaucracies that are both cynical and fuzzy-minded. The leaders don't know exactly what they want or how to achieve the vague goals they have set. What has happened in recent years in Asia, Africa, and Latin America is not encouraging.

As for us Latin Americans: we are face to face with what may well be our last chance historically. We are repeatedly reminded that we are part of the Third World. It should also be pointed out that ours is a unique, borderline situation; like other peoples in the Third World, we have a very low level of industrial development and are more or less completely dependent upon foreign powers (the United States in our case). At the same time, our economic and social situation is different, as is our history. The conquest and domination of Latin America by the Spanish and Portuguese bears little resemblance to that of Asia, and even less to that of Africa, conquered by other European peoples. Nor do our independence movements resemble those of these nations. Unlike what happened in India or Southeast Asia, none of the great pre-Columbian civilizations resisted domination; nor has any non-Christian religion survived among our peoples. The steppingstone to modernity in Latin America is Christianity, not Mohammedanism or Buddhism or Hinduism. The leap into modernity is a natural one for us, in a manner of speaking: modernity began as a criticism of Christianity; it is the daughter of Christianity, not of Islam or of Hinduism. For us, Christianity is a path rather than an obstacle; it involves a *change*, not a *conversion*, as it does in Asia and Africa. The same must be said of the influence that European political thought, especially that of France, has had on our wars of independence and our republican institutions. They were a matter of choice, not a heritage of colonial domination. And, finally, the nature of social conflict is different in our case. However incomplete, imperfect, and riddled with injustices social and cultural integration may be in Latin America, in our countries there are not two societies with opposite values at loggerheads with each other, as in most Asiatic and African countries. There are admittedly minorities and customs that are holdovers from the pre-Hispanic period, but they are not as serious or as burdensome as the caste system in India, tribal loyalties in Africa, and nomadism in other regions.

The history of Latin America has made it a case apart. What we really are is an eccentric, backward part of the West.

The subject of Latin America requires separate analysis, and I have therefore refrained from dealing with it at length in the course of these scattered remarks and comments. Many years ago, in the final pages of another book, I pointed out that

> No one has bothered to take a good look at the blurred and formless face of agrarian and nationalist revolutions in Latin America in order to try to understand them for what they are: a universal phenomenon that calls for a new interpretation . . . What is even more depressing is the silence of the Latin American *intelligentsia*, which is living in the center of this whirlwind . . .*

The Cuban Revolution, which took place after these lines were written, makes such reflection even more urgent. For the present, I will merely say that the task before us is not only to do away with an unjust and anachronistic state of affairs which condemns us to dependency on foreign powers in the international sphere, and on the domestic scene to an endless cycle: dictatorship, followed by anarchy, and a return to dictatorship. Even more importantly, we must also endeavor to recover our true past, which was shattered, dispersed, and sold the day after we won our independence. Latin America has been dismembered: nineteen pseudo-nations created by our "liberators," by oligarchies and, later, by imperialism. The change of our social structures and the recovery of our past—that is to say Latin American unity—are not two different tasks: they are one and the same thing. The present political division of our continent makes no sense either historically or economically. Almost none of our countries, with the exception of the very largest of them, is a viable economic unit by itself. The same is true in the area of politics: the one thing that can save us is an association free of all non-Latin American influence.

* *El laberinto de la solitud* (1959; English translation, *The Labyrinth of Solitude*, 1961.)

I do not know whether the peoples of Latin America will adopt the model of the Mexican or the Cuban Revolution. For different reasons, both these revolutions seem to me to have grave shortcomings. They are not really models but almost accidental forms that two popular movements were forced by internal and external circumstances to assume. In the beginning both lacked a precise ideology. In all likelihood, the other peoples of our continent will invent different forms. This is the great task confronting Latin America, one that will test the political imagination of our peoples: viable forms of revolt or reform (whichever best fits the case) must be discovered and new institutions and forms of human community must be created. Development does not merely mean quantitative progress: above all else, it is, or should be, a solution to the over-all problem of social life, including both work and leisure, being together and being by ourselves, individual freedom and popular sovereignty, food and music, contemplation and love, physical and emotional needs . . . Economic development and the reform of social and juridical structures would be useless without political confederation, without a Latin American alliance. If we fail, we will continue to be what we are now: a hunting and fishing preserve—whether for Americans, as today, or their Russian or Chinese successors.

Cyclical time was fatalistic: the bottom will eventually be the top, the way down is the way up. In order to break the cycle, man had no other recourse than to deny reality, the reality of the world and the reality of time. The most radical and consistent criticism was that of Buddhism. But Buddhism, which began as a criticism of time, soon became a prisoner of circular time. In the West the idea of rectilinear time was based on the notion of identity and homogeneity. It denied, in the first instance, that man's nature is plural, that the self is always *other*. In the second instance, it denied the *others*: colored peoples, yellow peoples, madmen, lovers—all those who were different in some way or other. The answer to circular time was either sanctity or cynicism: Buddha or Diogenes; the answer to rectilinear time was revolution or rebellion: Marx or Rimbaud. I do not know what the form of our age is: all I know is that it is a revolt. Satan does not want God to disappear: he wants to dethrone him, to speak with him as an equal, to re-establish the original relation, which was neither subjection nor annihilation of the other, but complementary opposition. Rectilinear time represented an attempt to eliminate dissimilarities, to suppress differences; contemporary revolt aspires to give *otherness* a place in historical life again.

A new form is emerging amid the present confusion, a moving pattern that is ceaselessly forming and re-forming. Like atoms and cells, this form is dynamic because it is the daughter of the fundamental opposition: the binary relation between the *I* and the *thou*, between us and them. I do not have an idyllic view of dialogue: since it is a confrontation of two points of view whose difference is irreducible, it is more often a struggle than an embrace. This dialogue is history itself: it does not exclude violence, but at the same time it is not merely violence. The revolt of Latin America is not simply an economical and political phenomenon; it is a historical movement and it encompasses those areas rather vaguely defined by the word *civilization*: a style, a language, a vision. Rodó and Darío were not mistaken in their belief that there was a fundamental incompatibility between Latin America and the United States. We are both eccentric offshoots of Europe; we have been shaped by different pasts and our present is no less antagonistic. This incompatibility is not only a product of different systems, ideologies, or techniques but also of something that is irreducible to all of these—something that can only be expressed as a symbol or a metaphor: what was once called a *soul*, that of men and that of civilizations. We fight to preserve our souls; we speak so that the other may recognize our soul and so that we may recognize ourselves in his soul, which is different from ours. The powerful conceive of history as a mirror: in the battered faces of others—the insulted and injured, the conquered or the "converted"—they see their own face reflected. This is the dialogue of masks, that double monologue of the victimizer and the victimized. Revolt is the criticism of masks, the beginning of genuine dialogue. It is also the creation of our own faces. Latin America is beginning to have a face.

CONJUNCTIONS
AND
DISJUNCTIONS

*Translated from the Spanish
by Helen R. Lane*

The Phenomenon,
engraving by José Guadalupe Posada
(Mexico, Instituto Nacional de Bellas Artes)

The Toilet of Venus, Velázquez (London, National Gallery).
Photo: National Gallery

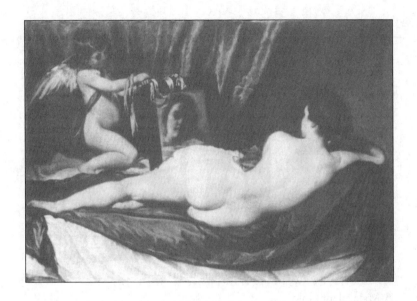

CONTENTS

1 The Metaphor

Its Terms. 181
Incarnation and Dissipation 185

2 Conjugations

A Malevolent Gold 191
Pyres, Mausoleums, Sanctuaries 194
Conjugations 202

3 Eve and Prajnaparamita

The Yakshi and the Virgin 209
The Judgment of God and the Games of Gods 219

4 Order and Accident

Sexual Alchemy and Erotic Courtesy. 245
Order and Accident 254
The Bride Stripped Bare by Her Bachelors 262

1 THE METAPHOR

ITS TERMS

There is a woodcut by Posada that shows a figure in a circus: a dwarf seen from the back, but with his face turned toward the spectator, and shown with another face down by his buttocks. Quevedo is no less explicit, and one of his juvenile works bears the title *Gracias y Desgracias del Ojo del Culo* [*Graces and Disgraces of the Eye of the Ass*]. It is a long comparison between an ass and a face. The superiority of the former lies in its having only one eye, as did the Cyclopes that "descended from the gods of sight."

Posada's woodcut and Quevedo's metaphor seem to say the same thing: that asses and faces are identical. There is a difference nonetheless: the woodcut shows that the ass is a face, whereas Quevedo affirms that the ass is like the face of the Cyclopes. We pass from the human world to the mythological world: if the face is bestial, as is the ass, the bestiality of both is divine or demoniacal. If we want to know what the face of the Cyclopes is like, the best thing is to ask Góngora. Let us listen to Polyphemus as he looks in the water and discovers his face:

> miréme y lucir vi un sol en mi frente
> cuando en el cielo un ojo se veía
> neutra el agua dudaba a cual fe preste:
> o al cielo humano o al cíclope celeste.

> [I looked at myself and saw a sun shining in my forehead
> while an eye was visible in the sky
> the neutral water doubted which was real:
> the human sky or the celestial Cyclops.]

Polyphemus sees his deformed face as *another* firmament. Transformations: the "eye" of the ass—that of the Cyclops—that of the sky. The sun dissolves the face-ass, soul-body dualism in a single dazzling, total image. We regain our former unity, but this unity is neither animal nor human; it is Cyclopean, mythical.

There is not much purpose in repeating here everything that psychoanalysis has taught us about the conflict between the face and the ass, the (repressive) reality principle and the (explosive) pleasure principle. I will merely note here that the metaphor that I mentioned, both as it works upward and as it works downward—the ass as a face and the face as an ass—serves each of these principles alternately. At first, the metaphor uncovers a similarity; then, immediately afterward, it covers it up again, either because the first term absorbs the second, or vice versa. In any case, the similarity disappears and the opposition between ass and face reappears, in a form that is now even stronger than before. Here, too, the similarity at first seems unbearable to us—and therefore we either laugh or cry; in the second step, the opposition also becomes unbearable—and therefore we either laugh or cry. When we say that the ass is like another face, we deny the soul-body dualism; we laugh because we have resolved the discord that we are. But the victory of the pleasure principle does not last long; at the same time that our laughter celebrates the reconciliation of the soul and the body, it dissolves it and makes it laughable once again. As a matter of fact, the ass is sober-sided; the organs of laughter are the same as those of language: the tongue and the lips. When we laugh at our ass—that caricature of our face—we affirm our separation and bring about the total defeat of the pleasure principle. Our face laughs at our ass and thus retraces the dividing line between the body and the spirit.

Neither the phallus nor the ass has a sense of humor. Being sullen, they are aggressive. Their aggressiveness is the result of the smiling repression of the face. As Baudelaire discovered, long before Freud: smiles, and the comic in general, are the stigmata of original sin, or, to put the matter another way, they are the attributes of our humanity, the result of and the witness to our violent separation from the natural world. The smile is the sign of our duality; if at times we make fun of our own selves with the same acrimony with which we laugh at others every day, it is because we are in fact always two: the I and the other. But the violent emissions of the phallus, the convulsions of the vulva, and the explosions of the ass wipe the smile off our face. Our principles totter, shaken by a psychic earthquake no less powerful than earthquakes in the ground beneath our feet. Deeply disturbed by the violence of our sensations and mental images, we pass from seriousness to hearty laughter. The I and the other become one, and what is more, the I is possessed by the other. Hearty laughter is similar to the physical and psychological spasm: we burst out laughing. This explosion is the contrary of the smile, and I am not certain that it can be called comic. The comic spirit implies two persons; the one who is watching and the one who is being watched, whereas when we laugh heartily the distinction is erased or at least diminished. A burst of laughter not only suppresses the duality, it also obliges us to become one with laughter in general, with the great physiological and cosmic turmoil of the ass and the phallus—the volcano and the monsoon.

A burst of laughter is also a metaphor: the face becomes a phallus, a vulva, or an ass. On the psychological level, a burst of laughter is the equivalent of what the expressions of poets and satirists are on the verbal level. Its explosion is an exaggeration that is no less extreme than Góngora's poetic image and Quevedo's wit. Both are the doubles of physiological and cosmic violence. The result is a transmutation: we leap from the world of duality, ruled by the reality principle, into that of the myth of original unity. A fit of laughter is not merely a response to the pleasure principle, nor its copy or reproduction (even though it is both these things): it is the metaphor of pleasure. Hearty laughter is a (provisional) synthesis between the soul and body, the I and the other. This synthesis is a transformation or symbolic translation: we are like the Cyclopes once again. Once again: hearty laughter is a regression to a former state; we return to the world of our own childhood, either individual or collective, to myth and play. We return to the primordial unity—before there was a *you* and an *I*—in the form of a *we* that embraces every living being and every element.

The other response to carnal violence is seriousness, impassivity. This is the philosophical response, as the burst of laughter is the mythical response. Seriousness is an attribute of ascetics and libertines. Hearty laughter is a relaxation, asceticism a rigidity: it hardens the body so as to preserve the soul. I couple the libertine with the ascetic because libertinage is also a hardening, of the spirit first of all, and then of the senses.

An asceticism in reverse. With his usual acuity, Sade states that the libertine philosopher must be imperturbable and aspire to the insensibility of the ancient Stoics, to ataraxia. His erotic archetypes are stones, metals, cooled lava. Equivalences, equations: the phallus and the volcano, the vulva and the crater. Resembling an earthquake in his emotional ardor and fury, the libertine must be hard, as stony as the rocks and crags that cover the plain after an eruption. Freedom, the philosophic state par excellence, is synonymous with hardness.

Strangely enough—or rather, not so strangely—this coincides with *Vajrayana* Buddhism, which conceives of the wise man and the saint, the adept who has simultaneously attained wisdom and liberation, as a being made in the image and likeness of the diamond. *Vajrayana* is the "way" or doctrine of the bolt of lightning and the diamond. *Vajra* refers to a lightning bolt and also to the invulnerable, indestructible diamondlike nature both of the doctrine and of the state of beatitude that the ascetic attains to. At the same time *vajra* also stands for the male sex organ in Tantric rites and language. The vulva is the "house of *vajra*" and also wisdom. Series of metaphors composed of terms that now belong to the corporeal world, now to the incorporeal world: the lightning bolt and the phallus, the vulva and wisdom, the diamond and the beatitude of the liberated yogi. The series of material terms culminates in a metaphor that identifies the discharge of celestial fire with the hardness of the diamond—a petrification of the flame; the series of psychic terms ends with another image in which the carnal embrace is indistinguishable from the indifference of the ascetic during meditation—a transfiguration of passion into essence. The two metaphors in the end become one: a fusion of the macrocosm and the microcosm.

Pairs of contrasting concepts such as those I have just mentioned appear in all cultures. What seems significant to me is that in Tantric Buddhism the duality is manifested in this very fire/diamond, eroticism/indifference polarity. The final resolution of this double opposition in terms of the paired concepts diamond/indifference is no less notable. The supreme Buddha is *Vajrasattava*, the "adamantine essence" in Sanskrit; the Tibetans call him the "Lord of Stones." The surprising thing is that in its origin *vajra* (the lightning bolt) was the arm of Indra, the jolly, dissolute Vedic god. There is an arch that unites the two poles of the human spirit through the centuries. An arch which in this case goes from Indra, the god of storms and drunkenness, the god of the terrible burst of laughter that hurls all the elements into primordial confusion, to the impassible, imperturbable, adamantine Buddha, absorbed in the contemplation of his emptiness.

From the Vedic hymn to the manual on meditation, from the bolt of lightning to the diamond, from laughter to philosophy. The path from fire to stone, from passion to hardness, is analogous in the religious tradition of India and in European libertine philosophy. The difference is that the former offers us a total, though dizzying, vision of man and the world while the latter ends in a blind alley. In short, we live between the earthquake and petrification, between myth and philosophy. At one extreme, convulsive laughter pulls down the edifice of our principles and we run the risk of perishing beneath the ruins; at the other extreme, philosophy threatens us with mummification in life, whatever the mask we choose, whether it be that of Calvin or that of Sade. These are ruminations in the shadow of Coatlicue:* destruction through movement or through immobility. A theme for an Aztec moralist.

INCARNATION AND DISSIPATION

Since man has been man, he has been exposed to aggression, either that of others or that of his own instincts. The expression "since man has been man" means, first, since our birth, and second, since the species stood up on its feet and adopted the erect posture. In this sense our condition is not historical: the dialectic of the pleasure principle and the reality principle unfolds in a zone untouched by the social changes of the last eight thousand years. Nevertheless, there is a difference: ancient societies established institutions and used methods that absorbed and transformed the aggressive instincts more easily and with less danger to the species than those of today. On one hand, systems of transformation of obsessions, impulses, and instincts into myths and collective images; on the other hand, rites: the incarnation of these images in ceremonies and

* An Aztec goddess represented with a girdle of skulls.

festivals. I hardly need add that I believe neither in the superiority of those cultures that have preceded us nor in the superiority of our own culture. I fear that a "healthy society" is a utopia; and, if it is not, it is situated neither in the historical past nor in the future, at least the future such as we see it from the point of view of the present.* Nonetheless, it seems obvious to me that antiquity (or antiquities, for there are several of them) offered a gamut of possibilities for sublimation and incarnation that was richer and more effective than ours.

So-called primitive cultures have created a system of metaphors and symbols which, as Lévi-Strauss has shown, constitute a veritable code of signs that are both physical and intellectual: a language. The function of language is to point to meanings and communicate them, but we modern men have reduced the sign to its meaning, and communication to the transmission of information. We have forgotten that signs are physical things and work on the senses. Perfume transmits information that is inseparable from sensation. The same happens with taste, sound, and other sensory expressions and impressions. The rigor of the "logic of the senses" of primitive peoples amazes us by its intellectual precision, but the richness of their perceptions is no less extraordinary: where a modern nose distinguishes only a vague odor, a savage perceives a precise range of different smells. What is most astonishing is the method, the manner of associating all these signs, so that, in the end, they are woven into a series of symbolic objects: the world converted into a physical language. This is a double marvel: speaking with the body and converting language into a body.

Cyclic time is another way toward absorption, transformation, and sublimation. The date that recurs is a return of previous time, an immersion in a past which is at once that of each individual and that of the

---

* Claude Lévi-Strauss believes that, if a golden age ever existed, it must have been in the villages of the Neolithic period. He may be right. The State was still in the embryonic stage, there was almost no division of labor, metals (arms) were unknown, as was writing (a bureaucracy of scribes/a mass of slaves), and religion had not yet produced an organized clergy. Kostas Papaioannou told me almost the same thing a number of years ago, showing me little female fertility figures: happiness personified, a perfect accord with the world.

group. As the wheel of time revolves, it allows the society to recover buried, or repressed, psychic structures so as to reincorporate them in a present that is also a past. It is not only the return of the ancients and antiquity: it is the possibility that each individual possesses of recovering his living portion of the past. The purpose of psychoanalysis is to elucidate the forgotten incident, so that to a certain extent the cure is a recovery of memory. In ancient rites it is not memory that remembers the past but the past that returns. This is what I have called, in another context, the incarnation of images.

From this point of view, art is the modern equivalent of rites and festivals: the poet and the novelist construct symbolic objects, organisms that emit images. They do what the savage does: they convert language into a body. Though they do not cease to be signs, the words take on a body. Music also creates bodily languages, perceptible geometries. Unlike the poet and the musician, the painter and the sculptor make the body a language. Things become signs. The celebrated *Venus of the Mirror*, for example, is a variant of the sex/face metaphor. It is a response to Quevedo's verbal image and Posada's graphic metaphor: in Velázquez's painting, neither the face nor the genitals are humiliated. It is a moment of miraculous concord. The goddess—and there is nothing less celestial than this girl, lying stretched out on her own nudity, so to speak—turning her back on the spectator, as does Posada's dwarf. In the center of the painting, in the lower half, at the height at which we see dawn break, in the east, at precisely the place where the sun appears, is the perfect sphere of the girl's hips: a rump that is a celestial body. Above, in the upper horizon, at the zenith, in the center of the sky, is the face of the girl. Is it her face? More likely, as in the case of Góngora's Polyphemus, it is the reflection of it in the "neutral water" of a mirror. We are dizzied by it: the mirror reflects the face of an image, the reflection of a reflection; the crystallization of a moment which has already vanished in the real world.

Paintings: solitary rites of contemplation. Poems: a feast of phantoms, an invitation to watch reflections. Images take on flesh in art only to have it fall away in the act of reading or contemplating. What is more, the artist believes in art and not, like the primitive, in the reality of his visions. For Velázquez Venus is an image, for Góngora the solar eye of the Cyclops is a metaphor, and for Quevedo, the Cyclopean anus is one more witty conceit. In all three cases, there is something that does not belong to the realm of reality but to the realm of art. Poetic sublimation becomes more or less completely identical with the death instinct. At the same time, participation with others takes the form of reading. Primitive man also deciphers signs, he also reads, but his signs are a double of his body and the body of the world. The reading of primitive man is corporeal.

However mannered they may seem to us, Quevedo's conceit and Góngora's metaphor were still a living language. Though the seventeenth century may have forgotten that the body is a language, its poets managed to create a language that gives us the sensation of a living body—perhaps because it is so complicated. This body is not human: it is the body of Cyclopes and sirens, of centaurs and devils. A language that has suffered martyrdom and been possessed like a bewitched body. To measure the degree of abstraction and sublimation, we need only compare Quevedo's language with Swift's. Swift is a writer who is infinitely more free than the Spaniard, but his daring is almost exclusively intellectual. Swift would have been offended at Quevedo's sensual violence, especially on the scatological level. This is a matter not of morality but of taste: everything is permitted in the sphere of ideas and feelings, but not in that of sensibility. The eighteenth century, the libertine century, was also the inventor of good taste. Repression disappears in one zone only to appear in another, no longer wearing the mask of morality but the veil of aesthetics.

Swift's horror of female anatomy comes from Saint Augustine, and it is echoed by two modern poets: William Butler Yeats and Juan Ramón Jiménez. In his best poem, "Espacio" ["Space"], Jiménez writes: "Love, love, love is *the place of excrement*," recalling Yeats's lines: "But Love has pitched his mansion in/The place of excrement." Although Quevedo probably felt the same sort of repulsion—he was a woman-hater, a whore-chaser, and a Petrarchist—his reaction is more whole-hearted and, his pessimism notwithstanding, more healthy: "It [the eye of the ass as compared to the eyes of the face] is incomparably better, since in both men and women it is a close neighbor of the genital members; and this is a proof that it is better, according to the proverb that says: 'Tell me what sort of company you keep and I'll tell you who you are.'" In Quevedo's day, the system of symbolic transformations of Catholicism still offers the possibility of speaking physically of physical things—even at a time when the Counter Reformation is beating a retreat and even though it takes the form of satire and scatology. In spite of the fact that Swift is freer intellectually than Quevedo, his sensuality encounters prohibitions no less powerful than those imposed on the Spanish poet by Neo-Scholasticism, absolute monarchy, and the Inquisition.

As repression becomes less rational, the inhibitions imposed upon sensual language increase. The extreme is Sade. No one has treated such inflammatory subjects in such cold and insipid language. His verbal ideal—when he does not give way to frenzy—is an erotic geometry and mathematics: bodies as ciphers and logical symbols, the love-positions as syllogisms. Abstraction borders on insensibility on one hand, and on boredom on the other. I do not want to disparage Sade's genius, even if the aura of veneration that has surrounded him for a number of years now makes me feel as though I am blaspheming against the great blasphemer. But there is nobody and nothing that can cause me to say that he is a sensual writer. The title of one of his works defines his language and his style: *Philosophy in the Bedroom*. The flame of passion is rekindled in the nineteenth century, and those who light it are the Romantic poets, who believed in true love and in the sublimity of the passions. The Romantic tide bears us on to Joyce and the Surrealists, a process that goes in the opposite direction from Sade and the eighteenth century: from the diamond to the bolt of lightning, from ataraxia to passion, from philosophy in the bedroom to poetry out of doors. And, today, another glacial era threatens us: the cold war is followed by cold libertinage. The debasement of forms is symptomatic of the lowering of erotic tension. The pleasure principle, which is explosion and subversion, is also, and above all, rite, representation; a festival, a ceremony. Sacrifice and courtliness: Eros is imaginary and cyclical, the exact opposite of the "happening," which occurs only once.

The phallus and the cunt are symbolic objects, and they are also sources of symbols. They are the body's language of passion, a language that only sickness and death—not philosophy—silence. The body is imaginary, not because it lacks reality, but because it is the most real reality: an image that is palpable yet ever-changing, and doomed to disappear. To dominate the body is to suppress the images it emits—and this domination is the purpose of the practices of the yogi and the ascetic. Or it is to make its reality disappear—and this is what the libertine does. Both practices aim at having done with the body, with its images and its nightmares: with its reality. For the reality of the body is a shifting image pinned down by desire. If language is the most perfect form of communication, the perfection of language cannot help but be erotic, and it includes death and silence: the failure of language . . . Failure? Silence is not a failure, but the end result, the culmination of language. Why do we keep saying that death is absurd? What do we know about death?

Poetic metaphors and jokes express our dual reality. That the roots of the joke and those of art are the same has been said again and again since Freud wrote his famous essay on the subject. What people do not always remember is that this original similarity finally becomes opposition. Both the joke and the poem are expressions of the pleasure principle, which, for a moment, wins out over the reality principle. In both cases the triumph is imaginary; whereas the joke is transitory, in art there is a drive toward form. Is form a victory over death or a new trap of Thanatos? Perhaps it is neither. It is frenetic love, an exasperated and infinitely patient desire to freeze not the body but the movement of the body: the body moving toward death. The body jolted, driven by passion. I do not deny that art, like everything we do, is sublimation, culture, an homage to death. But it is a sublimation that seeks to incarnate: to return to the body. The joke is exemplary, and, whether it is cynical or satirical, it is moral. The ultimate morality lies in the fact that it is dissipated. Art is the opposite of dissipation, in the physical and spiritual sense of the word: it is concentration, desire that seeks incarnation.

2 CONJUGATIONS

A MALEVOLENT GOLD*

The pleasure principle is subversive. The ruling order, whatever it may be, is repressive: it is the order of domination. Social criticism frequently takes the form of a joke aimed at the pedantry of the educated and the ridiculous results of "good up-bringing." It is an implicit—and at times explicit—tribute to the wisdom of the ignorant. Two systems of values confront each other: the culture of the poor and that of the rich. The first is inherited, unconscious, and ancient; the second is acquired, conscious, and modern. The opposition between the two is only a variation of the old dichotomy between nature and culture. It is Rousseau and Hobbes all over again: artificial society is authoritarian and hierarchical; natural society is free and egalitarian. Sex is subversive not only because it is spontaneous and anarchical, but also because it is egalitarian: it has no name and no class. Above all, it has no face. It is not individual: it belongs to the species. The fact that sex has no face is the source of all the metaphors that I have mentioned, and also the source of our unhappiness. The sex organs and the face are separated, one below and one above; moreover, the former are hidden by clothes and the latter is uncovered. (Thus, covering the woman's face, as the Muslims do, is tantamount to affirming that she has no face: her face is a sex organ.) This separation, which has made us human beings, condemns us to labor, to history, and to the construction of tombs. It also condemns us to invent metaphors to do away with this separation. The sex organs and all their images—from the most complex down to jokes in a barroom—remind us that there was a time when our face was down close to the ground and to our genitals. There were no individuals, and all human creatures were a part of the whole. The face finds this memory unbearable, and therefore it laughs—

---

* "*Un or néfaste incite pour son beau cadre une rixe . . .*" ("A malevolent gold prompts a quarrel for its handsome frame . . .") (Mallarmé, first version of the *Sonnet en ix*)

or vomits. Our sex organs tell us that there was a golden age; for the face, this age is not the solar ray of light of the Cyclops but excrement.

Max Weber discovered a relation between the Protestant ethic and the evolution of capitalism. Certain psychoanalysts, among them Erich Fromm, have stressed the connection between capitalism and anal eroticism. Norman O. Brown has brilliantly synthesized these two discoveries and has shown that the "excremental vision" constitutes the symbolic essence of modern civilization. The contradictory and complementary analogy between the sun and excrement is so evident that it almost needs no proof. It forms a pair of signs that alternately condense into one and become disassociated, ruled by the same syntax of symbols as other signs: fire and water, open and closed, pointed and round, wet and dry, light and shade. The rules of equivalence, opposition, and transformation that structural anthropology uses are perfectly applicable to these two signs, on either the individual level or the social level.

Anal eroticism is a pregenital phase of individual sexuality that corresponds to the golden age in the realm of social myths. There is little need to mention the infantile games and fantasies having to do with excrement. As for the mythic images: if the sun is life and death, excrement is death and life. The former gives us light and heat, but an excess of it kills us; it is life that can kill. The latter is refuse that is also a natural fertilizer: death that can give life. Excrement is the double of the phallus as the phallus is a double of the sun. Excrement is the *other* phallus, the *other* sun. It is sun that has rotted, as gold is congealed light: sun materialized in good solid ingots. Amassing gold is hoarding life (sun), and retaining excrement. Spending accumulated gold is disseminating life, transforming death into life. In the course of history all these images have become more and more abstract as instincts became more and more sublimated. The face drew farther and farther away from the ass.

The ambivalence of excrement and its identification with the sun and with gold gave it a sort of symbolic corporeality—sometimes beneficial and sometimes harmful—among primitive peoples as well as in antiquity and in the Middle Ages. Norman O. Brown is primarily interested in its recent metamorphoses. The associations and disassociations of gold and excrement constitute the secret history of modern society.

The condemnation of excrement by the Reformation was the antecedent and the immediate cause of the capitalist sublimation: gold converted into banknotes and stock certificates. This transformation corresponds, on the level of symbols and beliefs, to the change, on the level of economy and day-to-day living, to the transition from a closed economy, based on things, to the open economy of the capitalist market, based on signs. Privies are the infernal place, by definition. The place where putrefaction occurs is the place where perdition occurs: this world. The condemnation of this world is the condemnation of putrefaction and of the passion for hoarding it and adoring it: the golden calf is excremental. This condemnation also has to do with waste. The connection between anal retention and a rational economy, which carefully calculates what is spent, is clear. Faced with choosing between hoarding and wasting, there was only one recourse: sublimation. The second step consisted in transforming this retention into a product: the hiding and sterilizing of the privy, and, at the same time, a metamorphosis of the cellar in which gold and riches were kept into the institution of the bank.

Even though the Protestant ethic dominated Mohammedans and Hindus for centuries, it failed to convert them. But it did manage to convert gold. It disappeared as a thing, lost its materiality and was transformed into a sign—and by a curious consequence of the Calvinist ethical system, into the sign of the elect. The miser is guilty of an infernal passion because he plays with the gold he hoards in his cellar as the child plays with its feces. The capitalist rational economy is useful and moral: it is the sacrifice by omission, the contrary of the sacrifice through waste and hecatomb. Divine recompense is not manifested in material goods but in signs: abstract money. At the same time that gold disappears from the dress of men and women and from altars and palaces, it becomes the invisible blood of mercantile society and circulates, odorless and colorless, in every country. It is not hoarded as in the Middle Ages, nor is it wasted and squandered: it circulates, it is created, it is counted and discounted, and thus it multiplies. It possesses a double virtue: it is both merchandise and a sign for all merchandise. The moralization of gold and its transmutation into a sign is parallel to the expulsion of dirty words from the language and to the invention and popularization of the English water closet. The bank and the toilet: typical expressions of capitalism.

Before Freud and his followers, Marx had already observed the magic character of gold in the civilization of antiquity. As for its relation with excrement, he said that capitalist society is "the domination of living men by dead matter." He should have added: the domination by *abstract* dead matter, since it is not material gold that asphyxiates us but rather the whole symbolic network that stands for it. In the countries that we call Socialist, more because this is a handy verbal label than because we are concerned about intellectual exactitude, individual profit has disappeared, and, consequently, the sign of gold has also disappeared. Nonetheless, power in these countries is not less but more abstract and stifling than in capitalist societies. The hidden connection between the anal aggressiveness and the abstract violence of the bureaucracies of the East should be studied. We would also have to determine what other infantile, pregenital erogenous zones this strange sublimation of the myth of the age of gold corresponds to, a sublimation that in reality is its negation. The transmutation of the primordial sun—the gold that was everybody's, when everything was gold—into the omniscient eye of the bureaucratic Police State is as impressive as the transformation of excrement into banknotes. But no one, so far as I know, has ever embarked upon an investigation of this subject. It is likewise a shame that none of us has ever examined from this point of view an artistic style which came into being precisely in the dawn of our era and which is the antithesis of both modern "socialism" and modern capitalism—a style that we might call "the excremental Baroque."

PYRES, MAUSOLEUMS, SANCTUARIES

The Counter Reformation, the "Jesuit style," and Spanish poetry of the seventeenth century are the other side of the coin of Protestant austerity and its condemnation and sublimation of excrement. Spain extracts gold from the Indies, at first from the altars of the devil (that is, from pre-Columbian temples) and later from the bowels of the earth. In both cases, it is a product of the lower world, the dominion of barbarians, Cyclopes, and the body. America is a sort of fabulous privy, except that now the operation does not consist in the retention of gold but in its dispersion. The dominant tone is not moral but mythical. The solar metal spreads over the fields of Europe in the form of senseless wars and mad undertakings, a proud excremental squandering of gold, blood, and passion: a monstrous, methodical orgy that is mindful of the ritual destructions of the American Indians, although much more costly. But the gold of the Indies also serves to cover the interiors of churches, like a solar offering. Altars and their golden vegetation of saints, martyrs, virgins, and angels blaze in the dark naves. They burn and slowly die. Gold more twilight than dawn because of the advancing shadow; a warm light and trembling reflections that evoke the ancient and ominous glories of the setting sun and excrement. Is this a life that brings on death or a death that brings on life? If gold and its physiological double are signs of the deepest and most instinctive tendencies of a society, they stand for just the opposite of productive accumulation in the Spanish and Hispano-American Baroque: they are profit that is sacrificed and burned up, the violent consumption of accumulated wealth. Rites of perdition and waste. Sacrifice and defecation.

The sun-excrement duality is polarized in the two great poets of the period, Góngora and Quevedo. The two of them are a sort of apotheosis of Spanish poetry: with them a great era of European literature comes to a close. I see their poems as a funeral ceremony, splendid burial rites of the sun-excrement. Although Góngora is the sun-poet, he does not hesitate to use the word *shit* when necessary; the most daring artist that poetry in the West has produced did not have what is called "good taste." There are also resplendent passages in Quevedo, the excremental poet. Speaking of a gold ring with the portrait of a woman inside it, he writes:

> En breve cárcel traigo aprisionado
> con toda su familia de oro ardiente,
> el cerco de la luz resplandeciente ...

> [In a tiny cell I have imprisoned
> with all its family of burning gold,
> the halo of resplendent light ...]

And farther on: "I have all the Indies in my hand." The gold of the New World and its infraterrestrial gleam as of a Cyclopean privy, but also the intellectual splendor of Neoplatonic eroticism: the beloved is light, the Idea. The Petrarchist heritage and the gold of the pre-Columbian idols, the medieval inferno and the glories of Flanders and Italy, the Christian heaven and the mythological firmament, with its stars, its flowers that "the great wild beasts with gleaming pelts" feed upon all glow in this etched flash of lightning. And that is why Quevedo also says, in another sonnet, without contradicting himself: "The voice of the eye, that we call a fart/the nightingale of male whores . . ." The anus as an eye that is also a mouth. All these images are possessed by the greed, the fury, and the glory of death. Their complexity and their obscenity have the grandeur of a ritual holocaust.

Excrement for Swift is a theme for moral meditation; for Quevedo it is a plastic material like rubies, pearls, and the Greek and Latin myths of the rhetoric of his age. Quevedo's pessimism is total: everything can be used to fan the flames. But this fire is a form, a style; the flames assume the shape of a verbal architecture and its sparks are intellectual: witticisms and conceits. Quevedo's example is not the only one. Throughout the Spanish Baroque period, both in the realm of poetry and that of the plastic arts, the opposition between gold and shadow, flame and darkness, blood and night reigns. These elements symbolize not so much the struggle between life and death as a mortal combat between two rival principles: this life and the other life, the world here and the world beyond, the body and the soul. The body tempts the soul; it seeks to consume it with passion so that it will hurl itself into the black pit. The soul, in turn, punishes the body; it punishes it with fire because it wishes to reduce it to ashes. The martyrdom of the flesh is somewhat the counterpart of the autos-da-fé and the burning of heretics. It is also the counterpart of the sufferings of the soul, crucified on the burning cross of the senses. In both cases, fire is purifying.

In this dialectic of light and shadow, of flame and smoldering coals, fire represents the same principle as the bolt of lightning in Tantric Buddhism: the transmutation, through meditation, of sexual passion into adamantine indifference corresponds to the transfiguration of flesh into spiritual light through fire in the Spain of the Counter Reformation. Another analogy: just as the ray of light (the phallus) must be transmuted into a diamond, so the tree (the human body) must be transformed into a cross. In both cases there is a reduction of the natural element (the ray of light, the tree) to its essential elements so as to change it into a sign (a cross and a stylized *vajra*). Martyrdoms and transfigurations of nature . . . But such is the power of passion, such is the body's capacity for pleasure, that the flames become a joy. Martyrdom does not extinguish pleasure—it heightens it. The contortions of the burning members hint at sensations in which delight and torture are intermingled. Not even the religious spirit was insensitive to the fascination of combustion. Our mystics' "I am dying because I am not dying" and their "pleasure at dying" are the opposite, the complement and the transfiguration, of the desperate "kill me's" and the "I am dying of pleasure's" of lovers. These are scorched souls and bodies. In our Baroque art, the spirit vanquishes the body, but the body seizes upon the opportunity to glorify itself in the very act of dying. Its disaster is its monument.

The pleasure principle, even in these homages to death that Baroque poems are, always takes refuge in form. We are condemned to die, and thus sublimation inevitably serves the death instinct. Since we are also condemned to live, the pleasure principle erects immortal monuments (or would-be ones) to death . . .

As I am writing this, I can see the mausoleums of the Lodi dynasty from my window—buildings the color of blood that is scarcely dry, cupolas blackened by the sun, the years, and the rains of the monsoon season, and others of marble, whiter than jasmin—and trees with fantastic foliage planted in meadows as geometric as syllogisms, and amid the silence of the pools and the blue enamel of the sky, the cawing of crows and the silent circling of birds of prey. A flock of parakeets, green streaks that appear and disappear in the quiet air like skyrockets, intersected by the dark wings of great bats. Some are returning to their nests to sleep; others have just awakened and fly drowsily. It is almost nightfall, and there is still a shadowy light. These tombs are not made of stone or gold: they are made of a lunar, vegetable material. Only the domes are visible now, great immobile magnolias. The sky dips down into the pool. There is no top or bottom: the world has been concentrated in this serene rectangle, a space which contains everything and is made up of nothing but air and a few fleeting images. The god of Islam is not my God, but it seems to me that the opposition between life and death is dissolved in these tombs. But not in Swift, not in Quevedo.

If we wish to find traces of the fusion of the face and the sex organs in the history of Spanish poetry, it is best to leave Góngora and Quevedo and seek another poet: Juan Ruiz, the "Archpriest of Hita." It will be said that I am forgetting, among others, Lope de Vega, Fernando de Rojas, and the great Francisco Delicado. I am not forgetting them. It is just that, after the sumptuous and terrible ceremonies of gold, excrement, and death, I must go out and breathe the brisk and euphoric air of the fourteenth century. That is why I have sought out the universal clergyman in his little city. Perhaps he is off on one of his erotic hunting expeditions and is wandering about in the neighboring mountains, populated not by nymphs and centaurs, but by robust, licentious highland girls. Or he may be back in town, walking about in the atrium of the church, accompanied by Trotaconventos. The cleric and the bawd are weaving amorous nets or unraveling those that duennas and nuns have set out for them:

> No me las enseñes más
> que me matarás.
> Estábase la monja
> en el monesterio,
> sus teticas blancas
> de so el velo negro.
> Más, que me matarás.[*]

[*] Diego Sánchez de Badajoz. (*Recopilación en metro*, 1554). Cited in *Lírica hispánica de tipo popular*, selección, prólogo y notas de Margit Frenk Alatorre (Mexico City, 1966).

[Don't show me any more
You'll kill me.
There the nun was
In the monastery,
Her white little breasts
Beneath the black veil.
No more, you'll kill me.]

In the *Libro de buen amor*, the book of passionate love, the scatology is not funereal, nor are the sex organs bloody and golden. There is neither exaggerated sublimation nor harsh realism, though the passions are most lively. There is not a trace of Platonism or of aristocratic hierarchies: the chatelaine is not an invulnerable castle, even though "she could not be swayed by any amount of money." This is great praise. The Archpriest really liked women; he knew that even though they are the dwelling place of death, they are also the banquet table of life. And this knowledge neither horrified him nor enraged him. No, we are not only descendants of Quevedo, nor in the case of us Mexicans, of the ascetic Quetzalcoatl and the ferocious Huitzilo-pochtli. We are also descendants of the Archpriest and his duennas and damsels, his Jewish and Moorish women—of them and of the naked girls of the Neolithic period, those little statues made of ears of dried corn unearthed in Tlaltilco, still intact and smiling at us.

Reading Quevedo in the garden of a fifteenth-century Muslim mausoleum may seem incongruous; but it is not incongruous to read the *Libro de buen amor* in these surroundings: its author lived among Muslims, many of whom, both men and women, were singers, dancers, and wandering minstrels. They are exactly like the ones who still wander about in Rajasthan or Uttar Pradesh, and sometimes, when they pass through New Delhi, they sit in a circle in the meadows surrounding the mausoleums, eating, sleeping, or singing. The historic closeness of Spain and Islam does not blot out the obvious and vast differences between the mausoleum and the book of the Spanish poet. At the moment, what I should like to emphasize is this: the mausoleum reconciles life with death, and thus it is the latter that wins out; the book joins death and life, and what wins out is life. In both cases, there is a dialogue between the two principles. It is not right, of course, to compare a book to a monument. What, then, is the Western counterpart of these tombs? I cannot really answer that question. I have never felt this lightness of touch and this serenity in any Christian cemetery. The cemeteries of the Greeks and Romans? Perhaps—except they do not seem to me to be as airy and as welcoming as these mausoleums. History weighs heavily there; here it disappears: it is a story, a legend. The answer lies outside of Europe and monotheism—here again in India, in the Hindu temples and the Buddhist chaityas. They are not tombs: the Indians burn their dead. Yet many of these sanctuaries contain bones of saints and even teeth and other relics of Buddha. In Indian temples, life does not fight death: it absorbs it. And life, too, melts away—as a day melts away into the year and a year into a century.

In Indian sanctuaries, existence is conceived as proliferation and manifests itself with an insistent, monotonous richness that is mindful of the irregularity and the persistence of wild vegetation; in Muslim mausoleums nature is submitted to a geometry that is at once implacable and elegant: circles, rectangles, hexagons. Even water is transformed into geometry. Imprisoned in canals and pools, it is laid out in geometric spaces: it is a vision; it falls on a stone fountain or murmurs between marble banks; it is divided into regular units of time: it is sound. It is a play of echoes and correspondences between time and space; the eye, delighted by the harmonic divisions of space, contemplates the reflection of the stone in the water; the ear, entranced by the repetition of the same rhyme, listens to the sound of the water falling on the stone. The difference between the Indian temple and the Muslim mausoleum is a radical one; on the one hand, we are in the presence of a monism that includes the pluralism of the natural world, and a very rich and complicated polytheism; on the other, we are in the presence of an intransigent monotheism that excludes any sort of natural plurality or even the slightest trace of polytheism. In Indian civilization there is an exaltation of the body; in Islam the body disappears in the geometry of stone and garden.

When we speak of the temples of India, we must make a distinction between Hindu and Buddhist sanctuaries. Inside India, Hinduism and Buddhism were the protagonists of a dialogue. This dialogue was

Indian civilization. The fact that it has now ended helps explain the prostration of this civilization for over eight centuries, and its inability to renew itself and change. The dialogue degenerated into the monologue of Hinduism, a monologue that soon assumed the form of repetition and mannerism until, finally, ossification set in. Islam, appearing just as Buddhism disappears in India, failed to take its place: the opposition between Hinduism and Buddhism is a contradiction within one and the same system, whereas that between Islamism and Hinduism is the confrontation of two different and incompatible systems. Something similar occurred later in the case of Christianity and, today, is occurring with the ideologies linked to this religion: democracy, socialism . . . The West has experienced nothing similar to an intrusion of a completely different religion; the non-Christian religions it confronted were versions of the same monotheism: Judaism and Islamism.

The orientalists and philosophers who have described Buddhism as a nihilism that denies life were blind: they never saw the sculptures at Bharhut, Sanchi, Muttra, and other similar places. If Buddhism is pessimistic—and I do not see how a critical system of thought can fail to be—its pessimism is radical and includes the negation of the negation: it denies death with the same logic with which it denies life. In the period when Buddhism flourished, this dialectical refinement allowed it to accept and glorify the body. But in the great Hindu temples of Khajuraho and even in Konarak—which is less rococo and really imposing in its beautiful vastness—eroticism reaches the point of being monotonous. Something is missing: happiness or death, a spark of real passion to animate the interminable garlands of undulating bodies and faces that smile in a sort of sugary beatitude. Ecstasy here is mass-produced, a mannered orgasm. Nor is nature present in these corporeal games, which are more complicated than impassioned. Hinduism is excessive not so much because of its intrinsic powers, which are considerable, as because it has digested all its heterodoxies and contradictions; its excessive affirmation lacks the counterweight of negativity—that critical element that is the creative nucleus of Buddhism. Thanks to the Buddhist negation, ancient India changed, transformed itself, and re-created itself; once its negation was extirpated or assimilated, India did not grow: it proliferated.

Its eroticism became superficial, epidermal: a tissue of sensations and contractions.

The entwined bodies of Khajuraho are like those commentaries of a commentary of a commentary of the *Brahma Sutra*: the subtleties of the argument do not always add up to real profundity, which is simple. The pullulation of breasts, phalluses, haunches, muscles, and ecstatic smiles are, ultimately, cloying. This is not true in the Buddhist monuments, not in Bharhut and above all not in Karli. The great reliefs sculptured in the face of the portals of Karli are naked, smiling couples, not goddesses or demons but beings like ourselves, although stronger and livelier. The radiant health of their bodies is natural, with the somewhat heavy solidity of mountains and the slow grace of broad rivers. They are natural, civilized beings: there is immense courtesy in their powerful sensuality and their passion is peaceful. They are planted there like trees—except that they are trees that smile. No other civilization has created such complete and such perfect images of earthly joy. For the first and only time, a high historical culture was able to rival the Neolithic and its little fertility figures, and not come off the worse from the comparison—the opposite pole from Islam and its geometry of reflections at the bottom of pools.

CONJUGATIONS

Capitalism and Protestantism, the Counter Reformation and Spanish poetry, Muslim mausoleums and Indian temples: why is it that no one has ever written a general history of the relations between the body and the soul, life and death, the sex organs and the face? Doubtless for the same reason that no one has written a history of man. We have, instead, histories of men, that is to say, of civilizations and cultures. This is not surprising: to date no one knows what "human nature" really is. And we do not know because our "nature" is inseparable from culture, and culture is cultures. For this reason the American anthropologist A. L. Kroeber has suggested a two-pronged investigation: first, making a universal inventory of the characteristic traits—material, institutional, and symbolic—of the different cultures and civilizations, traits aimed at "determining the perimeters of human culture;" and, second, making another inventory "among the subhuman animals, of forms of conduct that are similar or anticipatory of human cultural forms."* Using this catalogue as a base, we could begin to construct both a theory of culture and a theory of human nature. It may be that at the end of this task, which reminds me of that of Sisyphus, we will manage to situate, if not to define, our nature. It is obvious that it is to be found at the point of intersection between human culture and the animal subculture: but where is this point?

For the moment, we can merely repeat that soul and body, face and sex organs, life and death are different realities that have different names in each civilization, and, therefore, different meanings. This is not all: it is impossible to translate the central terms of one culture into those of another: *mukti* is not really liberation, nor is *nirvana* extinction. The same thing happens with the *tê* of the Chinese, the *dēmokratia* of the Greeks, the *virtus* of the Romans, and the *yugên* of the Japanese. When we seem to be speaking of the same things with an Arab or an Eskimo, we may be speaking of different things; and it is not inconceivable that the opposite might also be true. But even though we cannot reduce the different meanings of all these terms to a single univocal pattern, we at least know that they are somewhat analogous. We likewise know that they constitute the common preoccupation of all men and of all societies. The moment we examine this difficulty carefully, we see that we are faced not so much with a diversity of realities as a plurality of meanings. The objection may fairly be raised that if we do not know for certain what a word means, we will have even less of an idea of what reality is being referred to. This is true, but the criticism also applies just as much to our terms as to those of another culture: for us, too, the words life, soul, and body are changing words with changing meanings designating changing realities. If we accept the advice of the modern philosophy of language, we ought to follow it to the very end: what it advises us to do is shut our mouths and not say a single word. This may be the most rational thing to do, but not the wisest. So without denigrating logicians, I shall proceed . . .

Each of the words that we are here concerned with possesses, within its own linguistic area, more or less definite relationships with the others:

* Alfred L. Kroeber, *An Anthropologist Looks at History: Selected Essays* (Berkeley, 1963).

life with death, sex with spirit, body with soul. These relationships are not always bilateral: they may also be triangular, even circular. There is a biopsychic circuit that goes from life to sex to spirit to death to life. Nonetheless, the basic relationship is that between pairs. Whatever the particular meaning of the terms that compose it, this relationship is universal: it exists everywhere, and it has almost surely existed throughout human history. There is another factor that is no less decisive and determining: in each instance we are faced not with realities but with names. In view of all this, it is not going too far to believe that we may some day construct a universal syntax of civilizations, such as the one Lévi-Strauss and his school are constructing for primitive societies. I should like to point out that this syntax could be constructed even though we are as yet unable to study the semantic aspect in depth. We must first find out how the signs function, how they are interrelated, and then determine what they mean. This investigation would attack the problem from a perspective diametrically opposed to that suggested by Kroeber. The combination of these two investigations would be the point of departure for a true history of man.

Basically, the relationship between the terms can only be one of opposition or of affinity. Too much opposition cancels out one of the terms of which it is composed; too much affinity also destroys it. Thus the relationship is always threatened, either by an excessive conjunction or by a disjunction that also is excessive. The predominance of one of the terms disturbs the balance; absolute equality between the two terms produces neutralization, and, as a consequence, immobility. The ideal relationship demands a certain slight disequilibrium of forces and a relative autonomy of each term with respect to the other. This slight disequilibrium implies on the one hand a recourse to sublimation (culture) and on the other hand the possibility of injecting spontaneity into the culture (creation); and this limited autonomy is called freedom. The essential thing is for the relationship not to be a tranquil one: the dialogue between oscillation and immobility is what gives a culture life and life form. There is another condition, governed like the preceding ones by the rules that structural anthropology has discovered: the terms are not intelligible except in relation to each other; they cannot be understood if they are studied one by one. This is something that Chuang-tzu said long ago: the word life has meaning only when compared to the word death, the word heat when compared to the word cold, the word dry when compared to wet. Finally, since it is impossible to translate the terms that compose the relation in each civilization (soul/body, spirit/nature, *purusa/prakrti*, etc.), the best thing to do would be to use two signs from logic or algebra which would include them all. Or we might use the words *body* and *non-body*, providing it is understood that they have no meaning except to express a contradictory relation. *Non-body* means neither *ātman* nor *tê* nor *psyche*; it is simply the contrary of *body*. And *body* in turn has no special connotation: it simply denotes the contrary of *non-body*.

It seems to me that if these observations were pursued further and systematically formulated, a method of investigation based on them, applicable both to the study of societies and to that of individuals, might be worked out. I say individuals and not only societies because the signs *body* and *non-body* either conflict with each other or are reunited, both in individuals and in their work, as we have seen in the case of Velázquez and Posada. My proposition, let me add, is a very modest one; I am suggesting something less than a syntax or a morphology of cultures: a thermometer, a very simple instrument to measure the degrees of cold or heat of a mind and of a civilization. The temperature chart of a society over a rather long period of time is not the same, of course, as its history, but the curves upward or downward are a precious index of its vitality, its resistance, and its ability to face other ups and downs. The comparison of the temperature charts of different civilizations can teach us, or rather confirm, what we all know empirically: that there are cold civilizations, warm civilizations, and others in which there are sudden alternations of periods of chills and periods of fever. And how do civilizations die? Some of them, the cold ones, die of a sudden combustion; the warm ones die by a slow cooling process that produces first desiccation and then pulverization; others, which are overly secluded, perish the moment they are exposed to storms; and others sleep for whole millennia in the gentle warmth of a normal temperature or commit suicide in a delirium brought on by fever.

The relations between the signs that orient the life of civilizations have often been studied, although never in an explicit and systematic manner. We hardly need recall the work of Georges Dumézil on the Indo-Europeans and what he calls their "tripartite ideology." This is a hypothesis that is as daring as it is fruitful and one that opens a new path not only for studies of Indo-European mythology, but also for studies of different civilizations. Perhaps some day someone will dare to study the civilizations of the Far East (China, Korea, Japan) and pre-Columbian America from Dumézil's point of view. It is not inconceivable that such a study would verify what many of us suspect: that the tendency of both civilizations to think in quadripartite terms is something more than a mere coincidence. Perhaps duality, thinking in terms of pairs, is common to all men, and what distinguishes civilizations is the manner in which they combine the basic paired terms: in tripartite, quadripartite, or circular structures.

Another example, taken this time from within a definite historical period, is Huizinga's classic study on the waning of the Middle Ages. The Dutch historian describes the stormy relations between the pleasure principle and the death instinct, the repressions of the latter and the rebellions of the former, the function of waste and holocaust in tourneys, the eroticism, the avarice, and the prodigality of princes, and the incarnation of all these contradictory tensions in the antithetical figures of Louis XI and Charles the Bold. The alternate domination of each of these principles (signs) in the course of the history of a civilization might also be studied. This has already been done several times, and done brilliantly. One of the favorite areas of exploration is the contrast in the West between the exalted spiritual tone of the twelfth and thirteenth centuries and the sensual coloration of the Renaissance. And we owe to E. R. Dodds a masterful description of the progressive, asphyxiating domination of the concept of the *soul* on ancient Greek beliefs up until the time when the rebellion of the *body* rent the fabric of the Greek social ethic.* Dodds has also published another book, *Pagan and Christian in an Age of Anxiety* (London, 1965), which can be considered the complement of

---

* *The Greeks and the Irrational* (London, 1951).

his previous book. In it, he has undertaken the study of the period from Marcus Aurelius to Constantine. In his first book, he describes the rebellion of the irrational (the *body*) against the rigors of classical philosophy and its rational constructs; in the second, he examines the anguished irrational substratum of the twilight of ancient civilization and the transformation of these impulses into a new religious rationality (the *non-body*). Dodds's books are something more than that, of course, but what I wish to emphasize is the decisive role played by the signs that I have called the *body* and the *non-body*.

The comparison between different civilizations has been the province where Toynbee has reigned, or did until very recently. Before that it was the domain of Spengler, who has today been discredited, and not always with good reason. Among recent studies of this type there is one by Jacques Soustelle, *Les quatre soleils* (Paris, 1967), in which the French anthropologist offers a series of reflections on the possible fate of Western civilization. The most notable feature of the book is that the author views the future from the perspective of the cosmogonic conceptions of the ancient Mayas and Mexicans. I believe that this is the first time that anyone has contemplated universal history from the vantage point of Meso-American civilization. Soustelle points out the surprising modernity of pre-Columbian thought. I want to emphasize that this cosmogony in perpetual rotation, based on the alternate pre-eminence of the creative principle and the destructive principle, reveals a pessimism and a wisdom no less profound than Freud's. It is yet another example, and perhaps the clearest one, of the dynamic relation between the signs *body* and *non-body*. I might draw another analogy: in the Meso-American philosophy of movement, the notion of a cosmic catastrophe—the end of each "sun," or era, by a cataclysm—is equivalent to our modern notion of an Accident, both in the sciences and in our life in history. Another feature that brings the Meso-Americans even closer to us is the excessive increase of aggressive instincts in the final phase of this civilization. The sadism of the Aztec religion and its sexual puritanism, the institution of the "florid war," and the rigorous nature of Tenochca political conceptions are expressions of an exaggerated disjunction between the signs *body* and *non-body*. They correspond to our idea of technology as a will-to-power, to the high watermark of militant ideologies, to the puritanism of the countries of Eastern Europe, and to their counterpart, the cold and no less fanatic promiscuity of the West, and, finally, to the warlike spirit of all our enterprises, including those that are apparently most peaceful. Aesthetics itself is military in our culture: a matter of avant-gardes, advances, breaks, conquests. The parallel with Náhuatl art is surprising: the symbolic system of Aztec poetry—its metaphors, its similes, its vocabulary—was a sort of verbal double of the "florid war," which, in turn, was the double of cosmic war. The same analogical system governed sacred architecture, sculpture, and the other arts; they were all representations of universal movement: the war of the gods, of the stars, of men.

All these examples reveal that there is a sort of combinatory system governing the basic signs of each civilization and that the character of each society, including its future, depends on the relationship between these signs. Later, I will attempt to show, in a more concrete and systematic manner, the forms—or rather some forms—whereby the signs unite and separate. In no case does the relationship disappear, however pronounced the disjunction or the conjunction. The association of signs, whether it be strong or weak, is what distinguishes us humans from the other animals. Rather, it is what makes us complex, problematical, and unpredictable beings. Since the dialectic of opposition and fusion unfolds within all men in all periods of history, I shall use the comparative method. I shall use examples taken from the West, from India, and from China, since I believe that Indian civilization is the other pole of that of the West, the other version of the Indo-European world. The relationship between India and the West is that of an opposition within a system. The relationship of both with the Far East (China, Japan, Korea, and Tibet) is a relationship between two different systems. Chinese examples in these reflections are thus neither convergent nor divergent: they are excentric. (What is the other pole of the world of China and Japan? Perhaps it is pre-Columbian America.) Finally, it would be insulting the reader's good sense if I were to warn him that I am not attempting to reduce history to a combination of signs such as those of the *I Ching* hexagrams. Signs, whether those from heaven or those of modern science, do not foretell our destiny: nothing is written in advance.

3 EVE AND PRAJNAPARAMITA

THE YAKSHI AND THE VIRGIN

Whatever the word and the particular meaning of *body* and *non-body* within each civilization, the relationship between these two signs is not, and cannot be, anything but unstable. Although the relationship is unsteady and precarious, there are a few rare moments of dynamic equilibrium. These moments are not a time of truce but a time for contradictory and creative dialogue. I have mentioned Indian Buddhist art, which goes from Bharhut and Sanchi to Muttra, Karli, and Amaravati; a parallel example in the West would be the art of the Middle Ages, from the Romanesque to Gothic. In Buddhist art the accent is placed on the corporeal, out of complementary opposition to the critical intellectualism and the ascetic rigor of Buddhism; in the face of medieval Catholicism— which is more corporeal and less radical in its criticism of the world and of existence—the figures of virgins and saints express the spiritual and incorporeal element, through the workings of the same law of complementary opposition. The representative male and female fertility figures (*yaksa* and *yaksi*) and the erotic couples (*maithuna*) that cover the exterior parts of the chaityas surround the very sanctuary of emptiness: a disincarnated man, the Buddha; the virgins, saints, and angels of the medieval churches and cathedrals surround an incarnated god, Christ. The extreme of disincarnation is the portrayal of Buddha by his aniconic symbols: the stupa, the tree of illumination, the throne, the wheel of doctrine; the response to this abstraction is the vitality and the sensuality of the sculptures of the yakshis. The extreme of incarnation is the representation of the birth of Christ and the episodes of his life on earth, above all that of his passion and sacrifice; the response to the blood and the martyred body of the god is the ascent into heaven and the transfiguration of the body.

The great period of Buddhist art coincides with the appearance, around the first century A.D., of the first Prajnaparamita Sutra, the origin of the madhyamika tendency. This doctrine preaches a radical relativism which eventually brings it to the point of maintaining that absolute emptiness (*śūnyatā*) is the only reality. Since everything is relative, everything participates in absolute nonreality, everything is empty; and therefore a bridge is constructed between the phenomenal world (*samsāra*) and emptiness, between the reality of this world and its unreality. Reality and unreality are terms that are relative, interdependent, and opposed; at the same time they are identical. The art of the Middle Ages, in turn, is contemporary with Scholasticism, which delves into and refines the Aristotelian notion of degrees of being, as expressed in the moderate realism of Saint Thomas Aquinas. Thus the two religions postulate the existence of various levels of ontological reality, the first moving in the direction of emptiness and the second in the direction of a fullness of being. These levels are degrees, or mediations, between the corporeal and the spiritual, the pleasure principle and the death instinct. In this way, they open up a whole gamut of possibilities for combining the contradictory signs. Both in Buddhist sanctuaries and in Christian cathedrals grotesque monsters and licentious and comic representations appear side by side with images of Buddha or Christ and their symbols. Between the lower world and the upper world there is a gradation of modes of being—or of modes of emptiness. In both cases the equilibrium is based on a slight disequilibrium: corporeality and sensuality in Buddhism, and spiritual transfiguration of bodies in medieval Catholicism. A religion that denies the reality of the body exalts it in its most striking form, eroticism; but a religion that has made incarnation its central dogma spiritualizes and transfigures the flesh.

The divergent evolution of these two movements—the dialectic inherent in the contradictory relation between the signs *body* and *non-body*—can be clearly seen in both religions. Buddhism is born in nonpriestly and aristocratic surroundings: Gautama belonged to the royal clan of the sakya and hence was a member of a warrior caste; his preaching from the start was well received by the nobles and above all by merchants, so that it soon became a religion of renunciation practiced by an urban, cosmopolitan, and well-to-do class; in its ultimate Indian expression, Tantrism, it is transformed into a religion of wandering mystics outside of society, and flourishes in the lower castes. Christianity is born in priestly and proletarian surroundings: Jesus is the son of a carpenter and a descendant of the House of David; the first Christians belong to the world that lives on the social periphery of the Roman Empire; later, Christianity was the official religion of an empire and, later still, it adopted an imperial organization itself; in its final form, Protestantism, it became the ascetic religion of capitalism.

Christianity ends where Buddhism begins. This latter, when it first began its career as a universal religion, was just one sect more among those that had undertaken to criticize the Brahmanical religion and reconsider the tradition of the Upanishads in the sixth century B.C. In this context the figures of Gautama, Mahavira, and other religious reformers recall the theologians of the first days of the Reformation—Luther, Zwingli, and Calvin. But in the course of its history, Buddhism wanders further and further away from its original critical and moral tendencies and progressively stresses its ritual and metaphysical features: the Mahayana philosophical systems, the cult of the image of Buddha, the appearance of Bodhisattvas as saviors of men, the doctrine of the universal compassion of the Buddhas, the increasing formality and complexity of Buddhist ritual and ceremony. The steps were: a criticism of the traditional religion; a religious philosophy; a metaphysical religion; a ritualistic religion. A contrary evolution can be observed in the case of Christianity: it is born as a doctrine of salvation and an announcement of the end of the world, that is to say, as a real religion and not only as a criticism or a reform of Judaism; it confronts pagan thought and creates a philosophy thanks to the Church Fathers; it constructs a great metaphysical system in the Middle Ages; it passes during the Reformation from metaphysics to criticism and from ritual to ethics. Analogous movements but in opposite directions: in Buddhism, from criticism and ethics to metaphysics and liturgy; in Christianity from metaphysics to ethics, and in the ritual sphere, a fading away of the notion of the eucharist, and the supremacy of the evangelical word (ethics) over the divine presence (the sacrament). Incarnation and disincarnation.

The evolution of artistic styles does not seem initially to display the same correspondence. Nevertheless, if the visual field is marked off with a fair degree of precision, the reverse-image symmetry appears once again, although not with the same clarity as it does in the evolution of these two religions. The first difficulty is that neither Christian art nor Buddhist art coincides, respectively, with the spatial and temporal limits of Western or Indian civilization. The area of comparison must therefore be carefully defined: in one case we must consider the Christian art of the West, excluding the art of primitive Christianity (the Greco-Roman appendage), and Byzantine, Coptic, and Syrian art; in the other case, we must consider Indian Buddhist and Hindu art, excluding the art of China, Korea, and Japan, though not the art of Nepal, Ceylon, Java, Cambodia, and Burma, which from the point of view of artistic styles are part of Indian civilization. (Tibet occupies an intermediate place that is a case in itself.) The second obstacle standing in the way of comparison is the different evolution of the two civilizations. We must again set limits: does the Vedic world represent what Greco-Roman civilization represents for the West, or is it simply the first period of Indian civilization? However we answer this question, it is clear that around the sixth century B.C. something new begins in India—either a distinct phase of Vedic civilization or a new civilization.*

Kroeber distinguishes two phases in Western civilization: medieval Catholic and modern. The high point reached in the late Middle Ages was followed by a period of disruption and confusion, which was followed by a revolutionary recombination of the elements of our civilization, a new period: the period in which we are still living and which, it appears, is coming to an end. In the West there occurred what Kroeber calls "a

---

* The connection between the civilization of the Indus and that of India is doubtful, to say the least. Apart from the fact that they are separated by a millennium or more, that of the Indus appears to be more akin to the Mesopotamian world, and, specifically, to the Sumerian-Babylonian world. Nonetheless, there appear to be certain features in Hinduism that may have come from Mohenjo-daro and Harappa, such as the cult of Siva and the Great Goddess. There are some scholars who believe that yoga practices and the caste system have the same pre-Aryan origin.

reconstitution within civilizations." There are differences between the Newtonian universe and the Einsteinian, but they are the same universe; the universe of Saint Thomas and Abelard is another universe, different from ours. India from the sixth century B.C. to the thirteenth century experienced nothing similar to the Renaissance, the Reformation, the Enlightenment, and the Industrial Revolution. There was no "reconstitution," only repetition, mannerism, self-imitation, and, finally, sclerosis. It was not the invasions of white Huns that put an end to Indian civilization but that civilization's inability to reconstruct itself or fecundate itself.

Two facts perhaps explain the slow petrification of India and its final crumbling in its Middle Ages: first, its Reformation (Buddhism) took place at the beginning of Indian civilization; second, the triumph of the Hindu Counter Reformation dislodged the merchant classes, the patrons of Buddhism, from the center of social life and put the local warlords and Brahmins in their place when the empire of the Guptas collapsed. This latter turn of events represented the end of the central monarchy and, therefore, of a Pan-Indian state: a consolidation of feudalism and the caste system. Indian civilization ended in what the historians call the Hindu Middle Ages. It can thus be said that in its main outline Indian history is a process that is the reverse image of what happened in the West . . . Therefore, in order for the comparison to make sense, it must deal with the first phase of Western civilization (medieval Catholicism) and Indian civilization from the sixth century B.C. onward. The disparity of time does not matter: what happened over a period of approximately two thousand years in India happened in less than a thousand years in the West.

The historians distinguish four periods in the art of the West: the formative, the Romanesque, the Gothic, and the flamboyant Gothic. The division of Indian art into periods is more uncertain and the vocabulary even vaguer. In general, three stages are mentioned: Buddhist, the Gupta and post-Gupta, and the Hindu medieval. The Buddhist period also can be, and should be, divided into two periods, both from the point of view of their duration and from the point of view of their stylistic changes: a formative period, not without certain resemblances with that of the West, which reaches its most perfect expression in the balustrades of the stupa of Bharhut; and another period at the zenith: Muttra, Sanchi (the toranas of the great stupa), Amaravati, Nagarjunanikonda, and Karli. The early period is preceded by a stage in which primitive Buddhism does not possess what can properly be called an artistic style; the flamboyant Gothic, the last stage in the West, is followed by a stylistic change that is a total break (the Renaissance) with medieval Christianity and a religious movement that does not even possess a style of its own: the Reformation.

The reliefs of Bharhut are the first great work of Indian art. The style of a whole civilization is born with these admirable sculptures, a style that neither historical and religious changes nor foreign influences—such as that of Gandhara—will modify in any substantial way and which will last until the thirteenth and fourteenth centuries. Before Bharhut, there is nothing that merits the name of a style: neither the stupas that come from the Vedic period nor the cosmopolitan art of the Maurya dynasty. The formative period of the art of the West also emerges from a zone that is vague as far as style is concerned: the influences of the barbarians, the Byzantines, and the Greco-Roman past. Carolingian art is an abortive attempt to resurrect an imperial style; that of the Mauryas is another abortive attempt to adopt a foreign imperial style.* The art of the West and that of India in their formative periods are as much a reaction against the two false universalisms that precede them (Carolingian art and the Greco-Persian cosmopolitanism of the Mauryas) as they are a transformation of the heritage that was more rightly theirs: in the one case the Greco-Roman past and the art of the barbarians, and in the other case, the Vedic stupa. These are two styles in search of themselves, which find themselves, respectively, in Cluny and in Bharhut. These

---

* Ananda K. Coomaraswamy maintains that there is no such Persian influence and that the pillars and capitals of Asoka are proof of a general relation to the art of Western Asia, especially Babylon and Assyria, rather than to that of Persepolis. To my mind, everything seems to indicate the contrary: the intimate relations of the Mauryas with the Seleucids; the presence of Persian and Greek artisans in Pataliputra, the capital of the Indian Empire; and, above all, the polish and high degree of perfection of these pillars and of the animal figures that crown the capitals, in the best tradition of the hybrid, official, and imperial art of the court of the Great King and his Greek successors.

external similarities make the spiritual oppositions of meaning and orientation more revealing. In Bharhut the balustrade around the aniconic symbol of the Disincarnated is a deliberate exaltation of sensual and profane life. The separation is absolute, but the representation of scenes in the previous lives of the Buddha (*jātakas*) constructs a bridge between the attributes of the sign *body* and the absence of attributes of the sign *non-body*. Byzantine art had so highly stylized the divine presence that it becomes an atemporal symbol; the arts of the barbarians also tended toward abstraction and ornamentation; in both tendencies, the sign takes precedence over the human figure, line over volume; this is antisculptural art. Medieval Christian art reinvents the art of sculpture, which is first and foremost the representation of the sacred figure: the body of the incarnated God. The first great work of Romanesque sculpture is perhaps the tympanum of the portal of Saint-Pierre de Moissac. It is a representation of the Last Judgment: the figure of the Lord—hieratic, radiant, immense—surrounded by tiny animated figures. The contrast is significant: in Bharhut Nothingness is god and everything adores it; in Saint-Pierre de Moissac Being is god and reigns over all.

The following two stages are the apogee of Buddhist art in India and mature Romanesque in the West. I have already mentioned the earthly sensuality of the yakshis of Karli, Muttra, and Sanchi; I now want to point to the vitality of Romanesque sculpture, which is sometimes demoniacal and sometimes divine. Either we find the body in its most elemental, sensual, and direct expression, or we find the body traversed by other-worldly forces and impulses that are not corporeal. The dissolution of reality is the counterpart in Buddhism of the resurrection of the flesh in Christianity. It is in this era that Buddha ceases to be represented only by his symbols and comes to be represented as a presence. This change is one of the consequences of the great religious revolution that Buddhism undergoes: the Prajnaparamita Sutras proclaim the doctrine of the Bodhisattvas; a little later, Nagarjuna and his followers elaborate and refine the notion of sunyata. Through the first of these developments an affective element is introduced into the austere Buddhist rigor: the figures of the Bodhisattvas who, moved by compassion, renounce Buddhism, or rather, transcend it: their mission is to save all living beings.* Through the second of these developments, Buddhism regains the world, thanks to the radical relativism of Nagarjuna. The bridge between existence and extinction ceases to be a bridge; nothingness is identical with phenomenal reality, and perceiving its identity and realizing it is to leap to the other shore, to attain "perfect wisdom" (*prajñāpāramitā*). Romanesque art links the ideas of order and rhythm. It conceives of the church as a space that is the sphere of the supernatural. But it is a space on this earth: the church does not seek to escape the earth; rather, it is the place where Presence manifests itself, a place laid out by reason and measured by rhythm. The old Greek and Mediterranean spirit, with its fondness for both the human form and for geometry, is still there, but it is now expressed in a new language. In India, a strict and devastating rationality breaks through the limits between phenomenal reality and the absolute and recovers the sign *body*, which ceases to be the opposite of *non-body*. In the West reason traces the limits of the sacred space and constructs churches in the image of absolute perfection: it is the earthly dwelling place of the *non-body*. These are the two great moments of Buddhism and Christianity and in both a dynamic equilibrium, a plenitude is achieved, if not an impossible harmony between the two signs.

Gupta and post-Gupta art are the reverse image of the Gothic. The first difference is that the Gupta and post-Gupta period is, above all, the period of a Hindu Renaissance—especially as regards the cult of Vishnu. The great innovation in architecture is the invention of the prototype of the Hindu temple; Buddhist sculpture in this period is less interesting,[†] and the same must be said for architecture and painting (the late frescoes of Ajanta give us some idea of what this latter must have been like).

---

* The ideal of Hinayana Buddhism is the Arhant, the ascetic who reaches nirvana through concentration and meditation and abandons the phenomenological world (*saṁsāra*); Mahayana Buddhism exalts the figure of the Bodhisattva, in whom "perfect wisdom" unites with compassion; in its final form (*Vajrayāna*), Tantric Buddhism accentuates the passional element of Compassion. When I refer to Tantrism I shall write (com) Passion, although the Sanskrit word is the same: *karunā*.

† See *India*, by Hermann Goetz, Art of the World Series (London, 1959).

Unlike what happens in the West, one and the same artistic style serves to express different religious tendencies and institutions: Hinduism, Buddhism, Jainism. The same thing had happened before, except that in the first two periods Indian art was essentially Buddhistic, whereas in this period Buddhism not only coexists with Hinduism but in the end yields up its central place to it. In the West there is only one religion and a single style; in India there are various religions, with one and the same style. The change in the West is artistic; there is a transition from the Romanesque to the Gothic. In India there is no change, but rather the maturation of a style and the beginning of a mannerism; the real change is religious: there is a growing tendency toward theism* and Buddhism complicates its pantheon and vastly enlarges it. Gothic art is sublime: the cathedral is not the space visited by the divine Presence; rather, it ascends toward it. The sign *non-body* volatilizes the figures and the stone itself is overcome by a spiritual anguish. Gupta art is sensual even in its most spiritual expressions, such as the smiling, contemplative face of Vishnu or Buddha. The Gothic is an arrow or a tormented spiral; the Gupta style loves the curve that winds back upon itself or opens out and palpitates: fruits, hips, breasts.

The post-Gupta sensual spirituality—such as we see it at Ajanta, Elephanta, and Mahabalipuram—is already so sophisticated a style that it soon leads to the Baroque: the immense, phantasmagorical erotic cathedrals of Khajuraho and Konarak. The same thing happens in reverse with the flamboyant Gothic. In both styles the sinuous triumphs, and the line twists and untwists and twists again, creating a dense vegetation. This is the temple as a forest made up more of branches and leaves than of trunks: a superfluous proliferation either of the spiritual or of the corporeal. In both there is a mystico-erotic treatment of motifs. Sculptured flames: the sign of the *non-body* is all-powerful in the flamboyant Gothic; the sign of the *body* covers the walls of the Hindu temples.

All these similarities and contrasts can be summed up in one: that between primitive Buddhism and the Protestant Reformation. Two

---

* The term theism is ambiguous. In this case, it in no way implies the notion of a single god who is the Creator, as in the West.

religions without an artistic style of their own: the one because it had not yet created one, and the other because it had rejected what Roman Catholicism offered it. However austere it may be, a religion without a liturgy, without symbols, temples, or altars is not a religion. Therefore, primitive Buddhism used the style that was close at hand and modified it as best it could; Protestantism did the same. Although the sanctuaries of primitive Buddhism have not survived, the testimony of literary texts and archaeology gives us a fairly good idea of what they were like.*They could not have been too different from Protestant churches: the same sobriety and simplicity; the same horror of realistic images of the Crucified and the Illuminated; the same veneration for abstract symbols—the cross and the wheel, the book and the tree. This brief description of the development of Indian Buddhist art and medieval Christian art—one of which passes from disincarnation to incarnation and the other from incarnation to disincarnation—shows that at certain times the two of them almost completely coincide. But this is an accidental resemblance: each religion follows its own path and does not intersect the other either in time or in space. Each one traces a spiral without knowing that it is the reverse image of what the other is tracing, as if this were a more perfect and more complex instance of the play of symmetries that Lévi-Strauss has discovered in the mythological system of the Indians of the Americas. The conclusion we may draw from all this seems apparent: if these two religions have no contact with each other in history, they nonetheless intersect in these pages. And they intersect because the spirit of all men, in all times, is the theater of the dialogue between the sign *body* and the sign *non-body*. This dialogue *is* man.

The following schematic drawing shows the relationships—similarities and oppositions—between medieval Christian art and Indian Buddhist art:

The Roman numerals in the left-hand column (the West) designate: I. the formative (post-Carolingian) period; II. the Romanesque; III. the Gothic; IV. the flamboyant Gothic; and V. the Protestant Reformation (with no style of its own). In the right-hand column (India) the

---

* See *Histoire du bouddhisme indien*, by Etienne Lamotte (Louvain, 1958).

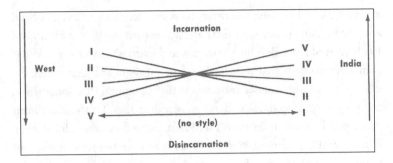

Roman numerals designate: I. primitive Buddhism (without a style of its own); II. the formative (post-Maurya) period; III. the art of Muttra, Sanchi, Andhra, and Western India; IV. Gupta and post-Gupta; and V. the Hindu Middle Ages.

THE JUDGMENT OF GOD AND THE GAMES OF GODS

The last and the most extreme expression of the Buddhist "corporization" is Tantrism; the final and most radical phase of Christian sublimation is Protestantism. The parallel between these two religious tendencies is impressive for two reasons: because it is an example of an excessive disequilibrium between the signs *body* and *non-body* and because this disequilibrium again takes the form of an inverse symmetry. The oppositions between Tantrism and Protestantism are much like those between light and shade, hot and cold, black and white. Both confront the insoluble conflict between body and spirit (which is emptiness for the Buddhist) and both resolve it by means of an exaggeration. Protestantism exaggerates the separation between body and spirit, to the benefit of the latter; Tantrism postulates the absorption of the body, also to the benefit of "spirit" (emptiness). Both are ascetic, but in Protestantism repression of the body predominates and in Tantrism reintegration of the body predominates. They are thus two attitudes that engender two obsessive types of sublimation: one moral and utilitarian, the other amoral and mystical.

There is a Hindu Tantrism and a Buddhist Tantrism. The manifestations of the two, whether in the sphere of ritual and contemplative practices (*sādhanā*) or in that of doctrine and speculation, are indistinguishable at times. The relationships between these two tendencies have not been entirely explained, and specialists are still debating whether Hinduism has borrowed from Buddhism (*sāktism* and *sivaism*) or vice versa. What is most probable is that they had a common origin and that they grew side by side simultaneously and never entirely commingled. Nonetheless, the most recent opinion tends to substantiate that Tantric Buddhism developed first and influenced Hinduism. According to André Bareau, Tantric Buddhist formulas (*dhāranī*) seem to have been translated into Chinese as early as the third century. The pilgrim Hsüan Tsang, who visited India four centuries later, reports that "Buddhist monks of the province of Uddiyana recited the same formulas." The two great centers of Buddhist Tantrism were the region of Uddiyana (the valley of Swat) in Western India, and the present states of Bengal, Bihar, and Orissa in the east. Hindu Tantrism is still practiced in these latter. Although the history of Tantrism remains to be written, it is evident that its two branches stem from a common trunk. The dialogue between Buddhism and Hinduism is transformed in Tantrism into something like a love duet: charmed by the same melody, the two protagonists take the words out of each other's mouth.

Agehananda Bharati observes that Hindu and Buddhist Tantrism have no new speculative features, nothing that is not already in the doctrines of Hinduism and in those of Mahayana Buddhism.* The originality of both lies in their practices, and above all in the emphasis they place on the efficacy of these practices: liberation (*mukti/sūnyatā*) is an experience that we may have here and now. Both sects agree that this experience consists in the abolition or fusion of contraries: masculine and feminine, subject and object, the phenomenal world and the transcendental world, this latter an absolute in the form of a fullness of being for the Hindu and ineffable emptiness for the Buddhist. Indian tradition had also spoken, in similar terms, of the abolition or fusion of opposites (*samanvaya*) and the ascent to a state of indescribable delight, not without analogy with that of our mystics: union with the absolute (*ānanda*) or dissolution in emptiness (*samatā*) or a regression to the principle of principles, to the inborn

* Agehananda Bharati, *The Tantric Tradition* (London, 1965).

(*sahaja*). The characteristic feature of Tantrism is the decision to abandon the conceptual sphere and that of everyday morality (good works and devotions) so as to enter a veritable "dark night" of the senses. Tantrism preaches a total experience, both carnal and spiritual, which must be felt and lived concretely in the ritual.

Both Buddhist and Hindu Tantrism take up—or more exactly, reincorporate—a very old tradition of orgiastic and fertility rites that probably antedates the arrival of the Aryans in the Indian subcontinent. The cult of the Great Goddess and an ascetic and phallic god, which some scholars identify as a proto-Shiva, had already made its appearance in the civilization of the Indus, as I stated before. This is a subterranean tradition that waters the religious subsoil of India and has continually nourished the official religions, even in our own day. Its position and its function within the religious universe might be compared to those of medieval witchcraft in the West, with certain decided differences. The hostility of official Indian religions toward pre-Vedic cults was far less strong than that of Christianity toward witchcraft; the persistence and the influence of this subterranean current was thus much greater in India than in Europe and continues to be so today. In Western culture, witchcraft and the other survivals of paganism were suppressed, or else fused with the corpus of Catholicism in a very attenuated and disfigured form; in India the age-old current not only secretly fed the official religions but even managed to carve out a sphere for itself within them—to the point of becoming, with Tantrism, a legitimate, although eccentric, path for achieving liberation from transmigrations and a state of joy and illumination. The attitudes of Indian and Christian established religions vis-à-vis their respective paganisms (*bodies*) are major and extreme examples of conjunction and disjunction.

It seems pointless to discuss the theme of the similarities between Tantric and Hindu Buddhism at any greater length. It is not pointless, however, to cite an observation of Agehananda Bharati: while the Hindu branch owes Buddhism a great part of its conceptual system and its philosophical vocabulary, the Buddhist branch owes to Hinduism many of the divinities in its female pantheon. This factor suggests that it is wisest to focus our attention on Tantric Buddhism as the other pole of Protestant Christianity. Moreover, Tantric Buddhism and Protestantism were radical and violent reactions to their respective religious traditions—the one against the negation of the sign *body* in Buddhism and the other against its affirmation in Roman Catholicism. For these reasons, and for others that will become evident, I shall refer almost exclusively to Tantric Buddhism in the remarks that follow. But I will also be obliged to deal with the revealing oppositions between the Hindu and the Buddhist attitudes, even at the risk of overcomplicating the exposition.

I shall begin by discussing the relationship of Tantric Buddhism and Protestantism with the religious traditions which they both inherit and transform: Mahayana Buddhism in the one case and Roman Catholicism in the other. The Buddhist tradition (I am simplifying, of course) is, in turn, the result of two others: the yoga tradition and that of the Upanishads. The first of these is corporeal and magic, the second speculative and metaphysical. The yoga tradition is probably older, corresponding to a pre-Aryan, aboriginal inheritance; the other is Aryan and is directly linked to the Brahmanical current, of which it is the expression and the criticism. Buddhism made its appearance at the beginning as a criticism of Brahmanism, but it is a criticism which embraces the tradition of the Upanishads, if only to deny it, this tradition being in turn critical and speculative. Within Buddhism the tendency to use reason and yoga, the practice of silent meditation and philosophical disputation, enter into a continuous dialogue: the asceticism of Hinayana yoga is countered by the dizzying Mahayana constructions (or rather destructions); the strict Hinayana philosophical criticism is countered by the soaring meditations of the Mahayana Bodhisattvas. It is a dialectic of conjunction: Buddhism tends to assimilate and absorb what is contrary rather than destroying it utterly. Borne on by the logic of its principles or impelled by the Indian fondness for suppressing contraries without destroying them, the Mahayana tendency preached the ultimate identity between the phenomenal world and emptiness, between samsara and nirvana. This metaphysical affirmation inevitably provoked a resurrection of the corporeal yoga current, in the form of a reverse asceticism: an eroticism. Thus Tantrism does not depart from Buddhism, nor is it, as has been said, a strange, magic, erotic intrusion which destroys the critical and speculative tradition. On the contrary, faithful to Buddhism, it is a new and more exaggerated attempt to reabsorb the corporeal, aboriginal yoga element within the great critical and metaphysical negation of Mahayana Buddhism.

Tantrism attempts an extreme fusion of the two traditions by way of a reabsorption of the older magic and corporeal element. The Protestant attitude toward Catholicism is the exact opposite. Catholicism is also the product of two traditions: Judaic monotheism and the Greco-Roman heritage. The second contains a speculative, corporeal, and orgiastic element, whereas Judaism is not metaphysical but moral and adores an aniconic god whose very name cannot be pronounced. Protestantism denies—or, in less extreme version attenuates—the Greco-Roman heritage and exalts an ideal image of primitive Christianity which is very close to the severity of Judaic monotheism. In other words: there is a separation of the two traditions and a preference for the anticorporeal and antimetaphysical tendency. Within the religious tradition of India, Buddhism is a sort of Reformation, and its criticism of Brahmanism culminates in a separation analogous to that of Protestantism from the Roman Church; nonetheless, the history of Indian Buddhism is a series of compromises, not so much with Hindu orthodoxy as with Hindu beliefs; the last and most thoroughgoing of these compromises is Tantrism. Protestantism, on the other hand, was and is an irreparable break. In the one case a loss of balance through conjunction; in the other a loss of balance through disjunction.

The attitudes toward food are revealing. The general rule of Protestantism is sobriety and an emphasis, therefore, on the simplicity and the nutritive value of food. There are no excessive fasts and no gastronomic orgies; it is a cuisine that is insipid and utilitarian. The Tantric banquet is above all an excess, and its utility, if such a word may be used, is other-worldly. There are two things that characterize the Western meal: the food is served in separate dishes and people are well behaved and reserved at table. Before the altar at the moment of communion, this reserve becomes silent meditation and veneration. In India, food is all mixed up on one plate, either out of asceticism or out of hedonism—the two poles of Hindu sensibility. The relation with food is more direct and more physical than in the West; the Indian eats with his hands (sometimes the plate is a leaf from a tree). Tantrism exaggerates this attitude and in the ritual feast people's table manners are deliberately coarse. This emphasizes the religious character of the act: a return to original chaos, and an absorption of the animal world. In the West the food is simple, and in the East there is an excess of condiments; it is nutritional utility versus a sacramental value, sobriety versus excess; distance and reserve with regard to food, closeness and voracity; a separation of dishes, a confusion of permitted and forbidden foods.

The determination of what is permitted and what is forbidden in the way of food is a violent and clear expression of the dichotomy between Protestant separation and Tantric fusion. The Protestant sacrament is almost immaterial, and unlike the Catholic rite, it accentuates the division between the body and the spirit. The Tantric banquet is a ritual violation of the dietetic and moral prohibitions of Hinduism and Buddhism. Not only do the faithful eat meat and drink alcohol; they also ingest foul substances. The *Hevajra Tantra* is explicit: "With the body naked and with bones as accoutrements, one should eat the sacrament in its foul and impure form." The sacrament is made up of minute portions of human flesh, and the flesh of cows, elephants, horses, and dogs, which the devout must mix, knead, purify, burn, and eat, at the same time ingesting the "five ambrosias." Neither the text nor the commentaries are explicit as to what these "ambrosias" really are: they might be either urine, excrement, semen, and other bodily substances, or the five products of the cow, or finally, the allegorical names of the five senses.* Whatever the interpretation of this and other passages, there is no doubt that the texts of the *Tantras*, whether Buddhist or Hindu, make the eating of impure food at the moment of consecration mandatory. Almost all the commentators insist on the symbolic nature of the ingredients, above all if they include excremental substances and human flesh, as is the case in the *Hevajra Tantra*. The commentators emphasize that the texts employ an allegorical language: the names of filthy substances and things really des-

---

* See The *Hevajra Tantra*. Translation and critical study by D. L. Snellgrove (London, 1951).

ignate ritual objects and spiritual concepts. But the explanation hardly appears valid: in many cases, the allegorical relation is precisely the contrary, that is, the names of concepts and ritual objects designate material substances and sexual organs and functions in the ciphered language of the text. For example *bala* (mental power) → *māmsa* (flesh) *kakhola* (an aromatic plant) → *padma* (lotus, vulva) *sūrya* (sun) → *rajas* (menstruation) *bodhicitta* (thought of illumination) → *śukra* (semen). The list could be extended.* I do not mean to say that the allegorical language of the *Tantras* consists only in attributing sexual meanings to words that designate spiritual concepts. The language of the *Tantras* is a poetic language and its meanings are always multiple. It also has a quality that I would call reversibility: each word can be converted into its contrary and later, or simultaneously, turn into itself again. The basic premise of Tantrism is the abolition of contraries—without suppressing them. This postulate brings on another: the mobility of the meanings, the continuous shifting of the signs and their meanings. Flesh is mental concentration; the vulva is a lotus that is emptiness that is wisdom; semen and illumination are one and the same thing; copulation is, as Mircea Eliade emphasizes, *samarasa*, the *identité de jouissance*, a fusion of subject and object, a return to the One.

It is not impossible that the rite may many times have been celebrated exactly as described. There is no use in hiding the nature of Tantric rituals; they are not only repulsive but sometimes downright criminal. In view of the reversibility that I have mentioned, it is pointless to discuss whether we are here confronted with symbols or realities: the symbols are experienced as realities and reality possesses a symbolic dimension—it is a metaphor of the absolute. But if the rite has as its object the attaining of a state of nonduality, either through fusion with being or through dissolution in the universal emptiness, it is also natural that it should attempt by every possible means to radically suppress the differences between the permitted and the forbidden, the agreeable and the filthy, the good and the accursed. The Tantric meal is a transgression. Unlike transgressions in

* Cf. *The Hevajra Tantra* and A. Bharati's book, *The Tantric Tradition*, already mentioned, especially the chapter devoted to "the intentional language" (*sandhābhāsā*).

the West, which are aggressions tending to destroy, or to abolish, the contrary, the transgression of Tantrism has as its aim to reintegrate—again, to *reincorporate*—all substances—including filthy ones such as excrement and forbidden ones such as human flesh.

The Hindu *Tantras* refer to the consumption of the five M's, that is to say, the five things forbidden by Brahmin orthodoxy, all of which begin with M: *mada* (wine), *matsya* (fish), *māmsa* (flesh), *mudrā* (beans?), and *maithuna* (copulation). The last two "ingredients" are strange. Bharati identifies *mudrā* as beans and supposes that the devout attribute an aphrodisiac power to this innocuous food. In the Buddhist rite, *mudrā* is the feminine partner, and it probably had the same meaning in the Hindu rite. Another possibility is that *mudrā* designated a drug or a portion of human flesh. The *Hevajra Tantra* justifies this hypothesis, since it very clearly mentions human flesh as sacred food, and does so several times. As for drugs: Bharati says that during the rite the devout drank a cup of *vijayā*, which is simply the Tantric name of bhānga, a potion made with ground *Cannabis indica* dissolved in milk and almond juice. It is very popular in the north of India, especially among holy beggars. It is not clear why copulation is included among the five M's, since it is neither an ingredient nor a food. What is more, and most important, it constituted the central part of the rite. These inconsistencies reveal that the Hindu Tantric tradition underwent a period of confusion and disintegration . . . The extreme immateriality of the Protestant sacrament emphasizes the separation between spirit and matter, man and the world, soul and body; the Tantric feast is a deliberate transgression, a breaking of the rules, the object of which is to attain the *reunion* of all the elements and all substances, to tear down walls, to go beyond limits, to erase the differences between the horrible and the divine, the animal and the human, dead flesh and living bodies, to experience *samarasa*, the identical flavor of all substances.

Protestant communion is individual, and as I have already said, it has retained only the barest trace of the material, corporeal nature of the sacrament. The Protestant rite tends to commemorate the word of Christ; it is not a re-production of his sacrifice as in the Catholic Mass. In the Tantric ceremony, all the castes mingle, the taboos of bodily contagion disappear, the sacrament is communal, clearly material and substantial. Immaterial food and individual communion/extremely material food and collective communion; separation and exaggeration of purity/mingling and exaltation of impurity. The caste system consists of a strict and hierarchical distinction between social groups founded on religious notions of purity and impurity. The higher the caste, the more severe the interdictions concerning sex and food, the greater the separation from the natural world and from other human groups. In the inferior castes the ritual prohibitions are more lax and the risks of contamination through contact with the profane, the bestial, or the filthy, are less. Purity is separation, impurity is union. The Tantric ceremony subverts the social order but it does so not for revolutionary but for ritual purposes: it affirms with even more emphasis than the official religions the primacy of the sacred over the profane. Protestantism was also a subversion of the social and religious order; however, it did not turn the old hierarchies upside down in order to return to the primordial mingling of all with all, but in order to proclaim the freedom and responsibility of the individual. It separated, it distinguished, it traced limits intended to preserve personal awareness and privacy. For the one the result was communality; for the other, individualism. A religious reform, Protestantism became a social and political revolution. A transgression of the religious order, Tantrism never abandons the sphere of symbols and rites: it was not (and is not) a rebellion but a ceremony. The social transgression of Tantrism completes the transgression with regard to food and does so with the same end in view: the conjunction of the signs *body* and *non-body*. The blending of flavors and substances into a single, indistinct flavor finds its exact equivalent in the dissolving of castes and hierarchies into a circle of adepts, the image of primordial indistinction.

The first modern references to Tantrism occur in a few scattered reports and memoirs of European travelers and residents. Almost all these reports date from the end of the eighteenth century and the beginning of the nineteenth. They are veiled allusions and, naturally, indignant ones; at other times the tone is more frank and more hostile: excited invective, execration mingled with horror—and with secret fascination. The fact that the authors of these reports were missionaries or civil servants of the

British Raj has caused modern opinion to regard them as lies and slanderous fabrications. But there is no reason totally to discard them. They may be partial, but there is a good deal of truth in them. The proof is that they often coincide with the texts. I am thinking in particular of the ritual assassination that some of these reports mention. Although the majority of modern commentators (both European and Hindu) say nothing about it, it is frankly described in the *Hevajra Tantra* and, as I understand it, in several other texts as well. The modern interpreters, following various traditional commentators, attempt to explain the mention of a corpse in the rite—either that of a murdered man or that of a dead man spirited away from the place of cremation—as another example of symbolism, similar to that of the impure substances. The distinction between a symbolic and a literal meaning is familiar to Tantric worshipers. As had to be the case in a system such as this, the distinction takes the form of a ritual division: the adepts "on the right hand" follow the allegorical interpretation, whereas the adepts "on the left hand" apply the text literally. Tantrism "on the left hand" is not only the most radical but actually the most Tantric: I have already said that what counts most in this religious system is not the doctrine but the practice (*sādhanā*). This difference between the rites "on the right hand" and those "on the left hand" is great but not irreconcilable. Everything is real in Tantrism—and everything is symbolic. Phenomenological reality is more than the symbol of the other reality: we touch symbols when we think we are touching bodies and material objects, and vice versa. By virtue of the same law of reversibility, all the symbols are real and tangible: concepts are bodies and even nothingness has a flavor. It is of no consequence whether the crime is real or figurative: reality and symbol fuse, and as they fuse they disappear.

Unlike the human sacrifices of the Aztecs and other peoples, the Tantric murder, whether real or feigned, is not so much a sacrifice as a ritual transgression. The sacrifice takes the form of an offering or a propitiation; in Tantrism the essential element is the crime, the transgression, the violation of the boundaries between what is permitted and what is forbidden. The *Hevajra Tantra* specifies that the victim of the actual murder must be a good man. Total transgression. The meaning of the act is exactly the opposite of the usual and predominant meaning of such an act in other religions. The same dialectic of transgression and reunion that rules the ingestion of impure foods and the confusion of castes in the circle of worshipers operates here. There is nothing similar in Protestantism. Its dialectic is not that of transgression—a violation that makes contraries overflow their boundaries and brings about their conjunction—but rather that of justice. Not the immolation of a victim, but the punishment of the guilty party. Justice re-establishes the limits that the crime has violated. It is a distribution, a reapportioning of rewards and punishments: a world in which each person occupies his proper place. The notion of sacrifice also refers to different realities and concepts. In Protestantism sacrifice is bloodless and moral; the model of Christian sacrifice is that of God, a voluntary victim: there is no other sacrifice than the sacrifice of ourselves. In the Tantric rite, the officiant is the one who sacrifices; in the Christian ceremony the worshiper, imitating Christ, offers himself as a sacrifice. His sacrifice is symbolic; it is a representation of the divine sacrifice. In Protestant Christianity, the sacrifice is above all an interiorization of the passion of Christ or its symbolic exteriorization, not in the ritual but in daily life: in the worshiper's labor and his social conduct. The sacrifice ceases to be corporeal. In Tantrism, there is a confusion between symbol and reality: the sacrifice may be real or figurative, whereas in Protestant Christianity there is a clear distinction between real blood and symbolic blood. In Tantrism, magical, physical values predominate; in Protestantism, moral values are supreme.

There is another opposition: the different attitudes toward death, or to be more exact, toward dead people. Although the thought and the presence of death are constantly with Christians, Protestantism soon abolished or attenuated its corporeal representations. Death became an idea, a thought that keeps the Christian awake nights and gnaws at his conscience: it lost its bodily presence and its symbolic representation. All the images, at once sumptuous and terrible, that obsessed medieval artists and those of the age of the Baroque in Catholic countries disappeared. The attitude toward the corpse, if not toward death, was similar to that adopted toward gold and excrement: it was hidden and it was sublimated. The dead man evaporated and death became a moral concept. I do not know whether the idea of metempsychosis aids Indians to bear the reality of death. Dying is a hard thing to face at all times and in all cultures. I fear that the function of this Indian belief is analogous to that of our beliefs: it is a device that protects a man against the horror he feels in the face of the fragility and wretchedness of existence, a projection of his fear of final extinction. Buddha himself condemned those nihilists who preached universal and absolute annihilation. In any case, the attitude of Indians toward the dead is more natural than that of Protestant Christians, but they do not delight in its physical, carnal representation as we Spaniards and Hispano-Americans do—except in Tantrism. The fondness of Mexicans for skeletons and skulls has no rival anywhere in the world except in the Buddhist art of Tibet and Nepal. There is a difference however: our skeletons are a satire on life and the living; theirs are alive and licentious. And there is something else: no image of Spanish and Hispano-American Catholicism, no allegory by Valdés Leal, and no skull by Posada possesses the meaning of the corpse which, according to certain informants, is the center around which the entire rite revolves in certain secret ceremonies, a meaning so real that it becomes hallucinatory, Philip Rawson's definition of the rite is sober and precise enough: "Sexual meditation among the corpses."* This is exactly the opposite of the Christian meditation on death and the dead.

The reaction of the first European travelers to Tantric practices is somewhat understandable: the violence of their censure is a reflection of the violence of the transgression. The diatribes of the Christian missionaries are no more passionate than those of the orthodox Brahmins and those of certain members of the Tibetan clergy. Lha lama Yesheö writes in the eleventh century:

> Since the development of rites of sexual union, people couple with no regard for their degree of kinship . . . The practices of you Tantrist village priests may seem startling to others if they hear of it in other kingdoms . . . but you are more greedy for flesh than falcons and wolves, more libidinous than donkeys and bulls, more avid for decomposition than houses in ruin or

---

* *Erotic Art of the East*, with an Introduction by Alex Comfort (New York, 1968).

the chest of a corpse. You are less clean than dogs and pigs. Having offered excrement, urine, sperm, and blood to pure gods, you will be reborn in [the hell of] a swamp full of putrefied corpses. How dreadful!*

This imprecation expresses the horror of the moral consciousness in the face of Tantrism. Morality—of whatever sort, be it Buddhist, Christian, or atheist—is dualist: *here* and *there*, good and evil, right and left. But Tantrism is not immoral: it attempts to transcend all dualisms and thus not even the adjective amoral fits it. The Tantric attitude, precisely because it is extremely religious, is not moral. In the sphere of the numinous there is no *here* or *there*, no *this* or *that*, no cardinal points or moral precepts. Tantrism is a superhuman effort to really go beyond good and evil. This lack of moderation may be mindful of Nietzsche. But Nietzsche's "nihilism" is philosophical and poetic, not religious. And it is solitary: the burst of laughter and the dance of the Superman above the abyss of the Eternal Return. The center, the heart of Tantrism, is something that Nietzsche rejects: ritual. Nonetheless, there is no return of past time without ritual, without incarnation and manifestation of the sacred date. Ritual is the Eternal Return. There is a contradiction in Nietzsche: the Superman, the "perfect nihilist," is a god without a religion (a ritual) and without a return; and there is a contradiction in Tantrism: it is a rite that never leads into history; it is merely a return, a repetition. Once again: what in the West is act and history is rite and symbol in India. India answered the idea of "changing the world" with another idea: dissipating it, turning it into a metaphor.

Tantrism tends to interpret and act out symbols literally. This literalness is naïve and terrible, as exact as a mathematical operation and as hallucinatory as a voyage in a dream. Tantrism is a system of incarnation of images, and this is why it alternately attracts us and repels us. The Abbé Dubois, who was one of the first to discuss the customs and practices of India, relates that in the "infamous feast" of Tantrism, the food was placed on top of a naked girl lying face up. Many friends and defenders

* Cited by R. A. Stein, in *La Civilisation tibétaine* (Paris, 1962).

of Indian civilization have called the abbot a liar. I do not know which makes me more indignant—Dubois's fury or the hypocrisy of the critics. The celebration of a feast in which a naked girl officiates—and that is the correct word—as the donor of the sacrament should not be criticized but praised. It is the incarnation of an image that appears in the poetry of every age: the body of the woman as an altar, a living table covered with living fruits, sacred and terrible. Novalis said that woman is the most exalted corporeal food: is this not what the Tantric ritual also says, though it does so in literal terms? The hunger and thirst of a holy meal, a feasting in honor of our mortality, a eucharist. During the Surrealist exposition dedicated to eroticism some years ago, there was a similar ceremony: a banquet in which the table was a naked woman. The Surrealists were unaware of the Indian antecedent. Images incarnate.

Like all the rest of Christianity, though much more noticeably, Protestantism lacks really erotic rites. Tantrism is above all a sexual ritual. The ceremony of Christian marriage is public but intercourse between bride and bridegroom is private. The Tantric ceremony consists of public copulation, either by several couples or a single couple in front of the circle of worshipers. It is practiced not with the wife, but with a *yogina* (a female practioner of yogi), in general one from an inferior caste. Among Christians the act is consummated in the bedroom, that is to say in a profane place; the *Tantras* specifically state that it must be celebrated in a temple or some consecrated site, preferably in places where the dead are cremated. Copulation atop ashes: destruction of the opposition between life and death, the dissolution of both in emptiness. The absorption of death by life is the reverse of Christianity; the vanishing of both in a third term, sunyata, is the reverse of Mediterranean paganism. We cannot help but admire this dialectic which, without denying the reality of life and the no less real evidence of death, reconciles them by dissipating them. And it reconciles them at the very height of the carnal act; the moment like a flash of lightning that is the most intense affirmation of time and also its negation. Copulation is the real and genuine union of samsara and nirvana, identity between existence and emptiness, thought and nonthought. Maithuna: two in one, the lotus and the lightning bolt, the vulva and the phallus, the vowels and the consonants, the right side of the body and the left, the world above and the world below.

The union of bodies and of opposing principles is also the realization of the hermaphrodite archetype. Reintegration through emptiness is equivalent to the union of the masculine and the feminine part in each of us. On identifying ourselves with emptiness, we also realize ourselves carnally and psychologically: we regain our feminine side, or our masculine side in the case of the woman. Tantrism takes as its point of departure the idea that in each man there is something feminine and in each woman something masculine. Instead of repressing and separating the feminine in man and the masculine in woman, Tantrism seeks to reconcile the two elements. The images of the Indian gods, even though they are always virile, radiate an almost feminine languor and softness. And though Indian goddesses have full breasts, wide hips, and thin waists, they radiate a gravity, an aplomb, a determination that is masculine. The contrast with the Christian West is marked. The results of our repression of femininity in man and of masculinity in woman have been the oceans of curves and the mountains of muscles in Rubens and the triangles and rectangles of the twentieth century.

Physical love is profane in Christian eyes; Tantrism knows nothing of what we call love, and its eroticism is sacramental. Protestantism accentuates the division between the sacred and the profane, the permitted and the forbidden, the masculine and the feminine; Tantrism aims at the absorption of the profane by the sacred, the destruction of the difference between the permitted and the forbidden, the fusion of the masculine and the feminine. The most extreme opposition has to do with the functions of ingestion and of excretion. The central rule of the Tantric sexual rite has to do with the withholding of sperm, not for moral reasons and even less for hygienic reasons, but because the entire act is aimed at the transmutation of semen and its fusion with emptiness. Thus in Tantrism the retention of semen corresponds to the real or symbolic ingestion of excrement; in Protestantism, rapid ejaculation corresponds to the real or symbolic retention of excrement. Seminal retention implies an eroticization of the entire body, a regression to the infantile games and pleasures that psychoanalysis calls polymorphous, pregenital, and perverse. Rapid ejaculation is the triumph of destructive and self-destructive genital eroticism, leading to frigidity in the woman and frustrated pleasure in the man. Ejaculation is linked to death; seminal retention is a regression to a previous state of sexuality. The triumph of death or regression to the undifferentiated sexuality of childhood: in both cases there is selfishness, fear, scorn of the partner. Disjunction and conjunction vitiate the pleasure principle, harm life in its very center.

Protestantism exaggerated the Christian horror of the body. The cause of our perdition, the decent thing is not to mention it, except in the neutral terms of science. For Tantrism the body is the real double of the universe which, in turn, is a manifestation of the adamantine and incorruptible body of Buddha. It propounds a symbolic anatomy and physiology that would be too lengthy and tedious to explain here. I shall merely say that it conceives of the body as a microcosm with six nodes of sexual, nervous, and psychic energy; these centers (*cakras*), from the genital organs to the brain, are connected by two veins (*rasanā* and *lalanā*). The human body is seen as a mandala which serves as an "aid" to meditation and as an altar on which a sacrifice is consumed. The two veins start at the sacred plexus, in which the penis (*linga*) and the vulva (*yoni*) are located. The first vein runs up the right side and polarizes the masculine aspect; the second runs up along the left side and symbolizes the feminine aspect. *Rasanā* is identified with (com) Passion (*karuna*) and with method (*upāya*); *lalanā* with emptiness and wisdom (*prajñā*). The chain of correspondences ramifies to the point of representing a veritable semantic constellation: *rasanā* (the tongue) → *prāna* (the breath of life) → *vyañjana* (the series of consonants) → the Jamuna River/*lalanā* (a dissolute woman) → *candra* (moon) → *apāna* (exhalation) → *svara* (the series of vowels) → the mother (the river) Ganges. There are many crudely material equivalences and linkages of spiritual concepts and sexual realities: *mahamāmsa* (human flesh) → *alija* (the mystical vowels)/*vajra* (a lightning bolt) → *linga* (penis) → *upāya* (meditation). Two notions of Mahayana Buddhism which are really conceptual, the compassion of the Bodhisattva and the action of thought during meditation (*upāya*) , take on a predominant erotic symbolism and become homologues of phallus and sperm; *śūnyatā* (emptiness) and *prajñā* (wisdom) evoke the female sexual organs.

During coitus, the couple tries to fuse the masculine and the feminine elements—to transcend the duality. The sexual act is a homologue of meditation and both are homologues of reality, which has been divided up into *this* and *that* but which in and of itself is only empty transparency. A third vein—*avadhūti*—runs between these two veins. The locus of union and intersection, it is the homologue of the *yogina*, the ascetic-libertine woman who "is neither subject nor object." The union of the two currents of energy in the central vein is realization, consummation. A commentary of the poems of Sahāra and Kānha says: "In the moment of great delight, the thought of illumination is born, that is, semen is produced." The great delight (*mahāsukha*) is also *sahaja*, the return to the innate. The horizontal union, between the feminine and masculine, corresponds to another union which is vertical: the union of semen (*śukra*) with the thought of illumination (*bodhiccita*). The transmutation is achieved by union with the feminine principle, in a moment which is the apex or conjugation of all energy. Instead of being spent, the drop of semen (*bindu*) thus transubstantiated ascends along the backbone until it shatters in a silent explosion: it is a lotus opening at the top of the skull. "Reflection is Consummation": *bindu* is *bodhiccita*, thought without an object, emptiness. Seminal retention is an alchemical and mystical operation: it is not meant to preserve the relation between body and soul but rather to dissolve the first in emptiness. The repressive disjunction in Protestantism and the explosive conjunction in Tantrism ultimately coincide.

A religious geography lies beside this magic physiology that I have briefly described. "Here in the body are the sacred rivers Jamuna and Ganges, here are Pragaya and Benares, the Sun and the Moon. In my wanderings, I have visited many sanctuaries, but none more holy than that of my body" (Poem of Sahāra). If the body is earth, the sacred earth, it is also language, and a symbolic language: in each phoneme and each syllable there lies a seed (*bīja*) that emits a vibration and a hidden sense when it is actualized in speech. *Rasanā* represents the consonants and *lalanā* the vowels. The two veins, or canals, of the body are now the masculine and feminine aspects of speech. Language occupies a central place in Tantrism; it is a system of incarnated metaphors. Throughout these pages I have referred to the play of echoes, correspondences and equivalences of the ciphered language of the *Tantras* (*sandhābhāsā*). The ancient commentators referred to this erotico-metaphysical hermeticism as "the twilight language": modern commentators, following Mircea Eliade, call it the "intentional language." But the specialists do not say (or else say it like somebody walking on red-hot coals) that this language is essentially poetic and obeys the same laws as poetic creation.

Tantric metaphors are not only intended to hide the real meaning of the rites from intruders; they are also verbal manifestations of the universal analogy that is the basis of poetry. These texts are governed by the same psychological and artistic necessity that caused our Baroque poets to build a language of their own within the Spanish language, the same necessity that inspired the language of Joyce and the Surrealists: the conception of writing as the double of the cosmos. If the body is a cosmos for Sahāra, his poem is a body—and this verbal body is *śūnyatā*. The closest and most impressive example of this is the *trobar clus* of the Provençal poets. The hermeticism of Provençal poetry is a verbal veil: opaque for the ignorant and transparent for the lover who gazes on the nakedness of the lady. One has to be in on the secret: I say *be in on* it and not *know* it. There must be participation: weaving the veil is an act of love and unraveling it is another. The same thing happens in the case of the hermetic language of the *Tantras:* in order to decipher it, it is not enough to know the key but to make one's way into the forest of symbols, to be a symbol among symbols. Poetry and Tantrism are alike in that they are both concrete, practical experiences.

The language of Protestant Christianity is critical and exemplary, a guide to meditation and action; the language of the *Tantras* is a microcosm, the verbal double of the universe and the body. In Protestantism, language obeys the laws of rational and moral economy and even-handed justice; in Tantrism, the cardinal principle is that of wealth lavishly spent: an offering, a gift, and also luxury—goods destined to be consumed or dissipated. The "productivity" of the Tantric language belongs to the realm of imitative magic: its model is nature, not work. In Protestantism there is a separation between language and reality: the Holy Scriptures are conceived of as a collection of moral principles; in Tantrism there is a union of language and reality: scripture is *lived* as a body that is an analogue of the physical body—and the body is *read* as a scripture.

Alongside this "intentional language" are magic formulas composed by the syllables that I have already mentioned apropos of the *rasanā* and the *lalanā* as the symbolic rubrics of the consonants and the vowels. These syllables do not go to make up words and Bharati calls them, in a rather forced way, "morphemes or quasimorphemes." The syllables (*bījas*) combine with each other and form sound units: *mantras*. Neither *bījas* nor *mantras* has any conceptual meaning; nonetheless each is extremely rich in emotional, magic, and religious meanings. In Bharati's view, the nucleus of Tantrism, its essence as a rite and as a practice, lies in the *mantras*. They are the heart of the religions of India. The *mantra* is the other face of yoga and, like yoga, it is not intellectual but practical and nondiscursive. It is a means of obtaining certain powers. The recitation of the *mantra*, whether silent or aloud, lays down a bridge between the reciter and the macrocosm, as do the breathing exercises of the yogi. But the *mantra* is above all a ritual instrument, to be used either in collective rites or personal worship. There is another aspect to which specialists, in my opinion, have not paid enough attention: the *mantras* are indicative signs, sonorous signs of identification. Each divinity, each guru, each disciple, each worshiper, each concept, and each moment of the ritual has a *mantra* appropriate to it. The poet Kānha has expressed it better than this complicated explanation I have given: the syllables (*bījas*) clasp the naked ankle of the *yogina* like a bracelet. They are sonorous attributes.

Neither Christian prayers and litanies nor abracadabras and other magic formulas are the equivalent of the *mantras*. Perhaps poetry is, or is rather one of its manifestations—which Alfonso Reyes once called "*jitanjáfora*," the nonconceptual explosion of the syllables, the joy, anguish, ecstasy, the anger, the desire expressed in them. It is a language beyond language, as in the poems of Kurt Schwitters, the interjections of Artaud, the serpentine, feline syllables of Michaux, the ecstatic vowels of Huidobro. No, my comparison is omitting the essential, the element that distinguishes the *mantras* from every sort of Western poetic expression: the

Indians do not invent these "sonorous jewels"—the guru passes them on to the disciple. Nor are they poems: they are verbal amulets, linguistic talismans, sonorous scapulars. A symbolic and hermetic language—genital words, phonetic and semantic couplings, jingling *mantras*—versus the verbal simplicity of Protestant Christianity and its neutral and abstract moral vocabulary. A language that distinguishes between the act and the word, and between the signifying sign and what it signifies/language that blurs the distinction between the word and the act, that reduces the sign to a mere signifier, that multiplies and changes the meanings of these signs, that conceives of itself as a game that is identical to that of the universe, in which the right side and the left side, the feminine and the masculine, fullness and emptiness, are one and the same—a language that means everything, and nothing.

The word *Prajñāpāramitā* designates one of the cardinal concepts of Mahayana Buddhism. It is the "supreme wisdom" of the Bodhisattvas and the person who has achieved it is already on the "other shore," on the other side of reality. It is the first and the last emptiness. Both the beginning and the end of knowledge, it is also a divinity in the Buddhist pantheon. There are innumerable images in stone, metal, and wood of Our Lady *Prajñāpāramitā*, and the beauty of some of them is unforgettable. I confess that the incarnation in the majesty of a female body of a concept as abstract as that of wisdom in emptiness never ceases to amaze me. A pure idea and a corporeal image, *Prajñāpāramitā* is also a vision and a sound: it is "a red, eight-petaled lotus," made up of vowels and consonants "that arises from the syllable Ah . . ." It is more: a sound and a color, a word reduced to its luminous vibration, an image of stone in a posture of voluptuous meditation, and a metaphysical concept, *Prajñāpāramitā* is at the same time a woman: the *yogina* of ritual. The female partner in the rite is an initiate, almost always of an inferior caste or an impure profession: the *candali* or the *dombī* (laundress). Kānha says in one of his songs to emptiness: "You are the *candali* of passion. Oh *dombī*, no one is more dissolute than you." *Candali* here means the "mystic heat" of the Tibetans: the union of the sun and the moon, the humor of the woman and the sperm of the man, the lotus of Perfect Wisdom and the lightning bolt of (com) Passion, melted and dissolved in one sudden burst of flame.

Phenomenal reality is identical to essential reality: the two are emptiness. Samsara is nirvana.*

Within the Tantric system, the Buddhist and Hindu branches are opposed in the same way that orthodox or traditional Hinduism and Buddhism are opposed. The first great contrast is that while in Hindu Tantrism the active principle is feminine (*Sakti*), in Buddhist Tantrism it is masculine (the adamantine Buddha, *Vajrasattava*). In Tibetan representations of ritual copulation (*yab yum*), the masculine divinity has a terrible and even ferocious look about him, whereas his partner (*dākinī*) has a fragile, though well-rounded, beauty; in Hindu images, the most energetic representation of the active principle, often fierce and terrible as well, is Sakti, the feminine pole of reality. At first glance, the Hindu notion contradicts the ideas about women that most societies have had. Nonetheless, this is not illogical: the absolute (represented by Siva) is the subject absorbed in the dream of its infinite solipsism; the appearance of Sakti is the birth of the object (nature, the concrete world) which rouses the subject from its lethargy. Iconography represents Sakti dancing on the sleeping body of Siva, who half opens his eyes. In Judaism there are not only any number of virile and heroic women; there is also our mother, Eve, who wakes Adam from his dream of paradise and obliges him to confront the real world: work, history, and death. In the Bible story, the woman is created from the rib of the sleeping man, as Sakti is born of Siva's dream and also wakes her companion. Eve and Sakti are nature, the objective world. My interpretation may seem to be far-fetched. It is not, but it would not matter if it were: there is another important factor which explains the apparent singularity of saktism.

The reason for attributing to Sakti values such as activity and energy, which may appear to be masculine virtues par excellence—although they really are not—is of a formal nature. It belongs to what we might call the

---

* With regard to the poems of Kānha and Sahāra see: *Les Chants mystiques de Kānha et Sahāra*, edited and translated by M. Shabidullah (Paris, 1921). See also the two books of Shashibhusan Das Gupta: *An Introduction to Tantric Buddhism* (Calcutta, 1958) and *Obscure Religious Cults* (Calcutta, 1962). *Buddhist Texts Through the Ages* (London, 1954), a collective work by Edward Conze *et al.*, contains the text of the lovely evocation of *Prajñāpāramitā* and Sahāra's poem.

law of symmetry, or correspondence, between symbols: the position of one symbol determines the position of the opposite symbol. In Buddhism, the active principle is masculine (*upāya*) but the consummation of the ritual—the abolition of duality—possesses a marked feminine tonality. The two central metaphysical concepts, śūnyatā and *Prajñāpāramitā*, are conceived of as feminine. The abolition of the duality implies the disappearance of the feminine and masculine poles, but this dissolution in Buddhism has a feminine sign. It could not be otherwise, given the position of the symbols. From the beginning, Buddhism affirmed that the supreme good (nirvana) was identical with the cessation of the ebb and flow of existence, and, in its highest form, with emptiness. In Mahayana Buddhism, emptiness was also represented by the round Zero, the image of the woman. For the Hindu, supreme beatitude is the union with being, with the nondual, the One. The coloration is masculine: the One extolled is phallic; it is the quiet, ecstatic linga, full of itself. The Buddhist conceives of the absolute as an object, and thus converts it into a homologue of the feminine pole of reality; the Hindu thinks of it as a subject and associates it with the masculine pole. Two sacred forms condense these images: the stupa and the linga—the Zero and the One. The activity engaged in to attain the (masculine) One cannot be anything but feminine (*Sakti*). Since activity is masculine, Sakti must express not only femininity in its most ample form—round breasts, a narrow waist, and powerful hips—but this femininity that is full to overflowing with itself must emit effluvia, masculine radiations. The same need for symbolic symmetry explains the femininity of the Buddhas and Bodhisattvas; they are the active masculine principle which has conquered and assimilated passivity. *Upāya* corresponds to śūnyatā; Sakti corresponds to Siva. The play of correspondences embraces the whole system. If we attribute the cipher zero to femininity, whether active or passive, and the cipher one to masculinity, which also may be either active or passive, the result will be as follows: in Buddhism 1 (active) → 0 (passive); in Hinduism 0 (active) → 1 (passive). From the point of view of their respective ideals of beatitude, the opposition between Buddhist Tantrism and Hindu is 0 (passive)/1 (passive). The means to achieve these goals have the same antithetical opposition: 1 (active)/0 (active). The inverse symmetry that rules each branch is reproduced in the relations between the two. It is the logic of the system, and doubtless the logic of every symbolic system.

The other opposition is no less radical and affects what is the nucleus of Tantrism, the attitude toward seminal ejaculation, with its polarity between feminine and masculine. Unlike Tantric Buddhism, there is no retention of sperm in Hindu Tantrism. Despite the studies that have been devoted to the subject for more than twenty-five years, the first to mention this fact was Agehananda Bharati in a recent work (*The Tantric Tradition* was published in 1965). Bharati was also the first, and to my knowledge the only one, to treat this antithetical relation in a systematic way. The release of sperm is equivalent to a ritual sacrifice, as can be seen in this passage from a Tantric text (*Vāmamārga*): "[The worshiper], while continuing to mentally recite his *mantra*, abandons his sperm with this invocation: 'On with light and ether, [as if they were] my two hands. I am the triumphant . . . I who have consumed *dharma* and *non-dharma* as the portions of the sacrifice, lovingly offer this oblation into the fire . . .'" *Dharma* and *non-dharma* seem to me to designate here, respectively, what is permitted and what is prohibited by orthodox Hinduism. The final mention of fire, which is identified with the female body, refers to one of the oldest rituals of India: the fire sacrifice. The Hindu Tantric ceremony reincorporates and revives the Indian tradition. The Vedic religion was based on the notion of ritual sacrifice. This is something, as Bharati aptly observes, that has been the cardinal element of the Hindu religion from the Vedic period to the present. Buddhism, on the other hand, appeared precisely as a criticism of the Brahman ritualism and its obsessive penchant for sacrifice. It is true that in the course of its history it created rituals that rival those of Hinduism, but the notion of sacrifice is not central in them. Buddhism puts the accent on the renunciation of the world; Hinduism conceives of the world as a rite whose center is sacrifice. There is asceticism in the former, and ritualism in the latter; seminal retention and release of sperm.

The inverse symmetry which rules the masculine/feminine, active/passive, being/emptiness polarity is repeated in the attitude toward ejaculation, except that now it is manifested in the form of retention/release, renunciation/sacrifice, interiorization/exteriorization. The process is the same: retention of semen = dissolution of the subject in emptiness (the object); release of semen = union of the object with being (the subject). In this dialectic we encounter the same affirmations and negations that define Buddhism and Hinduism: negation of the soul and the *I* versus affirmation of being (*ātman*); a monism without a subject versus a monism that reduces everything to the subject. Although the opposition between Protestant Christianity and Tantrism is of another order, it takes on the same form of reverse symmetry. The relation can be seen more clearly in the case of the basic physiological functions of ingestion and excretion of the two substances—excrement and semen—and their symbols. The symbolic retention of excrement in Protestant Christianity is the equivalent, in an opposite and contrary sense, of its ingestion in Hindu and Buddhist Tantrism (impure foods). With regard to seminal ejaculation, the attitude of Tantrism is unproductive and primarily religious: retention and release are homologues, the first of dissolution in the supreme emptiness and the second of the union with the fullness of being; in Protestantism, the meaning is productive and moral: the procreation of children. In Tantrism, copulation is a religious violation of moral rules; in Protestantism it is a legitimate practice (if it is done with one's spouse) which is intended to fulfill the Biblical religious precept. Tantrism destroys morals through religion; Protestantism transforms religion into morals. Sperm in Tantrism is transmuted into a sacred substance that becomes immaterial in the end, either because the sacrificial fire consumes it or because it is transfigured into the "thought of illumination." In Protestantism, semen engenders children, a family: it becomes social and is transformed into action upon the world.

Protestantism called for the free interpretation of sacred books and one of the first problems it had to face was that of the meaning of the sacred text: what do the paradoxes of the Gospels and the frequently immoral myths and stories of the Bible really mean? The Protestant interpretation is a moral and rational criticism of mythic language. Tantrism also accepts freedom of interpretation, but its exegesis is symbolic: it transforms the metaphysics of Mahayana Buddhism into a bodily analogy and thus goes from criticism to myth. Protestant language is clear; the language of the *Tantras* is "the twilight language," an idiom in which each word has four or five meanings at once. Protestantism separates myth and morals; Tantrism fuses morals and metaphysics in a mythical language. Protestantism reduces ritual to a minimum; Tantrism is mainly a ritual. In a penetrating study, Raimundo Panikar has shown that Christianity is above all an *orthodoxy* and Hinduism an *orthopraxy*; and although this distinction may not be entirely applicable to Hinayana Buddhism, it is to Mahayana Buddhism. Protestantism and Tantric Buddhism exaggerate the tendencies of their respective religious traditions: there is criticism of the texts and of orthodoxy in the former and ritualization of ideas in the latter. There is concern for public opinion in the former and an obsession with practices in the latter; there is clear language and public discussion in the former and a figurative language and secret ceremonies in the latter. Tantrism is esoteric and the doctrine is transmitted in secret; Protestantism proselytizes openly, through example and through the sermon intended for everyone. The former involves hidden, closed sects, the latter open sects that live in the light of day.

The negation of the body and of the world is transformed into a utilitarian ethic and social action in Protestantism; the absorption of the body in emptiness culminates in the cult of waste and asocial activity in Tantrism. The one exalts the economical and the useful; the other is indifferent to progress and cancels out social and moral distinctions. The one involves solitary introspection—holdovers and remains of sin and virtue—and a silent confrontation with a terrible, just God: the world as process, judgment, and sentence. Good and evil, the useful and the harmful, like *being* and *non-being*, are empty words, illusions for Tantrism: the yogi is a free man who has gone beyond the dualist trap. Protestantism represents the tribunal of conscience; Tantrism the erotic play of the cosmos within consciousness. There is pessimism, moralism, and utilitarianism in the one, and pessimism, amoralism, and nonproductive contemplation in the other. Protestantism represents an organized social life: the priest marries, heads a family, and his church is in the center of the town; Tantrism represents a mystical individual life: the adept is celibate, has no house, and lives on the periphery of the world. The pastor and the wandering ascetic: the one clean-shaven and dressed in black, occupies himself with philanthropic tasks; the other,

4 ORDER AND ACCIDENT

SEXUAL ALCHEMY AND EROTIC COURTESY

The Sinologist R. H. Van Gulik, to whom we owe various works (among them the triple, intriguing, detective story, *Dee Goong An*), published before his death a fundamental book on sexual life in ancient China.* The Dutch diplomat puts forward a new hypothesis concerning the origin of Tantrism: the central idea—the retention of semen and its transmutation—comes from Taoism. This is not the place to discuss his arguments, nor does my limited knowledge of the subject permit me to take part in the debate. I merely wish to point out that in several Hindu Tantric texts there is mention of *Cīna* (China) and *Mahācīna* (Mongolia? Tibet?) as favored regions for practices of sexual meditation. Bharati cites a curious detail: the offering to Siva of a hair from the pubis of the Sakti, pulled out during the ritual copulation and still wet with semen, is called *mahācīna sādhanā*. But it must not be forgotten that the texts to which I am here referring are recent, whereas Vajrayana Buddhism goes back at least as far as the sixth century A.D. The solution of the problem depends, perhaps, on the solution of another problem: the origin of yoga. Is it pre-Aryan and indigenous to India, as the majority of specialists believe today, or does it come from Central Asia (shamanism) as others believe? The presence of yoga elements in primitive Taoism, first pointed out by Maspero, only increases our perplexity. The origin of yoga is as obscure as that of the idea of the soul among the

---

* *Sexual Life in Ancient China* (Leiden, 1961). The book deals with a longer period than that indicated by the title, since it ends in the seventeenth century with the Ming dynasty. One observation in passing: Van Gulik translates the scabrous passages of the Chinese texts into Latin, as if knowledge of this language were a certificate of morality. Snellgrove forbears to translate several fragments of the *Hevajra Tantra* which he considers particularly scatological; fortunately they are few in number. But this latter way of going about things is more serious: almost all of us can get something out of Latin, whereas this is not true when the passage is in Tibetan or hybrid Sanskrit.

Greeks. In any case, there is one thing that no one questions: the great age and the universality of the belief that the retention of sperm is a saving up of life, a storing up of life. Chastity thus becomes a sort of recipe for immortality. The Chinese alchemical texts and the curious *Bed Treatises* offer more than one analogy with the Indian *Tantras*. These similarities are not coincidences; rather they reveal precise influences, either because they are an Indian borrowing from China (as Van Gulik maintains) or because the interchange was much more complicated: a Chinese influence in India; a re-elaboration within the Indian religious context; and a return to China. Once the relation between the Chinese texts and the Indian ones has been accepted, what I am interested in emphasizing is their differences. These seem to me to be more significant than their similarities.

Chinese eroticism is as old as the four legendary emperors. Erotology, in the specialized sense of the word, is also very old and is related both to alchemy and medicine. Van Gulik mentions six *Bed Treatises* dating from the Han period, all of which have disappeared because of the jealousy of the neo-Confucians and the puritanism of the Manchu dynasty. But texts from the Sui, T'ang, and Ming dynasties have come down to us. The collective names of these little works were *Fang-nei* (literally, "in the bed") and *Fang-shi* ("the subject of the bed"). They were extremely popular books. Abundantly illustrated, they constituted a sort of everyday manual, used principally by newlyweds and bachelors. The literary form is didactic, like that of our catechisms: the question-and-answer method. The persons who figure in the dialogue are usually the mythical Yellow Emperor and a girl who initiates him into sexual secrets. The female speaker is sometimes called *Su-nü*, the Simple Girl, sometimes *Hsü an-nü*, the Dark Girl, and sometimes *Ts'ai-nü*, the Chosen Girl. Although these works are inspired by Taoism, in the beginning the followers of Confucius did not violently oppose their diffusion.

In order to understand the nature of these texts, the basic Chinese conception of society, nature, and sex must be kept in mind. The principle is the same for both Confucians and Taoists: the archetype of human order is the cosmic order. Nature and its changes (*T'ien tao*), the light-and-shadow, heaven-and-earth, dragon-and-tiger duality is the basis of the *I Ching* (*The Book of Changes*), as well as of Confucian ethics and politics, the speculations of Lao-tzu and Chuang-tzu, and the elucubrations of the *yang* and *yin* school. No less important is the age-old idea that man produces semen in limited quantities, whereas the woman produces *ch'i*, the vital humor, in unlimited quantities. Thus, man must appropriate *ch'i* and conserve his semen as much as possible. The origin of seminal retention is pragmatic in China, while exactly the opposite is true in India. In the *Bed Treatises* the methods for retaining semen and transforming it into a vital principle are enumerated and described in minute detail. Likewise, the propitious days for conception are indicated, generally during the week following the end of menstruation.

Immortality, strictly speaking, is not a Confucian notion. Fan Hsün Tzŭ asks Mu-shu: "Our ancestors said: 'dead but immortal.' What did they mean?" Mu-shu answers:

In Lu, there lived a high dignitary called Tsang-Wen-Chung. After his death, his words remained. This is what the ancient proverb means. I have heard that it is best to build on virtue, then on action, and then on words. This is what we may call immortality. As for the preservation of the family name and the continuing of sacrifices to one's ancestors: no [civilized] society can disregard these practices. They are praiseworthy but they do not give immortality.*

Yet the permanence of the family, the society, and the State are a sort of social and biological immortality for Confucius and his disciples. Man is society and society is nature: a biological, historical, and cosmic continuity. For this reason, the *Bed Treatises* have only a secondary value: they are rules of sexual conduct intended to prevent premature old age, preserve male vitality, and guarantee fruitful coitus—erotology as a branch of family morality and, by extension, of good government. It must also be said that the advice in the treatises was really very useful if

---

* *Tso Chuan* (Commentaries by Tso on the *Annals of Autumn and Spring*), in *A Source Book in Chinese Philosophy*, compiled and translated by Wing-tsit Chan (Princeton, New Jersey, 1963).

we remember that the Chinese family was polygamous; what these books basically preached was sensible control of masculine sexuality. The Confucian mistrust of them, later becoming frank hostility, stemmed from the same preoccupation with the stability and sanctity of the family. The books of erotology were something more than treatises on hygiene: they were manuals of pleasure, an encyclopedia of major or minor perversions, apologies for licentiousness, and, what was worse, for unruly passions. As they were avidly read, not only by men but by women, they disturbed the natural harmony of the relations between the sexes, that is, the subordinate position of the woman.

Taoism, from the beginning, presented itself as an art, or method, of attaining immortality, or longevity at least, along with a state of accord with the cosmos. But as it is primarily a method and only secondarily a philosophy, it is similar to yoga. The similarity is even more evident if we take notice of the fact that both Taoist adepts and practitioners of yoga used certain bodily techniques to "nourish the vital principle," and that breathing exercises were the most important of these. Among the Taoist practices for attaining immortality the most important were doubtless those having to do with the retention of sperm. I have already mentioned the universality of the identification of semen with the vital powers, which is age-old. This idea can become obsessive: in modern India most people believe that every loss of semen, either through copulation or through involuntary emission, shortens one's life span. Many Westerners have the same fear, though it may be an unconscious one. In antiquity, semen was made divine by making it the homologue of the vital principle: it was spirit, a divine, creative power. This belief contributed a great deal to the origin and the development of asceticism: chastity was not only a method of storing up life but also a method of transmuting sperm into spirit and creative power. Is that not the meaning of the myths of the birth of Aphrodite and Minerva? Seminal retention for the Taoist adept was only half the operation: the other half consisted in the appropriation of *ch'i*, which was considered to be the purest manifestation of the *yin* essence. I mean *essence* here more in the material sense than in the philosophical, for it is more a fluid than an idea. From its very beginning Chinese civilization conceived of the cosmos as an order based on the dual rhythm—union, separation, union—of two powers, or forces: heaven and earth, masculine and feminine, active and passive, *yang* and *yin*. Assimilating *yin* (*ch'i*) and uniting it to *yang* (nonejaculated sperm) is the equivalent of converting oneself into a cosmos identical to the outer cosmos, governed by the rhythmical embrace of the two vital principles.

Like Tantrism, and for the same ritual and poetic reasons, Taoism invented a secret system of expressions and symbols. The English critic Philip Rawson describes it as a "sexual cryptography."* The difference as compared with Tantrism is this: Tantric symbols and expressions are concepts and obey rigorous distinctions of a philosophical nature; Taoist images are fluid and closer to poetic imagination than to rational discourse. Taoism is not governed by an intellectual dialectic but by the law of the association of images: it is a poetic structure that grows like a plant, a tree. In Tantrism, the human body and that of the cosmos are conceived of as a geometry of concepts, a spatial logic; in Taoism, they are conceived of as a system of metaphors and visual images, a tissue of allusions that perpetually comes unraveled and is continually rewoven. The patron saint of longevity in the Taoist list of saints is Shou Lou: this person appears in paintings and engravings as a smiling centenarian with an enormous head—"full of semen," as Rawson emphasizes—holding a peach (the image of the vulva) in his right hand, with his index finger pressing down on the cleft of the fruit. Tantrism brings us face to face with precise symbols, Taoism with allusive and elusive images. The chain of associations inspired by natural forms is very long and very suggestive: a half-opened pomegranate → a peony → a shell → a lotus → a vulva. Dew, fog, clouds, and other vapors are associated with the female fluid, as are certain classes of mushrooms. The same thing happens with masculine attributes: a bird, a ray of light, a deer, a tree of jade. The image of the human body as the double of the cosmic body appears often in poems, essays, and paintings. A Chinese landscape is not a realistic representation, but a metaphor of cosmic reality: the mountain and the valley, the waterfall and the abyss, are man and woman, *yang* and *yin* in conjunction or disjunction. The *Great Medicine of the Three Mountain Peaks* is to

* See *Erotic Art of the East* (New York, 1968).

be found in the body of the woman and is composed of three juices, or essences: one from the woman's mouth, another from her breasts, and the third, the most powerful, from the *Grotto of the White Tiger*, which is at the foot of the *Peak of the Purple Mushroom* (the mons veneris). According to Rawson these half-poetic, half-medicinal metaphors explain the popularity of cunnilingus among the Chinese: "The practice was an excellent method of imbibing the precious feminine fluid." Tantric corporeal geography refers to religious sites; it is a guide for the pilgrimages of the devout: sacred rivers such as the Ganges and the Jamuna, holy cities such as Benares and Bodhigaya. In China, the body is an allegory of nature: brooks, ravines, mountain peaks, clouds, grottoes, fruits, birds.

The methods of seminal retention and appropriation of *ch'i* were inseparable from alchemy and the practices of meditation. Van Gulik mentions various alchemical texts in which the operations and the transformations of substances were compared to copulation. One of them, entitled *The Pact of the Triple Equation*, is based on a universal analogy: the transmutation of cinnabar into mercury, that of semen into a vital principle during *coitus reservatus*, and the transformation of the various elements according to the combinations of the hexagrams of the *I Ching*. The principle of "two in one"—in an inverse symmetry to the "one in two" of the androgynous archetype—inspires both alchemy and mystical eroticism everywhere: the concept of the body as the analogical double of the macrocosm has barely been conceived when alchemy stretches a bridge between the two. Even a poet who displayed no particular inclination toward Taoist mysticism, Po Chü-i, wrote a poem on the alchemical embraces of the green dragon (the man) and the white tiger (the woman).

In its extreme forms Taoism also practiced public copulation in the Tantric manner. Not out of libertinage—although this, too, is ascetic—but in order to appropriate the vital principle and win immortality or, as I have stated, longevity. One of the most dramatic episodes in ancient Chinese history is the revolt called the Rebellion of the Yellow Turbans. The name refers to a Taoist sect that succeeded in organizing a vast portion of China into a sort of militant and religious communal social system at the end of the Han period. Although we do not have anything but the accounts of the enemies of the Yellow Turbans, it appears that the movement won the passionate loyalty of the people and of certain groups belonging to the intelligentsia. It is also certain that the rebels were practitioners of sexual Taoist mysticism and practiced collective rites of copulation. The rite has survived in semisecrecy down to the present day. In 1950 the government of the Popular Republic of China discovered and broke up a sect (the *l-kuan-tao*) whose worshipers still practiced the ancient sexual ceremonies of magic Taoism.

Indian eroticism presents no similarities. For the Indians, the three central human activities are pleasure (*kāma*), interest (*artha*), and the spiritual and moral life (*dharma*). Eroticism is part of the first of these. As in the case of the Chinese treatises, the first book, the famous *Kama Sutra*, is not the beginning, but the continuation, and the culmination, of a very old tradition. Although its technical content is similar to that of the Chinese texts—positions, aphrodisiacs, magic recipes, a list of anatomical and temperamental compatibilities—there are marked differences. It is not a treatise on conjugal sexual relations; it embraces the whole gamut of carnal commerce between men and women: the seduction of unmarried girls as well as dealings with courtesans, widows, and married and divorced women. There is another major difference: a whole chapter is expressly devoted to adultery. The theme of the book is frankly pleasure, and stolen sexual delights rather than those enjoyed at home, pleasure conceived of as an art—an art of civilized people. The dominant tone is primarily technical: how to come by sexual enjoyment and how to give it; and aesthetic: how to make life more beautiful and how to make sensations more intense and more lasting. There is not the slightest concern either for health (except as a condition of pleasure), or for the family, or for immortality. Morality and mysticism, politics and religion play no part in this text.

I do not know of any book less utilitarian and less religious than the *Kama Sutra*. The same thing is true of the other texts of Indian eroticism, such as the *Kokasatra* and the *Anangaranga*. None of them mentions seminal retention, although they do recommend that the sexual act be as prolonged as possible, and appropriate advice for doing so is provided. They are books having to do with erotic aesthetics and good bedroom manners: their equivalent, in another context, would be Castiglione's *Il*

Cortegiano. The Chinese books were part of medicine, and ancient book catalogues listed them under that heading. The Indian books were a branch of the worldly arts, such as the art of cosmetics and perfumes, archery and cooking, music and singing, dance and mime. There is another important difference; they were not aimed either at the religious man or the head of a family but at the dandy and the rich courtesan. Both types are the heroes of the stories, novels, and poems of the great *kāvya* literature. Louis Renou observes that the treatises on eroticism were very useful for writers, poets, and dramatists, who needed to know the theory of *kāma* as well as that of rhetoric (*alamkara*) and grammar. All the refined literature of Classic India attests to a very great familiarity with the erotic tradition.* These, then, were manuals of sexual technique, books on erotic courtesy, catechisms of indolent, refined elegance: pleasure as a branch of aesthetics.

The comparison between Chinese erotic alchemy and Tantric texts reveals differences of another sort that are no less marked. Alchemy plays an important part in the *Tantras*, and as in Taoism its object is to unite the masculine and feminine fluids. But the union serves different ends in each case. In Tantrism it is a means to attain illumination, and secondarily, certain magic powers (*siddhi*); in Taoism immortality is the essential aim. The goal of the Taoist is to reconquer the natural state because, among other things, being immortal means being reunited with the rhythmic movement of the cosmos, being ceaselessly re-engendered, like the year and its seasons, the century and its years. Taoist quietism is inactive, but not immobile: the wise man is like nature, which imperturbably and tirelessly goes its rounds, ever changing and ever returning to its beginning without a beginning. The ideogram of sexual union in the *I Ching* is *Chi-chi*, with the trigram *K'an* (water, cloud, woman) above and the trigram *Li* (fire, light, man) below. It is a moment and a situation within the natural order: the Chinese does not aspire to immobilize it as the Indian does, but rather to repeat it in the instant indicated by the conjunction of the signs. If the universe is cyclical and fluid, immortality must be a life that ebbs and flows. Discourse is the way of the west, recurrence the way of China.

---

* *L'Inde classique* (Paris, 1953).

The Indian denies the flow of things and the passage of time; all his practices and meditations tend to abolish discourse and recurrence: his aim is to stop the wheel of transmigrations. The Taoist flows along with the flux of the cosmos: to be immortal is to go around the circle once more, and at the same time remain motionless in its center. It is a paradox that is as valuable as the Christian paradox or the Buddhist. And it is incomparably wiser than the mad dash of our progress, that blind race from one unknown point to another that is equally unknown. The Taoist *hsü* is a state of calm, freedom, and nimbleness, untouched by the commotion of the world outside. It is not the emptiness of Buddhism, although it is also a state of emptiness. Rather it is the fluid, the nondetermined, that which changes without changing, that which never stops and yet is motionless. Union, yet distance too, like the fog in a Sung landscape or this line of Su Tung-p'o's: "Boatmen and water birds dream the same dream."* They dream the same dream but they are not the same. Three attitudes: the Indian denies the natural time of the Taoist and the historical time of Confucius, and sacrifices them on the altar of emptiness or nonduality; Confucius absorbs natural time and its essence, the *ch'i*, so as to transform it into historical time: family, society, the State; the Taoist denies historical time and culture so as to follow the rhythm of natural time. The differences between the Confucian and the Taoist attitudes are divergences; the differences between them and the Indian attitude, whether religious or profane, is a real opposition that makes the similarities insignificant. The surprising thing is not that there were borrowings from one civilization to the other but that one and the same practice, the retention of semen, was the object of such diametrically opposed elaborations and doctrines.

Tantrism denies historical time and natural time. The conjunction between the signs *body* and *non-body* are equivalent to a disembodiment, despite the exaggerated materialism of its practices. Taoism denies historical time: it aspires to reincorporate itself in cosmic time and be one with the cyclical rhythm of heaven and earth which alternately embrace each other and separate. It is another case of conjunction, although less

* *Su Tung-P'o: Selections from a Sung Dynasty Poet*, translated by Burton Watson (New York, 1965).

extreme than that of Tantrism. Less extreme and more fecund. Apart from the Taoist classics, which must be numbered among the most beautiful and profound books of any civilization, this doctrine has been like a secret river that has flowed for centuries. It inspired almost all the great poets and calligraphers and we owe to it the best Chinese painting, not to mention its influence on Ch'an Buddhism. Above all, it was for centuries the counter-weight to Confucian orthodoxy: thanks to Taoism, Chinese life was not only an immense, complicated ceremony, a tissue of genuflections and duties. Chuang-tzu was the salt of this civilization—the salt and the open door to the infinite. It is therefore unfair to compare Taoism with Tantrism, which is really only the last phase of Buddhism; the comparison really ought to be drawn between Taoism and the great Mahayana schools (*Mādhyamika* and *Vijñāna*). The Buddhist conjunction is active and deliberate, the Taoist passive and unconscious. Buddhism created a strict logic which is no less complex than modern symbolic logic; Taoism was asystematic and aesthetic. In the Buddhist conjunction the sign *non-body* takes on the logical form of the principle of identity: nirvana is samsara; in the Taoist conjunction skepticism and humor dissolve the *non-body*: it is more poetics than metaphysics, more a feeling about the world than an idea. The inability of Taoism to elaborate systems with the richness and complexity of Buddhism saved it: it did not become immobilized in a dogmatic system and was like "the water of the valley" that reflects all the changes of heaven in its quiet waters. This also prevented it from criticizing itself, denying itself, and transforming itself. It slowly declined until it merged and became one with the coarsest superstitions of the vulgar. Taoism ceased to flow and stagnated.

ORDER AND ACCIDENT

The Confucian attitude toward sex is moral but not metaphysical. It neither deifies nor condemns the phallus. The body is neither evil nor sinful: it is dangerous. We must control it and moderate it. Control and moderation do not mean repression or suppression, but harmony. The model of harmony is the immutable principles that govern the conjunctions and disjunctions of heaven and earth. Virtuous society is governed by the same laws: the emperor is the mirror of the cosmos. If the emperor is the son of heaven, the father of a family is the sun of his house. To regulate the emission of semen and absorb the feminine vital principle is to conform to the universal harmony and contribute to the general health of society. Conjugal copulation is a part of good government, like etiquette, the worship of family ancestors, the imitation of the classics, and the observance of the rites. The primordial essence of man is good because it is no different from the intrinsic goodness of nature. This innate goodness is also called order, whether it be cosmic or social. The sexual act fulfills the goal of the institution of the family—to have sons and educate them—which in turn merely reflects and fulfills the order of nature among men. Procreation and education are phases of the same process. During copulation, on favorable days with the proper woman, crude nature, natural time, is absorbed and transmuted into social, historical nature: sons. Education is the process of socialization and integration of biological offspring into the family and the family into the empire. In both cases, it is not a question of changing nature but of returning to the natural order. This is what constitutes what I have called, somewhat inaccurately, transmutation. The passionate and chaotic time of sex is converted into historical, social time. History and society are merely nature that has been beautified and returned to its pristine, primordial state.

I have used the word *history* a number of times in the preceding paragraph. I confess that this is an intrusion of a concept that is foreign to Confucius's system. Let me clarify matters, then, by saying that history must be understood to be culture on one hand, and archetypal antiquity on the other hand. The happy state of antiquity can return if men become as cultivated as their forebears. The word *tê* is generally translated as *virtue*, but according to Arthur Waley, the ancient Chinese also called the act of planting seeds *tê*.[*] Therefore *tê* is power: the inherent possibility of growth. Virtue is innate in man because it is a seed, and as such it requires cultivation. The model of cultivation, that is to say of culture, is the action of nature, the great producer of seeds, the mother of virtues. The transformation of semen into virtuous social life—either because its emission during conjugal copulation engenders sons or because its

* *The Way and Its Power* (London, 1934).

retention prolongs life—is cultivation rather than transformation. In this sense the sexual act is similar to the other acts of civilized man: in all of them natural time is cultivated and made to coincide with its hidden principle. This principle is *T'ien tao*: the cosmic order.

The central idea behind Confucian thought seems to deny the relationship between the signs *body* and *non-body*. What is more, one has the impression that these signs are not even present in this vision of the world. In fact, what I have called *non-body* is *tê*, virtue, and for Confucius this virtue is nothing other than nature. As for the body, it also is nature and the producer of *tê*. Everything is reduced to a difference of modes of existence and not of essence: the individual biological body, the family social body, the imperial political body, the body of the cosmos. But the same thing might be said, although in the opposite sense, of Buddhism and Christianity: everything is emptiness and everything is spirit. If we consider the real meaning of *tê*, we notice immediately that it is not nature but culture. The opposite term, corresponding to samsara and to sin, is barbarism, the life of the savage. *Non-body* is culture, the virtuous social life. The relation between the signs is the same as in the other civilizations, although its particular meaning is different. What happens (and this explains the confusion) is that the Confucian *non-body*—and even more markedly that of Taoism—is much closer to the body and to nature than Buddhist emptiness and Christian divinity. For this reason, even if sublimation occurred as in the other civilizations, the process that resulted in imbalance between the signs was different.

In a famous study, Max Weber described the analogies between Protestantism and the Confucian mandarin class. He also pointed out their essential difference: the former transforms the world; the latter enjoys and uses its fruits. But in my opinion the major similarity consists in the transmutation of natural time—excrement in the one case and semen in the other—into historical and social time. This similarity, as will be seen later, conceals a difference. Confucius's conception of society is inspired by the natural production of things through the action of an immutable order. This is the meaning of *tê* and of culture. The virtuous society, culture, is society that produces itself and repeats itself like nature. Nature is reintegrated, semen is reabsorbed, and life is multiplied and regulates itself.

Order, control, hierarchy: a harmony that excludes neither inequalities nor punishments. There is no disjunction, as in Protestantism, and the conjunction is never extreme, as in Tantrism. But Confucianism was not invulnerable (no idea and no institution is) to the double onslaught of sex and death. In Confucianism, the sublimation is expressed as a neutralization of the signs through a progressive paralysis, an immobility that gives the illusion of movement so as to become more perfect: nature becomes culture and culture in turn puts on the mask of a false nature which then is converted into culture and so on. Each time around, nature is less natural and culture more rigid and formal. China preserves itself through recurrence, but it does not deny itself and therefore it does not go beyond itself. The final petrification was inevitable. Petrification and beginning all over again yet another time: yesterday the First Emperor of the Ch'in and today his reincarnation, Chairman Mao. A total, absolute beginning over again, since it not only embraces the present and the future but also the past—through the burning and destruction of the classics yesterday and through the distortion of Chinese civilization and the imposition of the "Maoist interpretation" of history today. These are maniacal confiscations of the past, ever destined to be confiscated in turn by that power which is both the clearest expression of the future and the abolition of all time: forgetfulness. The process of sublimation in Confucianism was culture: an imitation of nature and of the classics; in Protestantism it was moral repression. The two attitudes are expressed plastically, so to speak, in their opposite reactions to semen and excrement.

In India and China, conjunction was the mode of relationship between the signs *body* and *non-body*, and in the West, disjunction. In its final phase Christianity exaggerates the separation: the body and nature are condemned in the Protestant ethic. The other pole of the relation (spirit, soul) is something very far removed from the Tao of Lao-tzu, the vacuity of Nagarjuna, or the natural order of Confucius: the reign of ideas and incorruptible essences. There is a divorce between heaven and earth: virtue lies in the sacrifice of nature so as to merit heaven. In its final phase, Christianity engenders modern areligious society and shifts from a vertical relationship between the terms to a horizontal one: heaven becomes history, the future, progress; and nature and the body, without ceasing to be enemies, cease to be objects of condemnation and become subjects of conversion. History is not circular and recurrent, as in China; nor is it an interval between the Fall and the End, as in medieval society, nor is it a struggle between equals as in Greek democracy: it is action opening out into the future, a colonization of what is to come.

Ancient Christianity, a twin of Islam in this regard, conceived of historical action as a crusade, a holy war, and the conversion of infidels. Modern Westerners transfer the conversion to nature: they operate on it, against it, with the same zeal and with better results than the crusaders against the Muslims. The transformation of excrement into abstract gold was only a part of the immense task of taming the natural world, of finally dominating contaminated and contaminating matter, of consummating the rout of this potent and rebellious element. The conquest, domination, and conversion of nature has theological roots, although those who today are undertaking it are areligious men of science and even atheists. Contemporary society has ceased to be Christian, but its passions are those of Christianity. Despite the fact that our science and our technology are not religious, they have a Christian stamp: they are inspired by the pious frenzy of the crusaders and the conquistadors, directed today not toward the conquest of souls but of the cosmos. China conceived of culture as the cultivation of nature; the modern West conceived of it as dominion over it; the one was cyclical and recurrent, the other dialectical: it denies itself each time it affirms itself and each one of its negations is a leap into the unknown.

The West represents extreme disjunction and no less extreme violence. There are bound to be some who will question the first-mentioned trait and observe that our era is *materialist*. Others will say that the violence of the West is no greater than that of the Assyrians, the Aztecs, and the Tartars, the only difference being that it is a creative violence: it has covered the earth with splendid constructions and has populated space with machines. I shall answer briefly. It is true that the thought of the West, and above all its science, has been less and less spiritualist since the sixteenth century. The traditional meaning of the sign *non-body* has slowly changed: it had a religious sense (divinity) at first, then a philosophical one (idealism), later a critical sense (reason), and, finally, a materialist one. This latter deserves an explanation. It would be difficult to call atomic particles or biological cells *ideas* or *spirit*. But they are not objects, things, in the sense of the ancient materialism: they are nodes of relations. We are confronted by materialism, to go on using this imprecise term, which opposes the concrete reality of the sign *body* with the same rigidity as it once did spirit. In order to know nature—in reality in order to dominate it—we have changed it; it has ceased to be a corporeal presence and become a relation. Nature has become intelligible up to a certain point, but it has also become intangible. It is no longer a body: it is an equation, a relation that is expressed in symbols and is therefore identical to thought or reducible to its laws. The scientific solipsism is a variant of the linguistic solipsism. Wittgenstein said of this latter that it was legitimate and coherent: "The world is my world: this is shown by the fact that the limits of language stand for the limits of my world . . . I am my world." Except that this "I am" is not the body but my language— a language that is less and less mine: the language of science.

The abstract nature of our materialism also shows up in our human sciences. The "social things" of Emile Durkheim and Marcel Mauss are not really objects but institutions and symbols worked out by an entelechy that is called society. It is hardly worth the trouble to cite another example: that of historical or dialectical materialism. The first expression indicates that we are in the presence of a historical matter, made by men. It is not the body: it is history. As for the second: no one has yet been able to explain the relation between matter and dialectic. No: our matter is not corporeal, nor is our materialism carnal. The old spirit has changed its name and address. It has simply lost some attributes and gained others. Psychoanalysis itself is part of the sublimation, and, therefore, of the neurosis, of Western civilization. In fact, the boundaries between neurosis and sublimation are very tenuous: the first traps us in an imaginary blind alley and the second opens up an exit for us that is equally imaginary. The therapy of psychoanalysis is equivalent, in the individual, to collective sublimations. Norman O. Brown cites a sentence of Freud's that saves me from having to continue this demonstration: "Neuroses are asocial structures. They attempt to realize by private means what is realized in society by collective means." These collective means are the sublimations we call art, religion, philosophy, science, and psychoanalysis. But these sublimations, included under the sign *non-body*, also lead societies into blind alleys when the relationship with the sign *body* is broken or debased. This is what happens in the West, not in spite of our materialism but because of it. Ours is an abstract materialism, a sort of Platonism in reverse, as disincarnated as the emptiness of Buddha. It no longer even provokes a response from the body: it has slipped into it and sucks its blood like a vampire. All we need do is leaf through a fashion magazine to see the sorry state to which the new materialism has reduced the human form: the bodies of these girls are the very image of asceticism, privation, and fasting.

The disjunction of the West, unlike conjunction in the East, prevents the dialogue between *non-body* and *body*. For the Christian West, foreign societies were always the incarnation of evil. Whether savage or civilized, they were manifestations of the inferior world, the body. And the West treated them with the same rigor with which ascetics punished their senses. Shakespeare says it straight out in *The Tempest*. The difference in attitudes between the colonization of America by the Hispano-Portuguese Catholics and that of Anglo-Saxon Protestants is only an expression of their basic attitudes toward the body. The possibility of mediation between the *body* and the *non-body* still existed for the Catholicism of the Counter Reformation; the consequence was conversion and interbreeding. For Protestantism the gap was unbridgeable, and the result was the extermination of American Indians or their incarceration on "reservations."

We transfer our aggressive tendencies: it is others who threaten us, pursue us, seek to destroy us. The others are also, and primarily, the Other: gods, natural forces, the whole universe. In every civilization, including the first period of our own (medieval Catholicism), earthquakes, epidemics, floods, droughts, and other calamities were seen as a supernatural aggression. At times they were taken to be the manifestations of the wrath, the caprice, and even the mad joy of the divinities, and at other times as punishments for the sins, the excesses, or the failings of men. One recourse was to placate or buy the benevolence of the deity with sacrifices, good works, rites of expiation, and other practices; another was the transfiguration of the penalty through ethical or philosophical sublimation, as in Sophocles's *Oedipus* or in the vision of Arjuna on the battlefield in which he comes to see Vishnu as the indifferent giver of life and death. Man can reconcile himself with his misfortune in both ways, through rites or through philosophical resignation. This reconciliation, whether illusory or not, had a specific virtue: it inserted misfortune in the cosmic and human order, made the exception intelligible, and gave the accidental a meaning. Modern science has eliminated epidemics and has given us plausible explanations of other natural catastrophes: nature has ceased to be the depository of our guilt feelings; at the same time, technology has extended and widened the notion of accident, and what is more, it has given it an absolutely different character. I doubt that the number of victims of falls from a horse and snake bite was greater, even proportionally, than the number of deaths caused by automobiles that overturn, trains that are derailed, or planes that crash. Accidents are part of our daily life and their shadow peoples our dreams as the evil eye keeps shepherds awake at night in the little hamlets of Afghanistan.

Apart from the individual, everyday accident, there is the universal Accident: the bomb. The threat of planetary extinction has no date attached to it: it may be today or tomorrow or never. It is extreme inde-termination, even more difficult to predict than the wrath of Jehovah or the fury of Siva. The Accident is the imminently probable. Immi-nent because it can happen today; probable not only because gods, spirit, cosmic harmony, and the Buddhist law of plural causality have disap-peared from our universe but also because, simultaneously, the confident determinism of the science of the nineteenth century has collapsed. The principle of indetermination in contemporary physics and Gödel's proof in logic are the equivalent of the Accident in the historical world. I do not mean to say that they are the same: I merely say that in the three cases axiomatic, deterministic systems have lost their consistency and revealed an inherent defect. But it is not really a defect: it is a property of the system, something that belongs to it as a system. The Accident is not an exception or a sickness of our political regimes; nor is it a correctable defect of our civilization: it is the natural consequence of our science, our politics, and our morality. The Accident is part of our idea of progress as

Zeus's concupiscence and Indra's drunkenness and gluttony were respectively part of the Greek world and of Vedic culture. The difference lies in the fact that Indra could be distracted with a sacrifice of *soma*, but the Accident is incorruptible and unpredictable.

Converting the Accident into one of the cogs of the historic order is no less prodigious a feat than demonstrating that neither the human brain nor computers can prove that the axioms of geometry and arithmetic—the bases of mathematics and the model of logic—are absolutely consistent. But the consequences are different: Gödel's proof leaves us perplexed; the Accident terrifies us. The sign *non-body* has always been repressive, threatening men with eternal hell, the circle of transmigrations, and other punishments. It now promises us total and accidental extinction without distinguishing between the righteous man and the sinner. The Accident has become a paradox of necessity: it possesses the fatality of necessity and at the same time the indetermination of freedom. The *non-body*, transformed into materialist science, is a synonym for terror: the Accident is one of the attributes of the reason that we adore, the terrible attribute, like the halter of Siva or the lightning bolt of Jupiter. Christian morality has given its powers of repression over to it, but at the same time this superhuman power has lost any pretention of morality. It is the return of the anguish of the Aztecs, without any celestial signs or presages. Catastrophe has become banal and laughable because in the final analysis the Accident is only an accident.

THE BRIDE STRIPPED BARE BY HER BACHELORS

The internal responses to Western repression have been as violent as the external reactions against its colonial oppression. They assumed bizarre and fantastic forms from the very beginning. Van Gulik emphasizes that an examination of the *Bed Treatises* turns up a very small number of sexual perversions and deviations. Anyone who has read Chinese erotic novels will agree with the Dutch Sinologist. The same is true of the literature and the art of India—be it sculpture, the novel, poetry, or books on erotology. The exception is the Tantric texts, but even in them the bloody scatological rites have as their precise object the reabsorption of the destructive instinct. The relation of conjunction prevented the excessive growth of sadism and masochism in ancient Asia. No other civilization, with the possible exception of the Aztecs, offers an art that rivals that of the West in sexual ferocity. And we differ in one way from the Aztecs: their art was a religious sublimation; ours is profane. When I speak of cruelty, I am not referring to the bloody representations of the religious art of the end of the Middle Ages or of those of the Counter Reformation in Spain: I am referring to modern art, from the eighteenth century to the present. Sade is unique, and he is so because the West has been unique in this respect. The relation between *non-body* and *body* assumes the form of torture and orgasm in European erotic books: death as a spur to pleasure and mistress of life. From Sade to the *Story of O*, our eroticism is a funeral hymn or a sinister pantomime. In Sade, pleasure leads to insensibility: the sexual explosion is followed by the immobility of cooled lava. The body becomes a knife or a stone; matter, the natural world that breathes and palpitates, is transformed into an abstraction: a sharp-edged syllogism that suppresses life and, finally, slits its own throat. It is a strange condemnation: it kills itself and thus comes back to life, only to kill itself again.

In areas less overtly aggressive than the modern erotic novel, violence explodes with the same energy, although with less fantastic cruelty. Consider the fight for free love, sexual education, the abolition of laws that punish erotic deviations, and other campaigns of this sort. What scandalizes me is not the legitimacy of these aspirations but the combative and bellicose stance their proponents adopt. The rights of love, the fight for sexual equality between men and women, the freedom of instincts: this vocabulary is that of politics and war. The analogy between eroticism and combat appears in all civilizations, but in none of them except our own does it take on the form of revolutionary protest. The erotic contest is a game, a spectacle for the Indian or the Chinese; for the Westerner, the war metaphor immediately takes on a military and political meaning, and is followed by a series of proclamations, regulations, norms, and duties. The fanaticism of our rebels is the counterpart of Puritan severity; there is a morality of dissolution as there is a morality of repression, and both of them make equally exorbitant demands on their proponents.

Our attitude toward sexual deviation is another example. Chinese literature does not deal with the theme of masculine homosexuality at any great length, and when it does, it does so only in passing; as for feminine homosexuality, its attitude is benevolent. It is a matter of vital economy rather than a moral problem: copulation between men is not heinous; it is harmful because if it is practiced to excess the opportunity of appropriating the precious feminine *ch'i* is lost. References to the subject in the literature and the art of India are even scantier, although erotic prints with lesbian themes are common. It is clear that both civilizations were not unaware of these deviations. If they did not exalt them as the Greeks, the Persians, and the Arabs did, neither did they persecute them with the frenzy of the West. The "heinous sin" is another feature peculiar to Christianity. In Delhi and other cities and towns of Uttar Pradesh and Rajasthan, there are musicians and dancers, members of a sect, who wander about the streets and public squares dressed as women. They are itinerant artists who practice male prostitution as a side line. They are present—in fact, custom makes their presence almost obligatory—when births or marriages are celebrated, both among Hindus and, Muslims. In the Victorian India of our day—which has been deformed by the double heritage of English and Muslim puritanism—nobody talks about them but neither does anybody dispense with their songs and dances when a child is born or somebody in the family gets married. In the West, homosexuals tend to be vindictive, and their rites are something like meetings of conspirators and plotters. In the East, another habit that is considered more a hygienic mental and physical practice than an abomination is masturbation. When we deal with sexual practices—whether solitary, heterosexual, or homosexual—our tendency is to reform rather than to conform. Discord is the complement of the Accident.

The history of the body in the final phase of Western culture is that of its rebellions. In no other era and in no other civilization has the erotic impulse manifested itself as a purely or predominantly sexual subversion. Eroticism is something more than a mere sexual urge; it is an expression of the sign *body*. But the sign *body* is not independent; it is a *relationship* and it always has to do with the sign *non-body*, whether it is a movement toward it or away from it. This rebellion in the West seems to indicate that the disjunction between the signs has become so extreme that the relation tends to disappear almost entirely. The situation is reminiscent, in a reverse sense, of the Cathar heresy, with its emphasis on chastity and its denial of procreation. Yesterday there was an attempt to dissolve the sign *body*, and today an attempt to dissolve the *non-body*. But does the relation really disappear? I have my doubts in both cases. As for the Cathars: even if we do not consider Provençal poetry to be a ciphered expression of Catharism, as Denis de Rougemont maintains, the influence of this movement on the conception of "courtly love" is obvious. In this poetry, neither of the two signs is negated: the ambiguous exaltation of adultery and the ideal lady, the rite of contemplation of the beloved who allows herself to be seen naked provided she is not touched, and the sort of idealization of *coitus reservatus* (known as *asang*) simultaneously affirm the *body* and the *non-body*.* It could not be otherwise: the one cannot live without the other. Their unions and separations are the substance of eroticism—that which distinguishes them from mere sexuality. There is no eroticism without reference to the *non-body*, as there is no religion without reference to the *body*. Pure sexuality does not exist among human beings or, probably, among the higher animals. It is a human myth—and a reality among the lower animal species. The function of eroticism in all societies is twofold: it is a sublimation and an imaginary transmutation of sexuality and thus serves the *non-body*, and it is a ritualization and an actualization of images and thus serves the *body*. The bodily rite comes under the sign of the *non-body*, as can be seen in Tantrism; the erotic image, as we all know from our own experience, comes under the sign of the *body*. In the image, the *body* loses its corporeal reality; in the rite, the *non-body* incarnates. The relation between the two signs continues to exist, whether it is a question of traditional images and collective rites or of individual fantasies and private games. Consequently, if the new sexual morality in fact lacks any reference to the *non-body*, it must be inter-

* *Asang* was one of the degrees of "courtly love" in which the lovers went to bed together naked, but did not consummate the sexual act. (Cf. *L'Erotique des troubadours*, by René Nelli [Toulouse, 1963].) Nelli sees this as a transposition and a purification of the chivalrous "proof of love."

preted as a nostalgia for animal life, a renunciation of human culture and therefore of eroticism. This is not the case, however. It is a morality: a new attempt of the *non-body* to slip into the body, detach its image, and convert it into an abstract reality. Catharism was the spirit's aversion toward the body; the new sexual morality is a perversion of the body by the spirit.

It is no less disturbing that the rebellion of the senses has taken the form of a social and political demand. Placing sex on the list of the rights of man is as paradoxical as regulating conjugal copulation through the standards of good government. There is a difference: Confucian good government tended to preserve society and referred to a reality that was at once natural and ideal: heaven and its cycle (*T'ien tao*); sexuality as a right tends to change society and refers to a reality that is merely abstract and ideal. We do not seek sexual freedom in the name of the body, which is not a subject with rights; we change it into a political entity. The erotic movements of other civilizations, such as late Taoism and Tantrism, were religious; in other cases—"courtly love" and Romantic passion are the examples closest to hand—they were born and survived on the frontiers of aesthetics, religion, and philosophy. In the West, eroticism has been intellectual and revolutionary since the eighteenth century. The libertine philosophers were primarily atheists and materialists, and only secondarily sensualists and hedonists. Their erotic philosophy was the consequence of their materialism and their atheism—a part of their polemic against the repressive powers of the monarchy and the Church. The combat between the signs *body* and *non-body* turned into a debate, and the struggle shifted from the sphere of images, symbols, and rites to that of ideas and theories. The passage from religion to philosophy and from aesthetics to politics was the beginning of the disincarnation of the body. *The 120 Days of Sodom* is a treatise on revolutionary philosophy, not a manual of sexual good manners such as the *Kama Sutra* or a guide to illumination such as the *Hevajra Tantra*. The ancients knew of the practices that Sade describes, so what was really new was not recording their existence but transforming them into opinions: they ceased to be abominations or sacred rites, depending on the civilization, and became ideas.

The new phenomenon is not eroticism but the supremacy of politics. Religious and philosophical ideas were preached in the past but in a strict sense they were not political ideas. Public action was a matter of morals or of convenience: an art, a technique, or a sacred duty, as in the Roman Republic. All this had little or nothing to do with the conception of politics as theory. Our politics by contrast is fundamentally a theory, a vision of the world. Sade's eroticism is a revolutionary philosophy, a kind of politics: he brandishes aberrant practices the way an orator draws up a long list of the people's grievances against the government. It is true that politics was a central activity among the Greeks, the attribute that distinguished the citizen from the slave and the barbarian. But it was not a method for changing the world. Its aim was individual and collective: in the first place, to distinguish oneself in the eyes of others either by the persuasion of one's virtuous example or the cleverness of one's rhetoric and thus gain fame, achieve renown, and, in short, realize the ideal of the citizen; in the second place, to contribute to the health of the *polis*, whatever meaning is given to *health* and *polis*: the independence of the city or its power, the freedom of its citizens or their happiness. The political doctrines of Plato, Aristotle, and the Stoics are not a theory of the world but the projection of their respective theories into the sphere of society and the State. For the Encyclopedists and later for Marx, theory is not only inseparable from practice, but theory, as theory, is already practice, action on the world. Theory, *simply because it is theory*, is political. In a society, such as the Chinese, preoccupied above all else with the preservation of the social order and the continuity of culture—preoccupations which are not exclusively political though they may appear to be so—censorship itself was an imperial function: the throne named ministers and censors as a gardener uses both fertilizer and clippers. Politics was part of cosmology (the law of heaven) and of the art of cultivation. In our society science and culture are expressions of classes or of civilizations: they are history, and, in the last analysis, politics. When I say that politics for us is a vision of the world, I am being a bit inaccurate: our idea of the world is not a vision but a judgment and thus it is also an action, a practice. The image of the world, or rather, *the idea of the world as an image*, has given way to another idea, another image: that of revolutionary theory. Our idea of the world is *to change the world*. Politics is a synonym of revolution.

When they attempted to translate the word *revolution*, the Chinese could find no better expression than *ko-ming*.* *Ko-ming* means "change of mandate," and by extension, change of dynasty. Whose mandate? Not that of the people but that of Heaven. The Mandate of Heaven (*T'ien ming*) means that the principle that governs nature (*T'ien tao*) has descended upon a prince. In *The Book of History*, Duke Chou says: "Heaven caused the ruin of the Yin dynasty. They lost the Mandate of Heaven and we, the Chous, received it. But I do not dare to assert that our descendants will keep it." The method for conserving the mandate is Confucian virtue. Nothing is further from our democratic ideas or from the conception of the right to the throne by blood ancestry. Naturally, this doctrine met with opposition, not from philosophers who were expressing the will of the people (there were none), but from apologists for imperial authority. Ancient China evolved a doctrine which served as the other pole of the asocial and individualist attitude of Taoism. This doctrine, a legalism or realism (*Fa-chia*), can be briefly summarized as follows: since the relation between names and the realities that they designate (*hsing-ming*: forms and names) changes and depends on circumstances, the theory of the immutable laws of heaven (*T'ien tao*) does not apply in any way to the art of governing men; it is incumbent upon the prince to give each name a single meaning and thus govern: once what is good and what is evil, what is useful and what is harmful to the State is defined, rewards and punishments can be doled out justly. Han Fei-tzu exhorts his lord: "Discard the benevolence of Yen [a legendary monarch] and forget the wisdom of Tzu Kung [a disciple of Confucius]. Arm the states of Hsü and Lu so that they may face an army of ten thousand war chariots and then the people of Ch'i and Ching will not be able to treat us as they please, as is the case now."† In this way the authority of tradition—the immutable meaning

* See *Confucian China and Its Modern Fate: The Problem of Monarchical Decay*, Vol. II, by Joseph R. Levenson (London, 1964).
† *Han Fei-tzu: Basic Writings*, translated by Burton Watson (New York, 1964). See also: *Three Ways of Thought in Ancient China*, by Arthur Waley (London, 1939).

of names—was rejected, and along with it the theory of the Mandate of Heaven: authority has no other origin than the prince, the arbiter of names and of rewards and punishments. The doctrine of the Mandate of Heaven affirms, on the contrary, that names and meanings are immutable: what changes are the princes. If the theory justifies the change of regime and also obliges the virtuous man to assassinate the prince who violates his Mandate, it prevents the changing of the system at the same time. Levenson comments: "*T'ien ming* doctrine really was an expression of conflict with the emperor, though a bureaucratic, not a democratic expression . . . a defense of gentry-literati in their conflict-collaboration with the emperor in manipulating the state." This is exactly the opposite of Saint-Just's doctrine: when Louis XVI was executed, it was primarily to deal a death blow to the monarchic principle.

In the West, revolution means not only a change of system but also something else, which is unprecedented: the changing of human nature. In medieval Christian society as in others, the transmutation of man was a religious process; not even philosophers, except for those dealing with religious philosophies such as Platonism, dared intervene in this sphere. But Christianity in its decline transferred the traditional mission of all religions to revolutionary parties: today it is they, not grace or the sacraments, who are the agents of the transmutation. This shift coincides with another in the spheres of art and poetry. In the past the primary and ultimate aim of art was the celebration or the condemnation of human life; beginning with the German Romantics and becoming even more energetic after Rimbaud, poetry set itself the task of *changing life*. Social revolution and revolutionary art became religious undertakings, or at least what antiquity always considered the exclusive province of religion. In this dividing up of the spoils of religion, revolution got as its share ethics, education, law, and public institutions: the *non-body*. Art's share was symbols, ceremonies, images—everything which I have called the incarnation of images: the sublimated, though perceptible, expression of the sign *body*.

The rebellion of the senses, as part of the general change, has sometimes taken the form of social demands and sometimes the form of poetic rebellion—or better stated, the fusion of poetry with philosophical-moral revolt and with eroticism, according to the Romantic and

Surrealist conception. This is one of the facets—or, more exactly, one of the roots—of the ambivalence of modern art, perpetually torn as it is between the expression of life, either to celebrate or condemn it, and the reform of life. Artists and poets of the modern era have worked together with revolutionaries at the task of destroying the old images of religion and monarchy, but they could not go along with them in their substitution of pure ideological abstractions for these symbols. The crisis begins with the German Romantics, torn between their initial sympathy for the French Revolution and their corporeal and analogical idealism. We owe to Novalis some of the most luminous maxims on eroticism and the relations between man's body and the body of the cosmos; but he is also the author of one of the most reactionary essays of the period: *Europe and Christianity*. The conflict, far from dying out, has become even more acute in the last fifty years. It is not necessary to call to mind the drama of Surrealism, the suicide of Mayakowski, or the moral martyrdom of César Vallejo. When the Peruvian poet, at the height of his Communist "engagement," castigates the "Bolshevik bishops," he does not reproach them so much for their theology of high bureaucrats as for not having been able to transform the idea of proletarian fraternity into a genuine communion: a rite that has no god but does have sacraments. This was a nostalgia for the symbol incarnated in the Eucharist.

The two revolutions of the West, the French Revolution and the Russian, enthroned the sign *non-body*, and in both of them this sign was transformed into a revolutionary agent and a teacher of society. The rebellion of the senses was sublimated and made into a moral force. In its most radical forms, it was transformed into a fight for erotic rights, either of women or of sexual minorities. In its moderate expressions it was channeled into action in favor of sexual education and hygiene, the securing of more rational legislation concerning monogamous marriage, the adoption of divorce laws, the suppression of barbarous punishments for sexual deviations, and other similar reforms. None of this was or is what our exasperated senses are asking for: they are asking for images, symbols, rites—forms of our desires, of our obsessions that are imaginary yet also real, ceremonies in which these images may be incarnated without ceasing to be images. The new materialism claims, as emphatically as the religions of antiquity, to possess the key to the universe. This may be true, but it is also certain that it has not been able to give us an image of this world or of other worlds. Its universe has no body and its material is as abstract and incorporeal as an idea. Its science tells us more about how the genital organs function than all the *Kama Sutras* and *Bed Treatises* ever have. But it has not given us an eroticism: in its manuals the words *pleasure* and *imagination* have been replaced by *orgasm* and *health*. Its recipes are techniques for preserving sexual power, regulating procreation, cleaning all the cobwebs of fear out of our psyche, and exorcising the phantoms of the father and the mother. They teach us how to be normal, not how to fall in love or be passionate. There is nothing further removed from an art of loving. By explaining how the body is made and how it functions, they have abolished its image. Then there is the popularity of sports, which has created a confusion between vigor and beauty, physical skill and erotic wisdom. The reaction of young people in our day, with their predilection for loud clothes, fantastic adornments, decadent or wild hairdos and make-up, and even personal uncleanliness, is not surprising. It is better to smell bad than to use toilet water advertised over television . . . The freedom of industrial society is gray; the freedom that makes passion a hygiene is false. The positions of bodies in the *Kama Sutra* are always shown against an imaginary landscape, the conventional décor of kāvya poetry; the backgrounds in contemporary erotology are either awkwardly portrayed or macabre.

Not everything is hygiene and "comfort" in industrial society. Apart from the lack of fantasy and voluptuousness, there is also the debasement of the body. Science has reduced it to a series of molecular and chemical combinations, capitalism to a utilitarian object—like any other that its industries produce. Bourgeois society has divided eroticism into three areas: a dangerous one, governed by the penal code; another for the department of health and social welfare; and the third for the entertainment industry. Orgasm is the universal goal—one more product of the system, and more hastily consumed and ephemeral than the others. The Protestant ethic sublimated excrement; capitalism has introduced the principle of rational production into the realm of eroticism. In the Communist countries the old Christian morality has been supplanted by a sort of neo-Confucianism that is less cultured and more obtuse than that of the Ch'ings. When I speak of Soviet puritanism, I am referring to the relatively tolerant period inaugurated by Khrushchev. In Stalin's time, the regime experienced a terror no less irrational than that of the Accident: Political Deviation. But the terror of the Accident has been more on the order of a psychological phenomenon, whereas that of Deviation immediately entered the realm of facts. Man's paradises are covered with gibbets. The first rule of a really free education would be to instill a repugnance for all doctrines of "obligatory happiness" in children. In the first half of the twentieth century, the sign *non-body*, not content with adopting the neutral procedures of science and applying the efficient methods of mass production to sexuality, has again donned its old costume of the hangman and intervened in politics, at times as the administrator of the Third Reich and at others as Commissar of the people.

Persecuted by the idolaters of abundance and by revolutionaries, the sign *body* took refuge in art. The remains of the body, that is: a form disfigured by repression and anger, and tortured by the feeling of guilt and irony. In the art of the past the deformations of the human figure were ritual; in our day they are aesthetic or psychological: the aggressive rationalism of Cubism, and the no less aggressive emotionality of Expressionism. It is subjectivity—rational, sentimental, or simply ironic, but always guilt-ridden—taking its revenge. I am not forgetting that there has been a secret tradition of exaltation of the body, from Rousseau and Blake to Matisse, Joyce, and certain poets; nor am I forgetting that every time that it comes to the surface in history, it is repressed or absorbed by the ruling ethicaesthetic. The truth is that contemporary art has not given us an image of the body: this is a mission that we have turned over to couturiers and public-relations men. This is not a defect of today's art but of our society. Art reveals, celebrates, or consecrates the image of the body that each civilization invents. No, the image of the body is not invented: it springs forth, it ripens like a fruit, it is born like a sun from the body of the world. The image of the body is the double of that of the cosmos, the human response to the universal nonhuman archetype. Each civilization has seen the body in a different way because each one has had a different idea of the world. The body and the world embrace each other or tear each other apart; they reflect each other or deny each other: the virgins of Chartres smile like Cretan maidens, but their smiles are different—they smile at another world, at the other world. The universe unfolds in the body, which is its mirror and its creature. Our era is critical; it has destroyed the old image of the world and as yet has not created another. That is why we do not have a body. We have an art of disincarnation, as in Mallarmé, or an art that howls with laughter and sends a shiver up our spines, as in the painting of Marcel Duchamp. The ultimate image of the Christian Virgin, the ideal lady of Provençal culture and the Great Goddess of Mediterranean culture is *The Bride Stripped Bare by Her Bachelors, Even*. This painting is divided into two parts: at the top is the goddess, turned into a motor; at the bottom are her worshipers, her victims, and her lovers—not Acteon, Adonis, and Mars, but nine puppets wearing the uniforms of policemen, hotel porters, and priests. It is semen, the vital essence of the Taoists, turned into a sort of erotic gasoline which bursts into flame *before* the body of the Bride is touched. From ritual to an electric toy: an infernal piece of buffoonery.

The idea of revolution was the great invention of the West in its second phase. Societies of the past did not have real revolutions but *koming*, changes of mandate and dynasty. Apart from these changes, they experienced profound transformations: births, deaths, and resurrections of religions. In this respect, too, our era is unique: no other society has ever made revolution its central idea. If this second phase of Western civilization comes to an end, as many people believe and as the reality that we all live tells us, the clearest sign that the end is approaching will be what Ortega y Gasset prophetically called "the twilight of revolutions." It is true that we have never had so many; it is also true that none of them fits the Western conception of what a revolution is. Like the first Christians waiting for the Apocalypse, modern society has been waiting for the arrival of the revolution since 1840. And revolution is coming: not the one that we have been waiting for, but another one, each time another one. Faced with this unexpected reality which cheats us, theologians speculate and try to prove, like Confucian mandarins, that the Mandate of Heaven (the idea of revolution) is the same; what is happening is that the prince (concrete revolution) is unworthy of the mandate. But there comes a time

The idea of process implies that things happen one after the other, either in the form of sudden leaps and bounds (revolution) or in the form of gradual changes (evolution). Progress is a synonym of process because it is thought that every change results sooner or later in an advance. Both modes of succession, the revolutionary and the evolutionary, correspond to a vision of history as a march toward something—we are not exactly certain where this something is, except that this *where* is better than the situation today, and that it lies in the future. History is envisioned as a continuous, never-ending colonization of the future. There is something infernal about this optimistic vision of history; the philosophy of progress is really a theory of the condemnation of man, who is doomed perpetually to move forward, knowing that he will never arrive at his final destination. This way of thinking is rooted in the Judeo-Christian tradition, and its mythical counterpart is the expulsion from Eden. In the garden of paradise, a present without a single flaw shone brightly; in the deserts of history, the only sun that guides us is the fleeting future. The subject of this continual pilgrimage is not a nation, a class, or a civilization, but an abstract entity: humanity. As the subject of history, "humanity" lacks substance; it is never present in person: it acts by means of its representatives, this people or that, this class or that. Persepolis, Rome, or New York, the monarchy or the proletariat, in turn *represent* humanity at one moment or another of history as a member of the legislature represents his electors, and as an actor represents the character he is playing.

History is a theater in which a single person, humanity, becomes many: servants, masters, bourgeois, mandarins, clergymen, peasants, workers. The incoherent shouting of all these voices turns into a rational dialogue, and this dialogue into a philosophical monologue. History is a discourse. But the rebellions of the twentieth century have violated both the rules of dramatic action and those of representation. We have unforeseen irruptions that disturb the linear nature of history: what should have happened has not occurred and what should have happened later happens now. If Chinese peasants or Latin-American revolutionaries are today the representatives of the subject "humanity," who or what do American and European workers, not to mention the Russian proletariat, represent? Both the events and the actors betray the text of the play. They write another text, or rather invent one. History becomes improvisation. This is the end of discourse and rational legibility.

What might be called *the inversion of historic causality* has its counterpart in the breaks in the linear order. I shall cite an example. It used to be supposed that revolution would be the consequence of the contradiction between the forces of production created by capitalism and the system of capitalist ownership. The fundamental opposition was: industrial production/private capitalist ownership. This real, material opposition could be expressed in terms of a logical dichotomy between reason (industrial production) and unreason (private capitalist ownership). Socialism would be the result of economic development; at the same time it would be the triumph of reason over the irrationality of the capitalist system. Necessity (history) possessed the rigor of logic; it was reason incarnate. Both history and reason were identified with morality: socialism was justice. And, finally: history, reason, and morality became one with progress. But modern revolts, including the Russian one, have not been the consequence of economic development, but of the absence of development. None of these revolts broke out because there was an irreconcilable contradiction between the system of industrial production and the system of capitalist ownership. On the contrary: in these countries the contradiction went through an initial phase and was therefore socially and historically productive. The results of these movements were also paradoxical. In Russia there was a leap from an incipient industrial capitalism to the system of state ownership. By doing away with the stage of free competition, unemployment, monopolies, and other disasters of capitalism were avoided. At the same time, the political and social counterpart of capitalism—free labor unions and democracy—was literally ignored. No longer a consequence of development, socialism has been a method of fostering it. Therefore it has had to accept the iron law of development: the storing up, the accumulation of capital (modestly called "the accumulation of Socialist capital"). Any accumulation brings on the expropriation of plus-value and an exploitation of the workers; the difference between capitalist and "Socialist" accumulation has been that in the first case the workers could group together and defend their interests, and in the second, because of the absence of democratic institutions, they were (and are) exploited by their "representatives." Socialism, which had ceased being synonymous with historical reason, has also ceased being synonymous with justice. It has lost its philosophical dignity and its moral halo. The so-called "historical laws" have disappeared completely. The rationality inherent in the historical process has proven to be merely one more myth. Or, better: a variation of the myth of linear time.

The linear conception of history makes three things necessary: First of all, there must be only one time: a present continually impelled toward the future. Second, there must be only one leading thread: universal history must be considered to be the manifestation of the Absolute in time, the expression of the class struggle or some other similar hypothesis. The third requirement is the continuous action of a protagonist who is also unique: humanity and its successive transitory masks. The revolts and rebellions of the twentieth century have demonstrated that the subject of history is multiple and that it is irreducible to the notion of class struggle as well as to the progressive and linear succession of civilizations (the Egyptians, the Greeks, the Romans, etc.). The plurality of protagonists has also demonstrated that the leading thread of history is also multiple: it is not a single strand but many, and not all of them are straight ones. There is a plurality of personages and a plurality of times on the march toward many *wheres*, not all of them situated in a future that vanishes the instant we touch it.

The decline of the future is a phenomenon that manifests itself, naturally, in the very place where it shone like a real sun: modern Western society. I will give two examples of its decline: the crisis of the notion of an avant-garde in the realm of art, and the violent irruption of sexuality. The extreme form of modernity in art is the destruction of the object; this tendency, which began as a criticism of the notion of the "work of art," has now culminated in a negation of the very notion of art. Things have come around full circle: art ceases to be "modern": it is an instantaneous present. As for sexuality and time: the body has never believed in progress; its religion is not the future but the present.

The emergence of the present as the central value is visible in many areas of contemporary sensibility: it is a ubiquitous phenomenon. Nonetheless, it is most clearly seen in the youth movement. If the rebellion of the underdeveloped countries denies the predictions of revolutionary thought about the logic of history and the universal historical subject of our time (the proletariat), the rebellion of youth dethrones the primacy of the future and discredits the suppositions of revolutionary messianism and of liberal evolutionism: what excites young people is not the progress of the entelechy called humanity but the realization of each concrete human vocation, here and now. The universality of the rebellion of youth is the real sign of the times: *the signal of a change of time*. This universality must not cause us to forget that the movement of youth has a different meaning in each country: negation of the society of abundance and opposition to imperialism, racial discrimination, and war in the United States and in Western Europe; the struggle for a democratic society against the oppression of Communist bureaucracies and against Soviet interference in the "Socialist" countries of Eastern Europe; the opposition to Yankee imperialism and local oppressors in Latin America. But these differences do not blur the most decisive fact: the style of the rebellion of youth rejecting the institutions and the moral and social systems that hold sway in the West. All these institutions and systems go to make up what is called *modernity*, in contrast to the medieval world. All of them are the offspring of linear time and all of them are being rejected today. Their rejection does not come from the past but from the present. The double crisis of Marxism and the ideology of liberal and democratic capitalism has the same meaning as the rebellion of the underdeveloped world and the rebellion of youth: they are the expressions of the end of linear time.

The twilight of the idea of revolution corresponds to the rapidity with which revolutionary movements are being transformed into rigid systems. The best definition I know of this process came from a guerrilla in Michoacán: "All revolutions degenerate into governments." The situation of the other heir of Christianity, art, is no better. But its prostration is not a consequence of the intolerant rigidity of a system but of the promiscuity of its various tendencies and manners. There is no art that does not create a style, and there is no style that does not eventually kill art. By injecting the idea of revolution into art, our era has created a plurality of styles and pseudostyles. This abundance turns into another abundance: that of styles that die aborning. Schools proliferate and propagate like mushrooms until their very abundance finally erases the differences between one tendency and another; movements live about as long as insects do, a few short hours; the aesthetic of novelty, surprise, and change turns into imitation, tedium, and repetition. What is left for us? First, the weapon of dying mortals: humor. As the Irish poet Patrick Kavanagh said to the doctor paying him a visit: "I'm afraid I'm not going to die . . ." We can sneer at death and thus exorcise it. We can still begin over again.

What excites me about the rebellion of youth even more than their generous but nebulous politics is the reappearance of passion as a magnetic reality. We are not just witnessing another rebellion of the senses: we are confronting an explosion of emotions and feelings. This is a search for the sign *body*, not as a cipher of pleasure (although we must not be afraid of the word *pleasure*: it is beautiful in every language), but as a magnet that attracts all the contradictory forces that haunt us. It is a point of reconciliation of man with others and with himself; it is also a point of departure leading, beyond the body, to the Other. Young people are discovering values that excited figures as different as Blake and Rousseau, Novalis and Breton—spontaneity, the negation of artificial society and its hierarchies, fraternity not only with men but with nature, the ability to be enthusiastic and also to be indignant, and the amazing ability to be amazed. In brief: they are discovering the heart. In this sense, the rebellion of youth is different from those that preceded it in this century, with the exception of that of the Surrealists. The tradition of these young people is more poetic and religious than philosophical and political; like Romanticism, with which it has more than one similarity, their rebellion is not so much intellectual dissidence as a passionate, vital, libertarian heresy. The ideology of the young is often a simplification and an acritical reduction of the revolutionary tradition of the West, which itself was scholastic and intolerant. The systematic spirit has infected many groups that arrogantly advocate authoritarian and obscurantist programs, such as Maoism and other theological fanaticisms. Embracing "Chinese Marxism" as a political philosophy and attempting to apply it to industrial societies of the West is at once grotesque and disheartening. It is not the ideology of youth but their attitude, their sensibility more than their thought, that is really new. I believe that, in them and through them, another possibility for the West is opening up, if only obscurely and confusedly as yet, something that has not been foreseen by ideologists and that only a handful of poets has glimpsed. Something still without form, like a world dawning. Or is this only an illusion of ours and these disturbances the last sparks of a dying hope?

Hearing any participant or eyewitness of the rebellion of young people in Paris in May 1968 is an experience that puts our ability to judge things objectively to the test. In all the accounts I have heard there is one surprising note: the tone of the revolt, at once passionate and disinterested, as if action had been confused with representation: it was like a mutiny that turned into a Festival and a political discussion that turned into a ceremony; epic theater and at the same time public confession. The secret of the fascination that this movement exercised on all those (including the spectators) who were present at its demonstrations lay in its attempt to unite politics, art, and eroticism. There was a fusion of private and collective passion, a continuous ebb and flow between the marvelous and the everyday, the lived act as an aesthetic representation, a conjunction of action and its celebration. There was a reuniting of man with his image: mirror reflections focused in another luminous body. It was a true conversion: not only a change of ideas but of sensibility; more than a change of being, it was a *return to being*, a social and psychic revelation that for a few days broadened the limits of reality and extended the realm of the possible. It was a return to the source, to the principle of principles: being oneself by being with everyone. It was a discovery of the power of language: my words are yours; speaking with you is speaking with myself. It was a reappearance of everything (communion, transfiguration, the transformation of water into wine and of words into a body) that religions claim as their own though it is anterior to them and constitutes the other dimension of man, his other half and his lost kingdom— man perpetually expelled and torn away from time, in search of *another* time, a prohibited, inaccessible time: the present moment. Not the eternity of religions but the incandescence of the instant: a consummation and an abolition of dates. What is the way to enter such a present? André

Breton once spoke of the possibility of incorporating an extra-religious sense of the sacred, made up of the triangle of love, poetry, and rebellion, into modern life. This *sacred* cannot emerge from anything but the depths of a collective experience. Society must manifest it, incarnate it, live it, and thus live and consume itself. Revolt as the path to Illumination. Here and now: a leap to the other shore.

And a nostalgia for Festival. But Festival is a manifestation of the cyclical time of myth; it is a present that returns, whereas we live in the linear and profane time of progress and history. Perhaps the revolt of youth is an empty festival, the summons, the invocation of an event that will always be a future event and never a present one, that never will simply *be*. Or perhaps it is a commemoration: the revolution no longer appears to be the elusive imminence of the future but rather something like a past to which we cannot return—yet which we cannot abandon either. In either case, it is not here, but there, always beyond our reach. Possessed by the memory of its future or of its past, by what it was or what it could have been—no, not possessed but rather deserted, empty, the orphan of its origin and its future—society mimics them. And by mimicking them, it exorcises them: for a few weeks it denies itself through the blasphemies and the sacrilege of its young people and then affirms itself more completely and more perfectly in the ensuing repression. A mimetic magic. A victim anointed by the ambiguous fascination of profanation, youth is the sacrificial lamb of the ceremony: after having profaned itself through it, society punishes itself. It is a symbolic profanation and castigation and at the same time a representation. The events on October 2, 1968, in the Plaza de Tlatelolco in Mexico City evoked (repeated) the Aztec rites: several hundred boys and girls sacrificed, on the ruins of a pyramid, by the army and the police. The literalness of the rite—the reality of the sacrifice—emphasized in a hideous way the unreal and expiatory nature of the repression: the Mexican powers-that-be punished their own revolutionary past by punishing these young people.

In every case and in every country workers have participated in the movement only as unwilling and temporary allies. This indifference is difficult to explain unless we accept one of the two following hypotheses: either the working class is not a revolutionary class or the revolt of youth does not fit within the classical framework of the class struggle. These two explanations are really one and the same: if the working class is no longer revolutionary, and if social conflicts and struggles become more acute instead of dying out; if the recrudescence of these struggles does not coincide with an economic crisis but rather with a period of abundance; and if a new world class of the exploited has not appeared to take the place of the proletariat in its revolutionary mission, then it is obvious that the theory of class struggle cannot account for contemporary phenomena. It is not that it is entirely false: it is inadequate, and we must seek another principle, another explanation. There are those who will tell me that the underdeveloped countries are the new proletariat. I need hardly point out in reply that the phenomenon of colonial dependence is not new (Marx was familiar with it); moreover, these countries do not constitute a class because of their social, economic, and historical heterogeneity. For this reason they do not have and cannot set up programs and universal plans as an international class, a party, or a church can.

The idea that intellectuals and technicians constitute the new class is more interesting, but unfortunately it has the defect that those groups are neither homogeneous nor can they be considered as a real proletariat—they are not a universal exploited class. As for young people: no dialectical skill and no trick of the imagination can transform them into a social class. From the viewpoint of revolutionary doctrines, what is really almost beyond explanation is the attitude of young people: they have nothing to gain, no philosophy has named them agents of history, and they embody no universal historical principle. This appears to be a strange situation: they are outside the real drama of history in the same way that the Biblical lamb was outside of the dialogue between Jehovah and Abraham. But it no longer seems strange if we observe that, like the rite as a whole, the victim is a representation, or, more precisely, a hypostasis of the revolutionary classes of the past.

The modern world was born with the democratic revolution of the bourgeoisie which, so to speak, nationalized and collectivized politics. By opening to the collectivity a sphere that up until that time had been the closed preserve of a few, it was thought that general politicization (democracy) would immediately result in the distribution of power among everyone. Although democracy—because of the bureaucratic nature of political parties, economic monopolies, and the manipulation of the means of information—has become a method of a few to control and garner power, we are haunted by the phantoms of the principles, beliefs, ideas, and forms of living and feeling that gave rise to our world. Nostalgia and remorse—this is probably why society indulges in costly and sometimes bloody revolutionary rituals. The ceremony commemorates an absence, or more precisely, it at once convokes, exorcises, and punishes an Absent Guest. The Absent Guest has a public name and another secret name: the first is Revolution and refers to the linear time of history; the other is Festival and evokes the circular time of myth. They are one and the same: the return of Revolution is Festival, the recurring principle of principles. But they do not really return: it is all pantomime, and on another day fasting and penitence. It is the Festival of the goddess Reason—without Robespierre and without the guillotine but with tear gas and television. It is the Return as a verbal orgy, a saturnalia of commonplaces, the nausea that Festival brings.

Or is the rebellion of youth yet another sign that we are living *an end of time*? I have already expressed my belief: modern time—linear time, the homologue of the ideas of progress and history, ever propelled into the future, the time of the sign *non-body*, of the fierce will to dominate nature and tame instincts, the time of sublimation, aggression, and self-mutilation—is coming to an end. I believe that we are entering another time, a time that has not yet revealed its form and about which we can say nothing except that it will be neither linear time nor cyclical time. Neither history nor myth. The time that is coming, if we really are living a change at times, a general revolt and not linear revolution, will be neither a future nor a past, but a present. At least this is what contemporary rebellions are confusedly demanding. Nor do art and poetry seek anything different, although artists and poets sometimes do not know this. The return of the present: the time that is coming is defined by a *here* and a *now*. It is a negation of the sign *non-body* in all its Western versions: religious or atheist, philosophical or political, materialist or idealist. The present does not project us into any place beyond, any motley, other-worldly eternities or abstract paradises at the end of history. It projects us into the medulla, the invisible center of time: the here and now. A carnal time, a mortal time: the present is not unreachable, the present is not forbidden territory. How can we touch it, how can we penetrate inside its transparent heart? I do not know, and I do not believe anybody knows . . . Perhaps the alliance of poetry and rebellion will give us a vision of it. I see in their conjunction the possibility of the return of the sign *body*: the incarnation of images, the return of the human figure, radiant and radiating symbols. If contemporary rebellion (and I am not thinking only of that of young people) is not dissipated in a succession of raucous cries and does not degenerate into closed, authoritarian systems, if it articulates its passion through poetic imagination, in the widest and freest sense of the word poetry, our incredulous eyes may behold the awakening and the return to our abject world of that corporeal and spiritual reality that we call *the presence of the beloved*. Then love will cease to be the isolated experience of an individual or a couple, an exception or a scandal. The word *presence* and the word *love* have appeared in these reflections for the first and the last time. They were the seed of the West, the origin of our art and of our poetry. In them is the secret of our resurrection.

THE MONKEY
GRAMMARIAN

*Translated from the Spanish
by Helen R. Lane*

HANUMĀN, HANUMAT, HANŪMAT. A celebrated monkey chief. He was able to fly and is a conspicuous figure in the *Rāmāyana* . . . Hanumān leaped from India to Ceylon in one bound; tore up trees, carried away the Himalayas, seized the clouds and performed many other wonderful exploits . . . Among his other accomplishments, Hanumān was a grammarian; and the *Rāmāyana* says: "The chief of monkeys is perfect; no one equals him in the sāstras, in learning, and in ascertaining the sense of the scriptures (or in moving at will). It is well known that Hanumān was the ninth author of grammar."

—John Dowson, M. R. A. S.,
A Classical Dictionary of Hindu Mythology

1

The best thing to do will be to choose the path to Galta, traverse it again (invent it as I traverse it), and without realizing it, almost imperceptibly, go to the end—without being concerned about what "going to the end" means or what I meant when I wrote that phrase. At the very beginning of the journey, already far off the main highway, as I walked along the path that leads to Galta, past the little grove of banyan trees and the pools of foul stagnant water, through the Gateway fallen into ruins and into the main courtyard bordered by dilapidated houses, I also had no idea where I was going, and was not concerned about it. I wasn't asking myself questions: I was walking, merely walking, with no fixed itinerary in mind. I was simply setting forth to meet . . . what? I didn't know at the time, and I still don't know. Perhaps that is why I wrote "going to the end": in order to find out, in order to discover what there is after the end. A verbal trap; after the end there is nothing, since if there were something, the end would not be the end. Nonetheless, we are always setting forth to meet . . . even though we know that there is nothing, or no one, awaiting us. We go along, without a fixed itinerary, yet at the same time with an end (what end?) in mind, and with the aim of reaching the end. A search for the end, a dread of the end: the obverse and the reverse of the same act. Without this end that constantly eludes us we would not journey forth, nor would there be any paths. But the end is the refutation and the condemnation of the path: at the end the path dissolves, the meeting fades away to nothingness. And the end—it too fades away to nothingness.

Setting forth once more, embarking upon the search once again: the narrow path that snakes among livid rocks and desolate, camel-colored hills; white houses hanging suspended from cliffs, looking as though they were about to let go and fall on the wayfarer's head; the smell of sweating hides and cow dung; the buzz of afternoon; the screams of monkeys leaping about amid the branches of the trees or scampering along the flat rooftops or swinging from the railings of a balcony; overhead, birds circling and the bluish spirals of smoke rising from kitchen fires; the almost pink light on the stones; the taste of salt on parched lips; the sound of loose earth slithering away beneath one's feet; the dust that clings to one's sweat-drenched skin, makes one's eyes red, and chokes one's lungs; images, memories, fragmentary shapes and forms—all those sensations, visions, half-thoughts that appear and disappear in the wink of an eye, as one sets forth to meet . . . The path also disappears as I think of it, as I say it.

Hanumān, drawing on paper, Rajasthan, 18th century. Collection of Marie José Paz (photograph by Daniel David).

2

Through my window, some three hundred yards away, the dark green bulk of the grove of trees, a mountain of leaves and branches that sways back and forth and threatens to fall over. A populace of beeches, birches, aspens, and ash trees gathered together on a slight prominence, their tops all capsizing, transformed into a single liquid mass, the crest of a heaving sea. The wind shakes them and lashes them until they howl in agony. The trees twist, bend, straighten up again with a deafening creak and strain upward as though struggling to uproot themselves and flee. No, they do not give in. The pain of roots and broken limbs, the fierce stubbornness of plants, no less powerful than that of animals and men. If these trees were suddenly to start walking, they would destroy everything in their path. But they choose to remain where they are: they do not have blood or nerves, only sap, and instead of rage or fear, a silent tenacity possesses them. Animals flee or attack; trees stay firmly planted where they are. Patience: the heroism of plants. Being neither a lion nor a serpent: being a holm-oak, a pirutree.

Clouds the color of steel have filled the sky; it is almost white in the distance, gradually turning darker and darker toward the center, just above the grove of trees, where it gathers in violent, deep purple masses. The trees shriek continuously beneath these malevolent accumulations. Toward the right the grove is a little less dense and the leafy intertwining branches of two beeches form a dark archway. Beneath the arch, there is a bright, extraordinarily quiet space, a sort of pool of light that is not completely visible from here, since the horizontal line of the neighbors' wall cuts across it. It is a low wall, a brick surface laid out in squares like graph paper, over which there extends the cold green stain of a rose-bush. In certain spots where there are no leaves, the knotty trunk and the bifurcations of its spreading branches, bristling with thorns, can be seen. A profusion of arms, pincers, claws and other extremities studded with spiny barbs: I had never thought of a rosebush as an immense crab. The patio must be some forty yards square; it is paved in cement, and along with the rosebush, a minuscule meadow dotted with daisies sets it off. In one corner there is a small table of dark wood which has long since fallen apart. What could it have been used for? Perhaps it was once a plant stand. Every day, for several hours, as I read or write, it is there in front of me, but even though I am quite accustomed to its presence, it continues to seem incongruous to me: what is it doing there? At times I am aware of it as one would be aware of an error, or an untoward act; at other times I see it as a critique. A critique of the rhetoric of the trees and the wind. In the opposite corner is the garbage can, a metal container three feet high and a foot and a half in diameter: four wire feet that support a cylinder with a rusty cover, lined with a plastic sack to hold the refuse. The sack is a fiery red color. Crabs again. The table and the garbage can, the brick walls and the cement paving enclose space. Do they enclose it or are they doors that open onto it?

Beneath the arch of the beeches the light has deepened, and its fixity, hemmed in by the heaving shadows of the foliage, is very nearly absolute. As I gaze at it, I too remain completely at rest. Or better put: my thought draws back in upon itself and remains perfectly still for a long moment. Is this repose the force that prevents the trees from fleeing and the sky from

Five-headed Hanumān, painting, Jammu, 18th century.

falling apart? Is it the *gravity* of this moment? Yes, I am well aware that nature—or what we call nature: that totality of objects and processes that surrounds us and that alternately creates us and devours us—is neither our accomplice nor our confidant. It is not proper to project our feelings onto things or to attribute our own sensations and passions to them. Can it also be improper to see in them a guide, a way of life? To learn the art of remaining motionless amid the agitation of the whirlwind, to learn to remain still and to be as transparent as this fixed light amid the frantic branches—this may be a program for life. But the bright spot is no longer an oval pool but an incandescent triangle, traversed by very fine flutings of shadow. The triangle stirs almost imperceptibly, until little by little a luminous boiling takes place, at the outer edges first, and then, with increasing fury, in its fiery center, as if all this liquid light were a seething substance gradually becoming yellower and yellower. Will it explode? The bubbles continually flare up and die away, in a rhythm resembling that of panting breath. As the sky grows darker, the bright patch of light dims and begins to flicker; it might almost be a lamp about to go out amid turbulent shadows. The trees remain exactly where they were, although they are now clad in another light.

Fixity is always momentary. It is an equilibrium, at once precarious and perfect, that lasts the space of an instant: a flickering of the light, the appearance of a cloud, or a slight change in temperature is enough to break the repose-pact and unleash the series of metamorphoses. Each metamorphosis, in turn, is another moment of fixity succeeded by another change and another unexpected equilibrium. No one is alone, and each change here brings about another change there. No one is alone and nothing is solid: change is comprised of fixities that are momentary accords. Ought I to say that the form of change is fixity, or more precisely, that change is an endless search for fixity? A nostalgia for inertia: indolence and its frozen paradises. Wisdom lies neither in fixity nor in change, but in the dialectic between the two. A constant coming and going: wisdom lies in the momentary. It is transition. But the moment I say *transition,* the spell is broken. Transition is not wisdom, but a simple going toward . . . Transition vanishes: only thus is it transition.

3

I did not want to think again about Galta and the dusty road that leads to it, and yet they are coming back now. They return furtively, despite the fact that I do not see them, I feel that they are here again, and are waiting to be named. No thought occurs to me, I am not thinking about anything, my mind is a real "blank": like the word *transition* when I say it, like the path as I walk along it, everything vanishes as I think of Galta. As I think of it? No, Galta is here, it has slithered into a corner of my thoughts and is lurking there with that indecisive existence (which nonetheless is demanding, precisely on account of its indecision) of thoughts not completely thought through, not wholly expressed. The imminence of presence before it presents itself But there is no such presence—only an expectation comprised of irritation and impotence. Galta is not here: it is awaiting me at the end of this phrase. It is awaiting me in order to disappear. In the face of the emptiness that its name conjures up, I feel the same perplexity as when confronted with its hilltops leveled off by centuries of wind and its yellowish plains on which, during the long months of drouth, when the heat pulverizes the rocks and the sky looks as though it will crack like the earth, the dust clouds rise. Reddish, grayish, or dusky apparitions that suddenly come gushing forth like a waterspout or a geyser, except that dust whirlwinds are images of thirst, malevolent celebrations of aridity. Phantoms that dance like whirling dervishes, that advance, retreat, fall motionless, disappear here, reappear there: apparitions without substance, ceremonies of dust and air. What I am writing is also a ceremony, the whirling of a word that appears and disappears as it circles round and round. I am erecting towers of air.

But it is on the other side of the mountain range that dust storms are frequent, on the great plain, not amid these slopes and ravines. Here the terrain is much rougher and more broken than on the other side, although it availed Galta nothing to take shelter beneath the skirts of the mountain range. On the contrary, its situation exposed it even more to the inroads of the desert. All these undulating surfaces, winding ravines, and gorges are the channels and beds of streams that no longer exist today. These sandy mounds were once covered with trees. The traveler makes his way among dilapidated dwellings: the landscape too has crumbled and fallen to ruins. I read a description dating from 1891: "The way the sandy desert is encroaching on the town should be noticed. It has caused one large suburb to be deserted and the houses and gardens are going to ruin. The sand has even drifted up the ravines of the hills. This evil ought to be arrested at any cost by planting." Less than twenty years later, Galta was abandoned. Not for long however: first monkeys and then bands of wandering pariahs occupied the ruins.

It is not more than an hour's walk away. One leaves the highway on one's left, winds one's way amid rocky hills and climbs upward along ravines that are equally arid. A desolation that is not so much grim as touchingly sad. A landscape of bones. The remains of temples and dwellings, archways that lead to courtyards choked with sand, façades behind which there is nothing save piles of rubble and garbage, stairways that lead to nothing but emptiness, terraces that have fallen in, pools that have become giant piles of excrement. After making one's way across this rolling terrain, one descends to a broad, bare plain. The path is strewn with sharp rocks and one soon tires. Despite the fact that it is now four o'clock in the afternoon, the ground is still burning hot. Sparse little bushes, thorny plants, vegetation that is twisted and stunted. Up ahead, not far in the distance, the starving mountain. A skin of stones, a mountain covered with scabs. There is a fine dust in the air, an impalpable substance that irritates and makes one feel queasy. Things seem stiller beneath this light that is weightless and yet oppressive. Perhaps the word is not *stillness* but *persistence:* things persist beneath the humiliation of the light. And the light persists. Things are more thinglike, everything is persisting in being, merely being. One crosses the stony bed of a little dry stream and the sound of one's footsteps on the stones is reminiscent of the sound of water, but the stones smoke, the ground smokes. The path now winds among conical, blackish hills. A petrified landscape. This geometrical severity contrasts with the deliriums that the wind and the rocks conjure up, there ahead on the mountain. The path continues upward for a hundred yards or so, at a not very steep incline, amid heaps of loose stones and coarse gravel. Geometry is succeeded by the formless: it is impossible to tell whether this debris is from the dwellings fallen to ruins or whether it is what remains of rocks that have been worn away, disintegrated by the wind and the sun. The path leads downward once again: weeds, bilious plants, thistles, the stench of cow dung and human and animal filth, rusty tin oil drums full of holes, rags with stains of menstrual blood, a flock of vultures around a dog with its belly ripped to pieces, millions of flies, a boulder on which the initials of the Congress Party have been daubed with tar, the dry bed of the little stream once again, an enormous nim-tree inhabited by hundreds of birds and squirrels, more flat stretches of ground and ruins, the impassioned flight of parakeets, a mound that was perhaps once a cenotaph, a wall with traces of red and black paint (Krishna and his harem of cowherds' wives, royal peacocks, and other forms that are unrecognizable), a marsh covered with lotuses and above them a cloud of butterflies, the silence of the rocks beneath the luminous vibrations of the air, the breathing of the landscape, terror at the creaking of a branch or the sound of a pebble displaced by a lizard (the constant invisible presence of the cobra and that other, equally impalpable presence, which never leaves us, the shadow of our thoughts, the reverse of what we see and speak and are), until finally, again walking along the bed of the same dry stream, one reaches a tiny valley.

Behind, and on either side, the flat-topped hills, the landscape leveled by erosion; ahead, the mountain with the footpath that leads to the great sacred pool beneath the rocks, and from there, via the pilgrim path, to the sanctuary at the summit. Scarcely a trace of the abandoned dwellings remains. Along the path here there are three towering, ancient banyan trees. In the shade of them—or rather: immersed in their depths, hidden in the semidarkness of their bowels, as though they were caves and not trees—are a group of lively children dressed in rags. They are watching over a dozen skinny cows resigned to the martyrdom inflicted on them by the flies and cattle ticks. There are also two kid goats and a multitude of crows. The first band of monkeys makes its appearance. The children throw stones at them. Green and gleaming beneath the steady light, two huge pools of pestilential water. Within a few weeks the water will have evaporated and the pools will be beds of fine dust on which the children and the wind will toss and tumble.

4

Fixity is always momentary. But how can it *always* be so? If it were, it would not be momentary—or would not be fixity. What did I mean by that phrase? I probably had in mind the opposition between motion and motionlessness, an opposition that the adverb *always* designates as continual and universal: it embraces all of time and applies to every circumstance. My phrase tends to dissolve this opposition and hence represents a sly violation of the principle of identity. I say "sly" because I chose the word *momentary* as an adjectival qualifier of *fixity* in order to tone down the violence of the contrast between movement and motionlessness. A little rhetorical trick intended to give an air of plausibility to my violation of the rules of logic. The relations between rhetoric and ethics are disturbing: the ease with which language can be twisted is worrisome, and the fact that our minds accept these perverse games so docilely is no less cause for concern. We ought to subject language to a diet of bread and water if we wish to keep it from being corrupted and from corrupting us. (The trouble is that a-diet-of-bread-and-water is a figurative expression, as is the-corruption-of-language-and-its-contagions.) It is necessary to unweave (another metaphor) even the simplest phrases in order to determine what it is that they contain (more figurative expressions) and what they are made of and how (what is language made of? and most important of all, is it already made, or is it something that is perpetually in the making?). Unweave the verbal fabric: reality will appear. (Two metaphors.) Can reality be the reverse of the fabric, the reverse of metaphor—that which is on the other side of language? (Language has no reverse, no opposite faces, no right or wrong side.) Perhaps reality too is a metaphor (of what and/or of whom?). Perhaps things are not things but words: metaphors, words for other things. With whom and of what do word-things speak? (This page is a sack of word-things.) It may be that, like things which speak to themselves in their language of things, language does not speak of things or of the world: it may speak only of itself and to itself. ("Thoughts of a dry brain

Hanumān, Western India,
17th century.

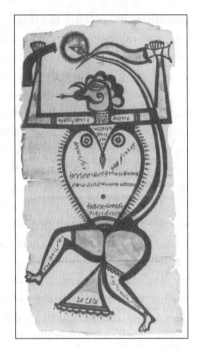

in a dry season.")* Certain realities cannot be expressed, but, and
here I quote from memory, "they
are what is manifested in language
without language stating it." They
are what language does not say and
hence says. (What is embodied in
language is not silence, which by
definition says nothing, nor is it
what silence would say if it were
to speak. If it were to cease to be
silence, and instead be . . .) What is
said in language without language
saying it is saying (that is to say?):
what is really said (that which
makes its appearance between one phrase and another, in that crack that
is neither silence nor a voice) is what language leaves unsaid (fixity is
always momentary).

To return to my initial observation: by means of a succession of
patient analyses and in a direction that is the opposite of that of the
normal activity of a speaker, whose function is to produce and construct
phrases, whereas here it is a question of taking them apart and uncou-
pling them (de-constructing them, so to speak) we ought to make our
way back upstream against the current, retrace our path, and proceeding
from one figurative expression to another, arrive back at the root, the
original, primordial word for which all others are metaphors. *Momentary*
is a metaphor—for what other word? By choosing it as the adjectival
qualifier of fixity, I fell into that frequent confusion whereby spatial properties are attributed to time and temporal properties to space, as when we
say "all year long," "the march of time," "the sweep of the minute hand,"

* From "Gerontion" by T. S. Eliot.

and other expressions of this sort. If I substitute direct statement for the figurative expression, the result is nonsense or a paradox: fixity is (always) *movement*. Fixity in turn thus proves to be a metaphor. What did I mean by that word? Perhaps this: *that which does not change*. Hence the phrase might have been: that which does not change is (always) movement. This is not satisfactory either however: the opposition between nonchange and movement is not clear, and the ambiguity reappears. Since movement is a metaphor for *change*, the best thing will be to say: nonchange is (always) change. It would appear that I have finally arrived at the desired disequilibrium. Nonetheless, change is not the primordial, original word that I am searching for: it is a form of *becoming*. When *becoming* is substituted for *change*, the relation between the two terms is altered, so that I am obliged to replace nonchange by *permanence*, which is a metaphor for *fixity*, as *becoming* is for *coming-to-be*, which in turn is a metaphor for *time* in all its ceaseless transformations . . . There is no beginning, no original word: each one is a metaphor for another word which is a metaphor for yet another, and so on. All of them are translations of translations. A transparency in which the obverse is the reverse: fixity is always momentary.

I begin all over again: if it does not make sense to say that fixity is *always* momentary, the same may not be true if I say that it *never* is. This morning's sunlight has fallen uninterruptedly on the motionless surface of the little table made of dark wood that is standing in one corner of the neighbors' patio (it finally has a function in these pages: it is serving me as an example in a dubious demonstration) during the brief period when the cloudy sky cleared: some fifteen minutes, just long enough to demonstrate the falsity of the phrase: fixity is never momentary. Perched on a thin wire of shadow, the silver and olive-colored thrush, itself a tapered shadow transformed into light standing out between and against the various glints of broken shards of bottles set into the top of a wall, at the time of day when reverberations depopulate space, a reflection among other reflections, a momentary sharp brightness in the form of a beak, feathers, and the gleam of a pair of eyes; the gray triangular lizard, coated with a powder so fine that its green tint is scarcely visible, quietly at rest in a crack in another wall on another afternoon in another place: not a variegated stone, but a bit of animal mercury; the coppice of cool green foliage on which, between one day and the next, without forewarning, there appears a flame-colored stain that is merely the scarlet armorial emblem of autumn and that immediately passes through different states, like the bed of coals that glows brightly before dying away, from copper to wine-red and from tawny to scorched brown: at each moment and in each state still the same plant; that butterfly I saw one noon in Kasauli, resting motionless on a sunflower, yellow and black like itself, its wings spread, a very thin sheet of Peruvian gold in which all the sun of the Himalayas might well have been concentrated—they are fixed: not there, but here in my mind, fixed for an instant. Fixity is always momentary.

My phrase is a moment, the moment of fixity in the monologue of Zeno the Eleatic and Hui Shih ("I leave today for Yüeh and I arrive yesterday"). In this monologue, one of the terms finally devours the other: either motionlessness is merely a state of movement (as in my phrase), or else movement is only an illusion of motionlessness (as among the Hindus). Therefore we ought not to say either *always* or *never*, but almost always or almost never, merely from time to time or more than is generally supposed and less than this expression might indicate, frequently or seldom, consistently or occasionally, we don't have at our disposal sufficient data to state with certainty whether it is periodic or irregular: fixity (always, never, almost always, almost never, etc.) is momentary (always, never, almost always, almost never, etc.) fixity (always, never, almost always, almost never, etc.) is momentary (always, never, almost always, almost never, etc.) fixity . . . All this means that fixity never is entirely fixity and that it is always a moment of change. Fixity is always momentary.

5

I must make an effort (didn't I say that I would now really go to the very end?), leave the spot with the pools of water, and arrive, some thousand yards farther on, at what I call the Gateway. The children accompany me, offer to act as guides, and beg me for coins. I stop to rest alongside a little tree, take out my pocket knife, and cut a branch off. It will serve me as a walking stick and as a standard. The Gateway is a stretch of wall, tall but not very long, that bears faint traces of black and red paint. The entryway is situated in the center of the wall, and is topped by a great Moorish arch. Above and on either side of the arch are two courses of balconies that call to mind those of Seville or Puebla, Mexico, except that these are made of wood rather than of forged iron. Beneath each balcony, there is an empty vaulted niche. The wall, the balconies, and the arch are the remains of what must have been a small palace dating from the end of the eighteenth century, similar to the many others all over the other side of the mountain.

Near the Gateway is a huge banyan tree that must be very old, to judge from the number of its dangling aerial roots and the intricate tangles in which they descend to the ground from the crown, there to attach themselves firmly, ascend again, jut out, and intertwine, like the lines, cables, and masts of a sailing vessel. But the banyan-sailboat is not rotting away in the stagnant waters of some bay, but here in this sandy soil instead. In its branches, the devout have fastened colored ribbons, all of them now faded by the rain and the sun. These discolored bits of cloth give it the pitiful air of a giant swathed in dirty bandages. Leaning against the trunk and resting on a small whitewashed platform is a stone about a foot and a half high; its shape is vaguely human, and it is daubed all over with thick, shiny, blood-red paint. At the foot of the figure are yellow petals, ashes, broken earthenware pots and other debris that I am unable to identify. The children leap about and point to the stone, shouting "Hanumān, Hanumān!" On hearing them shouting, a beggar suddenly emerges from the rocks to show me his hands eaten away by

The palace of Galta, with traces of red and black paint (photograph by Eusebio Rojas).

leprosy. The next moment, another mendicant appears, and then another and another.

I move away, walk through the arch, and enter a sort of little square. To the extreme right, a disorderly perspective of collapsing buildings out of plumb; to the left, a wall that repeats the Gateway on a more modest scale: traces of red and black paint, two courses of balconies, and an entryway topped by a graceful arch that affords a glimpse of a vast courtyard choked with hostile vegetation; across the way, a wide, winding street paved with stones and lined with houses in nearly total ruins. In the center of the street, some hundred yards away from where I am now standing, there is a fountain. Monkeys leap over the wall of the Gateway, scamper across the little square, and climb up onto the fountain. They are soon dislodged by the stones that the children throw at them. I walk toward the fountain. Ahead of me is a building that is still standing, without balconies but with massive wooden doors thrown wide open. It is a temple. Alongside the entrances are various booths with

The sacred pool of the sanctuary of Galta (photograph by Eusebio Rojas).

canvas awnings in which a few oldsters are selling cigarettes, matches, incense, sweets, prayers, holy images, and other trinkets and baubles. From the fountain one can glimpse the main courtyard, a vast rectangular space paved in flagstones. It has just been washed down and is giving off a whitish vapor. Around it, beneath a little rooftop supported by pillars, are various altars, like stands at a fair. A few wooden bars separate one altar from another, and each divinity from its worshipers. They are more like cages than altars. Two fat priests, naked from the waist up, appear in the entrance and invite me to come in. I decline to do so.

On the other side of the street is a building in ruins but handsome nonetheless. The high wall once again, the two courses of balconies reminiscent of Andalusia, the arch, and on the other side of the arch a stairway possessed of a certain secret stateliness. The stairway leads to a broad terrace surrounded by architectural features that repeat, on a smaller scale, those of the main archway. The lateral arches are supported by columns carved in random, fantastic shapes. Preceded by the monkeys, I cross the street and walk through the arch. I halt, and after a moment of indecision, begin slowly ascending the stairway. At the other end of the street the children and the priests shout something at me that I do not understand.

If I go on in this direction . . . because it is possible not to, and after having declined the invitation of the two obese priests, I could just as well walk on down the street for some ten minutes, come out in the open countryside, and start up the pilgrim path that leads to the great sacred pool and the hermitage at the foot of the rock. If I go on, I will climb the stairway step by step and reach the great terrace. Ah, here I am, breathing deeply in the center of this open rectangle which offers itself to one's gaze with a sort of logical simplicity. The simplicity, the necessity, the felicity of a perfect rectangle beneath the changes, the caprices, the violent onslaughts of the light. A space made of air, in which all forms have the consistency of air: Nothing has any weight. At the far side of the terrace is a great niche: again the shapeless stone daubed with fiery red pigment and at its feet the offerings: Yellow flowers, ashes from burned incense. I am surrounded by monkeys leaping back and forth: Robust males that continually scratch themselves and growl, baring their teeth if anyone approaches them, females with their young hanging from their teats, monkeys that drive other monkeys away, monkeys that dangle from the cornices and balustrades, monkeys that fight or play or masturbate or snatch stolen fruit from each other, gesticulating monkeys with gleaming eyes and tails in perpetual motion, howling monkeys with hairless bright-red buttocks, monkeys, monkeys, hordes of monkeys.

I stamp my feet on the ground, I shout at the top of my lungs, I run back and forth, I brandish the stick that I have cut down in the place with the pools of water and make it sing like a whip, I lash out with it at two or three monkeys who scamper away shrieking, I force my way through the others, I cross the terrace. I enter a gallery with a complicated wooden balustrade running the length of it, the repeated motif of which is a female monster with wings and claws that calls to mind the sphinxes of the Mediterranean (between the balusters and the moldings there appear and disappear the curious faces and the perpetually moving tails of the monkeys that keep cautiously following me at a distance), I enter a room in semidarkness, and despite the fact that I am more or less obliged to grope my way along in the deep shadows I can divine that this enclosed area is as spacious as an audience chamber or a banquet room, and presume that it must have been the main court of the harem or the throne room, I catch a glimpse of palpitating black sacks hanging from the ceiling, a flock of sleeping bats, the air is a heavy, acrid miasma, I go out onto another smaller terrace, how much light there is!, the monkeys reappear at the other end, looking at me from a distance with a gaze in which curiosity is indistinguishable from indifference (they are looking at me from across the distance that separates their being monkeys from my being a man), I am now at the foot of a wall stained with damp patches and with traces of paint, most likely it is a landscape, not that of Galta but another, a green and mountainous one, almost certainly it is one of those stereotyped representations of the Himalayas, yes, these vaguely conical and triangular forms represent mountains, Himalayas with snow-capped peaks, steep crags, waterfalls and moons above a narrow gorge, fairy tale mountains where wild beasts, anchorites, and marvels abound, in front of them there rises and falls, swells with pride and humbles itself, a mountain that creates and destroys itself, a sea shaken with violent

pierces mineral clouds, he sweeps like a tropical hurricane into the blur of shapeless stains that disfigure this entire end of the wall, representations perhaps of Lankā and its palace, perhaps there is painted here everything that Hanumān did and saw there after having bounded across the sea in one leap—an indecipherable jumble of lines, strokes, spirals, mad maps, grotesque stories, the discourse of monsoons inscribed on this crumbling wall.

6

Stains: thickets: blurs. Blots. Held prisoner by the lines, the liane of the letters. Suffocated by the loops, the nooses of the vowels. Nipped by the pincers, pecked by the sharp beaks of the consonants. A thicket of signs: the negation of signs. Senseless gesticulation; a grotesque rite. Plethora becomes hecatomb: signs devour signs. The thicket is reduced to a desert, the babble to silence. Decayed alphabets, burned writings, verbal debris. Ashes. Inchoate languages, larvae, fetuses, abortions. A thicket: a murderous pullulation: a wasteland. Repetitions, you wander about lost amid repetitions, you are merely a repetition among other repetitions. An artist of repetitions, a past master of disfigurations, a maestro of demolitions. The trees repeat other trees, the sands other sands, the jungle of letters is repetition, the stretch of dunes is repetition, the plethora is emptiness, emptiness is a plethora, I repeat repetitions, lost in the thicket of signs, wandering about in the trackless sand, stains on the wall beneath this sun of Galta, stains on this afternoon in Cambridge, a thicket and a stretch of dunes, stains on my forehead that assembles and disassembles vague landscapes. You are (I am) is a repetition among other repetitions. You are is I am; I am is you are: you are is I. Demolitions: I stretch out full length atop my triturations, I inhabit my demolitions.

Hanumān, a stone sculpture at the edge of the path to Galta. The devout write out a prayer or trace a sign on a piece of paper and paste it on the stone, which they then cover with red paint (photograph by Eusebio Rojas).

7

An indecipherable thicket of lines, strokes, spirals, maps: the discourse of fire on the wall. A motionless surface traversed by a flickering brightness: the shimmer of transparent water on the still bottom of the spring illuminated by invisible reflectors. A motionless surface on which the fire projects silent, fleeting, heaving shadows: beneath the ripples of the crystal-clear water dark phantoms swiftly slither. One, two, three, four black rays emerge from a black sun, grow longer, advance, occupy the whole of space, which oscillates and undulates, they fuse, form once again the dark sun of which they were born, emerge once again from this sun—like the fingers of a hand that opens, closes, and opens once again to transform itself into a fig leaf, a trefoil, a profusion of black wings, before vanishing altogether. A cascade of water silently plunges over the smooth walls of a dam. A charred moon rises out of a gaping abyss. A boat with billowing sails sends forth roots overhead, capsizes, becomes an inverted tree. Garments that fly in the air above a landscape of hills made of lampblack. Drifting continents, oceans in eruption. Surging waters, wave upon wave. The wind scatters the weightless rocks. A telamon shatters to bits. Birds again, fishes again. The shadows lock in embrace and cover the entire wall. They draw apart. Bubbles in the center of the liquid surface, concentric circles, submerged bells tolling in the depths. Splendor removes her garments with one hand, without letting go of her partner's rod with the other. As she strips naked, the fire on the hearth clothes her in copper-colored reflections. She has dropped her garments to one side and is swimming through the shadows. The light of the fire coils about Splendor's ankles, mounts between her thighs, illuminates her pubis and belly. The sun-colored water wets her fleecy mound and penetrates the lips of her vulva. The tempered tongue of the flames on the moist pudenda; the tongue enters and blindly gropes its way along the palpitating walls. The many-fingered water opens the valves and rubs the stubborn erectile button hidden amid dripping folds. The reflections, the flames, the waves lock in embrace and draw apart. Quivering shadows above the space that pants like an animal, shadows of a double butterfly that opens, closes, opens its wings. Knots. The surging waves rise and fall on Splendor's reclining body. The shadow of an animal drinking in shadows between the parted legs of the young woman. Water: shadow; light: silence. Light: water; shadow: silence. Silence: water; light: shadow.

8

Stains. Thickets. Surrounded, held prisoner amid the lines, the nooses, the loops of the liane. The eye lost in the profusion of paths that cross in all directions amid trees and foliage. Thickets: threads that knot together, tangled skeins of enigmas. Greenish-black coppices, brambles the color of fire or honey, quivering masses: the vegetation takes on an unreal, almost incorporeal appearance, as though it were a mere configuration of shadows and lights on a wall. But it is impenetrable. Sitting astride the towering wall, he contemplates the dense grove, scratches his bald rump, and says to himself: delight to the eye, defeat of reason. The sun burns the tips of the giant Burmese bamboos, so amazingly tall and slender: their shoots reach to a height of 130 feet, and they measure scarcely ten inches in diameter. He moves his head, extremely slowly, from left to right, thus taking in the entire panorama before him, from the giant bamboos to the undergrowth of poisonous trees. As his eyes survey the dense mass, there are inscribed on his mind, with the same swiftness and accuracy as when letters of the alphabet typed on a machine by skilled hands are imprinted on a sheet of paper, the name and characteristics of each tree and each plant: the betel palm of the Philippines, whose fruit, the betel nut, perfumes the breath and turns saliva red; the doum palm and the nibung, the one a native of the Sudan and the other of Java, both of them supple trees that bend and sway gracefully; the kitul palm, from which the alcoholic beverage known as "toddy" is extracted; the talipot palm: its trunk is a hundred feet tall and four feet wide, and on reaching the age of forty it develops a creamy inflorescence that measures some twenty feet across, whereupon it dies; the guaco, celebrated for its curative powers under the name lignum vitae; the gutta-percha tree, slender and modest; the wild banana, *Musa Paradisiaca,* and the traveler's tree, a vegetable fountain: it stores in the veins of its huge leaves quarts and quarts of potable water that thirsty travelers who have lost their way drink eagerly; the upa-tree: its bark contains ipoh, a poison that causes swelling and fever, sets the blood on fire, and kills; the Queensland shrub, covered with flowers resembling sea anemones, plants that produce dizziness and delirium; the tribes and confederations of hibiscuses and mallows; the rubber tree, confidant of the Olmecs, dripping with sap in the steamy shadows of the forest; the flame-colored mahogany; the okari nut tree, delight of the Papuan; the Ceylon jack, the fleshy brother of the breadfruit tree, whose fruits weigh more than fifty pounds; a tree well known in Sierra Leone: the poisonous sanny; the rambutan of Malaya: its leaves, soft to the touch, hide fruits bristling with spines; the sausage tree; the daluk: its milky sap causes blindness; the bunya-bunya araucaria (better known, he thought with a smile, as the monkey-puzzle tree) and the South American araucaria, a bottle-green cone two hundred feet high; the magnolia of Hindustan, the champak mentioned by Vālmīki on describing the visit of Hanumān to the grove of Ashoka, on the grounds of the palace of Rāvana, in Lankā; the sandalwood tree and the false sandalwood tree; the datura plant, the source of the drug of ascetics; the gum tree, in perpetual tumescence and detumescence; the kimuska, that the English call "flame of the forest," a passionate mass of foliage ranging from bright orange to fiery red, rather refreshing in the dryness of the endless summers; the ceiba and the ceibo, drowsy, indifferent witnesses of the spectacle of Palenque and Angkor; the mamey: its fruit a live coal inside a rugby ball; the pepper plant and its first cousin the terebinth; the Brazilian ironwood tree and the giant orchid of Malaya; the nam-nam and the almond trees of Java, that are not almond trees but huge carved rocks; certain sinister Latin American trees—which I shall not name in order to punish them—with fruits resembling human heads that give off a fetid odor: the vegetable world repeats the horror of the shocking history of that continent; the hora, that produces fruits so light that the breezes transport them; the inflexible breakaxe tree; the industrious bignonia of Brazil: it builds suspension bridges between one tree and another, thanks to the hooks with which it climbs and the tendrils with which it anchors itself; the snakewood, another acrobat climber, also skilled in the use of hooks, with markings like a snake skin; the oxypetal coiled up amid blue roots; the balsam fig with its strangling aerial roots; the double coconut palm, thus called because it is bisexual (and also known as the sea coconut since its bilobate or trilobite fruits, enveloped in a huge husk and mindful of huge genital organs, are found floating in the Indian Ocean): the male inflorescence is shaped like a phallus, measures three feet in length, and smells like a rat, whereas the female inflorescence is round, and when artificially pollenized, takes ten years to produce fruit; the goda kaduro of Oceania: its flat gray seeds contain the alkaloid of strychnine; the ink-bush, the rain tree; the ombu: a lovely shadow; the baobab; rosewood and the Pernambuco ironwood; ebony; the bo tree, the sacred fig beneath whose shade the Buddha vanquished Mara, a plant that strangles; the aromatic karunbu neti of the Moluccas, and the amomum that produces the spice known as grains of paradise; the bulu and the twining dada kehel . . . The Great Monkey closes his eyes, scratches himself again and muses: before the sun has become completely hidden—it is now fleeing amid the tall bamboo trees like an animal pursued by shadows— I shall succeed in reducing this grove of trees to a catalogue. A page of tangled plant calligraphy. A thicket of signs: how to read it, how to clear a path through this denseness? Hanumān smiles with pleasure at the analogy that has just occurred to him: calligraphy and vegetation, a grove of trees and writing, reading and a path. Following a path: reading a stretch of ground, deciphering a fragment of world. Reading considered as a path toward . . . The path as a reading: an interpretation of the natural world? He closes his eyes once more and sees himself, in another age, writing (on a piece of paper or on a rock, with a pen or with a chisel?) the act in the *Mahanātaka* describing his visit to the grove of the palace of Rāvana. He compares its rhetoric to a page of indecipherable calligraphy and thinks: the difference between human writing

Hanumān, Rajasthan,
18th century.

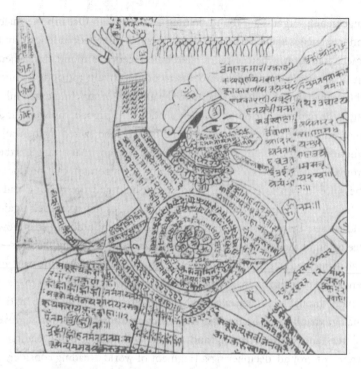

Hanumān, Rajasthan, 18th century: detail.

and divine consists in the fact that the number of signs of the former is limited, whereas that of the latter is infinite; hence the universe is a meaningless text, one which even the gods find illegible. The critique of the universe (and that of the gods) is called grammar . . . Disturbed by this strange thought, Hanumān leaps down from the wall, remains for a moment in a squatting position, then stands erect, scrutinizes the four points of the compass, and resolutely makes his way into the thicket.

9

Phrases that are liane that are damp stains that are shadows projected by the fire in a room not described that are the dark mass of the grove of beeches and aspens lashed by the wind some three hundred yards from my window that are demonstrations of light and shadow based on a vegetable reality at the hour of sunset whereby time in an allegory of itself imparts to us lessons of wisdom which the moment they are formulated are immediately destroyed by the merest flickers of light or shadow which are nothing more than time in its incarnations and disincarnations which are the phrases that I am writing on this paper and that disappears as I read them:

they are not the sensations, the perceptions, the mental images, and the thoughts which flare up and die away here, now, as I write or as I read what I write:

they are not what I see or what I have seen, they are the reverse of what is seen and of the power of sight—but they are not the invisible: they are the unsaid residuum;

they are not the other side of reality but, rather, the other side of language, what we have on the tip of our tongue that vanishes before it is said, the other side that cannot be named because it is the opposite of a name:

what is not said is not this or that which we leave unsaid, nor is it neither-this-nor-that: it is not the tree that I say I see but the sensation that I feel on sensing that I see it at the moment when I am just about to say that I see it, an insubstantial but real conjunction of vibrations and sounds and meanings that on being combined suggest the configuration of a green-bronze-black-woody-leafy-sonorous-silent presence;

no, it is not that either, if it is not a name, it surely cannot be the description of a name or the description of the sensation of the name or the name of the sensation:

a tree is not the name tree, nor is it the sensation of tree: it is the sensation of a perception of tree that dies away at the very moment of the perception of the sensation of tree;

names, as we already know, are empty, but what we did not know, or if we did know, had forgotten, is that sensations are perceptions of sensations that die away, sensations that vanish on becoming perceptions, since if they were not perceptions, how would we know that they are sensations?;

sensations that are not perceptions are not sensations, perceptions that are not names—what are they?

if you didn't know it before, you know now: everything is empty;

and the moment I say everything-is-empty, I am aware that I am falling into a trap: if everything is empty, this everything-is-empty is empty too;

no, it is full, full to overflowing, everything-is-empty is replete with itself, what we touch and see and taste and smell and think, the realities that we invent and the realities that touch us, look at us, hear us, and invent us, everything that we weave and unweave and everything that weaves and unweaves us, momentary appearances and disappearances, each one different and unique, is always the same full reality, always the same fabric that is woven as it is unwoven: even total emptiness and utter privation are plenitude (perhaps they are the apogee, the acme, the consummation and the calm of plenitude), everything is full to the brim, everything is real, all these invented realities and all these very real inventions are full of themselves, each and every one of them, replete with their own reality;

and the moment I say this, they empty themselves: things empty themselves and names fill themselves, they are no longer empty, names are plethoras, they are donors, they are full to bursting with blood, milk, semen, sap, they are swollen with minutes, hours, centuries, pregnant with meanings and significations and signals, they are the secret signs that time makes to itself, names suck the marrow from things, things die on this page but names increase and multiply, things die in order that names may live:

the tree disappears between my lips as I say it, and, as it vanishes, it appears: look at it, a whirlwind of leaves and roots and branches and a trunk amid the violent gusts of wind, a waterspout of green bronze sonorous leafy reality here on the page:

look at it over there, on the slight prominence of that stretch of ground: opaque amid the opaque mass of the trees, look at it, unreal in its brute mute reality, look at it unsaid:

the reality beyond language is not completely reality, a reality that does not speak or say is not reality;

and the moment I say that, the moment I write, letter by letter, that a reality stripped of names is not reality, the names evaporate, they are air, they are a sound encased in another sound and in another and another, a murmur, a faint cascade of meanings that fade away to nothingness:

the tree that I say is not the tree that I see, tree does not say tree, the tree is beyond its name, a leafy, woody reality: impenetrable, untouchable, a reality beyond signs, immersed in itself, firmly planted in its own reality: I can touch it but I cannot name it, I can set fire to it but if I name it I dissolve it:

the tree that is there among the trees is not the tree that I name but a reality that is beyond names, beyond the word reality, it is simply reality just as it is, the abolition of differences and also the abolition of similarities;

the tree that I name is not the tree, and the other one, the one that I do not name and that is there, on the other side of my window, its trunk now black and its foliage still inflamed by the setting sun, is not the tree either, but, rather, the inaccessible reality in which it is planted:

between the one and the other there appears the single tree of sensation which is the perception of the sensation of tree that is vanishing, but

who perceives, who senses, who vanishes as sensations and perceptions vanish?

at this very moment my eyes, on reading what I am writing with a certain haste in order to reach the end (which end? what end?) without having to rise from my chair to turn on the electric light, still taking advantage of the setting sun that is slipping down between the

Hanumān emerging out of Surasa's mouth. Lucknow, 20th century.
Surasa: she-devil.

branches and the leaves of the mass of beeches planted on a slight prominence,

(it might be said that this little mound is the pubis of this stretch of ground, so feminine is the landscape between the domes of the little astronomical observatories and the gentle undulations of the playing field of the college,

it might be said that it is the pubis of Splendor that grows brighter and then darker, a double butterfly, as the flames on the hearth flicker, as the tide of the night ebbs and flows),

at this very moment my eyes, on reading what I am writing, invent the reality of the person who is writing this long phrase; they are not inventing me, however, but a figure of speech: the writer, a reality that does not coincide with my own reality, if it is the case that I have any reality that I can call my own;

no, no reality is mine, no reality belongs to me (to us), we all live somewhere else, beyond where we are, we are all a reality different from the word I or the word we;

our most intimate reality lies outside ourselves and is not ours, and it is not one but many, plural and transitory, we are this plurality that is continually dissolving, the self is perhaps real, but the self is not *I* or *you* or *he*, the self is neither mine nor yours,

it is a state, a blink of the eye, it is the perception of a sensation that is vanishing, but who or what perceives, who senses?

are the eyes that look at what I write the same eyes that I say are looking at what I write?

we come and go between the word that dies away as it is uttered and the sensation that vanishes in perception—although we do not know who it is that utters the word nor who it is that perceives, although we do know that the self that perceives something that is vanishing also vanishes in this perception: it is only the perception of that self's own extinction,

we come and go: the reality beyond names is not habitable and the reality of names is a perpetual falling to pieces, there is nothing solid in the universe, in the entire dictionary there is not a single word on which to rest our heads, everything is a continual coming and going from things to names to things,

no, I say that I perpetually come and go but I haven't moved, as the tree has not moved since I began to write,

inexact expressions once again: *I began, I write,* who is writing what I am reading?, the question is reversible: what am I reading when I write: *who is writing what I am reading?*

the answer is reversible, the phrases at the end are the reverse of the phrases at the beginning and both are the same phrases

that are liane that are damp spots on an imaginary wall of a ruined house in Galta that are the shadows projected by the fire on a hearth lighted by two lovers that are the catalogue of a tropical botanical garden that are an allegory in a chapter in an epic poem that are the agitated mass of the grove of beeches on the other side of my window as the wind etcetera lessons etcetera destroyed etcetera time itself etcetera,

the phrases that I write on this paper are sensations, perceptions, images, etcetera, which flare up and die down here, in front of my eyes, the verbal residuum:

the only thing that remains of the felt, imagined, thought, perceived, and vanished realities, the only reality that these evaporated realities leave behind, a reality that, even though it is merely a combination of signs, is no less real than they are:

the signs are not presences but they configure another presence, the phrases fall into line one after the other on the page and as they advance they open up a path toward a temporarily final end,

the phrases configure a presence that disappears, they are the configuration of the abolition of presence,

yes, it is as though all these presences woven by the configurations of the signs were seeking its abolition in order that there might appear those inaccessible trees, immersed in themselves, not said, that are beyond the end of this phrase,

on the other side, there where eyes read what I am writing, and on reading it, dissipate it

10

He saw many women lying stretched out on mats, in diverse costumes and finery, their hair adorned with flowers; they had fallen asleep under the influence of the wine, after having spent half the night disporting themselves. And the stillness of that great company, now that their tinkling ornaments had fallen silent, was that of a vast nocturnal pool, covered with lotuses, with no sound now of swans or of bees . . . The noble monkey said to himself: *Here there have come together planets which, their store of merits having been exhausted, are fallen from the firmament.* It was true: the women glowed like incandescent fallen meteors. Some had collapsed in a heap, fast asleep, in the middle of their dances and were lying as though struck by a bolt of lightning, their hair and headdresses in disarray, amid their scattered garments; others had flung their garlands to the floor, and with the strings of their necklaces broken, their belt buckles unfastened, their skirts thrown back, looked like unsaddled mares; still others, having lost their bracelets and earrings, with their tunics torn to shreds and trampled underfoot, had the appearance of climbing vines trod upon by wild elephants. Here and there lunar reflections cast by scattered pearls criss-crossed between sleeping swans of breasts. Those women were rivers: their thighs the shores; the undulations of their pubes and bellies ripples of water in the breeze; their haunches and breasts the hills and mounds that the current flows round and girdles; their faces the lotuses; their desires the crocodiles; their sinuous bodies the bed of the stream. On ankles and wrists, forearms and shoulders, round the navel or at the tips of their breasts, there could be seen graceful scratches and pleasing purple bruises that resembled jewels . . . Some of these girls savored the lips and tongues of their female companions, who returned their kisses as though they were those of their master; their senses awakened though their spirits slumbered, they made love to each other, or lying by themselves, they clung with arms bedecked with jewels to a heap of their own garments, or beneath the dominion of wine and desire, some reclined against the belly of a companion or between her thighs, and others rested their head on the shoulder of a neighbor or hid their face between her breasts, and thus they coupled together, each with another, like the branches of a single tree. These slender women intertwined like flowering vines at the season when they cover the trunks of the trees and open their corollas to the March winds. These women twined together and wound their arms and legs about each other till they formed an intricate sylvan grove. (*Sundara Kund,* IX)

11

The transfiguration of their games and embraces into a meaningless ceremony filled them at once with fear and pleasure. On the one hand, the spectacle fascinated them and even excited their lust: that pair of giant lovers were themselves; on the other hand, the feeling of excitement that overcame them on seeing themselves as images of fire was allied with a feeling of anxiety, summed up in a question more apprehensive than incredulous: were they indeed themselves? On seeing those insubstantial forms silently appear and disappear, circle round each other, fuse and split apart, grope at each other and tear each other into bits that vanished and a moment later reappeared in order to form another chimerical body, it seemed to them that they were witnessing not the projection of their own actions and movements but a fantastic spectacle with no relation whatsoever to the reality that they were living at that moment. The ambiguous staging of an endless procession, made up of a succession of incoherent scenes of adoration and profanation, the climax of which was a sacrifice followed by the resurrection of the victim: yet another avid apparition that opened another scene different from the one that had just taken place, but possessed of the same insane logic. The wall showed them the metamorphosis of the transports of their bodies into a barbarous, enigmatic, scarcely human fable. Their actions were transformed into a dance of specters, this world reborn in the other world: reborn and disfigured: a cortege of bloodless, lifeless hallucinations.

The bodies that are stripped naked beneath the gaze of the other and their own, the caresses that knot them together and unknot them, the net of sensations that traps them and unites them as it disunites them from the world, the momentary bodies that two bodies form in their eagerness to be a single body—all this was transformed into a weft of symbols and hieroglyphs. They were unable to read them: immersed in the passionate reality of their bodies, they perceived only fragments of that other passion depicted on the wall. But even if they had paid close attention to the procession of silhouettes as it passed by, they would not have been able to interpret it. Despite having scarcely seen the cortege of shadows, they nonetheless knew that each one of their gestures and positions was inscribed on the wall, transfigured into a tangled jumble of scorpions or birds, hands or fish, discs or cones, transitory, shifting signs. Each movement engendered an enigmatic form, and each form intertwined with another and yet another. Coils of enigmas which in turn intertwined with others and coupled like the branches of a grove of trees or the tendrils of a creeping vine. In the flickering light of the fire the outlines of the shadows followed one upon the other, linked together in a chain. And just as they did not know the meaning of that theater of signs and yet were not unaware of its dark, passionate theme, so they knew that even though it was composed of mere shadows, the bower formed by its interweaving bodies was impenetrable.

Black clusters hanging from a ragged rock that is indistinct yet powerfully masculine, suddenly cracking asunder like an idol split apart with an axe: bifurcations, ramifications, disintegrations, coagulations, dismemberments, fusions. An inexhaustible flow of shadows and forms in which the same elements kept appearing—their bodies, their garments, the few objects and pieces of furniture in the room—combined each time in a different way, although, as in a poem, there were repetitions, rhymes, analogies, figures that appeared and reappeared with more or less the regularity of a surging sea: beds of lava, flying scissors, violins dangling from a noose, vessels full of seething letters of the alphabet, eruptions of triangles, pitched battles between rectangles and hexagons, thousands of dead victims of the London plague transmuted into clouds on which the Virgin ascends changed into the thousands of naked bodies locked in embrace of one of the colossal orgies of Harmony dreamed of by Fourier turned into the towering flames that devour the corpse of Sardanapalus, sea-going mountains, civilizations drowned in a drop of theological ink, screw propellers planted on the Mount of Calvary, conflagrations, conflagrations, the wind perpetually amid the flames, the wind that stirs up the ashes and scatters them.

Splendor leans back on the mat and with her two hands presses her breasts together but in such a way as to leave, down below, a narrow opening into which her companion, obeying the young woman's gesture of invitation, introduces his rod. The man is kneeling and Splendor's body lies outstretched beneath the arch of his legs, her torso half erect in order to facilitate her partner's thrusts. After a few vigorous assaults the rod traverses the channel formed by the young woman's breasts and reappears in the shadowy zone of her throat, very close to her mouth. She endeavors in vain to caress the head of the member with her tongue: its position prevents her from doing so. With a gesture that is swift but not violent, the man pushes upward and forward, making her breasts bound apart, and his rod emerges from between them like a swimmer returning to the surface, in reach now of Splendor's lips. She wets it with her tongue, draws it toward her, and guides it into the red grotto. The man's balls swell. A great splash. Concentric circles cover the surface of the pool. The clapper of the submerged bell tolls solemnly.

On the wall the body of the man is a bridge suspended over a motion-less river: Splendor's body. As the crackling of the fire on the hearth diminishes, the shadow of the man kneeling above the young woman increases in size until it covers the entire wall. The conjoining of the shadows precipitates the discharge. Sudden whiteness. An endless fall in a pitch-black cave. Afterwards he discovers himself lying beside her, in a half-shadow on the shore of the world: farther beyond are the other worlds, that of the objects and the pieces of furniture in the room and the other world of the wall, barely illuminated by the faint glow of the dying embers. After a time the man rises to his feet and stirs up the fire. His shadow is enormous and flutters all about the room. He returns to Splendor's side

Hanumān devouring the Sun and being followed by Indra. Alwar, Rajasthan.

and watches the reflections of the fire glide over her body. Garments of light, garments of water: her nakedness is more naked. He can now see her and grasp the whole of her. Before he had glimpsed only bits and pieces of her: a thigh, an elbow, the palm of a hand, a foot, a knee, an ear nestling in a lock of damp hair, an eye between eyelashes, the softness of backs of knees and insides of thighs reaching up as far as the dark zone rough to the touch, the wet black thicket between his fingers, the tongue between the teeth and the lips, a body more felt than seen, a body made of pieces of a body, regions of wetness or dryness, open or bosky areas, mounds or clefts, never the body, only its parts, each part a momentary totality in turn immediately split apart, a body segmented, quartered, carved up, chunks of ear ankle groin neck breast finger-nail, each piece a sign of the body of bodies, each part whole and entire, each sign an image that appears and burns until it consumes itself, each image a chain of vibrations, each vibration the perception of a sensation that dies away, millions of bodies in each vibration, millions of universes in each body, a rain of universes on the body of Splendor which is not a body but the river of signs of her body, a current of vibrations of sensations of perceptions of images of sensations of vibrations, a fall from whiteness to blackness, blackness to whiteness, whiteness to whiteness, black waves in the pink tunnel, a white fall in the black cleft, never the body but instead bodies that divide, excision and proliferation and dissipation, plethora and abolition, parts that split into parts, signs of the totality that end-lessly divides, a chain of perceptions of sensations of the total body that fades away to nothingness.

Almost timidly, he caresses the body of Splendor with the palm of his hand, from the hollow of the throat to the feet. Splendor returns the caress with the same sense of astonishment and recognition: her eyes and hands also discover, on contemplating it and touching it, a body that before this moment she had glimpsed and felt only as a disconnected series of momentary visions and sensations, a configuration of perceptions destroyed almost the instant it took shape. A body that had disappeared in her body and that at the very instant of that disappearance had caused her own to disappear: a current of vibrations that are dissipated in the perception of their own dissipation, a perception which is itself a dispersion of all perception but which for that very reason, because it is the perception of disappearance at the very moment it disappears, goes back upstream against the current, and following the path of dissolutions, recreates forms and universes until it again manifests itself in a body: this body of a man that her eyes gaze upon.

On the wall, Splendor is an undulation, the reclining form of sleeping hills and valleys. Activated by the fire whose flames leap up again and agitate the shadows, this mass of repose and sleep begins to stir again. The man speaks, accompanying his words with nods and gestures. On being reflected on the wall, these movements create a pantomime, a feast and a ritual in which a victim is quartered and the parts of the body scattered in a space that continually changes form and direction, like the stanzas of a poem that a voice unfolds on the moving page of the air. The flames leap higher and the wall becomes violently agitated, like a grove of trees lashed by the wind. Splendor's body is racked, torn apart, divided into one, two, three, four, five, six, seven, eight, nine, ten parts—until it finally vanishes altogether. The room is inundated with light. The man rises to his feet and paces back and forth, hunching over slightly and seemingly talking to himself. His stooping shadow appears to be searching about on the surface of the wall—smooth, flickering, and completely blank: empty water— for the remains of the woman who has disappeared.

A sādhu of Galta
(photograph by Eusebio Rojas).

12

On the wall of the terrace, the heroic feats of Hanumān in Lankā are now only a tempest of lines and strokes that intermingle with the purplish damp stains in a confused jumble. A few yards farther on, the stretch of wall ends in a pile of debris. Through the wide breach the surrounding countryside of Galta can be seen: straight ahead, bare forbidding hills that little by little fade away into a parched, yellowish expanse of flat ground, a desolate river valley subjected to the rule of a harsh, slashing light: to the left ravines and rolling hills, and on the slopes or at the tops piles of ruins, some inhabited by monkeys and others by families of pariahs, almost all of them members of the Balmik caste (they sweep and wash floors, collect refuse, cart away offal; they are specialists in dust, debris, and excrement, but here, installed amid the ruins and the rubble of the abandoned mansions, they also till the soil on neighboring farms, and, in the afternoon, they gather together in the courtyards and on the terraces to share a hookah, talk together, and tell each other stories); to the right, the twists and turns of the path that leads to the sanctuary at the top of the mountain. A bristling, ocher-colored terrain, sparse thorny vegetation, and scattered here and there, great white boulders polished by the wind. In the bends of the path, standing alone or in groups, powerful trees: pipals with hanging aerial roots, sinewy, supple arms with which for centuries they have strangled other trees, cracked boulders, and demolished walls and buildings; eucalyptuses with striped trunks and aromatic leaves; neem trees with corrugated, mineral-hard bark—in their fissures and forks, hidden by the acrid green of the leaves, there are colonies of tiny squirrels with huge bushy tails, hermit bats, flocks of crows. Imperturbable skies, indifferent and empty, except for the figures delineated by birds: circles and spirals of eaglets and vultures, ink spots of crows and blackbirds, green zigzag explosions of parakeets.

The muffled sound of rocks falling into a torrent: the cloud of dust raised by a flock of little black and tan goats led by two young shepherd boys, one of them playing a tune on a mouth organ and the other humming the words. The cool sound of the footsteps, the voices, and the laughter of a band of women descending from the sanctuary, loaded down with children as though they were fruit-bearing trees, barefoot and perspiring, their arms and ankles decked with many jangling bracelets— the dusty, tumultuous throng of women and the brilliant colors of their garments, violent reds and yellows, their coltlike gait, the tinkle of their laughter, the immensity of their eyes. Farther up, some fifty yards beyond the round fortified tower in ruins that once marked the outer limit of the city, invisible from here (one must branch off to the left and go around a huge rock that stands in the way), the terrain becomes more broken: there is a barrier of boulders and at the foot of them a pool surrounded by heterogeneous buildings. Here, the pilgrims rest after performing their ablutions. The spot is also a shelter for wandering ascetics. Among the rocks grow two much-venerated pipal trees. The water of the cascade is green, and the roar it makes as it rushes down makes me think of that of elephants at their bathtime. It is six o'clock; at this hour in the late afternoon the *sādhu*, the holy man who lives in some nearby ruins, leaves his retreat and, naked from head to foot, heads for the sacred pool. For years, even in the coldest days of December and January, he has performed his ritual ablutions as dawn breaks and as twilight falls. Although he is over sixty years old, he has the body of a young man and his gaze is clear. After his bath in the late afternoon, he recites his prayers, eats the meal that the devout bring to him, drinks a cup of tea and inhales a few puffs of hashish from his pipe or takes a little bhang in a cup of milk—not in order to stimulate his imagination, he says, but in order to calm it. He is searching for equanimity, the point where the opposition between inner and outer vision, between what we see and what we imagine, ceases. I should like to speak with the sadhu, but he does not understand my language and I do not speak his. Hence, I limit myself to sharing his tea, his bhang, and his tranquility from time to time. What does he think of me, I wonder? Perhaps he is now asking himself the same question, if perchance he thinks of me at all.

I feel someone watching me and turn around: the band of monkeys is spying on me from the other end of the terrace. I walk toward them in a straight line, unhurriedly, my stick upraised; my behavior does not seem to make them uneasy, and as I continue to walk toward them, they remain there, scarcely moving, looking at me with their usual irritating curiosity and their no less usual impertinent indifference. As soon as they feel me close by, they leap up, scamper off, and disappear behind the balustrade. I walk over to the opposite edge of the terrace and from there I see in the distance the bony crest of the mountain outlined with cruel precision. Down below, the street and the fountain, the temple and its two priests, the booths and their elderly vendors, the children leaping about and screeching, several starving cows, more monkeys, a lame dog. Everything is radiant: the animals, the people, the trees, the stones, the filth. A soft radiance that has reached an accord with the shadows and their folds. An alliance of brightnesses, a thoughtful restraint: objects take on a secret life, call out to each other, answer each other, they do not move and yet they vibrate, alive with a life that is different from life. A universal pause: I breathe in the air, the acrid odor of burned dung, the smell of incense and poverty. I plant myself firmly in this moment of motionlessness: the hour is a block of pure time.

Ten-armed Hanumān, Jodhpur, 19th century.

13

A thicket of lines, figures, forms, colors: nooses of curving strokes, maelstroms of color in which the eye drowns, a series of intertwined figures, repeated in horizontal bands, that totally confound the mind, as though space were being slowly covered line by line, with letters of the alphabet, each one different and yet related to the following one in the same way, and as though all of them, in their various conjunctions, invariably kept producing the same figure, the same word. Nonetheless, in each case the figure (the word) has a different meaning. Different and the same.

Above, the innocent kingdom of animal copulation. A plain covered with sparse, sunscorched grass, strewn with flowers the size of trees and with trees the size of flowers, bounded in the distance by a narrow red-tinged horizon—almost the trace of a scar that is still fresh: it is dawn or sunset—on which tiny, fuzzy white patches merge or dissolve, vague mosques and palaces that are perhaps clouds. And superimposed on this innocuous landscape, filling it completely with their obsessive, repeated fury, tongue thrust out, gleaming white teeth bared, immense staring eyes, pairs of tigers, rats, camels, elephants, blackbirds, hogs, rabbits, panthers, crows, dogs, donkeys, squirrels, a stallion and a mare, a bull, and a cow—the rats as big as elephants, the camels the same size as the squirrels—all coupling, the male mounted atop the female. A universal, ecstatic copulation.

Below: the ground is not yellow or dark gray but a bright parrot-green. Not the earthly kingdom of animals but the meadow-carpet of desire, a brilliant surface dotted with little red, white, and blue flowers, flowers-that-are-stars-that-are-signs (meadow: carpet: zodiac: calligraphy), a motionless garden that is a copy of the fixed night sky that is reflected in the design of the carpet that is transfigured into the pen-strokes of the manuscript. Above: the world in its myriad repetitions; below: the universe is analogy. But it is also exceptions, rupture, irregularity: as in the upper portion, occupying the entire space, outbursts of primal fury, vehement outcries, violent red and white spurts, five in the upper band and four in the lower one, nine enormous flowers, nine planets, nine carnal ideograms: a nāyikā, always the same one, like the repetition of the same luminous patterns in fireworks displays, emerging nine times from the circle of her skirt, a blue corolla spattered with little red dots or a red corolla strewn with tiny black and blue crosses (the sky as a meadow and both reflected in a woman's skirt)—a nāyikā lying on the carpet-garden-zodiac-calligraphy, reclining on a pillow of signs, her head thrown back and half hidden by a translucent veil through which her jet-black, pomaded hair can be seen, her profile transformed into that of an idol by her heavy ornaments—gold earrings set with rubies, diadems of pearls across the forehead, a diamond nose-pendant, chokers and necklaces of green and blue stones—sparkling rivers of bracelets on the arms, breasts with pointed nipples swelling beneath the orange *choli*, the body naked from the waist down, the thighs and belly a gleaming white, the shaved pubis a rosy pink, the labia of the vulva standing out, the ankles circled by bracelets with little tinkling bells, the palms of the hands and the soles of the feet tinted red, the upraised legs clasping the partner nine times—and it is always the same nāyikā, simultaneously possessed nine times in the two bands, five times in the upper one and four in the lower one, by nine lovers: a wild boar, a male goat, a monkey, a stallion, a bull, an elephant, a bear, a royal peacock, and another nāyikā—one dressed exactly like her, with the same jewels and ornaments, the same eyes of a bird, the same great noble nose, the same thick, well-defined mouth, the same face, the same plump whiteness—another self mounted atop her, a consoling two-headed creature set like a jewel in the twin vulvas.

A monkey of Galta
(photograph by Eusebio Rojas).

Asymmetry between the two parts: above, copulation between males and females of the same species; below, copulation of a human female with males of various species of animals and with another human female—never with a human male. Why? Repetition, analogy, exception. On the expanse of motionless space—wall, sky, page, sacred pool, garden—all these figures intertwine, trace the same sign and appear to be saying the same thing, but what is it that they are saying?

14

I halted before a fountain standing in the middle of the street, in the center of a semicircle. The tiny little stream of water flowing from the faucet had made a mud puddle on the ground; a dog with sparse, dark gray fur and patches of raw, bruised flesh was licking at it. (The dog, the street, the puddle: the light of three o'clock in the afternoon, a long time ago, on the cobblestones of a narrow street in a town in the Valley of Mexico, the body of a peasant dressed in white cotton work clothes lying in a pool of blood, the dog that is licking at it, the screams of the women in dark skirts and purple shawls running in the direction of the dead man.) Amid the almost completely ruined buildings forming the semicircle around the fountain was one that was still standing, a massive, squat structure with its heavy doors flung wide open: the temple. From where I was standing its inner courtyard could be seen, a vast quadrangle paved with flagstones (it had just been washed down and was giving off a whitish vapor). Around the edges of it, against the wall and underneath a roof supported by irregularly shaped pillars, some of stone and others of masonrywork, all of them whitewashed and decorated with red and blue designs, Grecian frets, and bunches of flowers, stood the altars with the gods, separated from each other by wooden bars, as though they were cages. At the entrances were various booths where elderly vendors were peddling their wares to the crowd of worshipers: flowers, sticks and bars of incense; images and color photographs of the gods (depicted by movie actors and actresses) and of Gandhi, Bose, and other heroes and saints; *bhasma*, the soft red paste with which the faithful trace religious signs on their foreheads at the moment in the ceremony when offerings are made; fans with advertisements for Coca-Cola and other soft drinks; peacock feathers; stone and metal lingas; boy dolls representing Durga mounted on a lion; mandarin oranges, bananas, sweets, betel and bhang leaves; colored ribbons and talismans; paperbound prayer books, biographies of saints, little pamphlets on astrology and magic; sacks of peanuts for the monkeys . . . Two priests appeared at the doors of the temple. They were fat and greasy, naked from the waist up, with the lower part of their bodies draped in a *dhoti,* a length of soft cotton cloth wound between their legs. A Brahman cord hanging down over their breasts, as ample as a wetnurse's; hair, pitch-black and oiled, braided in a pigtail; soft voices, obsequious gestures. On catching sight of me drifting amid the throng, they approached me and invited me to visit the temple. I declined to do so. At my refusal, they began a long peroration, but without stopping to listen to it, I lost myself in the crowd, allowing the human river to carry me along.

The devout were slowly ascending the steep path. It was a peaceful crowd, at once fervent and good-humored. They were united by a common desire: simply to get to where they were going, to see, to touch. Will and its tensions and contradictions played no part in that impersonal, passive, fluid, flowing desire. The joy of total trust: they felt like children in the hands of infinitely powerful and infinitely beneficent forces. The act that they were performing was inscribed upon the calendar of the ages, it was one of the spokes of one of the wheels of the chariot of time. They were walking to the sanctuary as past generations had done and as those to come would do. Walking with their relatives, their neighbors, and their friends and acquaintances, they were also walking with the dead and with those not yet born: the visible multitude was part of an invisible multitude. They were all walking through the centuries by way of the same path, the path that cancels out the distinction between one time and another, and unites the living with the dead. Following this path we leave tomorrow and arrive yesterday: today.

Although some groups were composed only of men or only of women, the majority were made up of entire families, from the great grandparents down to the grandchildren and great grandchildren, and including not only those related by blood but by religion and caste as well. Some were proceeding in pairs: the elderly couples babbled incessantly, but those recently wed walked along without exchanging a word, as though surprised to find themselves side by side. Then there were those walking all by themselves: the beggars with infirmities arousing pity or terror—the hunchbacked and the blind, those stricken with leprosy or elephantiasis or paralysis, those afflicted with pustules or tumors, drooling cretins, monsters eaten away by disease and wasting away from fever and starvation—and the others, erect and arrogant, convulsed with wild laughter or mute and possessed of the bright piercing eyes of illuminati, the sādhus, wandering ascetics covered with nothing but a loincloth or enveloped in a saffron robe, with kinky hair dyed red or scalps shaved bare except for a topknot, their bodies smeared with human ashes or with cow dung, their faces daubed with paint, and carrying in their right hand a rod in the shape of a trident and in their left hand a tin bowl, their only possession in this world, walking alone or accompanied by a young boy, their disciple, and in certain cases their catamite.

Little by little, we crossed hill and dale, amid ruins and more ruins. Some ran ahead and then lay down to rest beneath the trees or in the hollows of the rocks; the others walked along at a slow, steady pace, without halting; the lame and the crippled dragged themselves painfully along, and the invalids and paralytics were borne on stretchers. Dust, the smell of sweat, spices, trampled flowers, sickly-sweet odors, stinking breaths of air, cool breaths of air. Little portable radios, belonging to bands of young boys, poured forth catchy popular love-songs; small children clinging to their mother's breasts or skirts wailed and squalled; the devout chanted hymns; there were some who talked among themselves, some who laughed uproariously, and some who wept or talked to themselves—a ceaseless murmur, voices, cries, oaths, exclamations, outcries, millions of syllables that dissolved into a great, incoherent wave of sound, the

The nāyikā, the incarnation of the love of all creatures, miniature in an album, Rajasthan, c. 1780.

sound of humans making itself heard above the other sounds of the air and the earth, the screams of the monkeys, the cawing of the crows, the sea-roar of the foliage, the howl of the wind rushing through the gaps in the hills.

The wind does not hear itself but we hear it; animals communicate among themselves but we humans each talk to ourselves and communicate with the dead and with those not yet born. The human clamor is the wind that knows that it is wind, language that knows that it is language and the means whereby the human animal knows that it is alive, and by so knowing, learns to die.

The sound of several hundred men, women, and children walking along and talking: the promiscuous sound of gods, dead ancestors, unborn children and live ones hiding between their mother's bodice and her breast, with their little copper coins and their talismans, their fear of dying. The wind does not complain: man is the one who hears, in the complaint of the wind, the complaint of time. Men hears himself and looks at himself everywhere: the world is his mirror; the world neither hears us nor looks at itself in us: no one sees us, no one recognizes himself in man. To those hills we were strangers, as were the first men who, millennia ago, first walked among them. But those who were walking with me did not know that: they had done away with distance—time, history, the line that separates man from the world. Their pilgrimage on foot was the immemorial rite of the abolishing of differences. Yet these pilgrims knew something that I did not know: the sound of human syllables was simply one more noise amid the other noises of that afternoon. A different sound, yet one identical to the screams of the monkeys, the cries of the parakeets, and the roar of the wind. To know this was to reconcile oneself with time, to reconcile all times with all other times.

15

As he created beings, Prajāpati sweated and suffocated, and from his great heat and fatigue, from his sweat, Splendor was born. She made her appearance all of a sudden: there she was, standing erect, radiant, resplendent, sparkling. The moment they set eyes on her, the gods desired her. They said to Prajāpati: "Allow us to kill her: we can then divide her up and share her among all of us." He answered unto them: "Certainly not! Splendor is a woman: one does not kill women. But if you so wish, you may share her—on condition that you leave her alive." The gods shared her among themselves. Splendor hastened to Prajāpati to complain: "They have taken everything from me!" "Ask them to return to you what they took from you. Make a sacrifice," he counseled her. Splendor had the vision of the offering of the ten portions of the sacrifice. Then she recited the prayer of invitation and the gods appeared. Then she recited the prayer of adoration, backwards, beginning with the end, in order that everything might return to its original state. The gods consented to this return. Splendor then had the vision of the additional offerings. She recited them and offered them to the ten. As each one received his oblation, he returned his portion to Splendor and disappeared. Thus Splendor was restored to being.

In this liturgical sequence there are ten divinities, ten oblations, ten restitutions, ten portions of the group of the sacrifice, and the Poem in which it is said consists of stanzas of verses of ten syllables. The Poem is none other than Splendor. *(Satapatha-Brahmana,* 11-4-3)

The palace of Galta (18th century),
(photograph by Eusebio Rojas).

16

The word *reconciliation* appears and reappears. For a long time, I lighted my way with it, I ate and drank of it. *Liberation* was its sister and its antagonist. The heretic who abjures his errors and returns to the bosom of the church is reconciled with it; the purification of a sacred place that has been profaned is a reconciliation. Separation is a lack, an aberration. A lack: something is missing, we are not whole; an aberration: we have gone astray, we are not in the place where we belong. Reconciliation unites what was separated, it transforms the exclusion into conjunction, it reassembles what has been dispersed: we return to the whole and thus we return to the place where we belong. The end of exile. Liberation opens up another perspective: the breaking of chains and bonds, the sovereignty of free will. Conciliation is dependence, subjection; liberation is self-sufficiency, the plenitude of the one, the excellence of the unique. Liberation: being put to the proof, purgation, purification. When I am alone I am not alone: I am with myself; being separated is not being excluded: it is being oneself. When with everyone, I am exiled from myself; when I am alone, I am in the whole that belongs entirely to me. Liberation is not only an end of others and of otherness, but an end of the self. The return of the self—not to itself to what is the same, a return to sameness.

Is liberation the same as reconciliation? Although reconciliation leads by way of liberation and liberation by way of reconciliation, the two paths meet only to divide again: reconciliation is identity in concord, liberation is identity in difference. A plural unity; a selfsame unity. Different, yet the same; precisely one and the same. I am the others, my other selves; I in myself, in selfsameness. Reconciliation passes by way of dissension, dismemberment, rupture, and liberation. It passes by and returns. It is the original form of revolution, the form in which society perpetuates itself and re-engenders itself: regeneration of the social compact, return to the original plurality. In the beginning there was no One: chief, god, I; hence revolution is the end of the One and of undifferentiated unity, the beginning (re-beginning) of variety and its rhymes, its alliterations, its harmonious compositions. The degeneration of revolution, as can be seen in modern revolutionary movements, all of which, without exception, have turned into bureaucratic Caesarisms and institutionalized idolatry of the Chief and the System, is tantamount to the *decomposition* of society, which ceases to be a plural harmony, a *composition* in the literal sense of the word, and petrifies in the mask of the One. The degeneration lies in the fact that society endlessly repeats the image of the Chief, which is nothing other than the mask of *discomposure*: the disconcerting excesses, the imposture of the Caesar. But there never is a one, nor has there ever been a one: each one is an everyone. But there is no everyone: there is always one missing. We are neither a one together, nor is each all. There is no one and no all: there are ones and there are alls. Always in the plural, always an incomplete completeness, the *we* in search of its each one: its rhyme, its metaphor, its different complement.

I felt separated, far removed—not from others and from things, but from myself. When I searched for myself within myself, I did not find myself; I went outside myself and did not discover myself there either. Within and without, I always encountered another. The same self but always another self. My body and I, my shadow and I, their shadow. My shadows: my bodies: other others. They say that there are empty people: I was full, completely full of myself. Nonetheless, I was never in complete possession of myself, and I could never get all the way inside myself: there was always someone else there. Should I do away with him, exorcise him, kill him? The trouble was that the moment that I caught sight of him, he vanished. Talk with him, win him over, come to some agreement? I searched for him here and he turned up there. He had no substance, he took up no space whatsoever. He was never where I was; if I was there he was here; if I was here he was there. My invisible foreseeable, my visible unforeseeable. Never the same, never in the same place. Never the same place: outside was inside, inside was somewhere else, here was nowhere. Never anywhere. Great distances away: in the remotest of places: always way over yonder. Where? Here. The other has not moved: I have never moved from my place. He is here. Who is it that is here? *I* am: the same self as always. Where? Inside myself: from the beginning I have been falling inside myself, and I still am falling. From the beginning I am

Hanumān, Kalighat painting
(Bengal), 20th century.

always going to where I already am, yet I never arrive at where I am. I am always myself somewhere else: the same place, the other I. The way out is the way in: the way in—but there is no way in, it is all the way out. Here inside is always outside, here is always there, the other always somewhere else. There is always the same: himself: myself: the other. I am that one: the one there. That is how it is; that is what I am.

With whom could I reconcile myself: with myself or with the other— the others? Who were they, who were we? Reconciliation was neither an idea nor a word: it was a seed that, day after day at first and then hour after hour, had continued to grow and grow until it turned into an immense glass spiral through whose arteries and filaments there flowed light, red wine, honey, smoke, fire, salt water and fresh water, fog, boiling liquids, whirlwinds of feathers. Neither a thermometer nor a barometer: a power station that turns into a fountain that is a tree with branches and leaves of every conceivable color, a plant of live coals in winter and a plant of refreshing coolness in summer, a sun of brightness and a sun of darkness, a great albatross made of salt and air, a reflection-mill, a clock in which each hour contemplates itself in the others until it is reduced to nothingness. Reconciliation was a fruit— not the fruit but its maturity, not its maturity but its fall. Reconciliation was an agate planet and a tiny flame, a young girl, in the center of that incandescent marble. Reconciliation was certain colors interweaving so as to form a fixed star set in the forehead of the year, or floating in warm clusters between the spurs of the seasons; the vibration of a particle of light set in the pupil of the eye of a cat flung into one corner of noon;

the breathing of the shadows sleeping at the foot of an autumn skinned alive; the ocher temperatures, the gusts of wind the color of dates, a yellowish red, and the green pools of stagnant water, the river basins of ice, the wandering skies dressed in regal rags, the drums of the rain; suns no bigger than a quarter of an hour yet containing all the ages; spiders spinning translucent webs to trap infinitesimal blind creatures that emit light; foliage of flames, foliage of water, foliage of stone, magnetic foliage. Reconciliation was a womb and a vulva, but also the blinks of an eye, provinces of sand. It was night. Islands, universal gravitation, elective affinities, the hesitations of the light that at six o'clock in the late afternoon does not know whether to go or to stay. Reconciliation was not I. It was not all of you, nor a house, nor a past or a future. It was there over yonder. It was not a homecoming, a return to the kingdom of closed eyes. It was going out into the air and saying: *good morning*.

17

The wall was about two hundred yards long. It was tall, topped with parapets. Save for certain stretches that still showed traces of blue and red paint, it was covered with huge black, green, and dark purple spots: the fingerprints of the rains and the years. Just below the parapets, in a horizontal line running the length of the wall, a series of little balconies could be seen, each one crowned with a dome mindful of a parasol. The wooden blinds were faded and eaten away by the years. Some of the balconies still bore traces of the designs that had decorated them: garlands of flowers, branches of almond trees, little stylized parakeets, seashells mangoes. There was only one entrance, an enormous one, in the center: a Moorish archway, in the form of a horseshoe. It had once been the elephant gateway, and hence, its enormous size was completely out of proportion to the dimensions of the group of buildings as a whole. I took Splendor by the hand and we crossed through the archway together, between the two rows of beggars on either side. They were sitting on the ground, and on seeing us pass by they began whining their nasal supplications even more loudly, tapping their bowls excitedly and displaying their stumps and sores. With great gesticulations a little boy approached us, muttering something or other. He was about twelve years old, incredibly thin, with an intelligent face and huge, dark, shining eyes. Some disease had eaten away a huge hole in his left cheek, through which one could see some of his back teeth, his gums, and redder still, his tongue, moving about amid little bubbles of saliva—a tiny crimson amphibian possessed by a raging, obscene fit of agitation that made it circle round and round continuously inside its damp grotto. He babbled on endlessly. Although he emphasized his imperious desire to be listened to with all sorts of gestures and gesticulations, it was impossible to understand him since each time he uttered a word, the hole made wheezes and snorts that completely distorted what he was saying. Annoyed by our failure to understand, he melted into the crowd. We soon saw him surrounded by a group of people who began praising his tongue-twisters and his sly ways with words. We discovered that his loquacity was not mere nonsensical babble: he was not a beggar but a poet who was playing about with deformations and decompositions of words.

The main courtyard was a rectangular esplanade that had surely been the outdoor "audience chamber," a sort of hall outside the palace itself, although within the walls surrounding it, in which the princes customarily received their vassals and strangers. Its surface was covered with loose dirt; once upon a time it had been paved with tiles the same pink color as the walls. The esplanade was enclosed by walls on three sides: one to the south, another to the east, and another to the west. The one to the south was the Gateway through which we had entered; the other two walls were not as long and not as high. The one to the east was also topped with a parapet, whereas the one to the west had a gable-end roofed over with pink tiles. Like the Gateway, the entryway let into both the other walls was an arch in the form of a horseshoe, although smaller. Along the east wall there was repeated the same succession of little balconies as on the outer face of the Gateway wall, all of them also crowned with parasol domes and fitted out with wooden blinds, most of which had fallen to pieces. On days when the princes received visitors, the women would conceal themselves behind these blinds so as to be able to contemplate the spectacle below without being seen. Opposite the main wall, on the north side of the quadrangle, was a building that was not very tall, with a stairway leading to it which, despite its rather modest dimensions, nonetheless had a certain secret stateliness. The ground floor was nothing more than a massive cube of mortar, with no other function than to serve as a foundation for the upper floor, a vast rectangular hall bordered on all sides by an arcade. Its arches reproduced, on a smaller scale, those of the courtyard, and were supported by columns of random shapes, each one different from the others: cylindrical, square, spiral. The structure was crowned by a great many small cupolas. Time and many suns had blackened them and caused them to peel: they looked like charred, severed heads. From time to time there came from inside them the sound of parakeets, blackbirds, bats, making it seem as though these heads, even though they had been lopped off, were still emitting thoughts.

Hanumān, Rajasthan, 20th century.

The whole was theatrical, mere show. A double fiction: what those buildings represented (the illusions and nostalgias of a world that no longer existed) and what had been staged within their walls (ceremonies in which impotent princes celebrated the grandeur of a power on the point of ceasing to exist). An architecture in which to see oneself living, a substitution of the image for the act and of myth for reality. No, that is not precisely it. Neither image nor myth: the rule of obsession. In periods of decadence obsession is sovereign and takes the place of destiny. Obsession and its fears, its cupidity, its phobias, its monologue consisting of confessions-accusations-lamentations. And it was precisely this, obsession, that redeemed the little palace from its mediocrity and its banality. Despite its mannered hybridism, these courtyards and halls had been inhabited by chimeras with round breasts and sharp claws. A novelistic architecture, at once chivalrous and over-refined, perfumed and drenched with blood. Vividly lifelike and fantastic, chaotic and picturesque, unpredictable. A passionate architecture: dungeons and gardens, fountains and beheadings, an eroticized religion and an esthetic eroticism, the nāyikā's hips and the limbs of the quartered victim. Marble and blood. Terraces, banquet halls, music pavilions in the middle of artificial lakes, bedroom alcoves decorated with thousands of tiny mirrors that divide and multiply bodies until they become infinite. Proliferation, repetition, destruction: an architecture contaminated by delirium, stones corroded by desire, sexual stalactites of death. Lacking power and above all time (architecture requires as its foundation not only a solid space but an equally solid time, or at least capable of resisting the assaults of fortune, but the princes of Rajasthan were sovereigns doomed to disappear and they knew it), they erected edifices that were not intended to last but to dazzle and fascinate. Illusionist castles that instead of vanishing in this air rest on water: architecture transformed into a mere geometric pattern of reflections floating on the surface of a pool, dissipated by the slightest breath of air . . . There were no pools or musicians on the great esplanade now and no nāyikās were hiding on the little balconies: that day the pariahs of the Balmik caste were celebrating the feast of Hanumān, and the unreality of that architecture and the reality of its present state of ruin were resolved in a third term, at once brutally concrete and hallucinatory.

18

The grove of trees has turned black and become a gigantic pile of sacks of coal abandoned in the middle of the plot of ground by some unknown person for some unknown reason. A brute reality that says nothing except that it is (but what is it?) and that bears no resemblance to anything at all, not even to those nonexistent sacks of coal with which, ineptly, I have just now compared them. My excuse: the gigantic sacks of coal are as improbable as the grove of trees is unintelligible. Its unintelligibility—a word like a train always just on the point of going off the rails or losing one of its freight cars—stems from its excess of reality. It is a reality irreducible to other realities. The grove of trees is untranslatable: it is itself and only itself. It does not resemble other things or other groves of trees; neither does it resemble itself: each moment it is different. Perhaps I am exaggerating: after all, it is always the same grove of trees and its constant changes do not transform it into either a rock or a locomotive; moreover, it is not unique: the world is full of groves of trees like it. Am I exaggerating though? This grove does indeed resemble others, since otherwise it would not be called a grove of trees but would have another name; yet at the same time its reality is unique and would really deserve to have a proper name. Everyone deserves (we all deserve) a proper name, and no one has one. No one has ever had one and no one ever will have one. This is our real eternal damnation, ours and the world's. And this is what Christians mean when they speak of the state of "fallen nature." Paradise is governed by an ontological grammar: things and beings are its names and each name is a proper name. The grove of trees is not unique since it has a name that is a common noun (it is a fallen nature), but at the same time it is unique since it has no name that really belongs to it (it is innocent nature). This contradiction defies Christianity and dashes its logic to bits.

The fact that the grove of trees has no name, not the fact that I see it from my window, as the afternoon draws to a close, a blur against the bold sky of early autumn, a stain that little by little creeps across this page and covers it with letters that simultaneously describe it and conceal it—the fact that it does not have a name and the fact that *it can never have one*, is what impels me to speak of it. The poet is not one who names things, but one who dissolves their names, one who discovers that things do not have a name and that the names that we call them are not theirs. The critique of paradise is called language: the abolition of proper names; the critique of language is called poetry: names grow thinner and thinner, to the point of transparency, of evaporation. In the first case, the world becomes language; in the second, language is transformed into a world. Thanks to the poet, the world is left without names. Then, for the space of an instant, we can see it precisely as it is—an *adorable azure*. And this vision overwhelms us, drives us mad; if things are but have no name: *on earth there is no measure whatsoever.*

A moment ago, as it was burning in the solar brazier, the grove of trees did not appear to be an unintelligible reality but an emblem, a configuration of symbols. A cryptogram neither more nor less indecipherable than the enigmas that fire inscribes on the wall with the shadows of two lovers, the tangle of trees that Hanumān saw in the garden of Rāvana in Lankā and that Vālmīki turned into a fabric woven of names that we now read as a fragment of the *Rāmāyana*, the tattoo of monsoons and suns on the wall of the terrace of that small palace in Galta or the painting that describes the bestial and lesbian couplings of the nāyikā as an exception to (or an analogy of?) universal love. The transmutation of forms and their changes and movements into motionless signs: writing; the dissi-

Garuda, watercolor, Rajasthan, 19th century.

pation of the signs: reading. Through writing we abolish things, we turn them into meaning; through reading, we abolish signs, we extract the meaning from them, and almost immediately thereafter, we dissipate it: the meaning returns to the primordial stuff. The grove does not have a name, and these trees are not signs: they are trees. They are real and they are illegible. Although I refer to them when I say: *these trees are illegible*, they do not think of themselves as being referred to. They do not express anything, they do not signify: they are merely there, merely being. I can fell them, burn them, chop them up, turn them into masts, chairs, boats, houses, ashes; I can paint them, carve them, describe them, transform them into symbols of this or of that (even symbols of themselves), and make another grove of trees, real or imaginary, with them; I can classify them, analyze them, reduce them to a chemical formula or a mathematical equation and thus translate them, transform them into language—but *these* trees, the ones that I point to, the ones that are over there just beyond, always just beyond, my signs and my words, untouchable unreachable impenetrable, are what they are, and no name, no combinations of signs says them. They are unrepeatable: they will never again be what they are at this moment.

The grove is already part of the night. Its darkest, most nightlike part. So much so that I write, with no compunction, that it is a pile of coal, a sharp-pointed geometry of shadows surrounded by a world of vague ashes. It is still light in the neighbors' patio. An impersonal, posthumous light, for which the word *fixity* is most appropriate, even though we know that it will last for only a few short minutes, because it is a light that seems to resist the ceaseless change of things and of itself. The final, impartial clarity of this moment of transparency in which things become presences and coincide with themselves. It is the end (a provisory, cyclical end) of metamorphoses. An apparition: on the square cement blocks of the patio, astonishingly itself, without ostentation and without diffidence, the dark wooden table on top of which (as I only now discover) there is visible, on one corner, an oval spot with tiger markings, thin reddish stripes. In the opposite corner, the garbage can with the lid half open burns with a quiet, almost solid glow. The light runs down the brick wall as though it were water. A burned water, a water-that-

Hanumān, drawing on paper,
Rajasthan, 19th century.
(J. C. Ciancimino Collection.)

is-fire. The garbage can is overflowing with rubbish, and it is an altar that is consuming itself in silent exaltation: the refuse is a sheaf of flames beneath the coppery gleam of the rusty cover. The transfiguration of refuse—no, not a transfiguration: a revelation of garbage as what it really is: garbage. I cannot say "glorious garbage" because the adjective would defile it. The little dark wooden table, the garbage can: presences. Without a name, without a history, without a meaning, without a practical use: just because.

Things rest upon themselves, their foundation is their own reality, and they are unjustifiable. Hence they offer themselves to our sight, touch, hearing, taste, smell—not to our powers of thought. Not to think; to see, rather, to make of language a transparency. I see, I hear the footsteps of the light in the patio: little by little it withdraws from the wall opposite, projects itself onto the one on the left and covers it with a translucent mantle of barely perceptible vibrations: a transubstantiation of brick, a combustion of stone, an instant of incandescence of matter before it flings itself into its blindness—into its reality. I see, I hear, I touch the gradual petrification of language that no longer signifies but merely says: table, garbage can, without really saying them, as the table and the garbage can disappear in the patio that is now totally dark . . . The night is my salvation. We cannot *see* without risking going mad: things reveal us, without revealing anything, simply by being there in front of us, the emptiness of names, the incommensurability of the world, its quintessential muteness. And as the night accumulates in my window, I feel that I am not from here, but from there, from that world that has just been obliterated and is now awaiting the resurrection of dawn. I come from there, all of us come from there, and we shall one day return there. The fascination held for us by this other face, the seduction of this nonhuman side of the universe: where there is no name, no measure. Each individual, each thing, each instant: a unique, incomparable, incommensurable reality. To return, then, to the world of proper names.

19

A rose and green, yellow and purple undulation, wave upon wave of women, a surf of tunics dotted with little bits of mirrors like stars or spangled with sequins, the continual flowering of the pinks and blues of turbans, these thin long-shanked men are flamingos and herons, the sweat runs down the basalt of the cheekbones in rivers, wetting their mustaches that curve dangerously upward like the horns of an attacking bull, making the metal hoops they are wearing in their ears gleam, men with grave eyes as deep as a well, the flutter of feminine fabrics, ribbons, gauzes, transparencies, secret folds that conceal gazes, the tinkle of bracelets and anklets, the swaying of hips, the bright flash of earrings and amulets made of bits of colored glass, clusters of old men and old women and children driven along by the violent gust of wind of the feastday, devotees of Krishna in pale green skirts, with flowers in their hair and huge dark circles under their eyes, roaring with laughter, the main courtyard seethed with sounds, smells, tastes, a gigantic basket filled to overflowing with bright yellow, ocher, pomegranate, cinnamon, purple, black, wrinkled, transparent, speckled, smooth, glistening, spiny fruits, flaming fruits, cool refreshing suns, human sweat and animal sweat, incense, cinnamon, dung, clay and musk, jasmine and mango, sour milk, smells and tastes, tastes and colors, betel nut, clove, quicklime, coriander, rice powder, parsley, green and red peppers, honeysuckle, fetid pools, burned cow dung, limes, urine, sugarcane, spit bleeding from betel, slices of watermelon, pomegranates and their little cells: a monastery of blood; guavas, little caverns of perfume; peals of laughter, spilled whitenesses, ivory ceremonial rattles and exclamations, sighs of woe is me and shouts of get a move on, gongs and tambourines, the rustle of leaves of the women's skirts, the pattering rain of the naked feet on the dust, laughter and laments: the roar of water flinging itself over a precipice, the bound and rebound of cries and songs, the mingled chatter of children and birds, childgabble and birdprattle, the prayers of the beggargrims, the driveling supplications of the pilgrim-mendicants, the glug-glug of dialects, the boiling of languages, the fermentation and effervescence of the verbal liquid, gurgling bubbles that rise from the bottom of the Babelic broth and burst on reaching the air, the multitude and its surging tides, its multisurges and its multitudes, its multivalanche, the multisun beating down on the sunitude, povertides beneath the sunalanche, the suntide in its solity, the sunflame on the poverlanche, the multitidal solaritude

A mendicant (sādhu) dressed up as Hanumān at a fair in Ramtirth at Amritsar.

20

A quiet brightness projects itself on the wall across the way. Doubtless my neighbor has gone upstairs to his study, turned on the lamp next to the window, and by its light is peacefully reading *The Cambridge Evening News*. Down below, at the foot of the wall, the little pure-white daisies peep out of the darkness of the blades of grass and other tiny plants on the miniature meadow. Paths traveled by creatures smaller than an ant, castles built on a cubic millimeter of agate, snowdrifts the size of a grain of salt, continents drifting in a drop of water. The space beneath the leaves and between the infinitesimal plant stems of the meadow teems with a tremendous population continually passing over from the vegetable kingdom to the animal and from the animal to the mineral or the fantastic. That tiny branch that a breath of air faintly stirs was just a moment ago a ballerina with breasts like a top and a forehead pierced by a ray of light. A prisoner in the fortress created by the lunar reflections of the nail of the little finger of a small girl, a king has been dying in agony for a million seconds now. The microscope of fantasy reveals creatures different from those of science but no less real; although these are visions of ours, they are also the visions of a third party: someone is looking at them (is looking at himself?) through our eyes.

I am thinking of Richard Dadd, spending nine years, from 1855 to 1864, painting *The Fairy-Feller's Masterstroke* in the madhouse at Broadmoor, England. A fairly small painting that is a minute study of just a few square inches of ground—grasses, daisies, berries, tendrils of vines, hazelnuts, leaves, seeds—in the depths of which there appears an entire population of minuscule creatures, some of them characters from fairy tales and others who are probably portraits of Dadd's fellow inmates and of his jailers and keepers. The painting is a spectacle: the staging of the drama of the supernatural world in the theater of the natural world. A spectacle that contains another, a paralyzing and anxiety-filled one, the theme of which is expectation: the figures that people the painting are awaiting an event that is about to take place at any moment now. The center of the composition is an empty space, the point of intersection of all sorts of powers and the focal point on which all eyes are trained, a clearing in the forest of allusions and enigmas; in the center of this center there is a hazelnut on which the stone axe of the woodcutter is about to fall. Although we do not know what is hidden inside the hazelnut, we know that if the axe splits it in two, everything will change: life will commence to flow once more and the curse that has turned the figures in the painting to stone will be broken. The woodcutter is a robust young man, dressed in coarse cotton (or perhaps leather) work clothes and wearing on his head a cap from which there tumble locks of curly, reddish hair. With his feet firmly planted on the stony ground, he is grasping, with both hands, an upraised axe. Is this Dadd? How can we tell, since we can see the figure only from the back? Although it is impossible to be certain, I cannot resist the temptation to identify the figure of the woodcutter as being the painter. Dadd was shut up in the insane asylum because during

an outing in the country, in a violent fit of madness, he hacked his father to death with an axe. The woodcutter is readying himself to repeat the act, but the consequences of this symbolic repetition will be precisely the contrary of those that resulted from the original act; in the first instance, incarceration and petrification; in the second, on splitting the hazelnut apart, the woodcutter's axe breaks the spell. One disturbing detail: the axe that is about to put an end to the evil

The Fairy-Feller's Masterstroke, oil by Richard Dadd, 1855–1864 (Tate Gallery, London, photograph courtesy the gallery).

Detail of *The Fairy-Feller's Masterstroke.*

spell of petrification is a stone axe. Sympathetic magic.

We are able to see the faces of all the other figures. Some of them peek out of cracks and crevices in the ground and others form a mesmerized circle around the fateful hazelnut. Each of them is rooted to the spot as though suddenly bewitched and all of them create between them a space that is totally empty yet magnetized, the fascination of which is immediately felt by anyone contemplating the painting. I said *felt* when I should have said anticipated, for this space is a place where an apparition is imminent. And for that very reason it is, at one and the same time, absolutely empty and magnetized: nothing is *happening* except anticipation. The figures are rooted to the spot, and both literally and figuratively, they are plants and stones. Anticipation has immobilized them—the anticipation that does away with time but not anxiety. The anticipation is *eternal*: it abolishes time; the anticipation is *momentary*, an awaiting of what is imminent, what is about to happen from one moment to the next: it speeds up time. Fated to await the masterstroke of the woodcutter, the fairies gaze endlessly at a clearing in the forest that is nothing more than the focal point of their gaze and in which nothing whatsoever is happening. Dadd has painted the vision of the act of vision, the look that looks at a space in which the object looked at has been annihilated. The axe which, when it falls, will break the spell that paralyzes them, will never fall. It is an event that is always about to happen and at the same time will never happen. Between *never* and *always* there lies in wait anxiety, with its thousand feet and its single eye.

22

No painting can tell a story because nothing happens in it. Painting confronts us with fixed, unchangeable, motionless realities. In no canvas, not even excepting those that have as their theme real or supernatural happenings and those that give us the impression or the sensation of movement, does anything *happen*. In paintings things simply *are*; they do not *happen*. To speak and to write, to tell stories and to think, is to experience time elapsing, to go from one place to another: to advance. A painting has spatial limits, yet it has neither a beginning nor an end; a text is a succession that begins at one point and ends at another. To write and to speak are to trace a path: to create, to remember, to imagine a trajectory, to go toward . . . Painting offers us a vision, literature invites us to seek one and therefore traces an imaginary path toward it. Painting constructs presences, literature emits meanings and then attempts to catch up with them. Meaning is what words emit, what is beyond them, what escapes from between the meshes of the net of words and what they seek to retain or to trap. Meaning is not in the text but outside it. These words that I am writing are setting forth in search of their meaning, and that is the only meaning they have.

The palace of Galta (photograph by Eusebio Rojas).

24

Is it vision that lies at the end of the road? The neighbors' patio with its little dark wooden table and its rusty garbage can, the grove of beech trees on a prominence of the playing field of Churchill College, the spot with the pools of stagnant water and the banyan trees a hundred yards or so from what was once the entrance to Galta, are visions of reality irreducible to language. Each one of these realities is unique and to truly express it we would require a language composed solely of proper and unrepeatable names, a language that would not be a language: the double of the world, that would be neither a translation of it nor a symbol of it. Thus seeing these realities, truly seeing them, is the same as going mad: losing all names, entering the realm of the incommensurable. Or rather: returning to it, to the world before language exists. Hence, the path of poetic writing leads to the abolition of writing: at the end of it we are confronted with an inexpressible reality. The reality that poetry reveals and that appears behind language—the reality visible only through the destruction of language that the poetic act represents—is literally intolerable and maddening. At the same time, without the vision of this reality man is not man, and language is not language. Poetry gives us sustenance and destroys us, it gives us speech and dooms us to silence. It is the necessarily momentary perception (which is all that we can bear) of the incommensurable world which we one day abandon and to which we return when we die. Language sinks its roots into this world but transforms its juices and reactions into signs and symbols. Language is the consequence (or the cause) of our exile from the universe, signifying the distance between things and ourselves. At the same time it is our recourse against this distance. If our exile were to come to an end, language would come to an end: language, the measure of all things, *ratio*. Poetry is number, proportion, measure: language—except that it is a language that has turned in upon itself, that devours itself and destroys itself in order that there may appear what is other, what is without measure, the dizzying foundation, the unfathomable abyss out of which measure is born. The reverse of language.

Writing is a search for the meaning that writing itself violently expels. At the end of the search meaning evaporates and reveals to us a reality that literally is meaningless. What remains? The twofold movement of writing: a journey in the direction of meaning, a dissipation of meaning. An allegory of mortality: these phrases that I write, this path that I invent as I endeavor to describe the path that leads to Galta, become blurred, dissolve as I write: I never reach the end, and I never shall. There is no end, everything has been a perpetual beginning all over again. What I am saying is a continual saying of what I am about to say and never manage to say: I always say something else. A saying of something that the moment it is said evaporates, a saying that never says what I want to say. As I write, I journey toward meaning: as I read what I write, I blot it out, I dissolve the path. Each attempt I make ends up the same way: the dissolution of the text in the reading of it, the expulsion of the meaning through writing. The search for meaning culminates in the appearance of a reality that lies beyond the meaning and that disperses it, destroys it. We proceed from a search for meaning to its destruction in order that a reality may appear, a reality which in turn disappears. Reality and its radiance, reality and its opacity: the vision that poetic writing offers us is that of its dissolution. Poetry is empty, like the clearing in the forest in Dadd's painting: it is nothing but the *place* of the apparition which is, at the same time, that of its disappearance. *Rien n'aura lieu que le lieu.*

25

On the square-ruled wall of the terrace the damp stains and the traces of red, black, and blue paint create imaginary atlases. It is six in the afternoon. A pact between light and shadow: a universal pause. I breathe deeply: I am in the center of a time that is fully rounded, as full of itself as a drop of sunlight. I feel that ever since I was born, and even before, a before that has no when, I have been able to see the banyan tree at the corner of the esplanade growing taller and taller (a fraction of an inch each year), multiplying its aerial roots, interweaving them, descending to the earth by way of them, anchoring itself, taking root, rising again, descending again, and thus, for centuries, growing larger in a tangle of roots and branches. The banyan tree is a spider that has been spinning its interminable web for a thousand years. Discovering this causes me to feel an inhuman joy: I am rooted in this hour as the banyan tree is rooted in time immemorial. Nonetheless time does not stop: for more than two hours now Splendor and I have been walking through the great arch of the Gateway, crossing the deserted courtyard, and climbing the stairway that leads to this terrace. Time goes by yet does not go by. This hour of six in the afternoon has been, from the beginning, the same six o'clock in the afternoon, and yet minutes follow upon minutes with the same regularity as always. This hour of six in the afternoon little by little draws to a close, but each moment is transparent, and by the very fact of this transparency dissolves or becomes motionless, ceasing to flow. Six o'clock in the afternoon turns into a transparent immobility that has no depth and no reverse side: there is nothing behind it.

The notion that the very heart of time is a fixity that dissolves all images, all times, in a transparency with no depth or consistency, terrifies me. Because the present also becomes empty: it is a reflection suspended in another reflection. I search about for a reality that is less dizzying, a presence that will rescue me from this abysmal now, and I look at Splendor—but she is not looking at me: at this moment she is laughing at the gesticulations of a little monkey as it leaps from its mother's shoulder to the balustrade, swings by its tail from one of the balusters, takes a leap, falls at our feet a few steps away from us, looks up at us in terror, leaps again and this time lands on the shoulder of its mother, who growls and bares her teeth at us. I look at Splendor and through her face and her laugh I am able to make my way to another moment of another time, and there on a Paris street corner, at the intersection of the rue du Bac and the rue de Montalembert, I hear the same laugh. And this laugh is superimposed on the laugh that I hear here, on this page, as I make my way inside six o'clock in the afternoon of a day that I am creating and that has stopped still on the terrace of an abandoned house on the outskirts of Galta.

The times and the places are interchangeable: the face that I am now looking at, the one that, without seeing me, laughs at the monkey and its panic, is the one that I am looking at in another city, at another moment—on this same page. Never is the same when, the same laugh, the same stains on the wall, the same light of the same six o'clock in

Hanumān flying over the mountains, Jaipur, 19th century.

the afternoon. Each when goes by, changes, mingles with other whens, disappears and reappears. This laughter that scatters itself about here like the pearls of a broken necklace is the same laugh as always and always another, the laugh heard on a Paris street corner, the laugh of an afternoon that is drawing to a close and blending with the laugh that silently, like a purely visual cascade, or rather an absolutely mental one—not the idea of a cascade but a cascade become idea—plunges down onto my forehead and forces me to close my eyes because of the mute violence of its whiteness. Laughter: cascade: foam: unheard whiteness. Where do I hear this laughter, where do I see it? Having lost my way amid all these times and places, have I lost my past, am I living in a continuous present? Although I haven't moved, I feel that I am coming loose from myself: I am where I am and at the same time I am not where I am. The strangeness of being here, as though here were somewhere else; the strangeness of being in my body, of the fact that my body is my body and that I think what I think, hear what I hear. I am wandering far, far away from myself, by way of here, journeying along this path to Galta that I am creating as I write and that dissipates on being read. I am journeying by way of this here that is not outside and yet is not inside either; I am walking across the uneven, dusty surface of the terrace as though I were walking inside myself, but this inside of myself is outside: I see it, I see myself walking in it. "I" is an outside. I am looking at Splendor and she is not looking at me: she is looking at the little monkey. She too is coming loose from her past, she too is in her outside. She is not looking at me, she is laughing, and with a toss of her head, she makes her way inside her own laughter.

From the balustrade of the terrace, I see the courtyard below. There is no one there, the light has stopped moving, the banyan tree has firmly planted itself in its immobility. Splendor is standing at my side laughing, the little monkey is terrified and runs to hide in its mother's hairy arms, I breathe in this air as insubstantial as time. Transparency: in the end things are nothing but their visible properties. They are as we see them, they are what we see and I exist only because I see them. There is no other side, there is no bottom or crack or hole: everything is an adorable, impassible, abominable, impenetrable surface. I touch the present, I plunge my hand into the now, and it is as though I were plunging it into air, as though I were touching shadows, embracing reflections. A magic surface, at once insubstantial and impenetrable: all these realities are a fine-woven veil of presences that hide no secret. Exteriority, and nothing else: they say nothing, they keep nothing to themselves, they are simply there, before my eyes, beneath the not too harsh light of this autumn day. An indifferent state of existence, beyond beauty and ugliness, meaning and meaninglessness. The intestines spilling out of the belly of the dog whose body is rotting over there some fifty yards away from the banyan tree, the moist red beak of the vulture ripping it to pieces, the ridiculous movement of its wings sweeping the dust on the ground, what I think and feel on seeing this scene from the balustrade, amid Splendor's laughter and the little monkey's panic—these are distinct, unique, absolutely real realities, and yet they are also inconsistent, gratuitous, and in some way unreal. Realities that have no weight, no reason for being: the dog could be a pile of stones, the vulture a man or a horse, I myself a chunk of stone or another vulture, and the reality of this six o'clock in the afternoon would be no different. Or better put: *different* and *the same* are synonyms in the impartial light of this moment. Everything is the same and it is all the same whether I am who I am or someone different from who I am. On the path to Galta that always begins over and over again, imperceptibly and without my consciously willing it, as I kept walking along it and kept retracing my steps, again and again, this now of the terrace has been gradually constructed: I am riveted to the spot here, like the banyan tree trapped by its populace of intertwining aerial roots, but I might be there, in another now—that would be the same now. Each time is different; each place is different and all of them are the same place, they are all the same. Everything is now.

27

A rose and green, yellow and purple undulation, human tides, whitecaps of light on skin and hair, the inexhaustible flow of the human current that little by little, in less than an hour, inundated the entire courtyard. Leaning on the balustrade, we saw the pulse of the multitude throbbing, heard its swelling surge. A coming and going, a calm agitation that propagated itself and spread in eccentric waves, slowly filled the empty spaces, and as though it were an overflowing stream, mounted, patiently and persistently, step by step, the great stairway of the cubical building, partially in ruins, situated at the north corner of the parallelogram.

On the third and uppermost story of that massive structure, at the top of the stairway and below one of the arches crowning the building, the altar of Hanumān had been erected. The Great Monkey was represented by a relief carved in a block of black stone more than three feet high, approximately thirty inches wide, and half an inch thick, placed on, or rather, set into a platform of modest dimensions covered with a red and yellow cloth. The stone stood beneath a wooden canopy shaped like a fluted conch shell, painted gold. From the conch there hung a length of violet silk with fringes, also gilded, at the bottom. Two poles, mindful of wooden masts, stood on either side of the canopy, both of them painted blue and each of them bearing a triangular paper banner, one of them a green one and the other a white one. Scattered about on the bright red and yellow cloth covering the table of the altar were little piles of ashes from incense burned in honor of the image, and many petals, still fresh and moist, the remains of the floral offerings of the faithful. The stone was smeared with a brilliant red paste. Bathed in the lustral water, the nectar of the flowers and the melted butter of the oblations, the relief of Hanumān gleamed like the body of an athlete anointed with oil. Despite the thick red pigment, one could more or less make out the figure of the Simian, taking that extraordinary leap that brought him from the Nilgiri Mountains to the garden of the palace of Rāvana in Lankā; his left leg bent, his knee like a prow cleaving the waves, behind him his left leg extended like a wing, or rather, like an oar (his leap calls to mind flying, which in turn calls to mind swimming) and his long tail tracing a spiral: a line/a liana/the Milky Way, his one arm upraised, encircled by heavy bracelets, and the huge hand clutching a warclub, his other arm thrust forward, with the fingers of the hand spread apart like a fan or the leaf of a royal palm or like the fin of a fish or the crest of a bird (again: swimming and flying), his skull enclosed in a helmet—a fiery red meteor hurtling through space.

Like his father Vāyu, the Great Monkey "traces signs of fire in the sky if he flies; if he falls, he leaves a tail of sounds on the earth: we hear his roar but do not see his form." Hanumān, like his father, is wind, and that is why his leaps are like the flight of birds; and while he is air, he is also sound with meaning: an emitter of words, a poet. Son of the wind, poet and grammarian, Hanumān is the divine messenger, the Holy Spirit of India. He is a monkey that is a bird that is a vital and spiritual breath. Though he is chaste, his body is an inexhaustible fountain of sperm, and a single drop of sweat from his skin suffices to make the stone womb of a desert fecund. Hanumān is the friend, the counselor, and the inspirer of the poet Vālmīki. Since legend has it that the author of the *Rāmāyana* was a pariah suffering from leprosy, the pariahs of Galta, who particularly venerate Hanumān, have taken the name of the poet for their own and hence are called Balmiks. But on that altar, a black stone daubed with thick red pigment, bathed in the liquid butter of the oblations, Hanumān was above all the Fire of the sacrifice. A priest had lighted a little brazier that one of his acolytes had brought to him. Although naked from the waist up. he was not a Brahman and was not wearing the ritual cord around his neck; like the other officiants and like the majority of those present, he was a pariah. Turning his back to the worshipers who had crowded into the little sanctuary, he raised the brazier to the level of his eyes, and swinging it slowly up and down and in the direction of the eight points of the compass, he traced luminous circles and spirals in the air. The coals sizzled and smoked, the priest chanted the prayers in a whining nasal voice, and the other officiants, in accordance with the prescribed ritual, one by one cast spoonsful of melted butter into the fire: *The streams of butter gush forth (the golden rod in the center), they flow like rivers, they separate and flee like gazelles before the hunter, they leap about like women going to a love-tryst, the spoonsful of butter caress the burned wood, and the Fire accepts them with pleasure.*

With stones, little hammers, and other objects, the acolytes began to strike the iron bars hanging from the ceiling. A man appeared—wearing a coarse-woven garment, with a mask over his face, a helmet, and a rod simulating a lance. He may have represented one of the warrior monkeys who accompanied Hanumān and Sugriva on their expedition to Lankā. The acolytes continued to strike the iron bars, and a powerful and implacable storm of sound rained down on the heads of the multitude eddying about below. At the foot of the banyan tree a dozen *sādhus* had congregated, all of them advanced in years, with shaved heads or long tangled locks coated with red dust, wavy white beards, their faces smeared with paint and their foreheads decorated with signs: vertical and horizontal stripes, circles, halfmoons, tridents. Some of them were decked in white or saffron robes, others were naked, their bodies covered with ashes or cow dung, their genitals protected by a cotton pouch hanging from a cord that served as a belt. Lying stretched out on the ground, they were smoking, drinking tea or milk or bhang, laughing, conversing, praying in a half-whisper, or simply lying there silently. On hearing the sound of the bars being struck and the confused murmur of the priests' voices chanting hymns overhead, they all stood up and without forewarning, as though obeying an order that no one save them had heard, with blazing eyes and somnambulistic gestures—the gestures of someone walking in his sleep and moving about very slowly, like a diver at the bottom of the sea—they formed a circle and began to sing and dance. The crowd gathered round and followed their movements, transfixed, with smiling, respectful fascination. Leaps and chants, the flutter of bright-colored rags and sparkling tatters, luxurious poverty, flashes of splendor and wretchedness, a dance of invalids and nonagenarians, the gestures of drowned men and illuminati, dry branches of the human tree that the wind rips off and carries away, a flight of puppets, the rasping voices of stones falling in blind wells, the piercing voices of panes of glass shattering, acts of homage paid by death to life.

A sādhu in the sanctuary of Galta
(photograph by Eusebio Rojas).

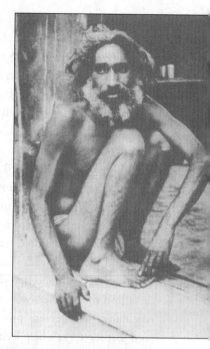

The multitude was a lake of quiet movements, one vast warm undulation. The springs had let go, the tensions were disappearing, to exist was to spread out, to overflow, to turn liquid, to return to the primordial water, to the ocean that is the mother of all. The dance of the *sādhus,* the chants of the officiants, the cries and exclamations of the multitude were bubbles rising from the great lake lying hypnotized beneath the metallic rain brought forth by the acolytes as they

A sādhu and pilgrim near Galta
(photograph by Eusebio Rojas).

struck the iron bars. In the sky overhead, insensible to the movements of the hordes of people jammed together in the courtyard and to their rites, the crows, the blackbirds, the vultures, and the parakeets imperturbably continued their flights, their disputes, and their lovemaking. A limpid, naked sky. The air too had ceased to move. Calm and indifference. A deceptive repose made up of thousands upon thousands of imperceptible changes and movements: although it appeared that the light had halted forever on the pink scar on the wall, the stone was throbbing, breathing, it was alive, its scar was becoming more and more inflamed until finally it turned into a great gaping red wound, and just as this smoldering coal was about to burst into flame, it changed its mind, contracted little by little, withdrew into itself, buried itself in its dying ardor, simply a black stain spreading over the wall now. It was the same with the sky, with the courtyard, with the crowd. Evening came amid the fallen brightnesses, submerged the flat-topped hills, blinded the reflections, turned the transparencies opaque. Congregating on the balconies from which, in other times, the princes and their wives contemplated the spectacles taking place on the esplanade, hundreds and hundreds of monkeys, with that curiosity of theirs that is a terrible form of the indifference of the universe, watched the feast being celebrated by the men down below.

28

When spoken or written, words advance and inscribe themselves one after the other upon the space that is theirs: the sheet of paper, the wall of air. They advance, they go from here to there, they trace a path: they go by, they are time. Although they never stop moving from one point to another and thus describe a horizontal or vertical line (depending on the nature of the writing), from another perspective, the simultaneous or converging one which is that of poetry, the phrases that go to make up a text appear as great motionless, transparent blocks: the text does not go anywhere, language ceases to flow. A dizzying repose because it is a fabric woven of nothing but clarity: each page reflects all the others, and each one is the echo of the one that precedes or follows it—the echo and the answer, rhyme and metaphor. There is no end and no beginning: everything is center. Neither before nor after, neither in front of nor behind, neither inside nor outside: everything is in everything. Like a spiral seashell, all times are this time now, which is nothing except, like cut crystal, the momentary condensation of other times into an insubstantial clarity. Condensation and dispersion, the secret sign that the now makes to itself just as it dissipates. Simultaneous perspective does not look upon language as a path because it is not the search for meaning that orients it. Poetry does not attempt to discover what there is at the end of the road; it conceives of the text as a series of transparent strata within which the various parts—the different verbal and semantic currents—produce momentary configurations as they intertwine or break apart, as they reflect each other or efface each other. Poetry contemplates itself, fuses with itself, and obliterates itself in the crystallizations of language. Apparitions, metamorphoses, volatilizations, precipitations of presences. These configurations are crystallized time: although they are perpetually in motion, they always point to the same hour—the hour of change. Each one of them contains all the others, each one is inside the others: change is only the oft-repeated and ever-different metaphor of identity.

Bharat transporting Hanumān to battlefield with his magic arrow, Oudh, 19th century.

The vision of poetry is that of the convergence of every point. The end of the road. This is the vision of Hanumān as he leaps (a geyser) from the valley to the mountaintop or as he plunges (a meteorite) from the star to the bottom of the sea: the dizzying oblique vision that reveals the universe not as a succession, a movement, but as an assemblage of spaces and times, a repose. Convergence is repose because at its apex the various movements, as they meet, obliterate each other; at the same time, from this peak of immobility, we perceive the universe as an assemblage of worlds in rotation. Poems: crystallizations of the universal play of analogy, transparent objects which, as they reproduce the mechanism and the rotary motion of analogy, are waterspouts of new analogies. In them the world plays at being the world, which is the game of similarities engendered by differences and that of contradictory similarities. Hanumān wrote on the rocky cliffs of a mountain the *Mahanātaka*, based on the same subject as the *Rāmāyana*; on reading it, Vālmīki feared that it would overshadow his poem and begged Hanumān to keep his drama a secret. The Monkey yielded to the poet's entreaty, uprooted the mountain, and threw the rocks into the sea. Vālmīki's pen and ink on the paper are a metaphor of the bolt of lightning and the rain with which

Hanumān wrote his drama on the rocky mountainside. Human writing reflects that of the universe, it is its translation, but also its metaphor: it says something totally different and it says the same thing. At the point of convergence the play of similarities and differences cancels itself out in order that identity alone may shine forth. The illusion of motionlessness, the play of mirrors of the one: identity is completely empty; it is a crystallization and in its transparent core the movement of analogy begins all over once again.

All poems say the same thing and each poem is unique. Each part reproduces the others and each part is different. As I began these pages I decided to follow literally the metaphor of the title of the collection that they were intended for, the Paths of Creation, and to write, to describe a text that was really a path and that could be read and followed as such. As I wrote, the path to Galta grew blurred or else I lost my bearings and went astray in the trackless wilds. Again and again I was obliged to return to the starting point. Instead of advancing, the text circled about itself. Is destruction creation? I do not know, but I do know that creation is not destruction. At each turn the text opened out into another one, at once its translation and its transposition: a spiral of repetitions and reiterations that have dissolved into a negation of writing as a path. Today I realize that my text was not going anywhere—except to meet itself. I also per-

Nude, photographic proof taken by an electronic process, 1968, Leon D. Harmon (artist) and Kenneth C. Knowlton (engineer), (University of California).

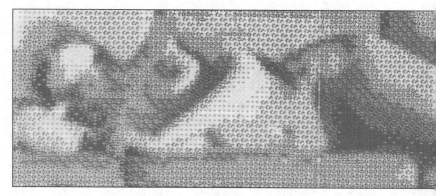

ceive that repetitions are metaphors and that reiterations are analogies: a system of mirrors that little by little have revealed another text. In this text Hanumān contemplates the garden of Rāvana like a page of calligraphy like the harem of the same Rāvana as described in the *Rāmāyana* like this page on which the swaying motions of the beeches in the grove opposite my window accumulate on this page like the shadows of two lovers projected by the fire on a wall like the stains of monsoon rains on a ruined palace of the abandoned town of Galta like the rectangular space on which there surge the wave upon wave of a multitude contemplated from the crumbling balconies by hundreds of monkeys like an image of writing and reading like a metaphor of the path and the pilgrimage to the sanctuary like the final dissolution of the path and the convergence of all the texts in this paragraph like a metaphor of the embrace of bodies. Analogy: universal transparency: seeing in this that.

29

The body of Splendor as it divides, disperses, dissipates itself in my body as it divides, disperses, dissipates itself in the body of Splendor:

breathing, warmth, outline, bulk that beneath the pressure of my fingertips slowly ceases to be a confusion of pulses and gathers itself together and reunites with itself,

vibrations, waves that strike my closed eyelids as the street lamps go out and dawn staggers through the city:

the body of Splendor before my eyes that gaze down on her as she lies between the sheets as I walk toward her in the dawn in the green light filtering through the enormous leaves of a banana tree onto an ocher footpath to Galta that leads me to this page where the body of Splendor lies between the sheets as I write on this page and as I read what I write,

an ocher footpath that suddenly starts walking, a river of burned waters seeking its path between the sheets, Splendor rises from the bed and walks about in the shadowy light of the room with staggering steps as the street lamps of the city go out:

she is searching for something, the dawn is searching for something, the young woman halts and looks at me: a squirrel gaze, a dawn gaze that lingers amid the leaves of the banyan tree along the ocher path that leads from Galta to this page, a gaze that is a well to be drunk from, a gaze in which I write the word reconciliation:

Splendor is this page, that which separates (liberates) and weaves together (reconciles) the various parts that compose it,

that which (the one who) is there, at the end of what I say, at the end of this page, and appears here as this phrase is uttered, as it dissipates,

The palace of Galta (18th century), (photograph by Eusebio Rojas).

the act inscribed on this page and the bodies (the phrases) that as they embrace give form to this act, this body:

the liturgical sequence and the dissipation of all rites through the double profanation (yours and mine), the reconciliation/liberation, of writing and reading

Cambridge, England, summer, 1970

MARCEL DUCHAMP: APPEARANCE STRIPPED BARE

*Translated from the Spanish
by Rachel Phillips and Donald Gardner*

CONTENTS

List of Illustrations 379
Foreword 380
The Castle of Purity 382
* Water Writes Always in * Plural 443
Chronology 504

ILLUSTRATIONS

Comb, *1916*. 392

Ball of Twine (With Hidden Noise), *1916*. 393

Air de Paris. 394

Why Not Sneeze Rrose Sélavy? *1921*. 395

The Large Glass, *or* The Bride Stripped Bare by Her
    Bachelors, Even, 1915–23. 401

Diagram based on The Large Glass Completed, 1965. 402

Portrait (Dulcinea), *1911*. 406

Typographic version of the Large Glass. 408

Tantric Imagery of Kali. 426

Door of Given: 1. The Waterfall, 2. The Illuminating 448
    Gas, 1946–66.

Tu m'. 450

*Window installation at Gotham Book Mart for publication
    of Andre Breton's Arcane 17.* 452

Cols alités (Bedridden Mountains), *1959*. 454

Photo of Duchamp and his wife at the foot of a waterfall. 458

The Triumph of Venus. 461

The Bride Stripped Bare by Her Bachelors, 1912 463

To Be Looked at (from the Other Side of the Glass)
    with One Eye, Close to, for Almost an Hour, *1918*. 475

Door of Given: 1. The Illuminating Gas, 2. The Waterfall,
    1948–49. 502

FOREWORD

■ In 1923 Marcel Duchamp left the *Large Glass (The Bride Stripped Bare by Her Bachelors, Even)* "finally unfinished." That was when the legend began: one of the most famous painters of our century had abandoned art to devote himself to chess. But in 1969, a few months after his death, critics and public discovered to their amazement that Duchamp had been working in secret for twenty years (1946-66) on a work that was probably no less important and complex than the *Large Glass*. It was an Assemblage called *Etant donnés: 1° la chute d'eau, 2° le gaz d'éclairage (Given: 1. The Waterfall, 2. The Illuminating Gas)*, and it is now housed in the Philadelphia Museum of Art, as are most of Duchamp's works. The title of the Assemblage alludes to one of the most important notes in the *Green Box*, that collection of ninety-three documents (photographs, drawings, and manuscript notes from 1911 to 1915) published in 1934 and constituting a sort of guidebook or manual to the *Large Glass*. And so the new work may be seen as another version of *The Bride Stripped Bare by Her Bachelors, Even*.

In the autumn of 1973 a large retrospective Duchamp exhibition was organized in the United States by the Philadelphia Museum of Art and the Museum of Modem Art of New York. At the request of both institutions I wrote for the occasion an essay on *Given: 1. The Waterfall, 2. The Illuminating Gas.* That essay complements another text of mine, written in 1966 and included in the "portmanteau book" *Marcel Duchamp, or the Castle of Purity* (New York, 1970). The present volume comprises both studies. The first, after a brief introduction to Duchamp's work, analyzes the *Large Glass;* the second examines the Assemblage and shows the relationship between these two works. When I was preparing this new edition I made a few scattered corrections in the first essay; in the process I added some thirty pages in which I try to uncover all the elements making up the *Large Glass,* the function of each one, and the relationships that unite them. I also revised the second essay and added another fifty pages. In these, my most recent reflections on the subject, I have tried to show where Duchamp's work belongs in the main tradition of the West—the physics and metaphysics not of sex but of love–and its meta-ironic relationship with that tradition.

It is above all the rigorous unity of Marcel Duchamp's work that surprises anyone reviewing it in its entirety. In fact, everything he did revolves around a single object, as elusive as life itself. From the *Nude Descending a Staircase* to the naked girl in the Philadelphia Assemblage, via the *Bride Stripped Bare by Her Bachelors, Even,* his life's work can be seen as different moments—the different appearances—of the same reality. Anamorphosis in the literal meaning of the word: to see this work in its successive forms is to return to the original form, the true source of appearances. An attempt at revelation, or, as he used to say, "ultrarapid exposure." He was fascinated by a four-dimensional object and the shadows it throws, those shadows we call realities. The object is an Idea, but the Idea is resolved at last into a naked girl: a presence.

—**O.P.**

Mexico, August 20, 1976.

THE CASTLE OF PURITY

Sens: on peut voir regarder.
Peut-on entendre écouter, sentir?

—M.D.

Perhaps the two painters who have had the greatest influence on our century are Pablo Picasso and Marcel Duchamp. The former by his works; the latter by a single work that is nothing less than the negation of work in the modern sense of the word. The transformations that Picasso's painting has gone through—metamorphoses would be a more accurate word—have astonished us consistently over a period of more than fifty years; Duchamp's inactivity is no less astonishing and, in its way, no less fruitful. The creations of the great Spanish artist have been incarnations and, at the same time, prophecies of the mutations that our age has suffered between the end of Impressionism and the Second World War. Incarnations: in his canvases and his objects the modern spirit becomes visible and palpable; prophecies: the transformations in his painting reveal our time as one which affirms itself only by negating itself and which negates itself only in order to invent and transcend itself. Not a precipitate of pure time, not the crystallizations of Klee, Kandinsky, or Braque, but time itself, its brutal urgency, the immediate imminence of the present moment. Right from the start, Duchamp set up a vertigo of delay in opposition to the vertigo of acceleration. In one of the notes in the celebrated *Green Box* he writes: "use *delay* instead of 'picture' or 'painting'; 'picture on glass' becomes 'delay in glass' . . ." This sentence gives us a glimpse into the meaning of his activity: painting is a criticism of movement, but movement is the criticism of painting. Picasso is what is going to happen and what is happening, he is posterity and archaic time, the distant ancestor and our next-door neighbor. Speed permits him to be two places at once, to belong to all the centuries without letting go of the here and now. He is not the movements of painting in the twentieth century; rather, he is movement become painting. He paints out of urgency and, above all, it is urgency that he paints: he is the painter of time. Duchamp's pictures are the presentation of movement: the analysis, the decomposition, the reverse of speed. Picasso's drawings move rapidly across the motionless space of the canvas. In the works of Duchamp space begins to walk and take on form; it becomes a machine that spins arguments and philosophizes; it resists movement with delay and delay with irony. The pictures of the former are images; those of the latter are a meditation on the image.

Picasso is an artist of an inexhaustible and uninterrupted fertility; the latter painted fewer than fifty canvases and these were done in under ten years: Duchamp abandoned painting, in the proper sense of the term, when he was hardly twenty-five years old. To be sure, he went on "painting" for another ten years, but everything he did from 1913 onward is a part of his attempt to substitute "painting-idea" for "painting-painting." This negation of painting, which he calls "olfactory" (because of its smell of turpentine) and "retinal" (purely visual), was the beginning of his true *work*. A work without works: there are no pictures except the *Large Glass* (the great delay), the Readymades, a few *gestures*, and a long silence. Picasso's work reminds one of that of his compatriot Lope de Vega, and in speaking of it, one should in fact use the plural: the works. Everything Duchamp has done is summed up in the *Large Glass*, which was "finally unfinished" in 1923. Picasso has rendered our century visible to us; Duchamp has shown us that all the arts, including the visual, are born and come to an end in an area that is invisible. Against the lucidity of instinct he opposed the instinct for lucidity: the invisible is not obscure or mysterious, it is transparent . . . The rapid parallel I have drawn is not an invidious comparison. Both of them, like all real artists, and not excluding the so-called minor artists, are incomparable. I have linked their names because it seems to me that each of them has in his own way succeeded in defining our age: the former by what he affirms, by his discoveries; the latter by what he negates, by his explorations. I don't know if they are the "greatest" painters of the first half of the century. I don't know what the word "greatest" means when applied to an artist. The case of Duchamp—like that of Max Ernst, Klee, De Chirico, Kandinsky, and a few others—fascinates me not because he is the "greatest," but because he is unique. This is the word that is appropriate to him and defines him.

The first pictures of Duchamp show a precocious mastery. They are the ones, however, that some critics describe as "fine painting." A short time afterward, under the influence of his elder brothers, Jacques Villon and the sculptor Raymond Duchamp-Villon, he passed from Fauvism to a restrained and analytical Cubism. Early in 1911, he made the acquaintance of Francis Picabia and Guillaume Apollinaire. It was undoubtedly his friendship with these two men that precipitated an evolution that had until then seemed normal. His desire to go beyond Cubism can already be seen in a canvas of this period; it is the portrait of a woman passing by: a girl glimpsed once, loved, and never seen again. The canvas shows a figure that unfolds into (or fuses with) five female silhouettes. As a representation of movement or, to be more precise, a decomposing and superimposing of the positions of a moving body it anticipates the *Nude Descending a Staircase*. The picture is called *Portrait (Dulcinea)*. I mention this detail because by means of the title Duchamp introduces a psychological element, in this case affectionate and ironic, into the composition. It is the beginning of his rebellion against visual and tactile painting, against "retinal" art. Later he will assert that the title is an *essential* element of painting, like color and drawing. In the same year, he painted a few other canvases, all of them striking in their execution and some of them ferocious in their pitiless vision of reality: analytical Cubism is transformed into mental surgery. This period closes with a noteworthy oil painting: *Coffee Mill*. The illustrations to three poems of Laforgue also come from this time. These drawings are interesting for two reasons: On the one hand, one of them anticipates the *Nude Descending a Staircase;* on the other, they reveal that Duchamp was a painter of *ideas* right from the start and that he never yielded to the fallacy of thinking of painting as a purely manual and visual art.

In a conversation he had in 1946 with the critic James Johnson Sweeney,[*] Duchamp hints at the influence of Laforgue on his painting:

* Quoted in *Marchand du sel*, écrits de Marcel Duchamp, introduction by Michel Sanouillet (Paris: Le Terrain Vague, 1958).

"The idea for the *Nude* . . . came from a drawing which I had made in 1911 to illustrate Jules Laforgue's poem *Encore à cet astre* . . . Rimbaud and Lautréamont seemed too old to me at the time. I wanted something younger. Mallarmé and Laforgue were closer to my taste . . ." In the same conversation, Duchamp emphasizes that it was not so much the poetry of Laforgue that interested him as his titles (*Comice agricole*, for example). This confession throws some light on the *verbal* origin of his creative activity as a painter. His fascination with language is of an intellectual order; it is the most perfect instrument for producing meanings and at the same time for destroying them. The pun is a miraculous device because in one and the same phrase we exalt the power of the language to convey meaning only in order, a moment later, to abolish it the more completely. Art for Duchamp, all the arts, obey the same law: meta-irony is inherent in their very spirit. It is an irony that destroys its own negation and, hence, returns in the affirmative. Nor is his mention of Mallarmé fortuitous. Between the *Nude* and *Igitur* there is a disturbing analogy: the descent of the staircase. How can one fail to see in the slow movement of the woman-machine an echo or an answer to that solemn moment in which *Igitur* abandons his room forever and goes step by step down the stairs which lead him to the crypt of his ancestors? In both cases, there is a rupture and a descent into a zone of silence. There the solitary spirit will be confronted with the absolute and its mask, chance.

Almost without realizing it, as if drawn by a magnet, I have passed over in a page and a half the ten years that separate his early works from the *Nude*. I must pause here. This picture is one of the pivotal works of modern painting: it marks the end of Cubism and the beginning of a development that hasn't yet been exhausted. Superficially—though his work is constant proof that no one is less concerned with the superficial than Duchamp—the *Nude* would seem to draw its inspiration from preoccupations similar to those of the Futurists: the desire to represent movement, the disintegrated vision of space, the cult of the machine. Chronology excludes the possibility of an influence: the first Futurist exhibition in Paris was held in 1912 and, a year before, Duchamp had already painted a sketch in oils for the *Nude*. The similarity, moreover, is only an apparent one: the Futurists wanted to suggest movement by means of a dynamic painting; Duchamp applies the notion of delay—or, rather, of analysis—to movement. His aim is more objective and goes closer to the bone: he doesn't claim to give the illusion of movement—a Baroque or Mannerist idea that the Futurists inherited—but to decompose it and offer a static representation of a changing object. It is true that Futurism also rejects the Cubist conception of the motionless object, but Duchamp goes beyond stasis and movement; he fuses them in order to dissolve them the more easily. Futurism is obsessed by sensation, Duchamp by ideas. Their use of color is also different. The Futurists revel in a painting that is brilliant, passionate, and almost always explosive. Duchamp came from Cubism and his colors are less lyrical; they are denser and more restrained: it is not brilliance that he is after but rigor.

The differences are even greater if we turn from the external features of the painting to considering its real significance, that is to say, if we really penetrate the vision of the artist. (Vision is not only what we see; it is a stance taken, an idea, a geometry—a *point of view* in both senses of the phrase.) Above all, it is one's attitude toward the machine. Duchamp is not an adept of its cult; on the contrary, unlike the Futurists, he was one of the first to denounce the ruinous character of modern mechanical activity. Machines are great producers of waste, and the refuse they leave increases in geometric proportion to their productive capacity. To prove the point, all one needs to do is to walk through any of our cities and breathe its polluted atmosphere. Machines are agents of destruction and it follows from this that the only mechanical devices that inspire Duchamp are those that function in an unpredictable manner—the antimachines. These apparatuses are the equivalent of the puns: the unusual ways in which they work nullify them as machines. Their relation to utility is the same as that of delay to movement; they are without sense or meaning. They are machines that distill criticism of themselves.

The *Nude* is an antimachine. The first irony consists in the fact that we don't even know if there is a nude in the picture. Encased in a metal corset or coat of mail, it is invisible. This suit of iron reminds us not so much of a piece of medieval armor as of the body of an automobile or a fuselage. Another stroke that distinguishes it from Futurism is the fact that it is a fuselage caught in the act not of flight but of a slow fall. It is a mixture of pessimism and humor: a feminine myth, the nude woman, is turned into a far more gloomy and threatening apparatus. I will mention, as a last point, a factor that was already present in his earlier works: rational violence, so much more ruthless than the physical violence that attracts Picasso. Robert Lebel says that in Duchamp's painting "the nude plays exactly the same role as the old drawings of the human skeleton in the anatomy books: it is an object for internal investigation."* For my part I would emphasize that the word "internal" should be understood in two senses: it is a reflection on the internal organs of an object and it is interior reflection, self-analysis. The object is a metaphor, an image of Duchamp: his reflection on the object is at the same time a meditation on himself. To a certain extent each one of his paintings is a symbolic self-portrait. Hence the plurality of meanings and points of view of a work like the *Nude:* it is pure plastic creation and meditation on painting and movement; it is the criticism and culminating point of Cubism; it is the beginning of another kind of painting and the end of the career of Duchamp as a pictorial artist; it is the myth of the nude woman and the destruction of this myth; it is machine and irony, symbol and autobiography.

After the *Nude,* Duchamp painted a few extraordinary pictures: *The King and the Queen Surrounded by Swift Nudes, The Passage from Virgin to Bride,* and *Bride.* In these canvases the human figure has disappeared completely. Its place is taken not by abstract forms but by transmutations of the human being into delirious pieces of mechanism. The object is reduced to its most simple elements: volume becomes line; the line, a series of dots. Painting is converted into symbolic cartography; the object into idea. This implacable reduction is not really a system of painting but a method of internal investigation. It is not the philosophy of painting but painting as philosophy. Moreover, it is a philosophy of plastic signs that is ceaselessly destroyed, as philosophy, by a sense of humor. The appearance of human machines might make one think of the automatons of De Chirico. It would be quite absurd to compare the two artists. The poetic value of the figures of the Italian painter comes from the juxtaposition

* Robert Lebel, *Sur Marcel Duchamp* (Paris: Trianon, 1959).

of modernity with antiquity; the four wings of his lyricism are melancholy and invention, nostalgia and prophecy. I mention De Chirico not because there is any similarity between him and Duchamp but because he is one more example of the disturbing invasion of modern painting by machines and robots. Antiquity and the Middle Ages thought of the automaton as a magical entity; from the Renaissance onward, especially in the seventeenth and eighteenth centuries, it was a pretext for philosophical speculation; Romanticism converted it into erotic obsession; today, because of science, it is a real possibility. The female machines of Duchamp remind us less of De Chirico and other modern painters than of the Eve Future of Villiers de L'Isle-Adam. Like her, they are daughters of satire and eroticism, although, unlike the invention of the Symbolist poet, their form doesn't imitate the human body. Their beauty, if this word can be applied to them, is not anthropomorphic. The only beauty that Duchamp is interested in is the beauty of "indifference": a beauty free at last from the notion of beauty, equidistant from the romanticism of Villiers and from contemporary cybernetics. The figures of Kafka, De Chirico, and others take their inspiration from the human body; those of Duchamp are mechanical devices and their humanity is not corporeal. They are machines without vestiges of humanity, and yet, their function is more sexual than mechanical, more symbolic than sexual. They are ideas or, better still, *relations*—in the physical sense, and also in the sexual and linguistic; they are propositions and, by virtue of the law of meta-irony, counterpropositions. They are symbol-machines.

There is no need to seek further for the origins of Duchamp's delirious machines. The union of these two words—"machine" and "delirium," "method" and "madness"—brings to mind the figure of Raymond Roussel. Duchamp himself has on various occasions referred to that memorable night in 1911 when—together with Apollinaire, Picabia, and Gabrielle Buffet—he went to a performance of *Impressions d'Afrique*. To his discovery of Roussel must be added that of Jean-Pierre Brisset.* In the conversation with Sweeney referred to earlier, Duchamp talks enthu-

---

* For Brisset see the *Anthologie de l'humour noir* by André Breton (Paris: Sagittaire, 1940).

siastically about both people: "Brisset and Rousseau were the two men I most admired at that time for the wildness of their imaginations . . . Brisset was preoccupied with the philological analysis of language—an analysis that consisted of spinning an unbelievable web of double entendres and puns. He was a kind of Douanier Rousseau of philology. But it was fundamentally Roussel who was responsible for my glass, *The Bride Stripped Bare by Her Bachelors, Even*. This play of his, which I saw with Apollinaire, helped me greatly on one side of my expression. I saw at once that I could use Roussel as an influence. I felt that as a painter it was much better to be influenced by a writer than by another painter. And Roussel showed me the way . . ."

The Bride is a "transposition," in the sense that Mallarmé gave the word, of the literary method of Roussel to painting. Although at that time the strange text in which Roussel explains his no less strange method, *Comment j'ai écrit certains de mes livres*, had not yet been published, Duchamp intuited the process: juxtaposing two words with similar sounds but different meanings, and finding a verbal bridge between them. It is the carefully reasoned and delirious development of the principle that inspires the pun. What is more, it is the conception of language as a structure in movement, this discovery of modern linguistics that has had so much influence on the anthropology of Lévi-Strauss and, later, on the new French criticism. For Roussel, of course, the method was not a philosophy but a literary method; equally, for Duchamp, it is the strongest and most effective form of meta-irony. The game that Duchamp is playing is more complex because the combination is not only verbal but also plastic and mental. At the same time, it contains an element that is absent in Roussel: criticism, irony. Duchamp *knows* that it is insane. Roussel's influence is not limited to the method of delirium. In the *Impressions d'Afrique*, there is a painting machine; although Duchamp did not fall into the trap of naïvely repeating the device literally, he resolved to suppress the hand, the brushstrokes, and all personal traces from his painting. Instead, ruler and compass. His intention wasn't to paint like a machine but to make use of machines for painting. However, his attitude does not show any affinity for the religion of the machine: every mechanism must produce its own antidote, meta-irony.

The element of laughter doesn't make the machines more human, but it does connect them with their center, which is man, with the source of their energy, which is hesitancy and contradiction. "Beauty of precision" in the service of indetermination: contradictory machines.

In the summer of 1912, Marcel Duchamp went to Munich for a time. There he painted several pictures that laid the groundwork for his "magnum opus," if it is permissible to use the terms of alchemy to describe the *Large Glass: Virgin (No. 1 and No. 2), The Passage from Virgin to Bride*, the Bride, and the first drawing on the theme of *The Bride Stripped Bare by Her Bachelors*, still without the adverb that makes the phrase stumble. The project of the *Large Glass* was on his mind from 1912 to 1923. Despite this central preoccupation, he was possessed by a will to contradiction that nothing and no one escaped, not even himself and his work, and there were long periods in which he almost totally lost interest in his idea. His ambiguous attitude to the work—whether to realize it or to abandon it—found a solution that contained all the possibilities that he could adopt toward it: to contradict it. This is, in my opinion, the meaning of his activity over all these years, from the invention of the Readymades and the puns and word games distributed under the female pseudonym Rrose Sélavy, to the optical machines, the short *Anémic Cinéma* (in collaboration with Man Ray), and his intermittent but central participation first in the Dada movement and later in Surrealism. It is impossible in an essay of this length to enumerate all Duchamp's activities, gestures, and inventions after his return from Germany.[*] I will mention only a few of them.

The first was his journey to Zone, a community in the Juras, again in the company of Apollinaire, Picabia, and Gabrielle Buffet. This excursion, to which we owe the title of the poem by Apollinaire that opens *Alcools*, already foretells the future explosion of Dada. The enigmatic marginal notes of the *Green Box* mention this brief journey, which was no less deci-

---

[*] Despite the time elapsed, the book by Robert Lebel that I have already quoted is still the most lucid study of Duchamp's life and development. On the puns, see *Duchamp du Signe* (Paris: Flammarion, 1975), which is a collection of his writings by Michel Sanouillet and Elmer Peterson. This volume completes and replaces *Marchand du Sel*.

sive than the one to Munich in the same year. In the personal evolution of Duchamp it has a significance analogous to his discovery of Roussel: it confirms his decision to break not only with "retinal" painting but also with the traditional conception of art and the common use of language (communication). In 1913 the first exhibition of modern art (the Armory Show) was held in New York and *Nude Descending a Staircase*, which was shown there, obtained an immediate and literally scandalous renown. It is significant—exemplary, I should say—that in the same year, Duchamp gave up "painting" and looked for employment that would allow him to dedicate himself freely to his investigations. Thanks to a recommendation from Picabia, he found work in the Bibliothèque Sainte-Geneviève.

Many notes, drawings, and calculations have been preserved from this period, almost all of them relating to the long-delayed execution of the *Large Glass*. Duchamp calls these notes *physique amusante*. They could also be called *comic calculations*. Here is an example: "a straight thread one meter long falls from a height of one meter onto a horizontal plane and, twisting *as it pleases*, gives us a new model for the unit of length." Duchamp carried out the experiment three times, so that we have three units, all three of them equally valid, and not just one as we have in our poor everyday geometry. The three threads are preserved in the position in which they fell, in a croquet box: they are "canned chance." Another example: "By *condescension* this weight is denser going down than going up." All these formulas have the aim of rendering useless our notions of left and right, here and there, East and West. If the center is in a state of permanent seism, if the ancient notions of solid matter and clear and distinct reason disappear and give place to indetermination, the result is general *disorientation*. Duchamp's intention is to get rid forever of "the possibility of recognizing or identifying any two things as being like each other": the only laws that interest him are the laws of exception, which apply only for one case and for one occasion only. His attitude to language is no different. He imagines an alphabet of signs to denote only the words that we call abstract ("which have no concrete reference") and concludes: "This alphabet very probably is suitable only for the description of this picture." Painting is writing, and the *Large Glass* is a text that we have to decipher.

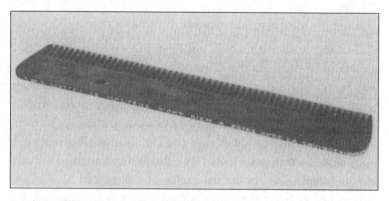

Comb, 1916. (Readymade.) Philadelphia Museum of Art: The Louise and Walter Arensberg Collection.

In 1913, the first Readymade appears: *Bicycle Wheel.* The original has been lost, but an American collector possesses a version of 1951. Little by little others arrive: *Comb, With Hidden Noise, Corkscrew, Pharmacy* (a chromolithograph), *Water & Gas on Every Floor, Apolinère Enameled* (an advertisement for Sapolin enamel), *Pocket Chess Set,* and a few others. There aren't many of them; Duchamp exalts the gesture without ever falling, like so many modern artists, into gesticulation. In some cases the Readymades are pure, that is, they pass without modification from the state of being an everyday object to that of being a "work of anti-art;" on other occasions they are altered or rectified, generally in an ironic manner tending to prevent any confusion between them and artistic objects. The most famous of them are *Fountain,* a urinal sent to the Independents exhibition in New York, and rejected by the selection committee; *L.H.O.O.Q.,* a reproduction of the *Mona Lisa* provided with a beard and mustache; *Air de Paris,* a 50-cc glass ampul that contains a sample of the atmosphere of that city; Bottlerack; Why Not Sneeze?, a birdcage that holds pieces of marble shaped like sugar cubes and a wooden thermometer . . . In 1915, to avoid the war and encouraged by the expectations that the *Nude* had aroused, he went to New York for a long period. He founded two pre-Dadaist reviews there, and with his friend Picabia and a handful of artists of various nationalities, he went about his work of stimulating, shocking, and bewildering people. In 1918, Duchamp lived for a few months in Buenos Aires. He told me that he spent the nights playing chess and slept during the day. His arrival coincided with a coup d'état and other disturbances that "made movement difficult." He made very few acquaintances—no one who was an artist, a poet, or a thinking individual. It is a pity: I don't know of anybody with a temperament closer to his own than Macedonio Fernández.

In the same year (1918) he returned to Paris. Tangential but decisive activity in the Dada movement. Return to New York. Preparatory work on the *Large Glass*, including the incredible "dust raising," which we can see today thanks to an admirable photograph by Man Ray. Explorations in the domain of optical art, static or in movement: *Rotorelief, Rotary Glass Plate (Precision Optics), Rotary Demisphere*, and other experiments that are among the antecedents of Op Art. Continuation and final abandonment of the *Large Glass*. Growing interest in chess and publication of a treatise on a move. Monte Carlo, and an abortive attempt to discover a formula that would enable him neither to lose nor to win at roulette. Participates in various exhibitions and manifestations of the Surrealists. During the Second World War settles finally in New York. Marriage to Teeny Sattler. Interviews, fame, influence on the new painting of England and America (Jasper Johns, Rauschenberg) and even music (John Cage) and dance (Merce Cunningham). The chess game goes on. And always the same attitude to good fortune or bad—meta-irony. In the summer of 1967, when I heard that they were going to hold a retrospective exhibition of his work in London, I asked him, "When will they have one in Paris?"

Ball of Twine (With Hidden Noise), *1916. (Readymade.) Philadelphia Museum of Art: The Louise and Walter Arensberg Collection.*

Air de Paris (Readymade.) Philadelphia Museum of Art: The Louise and Walter Arensberg Collection.

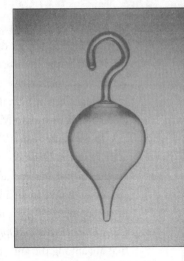

He answered me with an indefinable gesture and added, "No one is a prophet in his own country." Freedom personified, he is not even afraid of the commonplace, which is the bogey of most modern artists . . . This summary of his life leaves out many things, many encounters, various names of poets and painters and of women whom he found charming or who were charmed by him. It is impossible, however, not to mention the *Box in a Valise* (1941) and the *Green Box* (1934). The former contains miniature reproductions of almost all his works. The latter holds ninety-three documents—sketches, calculations, and notes from 1911 to 1915—and a colorplate of *The Bride*. These documents are the key, though incomplete, to the *Large Glass:* "I wanted to make a book, or rather, a catalog that would explain every detail of my picture."*

The Readymades are anonymous objects that the artist's gratuitous gesture, the mere fact of choosing them, converts into works of art. At the same time this gesture does away with the notion of art object. The essence of the act is contradiction; it is the plastic equivalent of the pun. As the latter destroys meaning, the former destroys the idea of value. The Readymades are not anti-art, like so many modern creations, but rather *an-artistic*. Neither art nor anti-art, but something in between, indifferent, existing in a void. The wealth of commentaries on their significance—some of them would certainly have made Duchamp laugh—shows that their interest is not plastic but critical or philosophical. It

---

* "Conversations avec Marcel Duchamp," a chapter of Alain Jouffroy's book, *Une Révolution du regard* (Paris: Gallimard, 1964). In 1967, after this essay was written, another collection of notes appeared that completes and amplifies those in the *Green Box*. The new collection is entitled *In the Infinitive*, also known as the *White Box*. It is not impossible that still more unpublished notes on the *Large Glass* and its speculations may be in existence.

would be senseless to argue about their beauty or ugliness, firstly because they are beyond beauty and ugliness, and secondly because they are not creations but signs, questioning or negating the act of creation. The Readymade does not postulate a new value: it is a jibe at what we call valuable. It is criticism in action: a kick at the work of art ensconced on its pedestal of adjectives. The act of criticism unfolds in two stages. The first belongs to the realm of hygiene, intellectual cleanliness—the Readymade is a criticism of taste; the second is an attack on the idea of the work of art.

For Duchamp, good taste is no less harmful than bad. We all know that there is no essential difference between them—yesterday's bad taste is the good taste of today—but what is taste? It is what we call pretty, beautiful, ugly, stupendous, marvelous, without having any clear understanding of its raison d'être: it is execution, construction, style, quality—the trademark. Primitive people don't have any idea of taste; they rely on instinct and tradition—that is to say, they repeat almost instinctively certain archetypes. Taste probably came into existence with the first cities, the state, and the division of classes. In the modern West it began in the Renaissance, but was unaware of itself until the Baroque period. In the eighteenth century it was the distinguishing mark of the courtier, and later, in the nineteenth, the sign of the parvenu. Today, since popular art is extinct, it tends to propagate itself among the masses. Its birth coincides

with the disappearance of religious art, and its development and supremacy are due, as much as anything, to the open market for artistic objects and to the bourgeois revolution. (A similar phenomenon, though it is not identical, can be seen

Why Not Sneeze Rrose Sélavy? *1921. (Readymade.) Philadelphia Museum of Art: The Louise and Walter Arensberg Collection.*

in certain epochs of the history of China and Japan.) "There's no law about tastes," says the Spanish proverb. In fact, taste evades both examination and judgment; it is a matter for samplers. It oscillates between instinct and fashion, style and prescription. As a notion of art it is skin-deep both in the sensuous and in the social meaning of the term: it titillates and is a mark of distinction. In the first case it reduces art to sensation; in the second it introduces a social hierarchy founded on a reality as mysterious and arbitrary as purity of blood or the color of one's skin. The process has become accentuated in our time: since Impressionism, painting has been converted into materials, color, drawing, texture, sensibility, sensuality—ideas are reduced to a tube of paint and contemplation to sensation.* The Readymade is a criticism of "retinal" and manual art; after he had proved to himself that he "mastered his craft," Duchamp denounced the superstition of craft. The artist is not the maker of things; his works are not pieces of workmanship—they are acts. There is a possibly unconscious echo in this attitude of the repugnance Rimbaud felt for the pen: *Quel siècle à mains!*

In its second stage, the Readymade passes from hygiene to the criticism of art itself. In criticizing the idea of execution, Duchamp doesn't claim to dissociate form from content. In art the only thing that counts is form. Or, to be more precise, forms are the transmitters of what they signify. Form projects meaning, it is an apparatus for signifying. Now, the significances of "retinal" painting are insignificant; they consist of impressions, sensations, secretions, ejaculations. The Readymade confronts this insignificance with its neutrality, its nonsignificance. For this reason it cannot be a beautiful object, or agreeable, repulsive, or even interesting. Nothing is more difficult than to find an object that is really neutral: "Anything can become very beautiful if the gesture is. repeated often enough; this is why the number of my Readymades is very limited . . ." The repetition of the act brings with it an immediate degradation, a relapse into taste—a fact Duchamp's imitators frequently forget.

---

* According to Duchamp all modern art is "retinal"—from Impressionism, Fauvism, and Cubism to abstract art and Op Art, with the exception of Surrealism and a few isolated instances such as Seurat and Mondrian.

Detached from its original context—usefulness, propaganda, or ornament—the Readymade suddenly loses all significance and is converted into an object existing in a vacuum, into a thing without any embellishment. Only for a moment: everything that man has handled has the fatal tendency to secrete meaning. Hardly have they been installed in their new hierarchy, than the nail and the flatiron suffer an invisible transformation and become objects for contemplation, study, or irritation. Hence the need to "rectify" the Readymade—injecting it with irony helps to preserve its anonymity and neutrality. A labor of Tantalus for, when significance and its appendages, admiration and reprobation, have been deflected from the object, how can one prevent them from being directed toward the author? If the object is anonymous, the man who chose it is not. And one could even add that the Readymade is not a work but a gesture, and a gesture that only an artist could realize, and not just any artist but inevitably Marcel Duchamp. It is not surprising that the critic and the discerning public find the gesture significant, although they are usually unable to say what it is significant of. The transition from worshiping the object to worshiping the author of the gesture is imperceptible and instantaneous: the circle is closed. But it is a circle that closes us inside it: Duchamp has leaped it with agility; while I am writing these notes, he is playing chess.

One stone is like another and a corkscrew is like another corkscrew. The resemblance between stones is natural and involuntary; between manufactured objects it is artificial and deliberate. The fact that all corkscrews are the same is a consequence of their significance: they are objects that have been manufactured for the purpose of drawing corks; the similarity between stones has no inherent significance. At least this is the modern attitude to nature. It hasn't always been the case. Roger Caillois points out that certain Chinese artists selected stones because they found them fascinating and turned them into works of art by the simple act of engraving or painting their name on them. The Japanese also collected stones and, as they were more ascetic, preferred them not to be too beautiful, strange, or unusual; they chose ordinary round stones. To look for stones for their difference and to look for them for their similarity are not separate acts; they both affirm that nature is the creator.

To select one stone among a thousand is equivalent to giving it a name. Guided by the principle of analogy, man gives names to nature; each name is a metaphor: Rocky Mountains, Red Sea, Hells Canyon, Eagles Rest. The name—or the signature of the artist—causes the place—or the stone—to enter the world of names, or, in other words, into the sphere of meanings. The act of Duchamp uproots the object from its meaning and makes an empty skin of the name: a bottlerack without bottles. The Chinese artist affirms his identity with nature; Duchamp, his irreducible separation from it. The act of the former is one of elevation or praise; that of the latter, a criticism. For the Chinese, the Greeks, the Mayans, or the Egyptians nature was a living totality, a creative being. For this reason art, according to Aristotle, is imitation; the poet imitates the creative gesture of nature. The Chinese artist follows this idea to its ultimate conclusion: he selects a stone and signs it. He inscribes his name on a piece of creation and his signature is an act of recognition—Duchamp selects a manufactured object; he inscribes his name as an act of negation and his gesture is a challenge.

The comparison between the gesture of the Chinese artist and that of Duchamp demonstrates the negative nature of the manufactured object. For the ancients nature was a goddess, and what is more, a breeding ground for gods—manifestations in their turn of vital energy in its three stages: birth, copulation, and death. The gods are born and their birth is that of the universe itself; they fall in love (sometimes with our own women) and the earth is peopled with demigods, monsters, and giants; they die and their death is the end and the resurrection of time. Objects are not born: we make them; they have no sex; nor do they die: they wear out or become useless. Their tomb is the trash can or the recycling furnace. Technology is neutral and sterile. Now, technology is the nature of modern man; it is our environment and our horizon. Of course, every work of man is a negation of nature, but at the same time it is a bridge between nature and us. Technology changes nature in a more radical and decisive manner: it throws it out. The familiar concept of the return to nature is proof that the world of technology comes between us and it: it is not a bridge but a wall. Heidegger says that technology is nihilistic because it is the most perfect and active expression of the will to power. Seen in this light the Readymade is a double negation: not only the gesture but the object itself is negative. Although Duchamp doesn't have the least nostalgia for the paradises or infernos of nature, he is still less a worshiper of technology. The injection of irony is a negation of technology because the manufactured object is turned into a Readymade, a useless article.

The Readymade is a two-edged weapon: if it is transformed into a work of art, it spoils the gesture of desecration; if it preserves its neutrality, it converts the gesture itself into a work. This is the trap that the majority of Duchamp's followers have fallen into: it is not easy to juggle with knives. There is another condition: the practice of the Readymade demands an absolute disinterest. Duchamp has earned derisory sums from his pictures—he has given most of them away—and he has always lived modestly, especially if one thinks of the fortunes a painter accumulates today as soon as he enjoys a certain reputation. Harder than despising money is resisting the temptation to make works or to turn oneself into a work. I believe that, thanks to irony, Duchamp has succeeded: the Readymade has been his Diogenes' barrel. Because, in the end, his gesture is a philosophical or, rather, dialectical game more than an artistic operation: it is a negation that, through humor, becomes affirmation. Suspended by irony, in a state of perpetual oscillation, this affirmation is always provisional. It is a contradiction that denies an significance to object and gesture alike; it is a pure action—in the moral sense and also in the sense of a game: his hands are clean, the execution is rapid and perfect. Purity requires that the gesture should be realized in such a way that it seems as little like a *choice* as possible: "The great problem was the act of selection. I had to pick an object without it impressing me and, as far as possible, without the least intervention of any idea or suggestion of aesthetic pleasure. It was necessary to reduce my personal taste to zero. It is very difficult to select an object that has absolutely no interest for us not only on the day we pick it but that never will and that, finally, can never have the possibility of becoming beautiful, pretty, agreeable or ugly . . ."

The act of selection bears a certain resemblance to making a rendezvous, and for this reason, it contains an element of eroticism—a desperate eroticism without any illusions: "To decide that at a point in the future (such and such a day, hour, and minute) I am going to pick a Readymade. What is important then is chronometry, the empty moment . . . it is a sort of rendezvous." I would add that it is a rendezvous without any element of surprise, an encounter in a time that is arid with indifference. The Readymade is not only a dialectical game; it is also an ascetic exercise, a means of purgation. Unlike the practices of the mystics, its end is not union with the divinity and the contemplation of the highest truth; it is a rendezvous with nobody and its ultimate goal is noncontemplation. The Readymade occupies an area of the spirit that is null: "This bottlerack, which still has no bottles, turned into a thing that one doesn't even look at, although we know it exists—that we only look at by *turning our heads* and whose existence was decided by a gesture I made one day. . . ." A nihilism that gyrates on itself and refutes itself; it is the enthroning of a nothing and, once it is on its throne, denying it and denying oneself. It is not an artistic act, this invention of an art of interior liberation. In the *Large Sutra on Perfect Wisdom*,[*] we are told that each one of us must strive to reach the blessed state of Bodhisattva, knowing full well that Bodhisattva is a nonentity, an empty name. That is what Duchamp calls the beauty of indifference—in other words, freedom.

The Bride Stripped Bare by Her Bachelors, Even is one of the most hermetic works of our century. It stands apart from most other modern texts—because this painting is a text—in that the author has given us a key: the notes of the *Green Box*. I have already said that it is an incomplete key, incomplete as is the *Large Glass* itself; furthermore, in their way the notes are also a riddle, scattered signs that we have to regroup and decipher. The *Bride* and the *Green Box* (to which we must now add the *White Box*) make up a system of mirrors that exchange reflections; each one clarifies and *rectifies* the others. There are numerous interpreta-

---

[*] *The Large Sutra on Perfect Wisdom*, translated by Edward Conze (London: Luzac and Co., 1961).

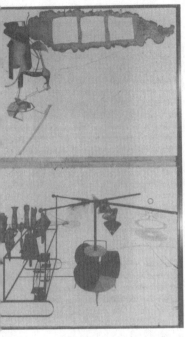

The Large Glass, *or* The Bride Stripped Bare
by Her Bachelors, Even, *1915–23. (Oil and lead
wire on glass.) Philadelphia Museum of Art:
Bequest of Katherine S. Dreier.*

tions of this enigmatic work. Some of them
show perspicacity.* I will not repeat them.
My purpose is a descriptive one: I want
to assemble some preliminary notes for a
future translation into Spanish. I will begin
with the title, *La Mariée mise à nu par ses
célibataires, même.* It is not easy to translate
this oscillating, convoluted phrase. First of
an *mise à nu* doesn't exactly mean denuded
or unclothed; it is a much more energetic
expression—stripped bare, exposed. It is
impossible not to associate it with a public
act or a ritual—the theater *(mise en scène)* or
an execution *(mise à mort).* The use of the word "bachelor" (célibataire),
instead of the seemingly normal "fiancé" or "suitor," sets up an unbridgeable separation between feminine and masculine; the bachelor is not even
a suitor, and the bride will never be married. The plural ("bachelors") and
the possessive adjective heighten the inferiority of the males; they bring
to mind the image of a herd, rather than polyandry.

The adverb "even" *(même)*, which Duchamp added later on, has been
discussed at great length. For one critic the allusion is transparent: "the

* One of the most noteworthy is Michel Carrouges' *Les Machines célibataires*
(Paris: Arcannes, 1951). The best descriptive synthesis of the painting is found
in André Breton's "Phare de la Mariée," in *Minotaur* (Paris, Vol. 2, No. 6, 1934).
The present essay was already written when two excellent studies appeared, both
containing complete and perceptive descriptions of the *Large Glass* and how it
works. The first is by John Golding, *The Bride Stripped Bare by Her Bachelors,
Even . . .* (London: Allen Lane, 1973). The second is Jean Suquet's *Miroir de la
Mariée* (Paris: Flammarion , 1974). Suquet has subsequently published another
essay, *Le Guéridon et la Virgule* (Paris: Christian Bourgeois, 1976), on a character
who was not painted in, but is essential to the *Large Glass*, the Juggler of Gravity.

This diagram is based on Duchamp's etching, The Large Glass Completed, *1965. By permission of the Museum of Modern Art, New York. Photo by Bacci.*

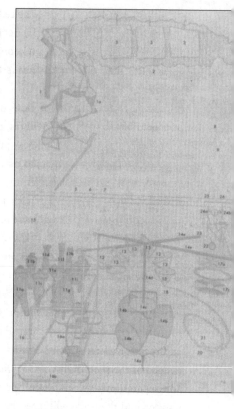

Bride loves me" *(m'aime)*. Duchamp has more than once denied this interpretation. In his conversations with Pierre Cabanne[*] he says again that he added the adverb precisely because it had no significance or connection either with the painting or with its title. The adverb, a magnificent demonstration of "adverbiality," meant nothing. In another interview he said that *même* reminded him of the famous double monosyllable of Bosse-de-Nage, Doctor Faustroll's monkey: Ha-Ha. The adverb *même* is the particle of hesitancy, the verbal capsule that contains those two solvents, irony and indifference. It is the "neither this nor that" of the Taoists. The adverb turns the *Large Glass* and its subject matter into a veritable act of exposition, in the photographic sense of the word, but in the liturgical and the worldly sense also. All the elements of the work are already there in the title: myth, barrack-room humor, eroticism, pseudoscience, and irony.

The name of each part also has a meaning—or rather, several meanings—and these complete the sense of the plastic composition. They complete and sometimes contradict it. They are signs that orient and disorient us, like the adverb *même*. The Bride's names are Motor-Desire,

[*] Pierre Cabanne, *Dialogues with Marcel Duchamp*, translated by Ron Padgett (New York: Viking. 1971).

Wasp, and Hanged Female. For H. P. Roché the Bride is a mixture of dragonfly and praying mantis. Carrouges, for his part, has discovered that *mariée* is the popular French name for a nocturnal butterfly, the *noctuelle*. The group of bachelors has a whole repertoire of gloomy names: Bachelor Apparatus, Nine Malic Molds *(Neuf Moules Malic)*, and finally, Cemetery of Uniforms and Liveries. At first there were eight males, but, no doubt for numerological reasons, Duchamp added another. Nine is a magic number; it has an aura. It is a multiple of three, and three is the number into which the Indo-Europeans concentrated their vision of the universe; it has been the focal point of their intellectual systems for thousands of years, from the days of Vedic India to modern Europe. The males are molds—the Spanish expression *machotes* suits them admirably—empty suits inflated by the illuminating gas that is their life's breath, their desiring soul. They represent nine families or tribes of men: gendarme, cuirassier, policeman, priest, busboy, stationmaster, department-store delivery boy, flunky, and undertaker. It is hard to imagine a more somber list. The Cemetery of Uniforms and Liveries is also called Eros' Matrix. One commentator has pointed out the ambivalence: the bachelors' tomb is their place of resurrection. The other meaning of matrix will not allow me to accept this interpretation completely—a matrix is a mold. The nine males are nine prototypes. Again we sense ambiguity, now confusing Platonic archetypes and mechanical molds.

The other parts have names that indicate their functions, though not without contradictions and ambivalences. Since I will discuss their positioning and their interaction later on, I will only list them here: Milky Way; Top Inscription, or Three Pistons; Nine Shots; Glider, Chariot, or Sleigh; Water Mill; Waterfall (invisible); Sieves, or Parasols; Capillary Tubes; Chocolate Grinder (made up of Bayonet, Necktie, Rollers, and Louis XV Chassis); Scissors; Bride's Horizon-Garment; Boxing Match (not painted); Oculist Witnesses; Handler of Gravity, or Juggler of Gravity, or Inspector of Space (not painted).

The Bride Stripped Bare by Her Bachelors, Even is a double glass, 109.25 inches high and 69.25 inches long, painted in oil and divided horizontally into two identical parts by a double lead wire. "Finally unfinished" in 1923, the *Large Glass* had its first public viewing in 1926, during the

International Exhibition of Modern Art at the Brooklyn Museum. It was broken when it was being returned from the museum to the house of its owner; the damage was not discovered until years later, and Duchamp did not repair the work until 1936. The dividing line, which serves both as horizon and as the Bride's transparent garment, was smashed; it is now merely a thin strip of glass held between two metallic bars. The scratched surface of the *Large Glass* is like the scarred body of a war veteran, a living map of campaigns endured. Duchamp confessed to Sweeney: "I love these cracks because they do not resemble broken glass. They have form, a symmetrical architecture. Better still, I see in them a strange purpose for which I'm not responsible, a design ready-made in a way that I respect and love." Like all radical skepticism, Duchamp's skepticism is open, and ends in the acceptance of the unknown. Not in vain did he take an interest in Pyrrho during his speculative period in the Bibliothèque Sainte-Geneviève. Chance is only one of the manifestations of a master plan that goes far beyond us. About this plan we know nothing, or next to nothing, except its power over us.

The upper half of the *Large Glass* is the Bride's domain. A complicated piece of machinery fills the far left. It is the Bride herself, or to be exact, the Bride in one of her personifications. In the central figure, which Duchamp called Hanged Female, Lebel has wanted to see "a sort of profile, in very schematic form, that could be that of a woman wearing a hat, whose face is covered by a veil." (A real widow, but whose?) Duchamp's commentary, which Lebel himself relayed, was rather enigmatic: "Voluntarily it might be the head, but accidentally what is seen is a nonvoluntary profile." The word "head" here does not indicate an anthropomorphic form but a position and probably a function within the ensemble. The vague similarities to a human form are accidental; the Bride is an apparatus, and her humanity lies neither in her shapes nor in her physiology. Her humanity is symbolic: the Bride is an ideal reality, a symbol manifested in mechanical forms, producing symbols in its turn. It is a symbol machine. But these symbols are distended and deformed by irony; they are symbols that distill their own negation. The way the Bride works is physiological, mechanical, ironic, symbolic, and imaginary all at the same time; the substance on which she runs is a secretion called "automobiline," her ecstasies are electric, and the physical force that moves her gears is desire.

The mystery surrounding the Bride comes not from a dearth but from an excess of information. The *Green Box* contains a fairly complete description of her morphology and of how she works. Frequently these notes are ambiguous and even contradictory; Duchamp's formula, beauty of precision, becomes a trap of uncertainties and confusions once it is subjected to the operation of meta-irony. It is hardly necessary to add that these uncertainties and confusions are an essential part of the Bride: they are her transparent veil. Furthermore, to really understand the painting we need not know exactly where her organs are, but we must have some idea of how they work. Having made that reservation, I shall now list, from top to bottom and from left to right, the different parts that comprise the apparatus.

At the top we can see a sort of hook. The Bride, in the proper sense of the term—the silhouette identified by Lebel as a female figure wearing a hat and veil—hangs from the hook. Though any anthropomorphic resemblance is deceptive, it is impossible not to notice a curious coincidence (if we can talk about coincidences in this realm): the painting *Portrait (Dulcinea)*, which dates from 1911, is a "simultaneist" vision of a stripping in five stages; the woman doing the striptease keeps her hat on throughout, like the Bride in the *Large Glass*.

Moving to the right, below the Milky Way, a groove* holds up a metallic shaft or stalk connected with the "desire-magnet" lower down. The desire-magnet contains in a cage the "filament substance" (invisible). This substance is the Bride's secretion, which materializes at her moment of "blossoming." The *Green Box* indicates that it "is like a solid flame . . . which licks the ball of the Handler of Gravity, displacing it as it pleases." The shaft of the desire-magnet is an axis, which is why its other name is "arbor-type." It is hard to decide if it is also called "motor with quite feeble cylinders," or if this expression denotes another part of the machinery.

---

* Paz comments here on the double meaning in Spanish of Duchamp's French word "*mortaise*." It translates into Spanish as *muesca* (groove) and *mortaja* (shroud). This ambiguity is lost in English. [Translator's note.]

Portrait (Dulcinea), 1911. (Oil on canvas.) Philadelphia Museum of Art: The Louise and Walter Arensberg Collection.

The arbor-type axis or spinal column is connected to a sort of syringe or lancet: this is the "wasp." The wasp has unusual characteristics: it secretes the "love gasoline" by osmosis; it possesses a sense of smell that allows it to perceive the "waves of unbalance" emitted by the black ball of the Juggler of Gravity; furthermore, it is endowed with a vibratory property that determines the pulsations of the "needle" and of a ventilation system. In turn this determines the "swinging to and fro of the Hanged Female with its accessories."

Below the wasp is the "tank of love gasoline or timid power." This erotic gasoline "distributed to the motor with quite feeble cylinders, in contact with the sparks of her constant life (desire-magnet) explodes and makes this virgin, who has attained her desire, blossom." The tank, also called an "oscillating bathtub," is what provides for the "hygiene of the Bride." Lower down, the "pulse needle" is balanced. It is mounted "on a wandering leash. It has the liberty of caged animals." The pulse needle is in the shape of a rather threatening pendulum, swinging over the void: the horizon-garment of the Bride.

The Bachelor-Machine is a "steam engine on a masonry substructure on this brick base, a solid foundation." The machine has "a tormented gearing," and it gives birth to its "desire-part." Thanks to the latter, the steam engine turns into a "desire motor." But this motor is separated from the Bride by a "cooler of transparent glass" that blends into the horizon-garment. In the *Large Glass* these items are hard to identify, and the Bride's architectonic masonry base does not appear.*

My description of the Bride is an interpretation. There are other versions of her morphology. For example, in Richard Hamilton's admirable "Typographic Letter" the "motor with quite feeble cylinders" and the tank of erotic gasoline appear below the Hanged Female. The position of the other parts is also slightly different in Hamilton's schema: on the right of the Hanged Female he places the wasp or "sex cylinder" with the cage of capillary tubes lower down, and below this the desire-magnet, which emits artificial sparks.

The *Green Box* tells us that the Bride is an agricultural machine, a plow (an allusion to Ceres?), a skeleton, an insect, a Hanged Female, a pendulum . . . "the Hanged Female is the form in *ordinary perspective* of a Hanged Female for which one could perhaps try to discover the *true form*." And so the forms of the Bride are only an appearance, one of her possible manifestations. Her true form, her real reality, is other. Duchamp has said that she is the projection of a three-dimensional object that in its turn is the projection of an (unknown) four-dimensional object. The Bride is the copy of a copy of the Idea. We are dealing with a mixture of speculations on non-Euclidean geometry, popular when Duchamp was young, and that current of Neoplatonism that has irrigated the soil and the subsoil of our civilization from the end of the fifteenth century onward. I am not talking of a conscious influence; as though they were our spiritual blood, the ideas stemming from Neoplatonic hermeticism circulate invisibly through us, blended into our ways of thinking and feeling. Alongside this Platonizing vision—that reality beyond the senses whose shadows we are—there appears another; Lebel thinks that the reality referred to as the fourth dimension is the moment of the carnal

---

* In *Given: 1. The Waterfall, 2. The Illuminating Gas*, (1946–66), the Assemblage discovered after Duchamp's death and now in the Philadelphia Museum of Art, the masonry construction and the brick wall are perfectly visible. Through an opening in the bricks the spectator sees the Bride, now in her three-dimensional shape, as a blond, naked girl reclining on a bed of twigs. Beyond her, on the wooded hillside, can be seen the silvery semicircle of the waterfall.

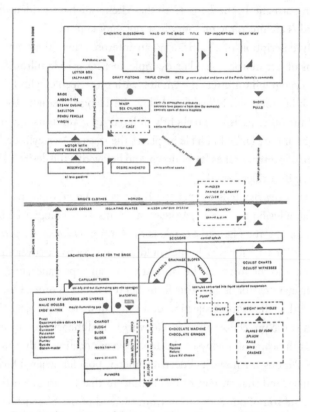

Typographic version of the Large Glass. *Courtesy of Richard Hamilton.*

embrace, during which the pair fuses time and space into one unique reality. The fourth dimension is the erotic dimension. But is there an embrace? Before that question is answered, it fades away, dissolved in the transparency of the *Large Glass*.

The Milky Way occupies the center of the upper half of the painting. It is a grayish cloud hanging from above, slightly pinkish at the extreme left (flesh-colored, Duchamp insists). The cloud seems to emerge from that part of the Hanged Female that I have called the head. Except that it doesn't come out like Minerva from Jupiter's broken forehead, but in a strange fashion from the Bride's occiput—if we may give an anatomical name to a machine part. Roché sees the cloud as a gaseous crocodile. For Michel Carrouges it is a gigantic caterpillar, an earlier version of the nocturnal butterfly *(noctuelle)* that is the Bride. This is a risky hypothesis, since the Milky Way, far from being an earlier form of the Bride, is rather an emanation from her in her moment of "cinematic blossoming."

Here I must interrupt my description to make a point. The accepted translation for *épanouissement*, the word Duchamp used, is "blossoming." There are several English equivalents for the French word,* as may be seen by checking dictionary entries—opening out, blooming, blowing (of flowers); beaming, brightening up (of the countenance); full bloom {of beauty}; expansion—but none that captures all its nuances. Duchamp uses the word in a figurative sense: the Bride blossoms, opens out, dilates with pleasure. It is not orgasm but the sensations that precede it. The *Green Box* is explicit: the blossoming "is the last state of the nude Bride before the orgasm that might make her fall . . ."

"Milky Way *flesh color* surrounds, unevenly densely, the 3 Pistons." Like the boards used in stadiums to mark up the scores or in airports to indicate the arrivals and departures of planes, the Pistons hang from three nails. Their other name is Nets. Duchamp hung a square piece of white cloth over an open window; the Nets are three photographs of that piece of material: "piston of the draft—that is, cloth accepted and rejected by the draft." The Nets or Pistons are also called Top Inscription because their function consists of transmitting to the Bachelors and to the Juggler of Gravity the Bride's discharges—her sensations, her commands. For Roché they are "the original Mystery, the Cause of Causes, a Trinity of empty boxes."

At the top right, below the Milky Way, there is a region of dots: the dents made by the Bachelors' Nine Shots. There are other parts not painted by Duchamp that must be kept in mind by anyone who wants to have an idea of how the machinery works. Below the region of the Nine Shots we ought to find the Cast Shadows, and below them the Image of the Sculpture of Drops. The Nine Shots were obtained by firing nine

---

* Paz makes this point vis-à-vis Spanish, but the statement holds true for English also. [Translator's note.]

times—three times from three different angles, making up the number of the Malic Molds—from a toy cannon loaded with matches soaked in fresh paint. On the far left, above the line indicating the horizon that separates the *Large Glass* into two halves, is the Bride's fallen, transparent garment. Naturally it is invisible. Farther down, in the realm of the Bachelors, appears the "air (or water) cooler" in transparent glass. It is also invisible. On the horizon itself, farther to the right, is the Wilson-Lincoln system. It can't be seen either. It is an optical trick based on those prisms that make us see the same face in two ways, looking like Wilson from one side and like Lincoln from the other. On the far right, still on the horizon, there is another character who has not been painted—the Juggler of Gravity. Had he ever been given a form, it would have been that of a spiral spring, resting on a small three-legged table, holding up a sort of tray on which a ball should roll (a black ball, as specified in a note in the *Green Box*). The Juggler of Gravity should dance on the horizon, the Bride's garment. Since he is a spring, he is elastic and grows upward until he bumps into the region of the Nine Shots and offers his black ball to the Bride, to the solid flame of her tongue.

In the lower half of the *Large Glass*, at the far left, we find the group of the Nine Malic Molds, or Cemetery of Uniforms and Liveries, or Eros' Matrix. All three names suit them because the Bachelors have no true personality. They are empty suits, hollow pieces inflated by the illuminating gas. "The Bachelors serve as an architectonic base of the Bride, which thus becomes a sort of apotheosis of virginity."

The differences between the Bride's and Bachelors' respective universes are vast. First of all, "the principal forms of the Bachelor-Machine are imperfect . . . that is, they are measurable . . . The principal forms of the Bride are more or less large or small, have no longer, in relation to their destination, a mensurability." (In the *White Box* an identical explanation appears under the heading "Perspective.") The region of the Bachelors is governed by the laws of classical perspective; the Bride's by a free geometry where "more or less" is the rule. A world of free forms, which cannot be measured and can be seen only with difficulty: the realm of indetermination, where causality has disappeared or, if it survives, obeys laws and principles that are different from those here below. The Bache-

lors' domain is that of measurements and causality, the region of our two-
and three-dimensional geometry and, therefore, of imperfect forms. This
opposition between our forms down here and hers up there is yet another
example of the way in which Duchamp places certain popular ideas of
modern physics—the fourth dimension and non-Euclidean geometry—
in the service of a metaphysics whose origin is Neoplatonic. For Plotinus
and for his fifteenth- and sixteenth-century followers, the One and its
emanations, the Ideas, were also free forms that escaped mensuration by
the senses. Geometry is the shadow of Ideas. Furthermore, it is the chink
through which we see the true forms. We see them without ever being
able to see them completely, we see them more or less.

There is another, equally telling difference between the Bride and
the Bachelors: "The Bride has a life-center; the Bachelors have not. They
live on coal or some other raw material, drawn not from them but from
their not-them." Being a liberated form, the Bride is self-sufficient; the
Bachelors, subject to geometry and perspective, are empty molds filled
by illuminating gas. They are uniforms and liveries: "The gas castings
so obtained would hear the litanies sung by the chariot, refrain of the
whole Bachelor-Machine. But *they* will never be able to go beyond their
Mask . . . as if enveloped, alongside their regrets, by a mirror reflecting
back to them their own complexity to the point of their being halluci-
nated rather onanistically."

The Nine Malic Molds are joined to the Sieve by means of a system
of capillary tubes that are none other than "the metrical units of capricious
length" calculated according to the method described above. The Sieve is
"a reverse image of porosity" and is made up of seven parasols arranged in
a semicircle. Dust is used in the parasols like "a kind of color (transparent
pastel)." Duchamp made "breeding grounds to raise dust on glass. Dust of
four months, six months, afterward hermetically closed up." The Sieve is
equipped with an aspirator pump, and each parasol has holes to facilitate
circulation. "The holes of the sieves should give *in the shape of a globe* the
figure of the . . . molds . . . by subsidized symmetry." The last parasol is
endowed with a "ventilator-mixer" that has the shape of a butterfly. By
virtue of its functions and the strange transformations that take place in
its inner galleries, the Sieve is a sort of Chamber of Metamorphoses.

Between the Nine Malic Molds and the Sieve is the Chariot, a little wagon on runners that is also known as the Sleigh. It appears in "the costume of Emancipation, hiding in its bosom the landscape of the Water Mill." The Mill is set in motion by a Waterfall. It is invisible, but the *Green Box* describes it as "a sort of waterspout coming from a distance in a semicircle, over the Malic Molds."* The runners of the Chariot slide on an underground rail. The metal of which the Chariot is made "is emancipated horizontally—that is, free of all gravity in the horizontal plane." The Water Mill is the wagon's propeller. Thanks to an ingenious mechanism that includes, among other devices, the fall of a bottle of Benedictine (or, in another version, four weights shaped like name-brand bottles), the Chariot is kept going with a fluctuating motion: "It goes, a weight falls and makes it go. It comes by the friction of the runners . . ." This second movement is a "phenomenon of inversion of friction . . . that is transformed into a returning force equal to the going force." Now we can perceive why the little wagon is made of emancipated metal.

Swinging to and fro, the Chariot recites endless litanies: "Slow life. Vicious circle. Onanism . . ." These litanies are the Bachelors' theme, the leitmotif of the celibate life here below. The Nine hear them and want to escape from themselves, to get rid of their masks—their liveries and uniforms—but they cannot . . . Another strange property: the weight of the bottle of Benedictine "by condescension . . . is denser going down than going up." Its density "is in perpetual movement, not at all fixed like that of metals." We can only call this property of the Benedictine bottle *philosophical:* its density is oscillating and thus "expresses the liberty of indifference," the only liberty to which we can aspire in this world of horizontal relationships.

The Chocolate Grinder occupies the center of the Bachelors' realm. Despite its position and size, its functions are rather limited. It is made up of a Louis XV Chassis, some rollers, a necktie provided "at the four corners with very sharp points," and the bayonet that holds up the Large Scissors. The continuous gyratory movement of the rollers is explained

---

* Though the Waterfall appears in the Assemblage in the Philadelphia Museum, the Nine Molds are not visible there.

by the action of a "principle of spontaneity," which is summed up in this formula: "The bachelor grinds his chocolate himself." A chocolate that "comes from one knows not where" and that "would deposit itself, after grinding, as milk chocolate." The Scissors open and close thanks to the seesaw motion of the Chariot, whose chanting keeps the movement rhythmical.

On the right-hand side of the Chocolate Grinder are the Oculist Witnesses. Once again, by an immediate association of ideas, the eyewitnesses of our religious and juridical traditions become another ambiguous breed. The Oculist Witnesses are represented by three circles, like those disks and diagrams on the charts used in optical establishments to test one's sight. Above the three circles there is a smaller one that ought to have been a magnifying glass. I shall come back to the Oculist Witnesses and the function of the glass when I deal with the overall movement that unifies all these elements—that is, when I get to their interrelated existence.

Below the Oculist Witnesses are the Drainage Slopes of Planes. They are in the shape of a toboggan "but more of a corkscrew." In the Bachelors' domain this part bears a certain resemblance to the Nine Shots in the Bride's. It is called the Region of Spray and ends in a movable Weight with nine holes in it. None of these details was painted. The same thing happens with another item, the last one, situated above the Oculist Witnesses and a little to their left: the Boxing Match. This has nothing to do with a fight between two pugilists in a ring, but with the banging of a "combat marble" against three targets mounted on three summits. Every time the marble reaches a summit, its impact releases a clockwork spring that makes two rams fan. I will refer to the consequences of their fall later on. For the time being, I want to point out that the system is governed by a red steel spring. Once the operation is over, the marble returns to its place and the indented clockwork wheels put the rams, which hold up the Bride's garment, back where they started.

---

* In Spanish "eyewitness" is *testigo ocular*. The "slight shift of letters and sounds" which, as Paz notes, turns Testigos Oculistas into *testigos oculares* is lost in English. [Translator's note.]

The reader should round out my description by seeing for himself. One does not have to go to Philadelphia to see the *Large Glass;* it can be adequately examined in some of the good reproductions published in recent years. In my opinion, the best and most faithful is that made in Plexiglas by Vicente Rojo, since it retains the transparency of the original.* To understand more clearly how the different parts of the machinery work, one must consult the 1965 sketch *(The Complete Large Glass)*, in which Duchamp numbered all the component parts of the work and traced in red ink those that are missing. Richard Hamilton has provided a clear guide in his "Typographic Letter" that accompanies the admirable translation of the *Green Box* by George Heard Hamilton (New York, 1960). I must also mention the schemata in Jean Suquet's book, Miroir de la Mariée, (1974) and of course, the two documents that have guided me in my exploration, the notes of the *Green Box* and the *White Box.*

The *Large Glass* is a picture of a bride's undressing. Her striptease is a spectacle, a ceremony, a physiological and psychological phenomenon, a mechanical operation, a physico-chemical process, an erotic and spiritual experience all rolled into one, and all governed by metairony. Music hall, church, a lonely girl's room, laboratory, factory where gases and explosives are made, a clearing in a wood at the foot of a waterfall, spiritual theater . . . The *Large Glass* is the painting of a recreative physics and of a metaphysics poised, like the Hanged Female, between eroticism and irony. Figuration of a possible reality that, because it belongs to a dimension different from ours, is essentially invisible. Also, and especially, an ecstatic representation of movement. What we see is a moment in a process, when the Bride reaches her "blossoming," itself the consequence of her stripping and the antecedent of her orgasm.

---

* In the portmanteau-book designed by Vicente Rojo *(Marcel Duchamp a El castillo de la pureza.* Mexico: Era, 1968). (Translated into English by Donald Gardner as *Marcel Duchamp, or the Castle of Purity,* New York: Grossman, 1970.) The Mexican edition contains the first version of this essay, a selection of texts by Duchamp, the Plexiglas reproduction of the *Large Glass,* three color plates, an envelope with nine reproductions of Readymades, a photo album with reproductions of autograph texts, and a souvenir portrait of Marcel Duchamp.

The notes of the two *Boxes*, like Duchamp's confessions, make it clear that the ceremony begins with the Bride and at her initiative. It is not in vain that she has a life-center. That vital center is the origin of the pulse-needle, which holds in equilibrium the sex cylinder, itself none other than the wasp. "At her base," says the *Green Box*, "the Bride is a tank of love gasoline or timid power." The Bride's autonomy, her sovereignty, is an attribute of her nature: "basically she is a motor, but before being a motor that transmits her timid power, *she is this very timid power*." The other name for this timid power is automobiline: love gasoline. Where does this gasoline come from? From the Bride herself—it is a secretion of the wasp. The Bride is a desiring motor that desires herself. Her essence, both in the chemico-physiological and in the ontological meanings of the word, is desire. This essence is, at one and the same time, a lubricant and her being in itself. Her essence, her being, is desire, and this desire, which cannot be reduced to feelings although it originates in them, is but a desire for being.

Another of the wasp's properties springs from her self-desiring self: she has a ventilation system, "an interior draft." It is no exaggeration to call this draft a *vital breath*, the Bride's soul or spirit. The draft is respon-sible for the vibratory movement of the pulse-needle. The sex cylinder, excited by the needle's vibration and lubricated by the gasoline, "spits at the drum the dew that is to nourish the vessels of the filament paste." As the reader will remember, the filaments are contained in a cage and are transformed at the moment of "blossoming" into a "solid flame." Up to this point we can trace the preparatory operations, the physiology and psychology of the Bride in her erotic awakening.

The draft of warm air that runs through the different parts of the machinery and sets them in motion is a metaphor for the desiring soul, and for sexuality also. Duchamp imagines the sighs and moans of desire as the snorts and backfiring of the motor of a car going up a hill . . . "faster and faster until it roars triumphantly." The draft—the Bride's desire, her amorous soul—reaches the Three Pistons, which are charged with transmitting her commands. There are no more than ten of these commands, and they may be reduced to only one. Two versions of this operation exist. In one, the draft is merely a warm vibration that, by unspecified channels, but in the form of electric discharges and sparks from the desire-magnet, reaches Eros' Matrix and awakens the Bachelors. In the second version—or is it a later stage of the ceremony?—the Bride's sighs and desires are air passing through the Three Pistons and being transformed into alphabetic unities. Thus the Pistons become the supports of the Top Inscription. A piece of the Hanged Female—it could be her brain—fills the function of an electric mailbox or matrix of letters. The mailbox contains an alphabet in which each sign or group of signs is an unrepeatable unity. We are dealing not with a phonetic but with an ideographic alphabet. Moreover, it has no synonyms and cannot be translated into any other language. A vocabulary-alphabet made up of "prime words, divisible only by themselves and by unity." The unities are written up on the Three Nets like the scores of games in stadiums. The writing of this mobile, instantaneous inscription of Desire is particular, but its reading universal.

Meanwhile, in the world below, life is slow, corrupt, and circular: the Chariot comes and goes, intoning its litanies; the bottle of Benedictine falls and returns to its place; the wheel of the Water Mill turns; the rollers grind their chocolate; the Scissors open and close. Then, shaken by the electric commands of the Bride, the Bachelors emerge from their stupor and wake up. The illuminating gas, coming who knows from where, inflates them. Pressure forces it to escape upward, through the capillary tubes. "By the phenomenon of stretching in the unit of length," the gas is "congealed, solidified, and transformed into elemental rods" or, according to another passage in the *Green Box*, "into thin, solid needles." Duchamp does not explain how the congealing of the gas is brought about. The needles, impelled by pressure, come out of their tubes, break, and become an infinity of "sequins lighter than air." Something like "retailed fog," made of myriads of sequins of "frosty gas." However, each sequin retains its "malic tint" and, therefore, tends to rise. Erotic desire is lighter than air and violates the laws of gravity. The sequin-gas is possessed by a "determination to rise." But as they rise, the sequins fall into the trap of the first parasol, which absorbs them. They enter the "labyrinth of the three directions."

The passage of the gas through the seven parasols is like a surprising derby. What is obvious here is ambivalence, the law which governs the

Large Glass and which is brought about by introducing into each phenomenon the solvent of *irony*. On one hand, the journey of the sequins is a descent to hell, a veritable pilgrimage to the underworld; on the other, it is an excursion to a fun fair, like those of our childhood, when we risked ourselves on the roller coaster or went into those booths filled with marvels—trapdoors, mirrors, ghosts, corridors, and caverns (today's modest equivalents of the specular labyrinths of the Baroque). Swept hither and yon, drawn in and blown out from one side to the other, the sequins lose their sense of direction and confuse the notions of right and left, up and down, backward and forward. They had kept their "malic" form, but the comings and goings, ups and downs, make them so seasick that they lose their individuality and forget their "determination to rise." The only thing left them is the "instinct for cohesion"; their gregarious impulse causes them to dissolve in an elemental liquid, "a vapor of inertia." And so they reach the end of their journey. As they emerge, they are awaited by the "butterfly-shaped ventilator-mixer," which, by turning, changes them into a substance that "resembles glycerine mixed with water." The gas has been transformed into a perfumer's item and into liquid explosive. In this state it hurls itself down the Slopes in the shape of a corkscrew and crashes three times. Clatter and splash.

The explosive liquid falls and is fired upward. But the Scissors literally cut its wings and force it to return and follow another path. The mission of the Scissors is to direct traffic, like traffic wardens when there are bottlenecks. The Weight with its nine holes collects the liquid, channels it, and takes it upward—a new voyage. The liquid seeps into the Oculists' hideout. Bedazzlement and metamorphosis: the Spray is turned into the Sculpture of Drops. A particularly choice metaphor: which of us, seeing water or steam gushing out from somewhere, has not wanted to see it turned suddenly into a sculpture? The Sculpture of Drops continues its flight, headed toward the upper half of the *Glass* "to meet the Nine Shots." But the drops sent back are not the real drops; this is a "mirrorical" trajectory and each drop has become its own image. Mutations: gas turned into solid needles turned into sequins lighter than air turned into inert vapor turned into liquid explosive turned into reflection in a mirror-glance.

The Sculpture of Drops is transformed from something that one looks at into something that looks. Like every act of looking, it is bounded by the horizon, that transparency that is the Bride's garment. Then it undergoes the effects of the Wilson-Lincoln system. The *Green Box* describes this transformation in a rather enigmatic way: "A mirrorical return. Each drop will pass the three planes at the horizon between the perspective and the geometrical drawing of two figures which will be indicated on these three planes by the Wilson-Lincoln system . . . The mirrorical drops, not the drops themselves but their image, pass between these two states of the same figure." The drops now are something else, though they have not ceased to be themselves. This is one of the themes or axes of the *Large Glass:* forms change, not essences. Universal anamorphosis: each form we see is the projection, the deformed image, of another one. The *White Box*, which makes a distinction between appearance and apparition, is explicit: what we see is almost always the *appearance* of objects—that is, "the retinal impression and other sensory consequences." The *apparition* is the object's mold, its archetypal pattern—its essence.

The "mirrorical drops" climb until they touch the region of the Nine Shots. There is an undoubted correspondence—and more, a *rhyme*—between the Image of the Sculpture of Drops and the Nine Shots. The former is the projection of the illuminating *gas* after its metamorphosis and its final transfiguration through the speculations of the Oculist Witnesses and the Wilson-Lincoln prism; the latter—the Bachelors' Nine Shots—is "the projection of the principal points of a three-dimensional body." The *Green Box* adds, "With maximum skill this projection will be reduced to a point. With ordinary skill," as is the case of the Bachelors, "the projection will be a demultiplication of the target." Desire is the common element, the source of both figures; rather, we might say that shots and "mirrorical drops" are only the projections of desire. A desire that *never* hits the mark. The *Green Box* says that "the coefficient of displacement"—that is to say the farther or the closer each shot is to the target—"is nothing but a souvenir." A strange, hermetic affirmation that, however, is not impossible to decipher: what we see is only a souvenir (vague, imprecise, unfaithful) of what it really *is*. Knowledge is remembrance. Amorous, desiring remembrance. A new appearance of Neoplatonism, voluntary or reflexive, in the *Large Glass*. True reality is elusive, not because it is changeable but because it lives in another sphere, in another dimension. We walk among shadows and illusions, and nothing that we see, touch, and think has real consistency. Between us and real reality intrudes the horizon—that horizon which is the limit of our gaze and which is none other than the Bride's transparent garment. The horizon of our memory. Deceptive transparency, light trick of the Wilson-Lincoln prism: the object we see from this side is not the one we see from the other. However, the object is one and the same. To desire is to remember this object, to take aim at its image.

It is no exaggeration to describe as celestial the region of the *Large Glass* that occupies the right-hand side of its upper half. Celestial not only because it borders on the Milky Way but also because the three elements that give it form are three constellations. All three are made of dots and luminous shadows, like those we see in astronomers' maps. The first is the region of the Nine Shots; the third is the Image of the Sculpture of Drops; the one in between is made by the Cast Shadows. Though it was not painted, we have a note dating from the same period as those of the two *Boxes*, in which Duchamp describes what its function was to have been. Duchamp imagines a method to "obtain a hypophysical analysis of the successive transformations of objects (in their form-outline)." It is the philosophical application, we might say, of the principle of the magic lantern, which so intrigued the minds of the seventeenth century. The object analyzed was to have been "constructed sculpturally in three dimensions," an aim compatible with Duchamp's intellectual preoccupations during those years. The note specifies "for the upper part of the *Glass* included between the horizon and the nine holes, cast shadows formed by the splashes/coming from below like some jets of water/that weave forms in their transparency.'" The correspondence between the Nine Shots, the Cast Shadows and the Image of the Sculpture of Drops is amazing. The

---

* The prototype of this idea is the last canvas painted by Duchamp, *Tu m'* (1918), which is still awaiting detailed analysis. The same is true of another prototype, that of the Oculist Witnesses, executed on glass in Buenos Aires, also in 1918, *To Be Looked at (from the Other Side of the Glass), with One Eye, Close to, for Almost an Hour.*

duality of the *Large Glass* begins to reveal its true meaning to us: down below, the world of here and now; up there, the world of real reality, essences, and ideas. Or to use the language of the *White Box:* up there *apparitions* (or their shadows *more or less* reflected by our senses) and down below *appearances*, what we touch and see, what we can measure and weigh. The forms up there are *relatively* real because they are only projections of the true forms that make up the fourth dimension. The world up there is not the projection of our desires; we are their projection. Our desire is nostalgia, the remembrance of that world.

While one portion of the Sculpture of Drops passes through the metamorphoses I have talked about, another crosses through the magnifying glass found above the three oculist circles. The glass turns the drops into a ray of light. Again the act of looking, through which the universal magnetism is conveyed. The magnifying glass throws the ray onto the combat marble. Struck by its luminous energy, the marble jumps up and hits the first summit. In this way it sets in motion the clockwork mechanism of the Boxing Match. The first fall of the rams that hold up the Bride's garment makes the Juggler of Gravity give a little jerk. The ball attacks again, "very hard": the rams fall again, the first one is unfastened, and the Juggler pirouettes. Attack number three, a "direct" attack this time: the second ram is unfastened; the Juggler jumps like the spring he is, and lifts his tray up to the "solid flame" in which the Bride's desire is manifest. The two rams pull the horizon-garment with them in their fall. Balanced on a shaky three-legged table resting on the garment, the Juggler of Gravity dances dangerously on its wobbling surface. With this dance the stripping reaches its climax.

The three "blossomings" accompany all these phenomena. The first is the result of the stripping by the Bachelors and is electrically controlled. Between the Bride and the Bachelors there is contact, though not at close quarters: sparks from the "desire-magnet;" explosions from the "motor with quite feeble cylinders;" the Bride's sighs, which make the fabric of the Three Pistons undulate in order to give her commands to the Bachelor-Machine; transformation of the filament substance into a "solid flame" that licks the black ball offered to it on a tray by the Juggler of Gravity; rattles from the car going up the slope; the movement of the gearbox and the serrated wheels . . . Duchamp compares this "blossoming" to the "throbbing jerk of the minute hand on an electric clock." The Bride accepts this stripping; she even provides the "love gasoline" to feed the sparks and "adds to the first focus of sparks the second focus of sparks of the desire-magnet." The first "blossoming" provokes the second, in which the desiring Bride voluntarily imagines her stripping. It is a sensation closely connected with the "arbortype," so that it is expressed "in boughs frosted in nickel and platinum."* To this "blossoming" corresponds the image of the automobile climbing the slope in first gear. The two "blossomings" are only one, the third a "mixture, physical compound of the two causes (Bachelors and imaginative desire) unanalyzable by logic." It is the "cinematic blossoming" that reveals itself as a flesh-colored Milky Way, "halo of the Bride, sum total of her splendid vibrations." When it reaches this point, says the *Green Box*, "the picture will be an inventory of the elements of this blossoming, elements of the sexual life imagined by her, the desiring Bride." There follows in the manuscript a revealing sentence that was later crossed out: "This blossoming has nothing to do with either the Bachelors or the stripping." In the "Bride's last stage before orgasm" the Bachelors disappear. The operation is circular: it begins in the Bride's Motor-Desire and ends in her. A self-sufficient world. It has no need even of spectators because the work itself includes them: the Oculist Witnesses. How can we not recall Velázquez and his *Meninas?*

The *Large Glass* is a design for a piece of machinery and the *Green Box* is therefore a bit like one of those sets of instructions that tell us how to put machines together and how they work. Since the former is a static illustration of a moment in the total operation, to understand it in its totality we must resort to the notes in the latter. Really the composition should have three parts: one plastic, another literary, and the third sonorous. Duchamp has made a few annotations for this third part: the litanies of the Chariot, the adagio of the Chocolate Grinder, shots or discharges, the noise of a car engine as it goes up a hill, and so forth. It

* The expression seemed unintelligible until the discovery of the Assemblage now in the Philadelphia Museum, in which the Bride appears reclining on a bed of twigs and leaves.

is a transposition of the moans and sighs of eroticism to the world of machines. On the other hand the *Large Glass* is also a mural (a portable one) representing the Apotheosis of the Bride, a picture, a satire of the machine mentality, an artistic experiment (painting in glass), a vision of love.

Of all possible interpretations, the psychoanalytical one is the most tempting and the easiest: onanism, destruction (or glorification) of the Virgin Mother, castration (the Scissors), narcissism, retention (anal symptoms), aggressiveness, self-destruction. A well-known psychiatrist ends his study—not devoid of brilliance—with the expected diagnosis: autism and schizophrenia. The drawback of such hypotheses is that their authors look at works only as symptoms or expressions of certain psychic tendencies; psychological explanation turns reality (the painting) into shadow, and shadow (the sickness) into reality. A personal encounter with Duchamp would have been enough to make one realize that his schizophrenia must have been of a very odd variety, for it did not prevent him from dealing with people or from being one of the most open men I knew. Furthermore, the rightness or wrongness of the diagnosis does not change the reality of the *Large Glass.* The realities of psychology and of art exist on different levels of meaning: Freud offers us a key to understanding Oedipus, but the Greek tragedy cannot be limited to the interpretations of psychoanalysis. Lévi-Strauss says that Freud's interpretation of the myth is nothing more than *another* version of it: in other words, Freud tells us, in the language that is appropriate to an age that has substituted logical thought for mythological analogy, the same story as Sophocles told us. Something similar could be said of the *Large Glass:* it is a version of the ancient myth of the great Goddess, Virgin, Mother, Giver and Exterminator of life. It is not a modern myth: it is the modern version—or vision—of the Myth.

In an interview with Jean Schuster, Duchamp tells us this story of the origin of his picture: "the fairground stalls of those days (1912) gave me the inspiration for the theme of the bride. They used to display dolls in the sideshows that frequently represented the partners of a marriage. The spectators threw balls at them, and if they hit the mark, they beheaded them and won a prize." The Bride is a doll; the people who throw the balls are her Bachelors; the Oculist Witnesses are the public; the Top Inscription is the scoreboard. The idea of representing the males as bachelors in uniform also has a popular origin. The bachelor keeps his virility intact while the husband disperses it and so becomes feminine. The husband, Tomás Segovia says, breaks the closed circle of the adolescents, and until he is redeemed by becoming a father, he is seen by his former comrades as a traitor to his own sex. This attitude expresses the adolescent's terror of woman and the fascinated revulsion that he feels for her hidden sexual organs. The uniform preserves his masculinity for two reasons: it belongs by right to men, is a sign that proclaims the separation between the two sexes, in such a way that women who put it on look like men; second, the uniform makes a group of the men, it turns them into a separate collectivity, bearing some resemblance to the ancient guilds and other secret male societies. So then, behind the modern masquerade another reality appears, archaic and fundamental: the separation between men and the Woman, the ambiguous cult the former profess and the dominion of the latter over them. We are moving from farce to sacred mystery, from popular art to the religious mural, from folk tale to allegory.

The *Large Glass* is a scene from a myth or, rather, from a family of myths related to the theme of the Virgin and the closed society of men. It would be curious to attempt a systematic comparison between the other versions of the myth and that of Duchamp. It is a task, however, beyond my ability and my purpose as translator of the text. I will limit myself to isolating certain elements. The first is the insurmountable separation between the males and the Bride and the dependency on her of the former; not only does the appeal of the Virgin wake the life in them but all their activity, a mixture of adoration and aggression, is a reflex action aroused by the energy which the woman emits and which is directed by her and toward herself. The spatial division into two halves is also significant: the here-below of the males—a messy and monotonous hell as the litanies of the Chariot tell us—and the solitary above-and-beyond of the Virgin, who is not even touched by the shots— the supplications of her Bachelors. The meaning of this division is plain; energy and decision is above, below there is passivity in its most contemptible form: the illusion of movement, self-deception (the males are led to believe that they exist only by way of a mirror that prevents them from seeing themselves in their comic unreality). The most noteworthy feature is the circular and illusory character of the operation: everything is born from the Virgin and returns to her. There is a paradox here: the Bride is condemned to remain a virgin. The erotic machinery that sets things in motion is entirely imaginary, as much because her males have no reality of their own as because the only reality which she knows and by which she is known is reflex: the projection of her Motor-Desire. The emanations that she receives, at a distance, are her own, filtered through a meaningless piece of machinery. At no moment of the process does the Bride enter into any relation with the true masculine reality or with the real reality: the imaginary machine that her Motor projects comes between her and the world.

In the version of the myth that Duchamp offers us there is no hero (the lover) who, by breaking the circle of males, setting fire to his livery or uniform, crossing the zone of gravity, conquering the Bride, and liberating her from her prison, will open her and break her virginity. It is not surprising that some critics, influenced by psychoanalysis, have seen in the *Large Glass* a castration myth, an allegory of onanism, or the expression of a pessimistic vision of love in which a true union is impossible. This interpretation is not false; it is inadequate. I hope to demonstrate that the theme of the *Large Glass* is another myth; in other words, that the myth of the Virgin and her Bachelors is the projection or translation of another myth. For the moment I will limit myself to emphasizing the circular nature of the operation: the Motor-Desire causes the Bride to rise out of herself, and this desire encloses her all the more completely in her own being. The world is her representation.

The Tantric imagery of Bengal represents Kali dancing in frenzy over two bodies that are as white as corpses. They are not dead; they are two ascetics covered with ashes. In one of her hands Kali grasps a sword, in another a pair of shears, in the third she holds a lotus, and in the last a cup. By her side are two little female figures who hold a sword in one hand and also hold a cup in the other. Around the five figures there is a profusion of bones and broken human limbs. A number of dogs are gnawing and licking them. The two white bodies are placed on top of each other and represent Shiva, the husband of Kali. The first of them has his eyes closed; he is fast asleep and unaware of what is happening; according to the traditional interpretation he is the absolute unconscious of itself. The other figure, a sort of emanation of the former, has his eyes half open and his body is hardly formed; he is the absolute already in a state of awareness or consciousness. The Goddess is a manifestation of Shiva and the three figures represent the stages of the manifestation: the unconscious passivity of the absolute, the phase of consciousness that is still passive, and the emergence of activity and energy. Kali is the world of phenomena, the incessant energy of this world, which is shown as destruction (sword and shears), as nourishment (the cup full of blood), and as contemplation (the lotus of the interior life). Kali is carnage, sexuality, propagation, and spiritual contemplation.

It is obvious that both the image and its philosophical explanation offer more than one parallel with the *Large Glass* and the *Green Box:* Kali and the Bride, the Oculist Witness and the two attendants, masculine passivity and feminine activity. The most obvious resemblance is that in both cases we are present at the representation of a circular operation that unveils the phenomenal reality of the world (strips it bare: ex-poses it) and simultaneously denies it all true reality. This parallel is not external but constitutes the essence or fundamental theme of both representations. The undeniable similarities between the Hindu image and the *Large Glass*, the *Green Box*, and my explanation of the Tantric tradition do not mean, of course, that there is a direct relation between them. Nor is the parallel a chance coincidence. They are two distinct and independent versions of the same idea—perhaps of a myth that refers to the cyclic character of time. Of course, neither Hindu tradition nor Duchamp was necessarily aware of this myth; the two versions are responses to the traditional images that both civilizations have made of the phenomenon of creation and destruction, woman and reality. I do not insist on this, because my purpose is not anthropological and the only thing that interests me in comparing these two images is to get somewhat deeper into the work of Duchamp.

There is another image of Kali that helps to clarify the resemblance. The Goddess is again dancing on the two pale Shivas. Seized by her delirium, she has decapitated herself; instead of the lotus, she is holding her own head in one of her hands, the mouth half open and its tongue hanging out. Three streams of blood gush from her neck: two of them into the cups of her attendants and the central one into her own mouth. The Goddess feeds the world and herself with her own blood in exactly the same way as the Bride sets her Bachelors in motion simply by gratifying herself and stripping herself bare. In the first case the operation is related to us in terms of myth and sacrifice; in the second, in pseudomechanical terms that, however, do not exclude the idea of sacrifice. The separation of the female body into two is equally striking: the Goddess and her head, the Bride and her Motor. This last point calls for further comment. The subdivision of the Goddess and the Bride into two parts—one active and the other receptive—is in its turn the consequence of another division; the Goddess and the Bride are projections or manifestations of something which Hindu imagery represents in the mode of myth (Shiva in his double form) and which Duchamp preserves invisibly, the fourth or archetypal dimension. Kali and the Bride are a representation and the real world is another representation, the shadow of a shadow. The circular movement is the reintegration of the energy dispersed by the dance or by desire, without any extraneous element enriching or changing it. Everything is imaginary. It is time to pass from myth to criticism.

Tantric Imagery of Kali.
Ediciones Era.

Neither the Hindu myth nor that of Duchamp is self-sufficient. To understand the Tantric image we have to resort to the methods of traditional exegesis and, in the case of the *Large Glass*, to the *Green Box*. The enigma of the two images consists in this: if Kali and the Bride are projections, or representations, what do they represent, what is the energy or entity that they are projecting? The Hindu myth gives a clear account of the origin of the Goddess. A frightful demon threatens the universe with destruction; the gods go in terror to the greater divinities, Shiva and Vishnu, to seek refuge; Shiva and Vishnu, on being informed of what is happening, become angry and swell with rage; the other gods imitate them, the assembly of divine angers fuses into a single image—the black Goddess with eight arms. Male power abdicates in favor of a female deity who will destroy the monster.* Philosophical commentary translates this story into metaphysical and ethical terms: energy and the world of phenomena are representations or manifestations of the absolute (unconscious and conscious, asleep and half awake). Energy is feminine for two reasons: woman is creation and destruction; the world of phenomena is Maya, illusion *(la ilusión)*. Duchamp's version of the myth is different from that of the Hindu commentator in that he rejects the metaphysical explanation and keeps silent. The Bride is a projection of the fourth dimension, but the fourth is, by definition, the unknown dimension.

Michel Carrouges concludes from this silence that he is an atheist. From the point of view of Christian tradition, his verdict is correct. But our believers and our atheists belong to one and the same family: the former affirm the existence of a single God, a personal Creator; the latter deny it. The negation of the latter makes sense only in the context of the Judeo-Christian monotheistic concept of God. As soon as it abandons these grounds, the discussion loses interest and turns into a quarrel inside a sect. In reality our atheism is antitheism. For a Buddhist atheist, Western atheism is only a negative and exasperated form of our monotheism. Duchamp has declared quite rightly on a number of occasions that "the genesis of the *Glass* is exterior to any religious or antireligious

* Heinrich Zimmer, *Myths and Symbols in Indian Art and Civilization* (New York: Pantheon, 1946).

preoccupation." (In this context the word "religion" refers to Christianity. The rites and beliefs of the East, for the most part, don't constitute what we would call a "religion"; this term should be applied only to the West.) Duchamp expresses himself even more clearly in a letter to Breton: "I don't accept discussions about the existence of God on the terms of *popular metaphysics*, which means that the word 'atheist,' as opposed to 'believer,' doesn't even interest me . . . For me there is something else that is different from *yes, no*, or from *indifferent*—for example: *absence of investigation in this area.*" Duchamp hasn't represented the Motor of the Motor-Desire because this would have meant dealing with a reality about which, as he himself honorably says, he knows nothing. Silence is more valid than dubious metaphysics or than error.

In Duchamp's silence we find the first and most notable difference between the traditional method of interpretation and the modern. The one affirms the myth and gives it a metaphysical or rational support; the other places it between parentheses. All the same, Duchamp's silence does have something to ten us: it is not an affirmation (the metaphysical attitude), nor a negation (atheism), nor is it indifference (skeptical agnosticism). His version of the myth is not metaphysical or negative, but ironic; it is criticism. On the one hand, it makes fun of the traditional myth. It reduces the worship of the Goddess, both in its religious and in its modern form, cult of the Virgin, or romantic love, to a grotesque mechanism in which desire becomes an internal-combustion engine, love becomes gasoline, and semen is gunpowder. On the other hand, criticism also makes fun of the positivist conception of love and, in general, of everything we call "modern" in the common use of the word: "scientism," positivism, technology, and so on. The *Large Glass* is a comic and infernal portrayal of modern love or, to be more precise, of what modern man has made of love. To convert the human body into a machine, even if it is a machine that produces symbols, is worse than degradation. Eroticism lives on the frontiers between the sacred and the blasphemous. The body is erotic because it is sacred. The two categories are inseparable: if the body is mere sex and animal impulse, eroticism is transformed into a monotonous process of reproduction; if religion is separated from eroticism, it tends to become a system of arid moral precepts. This is what has happened to Christianity, above all to Protestantism, which is its modern version.

Despite the fact that they are made of materials more lasting than our bodies, machines grow older more rapidly than we do. They are inventions and manufactured objects; our bodies are re-productions, re-creations. Machines wear out and after a time one model replaces another; bodies grow old and die, but the body has been the same from the appearance of man on the earth until now. The body is immortal because it is mortal; this is the secret of its permanent fascination—the secret of sexuality as much as of eroticism. The humorous element of *The Bride* does not lie only in the circular operation of her desire, but also in the fact that Duchamp, instead of painting brilliant and perishable bodies, painted opaque and creaking machines. The skeleton is comical because it is pathetic, the machine because it is icy. The first makes us laugh or weep; the second produces in us what I would call, following Duchamp, a *horror of indifference* . . . In short, Duchamp's criticism is two-edged: it is criticism of myth and criticism of criticism. The *Large Glass* is the culminating point of the tendency toward the irony of affirmation that inspires the Readymades. It is a critical myth and a criticism of criticism that takes the form of comic myth. In the first stage of the process, he translates the mythical elements into mechanical terms, and therefore denies them; in the second, he transfers the mechanical elements into a mythical context, and denies them again. He uses the myth to deny the criticism and criticism to deny the myth. This double negation produces an affirmation which is never conclusive and which exists in perpetual equilibrium over the void. Or as he has said: *Et-qui-libre? Equilibre.*

Some critics have found a theological significance in the division of the *Large Glass* into two halves—the realm of the Bride above and the fief of her bachelors below—and have pointed out that this duality corresponds to the ancient idea of a world above and a world below. Harriet and Sidney Janis have gone further. The lower part is a sort of hell, governed by the laws of matter and gravity, whereas the upper part is the region of the air and of levitation; the Bride is nothing other than an allegory of purified matter or, in Christian terms, of the Ascension of the

Virgin. The interpretation contains a grain of truth, but it is incomplete and based, moreover, on guesswork. Robert Lebel sees in the *Large Glass* an antiworld, the equivalent of the antimatter of contemporary physics, which reflects all Duchamp's fears and obsessions, especially those that are infantile or unconscious. Or, to put it in mythical terms, it is the manifestation of what the painter fears and hates just as the Goddess is the manifestation of the fear and anger of the gods. This antiworld is the "vomit, the monstrous and repulsive form of a Bachelor-Machine that is nothing other than an incestuous and masculine hell." It hardly seems necessary to observe that the *Large Glass* is *not* the representation of male desire but the projection of the desire of the Bride, which is in its turn the projection of an unknown dimension or Idea . . . Lebel adds that Duchamp's picture belongs to the same family as the *Garden of Earthly Delights* of Hieronymus Bosch. Although the comparison is correct, it has the same defect as the hypothesis of Harriet and Sidney Janis—it is incomplete. Christian religious painting is Trinitarian or tripartite: it consists of the world, of heaven, and of hell. The opposition of dualities is not Christian but Manichaean. Moreover, the division of the *Large Glass* into two halves is not exactly a division into heaven and hell; both parts are hell. The line of division doesn't allude to a theological separation ("the Bride is chaste with a touch of malice," the *Green Box* tells us), but one of power. The division is, if you like, of an ontological nature: the males have no existence in their own right; the Bride, on the other hand, enjoys a certain autonomy thanks to her Motor-Desire. But, as we have seen, the dual division is illusory like the whole painting; there comes a point when we have to reckon that, like the Bride and her Bachelors, we have been victims of an illusion. Duchamp has good reasons for painting images on glass: everything has been a representation and the characters in the drama and their circular actions are a projection, the dream of a dream.

The remarks I have made above do not mean that these critics haven't seen with some shrewdness a central feature of the *Large Glass*. This composition continues, in its own way, the great tradition of Western painting, and for this reason, it stands in violent opposition to what we have called painting since Impressionism. Duchamp has frequently referred to the aims that have inspired him: "It was my intention not to make a painting for *the eyes*, but a painting in which the tubes of color were a means and not an end in themselves. The fact that this kind of painting is called literary doesn't bother me; the word "literature" has a very vague meaning and I don't think it is adequate . . . There is a great difference between a painting that is only directed toward the retina and a painting that goes beyond the retinal impression—a painting that uses the tubes of color as a springboard to go further. This was the case with the religious painters of the Renaissance. The tubes of color didn't interest them. What they were interested in was to express their idea of divinity, in one form or another. With a different intention and for other ends, I took the same concept: pure painting doesn't interest me either in itself or as a goal to pursue. My goal is different, is a combination or, at any rate, an expression that only gray matter can produce.'" This long quotation spares me the need of any commentary. The *Large Glass* continues the tradition not because it shares the same ideals or exalts the same mythology but because, like it, it refuses to turn aesthetic sensation into an end in itself. It continues it, moreover, by being monumental—not only because of its proportions but also because the *Large Glass* is a *monument*. The divinity in whose honor Duchamp has raised this ambiguous monument is not the Bride or the Virgin or the Christian God but an invisible and possibly nonexistent being: the Idea.

Duchamp's enterprise was contradictory, and he saw it as such from the outset. For this reason irony is an essential element in his work. Irony is the antidote that counteracts any element that is "too serious, like eroticism," or too sublime, like the Idea. Irony is the Handler of Gravity, the question mark of *et-qui-libre?* The enterprise is contradictory for the following reason: how can one attempt a painting of ideas in a world that is impoverished of ideas? The Renaissance marked the beginning of the dissolution of the great Greco-Christian Idea of divinity, the last universal faith (in the limited sense of the term: "universal" meaning the community of European and Slavic peoples, the churches of East and West). It is true that the medieval faith was replaced by the imposing

---

* Conversation with Alain Jouffroy, in *Une Révolution du regard*.

constructions of Western metaphysics, but from the time of Kant, all these edifices have begun to crumble and from then on thought has been critical and not metaphysical. Today, we have criticism instead of ideas, methods instead of systems. Our only idea, in the proper sense of the term, is Criticism. The *Large Glass* is a painting of ideas because, as I think I have shown, it is a critical myth. But if it was only this, it would merely be one work more and the enterprise would be partially abortive. I should underline the fact that it is also and above all the Myth of Criticism; it is the painting of the *only modern idea*. Critical myth: criticism of the religious and erotic myth of the Bride-Virgin in terms of modern mechanical development and, simultaneously, a myth that burlesques our idea of science and technology. Myth of Criticism: painting-monument that relates one moment of the incarnations of Criticism in the world of objects and erotic relationships. Now, in the same way as religious painting implies that the artist, even if he is not religious, believes in some way in what he is painting, the painting of Criticism requires that the painting itself and its author be critics or that they participate in the critical spirit. As Myth of Criticism the *Large Glass* is a painting of Criticism and criticism of Painting. It is a work that turns in upon itself, that persists in destroying the very thing it creates. The function of irony now appears with greater clarity. Its negative purpose is to be the critical substance that impregnates the work; its positive purpose, as criticism of criticism, is to deny it and so to tip the balance onto the side of myth. Irony is the element that turns criticism into myth.

It would not be mistaken to call the *Large Glass* the Myth of Criticism. It is a picture that makes one think of certain works that prophesy and reveal the ambiguity of the modern world and its oscillation between myth and criticism. I am reminded of Ariosto's mock epic and of *Don Quixote*, which is an epic novel and a criticism of the epic. It is with these creations that modern irony is born; with Duchamp and other poets of the twentieth century, such as Joyce, the irony turns against itself. The circle closes; it is the end of one epoch and the beginning of another. The *Large Glass* is on the borders of two worlds, that of "modernity," which is in its death throes, and the beginnings of a new world, which hasn't yet taken shape. Hence its paradoxical position, similar to that of

Ariosto's poem and Cervantes' novel. *The Bride* continues the great tradition of Western painting that was interrupted by the appearance of the bourgeoisie, the open market for works of art, and the predominance of taste. This painting, like the works of the religious artists, is sign and Idea. At the same time, Duchamp breaks with this tradition. Impressionism and the other modern and contemporary schools continue the tradition of the craft of painting, although they eradicate the *idea* from the art of painting; Duchamp applies his criticism not only to the Idea but also to the very act of painting—the rift is total. It is a strange situation; he is the only modern painter who continues the tradition of the West and he is one of the first to break with what we have traditionally called the art, or craft, of painting. It could be argued that many artists of the present age have been painters of ideas: the Surrealists, Mondrian, Kandinsky, Klee, and many others. This is certainly true, but their ideas are subjective; their worlds, almost always fascinating, are private worlds, personal myths. Duchamp is, as Apollinaire conjectured, a *public* painter. No doubt someone will point out that other artists have also been painters of social ideas—the Mexican mural painters, for example. In its intentions the work of these painters belongs to the nineteenth century; it is program-painting, at times an art of propaganda and other times a vehicle of simplistic ideas about history and society. (Mexican mural painting is interesting because of its character and other values, as I have shown in another essay.*) The art of Duchamp is intellectual and what it gives us is the *spirit of the age*—Method, the critical Idea at the moment when it is meditating on itself, at the moment when it reflects itself in the transparent nothingness of a pane of glass.

The direct antecedent of Duchamp is not to be found in painting but in poetry: Mallarmé. The work that most closely resembles the *Large Glass* is *Un coup de dés*. It is not surprising; despite what the insular critics of painting think, it is almost always poetry that anticipates and prefigures the forms that the other arts adopt later. The affected piety of modern times that surrounds painting and often prevents us from *seeing* it is nothing other than idolatry for the object, adoration of a magic

---

* *Las peras del olmo* (Mexico City: Seix-Barral, 1957), pp. 244–64.

object which we can touch and which, like other objects, can be bought and sold. It is the elevation of the object in a civilization dedicated to producing and consuming objects. Duchamp refuses to put up with this superstitious blindness and has frequently emphasized the *verbal*, or poetic, origin of his work. When he talks about Mallarmé, he couldn't be more explicit: "A great figure. Modern art must return to the direction traced by Mallarmé; it it must be an intellectual, and not merely an animal, expression . . ."The similarity between the two artists springs not from the fact that they both show intellectual preoccupations in their work but from their radical nature—one is the poet and the other the painter of the Idea. Both of them come face to face with the same difficulty: there are no ideas in the modern world, only criticism. But neither of them takes refuge in skepticism and negation. For the poet, chance absorbs the absurd; it is a shot aimed at the absolute and which, in its changes and combinations, manifests or projects the absolute itself. It is the number which, in a state of perpetual motion, rolls from the beginning of the poem to the end and which resolves itself in what mayor may not be a constellation, the unobtainable *sum total in formation*. The role that chance plays in the universe of Mallarmé is the same as that assumed by humor and meta-irony in Duchamp. The theme of the picture and of the poem is criticism, the Idea which ceaselessly destroys and renews itself.

In *Los signos en rotación** (it is bad to quote oneself but worse to para-phrase) I endeavored to show how *Un coup de dés* is "a critical poem" and that "not only does it contain its own negation but this negation is its point of departure and its substance . . . the critical poem resolves itself in a conditional affirmation—an affirmation that feeds on its own nega-tion." Duchamp also turned criticism into myth and negation into an affirmation that is no less provisional than Mallarmé's. The poem and the picture are two distinct versions of the Myth of Criticism, one in the solemn mode of a hymn and the other in the mode of the comic poem. The resemblance can be seen more strikingly if we pass on from analogies of an intellectual order to the form of these two works. Mallarmé inau-

* *Los signos en rotación* (Buenos Aires, 1965).

gurated in *Un coup de dés* a poetic form that contains a plurality of readings—something very different from ambiguity or plurality of meanings, which is a property common to all language. It is an open form that "in its very movement, in its double rhythm of contraction and expansion, of negation that annuls itself and turns itself into an uncertain affirmation of itself, engenders its own interpretations, its successive readings . . . Sum total in perpetual formation: there is no final interpretation of *Un coup de dés* because the last word of the poem is not the final word." The incomplete state of the *Large Glass* is similar to the last word that is never final of *Un coup de dés;* it is an open space that provokes new interpretations and evokes, in its incomplete state, the void on which the work depends. This void is *the absence of the Idea.* Myths of Criticism: if the poem is a ritual of absence, the painting is its burlesque representation. Metaphors of the void. The hymn and the mural painting are open works that initiate a new type of creation; they are texts in which speculation, or the idea, or "gray matter" is the only character. An elusive character: Mallarmé's text is a poem in movement and Duchamp's painting is in a state of continual change. *The sum total in formation* of the poet is never complete; each one of its moments is definitive in relation to those that precede it and relative to those that come after; the reader himself is only one *reading* more, another instant in this never-ending tale, this constellation that is shaped by whatever is uncertain in each reading. Duchamp's painting is a transparent glass; as a genuine monument it is inseparable from the place it occupies and the space that surrounds it; it is an incomplete painting that is perpetually completing itself. Because it is an image that reflects the image of whoever contemplates it, we are never able to look at it without seeing ourselves. To sum up, the poem and the painting affirm simultaneously the absence of meaning and the necessity of meaning, and it is here that the meaning of both works resides. If the universe is a language, Mallarmé and Duchamp show us the reverse of language—the other side, the empty face of the universe. They are works in search of a meaning.

The influence of Duchamp's work and of his personality is part of the history of modern painting. If we omit the numerous and persistent offspring of that part of his work that is painting in the strict sense of the word—above all, of the *Nude Descending a Staircase*—and exclude also the equally numerous and not always successful Readymades, this influence is concentrated at three points: Dada, Surrealism, and contemporary Anglo-American painting. Picabia and Duchamp, as is well known, foresaw, prepared, and inspired the explosion of Dada; at the same time, they gave it elements and tendencies that were lacking in the work of the orthodox representatives of the movement. It is best to quote Duchamp on this point: "While Dada was a movement of negation and, by the very fact of its negation, turned itself into an appendage of the exact thing it was negating, Picabia and I wanted to open up a corridor of humor that at once led into dream-imagery and, consequently, into Surrealism. Dada was purely negative and accusatory . . . For example, my idea of a capricious metrical unit of length. I could have chosen a meter of wood instead of a thread and broken it in two; this would have been Dada." Duchamp's position in the Surrealist movement follows the same dialectic. In the full frenzy of Surrealism he returned to certain Dadaist gestures and kept alive a tradition of humor and negation that the movement, dominated as it was by the passionate and logical genius of Breton, would perhaps have discarded. His action was, in both cases, that of a precursor and contradictor.

The influence of Duchamp on Anglo-American painting has a different character. It is not a direct though distant activity, as in the epoch of Dada and militant Surrealism; it is an example. Contemporary American painting has gone through two distinct periods. In the first, the painters were influenced by the Mexican muralists and, a little later and more decisively, by the Surrealists: Ernst, Miró, Masson, Matta, Lam, and Tanguy. Among these names the most important were, in my opinion, Masson and Matta. This stage owed little to Duchamp. Abstract Expressionism was too olfactory and retinal to be the kind of painting he cared for. The second group, that of the young painters, would be unthinkable without his friendship, presence, and influence. It is necessary at this point to make a distinction between Pop Art in the proper sense of the term and the work of other young artists such as Jasper Johns and Robert Rauschenberg. Pop Art bears only a superficial resemblance to the *gesture* of Duchamp or, for that matter, to the attitude of Picabia, although it is closer to the second. Pop humor lacks aggression and its profanities are not inspired by negation or sacrilege but by what Nicholas Calas defines as the *why not?* Nor is it a metaphysical revolt; fundamentally it is passive and conformist. It is not a search for innocence or the "previous life," like the movement of the Beat poets, although like them, and with greater frequency, it falls into sentimentality. Its brusque recourse to brutality is just this—a way of countering this sentimentality. It is a typical national reaction. The Anglo-Americans swing between these two extremes with the same facility as the Spanish turn from anger to apathy and the Mexicans from the shout to silence. No one is less sentimental than Duchamp; his temperament is sober and his art *dry*. Picabia was exuberant and could laugh or weep copiously, but he never groaned or smirked before the public-as-mirror as the Pop Artist does. The common denominator of Duchamp and Picabia is their lucid desperation.. The great master of the Pop painters is, in fact, Kurt Schwitters. It is hardly necessary to remind oneself that he called his art of refuse and garbage *Merz*, an allusion to *Kommerz* (commerce), *Ausmerzen* (garbage), *Herz* (heart), and *Schmerz* (grief). It is an art of anguish saved by humor and fantasy but not exempt from self-pity. Finally, Duchamp and Picabia, like all the Dadaists and the Surrealists after them, lived in .perpetual conflict with the mass and with the minority; Pop Art, on the other hand, is a populism for the well-off.

In the case of Rauschenberg, Johns, and a few other artists, there is a difference. These two artists are extremely talented and their mental gifts are as great as their pictorial ones. Jasper Johns is, I think, the more concentrated and profound; his painting is rigorous—it is target practice and the target is metaphysical. Rauschenberg's sensibility is more on the surface and he has a great painterly instinct which he could turn into the beginnings of something important or which could relapse into mere good taste. Both of them have preoccupations similar to those of Duchamp, though in speaking of influence I mean affinity rather than exact derivation. They are two intrepid artists and their work is a continual exploration. Admittedly, I don't see either in them or in the others the prospect of that *total* work that the United States has been promising us for a century and a half. I am thinking as I write this not only of painting but equally of poetry. What Whitman prophesied neither Pound nor Williams, neither Stevens nor Cummings, neither Lowell nor Ginsberg has fulfilled. Lucid or visionary, almost always original and at times extraordinary, they are not the poets of midday but of twilight. Perhaps it is better so.

Being a public painter is not the same as being popular. Art, for Duchamp, is a secret and should be shared and passed on like a message between conspirators. Let us listen to him: "Today painting has become vulgarized to the utmost degree . . . While no one has the nerve to intervene in a conversation between mathematicians, we listen every day to after-dinner dissertations on the value of this painter or that . . . The production of an epoch is always its mediocrity. What is not produced is always better than what is." In another interview he confided to the poet Jouffroy: "The painter has already become completely integrated with actual society, he is no longer a pariah . . ." Duchamp doesn't want to end up either in the academy or among the beggars, but it is obvious that he would prefer the lot of the pariah to that of the "assimilated artist." His attitude to the current situation in art is not different from that which inspired the Readymades and the *Large Glass*. It is one of total criticism, and therefore, over and above all, criticism of modernity. The history of modern painting, from the Renaissance to our own times, could be described as the gradual transformation of the work of art into an artistic object: a transition from *vision* to the *perceptible thing*. The Readymades were a criticism both of taste and of the object. The *Large Glass* is the last genuinely meaningful work of the West; it is meaningful because by assuming the traditional meaning of painting, which is absent from retinal art, it dissolves it in a circular process and in this way affirms it. With it our tradition comes to an end. Or, rather, the painting of the future will have to begin with it and by confronting it, if painting has a future or the future a painting.

Meanwhile, imitations of the Readymades pile up in our museums and galleries. The isolated gesture is degraded into a dreary collective rite, a blasphemous game becomes passive acceptance, and the "objet-dart" turns into an inoffensive artifact. Since the Second World War the process has accelerated; painting and sculpture have been converted, like the other products of industrial society, into consumer goods. We are witnessing the end of the "perceptible thing," of retinal painting reduced to optical manipulation. What distinguished modern from classical art was—from Romantic irony to the humor of Dada and the Surrealists— the alliance of criticism and creation; the eradication of the critical element from works of art is equivalent to a veritable castration, and the abolition of meaning confronts us with a production no less insignificant, although much more numerous, than that of the retinal period. Finally, our epoch has replaced the old notion of *recognition* with the idea of publicity, but publicity dissipates into general anonymity. It is the revenge of criticism.

One of Duchamp's most disturbing ideas is crystallized in an often-quoted sentence: "The spectator makes the picture." Expressed with such insolent concision, it would seem to deny the existence of works of art and to proclaim an ingenuous nihilism. In a short text published in 1957 ("The Creative Act"),* he clarifies his idea a little. He explains here that the artist is never fully aware of his work. Between his intention and the realization, between what he *wants* to say and what the work actually *says*, there is a difference. This "difference" is, in fact, the work. Now, the spectator doesn't judge the picture by the intentions of its originator but by what he actually sees. This vision is never objective; the spectator interprets and "distills" what he sees. The "difference" is transformed into another difference, the work into another work. In my opinion Duchamp's explanation does not account for the creative act or process in its entirety. It is true that the spectator creates a work that is different from the one imagined by the artist, but between the two works, between what the artist *wanted* to do and what the spectator *thinks* he sees, there is a *reality:* the work. Without it, the re-creation of the spectator is impossible. The work makes the eye that sees it—or, at least it is a point of departure; out of it and by means of it the spectator invents another work. The value of a picture, a poem, or any other artistic creation is in proportion to the number of signs or meanings that we can see in it and the possibilities that it contains for combining them. A work is a machine for *producing*

* *Art News*, Vol. 56, No. 4. (New York, 1957).

meanings. In this sense Duchamp's idea is not entirely false: the picture depends on the spectator because only he can set in motion the apparatus of signs that comprises the whole work. This is the secret of the fascination of the *Large Glass* and the Readymades. Both of them demand an active contemplation, a creative participation. They make us and we make them. In the case of the Readymades the relation is not one of fusion but of opposition; they are objects made against the public, against ourselves. By one means or another Duchamp affirms that the work is not a museum piece. It is not an object of adoration nor is it useful; it is an object to be invented and created. His interest—indeed, his admiration and nostalgia—for the religious painters of the Renaissance has the same origin. Duchamp is against the museum, not against the cathedral; against the "collection," not against an art that is founded on life. Once more Apollinaire has hit the mark: Duchamp's purpose is to reconcile art and life, work and spectator. But the experience of other epochs cannot be repeated and Duchamp knows it. Art that is founded in life is socialized art, not social or socialist art; and still less is it an activity dedicated to the production of beautiful or purely decorative objects. Art founded in life means a poem by Mallarmé or a novel by Joyce; it is the most difficult art. An art that *obliges* the spectator or the reader to become himself an artist and a poet.

In 1923, Duchamp abandoned definitively the painting of the *Large Glass*. From then on his activity has been isolated and discontinuous. His only permanent occupation has been chess. There are some people who consider this attitude a desertion, and, inevitably, there are others who judge it as a sign of "artistic impotence." These people never stop to take note of the fact that Duchamp has placed in parentheses not so much art as the modern idea of the work of art. His inactivity is the natural prolongation of his criticism—it is meta-irony. I emphasize the distinction between art and the idea of the work because what the Readymades and Duchamp's other gestures denounce is the concept of art as an object— the "*objet d'art*"—that we can separate from its context in life and keep in museums and other safe deposits. The very expression "priceless work of art" reveals the passive and lucrative character—there is no contradiction in the terms—of our notion of the work. For the ancients as for

Duchamp and the Surrealists art is a means of liberation, contemplation, or knowledge, an adventure or a passion. Art is not a category separate from life . . . André Breton once compared his abandonment of painting with Rimbaud's break with poetry. Chess would be in these terms a sort of Harrar in New York, even more "execrable" than that of the poet. But Duchamp's inactivity is of a different order from Rimbaud's silence. The adolescent poet opposes a total negation to poetry and disowns his work; his silence is a wall and we don't know what lies behind this refusal to speak: wisdom, desperation, or a psychic change that converted a great poet into a mediocre adventurer. Duchamp's silence is open; he affirms that art is one of the highest forms of existence, on condition that the artist escapes a double trap—the illusion of the work of art and the temptation to wear the mask of the artist. Both of these petrify us; the first makes a prison of a passion, and the second a profession of freedom. To think that Duchamp is a vulgar nihilist is sheer stupidity: "I love the word 'believe.' Normally when people say *I know*, they don't know what they are saying; they believe that they know. I believe that art is the only activity by which man shows himself as an individual. By this activity he can transcend his animal nature—art opens onto regions that are not bound by time or space. To live is to believe—at least this is what *I believe*." Is it not strange that the author of the Readymades and the *Large Glass* should express himself in such a way and proclaim the supremacy of passion? Duchamp is intensely human, and it is contradiction that distinguishes men from angels, animals, and machines. Moreover, his "irony of affirmation" is a dialectical process that has the precise intention of undermining the authority of reason. He is not an irrationalist; he applies rational criticism to reason; his crazy and carefully reasoned humor is the backfired shot of reason. Duchamp is the creator of the Myth of Criticism, he is not a professor who makes criticism of the myth.

His friend Roché has compared him with Diogenes, and the comparison is correct. Like the cynic philosopher and like all of the very limited number of men who have dared to be free, Duchamp is a down. Freedom is not knowledge but what one has become after knowledge. It is a state of mind that not only admits contradiction but seeks it out for its nourishment and as a foundation. The saints do not laugh, nor

*WATER WRITES ALWAYS IN *PLURAL:*

Given   1.   the waterfall

   2.   the illuminating gas,

one will determine
we shall (determine) the conditions
for the instantaneous State of Rest (or allegorical appearance)
of a (succession) [of a group] of (various facts)
seeming to necessitate each other
under certain laws, in order to isolate the (sign)
the
of accordance between, on the one hand,
this State of Rest (capable of (innumerable eccentricities))
and, on the other, a choice of Possibilities
authorized by these laws and (also
(determining them).[†]

We are indebted to Apollinaire for three judgments on Marcel Duchamp, incompatible with one another, and all three true. In one of them he allotted his friend a mission: "to reconcile art and the people." In another he claimed that the young painter (Duchamp was about twenty-five when Apollinaire wrote this) was one of the few artists unafraid

---

[*] This expression appears in "*The*," Marcel Duchamp's first text in English, composed in New York in 1915. The article "the" was systematically replaced by an asterisk and gives the fragment its title.

[†] Marcel Duchamp, opening paragraph of the preface to the *Green Box*, translation by George Heard Hamilton, typography by Richard Hamilton, from *The Bride Stripped Bare by Her Bachelors, Even* (New York: Wittenborn, 1960).

of "being criticized as esoteric or unintelligible." The third judgment was no less peremptory nor, apparently, less arbitrary and contradictory: "Duchamp is the only painter of the modern school who today [autumn, 1912] concerns himself with the nude."*

The first claim, surprising at the time of its formulation, seems less so today. The Readymades evicted the "art object," replacing it with the anonymous "thing" that belongs to us all and to no one. Though they do not exactly represent the union of art and the people, they acted subversively against the fastidious privileges of artistic taste.

On the other hand *The Bride Stripped Bare by Her Bachelors, Even* does indeed bring about the union that Apollinaire predicted. It does so twice over: it not only adopts the highly publicity-conscious form of illustrations from catalogs of industrial machinery, but it was conceived by Duchamp as a monument whose theme is at once popular and traditional—the apotheosis of the Bride as she is being denuded.

Despite its twofold public character—graphic description of the workings of a machine and representation of an erotic ritual—the *Large Glass* is a secret work. Its composition is the projection of an object that we cannot perceive with our senses; what we see—outlines, mechanisms, diagrams—is only one of its manifestations in the mechanic-ironic mode. The painting is an enigma and, like all enigmas, is something not to be contemplated but deciphered. The visual aspect is only a starting point. Furthermore, there is another element that radically modifies the innocuous act of seeing a painting and turns it into a kind of initiation rite: the riddle is presented to us by a virgin who is also a machine. It is surely not necessary to recall the ancient and fateful connection between virgins and riddles. There is yet another similarity between the myth and the painting: like the heroes and the knights of old, we confront the enigma with only the innocence left to us and with a sure but hermetic guide—the notes of the *Green Box* and the *White Box*. The public monument to the Bride is transformed into a sexual and mental labyrinth; the

---

* All three quotations, Guillaume Apolinaire, *Les peintres cubists: Meditations estheques* (Paris: Figuere, 1913). English translation by Lionel Abel, *The Cubist Painters: Aesthetic Meditations* (New York: Wittenborn, Schultz, 1949), pp. 47-8.

Bride is a body made of reflections, allusions, and transparencies. Her clarity dazzles us, and I am afraid that, beside her, this text will seem like the gas lamp held by the naked woman in the Assemblage in the Philadelphia Museum of Art.

At once a scientific description, a monument to a virgin, and an enigma made up of fearful clarities, *The Bride Stripped Bare by Her Bachelors, Even* is a nude. And so it confirms Apollinaire's third assertion. Except that, once again, it is an assertion that belies itself even as we affirm it: the nude is a skeleton. Erotic myth and negation of the myth by the machine, public monument and secret creation, nude that is a skeleton, and skeleton that is a motor, the *Large Glass* opens out before us like the image of contradiction. But the contradiction is apparent rather than real: what we see are only moments and states of an invisible object, stages in the process of manifestation and concealment of a phenomenon. With that lucidity that is no less unique in him because it is constant, Duchamp alludes to the duplicity of his attempt in one of the first notes in the *Green Box*: "Perhaps make a *hinge picture*" (*tableau de charnière*). This expression, applicable to all his work, is particularly apt in the case of the *Large Glass*: we are facing a hinge picture that, as it opens out or folds back, physically and mentally, shows us other vistas, other apparitions of the same elusive object.

The *hinge* appears frequently in Duchamp. Thanks to the literal and paradoxical use of the idea of the hinge, Duchamp's doors and ideas open while remaining closed, and vice versa. If we have recourse to the same procedure, the expression "hinge picture," opening out (closing) on itself, reveals to us another expression that also appears in one of the early notes of the *Green Box*: "delay in glass" (*retard en verre*). Duchamp explains that this refers to a "sort of subtitle." Always explicit, even within his extreme succinctness, he adds that we must understand the word "delay" in the "indecisive reunion" of its different meanings. According to the Petit Littré dictionary, the meanings of *retard* are three in number: "What is or what happens too late; the delay of a watch, a dock, part of the movement that serves to slow it down or move it ahead; in harmony, the momentary delay when one starts to play one of the notes of a chord, but prolongs for a few moments the note of the preceding chord, a note that needs for its resolution the one which is delayed."* As it swings on its hinge, the "delay in glass," *The Bride* leads us on to another composition that is its *resolution*, as much in the musical sense as in any other. This composition, the final chord, is the Assemblage in the Philadelphia Museum. To see it is to hear the note held in abeyance in the *Large Glass*. Is the resolution the solution?

Although it has been described several times—in the noteworthy study by Anne d'Harnoncourt and Walter Hopps,† for example—I think it will serve some purpose here to give an idea of the work, since a photographic reproduction is not possible. As everyone knows, it is located in the Philadelphia Museum of Art beyond the large gallery where much of Duchamp's work is collected and where the *Large Glass* occupies the central spot. The visitor goes through a low doorway, into a room somewhat on the small side, completely empty. No painting on the white walls. There are no windows. In the far wall, embedded in a brick portal topped by an arch, there is an old wooden door, worm-eaten, patched, and closed by a rough crossbar made of wood and nailed on with heavy spikes. In the top lefthand corner there is a little window that has also been closed up. The door sets its material doorness in the visitor's way with a sort of aplomb: dead end. The opposite of the hinges and their paradoxes. A real condemned door. But if the visitor ventures nearer, he finds two small holes at eye level. If he goes even closer and dares to peep, he will see a scene he is not likely to forget. First of all, a brick wall with a slit in it, and through the slit, a wide open space, luminous and seemingly bewitched. Very near the beholder—but also very far away, on the "other side"—a naked girl, stretched on a kind of bed or pyre of branches and leaves, her face almost completely covered by the blond mass of her hair, her legs open and slightly bent, the pubes strangely smooth in contrast to the splendid abundance of her hair, her right arm out of the line of vision, her left slightly raised, the hand grasping a small gas lamp made of

---

* In English the third meaning is not apparent. [Translator's note.]
† "Etant donnés: 1° la chute d'eau, 2° le gaz d'éclairage. Reflections on a New Work by Macel Duchamp," *Philadelphia Museum of Art Bulletin*, Nos. 299, 300 (April–June and July–September, 1969).

metal and glass. The little lamp glows in the brilliant light of this motionless, end-of-summer day. Fascinated by this challenge to our common sense—what is there less clear than light?—our glance wanders over the landscape: in the background, wooded hills, green and reddish; lower down, a small lake and a light mist on the lake. An inevitably blue sky. Two or three little clouds, also inevitably white. On the far right, among some rocks, a waterfall catches the light. Stillness: a portion of time held motionless. The immobility of the naked woman and of the landscape contrasts with the movement of the waterfall and the flickering of the lamp. The silence is absolute. All is real and verges on banality; all is unreal and verges—on what?

The viewer draws back from the door feeling that mixture of joy and guilt of one who has unearthed a secret. But what is the secret? What, in fact, has he seen? The scene that takes place without taking place behind the door is no less enigmatic than the diagrams and outlines of the *Large Glass*. Seeking a sign to orient him in his perplexity, the visitor finds the title of the Assemblage affixed to the wall: *Etant donnés: 1° la chute d'eau, 2° le gaz d'éclairage.* (1946–1966). The contradictory relationship between public and secret art, monument and initiation rite, is repeated: the Assemblage leads us to its title, the title to the Preface of the *Green Box*, which begins with precisely the same pseudoscientific formula: *Etant donnés* . . . The formula leads us to the *Large Glass* and the *Large Glass* to our own image, which, as we gaze at the *Large Glass*, blends with the painted forms and the reflections of the outside world. The play of correspondences and reflections between the Assemblage and the *Large Glass* is upsetting, and it presents itself on the visual plane as well as the textual—the notes of the *Green Box* and those of the *White Box* are the verbal bridge between the two works. In both cases, the mere act of looking at a painting or an Assemblage is turned into the fact of viewing-through . . . In one case, through the obstacle of the door, which finally becomes the line of vision leading us to the landscape with the woman and the waterfall; in the other, through the glass on which the composition is painted and which, by reason of its very transparency, becomes an obstacle to our vision. Reversibility: seeing through opaqueness, not-seeing through transparency. The wooden door and the glass door: two

Door of Given: 1. The Waterfall, 2. The Illuminating Gas, 1946–66. *(Mixed media assemblage.) Philadelphia Museum of Art: Gift of the
Cassandra Foundation.*

opposite facets of the same idea. This
opposition is resolved in an identity: in
both cases we look at ourselves looking.
Hinge procedure. The question "What
do we see?" confronts us with ourselves.

Twenty-three years separate the
date when the *Large Glass* was definitively unfinished and the date when
the *Given* was begun. This long period
of retirement gave rise to the idea that
Duchamp had given up painting. The
truth is that after 1913, with only a few
exceptions like the *Tu m'* of 1918, his
work not only abandoned strictly pictorial procedures but also, without
ceasing to be visual, turned into the negation of what we have called
painting for more than two centuries. Duchamp's attitude toward the
pictorial tradition is also governed by the hinge principle: the negation
of painterly painting, which is the basic concept of the modern tradition
since Delacroix, implies negation of the avant-garde. This is a unique
position in the art of our era: Duchamp is at one and the same time the
artist who carries avant-garde trends to their final consequences, and the
artist who, in consummating them, turns them back on themselves and
so inverts them. Negation of "retinal" painting breaks with the modern
tradition and unexpectedly renews the bond with the central current
of the West, anathematized by Baudelaire and his twentieth-century
descendants: the painting of ideas.* A procedure analogous to that of the

---

* "The retinal shudder! Before, painting had other functions: it could be religious,
philosophical, moral . . . Our whole century is completely retinal, except for the
Surrealists, who tried to go outside it somewhat. And still, they didn't go so far!"

delay in glass, though in the diametrically opposite direction, the *accelera-tion* of the modern ends in its devaluation. In 1957 Duchamp was asked, "Do you believe in a forthcoming explosion of the modern spirit?" He replied, "Yes, but it is the word '*modern*' which has run itself out. Look at the *modern style* of the beginning of the century . . ."*

The general system governing Duchamp's work is the same as that which inspires the so-called Wilson-Lincoln effect—those portraits that represent Wilson when seen from the left and Lincoln from the right. The Wilson-Lincoln effect is a variant of the hinge principle: the pivot converted into the material and spiritual axis of the universe. Generalized reversibility, circularity of phenomena and ideas. Circularity includes the spectator, also; the Bride is enclosed in our glance, but we are enclosed in the *Large Glass* and included in the *Given.* We are part of both works. Thus there comes about a radical inversion of the position of the terms that intervene in creation and artistic contemplation and that, to a certain extent, constitute it: the artist's subjectivity (or the viewer's) and the work. A certain kind of relationship initiated by Romanticism ends with Duchamp.

The art and poetry of our time come into being precisely when the artist inserts subjectivity into the order of objectivity. This procedure sensitizes nature and the work, but at the same time, it makes them relative. Romantic irony has been the nourishment-poison of Western art and literature for almost two centuries. Nourishment, because it is the leavening of "modern beauty," as Baudelaire defined it: the bizarre, the unique. Or rather, objectivity torn apart by ironic subjectivity, which is always an awareness of human contingency, awareness of death. Poison, because "modern beauty," contrary to that of the ancients, is condemned to destroy itself; in order to exist, to affirm its modernity, it needs to negate what was modern scarcely as long ago as yesterday. It needs to negate itself. Modern beauty is bizarre because it is different from yester-

---

Duchamp quoted by Pierre Cabanne, *Dialogues with Marcel Duchamp,* translated by Ron Padgett (New York: Viking, 1971), p. 43.
* Jean Schuster, "Marcel Duchamp, vite," *Le Surréalisme, même* (Paris), No. 2, Spring 1957, p. 148.

Tu m'. (Oil on canvas with large brush attached.) Yale University Art Gallery: Bequest of Katherine S. Dreier.

day's, and for that very reason it is historical. It is change, it is perishable: historicity is mortality.

Duchamp's youth coincided with the explosion of the avant-garde movements; that is to say, with the last and most violent manifestation of the modern tradition ushered in by Romanticism. Duchamp has recalled more than once his youthful interest in Jules Laforgue, a poet thought little of in France but who has had a profound influence on Anglo-American poetry and on Latin-American as well. In Laforgue, modern subjectivity turns in on itself—he is a Symbolist poet who uses irony to gnaw away at the Symbolist aesthetic. It was natural that Laforgue should inspire Duchamp, as Mallarmé did later. Apart from the influences that he has revealed himself, others can be quoted. For example, this title of a Laforgue poem could be a phrase from the litany of the Chariot: "*Célibat, célibat, tout n'est que célibat.*" Another poem is called "Complainte de crépuscules célibataires." Human history, says Laforgue, is the "histoire d'un célibataire." Schopenhauer revised and corrected: the world is the representation of a bachelor self.

Duchamp submits Laforgue's irony to the disorienting action of the Wilson-Lincoln system and in this way changes it, literally turning it inside out. Modern irony, from Romanticism onward, is the action of the bite of subjectivity into the work; in the *Large Glass* and the *Given*, it is not the self that takes over the object, but the contrary: we see ourselves seeing through the opaqueness of the door of the Assemblage or the transparency of the *Large Glass*. The Wilson-Lincoln principle is revealed as a meta-irony, that is, as an "irony of affirmation," as opposed to the Romantic negation. Irony and subjectivity have become the axis of modern art. Duchamp makes this axis spin on itself, and he overturns the relationship between subject and object: his "laughing picture" laughs at us. The very notion of modernity is demolished. While continuing to be peculiar and different from yesterday's—continuing to be polemical and historical, i.e., modern—Duchamp's art undertakes the criticism of modernity and exchanges nods of recognition with the art of the past.

The negation of painterly painting was far from being a renunciation of art; the twenty-three years separating the *Large Glass* from *Given* were not empty—rather, they were years of search and preparation. The surprising thing is precisely the persistence of Duchamp's underground work, his patience and his coherence. Like Saint-Pol-Roux, who used to hang the inscription "The poet is working" from his door while he slept, Duchamp used to say that he was not doing anything except breathing—and when he was breathing, he was working. His obsessions and his myths were working him: inaction is the condition of inner activity. On various occasions Duchamp denounced the publicity surrounding modern art and maintained that artists should go underground. Here the hinge principle reappears: the man who drew a mustache on the *Mona Lisa* is the same man who, for twenty years, carried out work in secret. Contrary and complementary forms of his rupture with the world: public profanation and the descent to the catacombs, the slap in the face and silence.

Helped by Teeny, his wife and confidante, in assembling this clandestine production, Duchamp worked more or less continuously from 1946 to 1966, first in his study on Fourteenth Street, and later in modest premises in a commercial building on Eleventh Street. Early in 1969, three months after his death, Anne d'Harnoncourt and Paul Matisse dismounted the Assemblage, took the pieces to Philadelphia, and put them together again in the museum there. They used as a guide a notebook prepared by Duchamp and made up of precise instructions, diagrams, and more than a hundred photographs. An exceedingly difficult task, carried out with great skill and sensitivity.

The *Given* is a combination of materials, techniques, and different artistic forms. As for the former, some have been brought to the work with no modification—the twigs on which the nude is lying, the old door brought from Spain, the gas lamp, the bricks—and others have been modified by the artist. Equally varied are the techniques and forms of artistic expression: the artificial lighting and the theatrical illusion of the scene; the action of the invisible electric motor, which reminds us of the techniques of clockwork toy-making; sculpture, photography, painting, properly speaking, and even window dressing. All these techniques and forms draw together Duchamp's earlier experiences, for example, the window display at the Gotham Book Mart in New York in 1945, advertising Breton's *Arcane 17*, where a half-nude dummy was used. However, there is a difference between Duchamp's earlier works and the *Given*. In the former, he is trying to show what is behind or beyond appearance—the decomposition of movement in the *Nude Descending a Staircase*, a passionate game of chess in *The King and Queen Traversed by Swift Nudes*, the symbolic functioning of an erotic machine in the *Large Glass*—while

Window installation by Marcel Duchamp and Andre Breton for publication of Breton's Arcane 17, *at Gotham Book Mart, New York, 1945. Duchamp and Breton can be seen reflected in the glass. Photograph courtesy of Mme Duchamp.*

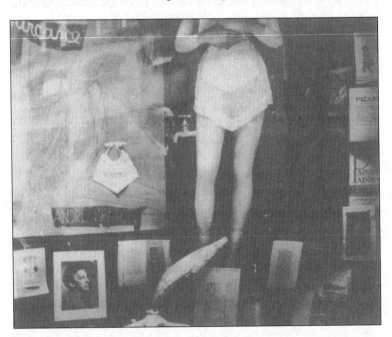

in the latter the artist seems to be satisfied with the appearance. In the *Large Glass*, the spectator must imagine the scene of the bride's delight at being stripped; in *Given* he sees her in the actual moment of fulfillment. The symbolic description of the phenomenon is followed by the phenomenon itself: the machine of the *Large Glass* is the representation of an enigma; the nude of *Given* is the enigma in person, its incarnation.

The bridge or hinge between the *Large Glass* and *Given* is a drawing from 1958: *Bedridden Mountains* [*Cols alités*], *Project for the 1959 Model of The Bride Stripped Bare by Her Bachelors, Even.* The drawing reproduces the *Large Glass*, but in the central region it adds a sketch of hills, with very fine, hardly visible lines. Furthermore, on the far right, after the Chocolate Grinder and as if it were a prolongation of one of the blades of the Scissors, Duchamp drew an electric pole with its wires and insulators. One of the notes in the *Green Box* indicates that the communication between the Bride and the Bachelors is electric, and in the 1958 drawing this idea—which refers rather to a metaphor: the electricity of thought, of the glance, and of desire—is expressed in the most direct and material form: a pole and its wires. And so we have two images of electricity: physical energy and psychic energy. By the title of the drawing Duchamp hints that the mountainous landscape is made up of passes (*Cols*), but that these passageways are bedridden, ailing (*alités*). As a result, they are scarcely passable, and communication between the realm of the Bachelors and that of the Bride is difficult. In *Given* communication is even more difficult, in spite of the fact that the landscape of wooded hills possesses an almost tactile reality—or perhaps for this very reason: we are dealing with the deceptive reality of *trompe l'oeil*. Last, the title alludes also to the law that governs the conception of the *Large Glass* and of *Given*: ironic causality. *Causalité/Cols alités:* a slight distension of the sounds takes us from the ailing passes of the hills to a universe in which chance and necessity exchange nods. The difference between "causality" and "casuality" lies in the different position of the same *u*. Knowledge is a disease of language.

The road from the *Large Glass* to *Given* is made up of reflections. It is a spiral which begins where it ends and in which over there is here. Identity emerges from itself in search of itself, and every time it

Cols alités (Bedridden Mountains),
1959. Collection Robert Lebel, Paris.

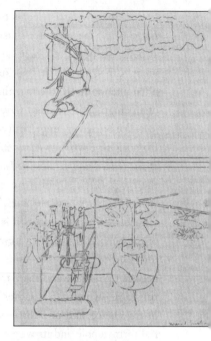

is about to meet itself, it bifurcates. But the echoes and correspondences between one and the other can be applied to all of Duchamp's work. We are facing a true constellation in which each painting, each Readymade, and each wordplay is joined to the others like the sentences of a discourse. A discourse ruled by rational syntax and delirious semantics. A system of forms and signs moved by their own laws. The landscape of *Given*, implicit in the *Large Glass*, is an echo or a rhyme of three other pictures in which the same combination of trees, sky, and water appears. One represents the landscape of his birthplace (B1ainville) and dates from 1902; another is the well-known Readymade of 1914, *Pharmacy;* the last is the 1953 *Moonlight on the Bay at Basswood.* The gas motif goes back to his adolescence; there is a drawing from 1903/04 that shows a gas lamp (*Hanging Gas Lamp*) with the brand name Bec Auer. The water/gas pair appears constantly in Duchamp's works, word games, and conversations, from the years when he was preparing the *Large Glass* until the year of his death. *Water and Gas on Every Floor* was an inscription found on the doors of new buildings in the Paris of his youth, which he used for the title page of the deluxe edition of Robert Lebel's monograph. Other correspondences could be quoted, but it might be better to concentrate on the water/gas duality: they are the two *authors* of the *Large Glass* and the *Given*, and their writing is in the plural.

In the note to the *Green Box* that serves as epigraph to this text and that gives its title to the Assemblage, it is clearly stated that the Waterfall and the Illuminating Gas literally produce the Bride. Water and gas are human and cosmic elements, physical and psychic. Eroticism and ironic causality at the same time, they come together and separate according to rigorous and eccentric laws. In the *Large Glass* they are invisible forces, and if it were not for the notes of the *Green Box*, we would not know that it is their action that sets the complicated and tragicomic mechanism running. Water and gas, says the *Green Box*, work in the *darkness* and in the *darkness* will emerge the "allegorical appearance," the Bride, like an "ultrarapid exposure."

Because they are elements pregnant with sexuality, erotic signs, it is not strange that one of the most assiduous exegetes of Duchamp's work has identified gas as a masculine and water as a feminine symbol. Two reasons prevent me from accepting this oversimplified interpretation. The first is the discredit into which the Jungian archetypes have fallen. Not because they are false but because people want to explain everything with them—and so nothing is explained. For that reason I prefer to call the Waterfall and the Illuminating Gas signs and not symbols. Symbols have lost their meaning by virtue of having so many contradictory meanings. On the other hand, signs are less ambitious and more agile; they are not emblems of a "conception of the world" but movable pieces of a syntax. The second reason: signs (and symbols) change their meaning and gender according to the context in which they are placed. They mean nothing by themselves; they are elements in a relationship. The laws that govern phonology and syntax are perfectly applicable in this sphere. No symbol has an immutable meaning; the meaning depends on the relation. We generally think of water as a feminine symbol, but as soon as it becomes running water—waterfall, river, stream, rain—it takes on a masculine tonality: it penetrates into the soil, or it gushes out of it. The same thing happens with air, although it is the masculine principle par excellence, from the Aztec Quetzalcoatl to the Christian Holy Ghost; the air that comes out of the orifices (the genitals, the mouth) of the archetypes of the great Jungian mother is feminine: the all-containing vessel. Air becomes feminine in the sylph and in the "cloud-damsels" of the Sirigiya frescoes. The cloud, image of indetermination, undecided between water and air, admirably expresses the ambivalent nature of signs and symbols. And why not mention fire, which is both Zeus's bolt and the feminine oven, the womb where men are cooked, according to the Nahuatl myth? The meaning of signs changes as their position in context changes. The best thing will be to follow the path of water and gas in the battle of reflections that the *Large Glass* and the *Given* interchange between themselves.

In the *Large Glass* gas appears as the determining element of the Bachelors. Not only does it inspire (inflate) them, but they expire it, in the double meaning of the word. They send it through the Capillary Tubes to the Sieves, where it undergoes an operation, in the surgical sense, emerging as an explosive liquid, to be immediately cut off and atomized by the Scissors; falling into the region of the Spray, it ascends once more and, sublimated by the Oculist Witnesses, who transform it into an image, is thrown into the Bride's domain, turned into a reflection of reflections. Despite all these adventures and misadventures, gas is invisible. In *Given* gas appears—and appears in its most direct and commonplace manifestation, in the form of a phallic gas lamp clutched by a naked girl. In the *Large Glass*, the Illuminating Gas is identified with the Bachelors—it is their desire; in the Assemblage the Bachelors disappear, or rather, are reabsorbed by the gas lamp. Onanism, leitmotif of the litanies of the Chariot, passes from the Bachelors to the Bride. But was the same thing not happening in the *Large Glass?* The *Given* confirms not only the imaginary nature of the operation—emphasized more than once by Duchamp—but also the nonexistence of the Bachelors: they are a projection, an invention of the Bride. In her turn the Bride is an epiphany of another invisible reality, the projection in two or three dimensions of a four-dimensional entity. And so the world is the representation not of a bachelor, as Laforgue said, but of a reality that we do not see and that appears sometimes as the rather sinister machine of the *Large Glass*, sometimes as a naked girl in her culminating moment of ecstasy.

In describing the physiology of the Bride, the *Green Box* mentions a substance that is not water, though it is a liquid and possesses certain affinities with gas: automobiline, the erotic gasoline that lubricates her organs and makes orgasm possible. The Bride is a "wasp" who secretes by osmosis the essence (gasoline) of love. The wasp draws the necessary doses from her liquid tank. The tank is an "oscillating bathtub" that provides for the Bride's hygiene, or, as Duchamp says somewhat cruelly, for her diet. In the *Given*, ideas become images, and the irony disappears: the tank is turned into the lake, and the "wasp-motor" into the naked girl, creature of the waters. But the best example of these changes—from the liquid state to the gaseous or vice versa, equivalent to mutations of gender—is the Milky Way of the *Large Glass*, manifestation of the Bride in the moment when, as she is being stripped, she reaches the fullness of delight. The Milky Way is a cloud, a gaseous form that has been and will again be water. The cloud is desire before its crystallization; it is not the body but its ghost, the *idée fixe* that has ceased to be an idea and is not yet perceptible reality. Our erotic imagination ceaselessly produces clouds, phantoms. The cloud is the veil that reveals more than it hides, the place where forms are dissipated and born anew. It is the metamorphosis, and for this reason, in the *Large Glass*, it is the manifestation of the threefold joy of the Bride as she is stripped bare: ultrarapid instantaneous communication between the machine state and that of the Milky Way.

This digression on automobiline and clouds should not make us forget that Duchamp does not talk about gas and water in general, but very precisely as Illuminating Gas and Waterfall. In the *Large Glass*, the Waterfall does not appear, but we know its form and location from the *Green Box:* "a jet of water coming from a distance in a semicircle, from above the Malic Molds." The Waterfall could be masculine, as much because it is in the domain of the Bachelors as because it is running water: "Flowing and moving waters," says Erich Neumann, "are bisexual and male and are worshiped as fructifers and movers.'" However, it is a masculinity dependent on the feminine sign: waterfalls and streams although "looked upon as masculine . . . have the significance of a son." In the *Large Glass* the Waterfall feeds the Bride's imagination and purposes, is part of the seduction mechanism of the Bachelors and cause of their ultimate failure. Moreover, it serves as a "cooler" between them and the Bride. In the Assemblage it is in the Bride's domain.

In the *Large Glass* the Waterfall is invisible, a force we do not see but which produces the movement of the Water Mill; in *Given*, the Water

---

* Erich Neumann, The *Great Mother*, Bollingen Series XLVII (Princeton: Princeton University Press, 1963), p. 48.

Mill disappears and the Waterfall is a visible presence. And who sees these apparitions and disappearances? The Oculist Witnesses, who are *inside* the *Large Glass*—and we ourselves who, by spying through the cracks in the Spanish door, incarnate the Witnesses as the nude incarnates the Bride. They (we) are the only ones who can tell us something (tell themselves) about the syntax of the Waterfall and the Illuminating Gas and about the text traced out in their conjunctions and metamorphoses.

In the *Large Glass*, the Oculist Witnesses occupy the extreme right of the Bachelors' domain. A little above the third witness there is a circle that represents the hole in the lock through which the voyeur peeps. The positioning of the Oculist Witnesses more or less corresponds to that of the holes in the door of the Assemblage. The spectator, like the Oculist Witnesses, is a voyeur; also, like them, he is an ocular witness, as much in the legal sense of being present in the case as in the religious sense of attesting to a passion or a martyrdom. We are reminded of the "Four Master Analysts of Ireland" in *Finnegans Wake*, with whom the Witnesses share more than one affinity. This is not the only analogy, moreover, between Joyce and Duchamp: the *Large Glass* and *Given* can be considered the visual equivalents of the Letter to Anna Livia Plurabelle, another "untitled Mamafesta memo-

Photo of Duchamp and his wife, Teeny, at the foot of a waterfall extraordinarily like the one in the Assemblage, *in 1965 near Figueras. The photograph was taken at Duchamp's request, without Denise Hare's knowing that it had any connection with the* Assemblage, *of which the world in general was unaware until Duchamp's death. Photo by Denise Browne Hare, courtesy of Ms. Hare.*

ralizing the Mosthighst." Just as ALP is at one and the same time the inspirer of the Letter and the Letter itself in its different versions, so the Bride is the invisible four-dimensional object *and* its momentary manifestations in the *Large Glass* and in the *Given*. Among the names given to Rrose Sélavy we find the ones given by Joyce to ALP: "Anna the Allmaziful, the Everliving, the Bringer of Plurabilities . . ." If the Letter contains its own interpretations and its own four Evangelists, the *Large Glass* and the *Given* contain their own viewers. The Oculist Witnesses form part of the *Large Glass*, and the spectator of the *Given*, by his very act of peeping, shares in the dual ritual of voyeurism and aesthetic contemplation. Or rather, without him the ritual would not take place. However, there is one difference between the *Large Glass* and the *Given*. It is not the first time that an artist includes in his painting those who look at it, and in my earlier study on Duchamp I recalled Velázquez and his *Meninas*. But what is representation in *Las Meninas* and in the *Large Glass* is an act in *Given;* we are really turned into voyeurs and also into ocular witnesses. Our testimony is part of the work.

The function of the Oculist Witnesses, despite their marginal position, is central: they receive the Spray from the Illuminating Gas, now converted into Sculpture of Drops, and transform it into a mirror image that they throw into the Bride's domain, in the zone of the Nine Shots. The Oculist Witnesses refine (sublimate) the Illuminating Gas turned Spray of explosive drops: they change the drops into a look—that is, into the most immediate manifestation of desire. The look passes through the obstructed passages (*cols alités*) of the Bride and reaches her. It arrives thus far not as reality, but as the image of desire. The vision of her nudity produces in the Bride the first blossoming, before orgasm. It is, as Duchamp emphasizes, an electric blossoming.* The function of the Oculist Witnesses is the sublimation of the Illuminating Gas into a visual image that they transport in a look capable of passing through obstacles. Desire is the "electricity at large" that the *Green Box* mentions. In *Given* electricity

* The second is the denuding voluntarily imagined by the Bride, and the third is the conjunction of the first two: the crown-blossoming in the form of a cloud or the Milky Way, which "cannot be analyzed by logic."

is literally everywhere: behind the backdrop (in the motor) and outside as the brilliant light that bathes the landscape and the naked figure.

Who are the Witnesses? Duchamp the artist (not the man) and ourselves, the spectators. There is often a tendency to see the Bride as a projection of Duchamp and, consequently, of the viewer. The contrary is also true: we are her projection. She sees her naked image in our desiring gaze, which is born from her and returns to her. Once again, the theme is viewing-through . . . We see the erotic object *through* the obstacle, be it door or glass, and this is voyeurism; the Bride sees herself naked in our gaze, and this is exhibitionism. Both are the same, as Schwarz has pointed out. But they are united not in Duchamp or in the viewer, but in the Bride. The circular operation starts from her and returns to her. The world is her representation.

The complementary opposite of voyeurism is clairvoyance. The Oculist Witnesses of the *Large Glass* and the beholder of *Given* are clairvoyants; their gaze passes through material obstacles. The relationship is circular, once again: if desire is second sight, clairvoyance is voyeurism transformed by the imagination, desire made knowledge. Eroticism is the condition of second sight. The erotic vision is creation as well as knowledge. Our gaze changes the erotic object: what we see is the image of our desire. "It is the spectators who make the picture." But the object also sees us; more precisely, our gaze is included in the object. My looking makes the painting only on condition that I accept becoming a part of the painting. I look at the painting, but I look at it looking at what I look at—looking at myself. The person peeping through the holes in the Spanish door is not outside the Assemblage: he is part of the spectacle. *Given* is realized by means of his look: it is a spectacle in which someone sees himself seeing something. And what does he really see? What do the Oculist Witnesses see? *They don't see.* It is the Bride who sees herself. The vision of herself excites her; she sees herself and strips herself bare in the look that looks at her. Reversibility: we look at ourselves looking at her, and she looks at herself in our look that looks at her naked. It is the moment of the discharge—we disappear from her sight.

The dialectic of the look that looks at nudity and nudity that looks at itself in this look irresistibly evokes one of the great myths of pagan

The Triumph of Venus. *Tray painting, School of Verona, early fifteenth century. Cliché Musées Nationaux, Paris.*

antiquity: Diana's bath and Actaeon's downfall. It is strange that to date no one has explored the disturbing similarities between this mythological episode and Duchamp's two great works. The subject matter is the same: the circularity of the look. Actaeon moves from hunter to hunted, from looking to being looked at.

But the correspondences, echoes, and rhymes are more numerous and precise than this comparison indicates. I will begin where the scene takes place: Ovid describes Diana's sanctuary as a valley wooded with pines and cypresses, surrounded by mountains. A waterfall tumbles down a rock, into a small lake, hardly more than a pool.* Ovid's description seems to anticipate the scene in *Given.*

Diana and the Bride: both are virgins, and Ovid uses a curious expression to describe the goddess's clothing: she is "the scarcely clad one." The Bride's virginity in no way implies frigidity or asexuality. The same is true of Diana: "In spite of the fact that she must be considered a virgin," says Dumézil, in the excavations of the sanctuary at Aricia, near Rome, votive offerings were found in the form of masculine and feminine organs, and images of "women clothed, but with their robes open in front."† Who corresponds to Actaeon in the *Large Glass* and the Assemblage? Not the Bachelors, since, apart from the fact that they do not exist in their own right, *they cannot see,* but the Oculist Witnesses. The

---

* Ovid, *Metamorphoses,* Book III, Loeb Classical Library (London and Cambridge, Mass., 1916), Vol. 1, p. 134.
† Georges Dumézil, *La Religion romaine archaïque* (Paris: Payot, 1966), p. 397.

similarity is more remarkable if we are aware that in both cases the visual violation is preceded by disorientation. According to Ovid, the young hunter reaches the sacred confine "wandering and with uncertain steps," that is to say, lost; before turning into the look of the Oculist Witnesses, the Illuminating Gas comes out of the Sieves unable to distinguish left from right; the visitor who goes up to the two holes in the door in the Philadelphia Museum of Art invariably does it after a moment of hesitation and disorientation.

The first study for the Bride (Munich, 1912) had as subtitle "Modesty Mechanism."Time and again Duchamp has emphasized the ambiguous nature of the Bride's modesty, a veil that uncovers her as it hides her, prohibition tinged with provocation. Warm, not cold modesty, and with a "touch of malice." Diana's attitude seems more resolutely and more fiercely chaste. Ovid expressly says that Actaeon's offense was an error, not a crime: it was not desire but destiny that led him to witness the goddess's bath. Nor is Diana an accomplice; her surprise and anger at the sight of Actaeon are genuine. But Pierre Klossowski in a splendid essay suggests that the goddess desires to see herself, a desire that implies being seen by someone else. For this reason, "Diana becomes the object of Actaeon's imagination."'This operation is identical to that of the Bride in the *Large Glass*, who sends herself her own nude image through the medium of the Oculist Witnesses, as Diana does through Actaeon. Klossowski indicates that the look stains, and that the virgin goddess *wishes* to be stained; for his part, Duchamp says that the Bride "warmly rejects (not chastely)" the Bachelors' offering. Lastly, as Diana throws water over Actaeon and transforms him into a deer, the Bride puts a cooler between the Bachelors and herself—the Waterfall.

In both cases we witness not the violation of the two virgins but its homologue: visual violation. But our look really does pass through the material obstacle—the door of the Assemblage, the boughs and leaves of the goddess's sanctuary—and so the transgression is as much psychic as material. Actaeon's punishment is to be turned into a deer—he who

---

* Pierre Klossowski, *Le Bain de Diane* (Paris: Jean-Jacques Pauvert Editeur, 1956), p. 55.

The Bride Stripped Bare by Her Bachelors, 1912. *Courtesy of Cordier &*
Ekstrom, Inc., New York. Photo by Geoffrey Clements.

stared is stared at—torn to pieces by his own dogs. "Seeing prohibited" is
a motif that Duchamp expresses in many ways, especially in his two windows: *Fresh Widow* (french window) and *The Brawl at Austerlitz*. Both
prevent us from seeing; they are windows not to see out of. In the title
of the former, there is, furthermore, an allusion to the guillotine—the
Widow, in popular French jargon—which immediately recalls the fate
of the Illuminating Gas cut to pieces by the Scissors, and of Actaeon by
his dogs.

According to a note from *In the Infinitive* (the *White Box*), the
real punishment consists of possession: "No obstinacy, *ad absurdum*, of
hiding the coition through a glass pane with one or many objects of the
shop window. The penalty consists in cutting the pane and in feeling
regret as soon as possession is consummated."* Except that voyeurism is

---

* Marcel Duchamp, *A l'infinitif* (the *White Box*, notes from 1912 to 1920) (New
York: Cordier & Ekstrom, 1966), p. 5.

not a solution either: if the punishment is eluded, the torture becomes greater. Nonconsummation, desiring without touching what is desired, is no less cruel a penalty than the punishment that follows possession. The solution is the conversion of voyeurism into contemplation—into knowledge.

The same note from *In the Infinitive* contains another curious confession, which is at the same time a lucid description of the circularity of the visual operation: "When one undergoes the examination of the shop windows, one also pronounces one's own sentence. In fact, one's choice is *round trip*." I have already pointed out the resemblance of the Actaeon myth and Duchamp's two works: the gazer is gazed at, the hunter hunted, the virgin strips herself in the look of him who looks at her. The "round trip" that Duchamp refers to exactly corresponds to the internal structure of the myth as well as of his two works. Actaeon depends on Diana; he is the instrument of her desire to see herself. The same thing happens with the Oculist Witnesses: as they look at themselves looking at her, they give the Bride back her image. It is all a round trip. Duchamp has said several times that the Bride is an appearance, the projection of an invisible reality. The Bride is an "instantaneous State of Rest," an "allegorical appearance." Klossowski indicates that Diana's essential body is also invisible: what Actaeon sees is an appearance, a momentary incarnation. In the theophanies of Diana and the Bride, Actaeon and the Oculist Witnesses—we ourselves—are included. The manifestations of Diana and the Bride demand that someone look at them. The subject is a dimension of the object: its reflexive dimensions, its glance.

There are other similarities worth mentioning. In the *Green Box* the Bride is often called Hanged Female (*Pendu femelle*). The machine outlined by Duchamp is literally suspended, hanging in space like a dead beast on a butcher's hook or a hanged man on a scaffold. The theme of the hanged man appears in many myths, but the sacrificial victim is invariably a god. There is, however, an exception: in the Peloponnesus, where the cult of Artemis was very popular, an effigy of the divinity was hung from a tree and was called Apanchomene (the Hanged Woman). One of the notes in the *Green Box* says that the Bride is an "agricultural machine"; further on, she is a "plowing tool." The plow is predominantly masculine—which is why Ceres was three times plowed. But there is another exception: in the festivals of Artemis Orthia, a plow was dedicated to the virgin goddess. There was also a flagellation of young men and a torch procession. (I will return to the latter detail.) In all these ceremonies, there were reminiscences of human sacrifice.

In order to label the Bride's axis, Duchamp uses the expression "arbor-type" (*arbre-type*). Diana is an arboreal divinity and was originally a dryad, like the yakshas of Hindu mythology. The tree that spreads its leaves to the heavens is a feminine tree, and its image, says Neumann, has fascinated all men: "It shades and shelters all living things and feeds them with its fruit which hang on like stars . . ."* The sky in which the tree-goddess stretches out its branches is not the day but the night sky—which is why leaves, branches, fruits, and birds are seen as stars. For his part, Dumézil observes that the name of Diana originally meant "the expanse of the heavens."† Referring to the blossoming (*épanouissement*) of the Bride, Duchamp indicates that in the arbor-type the bloom is *grafted on*, and is the Bride's aureole and the conjunction of her "splendid vibrations." This aureole or crown is none other than the Milky Way: the cloud that preserves in its bosom the lightning (Illuminating Gas) and the rain (Waterfall), the cloud that is the halfway point between the incarnation and the dissipation of the feminine form. The movable cipher of desire. Very significantly Ovid says that when Diana sees herself touched by Actaeon's gaze, she blushes like a cloud shot through by the sun . . . Finally, if Diana's tree is a figure of the mythical imagination, the alchemists saw it in the crystallization obtained by dissolving silver and mercury in nitric acid. It is the spirit of sal ammoniac. Duchamp would have liked this definition.

All the elements of the *Green Box* and the *Large Glass*—the Illuminating Gas, the arbor-type, the cloud or Milky Way, the Waterfall—appear in the Assemblage converted into visual semblances. The vision of the landscape and the Waterfall, with the naked woman (Milky Way) stretched on a bed of branches (the tree), would be a pacifying meta-

---

* Neumann, *The Great Mother*, p. 245.
† Dumézil, *La Religion romaine archaïque*, p. 396.

phor if it were not for the glow of the gas lamp lit in broad daylight. An incongruity that winks at us roguishly and destroys our idea of what an idyll should be. Torches appear in the ceremonies in honor of Diana, but nobody knows for sure why and for what purpose. The experts agree on only one point: they are not hymeneal torches. On the Ides of August, Dumézil says, processions of women would go to Aricia carrying torches. One of Propertius' loveliest elegies (II, 32) mentions these processions:

> Hoc utinam spatiere loco, quodcumque vacabis,
> Cynthia! sed tibi me credere turba vetat,
> cum videt accensis devotam currere taedis
> in nemus et Triviae lumina ferre deae.*

The relation between torch and goddess is clear in the case of divinities like Demeter and Persephone; it almost always symbolizes the union of the virgin mother and her son, as we see in Phosphora, "bearer of the torch." The flame is the fruit of the torch. Transposition of vegetal into cosmic images: the goddess is the tree of night, and her fruits and branches are the starry sky. The association between fire and sexuality is age-old, and the act of making fire has often been seen as homologous to the sexual act. Fire sleeps in wood and, like desire in a woman's body, is awakened by friction. It is impossible to miss the similarity between the arbor-type of the *Large Glass* and the tongue of flames into which the filament substance is converted, the girl in the Assemblage reclining on a surface of twigs and branches—bed and pyre all at the same time— holding up a lamp of burning gas, and the mythic images of the birth of fire. Though we are talking about a process that is determined by the action of the masculine element, in this case, according to Neumann, the masculine principle is subordinated to the feminine. In all the myths and rituals whose theme is the double relationship between the fruit-bearing

---

* "Ah that thou wouldst walk here in all thine hours of leisure! but the world forbids me trust thee, when it beholds thee hurry in frenzy with kindled torches to the Arician grove, and bear lights in honour of the goddess Trivia." *Elegies*, II, 32, translated by H. E. Butler, Loeb Classical Library (Cambridge, Mass.: Harvard University Press), p. 159.

earth and the light-producing darkness—the archetype of which would be the Eleusinian mysteries—"before and above all, woman experiences herself. Projected on the image of the Great Goddess, this experience is intimately linked with the principle of universal life."* Woman sees herself as a fountain of life. The masculine principle, dominated by the feminine, is a medium through which woman knows, fertilizes, and contemplates herself. The analogy with both Duchamp's works could not be more complete: the Nine Malic Molds of the *Large Glass*, inflated by gas, and the phallic lamp held by the girl are devices by means of which the Bride enjoys, sees, and knows herself.

The fire/log relationship unfolds into another: water/fire. Torches and candles are often thrown ceremonially into rivers and lakes; in the Catholic ritual of consecrating the baptismal font, the priest drops a burning candle into the water. This relationship is accurately reproduced in that of the Bride/Waterfall and the gas lamp burning in the light of day. There is the following difference between Duchamp's images and those of tradition: whereas the Bride is governed by the circularity of solitary desire, mythic and ritual images invariably evoke the idea of fertility. This is also true of the nocturnal processions of the Roman women to Diana's sanctuary in Aricia: though the torches the women carried were not hymeneal, they were associated with maternity and childbearing. Dumézil points out that Diana Nemorensis, although a virgin and incorporated into the severe Artemis, also had jurisdiction over procreation and birth. But whatever the differences between Duchamp's and the traditional images, the essential relationship remains unaffected—tree/fire and water/torch. Both are present in the two signs that *produce* the instantaneous appearance or ultrarapid exposure of the Bride: the Waterfall and the Illuminating Gas. There is another similarity: the darkness that, according to the *Green Box*, is required for the ultrarapid exposure and the shadows which in the Eleusinian mysteries, preceded *heurisis*: "Amid the total darkness the gong is struck, summoning Koré from the underworld . . . suddenly the torches create a sea of light and fire, and the cry is heard: Brimo has borne Brimos!"† Again I must point

---

* Neumann, *The Great Mother*, p. 318.
† Ibid.

out that the Greek ritual alludes to the birth of a god, whereas the torch held by the girl in the Assemblage does not evoke any idea of maternity or birth. The Bride begins and ends in herself.

I must still mention the relationship between Diana and Janus, the god of two faces, divinity of doors and hinges. As Dumézil says, his name marks him as a passage. Spatially speaking, he stands in doorways and presides as *janitor* over entrances and exits; in the temporal sense he is the beginning: his month is *Januarius*, the first month, standing between the year that is beginning and the one that has ended. He faces in two directions because every passage implies two places, two states, one left behind and one being approached. Janus is a hinge, a pivot. Though Dumézil says nothing about the relationship between them, we know that the Romans saw Diana as Janus' double. It seems unnecessary to stress the affinity between the Bride, the doors—in a word, the system of pivots that rules Duchamp's universe—and Janus and Diana, circular and double divinities whose end is their beginning and for whom obverse and reverse are one and the same. Divinities who ceaselessly unfold and reflect themselves, reflexive gods turning from themselves to themselves, Janus and Diana embody the circularity not only of desire but also of thought. A bifurcating unity, a duality that pursues unity only to bifurcate again. In them Eros becomes speculative.

The publication of *A l'infinitif* in 1966 and the appearance a year later of the *Entretiens* with Pierre Cabanne gave rise to commentaries on how Duchamp's artistic and philosophic preoccupations had been influenced by the notion of a fourth dimension. These commentaries were more or less personal variations on a well-known theme; it was no secret that the fourth dimension is one of the intellectual components of the *Large Glass*. Even the earliest studies on the work had picked up this thread. However, the matter deserves more careful scrutiny. Duchamp often talked about the contradiction implicit in his love-hate relationship with science. In the second of his conversations with Cabanne he refers to his interest in the representation of movement. It was an interest that he shared with most of the poets and artists of his time, as we see in the "simultaneism" of Barzun, Delaunay, Cendrars, Apollinaire, and others. Cabanne observed that this preoccupation with movement disappeared almost completely after *The Bride*. Duchamp attributed this change to his rediscovery of perspective: "The *Large Glass* constitutes a rehabilitation of perspective, which had then been completely ignored and disparaged." Of course, it was not a question of realistic perspective but "a mathematical, scientific perspective . . . based on calculations and dimensions." In the *Large Glass* visual representation is subordinated to a story—a legend, Breton used to say—except that anecdote and representation have undergone a radical transposition; instead of things and the sensorial consequences of our perception of them, the painting presents us with the measurements of things, the relationships between them, and the symbols of these relationships. A world *à l'infinitif*.

One of the first notes in the *Green Box* says, "In general the picture is the apparition of an appearance." Other notes explain to us that appearance is the conjoining of sensations—visual, tactile, auditory—at the moment when we perceive the object; apparition is the underlying, stable reality, never wholly visible: the system of relationships that is at once the mold and the essence of the object. Duchamp set himself to make an art of apparitions and not of appearances. It was a contradictory aim because painting has been up to now—all to the good—an art of appearances: the representation of what we see, with our eyes open or closed. But it is also good that a painter should decide to opt for invisible reality and to paint not things or images but relationships, essences, and signs. On condition, of course, that the painter in question is really a painter. It is exemplary but not strange that Duchamp should have risked taking this step: the very logic of his search urged him to jump from painting movement to painting all that lies beyond movement.

On the other hand, there is nothing less modern than this aim. As he said to Cabanne, "All painting, beginning with Impressionism, is antiscientific, even Seurat. I was interested in introducing the precise and exact aspect of science . . . It wasn't for love of science that I did this; on the contrary . . . irony was present." The art of the last two centuries has borne a common stamp: it has deified aesthetic values, which have been cut off from other values and turned into a self-sufficient, almost absolute reality in their own right. It is against this conception of art that Duchamp rebelled. He was unique in his negation of the modern tradition—painterly painting, retinal and olfactory painting. He was not unique in his rejection of the painting of appearances; the Cubists and Abstractionists also set themselves to paint essences and archetypes. The same must be said of his interest in theoretical speculations more or less inspired by the new physics: it was a general tendency among the artists of that era.

Poets and painters, especially those of the second generation of Cubists, had many heated discussions of the fourth dimension. In the bistros frequented by avant-garde artists, Maurice Princet, an imaginative, verbose insurance agent, used to hold forth on Lobachevski's and Riemann's geometry. In her memoirs Gabrielle Buffet tells us that "the three Duchamp brothers were enthralled by science and mathematics." Ribemont-Dessaignes, another who reported on that era, observes that the education of the Duchamps was more serious than that of many of their friends. Marcel never hid his affinities, and in the *White Box* he quotes Henri Poincaré and Elie Joufret, author of a *Four-dimensional Geometry*. It is actually from Joufret that the central idea of the *Large Glass* derives: the projection of a four-dimensional figure onto our space is a three-dimensional figure.* Jean Suquet has shown that some of Poincaré's concepts could be applied to the Bride: "The beings of hyperspace may be objects with precise definitions like those of ordinary space; we can conceive of them and study them but not represent them." Duchamp would have replied to Poincaré with a smile, "Except as freed forms." For many scientists and artists the new ideas of physics and mathematics were reflected, more or less deformed, in the mirror of the old Neoplatonism. León Hebreo used to say that "the body is the shadow of spiritual beauty" and Pico della Mirandola claimed that the intellect cannot see Venus in "her true form." Poincaré and Duchamp belonged to the same tradition, perhaps without knowing it.

Duchamp owes his age a debt. Like all true artists, in assuming it he denies it, and sometimes he transcends it. It is true that the *Large Glass* is an offshoot of certain concepts of the new physics, or rather, of the ver-

---

* The best study of this aspect of Marcel Duchamp appears in Jean Clair, *Marcel Duchamp ou le grand fictif* (Paris: Galilée, 1975).

sions of these concepts popularized in artistic and intellectual circles by professors and journalists. But an artist cannot be reduced to his sources any more than to his complexes. Here lies the limitation of the otherwise praiseworthy works of Jean Clair and Arturo Schwarz. Just as Shakespeare is not the sum of his readings, or Proust his asthma, Duchamp is not Gaston de Pawolowski's novel of scientific futurism or his hypothetical incestuous passion for Suzanne. I am not minimizing Schwarz's effort; his book is a monument of patience and devotion, invaluable for the information it contains.[*] Nor is Clair's essay to be overlooked.[†] But no one, not even Clair, would have dug up Gaston de Pawolowski if, in one of his conversations with Cabanne, Duchamp himself had not remembered this name and the impression the book had caused on him. Nor must we exaggerate: Pawolowski was not Duchamp's only source. Really they were both nourished by the works of such scientific disseminators as Poincaré and Joufret. Just as the generation after them talked about psychoanalysis and today's generation about linguistics, in those days they discussed physics and the new space-time. Even before them Jarry was mentioning the names of Riemann and Lord Kelvin with a certain familiarity, to say nothing of the popular successes of *The Time Machine*, *The Invisible Man*, *Tales of Space and Time*, and others of Wells' novels and stories.

Undoubtedly, Pawolowski's novel, *Journey to the Land of the Fourth Dimension*, is one of the sources of the *Large Glass*. But it must be recognized that the differences between the two works are greater than their similarities. Contrary to the long journey related by Pawolowski, the passage from one dimension to the other in the *Large Glass* is instantaneous. More important, it is illusory: *a round trip*. Pawolowski takes seriously the scientific ideas that he uses as scaffolding to construct a rather ingenuous fiction; in Duchamp's work these ideas have been distended by meta-irony until they are unrecognizable. Pawolowski's little novel is the curious work of an intelligent amateur; the *Large Glass* is the fulgurating

[*] Arturo Schwarz, *The Complete Works of Marcel Duchamp* (New York: Abrams, 1970).
[†] Jean Clair, *Marcel Duchamp ou le grand fictif*.

allegory of a voyage through space. Fulgurating implies faraway, radiant, and silent. Pawolowski wrote a work to entertain and to divulge ideas in vogue at the time; Duchamp used those ideas like a Readymade no less forcible than the Rembrandt he wanted to turn into an ironing board. It would be useless to look in *Journey to the Land of the Fourth Dimension* for all that makes of the *Large Glass* a unique work: irony and eroticism, intellectual complexity at one with simplicity of execution, philosophical courage, verbal economy. In a word, that "beauty of indifference" whose other name is freedom.

Apart from Roussel, Duchamp's true literary antecedent is Alfred Jarry. Most critics, following Duchamp, have underlined the similarity of his method and Roussel's. The resemblance between them extends to other characteristics: the same attempt to dehumanize by introducing artificial elements, the substitution of mechanical for psychological resources, and lastly the centrality of word games. In the *White Box* Duchamp talks about creating a "pictorial nominalism;" for Roussel, language has the consistency of things and things have the elasticity and malleability of words. The unusual constructions populating the pages of *Impressions d'Afrique* and *Locus Solus* are akin to Duchamp's plastic and linguistic inventions. His affinities with Jarry are of another kind. First and foremost, that distance between work and author that creates irony. There is no distance between Roussel and his work; the creating subject has been abolished or, more exactly, reduced to a process. Roussel *is* his method; Jarry and Duchamp cannot be reduced to theirs. There is humor, not irony, in Roussel; he does not look at himself in his creations, nor do his creations look at him; he does not make fun of them, nor they of him. Jarry is and is not Ubu; Duchamp is and is not Rrose Sélavy. Actually Duchamp is (in the plural) the Oculist Witnesses. The character Roussel creates is involuntary: it is his emanation or projection, not his invention. Therefore, it lacks self-criticism and even consciousness. Jarry's character is Jarry's invention, and this doubling creates a deceiving play of reflections. Of Ubu, Jarry, and Faustroll, who is most real? On the contrary, the man Roussel is no less unreal than the character Canterel. Duchamp's unfaithfulness to his *persona* irritated Breton several times and was indeed scandalous;

everyone thought he was playing chess and he was secretly building the Assemblage. He seemed possessed by the nihilistic fervor of the avant-garde, and actually he was moved by the paintings of the religious artists; he limited the number of his Readymades and he did not hesitate to authorize reproductions of them.

Roussel believed in science; Jarry and Duchamp used science as a weapon against science. Ubu says, *merdre* and Duchamp, *arrhe*. One defines pataphysics as the science of the particular, and the other wants "to lose the possibility of recognizing or identifying any two things as being like each other." Both would have liked to live in a world of unique objects and entities, where the exception alone would rule. Roussel lacked a vital and moral dimension common to Jarry and Duchamp; the subversion of the self . . . The best commentary on the *Large Glass* is *Ethernités*, the last book of the *Gestes et opinions du Docteur Faustroll*. A doubly penetrating commentary because it was written before the work was even conceived, and so does not refer to it at all. Furthermore, in a text dated 1899, an extraordinary composite of reason and humor, Jarry anticipates Duchamp. I am refering to the *Commentaire pour servir à la construction poétique de la machine à explorer le temps*. Jarry's temperament was richer and more inventive than Duchamp's. Also more baroque: he proceded by accumulation, arabesques, and ellipses. Duchamp is limpidity. The *Large Glass* and the *Given* owe their fascination to their elegance in the mathematical sense of the word—that is to say, their simplicity. Ambiguity achieved through transparency.

One whole section of the *White Box* refers to perspective. This confirms that the theme was central to Duchamp's interests during those years. It is significant that this period—Duchamp's sojourn in the Bibliothèque Sainte-Geneviève—saw the conception of the *Large Glass* and the calculations and speculations of both *Boxes*. It was his period of greatest intellectual productivity. The most remarkable notes are those alluding to a (hypothetical) fourth-dimensional perspective and its relationship with ordinary perspective. They also deal with the analogies between three-dimensional and two-dimensional space. For example, gravity and the center of gravity are properties of three-dimensional space that in the second dimension correspond to perspective and the vanishing point. These preoccupations undoubtedly gave rise to compositions such as *Tu m'* and *To Be Looked at (from the Other Side of the Glass) with One Eye, Close to, for Almost an Hour*, as well as the optical devices. Duchamp was also interested in "curious perspective," as anamorphosis was called in the seventeenth century. In the *White Box* there is an allusion to the mathematician Jean-François Niceron (1613–1646) of the Minorite Order and his treatise on perspective, *Thaumaturgus Opticus*. Niceron is one of the great theorists of anamorphosis, and the book quoted by Duchamp is the amplified Latin version of the first edition of *La perspective curieuse ou Magie artificielle des effets merveilleux.*[*] The recent studies of Jurgis Baltrušaitis on this theme unexpectedly illuminate this aspect of Duchamp's intellectual and artistic activity. It is remarkable that his interest in anamorphosis goes back to 1913, more than a half-century ago.

Perspective is an expedient designed to give us the illusion of a third dimension. Euclid established the basic principle: our field of vision is a pyramid whose apex is the viewer's eye. In the fifteenth century Leon Battista Alberti defined the picture as a transverse section of the visual pyramid. Objects seem to diminish or grow bigger as they move away from or toward the angle of the eye. Perspective is, therefore, the art of restoring appearances. Within perspective, says Baltrušaitis, resides an opposition: "It is science that fixes the exact dimensions and positions of forms in space; and it is the art of illusion which recreates them. Their history is not only that of aesthetic realism. It is also the story of a dream."

One of the simplest devices, used as much in painting as in architecture and in the theater, is what is known as accelerated perspective. It

---

[*] There are three editions of *La perspective curieuse;* the first dates from 1638 and the other two, both posthumous, from 1652 and 1663. Perhaps Duchamp consulted one of these volumes. *Thaumaturgus Opticus* is from 1646. The fundamental study, the only one in fact on this material is *Anamorphoses* (Paris; Olivier Perrin, 1969) by Jurgis Baltrušaitis. Apart from this truly fascinating work we are in debt to Baltrusaitis for having initiated, together with Arthur Van Schendel, director of the Rijksmuseum, the recent *Anamorphoses* exhibition held in Amsterdam (1975) and Paris (1976), also in New York (1977). The prologue for the excellent catalog for this exhibition was also written by Baltru-šaitis.

consists of showing objects as if they were farther away than they really are by diminishing their size or by elevating the visual horizon. The opposite procedure, delayed perspective, makes objects seem nearer than they are by augmenting their component parts. There comes a moment when the device is pushed to such extremes that the relationship between reality and representation is broken. The result is anamorphosis: perspective becomes perverted, we might say, and no longer reproduces reality. Either by acceleration, delaying tactics, or some other device like reflecting the image in a cylindrical mirror or elongating perspective by some other means, resemblance is lost. Instead of the image of the object, we see a confusion of lines and masses. But all we have to do is look from the intended angle—obliquely, for instance, or into a cylinder, or through two holes, as in the case of the Assemblage—for the realistic appearance to return. *Round trip.* Duchamp's trick: who has been put to the test of watching (from the other side of the glass) with one eye, close to, for almost an hour, *To Be Looked at (from the Other Side of the Glass) with One Eye, Close to, for Almost an Hour?*

Leonardo was interested in deformations of perspective. Dürer, too,

during his voyage to Italy was amazed by the "art of the secret perspective," and even conceived of a postern with one transparent pane that would calibrate the lengthening of visual rays in order to calculate the perspectives of anamorphosis. The famous Austrian Jesuit, Athanasius Kircher, who so greatly influenced Sor Juana Inés de la Cruz, perfected this postern. But the great center of speculation and experi-

To Be Looked at (from the Other Side of the Glass) with One Eye, Close to, for Almost an Hour, 1918. *Collection, the Museum of Modem Art, New York: Bequest of Katherine S. Dreier.*

mentation was the Minorite convent in Paris during the first half of the seventeenth century. Its leading spirit was the theologian and mathematician Father Marin Mersenne, fellow student and friend of Descartes, teacher of Jean-François Niceron. Interest in the "curious perspective" diminished during the eighteenth century, and anamorphosis became an elegant diversion; in the nineteenth it degenerated into a pornographic hobby and a political motif.

Baltrušaitis points out the dual nature of anamorphosis: "It is an evasion that implies a return; stifled in a torrent or whirlwind of confusion, the image emerges resembling itself when looked at sideways or reflected in a mirror . . . The destruction of the figure precedes its representation." The image is brought back to life from its tomb of jumbled lines. This reversibility turned the procedure into a sort of "proof by nine" of normal perspective or *costruzione legittima*, as the Italians called it. It soon became independent and appeared as often in paintings with religious themes as in erotic works. Its intrinsic duality explains its vogue: anamorphosis is an act of representation that hides the very object it represents. In a religious painting this property works like a double optics of revelation: the morass of lines and masses hides the sacred object, but when the canvas is seen from the appropriate angle, its jumble is clarified and takes on form, and the object appears. In a licentious painting anamorphosis makes us feel that we are peeping through the keyhole. In both cases it is *ultrarapid exposure*. For a mere instant we are the oculist witnesses.

Symbol of worldly vanity in Holbein's famous picture *The Ambassadors*, erotic image in others, in the seventeenth century anamorphosis gave rise above all to scientific and philosophical speculations. But in the seventeenth century science had not as yet cut itself off from magic, astrology, and other heritages of Neoplatonic hermeticism. The last representative of this trend was Kircher, whose mind was a prodigious blend of erudition and fantasy, science and occultism. I said earlier that Kircher modified Dürer's postern; he thought up an apparatus, which he called a mezopticon, composed of "a square standing on end, covered by a diaphanous cloth such as noblewomen use to veil their faces." Though its purpose was different—it was an optical apparatus and the cloth worked like a screen—the disposition and form of the mezopticon recall the Three Pistons of the *Large Glass.*

Mersenne's circle was more sober. Descartes was a guest of the Minorite convent on two occasions; there he became interested in the work of Niceron and of Emmanuel Maignon, another member of the group. Preoccupied with geometry and optics, they were all fascinated by the rational mystery of automata. A mystery because it came from a tradition going back to Hermes Trismegistus by way of Albertus Magnus and Cornelius Agrippa; rational because, as Salomon of Caus, another of these young sages, said, automata were "the reasoning embodiments of the forces of movement." (It might have been more accurate to say that they were—and are—the *moving embodiment of reason.*) Now, if automata, although lacking souls, were "moving embodiments of reason," perspective was also automatism, the mechanization of rational calculation. Automata and perspective were offshoots of the same science.

There is an amazing connection between these ideas and the conceptions that brought the *Large Glass* into being. I will point out two similarities that seem central to me. The first has to do with perspective, considered as a more than personal rationality in which neither the artist's hand nor his sensibility plays any part. The second is the invention of machines endowed with free will and movement, which function rationally without depending on a psychology. Reading certain fragments of the *Traité de l'homme,* we feel we are facing another version of *The Bride:* "And, truly, one can very well compare the sinews of the machine I'm describing with the pipes of the workings of these fountains; its muscles and tendons with the various mechanisms and contraptions that make them function; the animal humors with the activating water, whose heart is the source and whose brain concavities are its eyes." In the description of this garden with automata that twirl as in a mythological ballet, analogies with clockwork and water mills are unavoidable: "Moreover, breathing and other such natural and ordinary acts are, depending on the flow of its humors, like the movements of a clock or a mill, which are made perpetual by the mere flow of water." As Baltrušaitis comments, this is man thought of as a hydraulic machine.

Anamorphosis and automata are themes that can be seen as chapters in the history of physics or of philosophy. In the second case they are forms of illusion, images of our uncertain knowledge and our dependence on appearances. Beyond Cartesian doubt—the transparency of the *Large Glass*—reappears the Platonic distinction that is the axis of the speculations of the *White Box*: the difference between apparition and appearance. How can we distinguish one from the other? The fan of anamorphosis turns the Bride into a Hanged Female; twenty-five years later, it gives her back to us in the shape of a blond girl lying on a bed of twigs. Which, among all these *ultrarapid exposures*, is appearance and which is apparition? The fourth dimension is the heaven inhabited by apparitions, which are archetypes or molds of beings here below. The *White Box* calls it "a sort of mirror-image," a being made of reflections. Is apparition the appearance of another apparition hidden in another dimension? The *Large Glass* is a mirror and in its upper half float ("freed forms") the shadows of the fourth dimension. But what do we see in this transparency—our shadow or the Bride's? The Assemblage answers our question with a three-dimensional enigma. A lovable, visible, solid—but untouchable—image. Untouchable and untouched. We wander lost among appearances and apparitions. The human spirit is twofold; like the mirror, it is inhabited by essences and ghosts.

Duchamp's interest in optical phenomena, regarded as a dimension of physical science or as one extreme of philosophic doubt, became apparent early in his career. Early, constantly, and in a variety of forms: the problems of linear and anamorphic perspective, chronophotography and simultaneism, projecting the shadows of objects on a wall or screen, painting (delay) in glass, stereoscopic cinema, rotating sheets of glass (precision optics), revolving semi-spheres, rotoreliefs (optical disks), disks with puns inscribed spirally . . . In the section of the *Green Box* devoted to the Oculist Witnesses, he foresees "parts to look at cross-eyed like a piece of silvered glass in which are reflected the objects in the room." In the *White Box* he says that there are things, though he doesn't specify them, that must be looked at with only one eye, sometimes the right, sometimes the left. (He also talks of something considerably more difficult: to hear with only one ear, either the left or the right. . .) The notes I have mentioned refer to the Spray, and like the note in the *Green Box*, they are linked to the Oculist Witnesses and their function of transforming drops into "mirrorical images." And so they are connected with one of his most puzzling compositions: *To Be Looked at (from the Other Side of the Glass) with One Eye, Close to, for Almost an Hour.* This work is a prototype of the region of the *Large Glass* where the Oculist Witnesses are found. In its upper part, above the magnifying glass floats a pyramid that in its turn contains a series of triangular planes looking like other pyramids; they are the different transverse sections of the visual pyramid of classical perspective. Who looks cross-eyed through the lens? Whoever looks, when he does so, becomes an Oculist Witness. And what does he look at? The floating pyramid is the viewer's visual field and this visual field is the path toward the elusive object that is the Bride. The cruel path of perspective that is narrowed down to a point: the vanishing point. Like the "infinite Jura-Paris road" of the 1912 text, this path has a beginning but no end; the vanishing point is the place where everything disappears. Blending into the horizon, the Bride vanishes.

His preoccupation with the relationship between the second and third dimensions led him, from early on in his artistic career, to an interest in stereoscopy. This was a passion that never left him. In his youth, among the apparatuses designed to create the illusion of relief and depth, stereoscopic spectacles with one red lens and one green were popular, made sometimes of glass, sometimes of mica. *Pharmacy*, one of his first Readymades (1914), was actually "rectified" by adding two stains, one green and the other red. In 1920 he tried to create a stereoscopic film; his rotoreliefs and precision optics machines obey the same principle. There is a doubly "rectified" Readymade that has an undoubted and intimate relationship to the Oculist Witnesses and to *To Be Looked at (from the Other Side of the Glass) with One Eye, Close to, for Almost an Hour.* It appears in the same year and place as these two works: 1918 in Buenos Aires. It consists of two photos of the same scene: a calm sea, light and shade, a boat manned by a solitary boatsman faintly visible on the far right, the horizon and a clear separation of water and sky. In both photos Duchamp added a pyramid and its inverted projection, floating. Like the pyramid in *To Be Looked at*, the one in the Readymade is the visual field of the apparition and evanescence of the object that always eludes us—and is always present.

The *Given* is another example, the biggest and the best, of his enthusiasm for stereoscopies. There is an obvious relationship between this work of poetic illusionism and the theatrical monuments of Renaissance architecture, such as the Palladian Theater in Vicenza or Borromini's colonnade in the Palazzo Spada in Rome. It is also akin to the "optical chambers" of seventeenth-century Holland, and, of course, to the excellent dioramas in the Museum of Natural History in New York. Toward the end of his life, Duchamp made a sketch for an anaglyphic chimneypiece that was to produce a stereoscopic effect when seen through the appropriate spectacles. His close friends still recall his joy, shortly before his death, on again finding, in the same Parisian shop, the stereoscopic spectacles he was searching for in order to look at his sketch. Just like those of his youth . . .

All these experiments are one more expression of his preoccupation with what could be called the instability of the notions of right and left, here and there, inside and outside, behind and in front, up and down. These ideas are spatial forms of contradiction. But there is a point at which contradictions end: the hinge. They come to an end only to be reborn at once, transformed; the hinge is both the resolution of contradiction and its metamorphosis into another contradiction. The dialectic between apparition and appearance is reproduced in the hinge. Duchamp's optical experiments—and the same must be said of his linguistic experiments too—are applications of the general principle of the hinge. His works—paintings, Readymades, Assemblages, puns, speculations—form a system, and in this system the center, the hinge of hinges, is the *Large Glass*. The relationship between the Bride in the *Large Glass* and the woman in the *Given* has already been disentangled: both are appearances of the same apparition. This apparition is an unknown object that in turn reveals and hides itself, unfolds itself and winds itself up again in the folds and transparencies of the fourth dimension. Folds that are veils, now of water, now of glass. Are these veils made out of its thoughts or of ours? Whatever our response to this question, it is clear that the relationship uniting the Bride in the *Large Glass* with the girl in the *Given* is that of two images fused into one. It is not exaggerated to call this relationship stereoscopic. "Unknown reality" works like a stereoscope.

A similar relationship exists between the Bride in the *Large Glass*, the girl in the *Given*, and the Goddess of the ancient Mediterranean religions. This relationship is twofold. On the one hand, each of the three images is a moment in the rotation of an invisible and, by definition, unknown hinge, unknown at least to our senses and even to our reason; on the other hand, within its individual world each image is the center, the pivot. I will attempt to explore this second relationship. There is an obvious correspondence between each of the three feminine images and the worlds over which they reign. Actually the Bride and her landscape in the *Large Glass* correspond identically to each other. Moreover, this correspondence is made explicit: everything is a representation or projection of the Bride. In the Assemblage the identity is implicit: each one of the girl's physical attributes is, one might say, duplicated in the landscape. The wooded hill, the waterfall, and the lake are her mirror. In the mythic conception the oneness of the Goddess and her world is also presented like a sort of knot of images and reflections. The sacred place *is* the Goddess. Therefore, insists Jean Przyluzki, the location of the sanctuary is a *complete landscape*, made up, that is to say, of wood, hill, and water.* The forces of nature are concentrated in the divine presence, but in its turn the divine presence is spread throughout the physical space.

The evolution of the space occupied by the sanctuary will help us understand the function of the stereoscope in Duchamp's system. Once a fairly remote spot where the rites of the cult were celebrated, the sacred place gradually became the center of the world. It then becomes an ideal place: an Eden, a paradise outside physical reality. The center of the world—Eden—coincided with the Goddess; or rather, it *was* the Goddess. The holy tree of the sanctuary became the column of the temple, and the column became the axis of the cosmos. The four cardinal points originated from this center, returned to it, and disappeared in it. The column that was the Goddess, turning back on itself like the hinge, disappeared and was fused with its essence. This side and that side, right

* Jean Przyluzki, *La grande déesse* (Paris: Payot, 1950).

and left, the laws of perspective and gravitation canceled each other out. The identification of the center of the universe with the Goddess, of the Bride with her landscape, is resolved in another analogy: that of the stereoscope. But "stereoscope" is only one more name for the elusive object for which Duchamp searched all his life and which, in the notes of the *Green Box*, is called the *sign of the accordance*.

The opening paragraph of the preface to the *Green Box* reproduced as the epigraph to this study, is as much a program of the work to be realized as the definition of its purpose: "to isolate the sign of the accordance." This sign comes between the State of Rest (or allegorical appearance or ultrarapid exposure) and a series of Possibilities. The Appearance is the Bride in the darkness of the room, surprised in a moment of repose (though capable of "giving herself up to all the eccentricities"). The Possibilities can only be the other possible manifestations produced by the combined action of the Waterfall and the Illuminating Gas, according to the same laws as those that operate in the case of the ultrarapid exposure. In fact, the *sign of the accordance* is not something *between* Appearance and Possibilities but rather the relationship between them both. To clarify his idea Duchamp uses an "algebraic comparison." Let *a* be Appearance and *b* Possibilities; the relationship is not $a/b = c$ but the sign (a/b). "As soon as *a* and *b* are known, they become units and lose their relative numerical value; the sign that separated them remains *(the sign of the accordance)."* *The sign includes the three elements: a, b,* and the diagonal line: *a* and *b* are variables *(a* is an appearance and *b* the other possible appearances); the relationship symbolized by the diagonal line remains because it is an invariable. The line is separation and unity at one and the same time. An erotic algebra. Now let us move on to meta-ironic geometry.

If the diagonal line becomes a vertical axis turning on itself, it produces a line that always traces a circle, whether it turns in direction *a* (to the right) or *b* (to the left). Duchamp concludes that the figure produced by the original line, *whatever this may be*, cannot be described as right or left of the axis. And, furthermore, in proportion as the axis turns, obverse and reverse take on "a circular signification." The phenomenon affects not only the inside and the outside but the axis itself, for this loses its *"one-dimensional appearance."* The sign of the accordance, turning upon itself, is dissolved as appearance: it enters itself and is resolved in pure possibility. It is the *other* dimension. But we can say nothing about it. The only thing we know about the fourth dimension is that it is one dimension *more*. How can we name this dimension that consists of the reabsorption of all dimensions in a void that would have made Buddha himself smile with beatitude? We were looking for the sign of the concordance and we find a diagonal line that becomes a vertical line, a truly magic wand that makes everything around it disappear until it, too, reduced to a one-dimensional state, gyrates, gives one more pirouette, and disappears.

We must go back to the *Large Glass* and try to "isolate the sign of the accordance." This sign links "the allegorical appearance" in a state of "instantaneous rest" to the other possible manifestations or appearances of the Bride. The sign exists between virtuality and actuality; it separates them, it is a dividing line, and it connects them. Thanks to the powers of the magic wand, possibility is realized and—"ultrarapid exposure"—rests for a moment, turned into appearance. This appearance is an allegory of the other reality whose true form we do not know. Now we have seen the creature in two moments of its "instantaneous rest." Once hanging from a nail, handing out lascivious orders; we called her Hanged Female. Fifty years later we saw her again, naked in the open air, holding up a burning gas lamp; we dared not give her a name. The *sign of the accordance* is a diagonal line separating two signs (two destinies[*]): *a/b*. If we make it vertical, it becomes an axis that fuses here and there in one void as it turns, stereoscope and hinge like the tree-column which is the Goddess. If we move the vertical line down it becomes a horizontal line. In the middle of the line, just before my eyes, the vanishing point appears: the infinite road that goes from here to there, from the visual angle of the viewer to the Bride. What do I see? Literally, nothing.

The horizon is barely more than a fine line. On it, transparency behind transparency, is there water or glass? It is the Bride's garment. A diaphanous garment, a veil that uncovers her. A veil deceptive in its very

---

[*] Here Paz plays with the similarity in Spanish of *signo* (sign) and *sino* (destiny or fate, but also a popular derivation of *signo*). See his *Topoemas*, "Ideograma de libertad." (Translator's note.]

diaphaneity: what I see from this side is not exactly what I see from the other side. I always see something *else*. The Wilson-Lincoln system is no less efficacious and is simpler than the Cartesian doubt. Furthermore, this system is not outside man but inside him; it is not an optical mechanism but a condition of his spirit. It is the "question of shop windows" with which the *White Box* opens: the shop window proves the existence of the outside world but also its nonexistence. "When one undergoes the examination of the shop windows, one also pronounces one's own sentence. In fact, one's choice is *round trip*." The *White Box* ends thus: "No obstinacy, *ad absurdum*, of hiding the coition through a glass pane with one or many objects of the shop window. The penalty consists in cutting the pane and in feeling regret as soon as possession is consummated." The round trip of desire is no different from the gyrating of the vertical line, the stereoscope, the hinge, anamorphosis, puns, the Goddess's tree-column, and mathematical and philosophical speculations. Universal reversibility: the journey takes us there and back again.

The logic of the hinge rules this world. The *sign of the accordance* is only the most perfect expression of the hinge principle. What unites, separates; by uncovering the object, transparency interposes itself between that object and my gaze; the negation of the irony of affirmation denies the negation of the laugh; the dividing line between *a* and *b* is really the sign of their union: one cannot live without the other, but they are condemned to see each other without ever blending completely into each other. Apparition is dispersed in Appearance and each Appearance is reabsorbed as it spins upon itself, and returns, not to the Apparition, which is invisible, but to the place of Evanescence, the horizon.

In Duchamp's universe, the convergence of its three ruling sciences—eroticism, meta-irony, and metaphysics—is the *sign of the accordance*, and it envelops us also: it is the glass that separates us from the desired object but at the same time makes it visible. The glass of otherness and of sameness: we cannot break it or escape from it because the image that reveals us is our own image as we watch it watch. To a certain extent Possibilities and Appearance depend on us—and we on them. We are, while peeping through the glass or the holes in the door, one of the "various facts" that "under certain laws" condition "the instantaneous State of Rest or Allegorical Appearance."

Duchamp devalues art as craft in favor of art as idea; in its turn the idea constantly sees itself negated by irony. Duchamp's visual objects are the crystallization of an idea and the negation, the criticism, of that idea. The ambivalence of the glass, the sign that is separation/union, appears in this realm also. Duchamp did not hide his admiration for the works of art of the past that were incarnations of an Idea, almost always a religious one. The *Large Glass* is an attempt to resuscitate this tradition within a radically different context, both areligious and ironic. But from the seventeenth century onward our world has had no Ideas, in the sense in which Christianity had ideas during its time of apogee. What we have, especially from Kant onward, is Criticism. Even contemporary "ideologies," despite their pretentions of incarnating truth and despite the pseudoreligious fanaticisms they have engendered, present themselves as *methods*. Marxism itself does not claim to be anything more than a theoretical-practical method in which *praxis* is inseparable from criticism. Duchamp's art is public because he sets out to renew the tradition of art *at the service of the Mind;* it is hermetic because it is critical. Like the tree-goddess who is the center of the universe where the distinction between this side and that side disappears, the Bride in the *Large Glass* is the axis whose turning fuses all spaces into one. Plenitude and emptiness. Unlike the Goddess, the Bride is not a supernatural being but an Idea. But she is an Idea continually destroyed by herself: each one of her manifestations denies her, even as it realizes her. For this reason I dared to say, in my first study on Duchamp, that the Bride is the (involuntary) representation of the only Myth-Idea of the modern West: Criticism.

In the last few years Duchamp's work has received two kinds of interpretation, the psychological and the alchemical. I have already said what I think about the first of these: psychological interpretations often have an impoverishing effect. And they are also misleading. Freud himself warned us of the limitations of his method: it serves to give an account of the author's character and psychical conflicts, but not of the ultimate value and meaning of his work. In Duchamp's case Lebel cautioned us elegantly: "We beg the reader to note that we keep a safe distance from psychiatry, which others would not hesitate to requisition." Following a suggestion of Breton in "Phare de la Mariée,'" Lebel was one of the first to hint that, perhaps, in order to fully understand the *Large Glass,* it was necessary to have recourse to "the esoteric hypothesis." Later on, in a treatise on alchemy by Solidonius, Ulf Linde discovered an illustration of the disrobing of a virgin by two personages that is extraordinarily like the first version of *The Bride Stripped Bare by Her Bachelors* (Munich, 1912). From this discovery originates "the fashionable notion that alchemy provides a key to the iconography of the *Glass.*"† Hamilton sensibly calls into question the pertinence of the esoteric explanation, and insists that Duchamp never gave it credit. Indeed, when his friend Lebel questioned him expressly about this, he answered, "If I have practiced alchemy, it has been in the only way admissible nowadays—that is, without knowing it." A conclusive disavowal.

Certainly, as John Golding points out, the world of Duchamp's youth saw the end of Symbolism, and almost all the Symbolist poets and artists—as later happened with the Surrealists—were attracted by esoteric cults. In Jarry pataphysics walked arm in arm with alchemy and heraldry. But it is one thing to bring to light the particles of occultism, cabalism, and alchemy scattered throughout Duchamp's ideas, almost like dust specks and sediments, and another to say that the *Large Glass* and the Assemblage are works expressly and deliberately inspired by alchemy. We have only to read the notes of the two *Boxes* to agree with Richard Hamilton that "the subject of the *Large Glass* is space and time." This theme, in which physics embraces metaphysics, is closely linked to another: love. They are two inseparable themes that have been one from Plato onward. Love and knowledge have been the dual subject matter not only

* André Breton, "Phare de la Mariée," *Minotaure,* Vol. 2, No. 6 (December 1934), pp. 45–49.
† Richard Hamilton, "The Large Class," p. 58, in *Marcel Duchamp,* the catalog published jointly by the Philadelphia Museum of Art and the Museum of Modern Art in New York, edited by Anne d'Harnoncourt and Kynaston McShine to commemorate the extensive *Marcel Duchamp* exhibition in 1973. Also on this theme, see *The Machine as Seen at the End of the Mechanical Age* by K. C. Pontus Hultén (New York, 1968).

of Western thought, but of our poetry and art as well. Duchamp's work is appreciably more traditional than is commonly thought. Moreover, here lies one of the proofs of its authenticity. There are many profound relationships linking his two great works, the *Large Glass* and the Assemblage, with our traditions of erotic philosophy and poetry. I do not mean, of course, that Duchamp was inspired by the Provençal poets, nor do I claim him as an assiduous reader of Marsilio Ficino, León Hebreo, or Giordano Bruno. I think that his vision of love and his idea of the *other* dimension fit into our philosophic and spiritual tradition. They are part of it. René Nelli tells us that the Provençal concept of love has survived into the twentieth century, and the same is true of Neoplatonic hermeticism. In our erotic and spiritual lives both trends are still actively, though almost always invisibly, present.

Time and again the meaning of the division of the *Large Glass—Bride above, Bachelors below*—has been discussed. This duality does not refer to position alone, but also to number: unity above and plurality below. Whatever interpretation we may give to this opposition—later I will return to the unity/plurality theme—the division of the *Large Glass* corresponds to that of lady and troubadour in the courtly love tradition. The amatory code of Provence was a projection of the chivalric world onto the realm of sentiments and ideas, and it naturally reproduced, in the relationship between the lady and her swain, the hierarchic structure of medieval society. In its early days, Provençal love was a relationship between equals: the ladies and their suitors belonged to the same aristocratic circles; in its later stage—that of the great Provençal poetry—the troubadours almost always came from lower social strata than did their ladies.* Not all scholars accept this explanation. No matter; whatever the origin of the division, it is certain that in the classic era of courtly love, during the twelfth and thirteenth centuries, the concept predominating

---

* Cf. René Nelli, *L'Erotique des troubadours* (Toulouse: Edouard Privat, 1963). Also, Robert Briffault, *The Troubadours* (Bloomington, Ind.: Indiana University Press, 1965). The latter work is a translation by Briffault himself of his *Les Troubadours et le sentiment romanesque* (Paris, 1945), but with many changes and important additions.

in poetic texts is that of the *Large Glass:* the lady above, her lover below. It is less a social than a ceremonial and spiritual distinction; the lover is subordinated to the lady, whatever his condition and state.

Love was *service*. René Nelli says that "the barons and poets regarded themselves as their ladies' vassals and servants, obliged to bow down before them." A great lord, William IX, calls himself *obedienz*, and Cercamon, a troubadour of modest origins, proclaims himself *a coman* (servant) of his lady. Timidity was one of the lover's virtues, probably as a means of purifying and intensifying desire at the same time. The lover's timidity contrasts with the lady's boldness. From the earliest texts onward, Nelli says, "It is always the lady who takes the initiative and puts the lover to the test *(assaia, prueva)*." Cecco d'Ascoli used to say: *"La donna e umida."* The ministry of love was a pilgrimage from lower to higher. A journey that was a rite of purification like that of the Illuminating Gas and with a similar outcome: not physical possession but vision. Through a series of operations that are proofs of purification, the Illuminating Gas reaches a nonmaterial state: converted into an image, into "mirrorical drops," it is now only a gaze, a contemplation of the naked Bride; in his turn the troubadour passes through the different stages of his amorous ministry—each of them ending in a test—until sexual desire undergoes a sublimation like that of the gas: the troubadour at last attains the contemplation of his naked lady. Sight triumphs over touch. León Hebreo used to call this contemplation visual copulation.

The lady lives in the realm of the ideal, and the troubadour seeks the *other* reality in her and by means of the vision of her naked body—that reality of which she (and he) are images, likenesses. It is not difficult to perceive in this idea certain Platonic echoes, identical to those found in Duchamp, though there the mode is meta-ironic: love not as possession but as contemplation of an object that transports us to a higher sphere. *Instantaneous crossing.* The Provençal poets say little of their desire to possess the lady sexually, but none of them hides his desire to see her naked. The rites of amorous servitude ended with this contemplation. The ceremony of the disrobing was almost always clandestine, though the lady's maids and even her husband were sometimes present. The lover had to *spy* on his lady, like the spectator of the Assemblage. Just as the Bachelors never take off their uniforms—they couldn't, they are empty suits—the courtly lover watched, fully dressed, the ritual of the disrobing. As the dogma of the servitude of love demanded, the ceremony went through various stages. For example, the lady could allow herself to be seen either in transparent garments or completely in the nude. The last stage was the *asag* (test of love): the lover reached the bed and lay beside the naked lady, on top of the coverlet or underneath, without possessing her or without consummating the act completely *(coitus interruptus).* The texts also describe, though with no undue emphasis, the caresses the lady and her lover exchanged.

The value attributed to contemplation of the naked female body can be explained by the reason noted above: the identification of woman with Nature. Woman is her own landscape, whether we are dealing with the Goddess of mythology or with Duchamp's Bride or the Lady of the Provençals. I have already mentioned that in all these cases the lady took the initiative, and the ceremony could be realized only as she decreed. The Top Inscription was a social and psychological reality before it was an erotic pseudomechanism. In the *asag* the lady's decision was the condition *sine qua non* of the ceremony, and Nelli quotes various testimonies **to** this fact, among them the unequivocal text of a *trobairitz,* the Countess of Die, Provence's Sappho. It can be claimed that these analogies are less meaningful than the obvious contrast: whereas the ceremony of courtly love was a ritual of erotic sublimation, that of the *Large Glass* is a parody. But it is an ambivalent parody, love mocked by voyeurism, and at the same time voyeurism transformed into contemplation. We see a naked woman, a universe; like all universes, she is a mechanism; like all mechanisms, this one is "a moving embodiment of reason." Reason, which, in the girl in the Assemblage, is idea become presence. It is a fact worth repeating: Duchamp's work is a vast anamorphosis that unfolds before our eyes throughout the years. From the *Nude Descending a Staircase* to the naked girl in the Assemblage—different moments in the journey back toward original form.

* Nelli, *L'Erotique des troubadours.*

The *Green Box* tells us that the Bride "instead of being an asensual icicle, warmly rejects (not chastely)" the Bachelors. Nor was Provençal love a form of Platonism, though in its origins it was more or less indebted to Arabic erotica, itself impregnated with Platonic concepts. Briffault's information is invaluable on this score: until its last phase, when it was overcome and condemned by the Catholic Church, courtly love oscillated between sexual freedom and idealization. It was always a love outside marriage, a transgression consecrated by poetry and philosophy. In its essence, courtly love was a sublimated naturalism. Rather than a metaphysics, it was a physics of love. Nelli points out that this expression—*physics of love*—appears in the novel *Flamenca*. For the troubadours, love enters through the senses: "It wounds in two places, the ear and the eye." The metaphor is very old, and appears in early India as well as in Rome and Japan. The eyes are love's archers, and Provençal poetry is full of arrows, darts, and shafts that tear open and pierce bodies and souls. There are palpable correspondences with the *Large Glass:* the Nine Shots, the final fate of the Illuminating Gas, the Oculist Witnesses, the spectators peering through the holes in the door of the Assemblage. The 1948–49 relief, a "study" for the naked woman of the Assemblage, is another example of Duchamp's loyalty to the old metaphor, which in this case takes on a literal cruelty: the naked body is covered with tiny marks as if it had been pierced by arrows.

The metaphor of the arrows was only part of the physics of love. The "fire of the gaze" told a material truth: the eyes transmitted a warm, luminous fluid. As among the Neoplatonists and Duchamp himself, fire was associated with water: *en foc amoros arosat d'una douzor.* The cause of love is physical: a substance, an element that can be put into a philter or transmitted in a song. This substance is no garden-variety liquid, but a subtle fluid, like that warm draft which moves the cloth of the Three Pistons and which constitutes the Bride's sighs. Later on, erotic fluid became magnetic fluid; in Baroque poetry the magnet was as popular a symbol as Cupid's quiver in Latin: "If to the magnet of your graces, drawing me,/my breast acts as obedient steel . . ." says Sor Juana in a sonnet. Metaphors in Duchamp tend to become literal: erotic fluid is called automobiline, the Waterfall produces amorous electricity, the Illuminating Gas becomes explosive liquid.

Right from the start, Duchamp works a radical subversion: in the *Large Glass* the "physics of love" is a dazzling system of forces and relationships, a parody of "the heavenly mechanism." A literally *bedeviled* physics, ruled by laws that are *calembours*. A double negation: against the modern world of conditioned reflexes and psychic automatisms, Duchamp sets his imaginary physics of elastic principles, emancipated metals and freed forms; in opposition to physics, the science that for us occupies the place theology did in the Middle Ages, he invents ironic causality and subsidized symmetry. Through the double hole of this negation the Bride and Eros, the Oculist Witnesses, and we ourselves escape. Here a second stage begins, the operation of meta-irony in the proper sense of the term. All these grotesque phenomena produce a sublimation as does the amorous servitude of the Provençals: the Illuminating Gas becomes a stare and the Bride's orgasm transforms her into the Milky Way. Provençal erotica and Duchamp's own rely on physics. In both cases the operation consists of distilling the erotic fluid until it is transmuted into a gaze. The contemplation of a naked body in which alternately nature is revealed and the *other* reality hidden. The Bride's veil is her nakedness.

In the Middle Ages love was conceived of as a force at once psychic and material, the animating principle of human beings and celestial bodies. Love for Dante is not only an appetite, a propensity common to all creatures, but also a universal principle, physical and spiritual by turn, that binds things together, gives cohesion to the cosmos, and sets it in motion: "Neither the Creator nor His creatures . . . were ever without love/either natural or mind-directed, as you well know" (Purgatory, XVII). Natural love never errs, "but the other may err through bad intentions." The often-quoted line about the love that moves the sun and the other stars refers to divine power and to a physical force no less real than Newton's gravitation, though, like it, impalpable. The cosmological conceptions of the Middle Ages were dislodged by Copernicus and his followers. The change did not immediately affect ideas about love. The rediscovery of the works of Plato and Plotinus, oddly confused with the revelations of Hermes Trismegistus, gave rise to a tradition of *trattati d'amore*. In these treatises the influence of the new astronomy is nil. Giordano Bruno was the exception to this rule. For this reason—and for others that will soon be explained—it seems useful to recall some facts about Bruno himself.

The tradition of the love treatises begins with Marsilius Ficino's commentary on Plato's *Symposium* and culminates a century later with Bruno's *Eroici Furori* (1585). The theme of the latter work is intellectual love. His book has two parts, each one composed of five dialogues. Each dialogue is a commentary on some erotic sonnets written by Bruno himself. Critics have pointed out the similarities between this work and the *Vita Nuova:* "the author is not only the poet and the commentator but also the protagonist of his poems."* The relationship between the sonnets and the commentaries is like that between the *Large Glass* and the two *Boxes*. Bruno defines his book as "a natural and physical discourse," but warns that its language is erotic. In the dedication to the English poet Philip Sidney—the book was published during Bruno's stay in England—he claims as his model the *Song of Songs:* he wanted to deal with divine and intellectual themes in the language of earthly love. Nothing less like Bruno with his impassioned and contradictory genius, at once huge and puerile, than Duchamp: the freedom of indifference and meta-irony. And yet Duchamp's theme was also a "natural and physical discourse"—space and time—and his language was that of love in its most colloquial expressions. In the middle of the twentieth century his work is one more example of the interpenetration of the two themes that enthralled Bruno: love and knowledge.

For Bruno there are two sorts of furors. Some are irrational and lead us to bestiality, but others consist of the predisposition of the soul to "a certain divine abstraction." The latter, which are found in superior men, are again of two kinds. Some men, possessed by a god or a spirit, do noble

---

* Giordano Bruno, *Dialoghi italiani* (Florence, 1957). See also Frances A. Yates, *Giordano Bruno and the Hermetic Tradition* (New York: Vintage, 1969), and John Charles Nelson, *Renaissance Theory of Love* (New York: Columbia University Press, 1958).

deeds or utter marvelous words without knowing what they are doing or saying; others, and these are the best, are aware of their furor and, grown skillful in reflection and contemplation, "cease to be recipients and vehicles, and become true craftsmen and creators." The theme of his book is this type of furor. It is heroic as much because of the subject who experiences it—the craftsman and creator—as because of the object that inspires it, itself most lofty and most difficult: knowledge. Intellectual love is a heroic passion. This heroic furor moves the soul upward and impels it to climb Diotima's ladder from love of the beautiful body to the contemplation of spiritual beauty, and from this to union with the still uncreated. There is a clear division between above and below, but it is neither social nor ceremonial in kind as with courtly love, for it is essentially ontological. The spatial division is complemented by another, which derives from Plato and which the Gnostics adopted: that of light and dark. Our place is here below, but we do not wholly belong to darkness; our kingdom is the penumbra. We live among the shadows and reflections of the lights up there. The world up above, the world of light, is also and especially—here lies its ontological superiority—that of unity, while the world below is that of plurality. The Bride and her Bachelors. There is a continuous dialogue between above and below. This dialogue consists of the conversion of the one into the other, better yet, into the others, and of the others into the one. It is a process that Plato himself had defined as "deducing multiplicity from unity and reducing multiplicity to its unity." Deduction and reduction: the two central operations of the spirit. The emanations of unity moving downward: the engendering of earthly and visible things; heroic furor moving upward: the contemplation of forms, essences, ideas. Except that these ideas are also shadows, projections of the One hidden in the folds of its unity. Dialogue of apparitions and appearances, dialogue of shadows, dialogue of the Bride with herself.

Critical studies have hardly touched on the theme of colors and the place they occupy in Duchamp's erotic physics and in his physics of "distended laws." This is strange, for a whole chapter of the *Green Box* and another of the *White Box* are devoted to color. The distinction between apparition and appearance extends to color: there are, says the *Green Box*, native colors and apparent colors. Apparition is not only the mold

The theme of colors in Duchamp would need a separate study. Here I will point out only that "physical dye" is molecular *essence*. Dye is color in itself, the nature or being of the molecular object; at the same time it is a sort of negative print of real, visible color; lastly it is a secretion. Dye is found in all realms, from the ontological to the optical and from the optical to the botanical and the zoological. It is an essence, a definition, a color, and an odor. Thanks to "physical dye," colors are colors and, moreover, perfumes. Duchamp's molecules have the property of changing their nature as if they were subject to incessant punning. Perfumes from reds, blues, greens, or grays that slide toward yellow and even toward the "weaker maroons." Colors that are bred like silkworms or cultivated like asparagus. Fruit-bearing colors, except that "the fruit still has to avoid being eaten. It's this dryness of 'nuts and raisins' that you get in the ripe imputrescent colors. (Rarefied colors.)" The irony that distends physical laws and makes of the *Large Glass* "the mold design for a *possible reality*" also creates the uncorruptible beauty of indifference. Duchamp's colors exist not to be seen but thought: "There is a kind of *inopticity,* a kind of cold consideration in those colorings that only affect imaginary eyes . . . A bit like a present participle turning past." Verbal colors, mental colors we see with our eyes closed. Each color, the *White Box* insists, will have a *name.* A pictorial nominalism.

When I touched on the theme of the *physics of love* in Provence, I mentioned the duality fire/water, elements that are intertwined in the poetics of the troubadours. The Neoplatonic tradition also used these symbols. For those poets and philosophers, sight was the queen of the senses; by analogy, understanding and knowledge, intellection, were thought of as a sort of superior vision. Contemplation is seeing not with the eyes but with the mind. Therefore, the dividing line between the world up there and the one down here is precisely the line of the horizon, which limits our visual field. If our eyes are organs of contemplation, our heart is the seat of love. The dialogue between the eyes and the heart is the struggle between water and fire. In Duchamp the elements become part of an industrial, urban landscape ("water and gas on all floors") and in Bruno a mythic landscape, as we see in the lines of this sonnet, which anticipates Baroque rhetoric:

I who bear love's high banner,
Have hopes frozen and desires boiling:
I tremble, I freeze, I burn, and I shimmer,
I am mute, and fill the sky with burning cries:

From my heart I send sparks, and from my eyes I drip water;
I both live and die, and I laugh and lament:
The waters live, and the fire dies not,
So I have Thetis in my eyes, and Vulcan in my heart.

Death by water or by fire? The heroic lover is paralyzed by
contrary impulses, as is the Illuminating Gas as it emerges
from the Sieves of the "three-directional labyrinth":

I love another, I hate myself;
But if I put on feathers, the other changes to stone;
I put the other in heaven, if I put myself low;

Always the other flees, if I cease not to follow;
If I call, he does not respond;
And the more I search, the more he hides.*

The mixture of water and fire is explosive: the Illuminating Gas leaps
upward; the heroic lover also hurls himself, maddened by passion, after
the object of his desire. The theme of desire is that of the pursuit of a
ceaselessly fleeing object, whether this is a body, an idea, or an idea made
body. The pursuance of an ever-receding object implies an equally endless movement. This *metaphysical movement*, unlike material movement,
can only be perpetual and therefore circular. A race in which the subject
reaches its object only to let it go and run after it again. A hunt that has
no end.

Bruno's book reaches its moment of greatest tension and lucidity
with the image of the hunt. In the second dialogue of Part Two, we find
two surprising personifications of inaccessible divinity and its manifestation: Apollo and Diana. Bruno accentuates Diana's subordinate nature,

* Translated by Elizabeth Welles.

making her a projection of Apollo: "Diana is of the order of secondary intelligences who receive the splendor of the primary intelligence in order to communicate it to those who are deprived of a fuller vision . . . No one has been able to see the sun, universal Apollo, and his absolute light, but we can see his shadow, his Diana." The goddess is "the light that shines in the midst of the opacity of matter." She is the light shining on things and she is the things themselves: she is nature. Diana is her landscape. Bruno insists: "This Diana, who is being itself, this being that is truth itself, this truth that is nature itself . . ." Diana is different from the sun that she reflects, and is identical to it because "unity reveals itself in what it generates and in what is generated, the producer and the product." If the object of heroic love is identified with Diana, the subject can be none other than Actaeon. The hunter wanders through the woods looking for his object, his prey. In trees and in animals, in everything, he sees Diana's reflection: shadows of a shadow. As in Ovid's poem and in the Assemblage, water is of fundamental importance: it is the transparent labyrinth of the reflections that make up appearance—"In the water, a mirror of similitude, Actaeon sees the most beautiful form and face." Water fulfills the same function as the horizon because in it are united the "waters from above with those below . . . in it, seeing is possible." Again, like the line dividing the signs *a* and *b*, like the sign of the accordance and like the glass of the shop window, the water-horizon unites as it divides.

In Klossowski's commentary on the myth, Diana's desire to see herself leads her to see her reflection in Actaeon's gaze; Bruno inverts the process: Actaeon is transformed into the object of his desire and sees himself in the deer that his dogs—the Goddess's thoughts—must devour. But before this, the deer sees Diana naked at the water's edge. In Klossowski's interpretation, Diana desires herself and sees herself through Actaeon; in Bruno's, Actaeon is transformed into the very thing he desires. As a hunter he pursues a deer that, like everything else in the wood, is a reflection of Diana. And so, when Actaeon turns into a deer, he becomes part of the Goddess's nature. In both cases the process is circular, and in both, Actaeon, the subject, is only a dimension of Diana, the object. The same logic governs the *Large Glass* and the Assemblage. Actaeon, the Bachelors, and the viewer spying through the holes in the door are subjects transformed into the objects of an object: Diana sees herself naked in them.

The most remarkable similarity with the *Large Glass* occurs in the fourth dialogue of Part Two of *Eroici Furori*. The hero, the furious lover—the Actaeon who sees the deer he is hunting disappear at the horizon, where the moon, which is hunting him, appears—is multiplied into nine blind men. Each of the nine recites a poem in which he defines the type of blindness with which he is afflicted. The nine blind men represent nine of the lover's physical and psychological limitations; at the same time they are an allegory of negative theology: "We see *more* when we close our eyes than when we open them." The nine blind men are Bruno himself; they are also representations of the nine spheres that "Cabalists, wise men, Chaldeans, Platonists, and Christian theologians" have divided into nine orders of spirits. The number nine has immense prestige. Nine is three times three, and three is the number into which, according to Dumézil, the Indo-European vision of the world is concentrated. Nothing more natural than that Duchamp add one more Bachelor to Eros' Matrix, originally composed only of eight.

In the fifth dialogue the nine blind men finally receive the gift of sight. Their pilgrimage takes them to England, and there they meet some nymphs, daughters of Father Thames. In the presence of the nymph who leads the aquatic troupe and whose name is Una, the miracle occurs: a sacred urn, the gift of Ceres, opens of its own accord. Then the nine blind men are granted enlightenment, and contemplate the Goddess. But what do these blind men see when they are transformed into *illuminati*? What do the Bachelors see when they are turned into "mirrorical drops"? They see the transparency of the horizon, the nakedness of space—nothing. We cannot go beyond our horizon, the boundary of our visual field. The pyramid whose apex is our eyes has no base: it floats in an abyss. We see the nakedness of the Bride reflected in the glass water. We see the vanishing point.

Negative theology: in order to see, we must close our eyes. In the darkness, Diana surprised in the bath: *ultrarapid exposure*. A new concordance: all the Neoplatonic texts, beginning with Plotinus, say that the vision never arrives slowly, it is a sudden illumination. A *flash*. Instantaneous passage. The similarity with carnal copulation has been pointed out a thousand times, and I have already mentioned León Hebreo's energetic expression: visual copulation of the intellect with its object. Likewise all the texts affirm that union is imperfect. Imperfection is built into man's capacity to know and to see. Creatures of the third dimension, we live in penumbra and exist among appearances. Bruno says that this defect must not discourage the heroic lover: "It is enough to see divine beauty *on the limits of one's own horizon."* This sentence is a commentary anticipating the speculations of the two *Boxes,* and it could be considered another formulation of "the question of the shop windows."

Like the Illuminating Gas, the heroic lover climbs, and as he climbs, the object of his desire retreats along the horizon until it disappears. The One is folded back among its folds, the three-dimensional figure disappears in the mold-mirror of the fourth dimension. The One is not visible, or sayable, or thinkable. Like the vertical line of the *Green Box,* which, as it turns upon itself, loses even its *one dimension* and again becomes part of the nullity of space, the One is beyond all duality. It not even *is* because being necessarily implies nonbeing. The One exists before being. With our eyes glued to the horizon, that line of water hardened into glass, we pass from desire to contemplation—of what and of whom? The reply lies in Actaeon's sacrifice and in the fate of the Illuminating Gas: the subject becomes part of its own object. *Mors osculi,* that state in which death and life are conjoined. We cannot see the Goddess, but while the flash of the ultrarapid illumination lasts, says Bruno, "to see the goddess is to be seen by her."

The similarities between Duchamp's concepts and the two great erotic traditions of the West, courtly love and Neoplatonism, are many and perturbing. I have already stated my belief: these similarities are not the result of any direct or consciously sought influence. Duchamp had not read Bernard de Ventadour or Ficino. He did not need to read them: Duchamp is a link in a chain, he belongs to a tradition whose origins date back twenty-five hundred years. The similarities are no more significant than the differences, principally his subversive spirit, his ironic negation. This is the defining feature of modernity, and it appears in all poetic and artistic works from the end of the eighteenth century onward.

But Duchamp's irony is an irony of affirmation: meta-irony. It is this that distinguishes him from almost all his immediate predecessors and from most of his contemporaries. This is what distinguishes him, above all else, from Picasso. Picasso's nihilism is of a different moral and intellectual order from Duchamp's skepticism. Picasso's weakness—which will be seen more and more clearly as the years pass—lies not in his hand or in his eye, but in his mind. This great artist was also supremely incredulous, and therefore superstitious (which is why he could embrace communism at the very moment of Stalinism—that is, at the time when Marxism had lost its critical and rational values). Duchamp was a skeptic like Pyrrho; therefore he was free, and with a free spirit he accepted the powers of the unknown and the intervention of chance.

Where does Duchamp fit into twentieth-century art? He is thought of as avant-garde *à outrance*. He was. At the same time, his work came into being as a reaction *against* modern art, especially against the art of his time. In a few years he exhausted Fauvism, Futurism, and Cubism. Later on he turned against them. As to Abstractionism, he kept his distance; he never believed in form for form's sake, nor did he make an idol out of the triangle or the sphere. He was part of the Dada movement for what it denied, not what it affirmed—if it affirmed anything. He felt a deeper affinity for Surrealism, but though his participation in the movement was constant, it was always tangential. His most daring gesture— the invention of the Readymades—was ambivalent. The Readymades stand as criticism not of the art of the past, but of works of art, ancient or modern, insofar as they are considered as *objects*. This is exactly what sets him against *all* modern art. For Duchamp, there is no *art in itself*; art is not a thing but a medium, a cable for the transmission of ideas and emotions. If the *Large Glass* is an avant-garde work by virtue of its mechanical forms, it is not avant-garde in what these forms say—it is a legend, a grotesque, marvelous story. Modern art does not aspire to say, but to be: the *Large Glass* "says," it tells us something. In this, it resembles the art of the "religious painters of the Renaissance," as Duchamp insisted more than once. In the long quarrel between "order and adventure," his work also functions according to the hinge-principle. His meta-irony dissolves the Romantic and avant-garde opposition between subject and object. All this corroborates what I have been thinking and saying for a long time: when they are not a caricature of the authentic avant-garde of the first third of our century, the so-called avant-garde movements of the last thirty years are nostalgic and anachronistic.

Duchamp's work is a variation—yet another one—on a theme that belongs to the traditional art and thought of our civilization. It is a two-fold theme: love and knowledge. It has a single goal: to penetrate the nature of reality. It is a variation in meta-ironic mode: love leads us to knowledge, but knowledge is barely a reflection, the shadow of a transparent veil on the transparency of a glass. The *Bride* is her landscape, and we ourselves, who contemplate her naked, form part of that landscape. We are the eyes with which the Bride sees herself. Avid eyes by which she is stripped, eyes that close at the moment her garment falls on the glass horizon. The Bride and her landscape are a shadow, an idea, the outline of an invisible being on a mirror. A speculation. The Bride is our horizon, our reality; the nature of that reality is ideal or rather hypothetical: the Bride is a point of view. More exactly, she is the vanishing point. Real reality, the reality of the fourth dimension, is a *virtuality:* "not the Reality of the sensory appearance but the virtual representation of a mass (analogous to its reflexion in a mirror)." (*A l'infinitif.*)

The body of the Bride—the body of reality (its appearance)—"is the result of two forces: attraction in space and *distraction* in extension." The Bride is stretched out on her bed of branches and thus is extended, distended, distracted, and drawn away from her point of attraction: we, the mirrors that reflect her. The same movement unfolds in time: her body enjoys an "alternative freedom" with respect to the center of gravity. During certain intervals the body is free and not subject to attraction; at others it is determined by it. While these intervals last, the body is *outside* time. At least outside linear time, in another time. The Bride escapes among the figures and hands of the clock: she is a pendulum seen in profile. Like the line separating the signs *a* and *b*, which disappears as it spins on itself, time is dissolved; through this empty clarity, through this abyss of reflections, the Bride disappears. Time goes into itself and, like space and the sign of the accordance, becomes a virtuality. An ambiguous optical and mental reality, the Bride is also an imprecise auditive reality: "She is a virtual sound." An echo and a silence. But all these are negative ways of seeing her, hearing her, and thinking of her. If the Bride is a negative proof, she is a virtuality, she is a desire. The desire to be.

Like Mallarmé's poem *Un coup de dés*, the *Large Glass* and the Assemblage not only contain their negation, but this negation is their motor, their animating principle. In both works the moment of the apparition of the feminine presence coincides with the moment when she vanishes. Diana: pivot of the world, appearance that evaporates and appears again. Appearance is the momentary form of the apparition. It is the form which we apprehend with our senses and which vanishes through them. Apparition is not a form but a conjunction of forces, a knot. Apparition is life itself, and it is governed by the paradoxical logic of the hinge. The essential difference between the *Large Glass* and the Assemblage is that the Bride is presented in the former like an appearance that must be decoded, whereas, in the second, appearance is denuded to become a *presence* that is offered to our contemplation. There is no solution, Duchamp said, because there is no problem. We could say more precisely: the problem is resolved in presence, the Idea incarnate in a naked girl.

The Assemblage in Philadelphia is Duchamp's reconciliation with the world and with himself. But there is neither abdication nor renunciation; criticism and metairony do not disap-

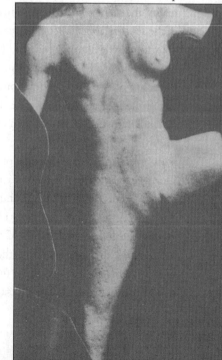

Door of Given: 1. The Illuminating Gas, 2. The Waterfall, *1948–49. (Painted leather over plaster relief, mounted on velvet.) Collection Mme Nora Martins Lobo, Sofia, Bulgaria. Photo by Jacques Faujour, © Centre G. Pompidou.*

pear. They are the gas lamp burning in the sunlight; its weak, flickering flame makes us doubt the reality of what we see. The lamp produces the *darkness* that Duchamp demanded for the ultrarapid exposure; it is the reflective element that makes the work enigmatic. The enigma lets us glimpse the other side of the presence, the single and double image: the void, death, the destruction of appearance, and simultaneously, momentary plenitude, vivacity in repose. The zero is full; plenitude opens up, it is empty. Feminine presence: the true waterfall in which is made manifest what is hidden, what is inside the convolutions of the world. The enigma is the glass that is separation/union: *The sign of the accordance.* We move from voyeurism to clairvoyance: the curse of sight becomes the freedom of contemplation.

—Mexico, December 27, 1972

CHRONOLOGY*

1887 Henri-Robert-Marcel Duchamp born near Blainville (Seine-Inférieure), in Normandy, on July 28 to Justin-Isidore (known as Eugène) Duchamp and Marie-Caroline-Lucie Duchamp (née Nicolle). Duchamp's maternal grandfather Emile-Frédéric Nicolle was a painter and engraver. His father was a notary, whose disapproval of an artist's career for his sons caused Duchamp's two elder brothers to change their name when they went against his wishes. Gaston (born 1875) called himself Jacques Villon and became a painter and engraver, while Raymond (born 1876) assumed the partial pseudonym Duchamp-Villon and became a sculptor. Their sister Suzanne (born 1889, and closest to Duchamp in age) also became a painter. Two more children completed the family: Yvonne (born 1895) and Magdeleine (born 1898).

Despite the striking difference in ages between the siblings, family ties were and remained close, with shared interests in music, art, and literature. Chess was a favorite pastime.

1902 Begins painting. Group of landscapes done at Blainville considered to be his first works.

1904 Graduates from the Ecole Bossuet, the lycée in Rouen.

Joins his elder brothers in Paris in October and lives with Villon in Montmartre on the Rue Caulaincourt. Studies painting at the Académie Julian until July 1905, but by his own account prefers to play billiards.

Paints family, friends, and landscapes in a Post-Impressionist manner.

1905 Following the example of Villon, executes cartoons for *Le Courrier Français* and *Le Rire* (continues this intermittently until 1910).

---

* From *Marcel Duchamp* edited by Anne d'Harnoncourt and Kynaston McShine. Copyright © 1973 The Museum of Modern Art, New York. All rights reserved. Reprinted by permission of the Museum of Modern Art.

Volunteers for military service. To obtain special classification, works for a printer in Rouen and prints a group of his grandfather's engraved views of that city. As an "art worker," receives exemption from second year of service.

Duchamp family moves into house at 71 Rue Jeanne d'Arc, Rouen, where they continue to live until the death of both parents in 1925.

1906 Resumes painting in Paris in October, living on the Rue Caulaincourt. With Villon, associates with cartoonists and illustrators.

1908 Moves out of Montmartre and establishes residence at 9 Avenue Amiral de Joinville, just outside of Paris in Neuilly, until 1913.

1909 Exhibits publicly for the first time at the Salon des Indépendants (two works). Three works included in the Salon d'Automne.

Exhibits at the first exhibition of the Société Normande de Peinture Moderne at the Salle Boieldieu in Rouen (December 20, 1909–January 20, 1910), organized by a friend, Pierre Dumont. Designs poster for the exhibition.

1910 Most important "early works" executed in this year. Paintings with a debt to Cézanne and Fauve coloring *(Portrait of the Artist's Father* and *Bust Portrait of Chauvel)* are followed by work with a new symbolic element *(Portrait of Dr. Dumouchel* and *Paradise)*.

Attends Sunday gatherings of artists and poets at his brothers' studios at 7 Rue Lemaître in Puteaux (a Parisian suburb adjacent to Neuilly). The group includes Albert Gleizes, Roger de La Fresnaye, Jean Metzinger, Fernand Léger, Georges Ribemont-Dessaignes, Guillaume Apollinaire, Henri-Martin Barzun, the "mathematician" Maurice Princet, and others.

About this time, meets Francis Picabia, probably introduced by Pierre Dumont. Shows four works at the Salon des Indépendants and five (including *The Chess Game*) at the Salon d'Automne.

Becomes Sociétaire of the Salon d'Automne and is thus permitted to enter paintings in the Salon without submission to jury.

1911 Continues work with symbolic overtones and begins paintings related to Cubism, with emphasis on successive images of a single body in motion. Aware of the chronophotographs of Etienne-Jules Marey and perhaps affected by similar ideas in the current work of Frank Kupka (his brothers' neighbor in Puteaux).

Shows *The Bush* and two landscapes at the Salon des Indépendants.

Executes a series of drawings and paintings analyzing the figures of two chess players (his brothers). Final painting executed by gaslight, as an experiment.

Marriage of his sister Suzanne to a pharmacist from Rouen. (The marriage ends in divorce a few years later.)

Exhibits again at Société Normande de la Peinture Moderne, Rouen. The Société sponsors an exhibition with the Cubist group in Paris at the Galerie d'Art Ancien et d'Art Contemporain, in which *Sonata* is included.

Shows *Young Man and Girl in Spring* and *Portrait (Dulcinea)* at Salon d'Automne.

Executes a group of drawings (of which three are known) inspired by poems of Jules Laforgue.

Toward the end of the year, paints *Sad Young Man in a Train* (a self-portrait) and oil sketch for *Nude Descending a Staircase.*

Duchamp-Villon asks his friends, including Gleizes, La Fresnaye, Metzinger, and Léger, to do paintings for the decoration of his kitchen at Puteaux. Duchamp executes *Coffee Mill*, his first painting to incorporate machine imagery and morphology.

1912 Climactic year of his most important oil-on-canvas works.

Paints *Nude Descending a Staircase*, which he submits to the Salon des Indépendants in March. Members of the Cubist hanging committee (including Gleizes and Henri Le Fauconnier) are disturbed by the painting and ask his brothers to intercede with him to at least alter the title. He withdraws the painting.

Attends opening of Futurist exhibition at Bernheim-Jeune gallery in February and pays several visits to the show.

During the spring, executes series of studies culminating in the mechanomorphic painting *King and Queen Surrounded by Swift Nudes.*

Nude Descending a Staircase is first shown in public at the Cubist exhibition at the Dalmau Gallery in Barcelona in May.

From friendship of Duchamp, Picabia, and Apollinaire there develop radical and ironic ideas challenging the commonly held notions of art. This independent activity precedes the official founding of Dada in Zurich, 1916.

With Picabia and Apollinaire, attends performance of Raymond Roussel's *Impressions d'Afrique* at the Théâtre Antoine, probably in May.

Crucial two-month visit to Munich during July and August, where he paints *The Passage from the Virgin to the Bride* and the *Bride,* and executes the first drawing on the theme of *The Bride Stripped Bare by the Bachelors.* Returns home by way of Prague, Vienna, Dresden, and Berlin.

Gleizes and Metzinger include him in their book *Du Cubisme,* published in Paris in August (*Sonata* and *Coffee Mill* reproduced).

In October, takes a car trip to the Jura mountains near the Swiss border with Apollinaire, Picabia, and Gabrielle Buffet. Records this stimulating event in a long manuscript note.

Begins to preserve notes and sketches jotted on stray pieces of paper which will eventually serve as a cryptic guide to the *Large Glass* and other projects, and which he will publish later in facsimile editions *(Box of 1914,* the *Green Box, A l'infinitif).*

Nude Descending a Staircase finally shown in Paris at the Salon de la Section d'Or (October 10–30) at the Galerie de la Boétie, organized by the Duchamp brothers and their friends. Five other works by Duchamp also included.

Walter Pach visits Duchamp and his brothers and selects four works by Duchamp for inclusion in the International Exhibition of Modern Art (the Armory Show).

1913 A year of critical change in the artist's career. Virtually abandons all conventional forms of painting and drawing. Begins to develop a personal system (metaphysics) of measurement and time-space calculation that "stretches the laws of physics just a little." Drawings become mechanical renderings. Three-dimensional objects become quasi-scientific devices: e.g., *Three Standard Stoppages,* a manifestation of "canned chance" that remained one of the artist's favorite works.

Experiments with musical composition based on laws of chance.

Begins mechanical drawings, painted studies, and notations that will culminate in his most complex and highly regarded work: *The Bride Stripped Bare by Her Bachelors, Even* (the *Large Glass),* 1915–23. Begins first preparatory study on glass: *Glider Containing a Water Mill in Neighboring Metals.*

Employed as librarian at the Bibliothèque Sainte-Geneviève, Paris.

Spends part of summer at Herne Bay, Kent, England, where he works on notes for the *Large Glass.*

In October, moves out of Neuilly studio back into Paris, to apartment at 23 Rue Saint-Hippolyte.

Mounts a bicycle wheel upside down on a kitchen stool as a "distraction," something pleasant to have in the studio. This object becomes a distant forerunner of the Readymades and also foreshadows a later preoccupation with rotating machines that produce optical effects.

In New York, *Nude Descending a Staircase* becomes the focus of national attention and controversy at the Armory Show (February 17–March 15) and travels with the show to Chicago and Boston. If is bought sight unseen by dealer Frederic C. Torrey from San Francisco for $324. Chicago lawyer Arthur Jerome Eddy buys *Portrait of Chess Players* and *King and Queen Surrounded by Swift Nudes* from the show. The architect Manierre Dawson buys the fourth work, *Sad Young Man in a Train,* thus giving the artist his first (perhaps greatest?) commercial success.

In winter of this year, draws full-scale study for the *Glass* on the plaster wall of the Rue Saint-Hippolyte studio.

Publication in Paris of Apollinaire's *Les Peintres cubistes,* with its prophetic assessment of Duchamp's contribution to modern art (*The Chess Game,* 1910, reproduced).

1914 Continues work on major studies for the *Large Glass: Chocolate Grinder, No.2; Network of Stoppages; Glider;* and another work on glass, *Nine Malic Molds.*

Collects a small group of notes and one drawing in the *Box of 1914*, of which three photographic replicas are made.

Buys a *Bottlerack* at a Paris bazaar and inscribes it. Adds touches of color to a commercial print and calls it *Pharmacy* (executed again in an edition of three, a favorite number for Duchamp). These constitute the first full-fledged appearances of the (still unnamed) genre Readymade, an unprecedented art form involving the infrequent selection, inscription, and display of commonplace objects chosen on the basis of complete visual indifference. Thus quietly begins a revolution whose effects continue to expand as artists propose the intrusion of wholly nonart elements into the aesthetic frame of reference.

With the outbreak of war, Villon and Duchamp-Villon are mobilized. Walter Pach, returning to France in autumn, urges Duchamp (exempt from service on account of his health) to visit the United States.

1915 Prior to first visit to New York, sends seven works (probably through Pach) to two exhibitions of modern French art at the Carroll Gallery there. Collector John Quinn purchases two paintings and a watercolor.

Sails on the S.S. *Pochambeau* to New York, arriving June 15, and greeted as a celebrity. Pach meets the boat, takes Duchamp directly to see Louise and Walter Arensberg, who at once become his close friends and enthusiastic patrons. In their apartment at 33 West 67th Street, Arensberg begins to assemble what will be the largest collection of Duchamp's work, assisted by the artist.

Lives with the Arensbergs for three months; moves to furnished apartment at 34 Beekman Place for month of October.

Later this fall, establishes a studio at 1947 Broadway (Lincoln Arcade Building). Acquires two large glass panels and begins work on the *Large Glass* itself.

Buys and inscribes two more manufactured objects (snow shovel and ventilator), for which he now coins term "Readymade."

Through efforts of Pach and Quinn, obtains job as librarian at French Institute for a brief period.

First published statement, "A Complete Reversal of Art Opinions by Marcel Duchamp, Iconoclast," in September issue of *Arts and Decora-*

tion (New York), followed by a number of brief interviews in the New York press.

Meets Man Ray, who becomes lifelong friend and fellow conspirator.

Circle of artists and poets with whom he mingles until 1918, often at lively gatherings at the Arensbergs, includes: Albert and Juliette Gleizes, Gabrielle Buffet and Picabia, Jean and Yvonne Crotti, John Covert, Charles Demuth, Charles Sheeler, Morton Schamberg, Joseph Stella, Marsden Hartley, Walter Pach, Louise and Allen Norton, Mina Loy, Arthur Cravan, Elsa Baroness von Freytag-Loringhoven, Isadora Duncan, William Carlos Williams, Beatrice Wood, Edgard Varèse, Marius de Zayas, Fania and Carl Van Vechten, and Wallace Stevens. Evenings at the Arensbergs involve vigorous debates on current art and literature, the planning of exhibitions and "little magazines," and much chess playing.

1916 Two Readymades are shown, together with five paintings and drawings (including both *Chocolate Grinders)*, in an exhibition of modern art at the Bourgeois Gallery, New York (April 3–29).

Included in "Four Musketeers" exhibition at Montross Gallery, New York (April 4–22), with Gleizes, Metzinger, and Crotti.

Henri-Pierre Roché arrives in New York and joins Arensbergs' circle. Roché becomes close friend of Duchamp, and they later collaborate in several ventures of buying and selling art on commission.

In October, moves from Lincoln Arcade Building into studio above Arensbergs at 33 West 67th Street. The Arensbergs gradually acquire ownership of the *Large Glass* in return for paying his rent.

About this time, makes a replica of the *Bicycle Wheel* (the original had remained in Paris) and hand-colors a full-scale photograph of the *Nude Descending a Staircase* for Arensberg. Importance of "original" or "unique" work of art thus brought into question.

As a founding member of the Society of Independent Artists, Inc., meets with Arensberg, Pach, John Sloan, George Bellows, and others to plan first exhibition with motto "No Jury. No Prizes. Hung in Alphabetical Order." Serves as chairman of hanging committee, with Bellows and Rockwell Kent.

Meets Katherine S. Dreier, also involved with Independents.

1917 Resigns from board of directors of Society of Independent Artists upon rejection of his Readymade *Fountain,* which he submitted under the pseudonym "R. Mutt" for their first annual exhibition. Arensberg also resigns in protest; *Fountain* is photographed by Alfred Stieglitz.

During Independents exhibition at the Grand Central Galleries, New York (April 10–May 6), organizes with Picabia a lecture in the galleries by Arthur Cravan, which ends in a scandalized uproar.

With aid of Roché, Arensberg, and Beatrice Wood, promotes the publication of two Dadaist reviews, *The Blind Man* and *Rongwrong.*

Becomes friendly with Carrie, Ettie, and Florine Stettheimer, three wealthy and cultivated sisters to whom he gives occasional French lessons. Other means of making a modest living include translations of French correspondence for John Quinn.

In October, takes a job for several months at French Mission for the War, as secretary to a captain.

1918 With execution for Katherine Dreier of *Tu m',* his first oil painting in four years, which takes him several months to complete, Duchamp gives up painting altogether.

When the United States enters the war, he moves to Buenos Aires, where he continues his creative activity for nine months. Sails from New York August 13 on the *S.S. Crofton Hall,* arriving in Argentina about a month later.

Takes a small apartment at 1507 Sarmiento and works on drawings for the *Large Glass.*

Executes third glass study, *To Be Looked at with One Eye, Close to, for Almost an Hour.*

Attempts to organize a Cubist exhibition in Buenos Aires; writes to Gleizes, Henri-Martin Barzun, and Marius de Zayas in New York, but the project does not materialize. Informs Arensbergs by letter that, "according to my principles," he will not exhibit his own work. He asks them not to lend anything of his to exhibitions in New York.

Plays chess avidly, and designs set of rubber stamps to record games and to permit him to play chess by mail.

Deeply distressed by death of Raymond Duchamp-Villon in France on October 9, which is followed a month later by the death of Apollinaire. Makes plans to return to France

1919 Joins chess club in Buenos Aires and plays constantly, to the point where he refers to himself as a "chess maniac."

Marriage of Suzanne Duchamp to Jean Crotti in Paris in April. Duchamp sends her instructions from Buenos Aires for *Unhappy Readymade* to be executed at long distance on the balcony of their Paris apartment.

Despite his desire not to exhibit, three drawings included in "Evolution of French Art" organized by Marius de Zayas at the Arden Gallery, New York, in May.

Returns to Europe, sailing June 22 from Buenos Aires on the S.S. *Highland Pride.*

Stays with Picabia in Paris until the end of the year, with intermittent visits to his family in Rouen.

Establishes contact with the Dada group in Paris and joins gatherings at the Café Certà near the Grands Boulevards; group includes André Breton, Louis Aragon, Paul Eluard, Tristan Tzara, Jacques Rigaut, Philippe Soupault, Georges Ribemont-Dessaignes, and Pierre de Massot.

Using reproduction of the *Mona Lisa* as a Readymade, executes scurrilous *L.H.O.O.Q.*, which becomes a talisman for the Dada movement.

1920 Returns to New York for the year in January, bringing *50 cc of Paris Air* as a present for Arensberg.

A version of *L.H.O.O.Q.* (without goatee) published by Picabia in March issue of *391* in Paris.

Takes a studio at 246 West 73rd Street, where, with the assistance of Man Ray, he executes *Rotary Glass Plates (Precision Optics),* his first motor-driven construction.

Collaborates with Man Ray on experimental anaglyphic film shot with two synchronized cameras. Man Ray photographs "dust breeding" on the *Large Glass.*

With Katherine Dreier and Man Ray, conceives and founds (on April 29) the Société Anonyme: Museum of Modern Art 1920. The pioneering activity of this organization presents eighty-four exhibitions by 1939 as well as numerous lectures and publications, and builds up a large permanent collection of international modern art. Duchamp serves first as chairman of the exhibition committee and later for many years as secretary to the Société.

Contributes work to first and third Group Exhibitions of the Société in its headquarters at 19 East 47th Street, New York.

Louis Eilshemius, discovered by Duchamp in the 1917 Independents, given his first one-man show by the Société.

Joins Marshall Chess Club, New York.

In winter, moves back into Lincoln Arcade Building, which witnesses birth of "Rrose Sélavy," a feminine alter-ego who lends her name henceforth to published puns and Readymades.

Photographed by Man Ray in his guise as a woman.

Another variation on the concept of the Readymade, *Fresh Widow,* is constructed to his design by a carpenter.

1921 With Man Ray, edits and publishes single issue (April) of *New York Dada,* including contributions by Tzara and Rube Goldberg.

In reply to invitation to enter Salon Dada (June 6–30) at the Galerie Montaigne in Paris, sends rude cable PODE BAL, dated June 1. Exhibition organizers are forced to hang placards bearing only catalog numbers (28–31) in space reserved for his work.

Sails for Europe on the *France* in June and spends next six months with the Crottis at 22 Rue la Condamine, Paris.

Man Ray arrives in Paris in July; Duchamp meets him at the station. During the summer, they continue film experiments with revolving spirals in Villon's garden at Puteaux.

First puns published in July issue of *391,* Paris.

As Rrose Sélavy, signs Picabia's painting *L'Oeil cacodylate*, which is shown at the Salon d'Automne and later hung in the Paris restaurant Le Boeuf sur le Toit.

Has hair cropped in the pattern of a comet (with a star-shaped tonsure) by Georges de Zayas.

Ownership of unfinished *Large Glass* passes to Katherine Dreier when Arensbergs move permanently to California in the late fall.

Writes Arensbergs of his plans to return to New York to complete the *Large Glass,* and mentions his intention to find a job in the movies "not as an actor, but rather as assistant cameraman."

1922 Sails for New York on S.S. *Aquitania* on January 28 to continue work on the *Large Glass* in the Lincoln Arcade studio. Occupied with silvering and scraping the Oculist Witnesses section of the *Glass.*

Gives French lessons.

With Leon Hartl, another French expatriate artist in New York, starts fabric-dyeing establishment that fails after about six months.

Designs layout for selection of art criticism by his friend Henry McBride. *Some French Moderns Says McBride* published by Société Anonyme, New York, in small edition.

Experiments with the secret truth of numbers, applied to games.

In a letter to Tzara in Paris, proposes lucrative scheme for marketing a gold insignia with the letters DADA as a "universal panacea" (the project was never realized).

Publication of first major critical essay on Duchamp, by André Breton, in October issue of *Littérature* (Paris).

Poet and medium Robert Desnos in Paris apparently receives puns "in a trance" from Rrose Sélavy in New York, and Breton publishes them in December issue of *Littérature.*

1923 Ceases work on the *Large Glass* and signs it, having brought it to a state of incompletion.

Returns to Europe in mid-February on the S.S. *Noordam* via Rotterdam.

Settles in Paris, where he remains until 1942, save for occasional trips around Europe and three brief visits to New York (1926–27, 1933–34, 1936).

Moves into the Hotel Istria, 29 Rue Campagne-Première. Man Ray has a studio nearby. Friendship with Brancusi.

Meets Mary Reynolds, an American widow living in Paris, and they establish a close friendship that lasts for several decades.

Works on optical disks, later used in *Anémic Cinéma*.

Travels to Brussels in March, where he spends several months, during which he participates in his first major chess tournament.

His passion for chess involves serious training and professional competition, which absorb increasing amounts of time for about the next ten years.

Member of the jury for this year's Salon d'Automne.

The idea reaches the public that Duchamp has ceased to produce art.

1924 In the course of several trips to Monte Carlo, invents a roulette system whereby one "neither wins nor loses."

Works all year on motorized *Rotary Demisphere*, commissioned by Paris collector Jacques Doucet.

Gives French lessons to Americans in Paris.

Death of John Quinn, New York, July 28.

Issues a major group of puns, published by Pierre de Massot in Paris as *The Wonderful Book: Reflections on Rrose Sélavy*.

Becomes chess champion of Haute-Normandie.

Appears with Man Ray, Erik Satie, and Picabia in René Clair's film *Entr'acte*, which is shown during the intermission of the Instantanéist ballet *Relâche* by Picabia and Satie, produced by the Swedish Ballet at the Théâtre des Champs-Elysées in December. Also appears in a brief tableau as Adam to Brogna Perlmutter's Eve, probably in a single evening performance of the review *Ciné Sketch* (on December 24?) during the short run of the ballet.

1925 Duchamp's mother dies on January 29; his father dies on February 3.

Participates in chess tournament, Nice, for which he designs poster.

Completes *Rotary Demisphere,* which he asks Doucet not to lend to any exhibition.

Continues to work on his roulette system.

1926 Incorporates optical experiments and puns into *Anémic Cinéma,* a seven-minute movie filmed in collaboration with Man Ray and Marc Allégret.

Sponsors sale of eighty paintings, watercolors, and drawings by Picabia at Hôtel Drouot, Paris, on March 8 (catalog introduction signed by Rrose Sélavy).

Begins speculative purchases and sales of art works, many on behalf of the Arensbergs, an activity ironically counter to his lifelong aversion to the commercial aspects of art.

Rents top-floor studio at 11 Rue Larrey in Paris, which he is to occupy for next sixteen years.

Société Anonyme commissions *Portrait of Marcel Duchamp* by Antoine Pevsner.

Travels to Milan and Venice in May. Assists Katherine Dreier in the organization of the International Exhibition of Modern Art sponsored by the Société Anonyme at the Brooklyn Museum (November 19, 1926–January 9, 1927). Exhibition includes 307 works by artists from twenty-three countries.

Sails on the *Paris* on October 13 to New York, where he arranges a Brancusi exhibition at the Brummer Gallery (November 17–December 15). Stays with Allen Norton at 111 West 16th Street. During exhibition meets Julien Levy.

Arranges showing for *Anémic Cinéma* at Fifth Avenue Theater.

The *Large Glass* shown publicly for first time at the International Exhibition in Brooklyn. This work is accidentally shattered in transit following the exhibition. Its condition remains undiscovered until the *Glass* is removed from storage by Katherine Dreier several years later.

1927 With Roché and Mrs. Charles Rumsey, and at Brancusi's request, arranges to buy John Quinn's collection of Brancusi sculpture before the public auction in February. Also buys back three of his own paintings before Quinn sale.

Brief visit to Chicago in January to arrange Brancusi exhibition at the Arts Club there (January 4–18).

Returns to Paris in late February and moves into 11 Rue Larrey studio, where he installs one door that serves two doorways. (The door is removed in 1963 and shown as an independent work of art.)

Continues chess activity in a pattern characteristic of the next five years: the winter months spent training in Nice and playing in a steady sequence of tournaments.

First marriage, on June 7 in Paris, to Lydie Sarazin-Levassor, twenty-five-year-old daughter of an automobile manufacturer. Formal church wedding. Bridal procession filmed by Man Ray. Marriage ends in divorce the following January.

1928 Chess continues, with tournaments in Hyères, Paris, The Hague, and Marseilles.

Arranges with Alfred Stieglitz for Picabia exhibition at the Intimate Gallery in New York.

1929 Visits Spain with Katherine Dreier.

Chess tournaments in Paris.

Begins work on chess book, detailed exposition of special end-game problems.

1930 Chess tournaments in Nice and Paris. Member of French team of the third Chess Olympiad, Hamburg. Duchamp draws with Frank Marshall, the US champion.

Nude Descending a Staircase shown for the first time since 1913 in exhibition of Cubism at De Hauke Gallery, New York, in April.

Apparent relaxation of determination not to exhibit. *Belle Haleine, Pharmacy, Monte Carlo Bond,* and two versions of *L.H.O.O.Q.* included in exhibition of collages, "La Peinture au Défi," organized by Louis Aragon at Galerie Goemans, Paris, in March.

Asked by Katherine Dreier to select works in Paris for a Société Anonyme exhibition in New York the following January. The selection includes Max Ernst, Joan Miró, Amédée Ozenfant, and Piet Mondrian.

Criticized by Breton in the *Second Manifesto of Surrealism* for abandoning art for chess.

1931 Important chess tournament in Prague. Becomes member of Committee of French Chess Federation and its delegate (until 1937) to the International Chess Federation.

1932 With Vitaly Halberstadt, publishes *L'Opposition et les cases conjugées sont réconciliées*. Layout and cover designed by Duchamp.

Chess tournament at La Baule. Plays in radio match against Argentine Chess Club of Buenos Aires. Wins Paris Chess Tournament in August, a high point in his chess career.

About this time, sees Raymond Roussel playing chess at nearby table at the Café de la Régence, Paris, but they do not meet.

Invents for Alexander Calder's movable constructions the name "mobiles" and encourages their exhibition at the Galerie Vignon in Paris. (Arp then names the static works "stabiles.")

1933 Last important international chess tournament, at Folkestone, England.

Translates Eugène Znosko-Borovsky's chess book into French: *Comment il faut commencer une partie d'échecs*, a study of opening moves that neatly counters his own interest in end games.

Sails for New York on October 25 to organize a second Brancusi exhibition at the Brummer Gallery (November 17–January 13, 1934).

1934 Returns to Paris in February.

Begins to assemble notes and photographs pertaining to the *Large Glass*. These are reproduced in a painstaking facsimile edition of three hundred, which he publishes in September in Paris: *La Mariée mise à nu par ses célibataires, même* (known as the *Green Box*).

1935 Produces a set of six *Rotoreliefs* in an edition of five hundred which he displays at the annual Paris inventors' salon, the Concours Lépine (August 30–October 8), with no commercial success. Refuses to allow Katherine Dreier to charge more than three dollars per set since they were so inexpensive to print.

Starts assembling material for the *Box in a Valise*, another special edition that is to include reproductions of all his major works.

Included in "Exposición Surrealista," Tenerife, Canary Islands.

Serves as captain of French team of First International Chess by Correspondence Olympiad. He is undefeated.

Designs a binding for Alfred Jarry's *Ubu Roi*, executed by Mary Reynolds.

Publication of André Breton's "Phare de la Mariée" (Lighthouse of the Bride), in winter issue of *Minotaure* (Paris)—the first comprehensive and illuminating essay on the *Large Glass*.

1936 Continues interest in optical phenomena with *Fluttering Hearts*, design for cover of issue of *Cahiers d'Art* (Paris), containing an important article on his work by Gabrielle Buffet.

Readymades including *Why Not Sneeze?* shown at the Exposition Surréaliste d'Objets at the apartment of the dealer Charles Ratton, Paris (May 22–29).

Four works included in the vast International Surrealist Exhibition in London at the New Burlington Galleries (June 11–July 4).

Sails May 20 on the *Normandie* for New York, to undertake the month-long painstaking restoration of the *Large Glass* at Katherine Dreier's house in West Redding, Connecticut.

In August, travels across the United States by train to San Francisco, and then visits the Arensbergs in Hollywood. Stops on return trip in Cleveland, where *Nude Descending a Staircase* is included in the Cleveland Museum of Art's Twentieth Anniversary Exhibition.

Sails for France on September 2.

Eleven works (largest selection to this date) included in *Fantastic Art, Dada, Surrealism*, the first major exhibition of its kind in the United

States, organized by Alfred H. Barr, Jr., at the Museum of Modern Art, New York (December 9, 1936–January 17, 1937).

1937 First one-man show held at the Arts Club of Chicago (February 5–27), while he remains in France. Nine works included. Preface to catalog by Julien Levy.

Designs glass doorway for André Breton's Galerie Gradiva, at 31 Rue de Seine, Paris.

Writes a chess column every Thursday for Paris daily journal *Ce Soir*, edited by Louis Aragon.

Continues work on reproductions for *Box in a Valise*.

Assists Peggy Guggenheim with her London gallery, Guggenheim Jeune. First show planned for Brancusi, then changed to drawings of Jean Cocteau.

1938 As "generator-arbitrator," participates in organization of the *Exposition Internationale du Surréalisme*, Galerie Beaux-Arts, Paris (January 17–February). Collaborates with Breton, Eluard, Salvador Dali, Ernst, Man Ray, and Wolfgang Paalen. Proposes ideas for elaborate installation, which includes a ceiling of twelve hundred coal sacks. Shows five works including *Rotary Demisphere* and *Nine Malic Molds* of 1914. Contributes mannequin (Rrose Sélavy) dressed only in his own hat and coat to row of artists' mannequins in the Rue Surréaliste. Leaves for England on the day of the opening. Eight works reproduced in the "Dictionnaire abrégé du surréalisme," a section of the exhibition catalog.

Prepares summer exhibition of contemporary sculpture for Guggenheim Jeune gallery, London. Selection includes Arp, Brancusi, Calder, Duchamp-Villon, Pevsner.

1939 Publishes volume of puns, *Rrose Sélavy, oculisme de précision, pails et coups de pieds en tous genres*, in Paris.

Monte Carlo Bond given by Duchamp to the Museum of Modern Art, New York (first work in a public collection).

Preoccupied with reproduction of the *Large Glass* on transparent plastic for *Box in a Valise*.

1940 Continues work on his *Valise*.

Summer with the Crottis in Arcachon, in the Occupied Zone of France.

Man Ray moves to the United States, settling in California.

Previously unpublished notes included in Breton's *Anthologie de l'humour nair*, which was intended to have a special cover by Duchamp.

1941 Official date of first publication of *Box in a Valise*. Individual *Valises* are assembled slowly over the years by Duchamp and various assistants, including Joseph Cornell, Xenia Cage, and Jacqueline Matisse.

As trustee, with Katherine Dreier, of the permanent collection of the Société Anonyme, authorizes its presentation to Yale University Art Gallery, New Haven, Connecticut. *Rotary Glass Plates* of 1920 included in this gift.

Obtains permanent pass for the "free zone" as a cheese dealer from his merchant friend Gustave Candel; travels between Paris and the south of France, moving the contents of the *Valises* to Marseilles, whence they will be sent to New York.

1942 Returns to the United States, where he resides for the rest of his life. Sails from Lisbon on the *Serpa Pinto*, arriving in New York on June 25.

Lives briefly in the Ernsts' apartment at 440 East 51st Street, then moves to 56 Seventh Avenue, where he stays with Frederick Kiesler.

Associates with Surrealist group of artists and writers temporarily living in New York during the war, including Breton, Ernst, Matta, André Masson, Wifredo Lam, and Yves Tanguy.

With Breton and Ernst, serves as editorial adviser for several issues of the review *VVV*, founded by David Hare in New York.

Peggy Guggenheim's gallery Art of This Century, which serves as a museum for her private collection and a gallery for temporary exhibitions, opens at 30 West 57th Street in October. Installation by Kiesler includes reproductions from Duchamp's *Valise* seen through holes in a revolving disk which the viewer turns with a wheel.

Collaborates with Breton, Sidney Janis, and R. A. Parker on catalog and exhibition of *First Papers of Surrealism*, shown at 451 Madison

Avenue, New York (October 14–November 7) and sponsored by the Coordinating Council of French Relief Societies. Designs spectacular and frustrating installation with a mile of string. Encourages Janis children to play energetic games in the gallery during opening (at which he is not present).

Meets John Cage through Peggy Guggenheim.

1943 Moves into top-floor studio at 210 West 14th Street, which he occupies for about twenty-two years.

With Breton, and Kurt Seligmann, designs show window at Brentano's bookstore on Fifth Avenue for publication of *La Part du diable* by Denis de Rougemont.

Takes part in a sequence of Maya Deren's uncompleted film *The Witch's Cradle*.

His collage *Genre Allegory* rejected by *Vogue* magazine as a design for a George Washington cover.

Large Glass placed on extended loan to the Museum of Modern Art, New York, and is part of international exhibition there, *Art in Progress* (first public appearance of the *Glass* since its repair in 1936). Remains on view until it is returned to Katherine Dreier in April 1946.

1944 Executes drawing of nude figure, first known sketch for his major last work, Etant donnés: *1° la chute d'eau, 2° le gaz d'éclairage*, on which he was to work in secret for twenty years.

Describes daily existence to Katherine Dreier: "Chessing, lessoning, starting a few boxes, my usual life."

Hans Richter begins his film *Dreams That Money Can Buy*, including sequence of Duchamp with his *Rotoreliefs*. Other collaborators are Calder, Ernst, Léger, and Man Ray.

Designs catalog for *Imagery of Chess* exhibition at Julien Levy Gallery in December and referees six simultaneous games of blindfold chess between champion George Koltanowski and Alfred Barr, Ernst, Kiesler, Levy, Dorothea Tanning, and Dr. Gregory Zilboorg.

The Société Anonyme publishes *Duchamp's Glass: An Analytical Reflection*, by Katherine Dreier and Matta.

1945 March issue of *View* (New York) devoted to Duchamp, providing first important illustrated anthology of writings on his work.

Family group exhibition of *Duchamp, Duchamp-Villon, Villon* at Yale University Art Gallery (February 25–March 25). Ten works shown. An exhibition of Duchamp and Villon organized by the Société Anonyme travels to college art galleries in Virginia, California, Pennsylvania, Minnesota, and Maine during 1945–46.

With Breton installs show window at Brentano's on Fifth Avenue for publication of Breton's *Arcane 17*. After protests from League of Women, installation is moved to Gotham Book Mart at 41 West 47th Street.

With Enrico Donati, installs show window at Brentano's for second edition of Breton's book *Le Surréalisme et la peinture.*

In December the Museum of Modern Art, New York, purchases *The Passage from the Virgin to the Bride* from Walter Pach (first painting to be bought by a museum).

1946 Begins twenty years of work on the tableau-assemblage *Etant donnés* in his 14th Street studio.

Guest director of the Florine Stettheimer exhibition at the Museum of Modern Art, New York (catalog by Henry McBride).

Serves, with Alfred Barr and Sidney Janis, on jury for *Bel Ami International Competition and Exhibition of New Paintings by Eleven American and European Artists* on the theme of the Temptation of St. Anthony. First prize awarded to Max Ernst.

First important extended interview, with James Johnson Sweeney, published in *The Museum of Modern Art Bulletin*, "Eleven European Artists in America."

Helps Katherine Dreier decorate her recently purchased house in Milford, Connecticut. Paints the small elevator installed in the entrance foyer with a trompe-l'oeil leaf pattern matching the wallpaper.

Visits Paris in the fall, where he and Breton design and prepare exhibition *Le Surréalisme en 1947* at the Galerie Maeght (July–August 1947). Duchamp's suggestions for the Labyrinth and Rain Room carried out by Kiesler. Returns to New York in December, long before the opening. Kiesler also executes photo-collage *The Green Ray* for the exhibition on Duchamp's behalf—"art by proxy."

1947 In collaboration with Enrico Donati in New York, designs catalog cover for *Le Surréalisme en 1947* and hand-colors 999 foam-rubber "falsies," labeled "Prière de Toucher," for the deluxe edition.

Applies for United States citizenship.

1948 Executes vellum-and-gesso study for nude figure in *Etant donnés*, which he gives to Maria Martins, the Brazilian sculptress.

Included in group exhibition with Joseph Cornell and Tanguy, *Through the Big End of the Opera Glass*, at the Julien Levy Gallery, New York, in December, for which he designs catalog.

1949 Participates in three-day session of the Western Round Table on Modern Art, held at the San Francisco Museum of Art, April 8–10. Other panelists are Gregory Bateson, Kenneth Burke, Alfred Frankenstein, Robert Goldwater, Darius Milhaud, Andrew Ritchie, Arnold Schönberg, Mark Tobey, and Frank Lloyd Wright, with George Boas as moderator; *Nude Descending a Staircase* shown in an exhibition assembled for the event at the museum. Afterward, visits Max Ernst in Sedona, Arizona, for a few days.

Largest group of works (thirty) exhibited to date included in *Twentieth Century Art from the Louise and Walter Arensberg Collection* at the Art Institute of Chicago (October 20–December 18).

Visits Chicago, with Arensbergs, at the time of the exhibition.

1950 Contributes thirty-three critical studies of artists (written 1943–49) to catalog of the Collection of the Société Anonyme, Yale University Art Gallery.

Takes brief trip in September to Paris, where Mary Reynolds is seriously ill. She dies on September 30.

As a trustee of the Arensbergs' Francis Bacon Foundation, joins in decision to donate the Arensbergs' collection of twentieth-century art and Pre-Columbian sculpture to the Philadelphia Museum of Art.

Appearance of first plaster erotic objects *(Not a Shoe, Female Fig Leaf)*.

1951 Publication of *Dada Painters and Poets: An Anthology*, edited by Robert Motherwell, New York. Includes contributions by and about Duchamp, who also gave advice and assistance to the editor.

1952 Helps to organize *Duchamp Frères et Soeur, Oeuvres d'Art*, an exhibition at the Rose Fried Gallery, New York (February 25–March).

Death of Katherine Dreier on March 29.

Collaborates with Hans Richter in the latter's film *8 X 8* based on chess. Sequences filmed in Southbury, Connecticut, with Ernst, Calder, Tanguy, Arp, Kiesler, Dorothea Tanning, Julien Levy, Jacqueline Matisse.

Gives address at banquet of New York State Chess Association on August 30.

Assists in organization of memorial exhibition of Katherine Dreier's own collection at Yale University Art Gallery in December. Writes preface for catalog. Miss Dreier's collection, which includes major works by Duchamp, is bequeathed to several museums including Yale University Art Gallery, the Museum of Modern Art, New York, and the Philadelphia Museum of Art. As an executor of her will, Duchamp plays an important role in the division of the collection.

1953 Assists with assembly and installation of the exhibition *Dada 1916–1923* at the Sidney Janis Gallery, New York. Shows twelve works. Designs catalog on single sheet of tissue paper which is crumpled into a ball before being distributed. Extended (unpublished) interview with Harriet, Sidney, and Carroll Janis.

Death of Picabia on November 30.

Death of Louise Arensberg on November 25, followed shortly by the death of Walter Arensberg on January 29, 1954.

Five works included in exhibition *Marcel Duchamp, Francis Picabia* at Rose Fried Gallery (December 7, 1953–January 8, 1954).

1954 Marries Alexina (Teeny) Sattler, who had previously been married to Pierre Matisse, on January 16 in New York. Duchamp thus acquired a new family of three stepchildren, Paul, Jacqueline, and Peter. Duchamp and his wife live in a fourth-floor walk-up apartment at 327 East 58th Street (formerly occupied by the Max Ernsts) for next five years.

Musée National d'Art Moderne in Paris acquires oil sketch of *Chess Players*, 1911, first work in a French public collection.

Publication in Paris of study by Michel Carrouges on Kafka, Roussel, and Duchamp, *Les Machines célibataires*, which provokes comment and controversy in French literary circles.

Opening of permanent exhibition of the Louise and Walter Arensberg Collection at the Philadelphia Museum of Art, which received this major bequest in 1950. Forty-three works by Duchamp included. Comprehensive catalog published. Installed by Henry Clifford with the assistance of Duchamp.

The *Large Glass*, bequeathed by Katherine Dreier, is permanently installed in the Arensberg galleries.

1955 Televised interview with James Johnson Sweeney at the Philadelphia Museum of Art, which is broadcast by NBC in "Wisdom Series" in January 1956.

Becomes a naturalized United States citizen. Alfred Barr, James Johnson Sweeney, and James Thrall Soby are witnesses at the ceremony.

About this time, begins to work on elaborate landscape for *Given*.

1956 Publication of *Surrealism and Its Affinities*, catalog by Hugh Edwards of the Mary Reynolds Collection of rare books, periodicals, and her own bookbindings, at the Art Institute of Chicago. Preface by Duchamp, who also designed the bookplate.

Sends remaining contents of unpublished *Valises* back to Paris, where various assistants continue the slow and painstaking work of their assembly.

1957 Major exhibition and catalog of *jacques Villon, Raymond Duchamp-Villon, Marcel Duchamp* at the Solomon R. Guggenheim Museum, New York (February 19–March 10), prepared by James Johnson Sweeney. Duchamp suggested the idea for the joint exhibition, advised on the selection, and designed the catalog. Exhibition later travels to Houston, Texas.

Delivers important lecture "The Creative Act" at convention (April 3–11) of the American Federation of Arts in Houston.

1958 Publication in Paris of *Marchand du Sel, écrits de Marcel Duchamp*, compiled by Michel Sanouillet. The most com prehensive collection to date of Duchamp's writings and statements, with bibliography by Poupard-Lieussou.

About this time, begins to spend summers in Cadaqués, on the Costa Brava, Spain; visits to Paris often included.

1959 Moves to apartment at 28 West 10th Street, New York, where he and his wife live until his death.

Assists in design and publication in Paris of *Sur Marcel Duchamp* by Robert Lebel. (English translation by George Heard Hamilton published in New York.) The most comprehensive and definitive work on Duchamp to that date. Includes a catalogue raisonné with 208 detailed entries and an extensive bibliography. Two new works executed for incorporation in deluxe edition: *Self-Portrait in Profile* and enamel plaque *Eau & gaz à tous les étages*. This publication celebrated in one-man exhibitions at the Sidney Janis Gallery, New York, Galerie La Hune, Paris, and the Institute of Contemporary Arts, London.

Enters the Collège de Pataphysique in France in the year 86 E.P. (*Ere pataphysique*) with the rank of Transcendent Satrap (the highest in this life) and the supplemental honor of being Maître de l'Ordre de la Grande Gidouille. (Note: E.P. in vulgar chronology is based on 1873, the year of Alfred Jarry's birth.)

With Breton, helps arrange the *Exposition Internationale du Surréalisme* at the Galerie Daniel Cordier, Paris (December 15, 1959–February 1960). Contributes *Couple of Laundress' Aprons* to *Boîte alerte*, special edition of catalog.

In Cadaqués for the summer, experiments with plaster casting from life *(With My Tongue in My Cheek, Torture-morte).*

1960 Publication in London of *The Bride Stripped Bare by Her Bachelors, Even,* first full English translation of the *Green Box,* by George Heard Hamilton with typographic layout by Richard Hamilton.

Exhibition *Dokumentation über Marcel Duchamp,* at the Kunstgewerbemuseum, Zurich (June 30–August 28).

Participates in symposium, "Should the Artist Go to College?" at Hofstra College, Hempstead, Long Island, New York, on May 13.

Elected to National Institute of Arts and Letters, New York, on May 25.

Collaborates with André Breton on direction of exhibition *Surrealist Intrusion in the Enchanter's Domain,* at the D'Arcy Galleries, New York (November 28, 1960–January 14, 1961). Designs catalog cover.

Contributes extended pun to broadside for Jean Tinguely's machine, *Homage to New York,* which destroyed itself in the Museum of Modern Art Sculpture Garden on March 17. Duchamp attends the event.

About this time a number of American artists, including Robert Rauschenberg, Jasper Johns, and Robert Morris, become interested in Duchamp's work and career, through reading Lebel's monograph, the translation of the notes of the *Green Box,* and visits to the Arensberg Collection in Philadelphia. Rauschenberg, for example, dedicates the combine painting *Trophy II,* 1960–61, to Teeny and Marcel Duchamp. Duchamp in turn takes an interest in contemporary manifestations; for example, attends Claes Oldenburg's *Store Days* performances in February—March 1962, and befriends younger artists in New York.

1961 Featured in *Art in Motion* exhibition and catalog, organized by Stedelijk Museum, Amsterdam (March 10–April 17), and Moderna Museet, Stockholm (May 17–September 3). Plays (and wins) chess by telegram with a group of students in Amsterdam on the occasion of the exhibition. First replica of *Large Glass* made by Ulf Linde included in exhibition and signed by Duchamp, who visits Stockholm for the occasion.

Participates in panel discussion "Where Do We Go from Here?" at the Philadelphia Museum College of Art on March 20. Other panelists are Larry Day, Louise Nevelson, and Theodoros Stamos, with Katharine Kuh as moderator. Delivers statement including the prophetic words "the great artist of tomorrow will go underground. "

Assists with reinstallation of Arensberg Collection at Philadelphia Museum of Art in May.

Interviewed by Katharine Kuh on March 29, and on September 27 by Richard Hamilton for BBC television *Monitor* program.

Featured in *The Art of Assemblage* exhibition and catalog organized by William Seitz at the Museum of Modern Art, New York (October 2–November 12). Exhibition travels to Dallas and San Francisco. Participates in symposium at Museum on October 19, delivering a brief prepared statement "Apropos of Readymades." Other panelists are Roger Shattuck, Robert Rauschenberg, and Richard Huelsenbeck, with Lawrence Alloway as moderator.

Receives honorary degree of Doctor of Humanities from Wayne State University, Detroit, Michigan, on November 29, and delivers an address. Lectured on his work at the Detroit Institute of Arts the previous day.

Dissertation completed by Lawrence D. Steefel, Jr., at Princeton University, New Jersey: *The Position of "La Mariée mise à nu par ses célibataires, même" (1915–1923) in the Stylistic and Iconographic Development of the Art of Marcel Duchamp.*

1962 Lectures on his work at Mount Holyoke College, Massachusetts, and at the Norton Gallery, Palm Beach, Florida.

1963 Designs poster for *1913 Armory Show 50th Anniversary Exhibition* at Munson-Williams-Proctor Institute, Utica, New York (February 17–March 31), and delivers lecture at the Institute on February 16. The exhibition travels to the Armory in New York (April 6–28).

Delivers lecture on his work, "Apropos of Myself," at Baltimore Museum of Art, Maryland, and Brandeis University, Waltham, Massachusetts.

Death of Jacques Villon, June 9.

Death of Suzanne Duchamp Crotti, September 11, whose husband Jean had died in 1958.

One-man exhibition (of replicas made by Ulf Linde) at Galerie Burén, Stockholm, in conjunction with publication of a major monograph, *Marcel Duchamp,* by Linde.

Continues to grant increasing numbers of interviews to critics and journalists.

First major retrospective exhibition, *By or of Marcel Duchamp or Rrose Sélavy,* organized by Walter Hopps at the Pasadena Art Museum (October 8–November 3). Duchamp designs poster and catalog cover; 114 works included. Visits California (with a side trip to Las Vegas) on the occasion of the exhibition.

1964 Galleria Schwarz, Milan, produces thirteen Readymades in editions of eight signed and numbered copies. One-man exhibition *Omaggio a Marcel Duchamp* at Galleria Schwarz (June 5–September 30) followed by European tour to Bern, Switzerland; London; the Hague and Eindhoven, the Netherlands; and Hannover, West Germany. Catalog includes contributions by Arturo Schwarz, Hopps, and Linde.

Jean-Marie Drot makes a film, *Game of Chess with Marcel Duchamp,* including extensive interview, for French television. Film wins first prize at the International Film Festival at Bergamo, Italy.

Delivers lecture "Apropos of Myself" at the City Art Museum of St. Louis on November 24.

1965 Major one-man exhibition, *Not Seen and/or Less Seen of/by Marcel Duchamp/Rrose Seiavy 1904–64,* at Cordier & Ekstrom Gallery, New Yark (January 14–February 13). Includes ninety items from the Mary Sisler Collection, many never exhibited previously. Catalog introduction and notes by Richard Hamilton; cover by Duchamp.

"Profiled" in the *New Yorker* magazine by Calvin Tomkins in February. The *New Yorker* article, plus three others (on John Cage, Jean Tingueiy, and Robert Rauschenberg), published by Calvin Tomkins as *The Bride and the Bachelors.*

Attends dinner on May 15 in honor of Rrose Sélavy, at Restaurant Victoria in Paris, sponsored by the Association pour l'Etude du Mouvement Dada.

During summer spent in Cadaqués, executes nine etchings of details of the *Large Glass,* which are published by Arturo Schwarz two years later.

In October, paintings representing the murder of Duchamp are shown by artists Aillaud, Arroyo, and Recalcati at the Galerie Creuze, Paris. Duchamp declines to sign a protest.

About this time, forced to vacate the 14th Street studio. Moves the nearly completed *Given* to a small room in a commercial building at 80 East 11th Street.

1966 Assists organization of *Hommage à Caissa* exhibition at Cordier & Ekstrom Gallery, New York (February 8–26), to benefit Marcel Duchamp Fund of American Chess Foundation.

Large Glass reconstructed, together with studies, by Richard Hamilton at the University of Newcastle-upon-Tyne, England. Exhibited in Mayas *The Bride Stripped Bare by Her Bachelors, Even, Again,* with photoreportage catalog.

First major European retrospective exhibition, *The Almost Complete Works of Marcel Duchamp,* organized by Richard Hamilton for the Arts Council of Great Britain at the Tate Gallery, London (June 18–July 31). Catalog by Richard Hamilton includes 242 items and "Elements of a Descriptive Bibliography" by Arturo Schwarz. Duchamp visits London on the occasion of the exhibition.

Tristram Powell makes a film, *Rebel Readymade,* for BBC television, which is shown on *New Release* on June 23.

Interviewed by William Coldstream, Richard Hamilton, Ronald Kitaj, Robert Melville, and David Sylvester at Richard Hamilton's home in London on June 19 for BBC (unpublished).

Special July issue of *Art and Artists* (London), with cover by Man Ray, devoted to Duchamp.

Publication of *The World of Marcel Duchamp*, by Calvin Tomkins and the Editors of Time-Life, Inc., New York.

Completes and signs last major work, *Given:* 1. *The Waterfall, 2. The Illuminating Gas*, 1946–66, in the secrecy of room 403, 80 East II th Street.

Nine works included in the *Dada Austellung* at the Kunsthaus, Zurich (October 8–November 7); the exhibition travels to the Musée National d'Art Moderne, Paris (November 30, 1966–January 30, 1967).

1967 Writes notes and assembles photographs in New York for book of instructions for dismantling and reassembling of *Given*.

Publication of important extended interviews by Pierre Cabanne, *Entretiens avec Marcel Duchamp*, in Paris. English translation by Ron Padgett published in New York (in 1971).

Publication by Cordier & Ekstrom Gallery, New York, of *A l'infinitif*, a limited boxed edition of seventy-nine unpublished notes dating from 1912–1920, reproduced in facsimile. Accompanied by English translation by Cleve Gray.

Publication in Milan by Arturo Schwarz of *The Large Glass and Related Works* (Volume I), including nine etchings by Duchamp of the *Glass* and its details.

Important family exhibition *Les Duchamps: Jacques Villon, Raymond Duchamp-Villon, Marcel Duchamp, Suzanne Duchamp-Crotti* at the Musée des Beaux-Arts, Rouen (April 15–June 1). Eighty-two works included. Catalog essay on Duchamp by Bernard Dorival.

First major showing in Paris at Musée National d'Art Moderne: *Duchamp- Villon, Marcel Duchamp* (June 6–July 2). Eighty-two works included. Catalog of Rouen exhibition, with alterations.

Exhibition *Editions de et sur Marcel Duchamp*, at Galerie Givaudan, Paris (June 8–September 30). Duchamp designs poster.

Begins work on nine etchings on theme of The Lovers for future publication by Arturo Schwarz.

One-man exhibition *Marcel Duchamp/Mary Sisler Collection* tours New Zealand and six museums in Australia during 1967–68.

Publication in Paris of monograph by Octavio Paz, *Marcel Duchamp ou le château de fa pureté.*

1968 Sometime prior to his departure for Europe this summer, takes Bill Copley to see the completed *Given* in his secret studio and expresses the wish that it join the large group of his works already in the Philadelphia Museum of Art. Copley feels that the Cassandra Foundation, with which he is at that time associated, could assist in making this possible.

Participates in *Reunion,* a musical performance organized by John Cage in Toronto, Canada, on February 5, during which Duchamp, Cage, and Teeny Duchamp play chess on a board electronically wired for sound.

Attends premiere performance (March 10) of Merce Cunningham's *Walkaround Time,* presented during the Second Buffalo Festival of the Arts Today at the State University College at Buffalo, New York. Music . . . *for nearly an hour* . . . composed by David Behrman, and played by John Cage, Gordon Mumma, David Tudor, and David Behrman. Decor based on the *Large Glass* supervised by Jasper Johns.

Featured in exhibition and catalog of *Dada, Surrealism, and Their Heritage,* organized by William S. Rubin at the Museum of Modern Art, New York (March 27–June 9). Thirteen works included. Duchamp attends opening. Exhibition travels to Los Angeles and Chicago.

Works on handmade anaglyph of the fireplace and chimney that he had had constructed in the Duchamps' summer apartment in Cadaqués.

Orders Spanish bricks for use around door of *Given* in permanent installation.

Dies on October 2 in Neuilly, during his customary summer and early fall visit to Paris and Cadaqués. Buried with other members of Duchamp family in the Cimetière Monumental at Rouen. At his request, his gravestone bears the inscription "D'ailleurs c'est toujours les autres qui meurent."

Publication of *To and from Rrose Sélavy*, by Shuzo Takiguchi, Tokyo, in a deluxe edition upon which Duchamp had collaborated, as did Jasper Johns, Jean Tinguely, and Shusaku Arakawa.

Publication of *Marcel Duchamp*, or *the Castle of Purity*, by Octavio Paz, in a boxed folio designed by Vicente Rajo (Mexico City: Era). French translation, Calerie Givaudan (Paris), 1968; Callimard, 1970. English translation, Cape Coliard (London) in association with Crossman Publishers (New York), 1970.

Featured in exhibition and catalog of *The Machine as Seen at the End of the Mechanical Age*, organized by Pontus Hultén for the Museum of Modern Art, New York (November 28, 1968–February 9, 1969). Thirteen works included. Exhibition travels to Houston and San Francisco.

1969 Publication by Arturo Schwarz in Milan of *The Large Class and Related Details* (Volume II), including nine etchings by Duchamp on theme of "The Lovers."

As Duchamp had hoped, his last major work, *Given*, enters the Philadelphia Museum of Art (as a gift from the Cassandra Foundation). The existence of the work remains a secret until it is finally installed in the museum. It is disassembled by Paul Matisse in collaboration with the museum staff, following Duchamp's written instructions, and transported in February from New York to Philadelphia. It is reassembled and installed in the small room Duchamp had suggested, at the rear of the galleries containing the Arensberg Collection. The room is opened to the public on July 7.

Publication of Arturo Schwarz's major monograph and catalogue raisonné, *The Complete Works of Marcel Duchamp*, accompanied by a volume of *Notes and Projects for the Large Glass*, which includes reproductions and English translations of 144 notes.

Featured in special summer issue of *Art in America*, New York. This section edited by Cleve Gray.

Publication of summer issue of *Philadelphia Museum of Art Bulletin* devoted to *Given*, "Reflections on a New Work by Marcel Duchamp," by Anne d'Hamoncourt and Walter Hopps. The first extended study of this work.

Since the public appearance of *Given* in 1969, and the resulting apparent "completion" of what the Tate Gallery exhibition called "The Almost Complete Works of Marcel Duchamp," exhibitions, books, and articles devoted to those works have proliferated. Suffice it to cite here the two most comprehensive exhibitions, whose catalogs also contain extensive bibliographical references:

September 22, 1973–April 21, 1974. *Marcel Duchamp.* Organized jointly by the Philadelphia Museum of Art and the Museum of Modern Art, New York. Also traveled to the Art Institute of Chicago. Contained 292 items.

January 31–May 2, 1977. *Marcel Duchamp.* Musée National d' Art Moderne, Centre National d'Art et de Culture Georges Pompidou, Paris. Contained 202 items.

The most complete anthology of Duchamp's writings to date appeared in 1973: *Salt Seller: The Writings of Marcel Duchamp,* ed. Michel Sanouillet and Elmer Peterson (New York: Oxford University Press). A revised and slightly expanded French edition *(Duchamp du Signe,* published by Flammarion) appeared in 1975. Duchamp's work never seems to be quite complete, however. Over 200 previously unpublished notes by Duchamp, dating from the same years as those in *The Green Box* and *A l'infinitif,* are currently being prepared for publication by the Musée National d'Art Moderne in Paris.

ON POETS
AND
OTHERS

CONTENTS

Foreword 539
Robert Frost: Visit To A Poet. 548
Walt Whitman 554
William Carlos Williams: The Saxifrage Flower 558
The Graphics Of Charles Tomlinson: Black And White 568
Jean-Paul Sartre: A Memento 577
Baudelaire As Art Critic: Presence And Present 589
André Breton, Or The Search For The Beginning 603
Henri Michaux. 613
Dostoevski: The Devil And The Ideologue. 625
Considering Solzhenitsyn: Dust After Mud 633
Gulag: Between Isaiah And Job 654
José Ortega y Gasset: The Why And The Wherefore 663
Luis Buñuel: Three Perspectives 674
Jorge Guillén 686
Two Notes On José Revueltas: Christianity And Revolution. 694
Luis Cernuda: The Edifying Word. 706

FOREWORD

■ When you meet Octavio Paz, you have the impression you're meeting *all* of him. He seems to contain all his ages. There is about him, and about the way he moves and laughs, often at himself, something of the adolescent. Here is the student striding through the streets of Mexico City at night arguing politics, discussing Dostoevski, with his schoolmates, joining the student strike in 1929. Here, too is the young idealist who went to the Yucatan in his early twenties to help found a school for the children of the sisal workers; and then went to Spain during the Civil War. Paz is recognizably the young disciple of the surrealist André Breton; and he retains the charismatic luster of controversial diplomat and teacher. Paz doesn't repudiate his past, and, unlike Nietzsche—whom he admires, and who systematically refused to revise his early work because, as he put it, "the young man he had been would have despised the older man he had become"—Paz is often willing to revise work he wrote four decades ago. It may be that poems are never finished, only abandoned—but still, Paz returns to some of them, drawing them a little farther along the road.

In many of the essays contained in this collection, Paz describes the relations of this young man—himself—with his elder and more established writers and philosophers. Robert Frost, Luis Cernuda, José Ortega y Gasset, William Carlos Williams, Ezra Pound, André Breton, all appear here to have been influences in Paz's life. In each of them he finds something to build on. And if ultimately he rejects them all, it is ruefully, an almost filial estrangement. Octavio Paz is a "pluralist." One of his favorite critical terms is *pluralism* in culture. Paz is deeply rooted in the cultures of the Spanish language. The poets and philosophers of France and England marked him, as did the various cultures and overwhelming erotic art of India. In each he finds ways of understanding his own culture. They show him different routes back to the beginning. French lucidity, even in revolution; English continuity, despite changes of the world outside; Indian mysticism, especially the mysticism of the body—all these help Paz home, to himself and his own culture, overlaid as it is by patterns of violence and repression.

Writing at the time of Breton's death, Paz notes: "All of us who had anything to do with Breton experienced a dual, dizzying feeling: fascination and a centrifugal impulse. I confess that for a long time I was kept awake by the worry that I might do or say something to provoke his reproof. I believe many of his friends had a similar experience . . . I should say that I write as if I were engaged in a silent dialogue with Breton: reply, answer, coincidence, disagreement, homage, all together. Even as I write this I experience that feeling." Under Breton's influence, Paz tried automatic writing and produced his great prose-poems. But it's interesting that in his valedictory essay on Breton, Paz quotes none of his master's poetry, only his critical statements. The English critic Jason Wilson suggests that Breton was an influence on Paz's poetics more than on the poetry itself, and I suspect he's right. In Paz there is a double impulse: first, an enthusiasm for ideas, especially ideas about poetry and poetic traditions. He is brilliant at recounting the history of artistic trends of this and last century, the modernist "tradition of discontinuity" called up in the titles of books such as *Conjunctions and Disjunctions* and *Alternating Current*. But at the other pole of his imaginative thought, T. S. Eliot has left a deep mark on his work. Eliot is in almost every way the opposite of Breton. Paz rejects Eliot's religion and politics; but he can't resist the actual poems and the literary essays.

Like other radical writers before him, Paz locates the intellectual poverty of much of Latin America in the fact that the eighteenth century—the great critical century, the Enlightenment—passed it by. While the United States was colonized by the spirit of the Reformation, Latin America suffered the Counter-Reformation. Without an Enlightenment, the critical disciplines that developed in France and England were not practiced in the Spanish colonies. Paz provides some benefits of the Enlightenment for Latin America. He is not alone in this, and he doesn't set out to write like Voltaire. But he produces social and literary criticism—for him the two are inseparable—which he has set in the French tradition of "moralism."

His most famous prose book is *The Labyrinth of Solitude*, published in 1950 and revised in 1959. In it he explores the Mexican psyche and tries to place Mexican history back within the Mexican himself. As he put it in an interview a decade ago, he wanted to "recover the consciousness" of a country that history had pushed aside. "One of the pivotal ideas of the book," he said, "is that there is a Mexico which is buried but alive. Or, more accurately, there is in Mexican men and women a universe of buried images, desires and impulses. I attempted a description—inadequate of course, little more than a glimpse—of the world of repressions, inhibitions, memories, appetites and dreams which Mexico has been and is." *The Labyrinth of Solitude* has fascinated two intellectual generations in Latin America. It is one of those rare keys to a culture that usually seems to be written by critics from the outside. Paz's rare achievement was to write as an insider, with passion *and* detachment. He has said, "Already at that time I thought as I do now, that history is a form of knowledge set between science properly speaking and poetry. Historical knowledge is not quantitative nor can the historian discover historical laws. The historian describes things like a scientist and has visions like a poet." His "history" is not in chronological sequence. Paz brings facts and images to the foreground and holds them still while he examines them minutely, tracing their origins, discovering their latencies. There are elements of autobiography in the images chosen. When Paz writes about the rituals for the day of the dead, the little offerings of sugar, day, and raffia are peculiarly vivid. He grew up near where these things were made and as a child strayed among the craftsmen's workshops. The relations between such images and the beliefs they reveal are teased out, now lovingly, now angrily. When Paz distinguishes firmly between ideas and beliefs, he follows his philosophical teacher José Ortega y Gasset. Ideas are changeable, in movement; beliefs are largely static and constant. "A man is defined more by what he believes than by what he thinks," Paz says. Paz *partly* believes, and in this he is typical of many modern writers. There is a withholding which is painful because the writer remains at the crossroads, his journey forever incomplete.

Skepticism and openness make it possible for Paz to see his world and his history freshly. Since the wars of independence, Latin Americans have tended to despise the earlier colonial periods. Paz emphasizes the decades of relative plenty and stability and the great cultural achievement of the colony. He underlines the political balances of power that existed between church and state. His aim isn't to apologize for the colonial system, but to restore a balance in our perception, to counter the automatic rhetoric that prevails in teaching and writing. Until the colonial period is integrated into the memory of Latin Americans, an essential part of the past remains repressed.

In *The Labyrinth of Solitude* Paz makes another unpopular point. He insists on the place of the brutal Emiliano Zapata in the Mexican Revolution, but he assigns to him an unexpected destiny. Zapata's project was an "attempt to return to origins." According to Paz, "the paradox of Zapatismo was that it was a profoundly traditionalist movement; and precisely in that traditionalism its revolutionary might resides. To put it more clearly, because it was traditionalist, Zapatismo was radically subversive." Zapata becomes for Paz a political talisman for his own poetic quest of *return*. Zapata's movement "signifies revelation, the emergence of certain hidden and repressed realities. It is revolution not as ideology but as an instinctive movement, an explosion which is the revelation of a reality prior to hierarchies, classes, property." I think the phrase "revolution not as ideology" is the key to his political writing.

In 1936, the Chilean poet Pablo Neruda arranged for Octavio Paz to go to Spain at the time of the Civil War. In Spain Paz did not like what he saw of the machinations of the Popular Front and its patrons. He began to question his kind of Marxist allegiances. His doubts were heightened by the Nazi-Soviet pact and later by his estrangement from Neruda. Ideological politics became for him the great seduction and the great tragedy of the writers of this and the last century. "The history of modern literature, from the German and English romantics to our own days, is the history of a long, unhappy passion for politics. From Coleridge to Mayakovski, Revolution has been the great Goddess, the eternal beloved and the great whore to poets and novelists. Politics filled Malraux's head with smoke, poisoned the sleepless nights of Cesar Vallejo, killed Garda Lorca, abandoned the old poet Antonio Machado in a village in the Pyrenees, locked Pound in an asylum, dishonoured Neruda and Aragon, has made Sartre a figure of ridicule, and has acknowledged Breton all too late. But we can't disown politics; it would be worse than spitting at the sky, spitting at ourselves." In one of his finest poems, the "Nocturne of San Ildefonso," he writes:

> The good, we sought the good:
> > to straighten out the world.
> We did not lack integrity:
> > we lacked humility.
> What we wanted we wanted without innocence.

His bitterness is hardly surprising. While Paz is a highly respected and loved poet, he remains a figure of controversy, and that controversy is political. The Latin American intellectual world is largely committed to the left in rather old-fashioned ways. And Paz represents another kind of radicalism. He began to define it when he published an article in the Argentinean magazine *Sur*, edited by Victoria Ocampo. She was the only editor brave enough to print it back in 1951. The article was on the Soviet labor camps. Paz had been collecting information about them with growing horror. If socialism was to claim any moral authority, it would have urgently to come to terms with the aberrations of Stalinism. When the piece appeared, Paz anticipated debate. Instead, it was greeted with public silence and with private abuse. Neruda was prominent among his accusers. He was "giving ammunition to the enemy"—namely the

United States. Better suppress the truth, common sense said. Paz writes in the same poem,

> Poetry,
> the bridge suspended between history and truth,
> is not a way towards this or that:
> it is to see
> the stillness within movement.

In those lines, he says something with which few of his fellow Latin American poets would agree. He refuses to put his art to use.

He remains a radical, but a radical who rejects ideologies. Paz sees his task in these terms: "The writer should be a sniper, he should endure solitude, he should know himself to be a marginal being. It is both a curse and a blessing that we writers are marginal." He also says: "Criticism is the apprenticeship of the revising imagination—imagination cured of fantasy and resolved to confront the world's reality. Criticism tells us that we ought to learn to dissolve the idols, learn to dissolve them in ourselves. We have to learn to be air, dream set free." This is no recipe for passivity. Paz has learned his own lesson. "Criticism reveals the possibility of liberty and this is an invitation to action." The failure of democracy in Latin America is a failure of criticism. Technological progress without a critical capacity gives us "more things, not more being."

Criticism is a discipline that keeps language to its meanings. "When a society becomes corrupt," he writes, "what first grows gangrenous is language. Social criticism, therefore, begins with grammar and the reestablishment of meanings." Even so, the true writer has an uneasy relationship with his language. For Paz the natural metaphor is an erotic one: "I believe the writer's attitude to language should be that of a lover: fidelity and, at the same time, a lack of respect for the beloved object. Veneration and transgression."

Opposite this caring and necessarily violent lover, he identifies the enemy—the enemy both of the individual and of the collective: the bureaucratic state perverted by ideology. This state he defines as *The Philanthropic Ogre* in one of his books of political essays: a cold, totalitarian monster that devours its children without appetite, mechanically, chewing hard.

Octavio Paz came up hard against that ogre at the end of his diplomatic career. From 1962 to 1968 he was Mexican ambassador to India. In 1968, the Olympic Games were staged in Mexico City, and radical students assembled huge demonstrations. One of them ended in a massacre—no one is quite sure how many people were killed. This outrage revealed to Paz what he had long suspected—the inability of the Mexican system to respond to democratic pressure. The written constitution remained a luminous fiction, the rhetoric of politics grew increasingly remote from the huge, hungry, unemployed sub-proletariat that had swamped the major cities. He could no longer represent the Mexican government. His resignation had considerable political effect. He spoke later of the "vitiated intellectual atmosphere" of Mexico. "Among us," he declared, "ideological simplifications dominate and our intellectuals do not show much respect for reality."

When he returned to Mexico two years later, he was a painful thorn in the side of the political establishment. But increasingly he also became an irritant to radical intellectuals. After his resignation he had been vested with great authority. Now he rejected the popular accolade and preferred to continue on his own way. His critical essays have not made comfortable reading for anyone. During the last ten years he has alienated many people in my generation and in the one before. They tend to see Paz as someone who has taken the conventional journey from left to right. They say his early work exceeds his later work in scope and quality. But for younger writers he is once again clearly a teacher and guide. He makes himself available, he encourages their work, he is a genuine solitary radical, a man in search of roots, and he responds to evidence of that search in others.

To be sure, the best early poems are major; but it is in the more recent collections and long poems, where he traces his way back through his culture, that he accomplishes what he set out to do over half a century ago. He carries less cultural luggage now—memory has done its sifting and what remains is the essential, the unforgettable, the things of which he is himself made. When he stepped away from political in-fighting and stood alone, he found his great subject not only in his Mexico's past but in his own. His life has spanned years of critical change in Latin America. He has seen the ends of a dozen dreams and his beloved cities dehumanized by overcrowding, pollution, destitution, almost as tragically as the cities of India. It is the end not only of dreams but of cultures and communities; in such places, how can the dream be set free?

Through his father and grandfather, Paz has the next best thing to a firsthand memory of nineteenth-century Mexico, when liberalism triumphed for a time. During this time the tensions which distort present-day Mexico did not exist. His most recent magazine is *Vuelta*, one of the most influential journals in Latin America. He is a wonderfully imaginative editor, one who invites into the Mexican arena an incongruous and stimulating range of intelligences from Europe and the rest of his own continent. For him, no subject is taboo. The title of the magazine implies turn, return, or turning back. His last major collection of poems, published in 1974, is also entitled *Vuelta*. In Emiliano Zapata, André Breton, and the writers and artists he admires, and in the religious and erotic traditions he explored during his years in India, he is looking for origins, sources, and the fresh resources that flow from them.

He spent his childhood in the village of Mixcoac, a suburb of Mexico City. It has an Aztec name and some broken walls survive from pre-conquest times. If you scratch about in your garden there you sometimes find potsherds. There are also colonial buildings—nothing very striking, but solid and permanent. There are examples of later architecture, too, and an inner ring road that reminds you that this is 1986 and nothing is safe against the ravages of technology. Nothing except memory and the sensitive eye registering its place in this visual anthology of popular Mexican history. Octavio Paz's grandfather, Ireneo, dominated the house where he grew up. Ireneo was a lawyer and a liberal reformer who fought against the French and wrote more than ten books. He edited a daily paper for thirty-eight years. To Paz the child, he was an old and disheartened man. He had fallen in, probably reluctantly, behind the strong man—the dictator Porfirio Díaz—and his cause was defeated by the revolution. Octavio Paz's father rebelled against Ireneo. Liberalism had failed. He supported something more radical, the revolution, and especially the agrarian reform which Zapata stood for. He was an agent and then a propagandist for Zapata. When the poet was a boy, old Zapatistas used to visit, bringing delicious, strange foods from their pueblos. They made a marked impression on the boy: they seemed to contain the turbulent history he was too young to remember. Paz's father, who became an alcoholic, died tragically in a train crash in 1935.

> My father went and came back through the flames.
>
> Among the sleepers and the rails
> > of a station swarming with flies and dust
> One afternoon we gathered up his pieces.
> > I was never able to speak with him.
> I find him now in dreams.
> That half-erased country of the dead.

The poet's mother was a Mexican of Spanish background. She was not cultured, but she was affectionate and supportive. He speaks of her tenderly as "a love letter with errors in the grammar."

In my opinion, his finest poem is "Pasado en Claro" which means "Fair Draft" or, as a translator has it, "A Draft of Shadows;" it was published in 1975. The energy of the language and the imaginative penetration of this poem set it in a class by itself. It evokes the long history of ritual, repression, and change in Mexico, but also Paz's own life, which in this context becomes ours as much as Wordsworth's does in *The Prelude*. He declares a debt to Wordsworth not only in the way the poem works but in the epigraph:

> Fair seed-time had my soul, and I grew up
> Foster'd alike by beauty and by fear.

Beauty and fear. In a sense, they are the twin poles not only of Paz's life but also of his work.

—Michael Schmidt

ROBERT FROST: VISIT TO A POET

After twenty minutes walking along the highway under a three o'clock sun, I came at last to the turning. I veered right and began to climb the slope. At intervals, the trees along the path provided a little coolness. Water ran down a small brook, through the undergrowth. The sand squeaked under my tread. Sun was everywhere. In the air there was a scent of green, hot growth, thirsty. Not a tree, not a leaf stirred. A few clouds rested heavily, anchored in a blue, waveless gulf. A bird sang. I hesitated: "How much nicer it would be to stretch out under this elm! The sound of water is worth more than all the poets' words." I walked on for another ten minutes. When I got to the farm, some fair-haired children were playing around a birch tree. I asked for the master; without interrupting their game, they replied, "He's up there, in the cabin." And they pointed to the very summit of the hill. I set off again. Now I was walking through deep undergrowth that came up to my knee. When I reached the top I could see the whole little valley; the blue mountains, the stream, the luminously green flatland, and, at the very bottom, the forest. The wind began to blow; everything swayed, almost cheerfully. All the leaves sang. I went toward the cabin. It was a little wooden shack, old, the paint flaked, grayed by the years. The windows were curtainless; I made a way through the underbrush and looked in. Inside, sitting in an easy chair, was an old man. Resting beside him was a woolly dog. When he saw me the man stood up and beckoned me to come around the other side. I did so and found him waiting for me at the door of his cabin. The dog jumped up to greet me. We crossed a little passage and went into a small room: unpolished floor, two chairs, a blue easy chair, another reddish one, a desk with a few books on it, a little table with papers and letters. On the walls three or four engravings, nothing remarkable. We sat down.

"Sure is hot. You want a beer?"

"Yes, I believe I do. I've walked half an hour and I'm worn out."

We drank the beer slowly. While I sipped mine, I took him in. With his white shirt open—is there anything cleaner than a dean white shirt?—his eyes blue, innocent, ironic, his philosopher's head and his farmer's hands, he looked like an ancient sage, the kind who prefers to observe the world from his retreat. But there was nothing ascetic in his looks, rather a manly sobriety. There he was, in his cabin, removed from the world, not to renounce it but to see it better. He wasn't a hermit nor was his hill a rock in the desert. The three crows hadn't brought him the bread he ate; he'd bought it himself in the village store.

"It's really a beautiful place. It almost seems real. This landscape is very different from ours in Mexico, it's made for men to look at. The distances are made for our legs, too."

"My daughter's told me the landscape of your country's very dramatic."

"Nature is hostile down there. What's more, we're few and weak. Man is consumed by the landscape and there's always the danger you might turn into a cactus."

"They tell me that men sit still for hours there just doing nothing."

"Afternoons you see them, completely still, by the roadsides or at the entrances to towns."

"Is that how they do their thinking?"

"It's a country that's going to turn to stone one day. The trees and the plants all tend to stone, just as the men do. And the animals, too: dogs, coyotes, snakes. There are little baked day birds and it's very strange to see them fly and hear them sing, because you never get used to the idea they're real birds."

"When I was fifteen, I wrote a poem. My first poem. And you know what it was about? *La noche triste.* I was reading Prescott then, and maybe reading him set me thinking about your country. Have you read Prescott?"

"That was one of my grandfather's favorite books, so I read him when I was a boy. I'd like to read him again."

"I like rereading books, too. I don't trust folk who don't reread. And those who read a lot of books. It seems crazy to me, this modern madness, and it'll only increase the number of pedants. You've got to read a few books well and frequently."

"A friend tells me they've invented a way of developing speed-reading. I think they're planning to introduce it into schools."

"They're mad. What you've got to teach people is to read slowly. And not to fidget about so much. And do you know why they invent all these things? Because they're scared. People are scared to pause on things, because that compromises them. That's why they flee the country and move to the cities. They're scared of being by themselves."

"Yes, the world's full of fear."

"And those with power exploit that fear. Individual life has never been so despised or authority so revered."

'Sure, it's easier to live as one, to decide as one. Even dying's easier, if you die at someone else's expense. We're invaded by fear. There's the common man's fear, and he hands himself over to the strong man. But there's also the fear the powerful feel; they don't dare to stay alone. Because they're scared, they ding onto power."

"Here people abandon the country to go work in factories. And when they come back they don't like the country anymore. The country's hard. You've always got to be alert, and you're responsible for everything and not just for a part, like in a factory."

"What's more, the country's the experience of solitude. You can't go to the films, or take refuge in a bar."

"Exactly. It's the experience of being free. It's like poetry. Life's like poetry, when the poet writes a poem. It begins as an invitation to the unknown: the first line gets written and what's to follow is unknown. It's unsure whether in the next line poetry's waiting for us, or failure. And that sense of mortal danger accompanies the poet in all his adventures."

"In each verse, a decision awaits us, and we can't choose to close our eyes and let instinct work on its own. Poetic instinct consists of an alert tension."

"In each line, in each phrase, the possibility of failure is concealed. The possibility that the whole poem, not just that isolated verse, will fail. That's how life is: at every moment we can lose it. Every moment there's mortal risk. Each instant is a choice."

"You're right. Poetry is the experience of liberty. The poet risks himself, chances all on the poem's all with each verse he writes."

"And you can't change your mind. Each act, each verse is irrevocable, forever. In each verse one is committed forever. But now folks have become irresponsible. No one wants to decide for himself. Like those poets who copy their ancestors."

"Don't you believe in the tradition?"

"Yes, but each poet's born to express something that's his own. And his first duty is to deny his ancestors, the rhetoric of those who've come before. When I started writing I found that the words of the old writers were no use to me; it was necessary for me to create my own language. And that language—which surprised and troubled some people—was the language of my community, the language that surrounded my childhood and adolescence. I had to wait a long time before I found my words. You've got to use everyday language . . ."

"But subjected to a different pressure. As if each word had been created only to express that particular moment. Because there's a certain fatality in words; a French writer says that 'images can't be looked for, they're found.' I don't think he means that chance presides over creation but that a *fated choice* leads us to certain words."

"The poet creates his own language. Then he ought to fight against *that* rhetoric. He should never abandon himself to his style."

"There are no poetic styles. When you get to style, literature displaces poetry."

"That was the case with American poetry when I started writing. That's where all my difficulties and my successes began. And now maybe it's necessary to fight against the rhetoric we've made. The world goes round and what was in yesterday is out today. You've got to make a little fun of all this. No need to take anything too seriously, not even ideas. Or rather, precisely because we're so serious and passionate, we ought to laugh at ourselves a little. Don't trust those who don't know how to laugh."

And he laughed with the laughter of a man who has seen rain, and also of a man who has got wet. We got up and went out for a little walk. We went down the hill. The dog leapt ahead of us. As we came out, he said to me:

"Most of all, don't trust those who don't know how to laugh at themselves. Solemn poets, humorless professors, prophets who only know how to howl and harangue. All those dangerous men."

"Do you read the contemporaries?"

"I always read poetry. I like reading the poems of young writers. And some philosophers. But I can't stand novels. I don't think I've ever read one through."

We walked on. When we got to the farmhouse, the children gathered round us. The poet was now telling me about his childhood, the years in San Francisco, and his return to New England.

"This is my country and I believe this is where the nation has its roots. Everything grew from here. Do you know that the state of Vermont refused to participate in the war against Mexico? Yes, everything grew from here. This is where the desire to immerse oneself in the unknown began, and the desire to stay alone with yourself. We ought to go back to that if we want to preserve what we are."

"It seems pretty hard to me. You're now a rich people."

"Years ago, I thought of going to a little country, where the noise that everyone makes just isn't heard. I chose Costa Rica; when I was getting ready to go I learned that there too an American company caned the tune. I didn't go. That's why I'm here, in New England."

We came to the turning. I looked at my watch: more than two hours had passed.

"I'd better be going. They're waiting for me down below, in Bread Loaf."

He stretched out his hand.

"You know the way?"

"Yes," I said, and we shook hands. When I'd gone a few steps I heard his voice:

"Come back soon! And when you get to New York, write to me. Don't forget."

I answered with a nod. I saw him climbing the path playing with his dog. "And he's seventy years old," I thought. As I walked back, I remembered another loner, another visit. "I think Robert Frost would like to have known Antonio Machado. But how would they have understood each other? The Spaniard didn't speak English, and the American doesn't know Spanish. No matter, they would have smiled. I'm sure they would have made friends straightaway." I remembered the house at Rocafort, in Valencia, the wild, neglected garden, the living room and the dust-covered furniture. And Machado, the cigarette in his mouth gone out. The Spaniard was also an old man retired from the world, and he too knew how to laugh and he too was absentminded. Like the American, he liked to philosophize, not in the schools but at the periphery. Sages for the people; the American in his cabin, the Spaniard in his provincial café. Machado too expressed a horror of the solemn and had the same smiling gravity. "Yes, the Anglo-Saxon has the cleaner shirt and there are more trees in his view. But the other's smile was sadder and finer. There's a great deal of snow in this fellow's poems, but there's dust, antiquity, history in the other's. That dust of Castile, that dust of Mexico, which as soon as you touch it dissolves between your hands . . ."

—Vermont, June 1945

WALT WHITMAN

Walt Whitman is the only great modern poet who does not seem to experience discord when he faces his world. Not even solitude; his monologue is a universal chorus. No doubt there are at least two people in him: the public poet and the private person who conceals his true erotic inclinations. But the mask—that of the poet of democracy—is rather more than a mask; it is his true face. Despite certain recent interpretations, in Whitman the poetic and the historical dream come together. There is no gap between his beliefs and social reality. And this fact is more important—I mean, more widely pertinent and significant-than any psychological consideration. The uniqueness of Whitman's poetry in the modern world cannot be explained except as a function of another, even greater, uniqueness which includes it: that of America.

In a book* which is a model of its genre, Edmundo O'Gorman has shown that our continent was never discovered. In effect, it is impossible to discover something which does not exist, and America, before its so-called discovery, did not exist. One ought rather to speak of the *invention* of America than of its discovery. If America is a creation of the European spirit, it begins to emerge from the sea-mists centuries before the expeditions of Columbus. And what the Europeans discover when they reach these lands is their own historic dream. Reyes has devoted some lucid pages to this subject: America is a sudden embodiment of a European utopia. The dream becomes a reality, a present; America is a present: a gift, a given of history. But it is an open present, a today that is tinged with tomorrow. The presence and the present of America are a future; our continent is, by its nature, the land which does not exist on its own, but as something which is created and invented. Its being, its reality or substance, consists of being always future, history which is justified not by the past but by what is to come. Our foundation is not what America

---

* *La idea del descubrimiento de America* (1951)

was but what it will be. America never was; and *it is, only if it is utopia,* history on its way to a golden age.

This may not be entirely true if one considers the colonial period of Spanish and Portuguese America. But it is revealing how, just as soon as the Latin Americans acquire self-consciousness and oppose the Spaniards, they rediscover the utopian nature of America and make the French utopias their own. All of them see in wars of independence a return to first principles, a reversion to what America really is. The War of Independence is a correction of American history and, as such, a restoration of the original reality. The exceptional and genuinely paradoxical nature of this restoration becomes dear if one notes that it consists of a restoration of the future. Thanks to French revolutionary principles, Latin America becomes again what it was at its birth: not a past, but a future, a dream. The dream of Europe, the place of choice, spatial and temporal, of all that the European reality could not be except by denying itself and its past. America is the dream of Europe, now free of European history, free of the burden of tradition. Once the problem of independence is resolved, the abstract and utopian nature of liberal America begins to show again in episodes such as the French intervention in Mexico. Neither Juarez nor his soldiers ever believed—according to Cosío Villegas—that they fought against France, but against a French usurpation. The true France was ideal and universal and more than just a nation, it was an idea, a philosophy. Cuesta says, with some justice, that the war with the French should be seen as a "civil war." It needed the Mexican Revolution to wake the country from this philosophical dream—which, in another way, concealed an historical reality hardly touched upon by the Independence, the Reform, and the Dictatorship—and discover itself, no longer as an abstract future but as an origin in which the three times needed to be sought: our past, our present, our future. The historical emphasis changed tense, and in this consists the true spiritual significance of the Mexican Revolution.

The utopian character of America is even purer in the Saxon portion of the continent. There were no complex Indian cultures there, nor did Roman Catholicism erect its vast nontemporal structures: America was—if it was anything—geography, pure space, open to human action.

Lacking historical substance—old class divisions, ancient institutions, inherited beliefs and laws—reality presented only natural obstacles. Men fought, not against history, but against nature. And where there was an historical obstacle—as in the Indian societies—it was erased from history and, reduced to a mere act of nature, action followed as if this were so. The North American attitude can be condemned in these terms: all that does not have a part in the utopian nature of America does not properly belong to history: it is a natural event and, thus, it doesn't exist; or it exists only as an inert obstacle, not as an alien conscience. Evil is outside, part of the natural world—like Indians, rivers, mountains, and other obstacles which must be domesticated or destroyed; or it is an intrusive reality (the English past, Spanish Catholicism, monarchy, etc.). The American War of Independence is the expulsion of the intrusive elements, alien to the American essence. If American reality is the reinvention of itself, whatever is found in any way irreducible or unassimilable is not American. In other places the future is a human attribute: because we are men, we have a future; in the Anglo-Saxon America of the last century, the process is inverted and the future determines man: we are men because we have a future. And whatever has no future is not man. Thus, reality leaves no gap at all for contradiction, ambiguity, or conflict to appear.

Whitman can sing confidently and in blithe innocence about democracy militant because the American utopia is confused with and indistinguishable from American reality. Whitman's poetry is a great prophetic dream, but it is a dream within another even greater one that feeds it. America is dreamed in Whitman's poetry because it is a dream itself. And it is dreamed as a concrete reality, almost a *physical* reality, with its men, its rivers, its cities and mountains. All that huge mass of reality moves lightly, as if it were weightless; and in fact, it is without historic weight: it is the future incarnate. The reality Whitman sings is utopian. By this I do not mean that it is unreal or exists only as idea, but that its essence, what enlivens it, justifies and makes sense of its progress and gives weight to its movements, is the future. Dream within a dream, Whitman's poetry is realistic only on this count: his dream is the dream of the reality itself, which has no other substance but to invent itself and dream itself. "When we dream that we dream," Novalis says, "waking is near at hand." Whitman was never aware that he dreamed and always thought himself a poetic realist. And he was, but only insofar as the reality he celebrated was not something given, but a substance crossed and recrossed by the future.

America dreams itself in Whitman because it was itself a dream, pure creation. Before and since Whitman we have had other poetic dreams. All of them—whether the dreamer's name is Poe or Daría, Melville or Dickinson—are more like attempts to escape from the American nightmare.

—Mexico, 1956

WILLIAM CARLOS WILLIAMS: THE SAXIFRAGE FLOWER

for James Laughlin

In the first third of our century, a change occurred in the literatures of the English language which affected verse and prose, syntax and sensibility, imagination and prosody alike. The change—similar to those which occurred about the same time in other parts of Europe and in Latin America—was originally the work of a handful of poets, almost all of them Americans. In that group of founders, William Carlos Williams occupies a place at once central and unique: unlike Pound and Eliot, he preferred to bury himself in a little city outside New York rather than uproot himself and go to London or Paris; unlike Wallace Stevens and e. e. cummings, who also decided to stay in the United States but who were cosmopolitan spirits, Williams from the outset sought a poetic Americanism. In effect, as he explains in the beautiful essays of *In the American Grain* (1925), America is not a given reality but something we all make together with our hands, our eyes, our brains, and our lips. The American reality is material, mental, visual, and above all, verbal: whether he speaks Spanish, English, Portuguese, or French, American man speaks a language different from the European original. More than just a reality we discover or make, America is a reality we speak.

William Carlos Williams was born in Rutherford, New Jersey, in 1883. His father was English, his mother Puerto Rican. He studied medicine at the University of Pennsylvania. There he met Pound—a friendship that was to last throughout his life—and the poet H. D. (Hilda Doolittle), who fascinated the two young poets. After taking his doctorate and a short period of pediatric study in Leipzig, in 1910 he settled definitively in Rutherford. Two years later he married Florence Herman:

a marriage that lasted a lifetime. Also for a lifetime he practiced a double vocation: medicine and poetry. Though he lived in the provinces, he was not a provincial: he was immersed in the artistic and intellectual currents of our century, traveled on various occasions to Europe, and befriended English, French, and Latin American writers. His literary friendships and enmities were varied and intense: Pound, Marianne Moore, Wallace Stevens, Eliot (whom he admired and condemned), e. e. cummings, and others, younger, like James Laughlin and Louis Zukofsky. His influence and friendship were decisive on Allen Ginsberg and also on the poetry of Robert Creeley, Robert Duncan, and the English poet Charles Tomlinson. (Poetic justice: a young English poet—and very English—praised by one who practiced almost his whole life a kind of poetic anti-Anglicism and who never tired of saying that the American language wasn't really English.) In 1951 he suffered his first attack of paralysis but survived a dozen years, dedicated to a literary program of rare fecundity: books of poetry, a translation of Quevedo, memoirs, lectures, and readings of his poems across the whole country. He died on 4 March 1963, where he was born and spent his life: in Rutherford.

His work is vast and varied: poetry, fiction, essays, theater, autobiography. The poetry has been collected in four volumes: *Collected Earlier Poems* (1906–1939), *Collected Later Poems* (1940–1946), *Pictures from Breughel* (1950–1962), and *Paterson* (1946–1958), a long poem in five books. Also there is a slim book of prose-poems which sometimes make one think of the automatic writing Breton and Soupault were engaged in around this time: *Kora in Hell* (1920). But in taking over a poetic form invented by French poetry, Williams changes it and converts it into a method of exploring language and the varied strata of the collective unconscious. *Kora in Hell* is a book which could only have been written by an American poet and ought to be read from the perspective of a later book which is the axis of Williams' Americanism, his *ars poetica: In the American Grain*. I will not consider his novels, stories, or theater pieces. Suffice it to say that they are extensions and irradiations of his poetry. The boundary between prose and verse, always hard to draw, becomes very tenuous in this poet: his free verse is very dose to prose, not as written but as spoken, the everyday language; and his prose is always rhythmic, like a coast bathed by poetic surf—not verse but the verbal flux and reflux that gives rise to verse.

From the time he started writing, Williams evinced a distrust of ideas. It was a reaction against the symbolist aesthetic shared by the majority of poets at that time (remember López Velarde) and in which, in his case, American pragmatism was combined with his medical profession. In a famous poem he defines his search: "To compose: not ideas but in things." But things are always beyond, on the other side: the "thing itself" is untouchable. Thus Williams' point of departure is not things but sensation. And yet sensation in turn is formless and instantaneous; one cannot build or do anything with pure sensations: that would result in chaos. Sensation is amphibious: at the same time it joins us to and divides us from things. It is the door through which we enter into things but also through which we come out of them and realize that we are not things. In order for sensation to accede to the objectivity of things it must itself be changed into a thing. The agent of change is language: the sensations are turned into verbal objects. A poem is a verbal object in which two contradictory properties are fused: the liveliness of the sensation and the objectivity of things.

Sensations are turned into verbal objects by the operation of a force which for Williams is not essentially distinct from electricity, steam, or gas: imagination. In some reflections written down in 1923 (included among the poems in the late edition of *Spring and All* as "dislocated prose"), Williams says that the imagination is "a creative force which makes objects." The poem is not a double of the sensation or of the thing. Imagination does not represent: it produces. Its products are poems, objects which were not real before. The poetic imagination produces poems, pictures, and cathedrals as nature produces pines, clouds, and crocodiles. Williams wrings the neck of traditional aesthetics: art does not imitate nature: it imitates its creative processes. It does not copy its products but its modes of production. "Art is not a mirror to reflect nature but imagination competes with the compositions of nature. The poet becomes a nature and works like her." It is incredible that Spanish-language critics have not paused over the extraordinary similarity between these ideas and those that Vicente Huidobro proclaimed in statements and manifestos. True, it's a matter of ideas that appear in the work of many poets and artists of that time (for example, in Reverdy, who initiated Huidobro into modern poetry), but the similarity between the North American and Latin American are impressive. Both *invert* in almost the same terms the Aristotelian aesthetic and *convert* it for the modern era: imagination is, like electricity, a form of energy, and the poet is the transmitter.

The poetic theories of Williams and the "Creationism" of Huidobra are twins, but hostile twins. Huidobro sees in poetry something homologous with magic and, like a primitive shaman who *makes* rain, wants to make poetry; Williams conceives of poetic imagination as an activity that completes and rivals science. Nothing is further from magic than Williams. In a moment of childish egotism, Huidobro said: "The poet is a little God," an expression that the American poet would have rejected. Another difference: Huidobro tried to produce verbal objects which were not imitations of real objects and which even negated them. Art as a means of escaping reality. The title of one of his books is also a definition of his purpose: *Horizonte cuadrado* (*Square Horizon*). Attempting the impossible: one need only compare the pictures of abstract painters with the images which microscopes and telescopes provide us to realize that we cannot get away from nature. For Williams the artist—it is significant that he was supported and inspired by the example of Juan Gris— *separates* the things of the imagination from the things of reality: cubist reality is not the table, the cup, the pipe, and the newspaper as they are but *another* reality, no less real. This *other* reality does not deny the reality of real things: it is *another* thing which is *the same thing* at the same time. "The mountain and the sea in a picture by Juan Gris," Williams says, "are not the mountain and the sea but a painting of the mountain and the sea." The poem-thing isn't the thing: it is something else which exchanges signs of intelligence with the thing.

The non-imitative realism of Williams brings him dose to two other poets: Jorge Guillén and Francis Ponge. (Again, I am pointing out coincidences, not influences.) A line of Guillén's defines their common repugnance for symbols: "the little birds chirp without design of grace." Do design and grace disappear? No: they enter the poem surreptitiously, without the poet's noticing. The "design of grace" is no longer in the real birds but in the text. The poem-thing is as unattainable as the poem-idea of symbolist poetry. Words are things, but things which mean. We cannot do away with meaning without doing away with the signs, that is, with language itself. Moreover: we would have to do away with the universe. All the things man touches are impregnated with meaning. Perceived by man, things exchange being for meaning: they are not, they mean. Even "having no meaning" is a way of meaning. The absurd is one of the extremes that meaning reaches when it examines its conscience and asks itself, What is the meaning of meaning? Ambivalence of meaning: it is the fissure through which we enter things and the fissure through which being escapes from them.

Meaning ceaselessly undermines the poem; it seeks to reduce its reality as an object of the senses and as a unique thing to an idea, a definition, or a "message." To protect the poem from the ravages of meaning, poets stress the material aspect of language. In poetry, the physical properties of the sign, audible and visible, are not less but more important than the semantic properties. Or rather: meaning returns to sound and becomes its servant. The poet works on the nostalgia which the signified feels for the signifier. In Ponge this process is achieved by the constant play between prose and poetry, fantastic humor and common sense. The result is a new being: the *objeu*. All the same, we can make fun of meaning, disperse and pulverize it, but we cannot annihilate it: whole or in living fragments and wriggling, like the slices of a serpent, meaning reappears. The creative description of the world turns, on the one hand, into a criticism of the world (Ponge as moralist); on the other, into *proeme* (the *précieux* Ponge, a sort of Graci´n of objects). In Guillén the celebration of the world and of things results in history, satire, elegy: again, meaning. Williams' solution to the amphibious nature of language— words are things and are meanings—is different. He is not a European with a history behind him ready made but one ahead and to be made. He does not correct poetry with the morality of prose or convert humor into a teacher of resignation in song. On the contrary: prose is a ground where poetry grows, and humor is the spur of the imagination. Williams is a sower of poetic seeds. The American language is a buried seed which can only come to fruition if irrigated and shone upon by poetic imagination.

Partial reconciliation, always partial and provisional, between meaning and thing. Meaning—criticism of the world in Guillén, of language in Ponge—becomes in Williams an active power at the service of things. Meaning *makes*, is the midwife of objects. His art seeks "to reconcile people and stones through metaphor," American man and his landscape, speaking being with mute object. The poem is a metaphor in which objects speak and words cease to be ideas to become sensible objects. Eye and ear: the object heard and the word drawn. In connection with the first, Williams was the master and friend of the so-called Objectivists: Zukofsky, Oppen; in connection with the second, of the Black Mountain school: Olson, Duncan, Creeley. Imagination not only sees: it hears; not only hears: it says. In his search for the American language, Williams finds (hears) the basic measure, a meter of variable foot but with a triadic accentual base. "We know nothing," he says, "but the dance: the measure is all we know." The poem-thing is a verbal object, rhythmical. Its rhythm is a transmutation of the language of a people. By means of language Williams makes the leap from thing and sensation to the world of history.

Paterson is the result of these concerns. Williams goes from the poem-thing to the poem-as-system-of-things. Single and multiple system: single as a city were it one man only, multiple as a woman were she many flowers. *Paterson* is the biography of a city of the industrial East of the United States and the history of one man. City and man are fused in the image of a waterfall that cascades down, with a deafening roar, from the stone mouth of the mountain. Paterson has been founded at the foot of that mountain. The cataract is language itself, the people who never know what they say and who wander always in search of the meaning of what they say. Cataract and mountain, man and woman, poet and people, preindustrial and industrial age, the incoherent noise of the cascade and the search for a measure, a meaning. *Paterson* belongs to the poetic *genre* invented by modern American poetry which oscillates between the *Aeneid* and a treatise on political economy, the *Divine Comedy* and journalism: huge collections of fragments, the most imposing example of which is Pound's *Cantos*.

All these poems, obsessed as much by a desire to *speak* the American reality as to *make* it, are the contemporary descendants of Whitman, and all of them, one way or another, set out to fulfill the prophecy of *Leaves of Grass*. And in a sense they do fulfill it, but negatively. Whitman's theme is the embodiment of the future in America. Marriage of the concrete and the universal, present and future: American democracy is the universalizing of national-bound European man and his rerooting in a particular land and society. The particularity consists in the fact that that society and that place are not a tradition but a present fired toward the future. Pound, Williams, and even Hart Crane are the other side of this promise: their poems demonstrate to us the ruins of that project. Ruins no less grand and impressive than the others. Cathedrals are the ruins of Christian eternity, *stupas* are the ruins of Buddhist vacuity, the Greek temples of the *polis* and of geometry, but the big American cities and their suburbs are the living ruins of the future. In those huge industrial waste-bins the philosophy and morality of progress have come to a standstill. With the modern world ends the titanism of the future, compared with which the titanisms of the past—Incas, Romans, Chinese, Egyptians—seem childish sand castles.

Williams' poem is complex and uneven. Beside magical or realistic fragments of great intensity, there are long disjointed chunks. Written in the face of and sometimes against *The Waste Land* and the *Cantos*, it gets out of hand in its polemic with these two works. This is its principal limitation: reading it depends on other readings, so that the reader's judgment turns fatally to comparison. The vision Pound and Eliot had of the modern world was somber. Their pessimism was instinct with feudal nostalgias and precapitalist concepts; thus their just condemnation of money and modernity turned immediately into conservative and, in Pound's case, Fascist attitudes. Though Williams' vision is not optimistic either—how could it be?—there are in it no reminiscences of other ages. This could be an advantage, but it is not: Williams has no philosophic or religious system, no coherent collection of ideas and beliefs. What his immediate tradition (Whitman) offered him was unusable. There is a kind of void at the center of Williams' conception (though not in his short poems) which is the very void of contemporary American culture.

The Christianity of *The Waste Land* is a truth that has been burned, cal-
cined, and which, in my view, will not put out leaves again, but it was
a central truth which, like light from a dead star, still *touches* us. I find
nothing like that in *Paterson*. Comparison with the *Cantos* is not to Williams's advantage either. The United States is an imperial power, and if
Pound could not be its Virgil he was at least its Milton: his theme is the
fall of a great power. The United States gained a world but lost its soul,
its future—that universal future in which Whitman believed. Perhaps
on account of his very integrity and morality, Williams did not see the
imperial aspect of his country, its demonic dimension.

Paterson has neither the unity nor the religious authenticity of *The
Waste* Land—even if Eliot's religious feeling is negative. The *Cantos*, for
their part, are an incomparably vaster and richer poem than Williams',
one of the few contemporary texts that stand up to our terrible age. So
what? The greatness of a poet is not measured by the extent but by the
intensity and perfection of his works. Also by their liveliness. Williams is
the author of the *liveliest* modern American poems. Yvor Winters rightly
says, "Herrick is less great than Shakespeare but probably he is no less
fine and will last as long as he . . . Williams will be almost as indestructible as Herrick; at the end of this century we will see him recognized,
along with Wallace Stevens, as one of the two best poets of his generation." The prophecy came true before Winters expected it to. As to his
ideas about New World poetry—is he really the most American of the
poets of his age? I neither know nor care. On the other hand, I know
he is the freshest, the most limpid. Fresh like a flow of drinking water,
limpid as that same water in a glass jug on an unpolished wooden table
in a whitewashed room in Nantucket. Wallace Stevens once caned him
"a sort of Diogenes of contemporary poetry." His lantern, burning in full
daylight, is a little sun of his own light. The sun's double and its refutation: that lantern illuminates areas forbidden to natural light.

In the summer of 1970, at Churchill College, Cambridge, I translated six Williams poems. Later, on two escapades, one to Veracruz and
another to Zihuatanejo, I translated others. Mine are not literal translations: literalness is not only impossible but reprehensible. Nor are they
(I wish they were!) re-creations: they are approximations and, at times,

transpositions. What I most regret is that I was unable to find in Spanish a rhythm equivalent to Williams'. But rather than embroil myself in the endless subject of poetry translation, I prefer to tell how I met him. Donald Allen sent me an English version of a poem of mine ("Hymn Among Ruins"). The translation impressed me for two reasons: it was magnificent, and its author was William Carlos Williams. I vowed that I would meet him, and on one of my trips to New York I asked Donald Allen to take me with him, as he had taken me before to meet cummings. One afternoon we visited him at his house in Rutherford. He was already half-paralyzed. The house was built of wood, as is common in the United States, and it was more a doctor's than a writer's house. I have never met a less affected man—the opposite of an orade. He was possessed by poetry, not by his role as a poet. Wit, calmness, that not taking yourself seriously which Latin American writers so lack. In each French, Italian, Spanish, and Latin American writer—especially if he is an atheist and revolutionary—a clergyman is concealed; among the Americans plainness, sympathy, and *democratic* humanity—in the true sense of this word—break the professional shell. It has always surprised me that in a world of relations as hard as that of the United States, cordiality constantly springs out like water from an unstanchable fountain. Maybe this has something to do with the religious origins of American democracy, which was a transposition of the religious community to the political sphere and of the dosed space of the Church to the open space of the public square. Protestant religious democracy preceded political democracy. Among us democracy was antireligious in origin and from the outset tended not to strengthen society in the face of government, but government in the face of the Church.

Williams was less talkative than cummings, and his conversation induced you to love him rather than admire him. We talked of Mexico and of the United States. As is natural we fell into talking about roots. For us, I told him, the profusion of roots and pasts smothers us, but you are oppressed by the huge weight of the future which is crumbling away. He agreed and gave me a pamphlet which a young poet had just published with a preface written by him: it was *Howl* by Allen Ginsberg. I saw him again years later, shortly before his death. Though ill health had battered him hard, his temper and his brain were intact. We spoke again of the three or four or seven Americas: the red, the white, the black, the green, the purple . . . Flossie, his wife, was with us. As we talked I thought of "Asphodel," his great love poem in age. Now, when I recall that conversation and write this, in my mind I pick the colorless flower and breathe its fragrance. "A strange scent," the poet says, "a *moral* scent." It is not really a scent at all, "except for the imagination." Isn't that the best definition of poetry: a language which does not say anything except to the imagination? In another poem too he says: "Saxifrage is my flower that splits open rocks." Imaginary flowers which work on reality, instant bridges between men and things. Thus the poet makes the world habitable.

—Zihuatanejo, 20 January 1973

THE GRAPHICS OF CHARLES TOMLINSON: BLACK AND WHITE

When I first read one of Charles Tomlinson's poems, over ten years ago, I was struck by the powerful presence of an element which, later, I found in almost all his creative work, even in the most reflective and self-contemplating: the outer world, a presence at once constant and invisible. It is everywhere but we do not see it. If Tomlinson is a poet for whom "the outer world exists," it must be added that it does not exist for him as an independent reality, apart from us. In his poems the distinction between subject and object is attenuated until it becomes, rather than a frontier, a zone of interpenetration, giving precedence not to the subject but to the object: the world is not a representation of the subject—the subject is the projection of the world. In his poems, outer reality—more than merely the space in which our actions, thoughts, and emotions unfold—is a climate which involves US, an impalpable substance, at once physical and mental, which we penetrate and which penetrates us. The world turns to air, temperature, sensation, thought; and we become stone, window, orange peel, turf, oil stain, helix.

Against the idea of the world-as-spectacle, Tomlinson opposes the concept—a very English one—of the world as event. His poems are neither a painting nor a description of the object or its more or less constant properties; what interests him is the process which leads it to be the object that it is. He is fascinated—with his eyes open: a lucid fascination—at the universal busyness, the continuous generation and degeneration of things. His is a poetry of the minimal catastrophes and resurrections of which the great catastrophe and resurrection of the world is composed. Objects are unstable congregations ruled alternately by the forces of attraction and repulsion. Process and not transition: not the place of departure and the place of arrival but what we are when we depart and what we have become when we arrive . . . The water-drops on a bench wet with rain, crowded on the edge of a slat, after an instant of ripening—analogous in the affairs of men to the moment of doubt which precedes major decisions—fall on to the concrete; "dropped seeds of now becoming then." A moral and physical evocation of the water-drops . . .

Thanks to a double process, at once visual and intellectual, the product of many patient hours of concentrated passivity and of a moment of decision, Tomlinson can isolate the object, observe it, leap suddenly inside it, and, before it dissolves, take the snapshot. The poem is the perception of the change, a perception which includes the poet: he changes with the changes of the object and perceives. himself in the perception of those changes. The leap into the object is a leap into himself. The mind is a photographic darkroom; there the images—"the gypsum's snow/the limestone stair/and boneyard landscape grow/into the identity of flesh" ("The Cavern"). It is not, of course, a pantheistic claim of being everywhere and being everything. Tomlinson does not wish to be the heart and soul of the universe. He does not seek the "thing in itself" or the "thing in myself" but rather things in that moment of indecision when they are on the point of generation or degeneration. The moment they appear or disappear before us, before they form as objects in our minds or resolve in our forgetfulness . . . Tomlinson quotes a passage from Kafka which defines his purpose admirably: "to catch a glimpse of things as they may have been before they show themselves to me."

His procedure approaches, at one extreme, science: maximum objectivity and purification, though not suppression, of the subject. On the other hand, nothing is further from modern scientism. This is not because of the aestheticism for which he is at times reproached, but because his poems are experiences and not experiments. Aestheticism is an affectation, contortion, preciosity, and in Tomlinson we find rigor, precision, economy, subtlety. The experiments of modern science are carried out on segments of reality, while experiences implicitly postulate that the grain of sand is a world and each fragment figures the whole; the archetype of experiments is the quantitative model of mathematics, while in experience a qualitative element appears which up to now has been rebel to measurement. A contemporary mathematician, René Thorn, describes the situation precisely and gracefully: "A la fin du XVIIième siècle, la controverse faisait rage entre tenants de physique de Descartes et de Newton. Descartes, avec ses tourbillons, ses atomes crochus, etc., expliquait tout et ne calculait rien; Newton, avec la loi de gravitation en $1/r^2$, calculait tout et n'expliquait rien." And he adds, "Le point de vue newtonien se justifie pleinement par son efficacité . . . mais les esprits soucieux de compréhension n'auront jamais, au regard des théories qualitative et descriptives, l'attitude méprisant du scientisme quantitatif." It is even less justifiable to undervalue the poets, who offer us not theories but experiences.

In many of his poems, Tomlinson presents us with the changes in the particle of dust, the outlines of the stain spreading on the rag, the way the pollen's flying mechanism works, the structure of the whirlwind. The experience fulfills a need of the human spirit: to imagine what we cannot see, give ideas a form the senses can respond to, *see* ideas. In this sense the poet's experiences are not less truthful than the experiments carried out in our laboratories, though their truth is on another level from scientific truth. Geometry translates the abstract relationships between bodies into forms which are visible archetypes: thus it is the frontier between the qualitative and the quantitative. But there is another frontier: that of art and poetry, which translates into sensible forms, that are at the same time archetypes, the qualitative relationships between things and men. Poetry—imagination and sensibility made language—is a crystallizing agent of phenomena. Tomlinson's poems are crystals, produced by the combined action of his sensibility and his imaginative and verbal powers—crystals sometimes transparent, sometimes rainbow-colored, not all perfect, but all poems that we can look through. The act of looking becomes a destiny and a profession of faith: seeing is believing.

It is hardly surprising that a poet with these concerns should be attracted to painting. In general, the poet who turns to plastic work tries to express with shapes and colors those things he cannot say with words. The same is true of the painter who writes. Arp's poetry is a counterpointing of wit and fantasy set against the abstract elegance of his painting. In the case of Michaux, painting and drawing are essentially rhythmic incantations, signs beyond articulate language, visual magic. The expressionism of some of Tagore's ink drawings, with their violence, compensates us for the sticky sweetness of many of his melodies. To find one of Valéry's watercolors among the arguments and paradoxes of the *Cahiers* is like opening the window and finding that, outside, the sea, the sun, and the trees still exist. When I was considering Tomlinson, I called to mind these other artists, and I asked myself how this desire to paint came to manifest itself in a meditative temperament such as his—a poet whose main faculty of sense is his eyes, but eyes which think. Before I had a chance to ask him about this, I received, around 1970, a letter from him in which he told me he had sent me one of the *New Directions Anthologies*, which included reproductions of some of his drawings done in 1968. Later in 1970, during my stay in England, I was able to see other drawings from that same period—all of them in black and white, except for a few in sepia; studies of cow skulls, skeletons of birds, rats, and other creatures which he and his daughters had found in the countryside and on the Cornish beaches.

In Tomlinson's poetry, the perception of movement is exquisite and precise. Whether the poem is about rocks, plants, sand, insects, leaves, birds, or human beings, the true protagonist, the hero of each poem, is change. Tomlinson hears foliage grow. Such an acute perception of variations, at times almost imperceptible, in beings and things necessarily implies a vision of reality as a system of cans and replies. Beings and things, in changing, come in contact: change means relationship. In those Tomlinson drawings, the skulls of the birds, rats, and cows were isolated structures, placed in an abstract space, far from other objects, and even at a remove from themselves, fixed and immovable. Rather than a counterpointing of his poetic work, they seemed to me a contradiction. He missed out some of the features which attract me to his poetry: delicacy, wit, refinement of tones, energy, depth. How could he recover all these qualities without turning Tomlinson the painter into a servile disciple of Tomlinson the poet?

The answer to this question is found in the work—drawings, collages, and *decalcomaía**—of recent years.

Tomlinson's painting vocation began, significantly, in a fascination with films. When he came down from Cambridge in 1948, he had not only seen "all the films;" he was also writing scripts which he sent to producers and which they, invariably, returned to him. This passion died out in time but left two enduring interests: the image in motion, and the idea of a literary text as support for the image. Both elements reappear in the poems and the collages. When the unions closed the doors of the film industry against him, Tomlinson dedicated himself energetically to painting. His first experiments, combining *frottage*, oil, and ink, date from that period. Between 1948 and 1950 he exhibited his work in London and Manchester. In 1951 he had the opportunity to live for a time in Italy. During that trip the urge to paint began to recede before the urge to write poetry. When he returned to England, he devoted himself more and more to writing, less and less to painting. In this first phase of his painting, the results were indecisive: *frottages* in the shadow of Max Ernst, studies of water and rocks more or less inspired by Cézanne, trees and foliage seen in Samuel Palmer rather than in the real world. Like other artists of his generation, he made the circuit round the various stations of modern art and paused, long enough to genuflect, before the geometric chapel of the Braques, the Légers, and the Grises. During those same years—getting on toward 1954—Tomlinson was writing the splendid *Seeing Is Believing* poems. He ceased painting.

The interruption was not long. Settled near Bristol, he returned to his brushes and crayons. The temptation to use black (why? he still asks himself) had an unfortunate effect: by exaggerating the contours, it made

---

* "*Decalcomanía* without preconceived object or *decalcomanía* of desire: by means of a thick brush, spread out black gouache, more or less diluted in places, upon a sheet of glossy white paper, and cover at once with a second sheet, upon which exert an even pressure. Lift off the second sheet without haste"—Oscar Domínguez, quoted in *Surrealism* by Roger Cardinal and Robert Stuart Short.

his compositions stiff. "I wanted to reveal the pressure of objects," he wrote to me, "but all I managed to do was thicken the outlines." In 1968 Tomlinson seriously confronted his vocation and the obstacles to it. I refer to his inner inhibitions and, most of all, to that mysterious predilection for black. As always happens, an intercessor appeared: Seghers. Tomlinson was wise to have chosen Hercules Seghers—each of us has the intercessors he deserves. It is worth noting that the work of this great artist—I am thinking of his impressive stony landscapes done in white, black, and sepia—also inspired Nicolas de Staäl. Seghers's lesson is: Do not abandon black, do not resist it, but embrace it, walk around it as you walk around a mountain. Black was not an enemy but an accomplice. If it was not a bridge, then it was a tunnel: if he followed it to the end it would bring him through to the other side, to the light. Tomlinson had found the key which had seemed lost. With that key he unlocked the door so long bolted against him and entered a world which, despite its initial strangeness, he soon recognized as his own. In that world black ruled. It was not an obstacle but an ally. The ascetic black and white proved to be rich, and the limitation on the use of materials provoked the explosion of forms and fantasy.

In the earliest drawings of this period, Tomlinson began with the method which shortly afterward he was to use in his collages: he set the image in a literary context and thus built up a system of visual echoes and verbal correspondences. It was only natural that he should have selected one of Mallarmé's sonnets in which the sea snail is a spiral of resonances and reflections. The encounter with surrealism was inevitable—not to repeat the experiences of Ernst or Tanguy but to find the route back to himself. Perhaps it would be best to quote a paragraph of the letter I mentioned before: "Why couldn't I make their world my world? But in my own terms. In poetry I had always been drawn to impersonality—how could I go beyond the self in painting?" Or put another way: how to use the surrealists' psychic automatism without lapsing into subjectivism? In poetry we accept the accident and use it even in the most conscious and premeditated works. Rhyme, for example, is an accident; it appears unsummoned, but, as soon as we accept it, it turns into a choice and a rule. Tomlinson asked himself:

what in painting is the equivalent of rhyme in poetry? What is *given* in the visual arts? Oscar Domínguez answered that question with his *decalcomanía*. In fact, Domínguez was a bridge to an artist closer to Tomlinson's own sensibility. In those days he was obsessed by Gaudí, and by the memory of the dining-room windows in Casa Batlló. He drew them many times: what would happen if we could look out from these windows on the lunar landscape?

Those two impulses, Domínguez's *decalcomanía* and Gaudí's architectural arabesques, fused: "Then, I conceived of the idea of cutting and contrasting sections of a sheet of *decalcomanía* and fitting them into the irregular windowpanes . . . Scissors! Here was the instrument of choice. I found I could *draw* with scissors, reacting *with* and *against* the *decalcomanía* . . . Finally I took a piece of paper, cut out the shape of Gaudí's window and moved this mask across my *decalcomanía* until I found my moonscape . . . The 18th of June 1970 was a day of discovery for me: I made my best arabesque of a mask, fitted it round a paint blot and then extended the idea of reflection implicit in the blot with geometric lines . . ." Tomlinson had found, with different means from those he used in his poetry but with analogous results, a visual counterpoint for his verbal world: a counterpointing and a complement.

The quotes from Tomlinson's letter reveal with involuntary but overwhelming clarity the double function of the images, be they verbal or visual. Gaudí's windows, converted by Tomlinson into masks, that is, into objects which *conceal*, serve him to *reveal*. And what does he discover through those window-masks? Not the real world: an imaginary landscape. What began on the 18th of June 1970 was a fantastic morphology. A morphology and not a mythology: the places and beings which Tomlinson's collages evoke for us reveal no paradise or hell. Those skies and those caverns are not inhabited by gods or devils; they are places of the mind. To be more exact, they are places, beings, and things revealed in the darkroom of the mind. They are the product of the confabulation—in the etymological sense of that word—of accident and imagination.

Has it all been the product of chance? But what is meant by that word? Chance is never produced by chance. Chance possesses a logic—is a logic. Because we have yet to discover the rules of something, we have no reason to doubt that there are rules. If we could outline a plan, however roughly, of its involved corridors of mirrors which ceaselessly knot and unknot themselves, we would know a little more of what really matters. We would know something, for instance, about the intervention of "chance" both in scientific discoveries and artistic creation and in history and our daily life. Of course, like all artists, Tomlinson knows something: we ought to accept chance as we accept the appearance of an unsummoned rhyme.

In general, we should stress the moral and philosophical aspect of the operation: in accepting chance, the artist transforms a thing of fate into free choice. Or it can be seen from another angle: rhyme guides the text but the text produces the rhyme. A modern superstition is that of art as transgression. The opposite seems to me more exact: art transforms disturbance into a new regularity. Topology can show us something: the appearance of the accident provokes, rather than the destruction of the system, a recombination of the structure which was destined to absorb it. The structure validates the disturbance, art canonizes the exception. Rhyme is not a rupture but a binding agent, a link in the chain, without which the continuity of the text would be broken. Rhymes convert the text into a succession of auditory equivalences, just as metaphors make the poem into a texture of semantic equivalences. Tomlinson's fantastic morphology is a world ruled by verbal and visual analogies.

What we call chance is nothing but the sudden revelation of relationships between things. Chance is an aspect of analogy. Its unexpected advent provokes the immediate response of analogy, which tends to integrate the exception in a system of correspondences. Thanks to chance we discover that silence is milk, that the stone is composed of water and wind, that ink has wings and a beak. Between the grain of corn and the lion we sense no relationship at all, until we reflect that both serve the same lord: the sun. The spectrum of relationships and affinities between things is extensive, from the interpenetration of one object with another—"the sea's edge is neither sand nor water," the poem says—to the literary comparisons linked by the word *like*. Contrary to surrealist practice, Tomlinson does not juxtapose contradictory realities in order to produce a mental explosion. His method is more subtle. And his intention is distinct from theirs: he does not wish to alter reality but to achieve a modus vivendi with it. He is not certain that the function of imagination is to transform reality; he is certain, on the other hand, that it can make it more real. Imagination imparts a little more reality to our lives.

Spurred on by fantasy and reined in by reflection, Tomlinson's work submits to the double requirements of imagination and perception: one demands freedom and the other precision. His attempt seems to propose for itself two contradictory objectives: the saving of appearances, and their destruction. The purpose is not contradictory because what it is really about is the rediscovery—more precisely, the re-living—of the original act of making. The experience of art is one of the experiences of Beginning: that archetypal moment in which, combining one set of things with another to produce a new, we reproduce the very moment of the making of the worlds. Intercommunication between the letter and the image, the *decalcomanía* and the scissors, the window and the mask, those things which are hard-looking and those which are soft-looking, the photograph and the drawing, the hand and the compass, the reality which we see with our eyes and the reality which doses our eyes so that we see it: the search for a lost identity. Or as Tomlinson puts it best: "to reconcile the I that is with the I that I am." In the nameless, impersonal I that is are fused the I that measures and the I that dreams, the I that thinks and the I that breathes, the I which creates and the I which destroys.

—Cambridge, Massachusetts, 1975

JEAN-PAUL SARTRE:
A MEMENTO

The death of Jean-Paul Sartre, after the initial shock this kind of news produces, aroused in me a feeling of resigned melancholy. I lived in Paris in the postwar years, which were the high noon of his glory and influence. Sartre bore that celebrity with humor and simplicity; despite the bigotry of many of his admirers which was irritating and funny at the same time, his simplicity, which was genuinely philosophical, disarmed more reticent spirits. During those years, I read him with furious passion: one of his qualities was the way he could elicit from his readers, with the same violence, rejection and assent. Often, as I read, I lamented that I did not know him personally, so I might tell him face to face my doubts and disagreements. A chance incident gave me that opportunity.

A friend, sent to Paris by the University of Mexico to finish his philosophical studies, confided to me that he was in danger of losing his academic grant if he did not publish soon an article on some philosophical theme. It occurred to me that a conversation with Sartre might be the matter for that article. Through some common friends we got near to him and proposed our idea. He accepted it and a few days later the three of us dined in the bar of the Pont-Royal The dinner interview lasted more than three hours, and during it Sartre was extremely lively, speaking with intelligence, passion, and energy. He also listened, and took the trouble to answer my questions and timid objections. My friend never wrote his article, but that first meeting gave me the opportunity to meet Sartre again at the same bar of the Pont-Royal. Our relationship ended after the third or fourth encounter: too many things divided us and I did not look him up again. I have defined these differences in some passages in my *Alternating Current* and *The Philanthropic Ogre*.

The subjects of those conversations were the topical ones of the time: existentialism and its relations with literature and politics. The publication in *Les temps modernes* of a fragment of the book on Genet which he was writing at the time led us to talk about that writer and about Saint Teresa. A parallel much to his liking since both, he said, in choosing Supreme Evil and Supreme Good ("le Non-Etre de l'Etre et l'Etre du non-Etre"), in fact had chosen the same thing. I was surprised that, guided only by a verbalist logic, he ignored precisely what was at the heart of his concerns and the foundation of his philosophical criticism: the subjectivity of Saint Teresa and her historical situation. In other words: the physical person that the Spanish nun had been, and the intellectual and affective horizon of her life, the religiosity of the Spanish sixteenth century. For Genet, Satan and God are words which signify cloudy realities, suprasensible entities: myths or ideas; for Saint Teresa, those same words were spiritual and sensible realities, incarnate ideas. And this is what distinguishes mystical from other expression: though the Devil is the Non-Person by substitution and though strictly, except in the mystery of the Incarnation, God is not a person either, for the believer both are tangible presences, humanized spirits.

During that conversation I made an uncomfortable discovery: Sartre had not read Saint Teresa. He spoke on hearsay. Later, in newspaper statements, he said he had been inspired by a comedy of Cervantes, *El rufián dieboso*, in the writing of *Le Diable et le Bon Dieu*, though he made it clear he had not read the piece, only a summary. This ignorance of Spanish literature is not unusual but widespread among Europeans and Americans: Edmund Wilson vaingloriously proclaimed that he had read neither Cervantes nor Calderón nor Lope de Vega. Nevertheless, Sartre's confession reveals that he did not know one of the highest moments in European culture: the Spanish drama of the sixteenth and seventeenth centuries. His lack of curiosity still astonishes me, since one of the great themes of the Spanish theater, the source of some of the best works of Tirso de Molina, Mira de Amescua, and Calderón, is precisely the one which troubled him all his life: the conflict between grace and liberty. In another conversation he confided to me his admiration for Mallarmé. Years later, reading what he had written on this poet, I realized that once again the object of his admiration was not the poems which Mallarmé actually wrote but his project of absolute poetry, that Book he never made. Despite what his philosophy declares, Sartre always preferred shadows to realities.

Our last conversation was almost entirely about politics. Commenting on the discussions at the United Nations about the Russian concentration camps, he told me: "The British and the French have no right to criticize the Russians on account of their camps, since they've got their colonies. In fact, colonies are the concentration camps of the bourgeoisie." His sweeping moral judgment overlooked the specific differences—historic, social, political—between the two systems. In equating Western colonialism with the repressive Soviet system, Sartre fudged the issue, the only one that could and should interest an intellectual of the left such as he was: what was the true social and historic nature of the Soviet regime? By evading the basic theme, he helped indirectly those who wanted to perpetuate the lies with which, up to that time, Soviet reality had been masked. This was a serious equivocation, if one can so describe an intellectual and moral fault.

True, in those days imperialism exploited the colonial population as the Soviet system exploited the prisoners in the camps. The difference was that the colonies were not a part of the repressive system of bourgeois states (there were no French workers condemned to forced labor in Algeria, nor were there British dissidents deported to India), while the population of the camps consisted of the Soviet people themselves: farmers, workers, intellectuals, and whole social categories (ethnic, religious, and professional). The camps, that is to say, repression, were (are) an integral part of the Soviet system. In those years, moreover, the colonies achieved independence, while the system of concentration camps has spread, like an infection, into all the countries in which Communist regimes rule. And there is something more: is it even thinkable that in the Russian, Cuban, and Vietnamese camps movements of emancipation should arise and develop, movements like those that have liberated the old European colonies in Asia and Africa? Sartre was not insensible to these arguments, but it was hard to convince him: he thought that we bourgeois intellectuals had no right to criticize the vices of the Soviet system while in our own countries oppression and exploitation survived. When the Hungarian Revolution broke out, he attributed the uprising in part to Khrushchev's imprudent declarations revealing the crimes of Stalin: one ought not to upset the workers.

Sartre's case is exemplary but not unique. A sort of moralizing masochism, inspired by the best principles, has paralyzed a large number of European and Latin American intellectuals for more than thirty years. We have been educated in the double heritage of Christianity and the Enlightenment; both currents, religious and secular, in their highest development were critical. Our models have been those men who, like a Las Casas or a Rousseau, had the courage to tell and condemn the horrors and injustices of their own societies. I would not wish to betray that tradition; without it, our societies would cease to be that dialogue with themselves without which there is no real civilization and they would become a monologue of power, at once barbarous and monotonous. Criticism served Kant and Hume, Voltaire and Diderot, to establish the modern world. Their criticism and that of their heirs in the nineteenth century and the first half of the twentieth was creative. We have perverted criticism: we have put it at the service of our hatred of ourselves and of the world. We have not built anything with it, except prisons of concepts. Worst of all: with criticism we have justified tyrannies. In Sartre this intellectual sickness turned into an historical myopia: for him the sun of reality never shone. That sun is cruel but also, in some moments, it is a sun of plenitude and fortune. Plenitude, fortune: two words that do not appear in his vocabulary . . . Our conversation ended abruptly: Simone de Beauvoir arrived and, rather impatiently, made him swallow down his coffee and depart.

Even though Sartre had made a brief trip to Mexico, he hardly spoke at all of his Mexican experience. I believe he was not a good traveler: he had too many opinions. His real journeys he took around himself, shut up in his room. Sartre's candor, his frankness and rectitude, impressed me as much as the solidity of his convictions. These two qualities were not at odds: his agility was that of a heavyweight boxer. He lacked grace but made up for it with a hearty, direct style. This lack of affectation was itself an affectation and could go beyond frankness to bluntness. Nonetheless, he welcomed the stranger cordially, and one guessed he was harsher with himself than with others. He was chubby and a little slow in movement; a round, unfinished face: more than a face, a ground plan of a face. The thick lenses of his spectacles made his person seem more remote. But one only had to hear him to forget his face. It's odd: though Sartre has written subtle pages on the meaning of the look and the act of looking, the effect of his conversation was quite the opposite; he annulled the power of sight.

When I recall those conversations I am surprised by the moral continuity, the constancy of Sartre: the themes and problems that impassioned him in his youth were those of his maturity and old age. He changed opinions often, yet, nevertheless, in all of his changes he remained true to himself. I remember I asked him if I was right to assume that the book on morality which he promised to write—a project he conceived as his great intellectual undertaking and which he never completed—would have to open out into a philosophy of history. He shook his head, doubtfully: the phrase "philosophy of history" seemed suspicious to him, spurious, as if philosophy was one thing and history another. Moreover, Marxism was already that philosophy, since it had penetrated to the core the sense of the historical movement of our time. He proposed within Marxism to insert the solid, real individual. We are our situation: our past, our moment; at the same time, we are something which cannot be reduced to those conditions, however much they determine us. In the introduction to *Les temps modernes* he speaks of a *total* liberation of man, but a few lines further on he says the danger consists in that "the man-totality" might disappear "swallowed up by class." Thus, he was opposed both to the ideology which reduces individuals to being nothing but functions of class, and to the one which conceived of classes as functions of the nation. He kept to this position throughout his life.

His philosophy of the "situation"—Ortega had said, more exactly, "circumstance"—did not seem to him a negation of the absolute but rather the only way to understand and realize it. In the same essay he said: "The absolute is Descartes, the man who eludes us because he has died, who lived in his epoch and pondered hour after hour with the means at hand, who loved in his childhood a cross-eyed girl, etc.; what is relative is Cartesianism, that wandering philosophy which they trundle out century after century . . ." I am not too sure that these peremptory statements would stand up to close scrutiny. Why must the "absolute" be a childhood passion for a cross-eyed girl (and why cross-eyed?) and why must the philosophy of Descartes (which is not exactly the Cartesianism Sartre depreciatingly alludes to) be relative beside that infantile passion? And why that word *absolute*, impregnated with theology? Neither passions nor philosophies are suited to that despotic adjective. There are passions for and toward the absolute and there are philosophies of the absolute but there are no passions or philosophies that are absolute . . . I have digressed. What I wanted to stress is that in that essay Sartre introduces among the social and historical determinants an element of indeterminacy: the human person, people. Thus, back in 1947, he had begun his long and unhappy dialogue with Marxism and Marxists. What task did he really set himself? To reconcile communism and liberty. He failed, but his failure has been that of three generations of leftist intellectuals.

Sartre wrote philosophical treatises and philosophical essays, books of criticism and novels, stories and plays. Profusion is not excellence. His were not an artist's gifts: often he gets lost in useless digressions and amplifications. His language is insistent and repetitive: hammering as argument. The reader ends up exhausted, not convinced. If his prose is not memorable, what is to be said of his novels and stories? He wrote admirable narratives but he lacked a novelist's power: the ability to create worlds, atmospheres, and characters. The same criticism could be made of his plays: we remember the ideas of *Les mouches* and *Huis clos*, not the shadow-characters which express them. In his search for solid man Sartre time after time was left clutching a fistful of abstractions. And his philosophy? His contributions were valuable but partial. His work is not a beginning but a continuation and, at times, a commentary of others. What would be left of it without Heidegger?

In his essays lively, dense pages abound, always a little overdone, powerful verbal waves seething with ideas, sarcasm, things that just occurred to him. The best of his writing, to my taste, is the most personal, the least "committed," those texts which are closer to confession than to speculation, like so many pages of *Les mots*, perhaps his best book: the words embody, play, return to their childhood. Sartre excelled in two opposing modes: analysis and invective. He was an excellent critic and a fiery polemicist. The polemicist damaged the critic: his analyses often turned into accusations, as in his books on Baudelaire and Flaubert or in his wild critiques of surrealism. Worse than the polemicist's axe were the moralist's rod and the schoolmaster's ruler. Often Sartre exercised criticism like a tribunal that distributes punishments and admonishments exclusively. His *Baudelaire* is at the same time penetrating and partial; more than a study, it is a warning, a lecture. Though the book on Genet sins by the opposite excess—there are moments at which it is a very Christian apologia for abjection as a way to salvation—it has pages which are hard to forget. When Sartre allowed himself to be led by his verbal gift, the result was surprising. If in talking of men he reduced them to concepts, ideas, and theses, he still transformed words into animate beings. A cruel paradox: he despised literature and was above all else a literary man.

He thought and wrote much and on many things. In spite of this diversity, much that he said, even when he erred, seems to me essential. Let me state it differently: essential *for us*, his contemporaries. Sartre lived the ideas, the battles and tragedies of our age with the intensity with which others live out their private dramas. He was a conscience and a passion. The two words do not contradict each other because his was the conscience of a passion; I mean, conscience of the passing of time and of man. More than a philosopher he was a moralist. Not in the sense of the traditions of the *Grand Siècle*, interested in the description and analysis of the soul and its passions. He was not a La Rochefoucauld. I call him moralist not on account of his psychological insight but because he had the courage to set himself throughout his life the only question which really matters: What reasons have we to live? Why and to what end do we live? Is it worthwhile living as we live?

We know the replies he gave to these questions: man, surrounded by nothing and non-sense, is little being. Man is not man: he is the project for man. That project is choice: we are condemned to choose, and our penalty is called history. We also know where that paradox of liberty as penalty led him. Time after time he supported the tyrannies of our century because he thought that the despotism of the revolutionary Caesars was nothing but the mask of liberty. Time after time he had to confess that he had erred: what seemed a mask was the concrete face of the Chiefs. In our century, revolution has been the mask of tyranny. Sartre saluted each triumphant revolution with joy (China, Cuba, Algeria, Vietnam) and afterward, always a little late, he had to declare that he had made a mistake: those regimes were abominable. If he was severe about the American intervention in Vietnam and the French policy in Algeria, he did not shut his eyes to the cases of Hungary, Czechoslovakia, and Cambodia. Nonetheless, for years he insisted on defending the Soviet Union and its satellites because he believed that, despite everything, those regimes embodied, even if in a deformed way, the socialist project. His criticism of the West was implacable and distills a hatred of his world and of himself; his preface to the book on Fanon is a fierce and impressive exercise in denigration which is, at the same time, a self-expiation. It is revealing that, in writing those pages, he did not perceive in the freedom movements of the so-called Third World the germs of political corruption which have transformed those revolutions into dictatorships.

Why did he strive so in order not to see and not to hear? I exclude of course the possibility of complicity or duplicity, as in the case of Aragon, Neruda, and so many others who, though they knew, kept silent. Obstinacy, pride? Penitential Christianity of a man who has ceased to believe in God but not in sin? Mad hope that one day things would change? But how *can* they change if no one dares denounce them, or if that denunciation, "so as not to play into the hands of imperialism," is conditioned and full of reservations and exonerating clauses? Sartre preached the responsibility of the writer, and, nonetheless, during the years when he exercised a kind of moral authority in the whole world (except the Communist countries), his successive and contradictory *engagements* were an example, if not of irresponsibility, then certainly of precipitateness and incoherence. The philosophy of "compromise" dissolved in contradictory public gestures. It is instructive to compare the changes in Sartre with the lucid and extremely coherent oeuvre of Cioran, a spirit apparently at the margins of our age but one who has lived and thought in depth and, for that reason, quietly. The ideas and attitudes of Sartre justified the opposite of what he set himself: the unembarrassed and generalized irresponsibility of the intellectuals on the left who during the last twenty years, in the name of revolutionary "compromise," tactics, dialectics, and other pretty terms, have eulogized and cloaked the tyrants and the executioners.

It would not be generous to continue with the catalogue of his obfuscations. How can we forget that they were the daughters of his love of liberty? Perhaps his love was not very clear-sighted on account of its very impetuous intensity. Moreover, many of those errors were ours: those of our age. At the end of his life he came around completely and joined up with his old adversary, Raymond Aron, in the campaign to charter a boat to transport the fugitives from the Communist tyranny of Vietnam. He also protested against the invasion of Afghanistan, and his name is one of those at the head of the manifesto of French intellectuals who petitioned their government to join the boycott of the Moscow Olympics. The shadows of Breton and Camus, whom he attacked with rage and little justice, should be satisfied . . . The aberrations of Sartre are one more example of the perverse use of the Hegelian dialectic in the twentieth century. His influence has been lamentable on the European intellectual conscience: the dialectic makes us see evil as the necessary complement of the good. If all is in motion, evil is a moment of the good; but a *necessary* moment and, fundamentally, good: evil serves the good.

In a deeper layer of Sartre's personality there was an antique moral fund marked, more than by dialectics, by the familiar inheritance of Protestantism. Throughout his life he practiced with great severity the examination of conscience, axis of the spiritual life of his Huguenot ancestors. Nietzsche said that the great contribution of Christianity to the knowledge of the soul had been the invention of the examination of conscience and of its corollary, *remorse*, which is at the same time self-punishment and the exercise of introspection. The work of Sartre is a confirmation, yet another confirmation, of the precision of this idea. His criticism, whether of American politics or of the attitudes of Flaubert, follows the intellectual and moral scheme of the examination of conscience: it begins as a watchfulness, a tearing off of the veils and masks, not in search of nakedness but of the hidden ulcer, and it ends, inexorably, in a judgment. For the Protestant religious conscience, to know the world is to judge it and to judge it is to condemn it.

By a curious philosophical transposition, Sartre substituted for the predestination and liberty of Protestant theology psychoanalysis and Marxism. But all the great themes which fired the reformers appear in his work. The center of his thought was the complementary opposition between the situation (predestination) and liberty; this too was the theme of the Calvinists and the nub of their argument with the Jesuits. Not even God is absent: the Situation (History) assumes his functions, if not his features and his essence. But the Situation of Sartre is a deity which, since it has to have all the faces, has none: it is an abstract deity. Unlike the Christian God, it does not assume human form, nor is it an accomplice in our destiny: we are its accomplices and it is fulfilled in us. Sartre inherited from Christianity not transcendence, the affirmation of another reality and of another world, but the negation of this world and abhorrence of our earthly reality. Thus, in the depth of his analysis, protests, and insults against bourgeois society, the old vindictive voice of Christianity resounds. The true term for his criticism is *remorse*. In accusing his class and his world, Sartre accuses himself with the violence of a penitent.

It is remarkable that the two writers of greatest influence in France in this century—I am talking of moral, not literary, influence—have been André Gide and Jean-Paul Sartre. Two Protestants rebelling against Protestantism, their family, their class and its morality. Two moralist immoralists. Gide rebelled in the name of the senses and of the imagination; more than to liberate man, he wanted to free the shackled passions in each man. Communism disillusioned him because he perceived that it substituted for the Christian moral prison one more total and fierce. Gide was a moralist but also an aesthete, and in his work moral criticism is allied to the cultivation of the beautiful. The word *pleasure* has on his lips a savor at once subversive and voluptuous. More an evangelist than a radical, Sartre despised art and literature with the fury of a Church father. In a moment of desperation he said: "Hell is other people." A terrible expression, since the others are our horizon: the world of men. For this reason, no doubt, he later maintained that the liberation of the individual came by way of collective liberation. His work sets off from "I" to the conquest of "we." Perhaps he forgot that the "we" is a collective "thou": to love the others one must first love the other, the neighbor. We need, we moderns, to rediscover the "thou."

In one of his first works, *Les mouches*, there is a phrase which has been cited often but which is worth repeating: "Life begins the other side of despair." Only, what's on the other side of despair isn't life but the ancient Christian virtue we call hope. The first time the word *hope*, in an explicit way, appears on Sartre's lips is in the last interview which *Le nouvel observateur* published shortly before his death. It was his last statement. A disjointed and moving text. At one point, with an unbuttonedness which some have found disconcerting and others simply deplorable, he declares that his pessimism was a tribute to the fashion of the time. Strange affirmation: the whole interview is shot through with a vision of the world at times disillusioned and at others—most often—emphatically pessimistic. In the course of his conversation with his young disciple, Sartre reveals a stoical and admirable resignation in confronting his coming death. This attitude justly acquires all of its value because it stands out against a black backdrop: Sartre confesses that his work has remained incomplete, that his political action was frustrated, and that the world he leaves is more somber than the one he found at birth. For this reason I was genuinely impressed by his calm hope: despite the disasters of our age, one day men will reconquer (or will they conquer for the first time?) fraternity. I found it strange, on the other hand, that he should say that the origin and foundation of that hope is in Judaism. It is the least universal of the three monotheisms. Judaism is a closed fraternity. Why was he once again deaf to the voice of his tradition?

The dream of universal brotherhood—and more, the enlightened certainty that that is the state to which all men are naturally and supernaturally predestined, if we recover original innocence—appears in primitive Christianity. It reappears among the Gnostics of the third and fourth centuries and in the millennialist movements which, from time to time, have shaken the West, from the Middle Ages to the Reformation. But that little disagreement doesn't matter. It is uplifting that, at the end of his life, without rejecting his atheism, resigned to death, Sartre should have taken up the best and most pure element in our religious tradition: the vision of a world of men and women reconciled, transparent to each other because there is no longer anything to conceal or to fear, returned to an original nakedness. The loss and recovery of innocence were the theme of another great Protestant, involved as Sartre was in the battles of his century, and who, on account of the excess of his love for liberty, justified the tyrant Cromwell: John Milton. In the last book of *Paradise Lost* he describes. the slow and distressing departure of Adam and Eve—and with them the departure of all of us, their children—toward the eventual innocent kingdom:

> The world was all before them, where to choose
> Their place of rest, and Providence their guide:
> They hand in hand, with wandering steps and slow,
> Through Eden took their solitary way.

When I wrote these pages and read through them, I thought once more of the man who inspired them. I was tempted to paraphrase him—homage and recognition—writing in his memory: *Liberty is other people.*

Mexico, April 1980

BAUDELAIRE AS ART CRITIC: PRESENCE AND PRESENT

In his first essay on the visual arts (the 1845 Salon), faced with a canvas that represents the emperor Marcus Aurelius at the moment when, about to die, he entrusts young Commodus to his Stoic friends, Baudelaire writes with characteristic impetuosity: "Here we see Delacroix in full, that is, we have before our eyes one of the most complete specimens of what genius can achieve in painting." A few lines further on, with one phrase, he gives the reason for his fascination with this historical-philosophical picture: "This heightening of the green and red pleases our soul." Not the theme nor the figures but the relation between two colors, one cool and the other warm. The presence which the painting summons up is not the historical or philosophical image but the accord between a blue and a flesh-hue, a yellow and a violet. The body and the soul—or the pagan and Christian traditions—reduced to a visual vibration: music for the eye. Ten years later, again considering the work of Delacroix, he is even more explicit and conclusive: "Above all one must emphasize, and this is very important, that seen from a great distance, a distance which makes it hard to analyze or even understand the subject, a Delacroix painting instantly produces on the soul a rich impression, happy or sad . . . it is as though this color—I beg pardon for these treacheries of language in expressing ideas of great delicacy—thinks for itself, independently of the objects it clothes." To see a picture is to hear it, to understand what it says. Painting, which is music, is also and above all else language.

The idea of language includes the idea of translation: the painter translates the word into visual images; the critic is a poet who translates lines and colors into words. The artist is the universal translator. True, that translation is a transmutation. This consists, as we know, of the interpretation of nonlinguistic signs by means of linguistic signs—or the reverse. Each of those "translations" is in fact another work, not so much a copy of as a metaphor for the original. Later I will touch on this theme; but here let me point out that Baudelaire, with the same vehemence with which he argues that analogy ("translation") is the only way of approaching the picture, insists that the color thinks, *independently* of the objects it clothes. My comments begin with an analysis of this point.

At the heart of sense experience, the analogy between painting and language is perfect. One consists of the combination of a limited series of sounds; the other of the combination of a series of lines and colors. Painting obeys the same rules of opposition and affinity which govern language; in the one, combination produces visual forms, in the other, verbal forms. Just as the word is a repository of a gamut of approximate meanings, one of which is actualized in the phrase according to its position in context, so a color has no value in itself: it is nothing but a relation, "the accord between two tones." Thus it cannot be absolutely defined: "Colors only exist relatively." It should be added that drawing is nothing but a system of lines, a conjunction of relationships. Now, as the sphere of the senses is abandoned—in language sound, color and line in painting—a notable difference emerges: a phrase (combination of words) is translated by another phrase; a picture (combination of colors and lines) is translated by a phrase. The transition from what can be grasped by the senses to what can be understood is not accomplished in the picture but outside it: the *meaning* unfolds in a nonpictorial sphere. Or, in other words, the language of painting is a system of signs that find their meaning in other systems. Baudelaire himself says it: color is a cloak or, to use the musical analogy again, an accompaniment.

All the pictorial works of all civilizations—except the merely decorative and those of the modern period—present two levels: one properly speaking pictorial, the other extra- or metapictorial. The first is made up of the relations between colors and lines; those relations construct or, more precisely, *weave* the second level: a real or imaginary object. The pictorial level refers us to a representation, and this refers us to a world which is no longer that of the painting. Of course, all representation is symbolic and the object depicted is never just a copy or representation of the original. Another peculiarity to note: the less representative the object, the less pictorial the painting tends to be, and the more to be confused with writing. For instance, in Islamic culture the arabesque, the colors on the walls at Teotihuacán and in the Mexican codices, the tantric painting in Buddhist and Hindu India. In this last, the colors and lines think and speak for themselves because, at the border between word and painting, they are articulated as a discourse. When we contemplate a roll of tantric paintings, we do not see a succession of scenes and landscapes as in Chinese painting, but rather we read a ritual. The painting frees itself from the tyranny of representation only to fall into the servitude of writing. Thus the pictorial values are not autonomous: they always build toward the representation of a real or ideal object. Without them, there would be no representation; without it, painting would have no meaning.

The object, what presents itself to the eyes or the imagination, never appears as it is. The form in which the presence appears is the representation. Being is invisible, and we are doomed to perceive it through a veil woven of symbols. The world is a cluster of signs. Representation signifies the distance between the full presence and our gazing: it is the sign of our changing and finite being in time, the mask of death. At the same time, it is the bridge across—if not to the pure and full presence—at least to its reflection: our answer to death and to being, to the unthinkable and the unspeakable. If representation does not abolish distance—the sense of a thing never entirely coincides with its being—it is the transfiguration of presence, its metaphor.

No civilization placed in doubt the relationship between the pictorial and the metapictorial, plastic values and representation. The more or less clear awareness of that relation precluded, it seems to me, the confusion between one level and another: what was distinctive, "worth seeing," was not the theme or the object represented but the painting itself, though invariably and necessarily in relation to what it represented. Color and line constituted the representation, and it gave them meaning. But as soon as painting begins to gain autonomy, this relation becomes contradictory. Even though the process begins in the Renaissance, from the critical point of view the beginning of the break is in Kant's aesthetics: the contemplation of the beautiful lays stress on the pictorial. At the same time, modern philosophy submits traditional certainties, systems, and beliefs to a radical analysis; the old meanings disperse and the representations with them. From Baudelaire on, the relation breaks: colors and lines cease to serve representative ends and aspire to mean in themselves. Painting no longer weaves a presence: it *is* presence. This break opens a double way which is also an abyss. If color and line are really a presence, they cease to be a language and the picture reverts to the world of things. That has been the fate of much contemporary painting. The other direction, foreseen by Baudelaire, can be stated in the formula: Color thinks, painting is a language. It is the other route of modern art, the way of catharsis.

In renouncing the representation that gave it meaning, painting becomes a clutch of signs projected on a space void of meanings. The old space where representation lived is deserted, or rather covered with riddles: what does the painting say? The relation between the spectator and the work suffers a radical inversion: the work is no longer the answer to the spectator's question but itself becomes a question. The answer (that is, the meaning) depends on who is looking at the picture. Painting suggests contemplation to us—not of what it shows but of a presence which the colors and forms evoke without ever entirely revealing: a presence that is in fact invisible. Painting is a language which cannot say, except by omission and allusion: the picture presents us with the signs of an absence.

The first consequence of the break was the substitution of literal for analogical interpretation, the end of criticism as judgment and the birth of poetic criticism. No less decisive was the masking of presence. Earlier painting not only alluded to a presence but, as it represented it, wove a transparency: not the embodiment of presence but its transfiguration. If representation gave meaning to painting, painting gave life to meaning: it filled it with life. By giving it form, it transformed it into a visible, palpable image. From Baudelaire on, painting thinks but does not speak, is language but does not mean; it is luminous matter and form, but it has ceased to be image. Baudelaire is original not only because he was among the first to formulate an aesthetic of modern art; it must also be said that he suggested to us an aesthetic of disembodiment.

All Baudelaire's critical writing is pervaded by a contradictory tension. The opposition between the pictorial and the metapictorial, in the end resolved to the advantage of the former, is reproduced too in the contradictory relationship between "the eternal and the ephemeral": the ideal model and the unique beauty. As in the case of color, the eternal and the ephemeral refuse to be defined separately. The eternal is what cannot be defined by the substitution of an epithet, what serves as the ground against which the modern stands out clearly. Baudelaire's descriptions are negative and tend to underline the static and undifferentiated character both of the eternal and of the classical ideal of beauty. By contrast, the modern and its equivalent in space—the unique and the bizarre— are dynamic and positive. They are the break—a break which ensures continuity; they are innovation—an innovation which reintroduces in the present an immemorial principle. Baudelaire's attitude once again implies an inversion of the traditional perspective. Before, the past, taken to be the repository of the eternal, defined the present; and it defined it strictly: artistic creation was an imitation of archetypes, whether these were works of antiquity or of nature itself. Now the eternal depends upon the present: on the one hand, the present is the criticism of tradition, so that each moment is, at the same time, a refutation of eternity and its metamorphosis into an ephemeral novelty; on the other hand, the eternal is not single but manifold and there are as many beauties as there are races, ages, and civilizations: "Every people is academic in its judgment of others, barbarous when others judge it." Recovery of the art of non-European peoples: "The beautiful is always the bizarre." But what is the bizarre? Again, it is nothing except a relationship.

It is not hard to understand why Baudelaire was reluctant to face definition: it is impossible to construct a system founded upon the value of the ephemeral and the particular because both are, by their very nature, what escapes definition, the unknown quantity which dissolves systems. Precisely because, though always present, the modern and the bizarre are unpredictable and changing realities, every system is unreal, even those which claim to be established on an eternal precept. The system is "a kind of condemnation which forces us into a perpetual recantation . . . To elude the horror of those philosophical apostasies, I have resigned myself proudly to modesty: I am content to feel." An aesthetic which renounces reflection, an art without a head? Rather, an aesthetic which inclines toward the horrors and marvels of succession, an art fascinated by the renewed appearance of the sign of death in every living form.

Given that the modern cannot be defined, Baudelaire gives us a list of contrasts. The antique is characterized by public ostentation; the modern by private life. In one, hierarchy and ceremony; in the other, democracy and simplicity. By their cut and color, antique clothes make life a spectacle and exalt whoever wears them; modern clothes, black or dark of hue, are the expression of universal equality and serve not to expose but to conceal. Antique fashion separates, points up, distinguishes; the modern is "an identical livery of desolation . . . an immense procession of grave-diggers, political grave-diggers, lover grave-diggers, bourgeois grave-diggers. We all celebrate a burial." Here once more the law of contrast or complementary opposition intervenes: in a uniformed society, those who concentrate in themselves a uniqueness are not representative individuals, as in ancient times, but eccentrics and marginal people: the dandy, the artist, criminals, harlots, the lonely man lost in the crowd, the beggar, the wanderer. Not the men of note, exceptional men. Modern beauty is strangeness. But then, what would Baudelaire have said if confronted with the socialization of dandyism in Carnaby Street? Our modernity is the opposite of his: we have turned eccentricity into a vulgar consumer value. Three moments in Western civilization: in the ancien régime, private life lived as ceremony; in the nineteenth century, lived as in a secret novel; in the twentieth century, private life lived publicly.

For Baudelaire, the modern is the opposite of publicity; it is the unusual, so long as it is private and even secret. Thus the importance of makeup and masks which at the same time reveal and conceal. In women, the modern is the "secret distinction," a kind of "infernal or divine heroism": the bedroom as a cave of witchcraft or the sanctuary of a bloody priestess. Also modern are "humor," melancholy, disdain, the desolated sensibility, synesthesia, spirituality, a taste for infinities, fantasy, the voyage—not to conquer territories but to flee the world of progress. In short: subjectivity, subjective beauty. Composed of opposites, the modern is also the reality of the street, the motley crowd, and fashions. There is an antique death and a modern one. Hercules commits suicide because "the burns from his tunic were unbearable," Cato because "he can do nothing more for liberty," and Cleopatra because "she loses her throne and her lover . . . but none of them destroys himself in order to change his skin in view of metempsychosis," as Balzac's hero does. What then is the modern if not the appetite for change—and more: the *consciousness* of change? The ancients had an idea of the past from which they judged the changes of the present; the moderns have an idea of change and from it they judge the past and the present. That consciousness has another name: *misfortune.* It is the mark which the elect wear on their brow, and in it the bizarre, the irregular, and the deformed, all those attributes of modern beauty, are summarized. The sign of the modern is a stigma: presence wounded by time, tattooed by death.

In ancient times, men could not escape eternity, whether pagan destiny or Christian providence; modern man is condemned to the present, to instability. There is no repose. It doesn't matter: there is an instant in which time, which cannot be restrained, turns on itself; an instant not outside time but before history and the *reverse* of the present. It is the original instant, and in it modernity discovers itself as antiquity without dates: the time of the savage. When it destroys the idea of eternal beauty, the modern opens the doors to the world of savages: the most modern art is thus the most ancient. Thence the greatness of Delacroix: his painting is "cannibal painting." With a kind of rabid enthusiasm, Baudelaire exalts the painter's "savagery," his affinity with the Aztec priest with his obsidian knife, the destructive "Molochlike" character of his work, like the "triumphal hymns" of fire. Delacroix's stains of color excite in the spirit the ferocity of certain tropical twilights, the density of the hot ash on the ruins. The original instant does not detain time: it is the other face of the present, just as barbarism is the other side of civilization. Prisoners of relation, one depends on the other: the savage is so only from the civilized perspective. Moreover, as Baudelaire's successors were not slow to prove, "savagery" is no less diverse than "the modern": there are as many artistic styles as there are primitive societies. Savagery is another illusion of modernity. At the same time, it is a criticism of modernity. Savagery, modernity, and tradition are manifestations of the art of criticism, that is to say, of polemical and historical art. When he introduces the notions of modernity and savagery into art, Baudelaire inserts criticism into the creation, invents critical art. Previously criticism preceded or followed creation; now it goes hand in hand with it and is, he would say, its condition. Just as criticism becomes a creation by analogy, so creation is also criticism because it is historical. In constant battle with the past, modern art is in conflict with itself. The art of our time lives and dies of modernity.

Both from the perspective of language and from that of history, Baudelaire's reflection opens out into an unsustainable paradox which is, nonetheless, the very reality of modern painting: the triumph of the pictorial is the equivalent of the disembodiment of presence, the victory of modernity is its ruin, the original moment does not dissolve but affirms history, the aesthetic of particularity refutes itself, and the creative accident turns into a mechanical repetition. Torn between these antithetical contraries, Baudelaire seeks in analogy a system which, without suppressing tensions, resolves them into a harmony. Analogy is the highest function of the imagination, since it fuses analysis and synthesis, translation and creation. It is knowledge of and at the same time a transmutation of reality. On the one hand, it is an arch that joins different historical periods and civilizations; on the other, it is a bridge between different languages: poetry, music, painting. In the first instance, if it is not "the eternal" it is what articulates all times and all spaces in an image which, ceaselessly changing, prolongs and perpetuates itself. In the second instance, it transforms communication into creation: what painting says without telling, turns into what music paints without painting, and what—without ever expressly mentioning it—the poetic word enunciates.

This differs from the old sense of analogy in this respect: the medieval artist had a universe with signs accessible to all and governed by a single code: Scripture; the modern artist has a repertory of heterogeneous signs and, instead of sacred writings, confronts a multitude of contradictory books and traditions. Thus modern analogy also flows out into the dispersal of meaning. Analogical translation is a rotating metaphor which engenders another metaphor which in turn provokes another and another: what do all these metaphors say? Nothing that the painting has not already said: presence is concealed to the extent that the meaning is dissolved.

In many of his poems and critical reflections, Baudelaire has stated unequivocally what the *ultimate sense* of analogy is. Particularly explicit are the pages he devotes to the music of Wagner. More than a reflection on analogy, those pages tell of a unique experience which we have no choice but to call *the disembodiment of presence*. When he hears the overture to *Lohengrin,* he feels himself released from "the fetters of gravity," so that, rocked by the music, he finds himself "in a solitude with an immense horizon and a vast diffuse light; immensity with no integrity other than itself. Soon I experience the feeling of an even livelier clarity; the intensity of the light increased so quickly that dictionary words would be inadequate to express that superabundance, endlessly reborn, of ardor and whiteness. Then I conceived clearly the idea of a soul moving in a luminous atmosphere, an ecstasy composed of voluptuousness and knowledge . . ." The sensations of altitude and voluptuousness are closely associated with those of the loss of body and of that white light which is the abolition of all color. Empty of itself, his being rests in an immensity which contains nothing but itself. Again and again the notion of time is changed into that of space which extends "to the remotest conceivable limits." The feeling of being at a frontier: space extends so far that in fact it is invisible and inconceivable: non-space, non-time. The ecstasy of knowledge consists in this annulment: immersed in the floating space, the poet becomes detached from his identity and fused with vacant extension. The critical art culminates in a final negation: Baudelaire contemplates, literally, *nothing.* Or rather, he contemplates a metaphor of nothingness. A transparency that, if it hides nothing, reflects nothing either—not even his questioning face. The aesthetic of analogy is the aesthetic of the annihilation of presence.

Baudelaire's thought gave a critical and aesthetic conscience to almost all the artistic movements of our time, from impressionism to the present. The idea of painting as an autonomous and self-sufficient language has been shared by the majority of artists of our time and was the foundation of abstract painting. A little more should be said about the value, at once polemical and magical, of the word *modernity* and of its descendants: the new, the avant-garde (though Baudelaire does not conceal his revulsion for this term). It is worth bearing in mind that a constant note in modern art has been the use of procedures and styles each time more remote from Renaissance and Greco-Roman traditions, everything from black art to pre-Columbian art, from the painting of children to that of schizophrenics; plurality of the ideas of beauty. The preeminence of spontaneity, the communication between waking and dream, the nostalgia for a word lost in the beginnings of time, and the exaltation of childhood are themes which reappear in impressionism, surrealism, and abstract expressionism. The reduction of beauty to the singular, the characteristic, or the monstrous: expressionism. The creative function of analogy, the aesthetic of surprise: Breton, Apollinaire.

In a sense, it could be said that modern art has fulfilled Baudelaire. It would also be right to say that it has contradicted him. These two statements are not mutually exclusive but complementary: the situation in 1967 is as much the negation of that of 1860 as its result. In recent decades the acceleration of changes has been such that it almost amounts to a refutation of change: immobility and repetition. The same happens with the increasing production of more and more works, each one pretending to be exceptional and unique: apart from the fact that most are the daughters of industrious imitation and not of imagination, they give us the impression of a huge heaping-up of heteroclite objects—the confusion of refuse. Marcel Duchamp asks himself: "We are drowned in a sea of paintings . . . where are the granaries and cellars which could contain them?" Modernity ends by negating itself: the vanguard of 1967 repeats the achievements and gestures of the 1917 vanguard. We are living through the end of the idea of modern art. Thus the first thing artists and critics would have to do would be to apply to that idea the rigorous criticism that Baudelaire applied to the notion of "tradition."

The aesthetics of modernity are contemporary with certain changes in the production, distribution, and evaluation of works. The autonomy of painting—its separation from the other arts and its claim to constitute itself as a self-sufficient language—is parallel to the birth of the museum, the commercial gallery, the professional critic, and the collector. It is a

dared to put themselves in the path of the bull, as bullfight aficionados say. In other words: they attack the system and its principles. In the first place, they revert to teamwork. Baudelaire in his lifetime, faced with the spectacle of hundreds of painters in search of an impossible and in the final account an inane originality, was pointing out how much better it would have been for them had they worked honorably in the studio of a master. Painting itself would have benefited: "A vast output is nothing more than a thought with a thousand arms." The *Groupe de recherche d'art visuel* substitutes the studio for the laboratory, artisanal production for research, the idea of the master-patron for the association of artists, and sets at the center of its concerns that *thought* of which Baudelaire speaks and which is nothing but another name for imagination. An end to the superstition attached to the profession: "Who possesses only ability is a dolt." An end to the fanaticism of the unique object, as much by the multiplication of specimens of each work as by making each one of them an object which invites us to contemplate and transform it. And an end to the idea of the spectator; instead, creative interplay: the *Groupe* suggests situations which provoke a joint reaction from those who participate.

The work dissolves into life, but life is resolved in *fiesta*. This word immediately evokes one of the myths of modernity: Baudelaire's savage, Breton's "far off man." Only now it's not a matter of reverting to the art of primitive men or of reviving their beliefs, but of finding, thanks specifically to our machines, a collective way to consume and to consummate time. Le Parc has said that a painting lasts as long as a look. That is true, if the look is a sign of intelligence which we pass over the work . . . I do not know if the works of the *Groupe* will end up in museums, as those of their predecessors have. It's a safe bet. It does not matter: I've cited the attempt by these young artists because their program seems to be a symptom, among others, of the disappearance of the "idea of modernity," as Baudelaire and his successors conceived it, from the impressionists to the abstract painters. I am sure that we are witnesses to the end of the "art object" and the conception of art as the mere production of objects. The notion of substance dissolves not only in contemporary philosophy and physics, but even in the world of economics: considerations of use displace increasingly valuation in terms of durability. I will add finally that my idea of the *fiesta* differs from that proposed by these young artists. The *fiesta* I dream of would not only be the sharing and consummation of the object, but, unlike that of the primitives, it would *have no object:* not commemoration of an anniversary nor a return to past time; it would be—I have no choice but to force language so that I can say it—the dissipation of time, *production of forgetfulness.*

The resurrection of the *fiesta* is one of the unravelings of contemporary art, as much in the domain of the visual as of the musical and verbal arts: a dissolving of the art object in the temporal current and the crystallization of historical time in a closed space. The *fiesta* suppresses, for a moment, the opposition between presence and representation, the atemporal and the historical, the sign and the object signified. It is a presentation but at the same time a consummation: presence embodies only to share itself out and to be consumed among the communicants. Thus, at one extreme, the quarrel between the eternal and the ephemeral is settled. But from the ashes of *fiesta* discord between the pictorial and the metapictorial revives. Is there another way?

Doubtfully and guided by the principle of analogy, which is also that of complementary opposition, I venture an hypothesis: the pole opposite to *fiesta* is contemplation. If the first supplies a lack in our mass society, the second satisfies another lack in our society of solitaries. The art of contemplation produces objects but it does not consider them things, rather signs: points of departure toward the discovery of another reality, whether of presence or absence. I write "toward the discovery" because in a society like ours art offers us neither meanings nor representations: it is art in search of meaning. An art in search of presence or of absence where meanings dissolve. This art of contemplation would redeem the notion of *oeuvre* except that, instead of perceiving in it an object, a thing, it would give it back its true function: of being a *bridge* between the spectator and that presence to which art always alludes without ever entirely naming.

After more than a century of modernism, our situation is rather like that of the character in *Kantan,* that Nō play admirably translated by Arthur Waley: a young walker finds accommodation in an inn and, tired from his journey, stretches out on a mat; while the innkeeper prepares him a handful of rice, he dreams that he accedes to the throne of China and that he lives, as though he were immortal, fifty years of glory: the few minutes it took for the rice to cook and for him to wake up. Like the Buddhist pilgrim, we can ask ourselves: has something changed? If we answer: nothing has changed because all the changes were made of the substance of the dream, we will implicitly affirm that we have changed. Before dreaming that dream we could not have answered thus; but to know that changes are chimerical, we should change. If we respond in the affirmative, we will incur a contradiction, too: our change consists in perceiving that all changes are illusory, our own being no exception. The art and criticism of the twentieth century have been prisoners of this paradox. Perhaps the only answer is not to ask the question, to get up and wander on in search of presence, not as if nothing had happened but as if everything had—that everything which is identical with nothing.

—Delhi, December 1967

ANDRÉ BRETON, OR THE SEARCH FOR THE BEGINNING

It is not possible to write about André Breton with unimpassioned language. What's more, it would be wrong to do so. For him, the powers of the word were indistinguishable from those of passion, and this, in its highest and tensest form, was nothing but language in a state of savage purity: poetry. Breton: the language of passion—the passion of language. His whole research, quite as much as—if not more than—an exploration of unknown psychic territories, was the repossession of a lost kingdom: the word of the beginning, man before men and civilizations. Surrealism was an order of chivalry and its whole enterprise was a *quête du graal.* The surprising evolution of the Spanish term *querer* expresses well the tone of the search: *querer* comes from *quaerere* (to seek, to inquire), but in Spanish it soon changed its meaning to signify impassioned will, desire. *Querer:* passional, amorous search. Search not toward the future or the past but toward that center of convergence which is, simultaneously, the origin and end of time: the day before the beginning and after the end. His outrage at "the infamous Christian idea of sin" is something more than a rejection of traditional Western values: it is an affirmation of man's original innocence. This distinguishes him from almost all his contemporaries and from those who followed him. For Bataille, eroticism, death, and sin are interchangeable signs which repeat in their combinations, with terrifying monotony, the same meaning: the nothingness of man, his irremediable abjection. For Sartre, too, man is the son of a curse, either ontological or historical, call it anxiety or salaried work. Both are rebel sons of Christianity. The origin of Breton is other. In his life and work he was not so much the heir of Sade and Freud as of Rousseau and Eckhart. He was not a philosopher but a poet and, what is more, in the old sense of the term, a man of honor. His intransigence on the idea of sin was a point of honor: it seemed to him that sin was, in effect, a *stain*, something which wounded not human *being* but human dignity. Belief in sin was incompatible with his notion of man. This conviction, which set him very violently against many modern philosophies and all religions, was at its root religious too: it was an act of faith. What is most strange—I should say admirable—is that he never abandoned that faith. He denounced frailties, faintings, and treacheries, but he never thought our guilt congenital. He was a party man without the least trace of Manichaeism. For Breton, sin and birth were not synonymous.

Man, even when degraded by the neocapitalism and pseudosocialism of our times, is a marvelous being because, sometimes, he *speaks*. Language is the mark, or the sign, not of his fall but of his essential irresponsibility. By means of the word we can accede to the lost kingdom and recover old powers. Those powers are not ours. The inspired man, the one who speaks in truth, says nothing that is his: language speaks through his mouth. Dream lends itself to the explosion of the word because it is an affective state: its passivity is the activity of desire. Dream is passionate. Here too his opposition to Christianity was religious in character: language, to speak to itself, annihilates conscience. Poetry does not save the "I" of the poet, it dissolves it in the vaster and more powerful reality of speech. The practice of poetry requires abandonment, renunciation of the "I." It is sad that Buddhism did not interest him: that tradition too destroys the illusion of the "I," though not for the benefit of language but of silence. (I should add that that silence is a quietened word, a silence which does not cease to emit meanings from more than two thousand years ago.) I am reminded of Buddhism because I believe that "automatic writing" is rather like a modern equivalent of Buddhist meditation; I do not think it is a method for writing poems, nor is it a rhetorical recipe: it is a psychic exercise, a convocation and an invocation destined to open the floodgates of verbal flow. Poetic automatism, as Breton himself stressed many times, is a neighbor of asceticism: it implies a state of difficult passivity which, in turn, requires the abolition of all criticism and self-criticism. It is a radical criticism of criticism, a placing of conscience under interdict. In its fashion, it is a way of purgation, a means of negation which tends to provoke the appearance of true reality: primordial language.

The basis of "automatic writing" is a belief in the identity between speaking and thinking. Man does not speak because he thinks but thinks because he speaks; or rather, speaking is not distinct from thought: to speak is to think. Breton justifies this idea with his observation: "Nous ne disposons spontanément pour nous exprimer que d'une *seule* structure verbale excluant de la manière la plus catégorique toute autre structure apparemment chargée du même sens." The first objection which could be raised against this cutting formula is the fact that both in daily speech and in written prose we are confronted with phrases which could be said in other words or with the same words in a different order. Breton could answer, rightly, that between one version and another not only does the syntactical structure change but the idea itself is modified, however imperceptibly. Every change in the verbal structure produces a change of meaning. In a strict sense, what we call synonyms are nothing but translations or equivalences within a language; and what we call translation is transfer or interpretation. Words such as *nirvana, dharma, tao,* or *jen* are in fact untranslatable; the same happens with *physics, nature, democracy, revolution,* and other Western terms which have no exact equivalent in languages alien to our tradition. The more intimate the relation between the verbal structure and the meaning—mathematics and poetry, to avoid talking of unarticulated languages such as music and painting—the more difficult translation becomes. At either extreme of language—exclamation and equation—it is impossible to separate the sign from its two halves: signifier and signified are the same. Breton thus opposes, perhaps without knowing it, Saussure: language is not only an arbitrary convention between sound and sense, something the linguists themselves are now coming to recognize.

Breton's ideas about language were magical in nature. Not only did he refrain from distinguishing magic and poetry, but he always thought that the latter was effectively a force, a substance or an energy capable of changing reality. At the same time, those ideas had a precision and penetration which I dare to call scientific. On the one hand, he saw language as an autonomous current endowed with its own power, a kind of universal magnetism; on the other, he conceived that erotic substance as a system of signs ruled by a double law of affinity and opposition, similarity and otherness. This vision is not far from that of the modern linguists: words and their constituent elements are fields of energy, like atoms and their particles. The attraction between syllables and words is not different from that of stars and bodies. The ancient notion of analogy reappears: nature is language, and language, for its part, is a double of nature. To recover natural language is to return to nature, before the fall and before history: poetry is the witness of original innocence. The *Social Contract* becomes, for Breton, a verbal, a poetic accord between man and nature, word and thought. From this perspective one can better understand that often repeated assertion: Surrealism is a movement of total liberation, not a poetic school. Poetry, the route to reconquering innocent language and renewing the original contract, is the scripture of the foundation of man. Surrealism is revolutionary because it is a return to the origin of the origin.

The earliest poems of Breton reveal the traces of an impassioned reading of Mallarmé. Not even at the moments of greatest verbal violence and freedom did he abandon that taste for the word, at once precise and precious. Iridescent word, language of reverberations. He was a "mannerist" poet in the good sense of the term; within the European tradition he belongs to that strain which descends from Góngora, Marino, Donne—poets whose work I do not know if he read and who, I fear, his poetic morality reproved. Verbal splendor, and violence of mind and passion. A strange alliance, but not all that uncommon, between prophecy and aestheticism which makes his best poems into objects of beauty and, at the same time, into spiritual testaments. That is, perhaps, the reason for his cult of Lautréamont, the poet who found the *form* of psychic explosion. Thence, too, his avowed repugnance for the simplistic brutality of Dada, though he judged it inevitable and welcome as a "revolutionary necessity." His reservations about other poets are different in nature. His admiration of Apollinaire contains a grain of reticence because for Breton poetry was the creation of reality by means of the word and not just verbal inventiveness. He loved novelty and surprise in art, but the term *invention* was not to his liking; on the other hand, in many of his texts the noun *revelation* glows with an unequivocal light. Saying is the highest form of activity: to reveal what is hidden, to waken the buried word, to provoke the emergence of our double, to create that other which we are and which we never entirely cease to be.

Revelation is resurrection, exposure, initiation. It is a word that evokes rite and ceremony. Except as a means of provocation, to outrage the public or incite rebellion, Breton despised openair spectacles. The fiesta should be celebrated in the catacombs. Each of the surrealist exhibitions revolved around a contradictory axis: scandal and secret, consecration and profanation. Consecration and conspiracy are kindred terms; revelation is also rebellion. The *other*, our double, denies the illusory coherence and security of our conscience, that pillar of smoke which supports our arrogant philosophical and religious constructions. The *others*, proletarians and colonial slaves, primitive myths and revolutionary utopias, threaten with no less violence the beliefs and institutions of the West. Breton extends his hand to both, to Fourier and to the Papuas from New Guinea. Rebellion and revelation, language and passion, are manifestations of a single reality. The true name of that reality is also double: innocence and marvel. Man is creator of marvels, is a poet, because he is an innocent being. Children, women, lovers, those inspired and even the mad are the embodiment of the marvelous. All they do is unexpected and unpremeditated. They don't know what they do: they're irresponsible, innocent. Magnets, lightning rods, highpower cables: their words and deeds are nonsensical and yet have a meaning. They are the scattered signs of a language in constant movement which spreads before our eyes a fan of contradictory meanings—resolved at last in a unique and ultimate sense. Through them and in them the universe talks to us and to itself.

I've repeated some of his words: revelation and rebellion, innocence and marvel, passion and language. There is another: magnetism. Breton was one of the centers of gravity of our age. Not only did he believe that men are governed by the laws of attraction and repulsion but that his person was itself an embodiment of those forces. All of us who had anything to do with him experienced that dual, dizzying feeling: fascination and the centrifugal impulse. I confess that for a long time I was kept awake by the worry that I might do or say something to provoke his reproof. I believe many of his friends had a similar experience. Just a few years ago Buñuel invited me to view, in private, one of his films. When it was over, he asked me: "Will Breton find it to be in the surrealist tradition?" I cite Buñuel not only as a great artist, but because he is a man of really exceptional integrity of character and freedom of spirit. These feelings, experienced by all those who visited Breton regularly, had nothing to do with fear of or respect for a superior (though I believe that, if there are superior men, Breton was one of them). I never saw him as a chief, still less as a Pope, to use the ignoble term popularized by certain fools. Despite my friendship with him personally, my activities with the surrealist group were tangential. Still, his affection and generosity always confused me, from the beginning of our relationship to the end of his days. I have never known why he put up with me: perhaps because I was from Mexico, a country he always loved? Beyond these private considerations, I should say that I write as if I were engaged in silent dialogue with Breton: reply, answer, coincidence, disagreement, homage, all together. Even as I write now I experience that feeling.

In my adolescence, during a period of isolation and exaltation, I read by chance some pages which, I learned later, form chapters of *L'amour fou*. In them Breton describes his climb to the summit of the Teides, in Tenerife. That text, read at almost the same time as Blake's *The Marriage of Heaven and Hell*, opened the doors of modern poetry to me. It was an "art of love," not in the trivial way of Ovid's, but as an initiation into something which later life and my experience of the Orient have confirmed: the analogy, or better said, the identity between woman and nature. Is the water feminine or is woman a surge of waves, a nocturnal river, a dawn beach tattooed by the wind? If we are a metaphor of the universe, the human couple is the metaphor par excellence, the point in which all forces meet, the seed of all forms. The couple is, again, reconquered time, time before time. Against wind and tide, I have tried to be true to that revelation; the word *love* preserves intact all its powers over me. Or as he says, "On n'en sera plus jamais quitte avec ces frondaisons de l'age d'or." In all his writing, first to last, this obstinate belief in a paradisiac age appears, joined to the vision of the primordial couple. Woman is bridge, place of reconciliation between the natural and human world. She is solid language, embodied revelation: "Le femme n'est plus qu'un calice débordante de voyelles."

Years later, I got to know Benjamin Péret, Leonora Carrington, Wolfgang Paalen, Remedios Varo, and other surrealists who had sought refuge in Mexico during the Second World War. Peace came and I saw Benjamin again in Paris. He took me to the café at Place Blanche. For a long time I saw Breton regularly. Though regular contact is not always beneficial to the exchange of ideas and feelings, more than once I felt that current which really joins speakers together, even if their points of view are not identical. I shall never forget, among all those conversations, one which we had in the summer of 1964, shortly before I was to return to India. I remember it not because it was the last but because of the atmosphere that surrounded it. This is not the occasion to recount that episode (one day, I promise myself, I will). For me it was an *encounter*, in the sense which Breton gave the word: predestination and, at the same time, election. That night, as we walked alone together through the neighborhood of Les Halles, the conversation veered toward a theme which preoccupied him: the future of the surrealist movement. I remember saying to him, roughly, that for me surrealism was the sacred illness of our world, like leprosy in the Middle Ages or the Spanish "illuminati" of the sixteenth century; a necessary negation of the West, it would live much as modern civilization did, independent of political systems and the ideologies that would predominate in the future. My exaltation impressed him, but he replied, "Negation lives as a function of affirmation and vice versa; I very much doubt that the world beginning now can be defined as affirmation or negation: we come into a neutral zone and the surrealist rebellion should express itself in forms which are neither negation nor affirmation . . ." It is not outrageous to suggest that this idea inspired the last exhibition of the group: absolute separation. This is not the first time Breton asked for the "concealment" of surrealism, but he seldom declared his wish so decisively. Perhaps he thought the movement would recover its fertility only if it demonstrated its ability to change itself into an underground force. Return to the catacombs? I don't know. I asked myself if in a society like ours, in which the old contradictions have vanished—not to the benefit of the principle of identity but by a kind of universal annulment and devaluation—what Mallarmé called "restricted action" still has meaning: is publishing still a form of action, or is it a way of dissolving it in the anonymity of publicity?

It is often said that the ambiguity of surrealism consists of the fact that it was a movement of poets and painters which, nonetheless, refuses to be judged by aesthetic criteria. Is this not the case with all past artistic trends and with all the works of the great poets and painters? "Art" is an invention of aesthetics, which, in turn, is an invention of philosophers. Nietzsche buried both and danced on their tomb: what we call art is a game. The surrealist desire to erase the borders between art and life is not new; what are new are the terms in which it expressed itself, and new also is the meaning of its action. Neither "artistic life" nor "vital art": to return to the word's origin, to the moment at which speaking is synonymous with creating. I do not know what future there is for the surrealist group; I am sure that the current which runs from German romanticism and from Blake to surrealism will not disappear. It will live at the margin. It will be the *other* voice.

Surrealism, critics say, is no longer the vanguard. Besides the fact that I dislike that military term, I do not believe that novelty, that being on the point of happening, is an essential characteristic of surrealism. Not even Dada had that frenetic cult of the new which the futurists, for example, postulated. Neither Dada nor surrealism worships machines. Surrealism profaned them: unproductive machines, "élevages de poussière," melting watches. The machine as a method of criticism of the worship of machine and of men who worship progress and its farces. Is Duchamp the beginning or the end of painting? By his oeuvre and even more by his attitude which denied the oeuvre, Duchamp concludes a period of Western art (that of painting properly speaking) and opens another which is no longer "artistic": the dissolution of art in life, language in the closed circle of the game of words, reason in its philosophical antidote—laughter. Duchamp dissolves the modern with the same gesture he uses to deny tradition. In the case of Breton, moreover, there is the vision of time not as a succession but as the constant, though invisible, presence of an innocent present. The future struck him as fascinating because it was the territory of the unexpected: not what will be according to reason, but what might be according to imagination. The destruction of the actual world would permit the appearance of real time, not historical but natural, not ruled by progress but by desire. This, if I have it right, was his idea of a Communist-libertarian society. He never thought that there was an essential contradiction between myths and utopias, poetry and revolutionary programs. He read Fourier as we can read the Vedas or the Popol Vuh, and the Eskimos' poems struck him as revolutionary prophecies. The most ancient past and the furthest future came together naturally in his spirit. Similarly: his materialism was not a vulgar "scientism," nor was his irrationality a hatred of reason.

The decision to embrace opposite terms—Sade and Rousseau, Novalis and Roussel, Juliette and Eloise, Marx and Chateaubriand—appears constantly in his writings and in his actions. Nothing is further removed from this attitude than the complacent tolerance of skepticism. In the world of thought he hated eclecticism, and in the world of eroticism he hated promiscuity. The best parts of his work—prose as well as verse—are those pages inspired by the idea of election and the correlative of fidelity to that election, whether in art or in politics, in friendship or in love. This idea was the axis of his life and the center of his conception of the single love: the luminosity of passion cut by liberty, an unalterable diamond. Our age has freed love from the prisons of the last century only to turn it into an anonymous pastime, one more consumer item in a society of extremely busy consumers. Breton's vision is the denial of almost everything which passes today for love and even for eroticism (another word carelessly handled like the paltriest coin). It is hard to understand completely his unreserved attachment to the work of Sade. True, he was moved and exalted by the absolute character of Sade's negation, but how to reconcile this with the belief in love, center of the golden age? Sade denounces love: it is a hypocrisy or, worse still, an illusion. His system is raving, not incoherent: his denial is no less complete than the affirmation of Saint Augustine. Both repudiate with identical violence all Manichaeism; for the Christian saint evil has no ontological reality; for Sade what lacks reality is what we call the good: his version of the *Social Contract* is the statutes of the Society of the Friends of Crime.

Bataille tried to turn Sade's monologue into a dialogue and set against absolute eroticism a no less absolute interlocutor: the Christian God. The result was silence and laughter: "atheology." The unthinkable and the unnameable. Breton set out to reintroduce love into eroticism or, more precisely, to consecrate eroticism by love. Again: his opposition to all religions implies a will to consecrate. And more, a will to reconcile. Commenting on a passage of the *Nouvelle Justine*—the episode in which one of the characters mixes his sperm with Etna lava—Breton observes that the act is a love homage to nature, "une façon, des plus folles, des plus indiscutables de l'aimer." True, his admiration for Sade was almost boundless and he always thought that "tant qu'on ne sera pas quitte avec l'idée de la transcendance d'un bien quelconque . . . la représentation exaltée du mal inné gardera la plus grande valeur révolutionnaire." With this reservation, in the dialogue between Sade and Rousseau, he inclines irresistibly to the latter, the friend of primitive man, the lover of nature. Love is not an illusion: it is the mediation between man and nature, the place in which earthly and spiritual magnetism cross.

Each facet of his work reflects the others. It is not the passive reflection of the mirror: it is not a repetition but a reply. Contrary beams of light, a dialogue of luminosities. Magnetism, revelation, thirst, and innocence and, at the same time, disdain. Haughty? Yes, in the noble sense of the word: a bird of prey, a bird of the heights. All the words of this family—haughty, high—suit him. He was raised up, exalted, his poetry exalts us, and, above all, he said that the bodies of woman and man were our only altars. And death? Each man is born and dies at various times. It is not the first time that Breton dies. He knew it better than anyone: each of his central books is the story of a resurrection. I know that it is different now and that we will not see him again. This death is no illusion. All the same, Breton lived certain moments, saw certain evidences which are the negation of time and of what we call a normal perspective on time. I call those instants poetic, though they are experiences common to all men: the only difference is that the poet remembers them and tries to embody them in words, sounds, colors. Whoever has lived those moments and is able to bend to their meaning knows that the "I" does not save itself because it does not exist. He knows too that, as Breton himself often stressed, the borders between dream and waking, life and death, time and timeless presence, are fluid and indecisive. We do not know what it really is to die, except that it is the end of the "I"—the end of prison. Breton broke that prison various times, enlarged or denied time, and, for an unmeasured moment, coincided with the *other* time. This experience, nucleus of his life and of his thought, is invulnerable and untouchable: it is beyond time, beyond death—beyond us. Knowing this reconciles me to his recent death and to all death.

—*Alternating Current*, 1967

HENRI MICHAUX

I.

In recent years, Henri Michaux has published three books in which he tells of his encounters with mescaline *(Misérable miracle* [1956]; *L'infini turbulent* [1957]; *Paix dans les brisements* [1959]). To this must be added a disturbing series of drawings—the majority in black and white, others in color—carried out shortly after each experience. Prose, poems, and drawings interpenetrate, extend, and illuminate one another. The drawings do not merely illustrate the texts. Michaux's painting has never been subsidiary to his poetry: it is a case of worlds that are at once autonomous and complementary. But in the case of the mescaline experience the lines and the words form an entity that is difficult to separate. Shapes, ideas, and sensations tangle about each other as though they were a single, dizzying creature. In a sense the drawings, far from being *illustrations* of the written word, are a kind of *commentary*. The rhythm and movement of the lines make one think of an unusual musical notation, except that we are faced not with a notation of sounds or ideas but of vertigos, lacerations, and regatherings of being. Incisions in the cortex of time, halfway between the ideographic sign and the magic inscription, characters and shapes "more perceptible than legible," these drawings are a critique of poetic and pictorial writing, that is, an extension of the sign and the image, something beyond word and line.

Painting and poetry are languages with which Michaux has striven to say something specifically unsayable. A poet, he began to paint when he perceived that this new medium would allow him to say what his poetry could no longer say. But is it a matter of saying? Perhaps Michaux has never set out to say. All of his attempts are directed at touching that zone, by definition inexpressible and unshareable, in which meanings vanish. A center null and replete, empty and full of itself at the same time. The sign and the signified—the distance between the object and the consciousness that contemplates it—evaporate in the overwhelming presence which alone exists. The work of Michaux—poems, real and imaginary journeys, paintings—is a long and sinuous expedition in the direction of some of our infinities—the most secret, the most fearful, and, at the same time, the most laughable—always in search of the *other* infinity.

Michaux travels in his languages: lines, words, colors, silences, rhythms. And he is not afraid to break the backbone of a word as the horseman who does not hesitate to wind a mount. To get—where? To that nowhere which is everywhere and here. Language-vehicle but also language-knife and miner's lamp. Language-cauterizer and language-bandage, language-fog and siren in the fog. Pickax against rock and lightning in the depths of night. Words become tools. Once more, extensions of the hand, the eye, thought. Nonartistic language. Cutting and severing words, reduced to their most immediate and aggressive function: opening a way for themselves. Yet it is a matter of paradoxical utility, since they are no longer at the service of communication but of the inexpressible. A nonhuman and maybe a superhuman enterprise. The extraordinary tension of Michaux's language is due to the fact that all his honed efficiency is governed by a will hurled into the encounter with something which is inefficient par excellence: that state of not knowing what absolute knowledge is, the thought which no longer thinks because it has merged with itself, the infinite transparency, the unmoving whirlwind.

Misérable miracle opens with these words: "This is an exploration. By means of the word, the sign, the drawing. Mescaline is what is explored." When I finished the book I asked myself if the result of the experience hadn't been the opposite: the poet Michaux explored by mescaline. Exploration or encounter? More the latter. Hand to hand with the drug, with the tremor of the earth, with the tremor of the being shaken by his inner foe—a foe that fuses itself with our own being, a foe indistinguishable and inseparable from us. Encounter with mescaline: encounter with ourselves, with the known-unknown. The double who wears our own face for a mask. The face which erases and transforms itself into an enormous mocking grin. The devil. The clown. That's not me. That is me. Martyrissible apparition. And when the face turns, there is no one. I too have left myself. Space, space, pure vibration. Great gift, present of the gods, mescaline is a window where the gaze slips away infinitely without finding anything but itself gazing. There is no I: there is a space, vibration, perpetual liveliness. Struggles, terrors, exaltations, panics, delights: is it Michaux or mescaline? It was all there in his earlier books. Mescaline was a *confirmation*. Mescaline: witness. The poet saw his inner space in the space outside. Transit from inner to outer—an outside which is interiority itself, the nucleus of reality. Atrocious, unspeakable spectacle. Michaux can say: I stepped out of my life to glimpse life.

It all begins with a vibration. Imperceptible movement which minute by minute gains momentum. Wind, a long whistling, whetted hurricane, torrent of faces, shapes, lines. Everything falling, advancing, climbing, vanishing, reappearing. Dizzying evaporation and condensation. Bubbles, bubbles, cobblestones, gravel. Stones of gas. Lines that intersect, rivers that join, infinite bifurcations, meanderings, deltas, deserts that advance, deserts that fly. Scatterings, agglutinations, fragmentations, re-formings. Broken words, coupling of syllables, fornication of meanings. Destruction of language. Mescaline rules by silence—and screams, screams without a mouth and we fall into its silence! Return to the vibrations, entry into undulations. Repetitions: mescaline is a "mechanism of the infinite." Heterogeneity, continual welling up of fragments, particles, pieces. Exasperated series. Nothing is fixed. Avalanches, rule of the uncountable number, execrable proliferation. Gangrened space, cancerous time. Is there no center? Shaken by the blast of mescaline, sucked at by the abstract whirlwind, the modern Westerner finds nothing to grasp. He has forgotten the names, God is no longer called God. For the Aztec and the Tarahumara Indian it was enough to pronounce the name for the divine presence to come down, in its infinite manifestations. Unity and plurality of the ancients. For us, lacking gods: Pullulation and Time. We have lost the names. We are left with "causes and effects, antecedents and consequences." Space full of insignificances. Heterogeneity is repetition, amorphous mass. Miserable miracle.

The first encounter with mescaline ends with the discovery of a "mechanism of the infinite." The infinite production of colors, rhythms, and forms reveals itself to be in the end a terrifying and laughable cascade of trifles. We are fairground millionaires. The second series of experiences

(L'infini turbulent) occasioned unexpected reactions and visions. Exposed to continuous physiological discharges and to an implacable psychic tension, being opened up. The exploration of mescaline, like a fire or an earthquake, was devastating; only the essential remained standing, what was, because infinitely frail, infinitely strong. What is this power called? Is it a faculty, a power, or, better said, an absence of power, the total helplessness of man? I think it is the last. That helplessness is our strength. At the final moment, when nothing remains in us—loss of the I, loss of identity—the fusion occurs with something alien which is, nonetheless, our own, the only thing that is truly ours. The hollow, the hole which we are in, is filled to overflowing, until it becomes a fountain. In the extreme drought water springs. Perhaps there is a point of union between man's being and that of the universe. For the rest, nothing positive: hole, abyss, turbulent infinity. State of abandonment, alienation—but not madness. Madmen are locked in their madness, which is, so to speak, an ontological mistake: taking the part for the whole. Equidistant from sanity and madness, the vision Michaux tells of is total: contemplation of the demonic and the divine—there is no alternative to those terms—as an inseparable reality, as the ultimate reality. Of man or of the universe? I don't know. Perhaps of universe-man. Man penetrated, overcome by the universe.

The demonic trance was above all the revelation of a transhuman eroticism—and thus infinitely perverse. A psychic violation, an insidious opening and extending and unfolding of the most secret parts of being. Nothing sexual. An infinitely sensual universe from which the human body and form had vanished. Not the "triumph of matter" or of flesh but the vision of the other side of the spirit. Abstract lust: "Dissolution—the right word which I understood in a flash . . . I revel in deliquescence." Temptation, in the literal sense of the word, the sense to which all great mystics (Christians, Buddhists, Muslims) have referred. Nonetheless, I confess that I do not entirely understand this passage. Perhaps Michaux's aversion stems less from contact with Eros than from the vision of cosmic confusion, that is, from the revelation of chaos. The depths of the being laid bare, the other side of the presence, the chaos is the primordial clay, the ancient disorder and, at the same time, the universal matrix. I experienced a similar sensation, though less intense, which affected only the most superficial areas of my consciousness, in the huge summer of India during my first visit in 1952. Fallen into the great panting mouth, the universe seemed to me an immense, multiple fornication. I glimpsed then the meaning of the architecture of Konarak and of ascetic eroticism. The vision of chaos is a kind of ritual bath, a regeneration by immersion in the original fountain, a genuine return to the "earlier life." Primitive men, Chinese Taoists, archaic Greeks, and other people do not fear the tremendous contact. The Western attitude is unhealthy. It is moral. Great isolator, great separator, morality splits man in two. To return to unity of vision is to reconcile body, soul, and world. At the end of the attempt Michaux recalls a fragment of a tantric poem:

> Inaccessible to impregnations,
> Enjoying all enjoyments,
> Touching all like the wind,
> Penetrated by all like the sky,
> The *yoguin* always pure
> Bathes in the perpetual river.
> Enjoys all enjoyments and nothing stains him.

The divine vision—inseparable from the demonic, since both are revelations of *unity*—began with the "apparition of the gods." Thousands, hundreds of thousands, one after another, in long queues, an infinity of august faces, horizon of beneficent presences. Astonishment and recognition. But first: sea swells of whitenesses. Everywhere whiteness, sonorous, shining. And light, seas of light. Later, the images of the gods disappeared, though the peaceful and enjoyable cascade of being did not stop welling out. Admiration: "I hold to the divine perfection of the continuance of Being throughout time, a continuance so beautiful—beautiful beyond the limits of knowledge—that the gods, as the *Mahabarata* says, the gods themselves grow jealous and come to admire it." Confidence, faith (in what? just faith), a sense of passing with the perfection that passes (and does not pass), tireless, equal with itself. An instant is born, rises, opens out, vanishes at the moment when another instant is born and rises. Joy after joy. Ineffable abandonment and security. The vision of the gods is followed by nonvision: we're at the center of time. This trip is a return: a falling away, an unlearning, return to birth. Reading these pages of Michaux I remembered something the painter Paalen showed me some years ago: a chunk of quartz on which the image of old Tlaloc, the rain god, was incised. He went to the window and let the sun shine through it:

> Touched by the light
> The quartz becomes a cascade.
> On the waters floats the god, a child.

The nonvision: outside reality, history, purposes, calculations, hatred, love, "beyond resolutions and irresolutions, *beyond choices,*" the poet returns to a perpetual birth and hears "the endless poem, without rhymes, without music, without words, which the Universe ceaselessly proclaims." The divine experience is participation in an infinite which is measure and rhythm. Inevitably the words water, music, light, great open space, resonant, come to the lips. The I vanishes but in the hollow it has left no other I takes its place. No god but rather the divine. No particular faith but rather the feeling that precedes and sustains all faith, all hope. No face but the being without face, the being which is all faces. Peace in the crater, reconciliation of man—what remains of him—with the total presence.

As he sets out on his experience, Michaux writes: "I intend to explore the mediocre human condition." That phrase—which can be applied as well to all of Michaux's work and to the work of any great artist—proved quite false in its second part. The exploration showed that man is not a mediocre creature. One part of him—walled up, obscured from the beginning of the beginning—is open to the infinite. The so-called human condition is a point at which other forces intersect. Perhaps our condition is not human.

—Paris, 1961

II. The Prince and the Clown

To see is an act that postulates the ultimate identity between the beholder and the beheld. A postulate which needs neither proof nor demonstration: the eyes, when they see this or that, confirm the reality of what they see quite as much as their own reality. Mutual recognition: I recognize myself in what I recognize. To see is the original, paradisiac tautology. Mirror happiness: I discover myself in my images. What I look at is what looks: myself. A coincidence which unfolds: I am an image among my images and each of them, showing that it is real, confirms that I am real as well. . . Soon, very soon, the coincidence breaks: I do not recognize myself in what I see nor do I recognize it. The world has taken leave of itself, gone I don't know where. There is no world. Or have I taken leave of myself? There is nowhere to go. There is a fault—in the geological sense: not a flaw but a fissure—and through it the images drain away. The eye recoils. One must extend a bridge, many bridges, between one shore of reality and the other, between beholder and beheld: language, languages. By those bridges we cross the null zones that divide this from that, here from there, now from before or after. But there are some who are obdurate—a few each century—who prefer not to move. They say that bridges do not exist or that movement is illusory; though we are ceaselessly restless and go from one place to another, in fact we have not changed places at all. Henri Michaux is one of those few. Fascinated, he approaches the edge of the precipice and, for many years now, gazes fixedly. What does he look at? The hollow, the wound, absence.

Whoever gazes at the fault is not seeking recognition. He does not look to confirm his reality in the reality of the world. Looking becomes a negation, an asceticism, a critical act. Looking as Michaux looks is to untie the knot of reflections into which the sense of sight has turned the world. To look in this fashion is to stanch the spring, the fountain of certainties at once radiant and meaningless, to break the mirror in which images, in self-contemplation, sip at themselves. To look with that gaze is to walk backward, unwalk the way one has come, go back until arrival at the end of all roads. To arrive at blackness. What is blackness? Michaux has written: "le noir ramene au fondement, a l'origine" ("black brings one back to the foundation, the origin"). But the origin is what draws further off as we approach it. It is a point on the line that describes a circle, and at that point, according to Heraclitus, beginning and periphery are confused together. Blackness is a foundation but also a precipice. Blackness is a well and the well is an eye. To gaze is not to recover the images that have fallen into the well of origin but to fall oneself into that well that is bottomless, without beginning. To fall into oneself, into one's eye, one's well. To contemplate in the pond, now waterless, the gradual evaporation of our shadow. Gazing thus is to witness the conjugations of blackness and the dispersions of transparency.

For Michaux painting has been a journey into himself, a spiritual descent. One trial, one passion. Also a lucid account of vertigo: during the interminable falling he kept his eyes open and was able to decipher, in the green and black stains on the sides of the well shaft, the inscriptions of fear, terror, madness. On a piece of paper, on his work table, by the light of a lamp, he saw a face, many faces: the solitude of the creature in threatening spaces. Journeys through the tunnels of the spirit and those of physiology, expeditions through the infinitesimal immensities of sensations, impressions, perceptions, representations. Histories, geographies, cosmologies of the countries of the interior, undefined, fluid, perpetually decomposing and gestating, with their ferocious vegetation, their spectral populations. Michaux is the painter of apparitions and disappearances. It is common, in considering his works, to praise his fantasy. I must confess that I am moved by their *accuracy*. They are true snapshots of horror, anxiety, dereliction. Or rather: we live among indefinable powers, but, though we do not know their true names, we know they take shape in sudden, momentary images, that they are horror, anguish, and despair *in person*. Michaux's creatures are unexpected revelations which, nonetheless, we recognize: we had already seen, in a gap of time, closing our eyes or turning our head, at an undefended moment, those atrocious and malevolent or suffering, vulnerable, and wounded features. Michaux does not invent: he sees. He astonishes us because he shows us what is hidden in the creases of our souls. All those creatures inhabit us, live and sleep with us. We are at the same time the fields they cultivate and their battlefields.

a refinement that does not exclude ferocity and humor. Fast, nervous painting, shaken by electric currents, painting with wings and beaks and claws. Michaux paints with the body, with all his senses together, mixed up, tensed, as if he wished to make the canvas the field of battle or of play for sensations and perceptions. Battle, play: also music. There is a rhythmic element in his painting. The hand sees, the eye hears. What does it hear? The surf of colors and inks, the whisper of lines which run together, the dry cries of the signs, insects that do battle on the leaves. The eye hears the circulation of the great impalpable forms in the empty spaces. Whirlwinds, whirlpools, explosions, migrations, floods, landslides, jungles, confabulations. Painting of movement, painting in movement.

The experience of drugs was also, in its way, a physical experience like the battle with his graphic materials. The result was, similarly, a psychic liberation. The well became a fountain. Mescaline released the flow of drawings, engravings, reflections, and notes in prose, poems. I have already spoken of Michaux's experiences of hallucinogenic drugs. As powerful as the action of the drugs—and more constant, since it has stayed with him through all of his adventures—has been the influence of humor. In current language the word *humor* has an almost entirely psychological meaning: a disposition of temperament and spirit. But humor is also a liquid, a substance, and thus it can be compared with drugs. In medieval and Renaissance medicine, the melancholy temperament depended not only on a disposition of spirit but on the combined influence of Saturn and black bile. The affinity between the melancholy temperament, a black "humor," and a predisposition to arts and letters fascinated the ancients. In the *Problems,* Aristotle affirms that in certain individuals "the seat of bile is near the seat of the intelligence and that is why fury and enthusiasm overcome them, as happens with Sybils and Bacchantes and with all those inspired by the gods . . . Melancholics surpass other men in letters, the arts and public life." Among the great melancholics Aristotle cites are, preeminently, Heraclitus and Democritus. Ficino picks up this idea and weaves it together with the astrological motif of Saturn: "Melancholy or black bile fills the head with vapors, fires the brain and oppresses the spirit night and day with gloomy and frightening visions . . ." From Ficino to Agrippa and from Agrippa to

Dürer and his *Melencholia I*, Shakespeare and *Hamlet*, Donne, Juana Inés de la Cruz, the romantics, the symbolists . . . in the West melancholy has been the disease of the contemplative and spiritual.

In the composition—chemical and spiritual—of Michaux's black ink there is a Saturnine element. One of his earliest works is called *Prince of Night* (1937). It is a sumptuous and funereal character who, inevitably, calls to mind Nerval's Prince of Aquitaine of the sonnet "El desdichado." From almost the same period there is another gouache, its double and replica: *Clown*. The relation between Prince and Clown is intimate and ambiguous. It is the relationship between the hand and the cheek: "Je le gifle, je le gifle, je le mouche ensuite par dérision." That is also the relation between the sovereign and the subject: "Dans ma nuit, j'assiège mon Roi, je me lève progressivement et je lui tords le cou. Je le secoue et le secoue comme un vieux prunier, et sa couronne tremble sur sa tête. Et pourtant, c'est mon Roi. Je les sais et il le sait, et c'est bien sûr que je suis à son service." But who is the king and who is the clown? The secret of the identity of each character and of their transformations is in the black ink's well. The apparitions spring from the black and return to it. In the Western pictorial tradition humor does not abound, and the modern works in which it appears can be counted on the fingers, from Duchamp and Picabia to Klee and from Max Ernst to Matta. Michaux's intervention in this domain has been decisive and brilliant. The phosphorescent beings that spring from his well of black ink are no less surprising than those which rise out of the amphoras where djins are bottled up.

Michaux's earliest attempts at graphics were line drawings and "alphabets." The *sign* attracted him from the outset. A sign freed of its conceptual burden and closer, in the oral domain, to onomatopoeia than to the word. Painting and writing are crossbred in Michaux without ever becoming confused. His poetry aspires to be pure rhythm, while his painting is shot through with the desire to say. In the first, a nostalgia for the line, in the second, for the word. But his poems, at the frontiers of Pentecost and silence, say; and his pictures, at the frontiers of saying, are silent. What his painting says cannot be translated to the language of poetry, and vice versa. All the same, both flow together: the same maelstrom fascinates them. World of apparitions, accumulations and dissolvings of forms, world of lines and arrows that riddle receding horizons: movement is continual metamorphosis, space unfolds, is dispersed, is scattered in animated fragments, joins back with itself, spins, is an incandescent ball which rolls across a blasted plain, stops at the edge of the paper, is a drop of ink pregnant with reptiles, is a drop of time that bursts and falls in a hard rain of seeds that lasts a thousand years. Michaux's creatures undergo all changes, from petrification to evaporation. Smoke hardens into mountain, stone is malleable and, if you blow on it, it vanishes, becomes a gust of air. Genesis, but genesis in reverse: forms, sucked at by the maelstrom, return to their origin. Forms falling toward their antique forms, embryonic, before the I and before language itself. Stains, jungles. Then, everything vanishes. Now we face the unlimited, what Michaux calls the "transreal." Before forms and names. The beyond of the visible which is also the beyond of the sayable. End of painting and of poetry. In a final metamorphosis Michaux's painting opens out and shows that, in truth, there is nothing to see. In that instant everything begins again: the unlimited is not outside but within us.

—Mexico D.F., 6 October 1977

DOSTOEVSKI: THE DEVIL AND THE IDEOLOGUE

A century ago, on 28 January 1881, Feodor Dostoevski died. From that time his influence has grown and spread, first in his own country, where during his lifetime he had already achieved fame, and afterward in Europe, America, and Asia. This influence has not been exclusively literary but also spiritual and vital: several generations have read his novels not as fictions but as studies of the human soul, and hundreds of thousands of readers throughout the world have in imagination talked and argued with his characters as if they were old acquaintances. His work has touched spirits as different as Nietzsche and Gide, Faulkner and Camus; in Mexico two writers read him with passion, no doubt because they belonged to his own intellectual family and recognized themselves in many of his ideas and obsessions: Vasconcelos and Revueltas. He is (or was) a writer preferred by the young: I still remember the endless conversations I carried on, when I was finishing my B.A., with some of my classmates on long walks which began at nightfall in San Ildefonso and ended after midnight in Santa Maria or on Avenida de los Insurgentes, looking out for the last tram. Ivan and Dimitri Karamazov fought it out in each one of us.

Nothing was more natural than that fervor: despite the century which divides us from him, Dostoevski is our great contemporary. Very few writers of the past have his presence: to read his novels is to read a chronicle of the twentieth century. But his presence is not that of intellectual or literary novelty. In his tastes and his aesthetic concerns he is a writer of another age; he is prolix, and, were it not for his oddly modern humor, many of his pages would be boring. His historical world is not ours. *Diary of a Writer* contains many passages which repel me with their Slavism and their anti-Semitism. His anti-European tirades remind me, though they are more inspired than these, of the ventings and resentments of Mexican and Latin American nationalism. His vision of history is sometimes profound but also confused: it lacks that understanding of event, at once quick and sharp, which delights us in a writer like Stendhal. Nor did he have the eye of Tocqueville, which sees through the surface of a society and an age. He was not, like Tolstoi, an epic chronicler. He does not tell us what happens but he obliges us to go down under ground so that we see *what is* happening really: he obliges us to see ourselves. Dostoevski is our contemporary because he guessed what the dramas and conflicts of our age would be. And he guessed not because he had the gift of prophecy or was able to see future events, but because he had the ability to get inside souls.

He was one of the first—perhaps *the* first—who took account of modern nihilism. He has left us descriptions of that spiritual phenomenon which are unforgettable and which, even today, shake us with their insight and their mysterious precision. The nihilism of antiquity was related to skepticism and epicureanism; his ideal was a noble serenity: to achieve equanimity despite the accidents of fortune. The nihilism of ancient India, which so impressed Alexander and his companions, according to Plutarch, was a philosophical attitude not without analogy to pyrrhonism and which culminated in the contemplation of vacuity. For Nāgārjuna and his followers, nihilism was the antechamber of religion. But modern nihilism, though it too is born of intellectual conviction, does not open out into philosophical impassivity or the beatitude of indifference; rather, it is an inability to believe or affirm something, a spiritual more than a philosophical failure.

Nietzsche imagined the coming of a "complete nihilist," embodied in the Superman, who plays, dances, and laughs in the spirals of the Eternal Return. The Superman's dance celebrates universal *insignificance,* the evaporation of meaning and the subversion of values. But the true nihilist, as Dostoevski saw more realistically, neither dances nor laughs: he goes from here to there—around his room or, it's the same to him, around the world—without ever being able to rest but also without being able to do anything. He is condemned to go round and round, talking to his phantoms. His sickness, like that of Sade's libertines or the *accidie* of

the medieval monks, attacked by the midday devil, is a continual dissat-
isfaction, an inability to love anyone or anything, a restlessness without
object, a disgust of the self—and a love of the self. The modern nihilist,
poor Narcissus, sees in the water's depth his reflection shattered into
pieces. The vision of his fall fascinates him: faced with himself, nausea
grips him, but he cannot look away. Quevedo guessed at this state in two
lines that are hard to forget: "las aguas del abismo/donde me enamoraba
de mi mismo" ("the waters of the abyss where I was falling in love with
myself").

Stavrogin, protagonist of *The Devils* (less literal—the old translation
The Possessed was more exact), writes to Daria Pavlovna, who loved him: "I
have set trials, everywhere, for my strength . . . During these trials, before
myself or before the others, that strength has always proven limitless.
But, what to do with it? This is what I never knew and still don't know,
despite all the courage you want to give me . . . I can feel the desire to
carry through a good deed and this pleases me; and yet I feel the same
pleasure when I want to do something bad . . . my feelings are petty, never
strong . . . I threw myself into the life of a libertine . . . but I do not love
or even like licentiousness . . . Do you believe because you love me, that
you could give some purpose to my existence? Do not be imprudent: my
love is as feeble as I am . . . Your brother told me one day that whoever
has no more ties with the earth loses his gods forthwith. That's to say, his
purposes. One can argue all of this indefinitely but I can only deny, deny
without the least grandeur of soul, without strength. In me, denial itself
is feeble. All is spongy, bland. Generous Kirilov couldn't bear *his idea*
and he blew off the top of his head . . . I could never lose my mind or
believe in an idea, the way he did . . . I could never, never, shoot myself in
the temple." How to define this situation? Dispiritedness, lack of spirit.
Stavrogin: the man whose soul has been removed.

Yet having written that letter, Stavrogin hangs himself in the garret.
The final paradox: the noose was made of silk and the suicide, with foresight, carefully, had soaped it. Fascination with death and fear of pain.
But the greatness of the nihilist resides not in his attitude nor in his
ideas but in his lucidity. His clarity redeems him from what Stavrogin
called his baseness or pettiness. Or is suicide, far from being an answer,

another test? If that is so, it is an inadequate test. No matter: the nihilist is an intellectual hero, since he dares to delve into his cloven soul, in the knowledge that he's engaged in a hopeless exploration. Nietzsche would say that Stavrogin was an "incomplete nihilist": he lacks knowledge of the Eternal Return. But perhaps it would be more precise to say that Dostoevski's character, like so many of our contemporaries, is an incomplete Christian. He has ceased believing but he has been unable to substitute others for the ancient certitudes or to live in the open, without ideas to justify or give meaning to his existence. God has disappeared, but evil has not. The loss of metaphysical referents does not extinguish sin: on the contrary, it gives it a kind of immortality. The nihilist is nearer to Gnostic pessimism than to Christian optimism and the hope of salvation. If there is no God there is no remission of sins, but evil is not abolished either: sin ceases to be an accident, a state, and becomes a permanent condition of men. It is a reversal of Augustinianism: evil is being. The utopian would like to bring heaven to earth, and make us gods; the nihilist knows himself condemned from birth; earth is already hell.

The portrait of the nihilist, is it a self-portrait? Yes and no: Dostoevski writes to escape nihilism not by suicide and negation but by affirmation and joy. The answer to nihilism, that disease of intellectuals, is the vital simplicity of Dimitri Karamazov or the supernatural joy of Alyosha. One way or the other, the answer is not in philosophy and ideas but in life. The refutation of nihilism in the innocence of the simple. Dostoevski's world is peopled by men, women, and children who are at once commonplace and prodigious. Some are anguished, others sensual, some sing in their abjection and others despair in their prosperity. There are saints and criminals, idiots and geniuses, women pious as a glass of water, and children who are angels tormented by their parents. (How different Dostoevski's vision of childhood is from Freud's!) A world of criminals and just men: for both the gates of the kingdom of heaven are open. All can save or lose themselves. The corpse of Father Zosima exhales a stench of corruption, revealing that, despite his piety, he did not die in the odor of sanctity; on the other hand, remembering the bandits and criminals who were his companions in prison in Siberia, Dostoevski says: "There man, quite soon, escapes all measure." Man, "improbable creature," can save himself at any moment. In this, Dostoevski's Christianity is kin to the ideas on liberty and grace of Calderón, Tirso de Molina, and Mira de Amescua.

For us, Dostoevski's saints and prostitutes, criminals and just men possess an almost superhuman reality; I mean to say, they are unusual beings, from another age. An age on its way to extinction: they belong to the preindustrial era. In this sense Marx was the more lucid: he foresaw the disintegration of the traditional bonds and the erosion of old ways of life by the combined action of the capitalist market and industry. But Marx did not predict the rise of a new type of men who, though calling themselves his heirs, would bring about in the twentieth century the ruin of socialist dreams and aspirations. Dostoevski was the first to describe this class of men. We know them well since in our day their number is legion: they are the sectarians and fanatics of ideology, proselytes of the Stavrogins and Ivans of our time. Their prototype is Smerdiakov, the parricide, disciple of Ivan and precursor of Stalin and so many others. The sectarians have inherited from the nihilists not their lucidity but their lack of belief. And they have converted lack of belief into a new and more base superstition. Dostoevski calls them the *possessed* because, unlike Ivan and Stavrogin, they are not aware that they are possessed by devils. That is why he compares them to the pigs in the Gospel (Luke 7:31–35). When they lose their old faith, they venerate falsely rational idols: progress, social and revolutionary utopias. They have forsworn their parents' religion, but not religion itself: instead of Christ and the Virgin Mary they adore two or three ideas out of a pamphlet. They're the ancestors of our terrorists. Dostoevski's world is that of a society sick with that corruption of religion which we call ideology. His world is the prefiguration of ours.

Dostoevski was a revolutionary in his youth. He was imprisoned for his activities, sentenced to death, and then pardoned. He spent several years in Siberia—the concentration camps of modern Russia are a perfected and amplified inheritance of the czarist system of repression—and on his return he broke with his radical past. He was conservative, Christian, monarchist, and nationalist. Even so, it would be wrong to reduce his work to an ideological definition. He was not an ideologue—though ideas have a cardinal importance in his novels—but a novelist. One of his protagonists, Dimitri Karamazov, says: *We should love life more than the sense of life*. Dimitri is an answer to Ivan, but not *the* answer: Dostoevski does not oppose one idea to another, but one human reality to another. As was not the case with Flaubert, James, or Proust, ideas are real for him, though not in themselves but as a dimension of existence. The only ideas that interested him were embodied ideas. Some come from God, that is to say, from the depth of the heart; others, the majority, come from the devil, that is to say, from the brain. As the soul was for medieval clergymen, conscience for the modern intellectual is a theater of war. The novels of Dostoevski, from this perspective, are religious parables, and his art is closer to Saint Augustine and Pascal than to modern realism. At the same time, on account of the rigor of his psychological analyses, his work anticipates Freud and, in certain ways, transcends him.

We owe to Dostoevski the most profound and comprehensive diagnosis of the modern disease: psychic schism, the divided conscience. His description is psychological and religious at the same time. Stavrogin and Ivan suffer visions: they see and speak to specters which are devils. At the same time, since both are modern, they attribute those apparitions to psychic blockages: they are projections of their troubled souls. But neither of them is very sure of that explanation. Time and again, in their conversation with their spectral visitants, they find themselves constrained to accept their reality in desperation: they really converse with the devil. The consciousness of the schism is diabolical: to be possessed means to know that the "I" is broken and there is a stranger who usurps our voice. Is that stranger the devil or ourselves? Whatever we reply, the identity of the person is divided. These passages are like hallucinations: Ivan's and Stavrogin's conversations with their devils are recounted with great realism and as if the subject were commonplace. Absurd situations and ironic reflections abound. By turns fear makes us laugh, then makes our blood run cold. We experience an ambiguous fascination: the psychological description turns imperceptibly into metaphysical speculation, this into religious vision, and, at last, religious vision into a story that mingles in an inexplicable way the supernatural and the everyday, the grotesque and the abysmal.

Dostoevski's devils are uniquely credible in modern literature. Since the eighteenth century the phantoms of our poems and novels have been unconvincing. They are comic figures, and the affectation of their language and attitudes is, at the same time, pompous and intolerable. The devils of Goethe and Valéry are plausible because of their extremely intellectual and symbolic character; acceptable too are those which present themselves in a deliberate and ironic manner as fantastic fictions: the devil in Nerval's *The Enchanted Hand* or the delicious *Devil in Love* of Cazotte. But modern devils brag of being devils and do all they can to let us know they come from there, from the underworld. They are the parvenus of the supernatural. Dostoevski's devils are modern, too, and don't resemble the old medieval and baroque devils, lascivious, extravagant, astute, and a little stupid. Dostoevski's devils are our contemporaries and possess a *clinical* reality, to put it that way. This is his great discovery: he saw the hidden resemblance between evil and infirmity, possession and reflection. His devils reason, and, as if they were psychoanalysts, they endeavor to prove their nonexistence, their imaginary nature. They tell us: I'm nothing but an obsession. And then: I am the nothing that manifests itself as obsession. I am your obsession; I am your nothing. They triumph over us (and themselves) thanks to these unanswerable arguments. Ivan and Stavrogin, two intellectuals, have no choice but to believe them: they are truly the devil since only the devil can reason in that way. But they would also be possessed by the devil if they clung to the belief that it's merely a matter of a sick mind's hallucinations. In either case, both are possessed by denial, the devil's essence. This is how the thought that terrorizes Ivan is fulfilled: to believe in the devil it is not necessary to believe in God.

There is one kind of person immune to the seduction of the devil: the ideologue. He is the man who has rooted out duality. He does not discuss: he demonstrates, indoctrinates, refutes, convinces, condemns. He calls others *comrades* but he never talks to them: he talks to *his idea*. Nor does he speak to the *other* which we all carry within us. He doesn't even suspect its existence: the *other* is an idealist fantasy, a petit-bourgeois superstition. The ideologue is the spiritual cripple: half of him is missing. Dostoevski loved the poor and the simple, the humbled and those who

CONSIDERING SOLZHENITSYN: DUST AFTER MUD

I have often heard it said that cowardice is the
mother of cruelty.

—Montaigne

In 1947, I was reading, with a chill in my soul, David Rousset's book on Hitler's concentration camps, *The Days of Our Death*. Rousset's book impressed me for two reasons: it was the account of a victim of the Nazis, but at the same time a lucid social and psychological analysis of that separate universe, the twentieth-century concentration camps. Two years later, Rousset published in the French press another declaration: the industry of homicide was flourishing in the Soviet Union as well. Many received Rousset's revelations with the horror and disbelief of one who suddenly discovers a hidden leprosy in Venus Aphrodite. The Communists and their comrades responded angrily: Rousset's allegations were a crude invention of the CIA and the propaganda services of American imperialism. "Progressive" intellectuals behaved no better than the Communists. In the magazine *Les temps modernes* Jean-Paul Sartre and Maurice Merleau-Ponty adopted a curious attitude (see issues 51 and 57 of that magazine, January and July 1950). Neither philosopher attempted to deny the deeds nor to minimize their seriousness, but both refused to draw the conclusions which the existence of the camps compelled on reflection: to what degree was Stalinist totalitarianism the result—as much as or more than of Russia's social backwardness and autocratic past—of the Leninist concept of the Party? Were not Stalin and his forced-labor camps the product of the terrorist, antidemocratic practices of the Bolsheviks from the time they took power in 1917?

Years later, Merleau-Ponty attempted to answer those questions in *The Adventures of Dialectics,* a partial corrective for a book which, at the end of his life, he very much regretted having written: *Humanism and Terror.* And Sartre: we know his views. Even in 1974 he asserts, though he deplores it, the inevitability both of violence and of dictatorship. Not of a class but of a group:

> . . . violence is necessary to change from one society to another but I do not know the nature of the order which, perhaps, will replace the present society. Will there be a dictatorship of the proletariat? To tell the truth, I don't believe so. There will always be a dictatorship exercised by representatives of the proletariat, which is something entirely different . . . *(Le monde,* 8 February 1974)

Sartre's pessimism has one advantage at least: it puts the cards on the table. But in 1950, trapped in a dilemma we now know was false, both French writers decided to condemn David Rousset: in denouncing the repressive Soviet system in the major bourgeois newspapers, their old companion had become a tool of the cold war and provided weapons for the enemies of socialism.

In those years I lived in Paris. The polemics on the Russian concentration camps moved and shook me: they put under interdict the validity of an historical enterprise that had kindled the minds of the best men of our time. The 1917 Revolution, as André Breton wrote some time before, was a fabulous beast similar to the zodiacal Aries: "Though violence nested between its horns, the whole of springtime opened in the depths of its eyes." Now those eyes observed us with the vacant gaze of the murderer. I made a summary and a selection of documents and testimonies which proved, without grounds for doubt, the existence in the USSR of a vast repressive system, founded on the forced labor of millions of human beings and integrated into the Soviet economy. Victoria Ocampo, the distinguished editor of the Argentinean magazine *Sur,* learned of my work and revealed her ethical consistency and integrity once again: she asked me to send the documentary evidence I had collected for publication in *Sur,* along with a brief explanatory note (see *Sur,* Number 19, March 1951). The reaction of progressive intellectuals was silence. No one mentioned my article, but a campaign of insinuation recurred, along with misleading suggestions initiated some years earlier by Neruda and his Mexican friends. It was a campaign that dogs me even today. The epithets change, but not the reproach: I have been successively a "cosmopolitan," "formalist," "Trotskyite," CIA agent, "liberal intellectual," and even a "structuralist at the service of the bourgeoisie"!

My commentary on the facts advanced the usual explanation: the Soviet concentration camps were a blemish that disfigured the Russian regime but did not amount to an inherent flaw in the system. To say that, in 1950, was a political error; to repeat it now, in 1974, would be something more than an error. What most impressed me, and the majority of those who in those years took an interest in the matter, was the economic function of the forced-labor camps. I believed that, unlike the Nazi camps—real extermination camps—the Soviet camps were a wicked form of exploitation, not without analogies to Stakhanovism. One of the "spurs of industrialization." I was wrong: now we know that the mortality rate in the camps, shortly before the Second World War, was 40 percent of the interned population, while the productivity of a camp laborer was 50 percent that of a free laborer (see Hannah Arendt, *Le Système Totalitaire*, p. 281, Paris, 1972). The publication of Robert Conquest's work on the great purges *(The Great Terror,* London, 1968) completes the accounts and testimonies of the survivors—the majority of them Communists—and closes the debate. Or, better said, opens it on another plane. The function of the camps was *something else.*

If the economic usefulness of the camps is more than doubtful, their political function presents peculiarities at once strange and repugnant. The camps are not a weapon in the battle against political enemies but an institution of punishment for the vanquished. The person who ends up in a camp is not an active opponent but a defeated man, defenseless and unable to offer further resistance. The same logic rules the purges and purifications: they aren't incidents in political and ideological battles but immense ceremonies of expiation and punishment. The confessions and self-accusations turn the defeated into the accomplices of their executioners, and thus the grave itself becomes a rubbish collector. Saddest of all, the majority of the internees were not (and are not) political opponents: they are "delinquents" from every level of Soviet society. In Stalin's time the population of the camps came to exceed fifteen million human beings. It has diminished since the liberal reforms of Khrushchev and today it varies between one and two million persons, of whom—according to the experts on these melancholy matters—only some ten thousand can be considered political prisoners, in the strict sense of the word. It is incredible that the rest—a million human beings—should be made up of delinquents, at any event in the sense we in our countries give to that term. The political and psychological function of the camps becomes clear: it is a matter of an institution of *preventive terror,* for lack of a better expression. The entire populace, even under the relatively more humane rule of Khrushchev and his successors, lives under threat of internment. A staggering transposition of the dogma of original sin: each Soviet citizen can be transported to a forced-labor camp. The communization of guilt includes the communization of punishment.

The publication of *The Gulag Archipelago,* and the campaign of defamation against Alexander Solzhenitsyn which culminated in his expulsion from the Soviet Union, tested again, as in 1950, the disposition and the independence of writers throughout the world. Among us in Latin America, a few protested, others kept silence; others disgraced themselves. A modish fellow who nowadays, on the official Mexican television network, sucks up to the bureaucracy that rules us and at the same time to the intellectuals that criticize it, didn't hesitate to pillory Solzhenitsyn: in the name of "abstract liberty" the Russian dissident had defamed the "most important social experiment of the twentieth century." According to this two-face, the Russian dissidents want to return to a free-enterprise system, while the defenders of real liberty are Brezhnev and Father Arrupe, Captain General of the Jesuits, who is a declared enemy of the capitalist system!

The majority of Mexican writers and journalists who have concerned themselves with Solzhenitsyn have done so with more discretion, dignity, and generosity. Nonetheless, few have spoken as frankly and courageously as José Revueltas. The Mexican novelist has revealed, once again, that revolutionary convictions are not at loggerheads with a love of truth and that a scrutiny of what occurs in countries called "socialist" itself requires a revision of the authoritarian legacy of Marxism. A revision which, I add in passing, ought to go beyond Lenin and probe the Hegelian origins of Marx's thought.

The writer of *Inventario*, the acute and almost always judicious chronicle of *Diorama De La Cultura*, probably with the intention of defending Solzhenitsyn against the snapping of the rabid pack, recalled that Lukács had, at the end of his life, considered Solzhenitsyn a true "socialist realist." I quote that paragraph:

Lukács presents the author of *The First Circle* as the most achieved exponent of socialist realism who has, socially and ideologically, the chance of discovering all the immediate and concrete aspects of society, and representing them artistically according to the laws of their own evaluation.

In the speech he wrote accepting the 1970 Nobel Prize, Solzhenitsyn spoke a few words which can summarize what Lukács meant by socialist realism, something quite distinct from those propaganda texts disguised as novels which are not realistic and much less socialist:

Literature is the memory of peoples; it transmits from one generation to the next the irrefutable experiences of men. It preserves and enlivens the flame of a history immune to all deformation, far from every lie.

Before this strange opinion, two comments occur to me. First: since its origins in 1934 "socialist realism" has been a literary-bureaucratic dogma of Stalinism, while Solzhenitsyn, a rebel writer, is more an heir to the realism of Tolstoi and Dostoevski, profoundly Slavic and Christian. Second: even if Solzhenitsyn were a "socialist realist" who does not know he is a "socialist realist," *The Gulag Archipelago* is not a novel but a work of history.

The Gulag Archipelago is not only a denunciation of the excesses of the Stalinist regime, however atrocious they may have been, but of the Soviet system itself, as it was established by Lenin and the Bolsheviks. There are two dates that form an essential part of the title of the book and its content: *1918–1956*. The work extends from the origins of the Soviet system of repression (the establishment of the Cheka in 1918) to the beginning of Khrushchev's regime. We know, moreover, that in other volumes not yet published the Russian writer concerns himself with repression in the contemporary period, that is, the period of Khrushchev and Brezhnev. Solzhenitsyn's opinions are, of course, open to dispute. See for example Roy Medvedev's criticism from the perspective of Marxism-Leninism. The Russian historian agrees that it would not be honest to conceal the serious errors of Lenin but thinks that those errors do not compromise entirely the Bolshevik historical project. Medvedev's position isn't very far from that which Merleau-Ponty and Sartre assumed in 1950, though he does not concur in the bigotry of the pious legend of the Bolsheviks. ("In Lenin and Trotsky," declared the editorial in *Les temps modernes* 51, "there isn't a single word that isn't sensible.") Halfway between Solzhenitsyn and Medvedev we find Sakharov, the great physicist and mathematician. His condemnation of Leninism is more decisive than Medvedev's, but in his criticism there is neither Slavophilia nor Christianity as in Solzhenitsyn's work. Sakharov is a liberal intellectual, in the true sense of the expression, and is closer to Herzen and Turgenev than to Dostoevski and Tolstoi.

This brief description reveals the variety of the Soviet dissidents' attitudes. A really remarkable feat is the survival—or more correctly, the continued vitality—of intellectual and spiritual currents predating the 1917 Revolution, and these, after half a century of Marxist-Leninist dictatorship, reappear and inspire men as different as the historian Andrei Amalrik and the poet Joseph Brodsky. Amalrik's historical analyses owe little to the Marxist method, and Brodsky's thought is profoundly marked by the Judaic-Christian philosophy of Leon Chestov. In fact, we are present at the resurrection of the old Russian culture. I indicated above the liberal and Europeanist affiliation of Sakharov, in the tradition of Herzen. On the other hand, Solzhenitsyn's thought is part of the tradition of that philosophical Christian current which Vladimir Soloviev (1853–1900) represented toward the end of the last century. The position the Medvedev brothers adopt is, too, an indication that a certain "Western Marxism," a social-democratic Marxism, closer to the thought of the Mensheviks than the ideas of Lenin and Trotsky, did not perish in exile with Plekanov and Martov.

The first sign of the resurrection of Russian culture, at least for us foreigners, was the publication of Pasternak's *Dr. Zhivago*. The reader will perhaps recall that in the early chapters there are allusions to the ideas and even to the persons of Soloviev and Vyacheslav Ivanov. The figure of Lara, a fusion of Russia and woman, instantly calls to mind the erotic-religious-patriotic vision of Soloviev and the cult of Sophia. Pasternak's fascination is not unique. In his youth Soloviev had so impressed Dostoevski that some of his characteristics reappear in Alyosha Karamazov. Later on the philosopher was to leave his mark on Aleksandr Blok and today he influences Solzhenitsyn. But the Russian novelist aligns himself more closely with the tradition of exalted religiousness and Slavophilia of a Seraph of Sarov and of a Tikhon Zadonsky, rather as the Patriarch Zosima is its incarnation in Dostoevski's novel (cf. *The Icon and the Axe*, James H. Billington, New York, 1968). In Solzhenitsyn there is no Russian imperialism; but there is a clear repugnance for the West, its rationalism, and its materialist democracy of soulless businessmen. On the other hand, Soloviev never concealed his sympathies with Roman Catholicism and European civilization. His two masters are, however strange it may seem, Joseph de Maistre and Auguste Comte. The actuality of Soloviev is extraordinary. Doubtless readers of *Plural* will recall the essay by the great Polish poet Czeslaw Milosz about one of his works: *Three Conversations on War, Progress, and the End of the World, with a Brief History of the Antichrist and Supplements (Plural*, 12 September 1972). In that celebrated work Soloviev prophesies, among other things, the Sino-Soviet conflict, a conflict in which he saw, not without reason, the beginning of the end.

To explore relations between the spiritual history of Russia and the contemporary dissidents is a labor beyond the limits both of this essay and of my ability. Nor have I set out to describe the ideas of Solzhenitsyn, still less to defend or attack them. The temper of that writer, the depth of his feelings, and the uprightness and integrity of his character awake spontaneously my admiration, but that admiration does not imply an adherence to his philosophy. True, as well as a moral sympathy, I feel a certain affinity with him too, a spiritual rather than an intellectual affinity. Solzhenitsyn is not only a critic of Russia and Bolshevism but of the modern age itself. What does it matter if that critique proceeds from presuppositions different from mine? Another Soviet dissident, the poet Brodsky, said to me recently in Cambridge, Massachusetts, "It all began with Descartes." I could have shrugged my shoulders and replied, "It all began with Hume . . . or Kant." I preferred to remain silent and reflect on the atrocious history of the twentieth century. I don't know when it all began; I ask myself, when will it end? Solzhenitsyn's critique is neither more profound nor more true than Thoreau's, Blake's, or Nietzsche's. Nor does it invalidate what, in our days, the great poets and rebels have said. I think of those irreducible and incorruptible figures—Breton, Russell, Camus, and a few others, some now dead, others surviving, who did not yield and have not yielded to the totalitarian blandishments of communism or fascism or the "comfort" of the consumer society. Solzhenitsyn speaks from another tradition, and this, for me, is impressive: his voice is not modern but ancient. It is an ancientness tempered in the modern world. His ancientness is that of the old Russian Christianity, but it is a Christianity which has passed through the central experience of our century—the dehumanization of the totalitarian concentration camps—and has emerged intact and strengthened. If history is the testing ground, Solzhenitsyn has passed the test. His example is not intellectual or political nor even, in the current sense of the word, moral. We have to use an even older word, a word which still retains a religious overtone—a hint of death and sacrifice: *witness*. In a century of false testimonies, a writer becomes the witness to man.

Solzhenitsyn's ideas—religious, political, and literary—are disputable, but I will not dispute them here. His book raises issues which go beyond, on the one hand, his political philosophy and, on the other, the ritual condemnation of Stalinism. This latter issue concerns me. The Bolshevik program, that is, Marxism-Leninism, is a universal program, and from that derives the interest, for non-Russian readers, of Solzhenitsyn's book. *The Gulag Archipelago* isn't a book of political philosophy but a work of history; more precisely, it is a *witnessing*—in the old sense of the word: the martyrs are witnesses—to the repressive system founded in 1918 by the Bolsheviks and which survives intact down to our days, though it has been relatively humanized by Khrushchev and does not today display the monstrous and grotesque traces of Stalinism.

The terror of the Jacobins was a temporary, emergency measure, an extraordinary recourse to meet the challenge of internal insurrection and external aggression at the same time. The Bolshevik terror began in 1918 and endures today: over half a century. In *The State and Revolution*, a book written in 1917, shortly before the attack on the Winter Palace, Lenin opposed the ideas of Karl Kautsky and the theses of the Second International—those tendencies seemed to him authoritarian and bureaucratic—and delivered an exalted eulogy of political liberty and of self-government by the workers. *The State and Revolution* contradicts many of Lenin's earlier opinions and, more decisively and significantly, all his practice from the time that his Bolshevik Party took power. Between the Leninist concept of the Bolshevik Party, "the vanguard of the proletariat," and the ardent semi-anarchism of *The State and Revolution* there is an abyss. The figure of Lenin, like all human figures, is contradictory and dramatic: the author of *The State and Revolution* was also the founder of the Cheka and the forced-labor camps, and the man who initiated the dictatorship of the Central Committee over the Party.

Would Lenin, had he survived longer, have accomplished the democratic reform of both the Party and the regime itself? We cannot know. In his so-called Will he suggested that, to avoid a bureaucratic dictatorship, the number of members of the Central Committee of the Politburo should be increased. Rather like applying a poultice to cure a cancer. The evil was not (and is not) only in the dictatorship by the Committee over the Party but of the Party over the country. In any case, Lenin's suggestion was not taken up: the Politburo of 1974 is composed, like that of 1918, of eleven members, over which a Secretary General reigns. Nor did the other Bolshevik leaders reveal an understanding of the political problem, and all of them confused in a common scorn what they called "bourgeois democracy" and human liberty. Thanks perhaps to the influence of Bukharin, Lenin adopted a political program called NEP, which saved Russia from the great economic crisis which followed the civil war. But neither Lenin nor Bukharin thought of applying the NEP's economic liberalism to political life. Let's listen to Bukharin: "Among us too other parties can exist. But here—and this is the fundamental principle that distinguishes us from the West—the only conceivable situation is this: one party rules, the others are in prison" *(Troud,* 13 November 1927). This statement is not exceptional. In 1921 Lenin said, "The place for the Mensheviks and Revolutionary Socialists, both those who admit to it and those who conceal it, is prison . . ." And to clear up any confusion between the economic liberalism of the NEP and political liberalism, Lenin writes to Kamenev in a letter dated 3 November 1922: "It is a big mistake to believe that the NEP has put an end to terror. We will have recourse to terror again and also to economic terror."

The majority of historians believe that the road which led to the Stalinist perversion began with the change from the dictatorship of the Soviets (councils of workers, farmers, and soldiers) to the dictatorship of the Party. Nonetheless, some forget that the theoretical justification of that confusion between the organs of the working class and the Party constitutes the very marrow of Leninism. Without the Party, Lenin said, there is no proletarian revolution: "The history of all nations shows that, by its own efforts, the working class is not capable of evolving beyond a syndicalist conscience." Lenin turns the working class into a minor, and makes the Party the true agent of history. In 1904, Trotsky commanded these ideas and anticipated the whole process, from the phase where the Party is above the proletariat to the phase in which the Central Committee is above the Party, and afterward to the phase in which the Politburo is above the Committee, until we reach the phase in which a dictator is above the Politburo.

Later Trotsky succumbed to the same aberration he had denounced. With his habitual clarity and coherence, in *Terrorism and Communism* (1920), he applied the Leninist ideas of the function of the "vanguard" of the Party:

> We have been accused more than once of substituting the Party dictatorship for the dictatorship of the Soviets. Nonetheless, we can affirm without risk of error that the dictatorship of the Soviets has not been possible without the dictatorship of the

Party . . . The substitution of the power of the working class by the power of the Party has not been a fortuitous or chance occurrence: the Communists express the fundamental interests of the working class . . . But, some cunning critics ask, who guarantees that it is precisely *your* Party that expresses the historical evolution? In suppressing or repressing the other parties, you have eliminated political rivalry, the source of positive contention, and thus you have deprived yourselves of the possibility of verifying the soundness of the political line you have adopted . . . This critique is inspired by a purely liberal idea of the course of the revolution . . . We have crushed the Mensheviks and the Revolutionary Socialists, and that judgment is enough for us. In any case our task is not to measure each moment, statistically, the importance of the groups that represent each tendency, but to make certain of the victory of our tendency, which is the tendency of the dictatorship of the proletariat . . .

To justify the dictatorship of the Party over the Soviets, Trotsky substitutes the quantitative and objective criterion—that is, the democratic criterion which consists in "measuring" what tendencies represent the majority and what the minority—with a qualitative, subjective criterion: the supposed ability of the Party to interpret the "true" interests of the masses, even if against the opinion and will of these.

In the last great political debate within the Bolshevik Party which ended with the destruction of the so-called Workers' Opposition (Tenth Party Congress, 1921), Trotsky said:

The Workers' Opposition has made fetishes of democratic principles. It has placed the right of the workers to elect their representatives above Party, to put it in those terms, as though the Party hadn't the right to impose its dictatorship, even if that dictatorship were temporarily to oppose the changing tendencies of workers' democracy. We must remember the historical revolutionary mission of the Party. The Party is obliged to maintain

> its dictatorship without bearing in mind the ephemeral fluctua-
> tions of spontaneous reactions among the masses and even the
> momentary vacillation of the working class . . . The dictator-
> ship does not rest at every moment on the formal principle of
> workers' democracy.

In his Will Lenin reproaches Trotsky for his arrogance ("he has too much confidence in himself") and his bureaucratic tendencies ("he is too much inclined not to consider any but the purely administrative side of things"). But Lenin did not remark that those tendencies of Trotsky's personality had been justified in and nourished by the same ideas as his own on the relationship between the Party and the working classes. The same can be said of the personal tendencies of Bukharin and Stalin: Leninism was their common theoretical and political foundation. I do not wish to compare two eminent but tragically and radically wrongheaded men, Bukharin and Trotsky, with a monster like Stalin. I only point out their common intellectual affiliation.

The Leninist notion of political power is inseparable from the notion of dictatorship; and this, in turn, is conducive to terror. Lenin was the creator of the Cheka, and the Bolsheviks of the historic period were the first to justify the execution of hostages, the mass deportations, and the liquidation of whole collectives. Before Stalin murdered the Bolsheviks, Lenin and Trotsky physically annihilated, by violent and lawless means, the other revolutionary parties, from the Mensheviks to the Anarchists and from the Revolutionary Socialists to the left-wing Communist opposition. Years later, in exile, Trotsky repented, though only in part, and conceded, in *The Betrayed Revolution* (1936), that the first thing that had to be done in Russia was to re-establish the legality of other revolutionary parties. Why only the *revolutionary* parties?

In Marxism there were authoritarian tendencies that had their origin in Hegel. Yet Marx never spoke of the dictatorship of a single party, but of something very different: temporary dictatorship of the proletariat in the period directly after the taking of power. Leninism introduced a new element: the notion of the revolutionary party, the vanguard of the pro-letariat, which implies in its name the course of society and history. The essence of Leninism is not in the generous ideas of *The State and Revolu-*

tion, which appears too in other socialist and anarchist authors, but in the concept of a party of professional revolutionaries which embodies the march of history. This party tends to turn itself inevitably into a caste, as soon as it conquers power. The history of the twentieth century has shown us time and again the inexorable transformation of revolutionary parties into pitiless bureaucracies. The phenomenon has repeated itself everywhere: dictatorship by the Communist Party of the society; dictatorship of the Central Committee over the Communist Party; dictatorship of the revolutionary Caesar over the Central Committee. The Caesar can be called Brezhnev, Mao, or Fidel: the process is the same.

The repressive Soviet system is an inverted image of the political system created by Lenin. The forced-labor camps, the police bureaucracy that administers them, the arrests without process of law, the judgments behind closed doors, the torture, the intimidation, the calumnies, the self-accusations and confessions, the general spying: all this is the consequence of the dictatorship of the sole Party and, within the Party of dictatorship, of one group and one man. The political pyramid that is the Communist system is reproduced in the inverted pyramid of their repressive system. In turn, the repression the Party exercises on the populace is reproduced in the heart of the Party itself: the elimination of external opposition is succeeded necessarily by the elimination of internal rivals and dissidents: the Bolsheviks followed the road of the Mensheviks, Anarchists, and Revolutionary Socialists. President Liu-Shao-Ch'i and his old enemy Marshal Lin Piao lie now together, mingled in the same historical opprobrium. Recourse to bloody purges and cultural revolutions is no accident: how else can the middle and upper echelons of Party directors be renewed, and how else could political disputes and rivalries be resolved? The suppression of internal democracy condemns the Party to violent periodic convulsions.

Even if we think economic structures are governed by us, it is impossible to ignore the decisive function of ideologies in historical life. Though according to Marx and Engels ideologies are mere superstructures, the truth is that these "superstructures" often outlive the "structures." Christianity outlived the bureaucratic and imperial regime of Constantine, medieval feudalism, the absolute monarchies of the seventeenth century, and the national bourgeois democracies of the nineteenth. Buddhism has

revealed even greater vitality. And what of Confucianism? It will probably survive Mao, as it has survived the Han, the Tang, and the Ming.
And, deeper than ideologies, there is another realm scarcely affected by
historical change: beliefs. Magic and astrology, to call on two well-worn
examples, have survived Plato and Aristotle, Abelard and Saint Thomas,
Kant and Hegel, Nietzsche and Freud. Thus, to explain the repressive
Soviet system we have to bear in mind various levels or strata of social
and historical reality. For Trotsky, Stalinism was above all a consequence
of the social and economic backwardness of Russia: the economic structure determined it. For other critics, it was rather the result of Bolshevik
ideology. Both explanations are, at the same time, exact and incomplete.
It seems to me that another factor is no less important: the very history
of Russia, its religious and political tradition, all that half-conscious, airy
element of beliefs, feelings, and images that constitutes what earlier historians called the *genius* (the soul) of society.

There is a clear continuity between the despotism exercised by Peter
and Catherine and that of Lenin and Trotsky, between the bloodthirsty
paranoia of Ivan the Terrible and Stalin. Stalinism and czarist autocracy
were born, grew, and fed upon Russian reality. The same must be said of
the bureaucracy and the police system. Autocracy and bureaucracy are
features which Russia probably inherited from Byzantium, along with
Christianity and the great art. Other features in Russian society are Oriental, and others have their origin in Slavic paganism. The history of
Russia is a strange mixture of sensuality and exalted spiritualism, brutality and heroism, saintliness and abject superstition. Russian "primitivism" has been described or analyzed many times, now with admiration and now with horror. It is, one must confess, a very unprimitive
primitivism: not only did it create one of the most profound, rich, and
complex literatures in the world, but it also represents a living and unique
spiritual tradition of our time. I am convinced that that tradition is called
to give life, like a spring, to the drought, the egoism, and the decay of the
contemporary West. The stories told by the survivors of the Nazi and
the Soviet concentration camps reveal the difference between Western
"modernity" and Russian "primitivism." In the case of the former, the
words ceaselessly repeated are *inhumanity, impersonality,* and *homicidal*

efficiency; while in the case of the latter, besides the horror and bestiality, words like *compassion, charity,* and *fraternity* stand out. The Russian
nation has preserved, as one can see from the contemporary writers and
intellectuals, a Christian foundation.

Russia is not primitive: it is *ancient.* Despite the Revolution, its
modernity is incomplete: Russia did not have an eighteenth century. It
would be useless to seek in its intellectual, philosophical, or moral tradition a Hume, a Kant, or a Diderot. This explains, at least in part, the
coexistence in modern Russia of precapitalist virtues and vices such as
indifference to political and social liberties. There is a similarity—as yet
little explored—between the Spanish and the Russian traditions: neither
they nor we, the Latin Americans, have a critical tradition because neither they nor we had in fact anything which can be compared with the
Enlightenment and the intellectual movement of the eighteenth century in Europe. Nor did we have anything to compare with the Protestant Reformation, that great seedbed of liberties and democracy in the
modern world. Thence the failure of the tentative democracies in Spain
and its old colonies. The Spanish empire disintegrated and with it our
countries too. Confronted with the anarchy which followed the dissolution of the Spanish order, we had no remedy but the barbaric remedy of
tyranny. The sad contemporary reality is the result of the failure of our
wars of independence: we were unable to rebuild, on modern principles,
the Spanish order. Dismembered, each part became a victim of the chiefs
of armed groups—our generals and presidents—and of imperialism,
especially that of the United States. With independence, our countries
did not begin a new phase: rather, the end of the Spanish world was hastened and achieved. When will we recover? In Russia there was no disintegration: the Communist bureaucracy replaced the czarist autocracy.

Like a good Russian, Solzhenitsyn would resign himself—he has
said recently—to seeing his country ruled by a nondemocratic regime
so long as it corresponded, however distantly, with the image that traditional thought created of the Christian sovereign, afraid of God and
loving his subjects. An idea, I mention in passing, that has its equivalent
in the "universal sovereign" of Buddhism (Asoka is the great example)
and in the Confucian idea that the emperor rules by heavenly mandate.

The Russian novelist's idea may seem fantastic, and to a certain degree it is. Nonetheless, it corresponds rather to a more realistic and deeper vision of the history of his country. And we, Spanish-Americans and Spaniards, is it not time that we examined more soberly and realistically our present and our past? When will we evolve our own political thought? A century and a half of petty tyrants, pronouncements, and military dictatorships—has this not opened our eyes? Our failure to adapt democratic institutions, in their two modern versions—the Anglo-Saxon and the French—ought to compel us to think on our own account, without looking through the spectacles of modish ideology. The contradiction between our institutions and what we really are is scandalous and would be comical were it not tragic. I feel no nostalgia for the Indian King or the Viceroy, for the Lady Serpent or the Grand Inquisitor, nor for His Most Serene Highness, or the Hero of Peace or the Great Chief of the Revolution. But these grotesque, frightening titles denote realities, and those realities are more real than our laws and constitutions. It is useless to close our eyes to them and more useless still to repress our past and condemn it to live on in history's subsoil; the life underground strengthens it, and periodically it reappears as a destructive eruption or explosion. This is the result of the ingenuity, hypocrisy, or stupidity of those who pretend to bury it alive. We need to *name* our past, to find political and juridical forms to integrate it and transform it into a creative force. Only thus will we begin to be free.

The system of sending delinquents against the common order along with political prisoners to Siberia was not a Communist but a czarist invention. The infamous Russian penal colonies were known throughout the world, and in 1886 an American explorer, George Kennan, devoted a book to this somber subject: *Siberia and the Exile System.* The reader need not be reminded of Dostoevski's *House of the Dead.* Less known is Anton Chekhov's *The Island, a Voyage to Sajalin.* But there is an essential difference: Dostoevski's and Chekhov's books were published legally in czarist Russia, while Solzhenitsyn had to publish his book abroad with the known risks. In 1890 Chekhov decided to travel to the celebrated penal colony of Sajalin and write a book on the Russian penitentiary system. Though it seems strange, the czarist authorities permitted his journey, and the Russian writer was able to interview the prisoners with considerable freedom (except for the political prisoners). Five years later, in 1895, he published his book, a complete condemnation of the Russian penal system. Chekhov's experience under czarism is unthinkable in any twentieth-century Marxist-Leninist regime.

As well as the circumstances of historical and national organizations, the place of individuals in the general order must be mentioned. Almost always these orders are interwoven with international realities and the national context. For example, in the case of Yugoslavia, Tito, as well as being the head of the Communist Party, led the nationalist resistance first against the Nazis and afterward against Stalin's attempts at intervention. Yugoslav nationalism contributed to the regime's relaxation of the terrible burden of the Russian and Leninist tradition: Yugoslavia humanized itself. It would be an error to ignore the beneficent influence of Tito's personality in that revolution. In each of the Communist states the Caesar imposes his style on the regime. In the time of Stalin, the color of the system was the rabid yellow and green of rage; today it is gray like Brezhnev's conscience. In China the regime is no less oppressive than in Russia, but its customs are not brutal or glacial: no Ivan the Terrible but Huang Ti, the first emperor. There is a striking resemblance between Huang and Mao, as Etiemble pointed out (see *Plural* 29, February 1974). Both rivals of Confucius and both possessed by the same superhuman ambition: to make time itself—past, present, and future—a huge monument that repeats its features. Time becomes malleable, history is a docile substance which takes on the kind and terrible imprint of the president-emperor. The first Cultural Revolution was the burning of the Chinese classics, especially the books of Confucius, ordered by Huang Ti in 213 B.C. Local variations on a universal archetype: the Caesar of Havana makes use of dialectics much as the old Spanish landowners used the whip.

The similarities between the Stalinist and Nazi regimes make it right for us to describe them both as totalitarian. That is the point of view of Hannah Arendt, but also of a man like Andrei Sakharov, one of the fathers of the Russian H-bomb:

> Nazism survived for twelve years; Stalinism twice as long. Besides the various common features, there are differences between them. The hypocrisy and demagogy of Stalin were

of a more subtle order, depending not on a frankly barbarous program like Hitler's but on a socialist ideology, a progressive, scientific, and popular ideology which was a useful screen to deceive the working class, and to anesthetize the vigilance of the intellectuals and of rivals in the struggle for power . . . Thanks to that "peculiarity" of Stalinism, the most terrible blows were delivered to the Soviet people and their most active, competent and honorable representatives. Between ten and fifteen million Soviet citizens, at least, have perished in the dungeons of the NKVD, martyred or executed, and in the camps for "Kulaks" and their families, camps "without right of correspondence" (those camps were the prototypes for the Nazi extermination camps), or dead of cold and hunger or exhausted by the inhuman labor in the glacial mines of Norilsk and Vorkuta, in the countless quarries and forest exploitations, in the construction of canals or, simply, from being transported in closed train cars or drowned in the "ships of death" on the Sea of Okhotsk, during the deportation of whole populations, the Tartars from Crimea, the Germans from the Volga, Calmuks and other groups from the Caucasus. *(La liberté intellectuelle en URSS et la Coexistence,* Paris, Gallimard, 1968)

The testimony of the celebrated Soviet economist Eugene Varga is no less impressive:

Though in Stalin's dungeons and concentration camps there were fewer cruel men and sadists than in Hitler's camps, it can be affirmed that no difference in principle existed between them. Many of those executioners are still at liberty and receive comfortable pensions *(Testament,* 1964: Paris, Granet, 1970).

However terrible the testimony of Solzhenitsyn, Sakharov, Varga, and many others, it seems to me that a crucial distinction ought to be made: neither the pre-Stalin period (1918–1928) nor the post-Stalin period (1956–1974) can be compared with nazism. Therefore one must distinguish, as Hannah Arendt does, between totalitarian systems properly speaking (nazism and Stalinism) and Communist bureaucratic dictatorships. Nevertheless it is clear that there is a causal relationship between Bolshevism and totalitarianism: without the dictatorship of the Party over the country and the Central Committee over the Party, Stalinism could not have developed. Trotsky thought the difference between communism and nazism consisted in the different organization of the economy: state property in the former and capitalist property in the latter. The truth is that, beyond the differences in the control of property, the two systems are similar in being bureaucratic dictatorships of one group which stands above class, society, and morality. The notion of a separate group is crucial. That group is a political party which initially takes the form of a gathering of conspirators. When it takes power, the conspirators' secret cell becomes the police cell, equally secret, for interrogation and torture. Leninism is not Stalinism but one of its antecedents. The others are in the Russian past, as well as in human nature.

Beyond Leninism is Marxism. I allude to the original Marxism, worked out by Marx and Engels in their mature years. That Marxism too contains the germs of authoritarianism—though to a far lesser degree than in Lenin and Trotsky—and many of the criticisms Bakunin leveled at it are still valid. But the germs of liberty which are found in the writings of Marx and Engels are no less fertile and powerful than the dogmatic Hegelian inheritance. And another thing: the socialist program is essentially a Promethean program of liberation of men and nations. Only from this point of view can (and ought) a criticism of the authoritarian tendencies in Marxism be made. In 1956 Bertrand Russell admirably summarized the stance of a free spirit confronting terrorist dogmas:

> My objections to modern Communism are far deeper than my objections to Marx. What I find particularly disastrous is the abandonment of democracy. A minority which leans for support on the activities of the secret police must necessarily become a cruel, oppressive and obscurantist minority. The dangers which irresponsible power engenders were generally rec-

ognized during the eighteenth and nineteenth centuries, but many, blinded by the external successes of the Soviet Union, have forgotten all that which was painfully learned during the years of absolute monarchy: Victims of the curious illusion that they form part of the vanguard of progress, they have reverted to the worst periods of the Middle Ages. *(Portraits from Memory,* New York, 1956)

The rejection of Caesarism and of Communist dictatorship does not in any way imply a justification of American imperialism, of racism, or of the atomic bomb; nor a shutting of the eyes before the injustice of the capitalist system. We cannot justify what happens in the West and in Latin America by saying that what happens in Russia and Czechoslovakia is worse: horrors there do not justify horrors here. What happens among us is unjustifiable, whether it is the prison detention of Onetti, the murders in Chile, or the tortures in Brazil. But nor is it possible for us to be blind to the misfortunes of the Russian, Czech, Chinese, or Cuban dissidents. The defense of so-called formal liberties is, day by day, the first political duty of a writer, whether in Mexico, in Moscow, or in Montevideo. The "formal liberties" are not, of course, all liberty, and liberty itself is not the sole human aspiration: fraternity, justice, equality, and security are also desirable. But without those formal liberties—of thought, expression, of association and movement, of saying "no" to power—there is no fraternity, no justice, nor hope of equality.

On this we ought to be unswerving and denounce implacably all equivocations, confusions, and lies. It is inadmissible, for example, that people who even a few months ago were calling the freedom of the press a "bourgeois trick" and were encouraging students, in the name of a radicalism both hackneyed and obscurantist, to violate the principle of academic freedom now form committees and sign manifestos to defend that very freedom of the press in Uruguay and Chile. Recently Günter Grass was putting us on our guard, recalling the pseudoradical frivolity of German intellectuals in the period of the Weimar Republic. While there was democracy in Germany, they never ceased to scoff at it as an illusion and a bourgeois plot, but when, fatally, Hitler came, they fled—not to

Moscow but to New York, doubtless to pursue there with increased ardor their critique of bourgeois society.

The moral and structural similarities between Stalinism and nazism should not make us forget their distinct ideological origins. Nazism was a narrowly nationalist and racist ideology, while Stalinism was a perversion of the great and beautiful socialist tradition. Leninism presents itself as a universal doctrine. It is impossible to be unmoved by the Lenin of *The State and Revolution*. Equally, it is impossible to forget that he was the founder of the Cheka and the man who unleashed terror against the Mensheviks and Revolutionary Socialists, his comrades in arms. Almost all Western and Latin American writers, at one point or another in our lives, sometimes because of generous but ignorant impulses, sometimes out of weakness under the pressure of the intellectual milieu, and sometimes simply to be modish, have allowed ourselves to be seduced by Leninism. When I consider Aragon, Eluard, Neruda, and other famous Stalinist writers and poets, I feel the gooseflesh that I get from reading certain passages in the *Inferno*. No doubt they began in good faith. How could they have shut their eyes to the horrors of capitalism and the disasters of imperialism in Asia, Africa, and our part of America? They experienced a generous surge of indignation and of solidarity with the victims. But insensibly, commitment by commitment, they saw themselves become tangled in a mesh of lies, falsehoods, deceits, and perjuries, until they lost their souls. They became, literally, soulless. This may seem exaggerated: Dante and his punishments for some wrongheaded political views? Who nowadays anyway believes in the soul? I will add that our opinions on this subject have not been mere errors or flaws in our faculty of judgment. They have been a sin in the old religious sense of that word: something that affects the whole being. Very few of us could look a Solzhenitsyn, or a Nadejda Mandelstam, in the eye. That sin has stained us and, fatally, has stained our writings as well. I say this with sadness, and with humility.

—Mexico, March 1974

GULAG: BETWEEN ISAIAH AND JOB*

Some writers and journalists, in Mexico and elsewhere in America and Europe, have criticized with a certain harshness things—some of them admittedly far of the mark—that Solzhenitsyn has said in recent months. The tone of these recriminations, ranging from the vindictive to the relieved "I told you so," is that of the man who has had a weight lifted from his shoulders: "Ah, that explains it all, Solzhenitsyn is a reactionary. . . " This attitude is another indication that the attacks against the revelations about the totalitarian Soviet system which the writer has made were accepted *à contre coeur* by many Western and Latin American intellectuals. It's hardly surprising: the Bolshevik myth, the faith in the essential purity and goodwill of the Soviet Union, above and beyond its failures and errors, is a superstition not easily eradicated. The ancient theological distinction between *substance* and *accident* continues to serve our century's believers with the same efficacy that it did in the Middle Ages: the substance is Marxism-Leninism and the accident is Stalinism. That's why, when Solzhenitsyn's early books were published, the brilliant, casuistical Lukács tried to turn their author into a "socialist realist," that is, a dissident *within* the Church. But Solzhenitsyn's emergence— not only his, but the appearance of many other independent Russian writers and intellectuals—was and is significant for precisely the opposite reason: they are dissidents outside the Church. Their repudiation of Marxism-Leninism is complete. This is what seems to me portentous: more than half a century after the October Revolution, many Russian

---

* This essay was published twenty months after Paz's first essay on Solzhenitsyn. It extends some of the arguments advanced in that piece and distinguishes between Solzhenitsyn the witness and Solzhenitsyn the social theorist.

spirits, perhaps the best—scientists, novelists, historians, poets, and philosophers—have ceased to be Marxists. A few have even returned—like Solzhenitsyn and Brodsky—to Christianity. It is a phenomenon incomprehensible to many European and American intellectuals. Incomprehensible and unacceptable.

I don't know if history repeats itself: I know that men change very little. There is no salvation outside the Church. If Solzhenitsyn is not a dissident revolutionary, he must be a reactionary imperialist. To condemn Solzhenitsyn, who dared to speak, is to absolve oneself—a self that has preserved its silence for years and years. The truth is that Solzhenitsyn is neither a revolutionary nor a reactionary: his is another tradition. When he repudiated Marxism-Leninism he repudiated too the "enlightened" and progressivist tradition of the West. He is as far from Kant and Robespierre as he is from Marx and Lenin. Nor does he feel drawn to Adam Smith or Jefferson. He is not liberal, not democrat, not capitalist. He believes in liberty—yes—because he believes in human dignity; he also believes in charity and comradeship, not in representative democracy nor in class solidarity. He would accept a Russia ruled by an autocrat, providing that autocrat were at the same time a genuine Christian: someone who believed in the sanctity of the human being, in the daily mystery of the other, who is our fellow creature. Here I ought to pause briefly to say that I disagree with Solzhenitsyn in this: Christians do not love their fellow creatures. And they do not love them because they have never *really* believed in otherness. History shows us how when they have found it they have converted it or destroyed it. At the root of Christians, as at the root of their descendants the Marxists, I perceive a terrible self-disgust which makes them hate and envy others, especially if those others are pagans. This is the psychological source of their missionary zeal and of the Inquisitions with which now one faction, now another, have darkened the planet.

Solzhenitsyn's Christianity is not dogmatic or inquisitorial. If his faith distances him from the political institutions created by the bourgeois revolution, it also makes him an enemy to the idolatry of Caesar and his embalmed corpse, and to the fanatic adherence to the letter of "holy writ," those two religions of Communist states. In short, Solzhenitsyn's world is a premodern society with its system of special laws, local liberties, and individual privileges of exemption. Yet, archaic though his political philosophy seems to us, his vision reflects with greater clarity than the critiques of his detractors the historical crossroads at which we find ourselves. I admit that often his line of reasoning fails to convince me and that his intellectual style is alien and contrary to my mental habits, my aesthetic tastes, and indeed my moral convictions. I am nearer to Celsius than to Saint Paul, I prefer Plotinus to Saint Augustine and Hume to Pascal. But Solzhenitsyn's direct and simple vision penetrates actuality and reveals to us what is hidden in the folds and creases of our days. Moral passion is a passion for truth and it provokes the appearance of truth. There is a prophetic element in his writings which I do not find in the work of any other of my contemporaries. Sometimes, as in Dante's tercets—though the Russian's prose is ponderous and his arguments prolix—I hear the voice of Isaiah and I recoil and rebel; at other times, I hear the voice of Job and I pity and accept. Like the prophets and like Dante, the Russian writer tells us of actuality from the other shore, that shore I dare not call eternal because I do not believe in eternity. Solzhenitsyn tells us what is happening, what is happening to us, what is violating us. He treats history from the double perspective of the now and the forever.

Apart from certain countries whose histories are separate from the general history of Europe toward the end of the seventeenth century (I'm thinking of Spain, Portugal, and the old American colonies of both nations), the West is living out the end of something which began at the close of the eighteenth century: that *modernity* which, in the political sphere, found expression in representative democracy, balance of power, the equality of citizens before the law, and the system of human rights and individual guarantees. As if it were an ironic and devilish confirmation of Marx's predictions—a confirmation in reverse—bourgeois democracy dies at the hands of its own historical creation. Thus Hegel's and his disciples' creative negation seems to fulfill itself in a perverse way: the infant matricide, destroyer of the old order, is not the universal proletariat but the new Leviathan, the bureaucratic state. Revolution destroys the bourgeoisie but not to liberate men—rather to enchain them more cruelly. The connection between the bureaucratic state and the industrial system, created by bourgeois democracy, is so close that a critique of the first implies necessarily a critique of the second.

Marxism is inadequate for our time because its critique of capitalism, far from including industrialism, includes an apology for its works. To laud technology and believe in industry as the greatest liberating agent of man—a belief common to capitalists and Communists—was logical in 1850, legitimate in 1900, understandable in 1920, but it is scandalous in 1975. Today we are aware that the evil is implicit not solely in the system of ownership of the means of production, but in the means of production themselves. Naturally it is impossible to renounce industry; it's not impossible to stop making a god of it, or to limit its destructiveness. Apart from the noxious ecological consequences, perhaps irreparable, the industrial system includes social dangers which no one now can be blind to. It is inhuman and dehumanizes all that it touches, from the "lords of the machines" to their "servants," as the economist Perroux calls those involved in the process: owners, technocrats, and workers. Whatever the political regime in which it evolves, modern industry automatically generates impersonal structures of labor and human relations no less impersonal, pitiless, and mechanical. Those structures and those relations contain a power, like the germ of the future organism, the bureaucratic state with its administrators, its moralists, its judges and psychiatrists and camps for labor reeducation.

Ever since it first appeared, Marxism has pretended to know the secret of the laws of historical evolution. It has not, throughout its history, abandoned this pretense and it is found in the writings of all the sects into which it has split, from Bernstein to Kautsky and from Lenin to Mao. Nonetheless, among its prophecies for the future there is no mention of the possibility which now seems to us most threatening and imminent: bureaucratic totalitarianism as the unraveling of the crisis of bourgeois society. There is one exception: Leon Trotsky. I mention him—though one swallow doesn't make a summer—because his case is full of pathos. At the end of his life, in the last article he wrote, shortly before he was murdered, Trotsky evoked—without much faith in it, just in passing, as one who shakes off a nightmare—the hypothesis that the Marxist view of modern history as the final triumph of socialism might be a hideous error of perspective. Then he said that, in view of the absence of proletarian revolutions in the West, during the Second World War or immediately after it the crisis of capitalism would resolve itself in the appearance of totalitarian collectivist societies whose earliest historical realizations were, in those days (1939), Hitler's Germany and Stalin's Russia. Since then, some Trotskyite groups (though dissidents within that movement, like those that publish *Socialisme ou Barbarie*) have directed their analysis into the area indicated by Trotsky, but they have not managed to devise a genuinely Marxist theory of totalitarian collectivism. The main obstacle in the way of a clear understanding of the phenomenon is their failure to recognize, as their teacher had, the class nature of the bureaucracy.*

Oddly, the only thing Trotsky thought of to confront the new Leviathan was—to elaborate a minimal program of defense of the workers! It's revealing that, despite his extraordinary intelligence, he did not consider two circumstances. The first is that he, with his dogmatic intolerance and his rigid conception of the Bolshevik Party as the instrument of history, had contributed powerfully to the construction of the world's first bureaucratic state. That irony is the more wounding if we remember that Lenin, in his Will, reproaches Trotsky for his bureaucratic leanings and his tendency to treat problems from the purely administrative angle. The second circumstance is the disproportion between the magnitude of the evil Trotsky perceived—a totalitarian collectivism instead of socialism— and the inanity of the remedy: a minimal plan of action. A curious vision of professional revolutionaries: they reduce the history of the world to the editing of a manifesto and the forming of committees. Bureaucracy and apocalypse.

The bureaucratic state is not exclusively found in countries called socialist. It happened in Germany and it could happen elsewhere: indus-

---

* I was too sweeping. We owe to Cornelius Costariadis and to Claude Lefort valuable and illuminating analyses of the historical nature of the Russian bureaucratic State that vastly overcome the limitations of the traditional Trotskyite critique. See my book *One Earth, Four or Five Worlds* (1985).

trial society carries it in its womb. The great multinational companies prefigure it, as do other institutions that form a part of Western democracies, like the American CIA. Nonetheless, if liberty is to survive the bureaucratic state, it ought to find a different alternative to the ones that capitalist democracies offer today. The weakness of these democracies is not physical but spiritual. They are richer and more powerful than their totalitarian adversaries, but they do not know what to do with their power and their wealth. Without faith in anything beyond immediate profit, they have time and time again entered into pacts with crime. This is what Solzhenitsyn has said—though in the religious language of another age—and this is what has scandalized the Pharisees. I'll add something I should have said before: Western democracies have protected and continue to protect all the tyrants and petty tyrants of the five continents.

It's often said that Solzhenitsyn has revealed nothing new. That is true: we all knew that in the Soviet Union forced-labor camps existed and that they were extermination camps for millions of human beings. What is new is that the majority of "left-wing intellectuals" has at last accepted that the paradise was in fact hell. This return to reason, I fear, is due not so much to Solzhenitsyn's genius as to the salutary effects of Khrushchev's revelations. They believed as they were told and they ceased to believe as they were told. Perhaps for this reason few—very few—of them have had the humble courage to analyze in public what went wrong and to explain the reasons that moved them to think and act as they did. The reluctance to admit error is such that one of those hardened souls, a great poet, said: "How could I, a writer, have avoided erring, when History itself erred?" The Greeks and the Aztecs knew that their gods sinned, but modern men surpass the ancients: History, that fleshed-out idea, like a scatterbrained matron goes on a spree with the first comer, whether his name is Tamburlaine or Stalin. This is where Marxism has come to rest, a system of thought that presents itself as "the critique of heaven."

In an article I wrote on the publication of the first volume of *The Gulag Archipelago*, I emphasized that the respect Solzhenitsyn inspires in me does not imply adherence to his ideas or to his stance. I approve his criticism of the Soviet regime and of the hedonism, hypocrisy, and myopic opportunism of the Western democracies; I repudiate his simplistic idea of history as a battle between two empires and two trends. Solzhenitsyn has not understood that the century of the disintegration and liquidation of the European imperial system has also been the century of the rebirth of the old Asiatic nations, such as China, and the rise of young countries in Africa and elsewhere in the world. Will those movements resolve themselves in a gigantic historical failure like the failure, up to now, of Brazil and the Spanish American nations, born a century and a half ago out of the Spanish and Portuguese disintegration? It is impossible to know, but the case of China seems to point in the other direction.

Solzhenitsyn's ignorance is serious because its true name is arrogance. It is, above all, a very Russian trait, as anyone who has had dealings with writers and intellectuals from that country, whether dissident or orthodox, knows. This is another of the great Russian mysteries, as all readers of Dostoevski know: in Russians arrogance goes hand in hand with humility, brutality with piety, fanaticism with the greatest spiritual liberty. The insensibility and blindness of a great writer and a great heart: Solzhenitsyn the brave and the pious has revealed a certain *imperial* indifference, in the ample sense of the word, in the face of the sufferings of peoples humiliated and subjected by the West. The strangest thing of all is that, being as he is a friend and witness to liberty, he should not have felt sympathy with the struggles of those peoples for freedom.

The case of Vietnam illustrates Solzhenitsyn's limitations. His and his critics'. Those groups who opposed, almost always with good and legitimate reasons, the American intervention in Indochina denied at the same time something undeniable: the conflict was an episode in the battle between Washington and Moscow. Not to see it—or to try not to see it—was to be blind to what Solzhenitsyn and (also) Mao saw: the defeat of the Americans encourages the aspirations toward Soviet hegemony in Asia and Eastern Europe. Those same groups—socialists, libertarians, democrats, anti-imperialist liberals—denounced justifiably the immorality and corruption of the South Vietnamese regime but did not say a single word about the actual nature of the one that ruled in North Vietnam. A witness beyond suspicion, Jean Lacouture, has called the Hanoi government the most Stalinist in the Communist world. Its leader, Ho Chi Minh, directed a bloody purge against Trotskyites and other dissidents of the left when he took power. The cruel measures adopted by the triumvirate which rules Cambodia have shocked and shamed Western supporters of the Khmer Rouge. All this proves that the left is snared in its own ideology; that is why it has not yet found the means of combating imperialism without succoring totalitarianism instead. But Solzhenitsyn himself is a victim of the ideological snare: he said that the war in Indochina was an imperial conflict, but he did not say that it was also—and above all else—a war of national liberation. This was what legitimized it. To ignore this fact is to ignore not only the complexity of all historical reality but also its human and moral dimension. Manichaeism is the moralist's trap.

Solzhenitsyn's opinions do not invalidate his testimony. *The Gulag Archipelago* is neither a book of political philosophy nor a sociological treatise. Its theme is something else: human suffering in its two most extreme aspects, abjection and heroism. It is not the suffering which nature or destiny or the gods inflict, but which man inflicts on his fellow man. The theme is as ancient as human society, ancient as the primitive hordes and as Cain. It is a political, biological, psychological, philosophical, and religious theme: evil. No one has yet been able to tell us why evil exists in the world and why evil abides in man. Solzhenitsyn's work has two virtues, both great: first, it is the account of something lived and suffered; second, it constitutes a complete and horrifying encyclopedia of political horror in the twentieth century. The two volumes which have appeared so far are a geography and an anatomy of the *evil* of our era. That evil is not melancholy or despair or *taedium vitae* but sadism without an erotic element: crime socialized and submitted to the norms of mass production. A crime monotonous as an infinite multiplication exercise. What age and what civilization can offer a book to compare with Solzhenitsyn's or with the accounts of the survivors of the Nazi camps? Our civilization has touched the extreme of evil (Hitler, Stalin), and those books reveal it. This is the root of their greatness. The resistance which Solzhenitsyn's books have provoked is explicable: those books are the evocation of a reality whose very existence is the most thorough refutation, desolating and convincing, of several centuries of utopian thought, from Campanella to Fourier and from More to Marx. Moreover, they are a life study of a loathsome society but one in which millions of our contemporaries—among them countless writers, scientists, artists—have seen nothing less than the adorable features of the Best of Future Worlds. What do they say to themselves now, if they dare to speak to themselves, the authors of those exalted travelogues to the USSR (one of them was called *Return from the Future*), those enthusiastic poems and those impassioned reports about "the fatherland of socialism"?

The Gulag Archipelago takes the double form of a history and a catalogue. The history of the origin, development, and proliferation of a cancer which began as a *tactical* measure at a difficult stage in the struggle for power and which ended as a social *institution* in whose destructive function millions of human beings participated, some as victims and others as executioners, guards, and accomplices. The catalogue: An inventory of the gradations—gradations also in the scale of being—between bestiality and saintliness. In telling us of the birth, the development, and the transformation of the totalitarian cancer, Solzhenitsyn writes a chapter, perhaps the most terrible chapter, in the general history of the collective Cain; in telling us the cases he has witnessed and those which other eyewitnesses have told him—witnesses in the evangelical sense of the word—he gives us a vision of man. The history is social; the catalogue individual. The history is limited: Social systems are born, evolve, and die; they're ephemeral. The catalogue is not historical: It relates not to the system but to the human condition. Abjection and its complement: the vision of Job on his dungheap has no term.

—Mexico, December 1975

JOSÉ ORTEGA Y GASSET: THE WHY AND THE WHEREFORE*

I write these lines with enthusiasm and with fear. Enthusiasm because I always admired José Ortega y Gasset; fear because—apart from my personal inadequacies—I do not believe one can summarize or judge in an essay a literary and philosophical oeuvre as vast and varied as his. A philosophy which can be summarized in a phrase is not a philosophy but a religion. Or its counterfeit: ideology. Buddhism is the most intellectual and discursive of religions; all the same, a sutra condenses the entire doctrine in the monosyllable *a*, the particle of universal negation. Christianity, too, can be stated in one or two phrases, such as "Love one another" or "My kingdom is not of this world." The same thing happens, at a lower level, with ideologies. For example: "Universal history is the history of the war of the classes" or, in the liberal camp, "Progress is the law of societies." The difference is that ideologies pretend to talk in the name of science. As Alain Besançon says: the religious man *knows that he believes* while the ideologue *believes that he knows* (Tertullian and Lenin). Maxims, tags, the sayings, and the articles of faith do not impoverish religion: they are seeds which grow and fruit in the heart of the faithful. Philosophy, by contrast, is nothing if not development, demonstration, and justification of an idea or an intuition. Without explication there is no philosophy. Nor, of course, criticism of the philosophical work.

To the difficulty of reducing to a few pages so rich and complex a body of thought as Ortega y Gasset's, one must add the actual character of his writings. He was a true essayist, perhaps the greatest in the Spanish

---

* This essay first appeared in a special issue of the Madrid daily paper *El País* dedicated to the memory of José Ortega y Gasset on the twenty-fifth anniversary of his death.

language; that is, he was a master of a genre which does not allow the simplifications of synopsis. The essayist must be diverse, penetrating, acute, fresh, and he must master the difficult art of using three dots . . . He does not exhaust his theme, he neither compiles nor systematizes: he explores. If he succumbs to the temptation to be categorical, as Ortega y Gasset so often did, he should introduce into what he says a few drops of doubt, a reserve. The prose of the essay flows in a lively way, never in a straight line, but always equidistant from the two extremes which ceaselessly lie in wait for it: the treatise and the aphorism. Two forms of freezing.

Like a good essayist, Ortega y Gasset came back from each of his expeditions through unknown lands with unusual discoveries and trophies but without having charted a map of the new land. He did not colonize: he discovered. This is why I have never understood the complaint of those who say he left us no complete books (that is, treatises, systems). Can one not say the same of Montaigne and of Thomas Browne, of Renan and of Carlyle? The essays of Schopenhauer are not inferior to his great philosophical work. The same thing happens, in our century, with Bertrand Russell. Wittgenstein himself, author of the most rigorous and geometrical book of philosophy of modern times, felt after writing it the need to write books more like the essay, acts of unsystematic reflection and meditation. It was fortunate that Ortega y Gasset did not succumb to the temptation of the treatise or the summa. His genius did not predispose him to define or to construct. He was neither a geometrician nor an architect. I see his works not as a collection of buildings but as a net of roads and navigable rivers. An oeuvre to be traveled through rather than resided in: he invites us not to stay but to move on.

He touched on an astonishing diversity of themes. More astonishing is how frequently those various subjects resolve themselves in genuine discoveries. Much of what he said is still worth remembering and discussing. I have already mentioned the extraordinary mobility of his thought: to read him is to walk briskly along difficult byways toward hardly glimpsed goals; sometimes one reaches the destination and sometimes one remains on the outskirts. No matter: what is important is the making of trails. But to read him is also to linger before this or that idea, to put the book aside

The world, as he explained many times, is inseparable from the "I." The unity or nucleus of the human being is an indissoluble relationship: the "I" is time and space; or: society, history—action. Thus it is not odd that among his best essays there are some on historical and political themes, such as *The Revolt of the Masses, The Theme of Our Time, The End of Revolutions* (full of extraordinary prophecies of what is happening today, though clouded by a cyclic idea of history which did not let him see completely the *unique* character of the revolutionary myth), *Man the Technician,* and so many others. Ortega y Gasset had, like Tocqueville, the highly rational ability to see what was coming. His lucidity contrasts with the blindness of so many of our prophets. If one compares his essays on contemporary historical and political themes with those of Sartre, one immediately perceives that he was more lucid and penetrating than the French philosopher. He was less often wrong, was more consistent, and thus saved himself (and us) all those rectifications which mar the work of Sartre and which ended with the late *mea culpa* of his last days. Comparison with Bertrand Russell, too, is not disadvantageous to Ortega y Gasset: the history of his political opinions, without being entirely coherent, does not abound in the contradictions and pirouettes of Russell's, who went from one extreme to the other. One can approve or reprove his political ideas, but one cannot accuse him—as one can the others—of inconsistency.

I may have been unfaithful to the tenor of his work in speaking of his *thought*. One ought rather to say, his *thoughts*. The plural is justified not because his thinking lacks unity but because it deals with a coherence inimical to system and which cannot be reduced to a chain of reasons and propositions. Despite the variety of the matter he dealt with, he did not leave us a dispersed oeuvre. On the contrary. But his genius was not interested in the form of theory, in the proper sense of the word, nor in the form of demonstration. He sometimes used the word *meditation*. It is exact, but *essay* is more general. Better said: *essays,* because the genre does not admit the singular. Though the unity of these essays is, dearly, of an intellectual order, their root is vital and even, I dare say, aesthetic. There is a way of thinking, a *style,* which is Ortega y Gasset's alone. In this method of operation which combines intellectual rigor with the aesthetic necessity of personal expression lies the secret of his work's unity.

Ortega y Gasset not only thought about this and that but also, from his earliest writings, decided that those thoughts, even those he took from his teachers and from the tradition, would bear his hallmark. To think was, for him, synonymous with expression. This was the opposite of Spinoza, who wanted to see his discourse, purged of impurities and accidents of the "I," as the verbal crystallization of mathematics, of the universal order. In this Ortega y Gasset was not far from the father of the essay, Montaigne. Many of Montaigne's ideas are drawn from antiquity and from some of his contemporaries, but his indisputable originality is not in the reading of Sextus Empiricus but in the way in which he lived and relived those ideas and how, in rethinking them, he changed them, made them his own and, thus, made them ours.

The number of ideas—what are called *ideas*—is not infinite. Philosophical speculation, for the last two and a half thousand years, has consisted of variations and combinations of concepts such as movement and identity, substance and change, being and entities, the one and the many, first principles and nothingness, etc. Naturally, those variations have been logically, vitally, and historically *necessary*. In the case of Ortega y Gasset this rethinking of the philosophical tradition and the thought of his age culminated in a question about the *why* and *how* of ideas. He inserted them into human life: thus they changed their nature, they were not essences which we contemplate in an unmoving heaven but instruments, weapons, mental objects which we use and live. Ideas are the forms of universal coexistence. He took the questioning of ideas further, to investigate what underlies and perhaps determines them: not the principle of sufficient reason but the domination of inarticulate beliefs. It is an hypothesis which, in another form, has reappeared in our days: the *beliefs* of Ortega y Gasset are, for Georges Dumézil, psychic structures, elemental in a society, present in its language and in its conception of the other world and of itself. The explanation for the immense influence Ortega y Gasset had on the intellectual life of our countries lies, no doubt, in this notion he had of ideas and concepts as *whys* and *hows*. They ceased to be entities beyond us and became vital spaces. His teaching consisted of showing us what ideas were for and how we could use them: not to know ourselves nor to contemplate essences but to open for ourselves a passage in our given circumstances, to converse with our world, with our past and with our kin.

Discourse with Ortega y Gasset was often a monologue. Many have regretted this, with some reason. Still, one must grant that that monologue taught us to think and made us talk, if not with ourselves, then with our Latin American history. He taught us that landscape is not a state of the soul and that we are not mere accidents of the landscape. The relationship between man and his environment is more complex than the antique relationship between subject and object. The environment is a "here" seen and lived from a "me"; that *from a me* is always a *from here*. The relation between one pole and another is, more than a dialogue, an interaction. Ideas are reactions, acts. This view, at once erotic and polemic of human destiny, does not open into any beyond. There is no transcendence beyond the act or the thought which, when it is carried out, is exhausted: then, under threat of extinction, one must begin again. Man is a being who continually makes and remakes himself. The great invention of man is men.

This is a Promethean and also a tragic view: if we are a perpetual self-creation, we are an eternal rebeginning. There is no rest: end and beginning are the same. And there is no human nature: man is not a given but something that makes and discovers itself. From the beginning of the beginning, cast out of himself and out of nature, he is a being in the air; all his creations—what we call culture and history—are nothing more than contrivances to keep him suspended in the air so that he will not fall back into the bestial inertia that preceded the beginning. History is our condition and our liberty: it is what we are in and what we make. Yet history does not consist of settled accounts, but of a suspension in the air, rootless, outside nature. I have always been staggered by this vision of man as a creature in permanent struggle against the laws of gravity. But it is a vision in which the other face of reality does not appear: history as an incessant production of ruins, man as fall and continual self-unmaking. I fear Ortega y Gasset's philosophy lacked the weight, the gravity, of death. There are two great absences in his work: Epictetus and Saint Augustine.

His intellectual endeavor found three outlets: his books, his teaching, and the *Revista de Occidente* with its publishing list. His influence left a deep mark on the cultural life of Spain and Latin America. For the first time, after a two-century eclipse, Spanish thought was heard and discussed in Latin American countries. Not only were our ways of thought and our funds of information renewed and changed; literature, the arts, and the sensibility of the age also show the marks of Ortega y Gasset and his circle. Between 1920 and 1935 in the enlightened classes, as they were called in the nineteenth century, a *style* predominated which came from the *Revista de Occidente*. I am sure that Ortega's thought will be discovered, and very soon, by younger Spanish generations. I cannot conceive a *healthy* Spanish culture without his presence. It will, of course, be a different Ortega y Gasset from the one we knew and read: each generation invents its authors. A more European Spain—such as the one currently on the drawing board—will feel greater affinity with the tradition which Ortega y Gasset represents, which is the tradition that has always looked toward Europe. But European culture is living through difficult years and cannot any longer be the fount of inspiration that it was at the outset of this century. Moreover, Spain is also American, as Valle-Inclán admirably saw, while Unamuno, Machado, and Ortega y Gasset himself were blind to it. Nor did the poets of the generation of 1927, though they discovered Neruda, feel or really understand Latin America. Thus the return to Ortega y Gasset will not be a matter of repeating but of amending him.

In this vast, rich, and diverse oeuvre I note three omissions. I have already mentioned two. The first is the look inward, introspection, which is always resolved in irony: he never saw himself and therefore, perhaps, did not know how to smile at his reflection in the mirror. Another is death, the undoing which is all doing. Ortega y Gasset's man is intrepid and his sign is Sagittarius; all the same, though he can look the sun in the face, he never looks at death. The third omission is the stars. In his mental heaven the lively and intelligent stars have vanished, the ideas and essences, the numbers turned light, the ardent spirits which enraptured Plotinus and Porphyry. His philosophy is of thought as action; to think is to do, build, make way, coexist: it is not to see or to contemplate. The work of Ortega y Gasset is a passionate thinking about this world, but from his world many other worlds are lacking, those which constitute the other world: death and nothing, reversals of life, history, and reason; the inner kingdom, that secret territory discovered by the Stoics and explored, before all others, by the Christian mystics; and the contemplation of essences or, as Sister Juana Ines de la Cruz put it, in the only truly philosophical poem in our language, "First Dream," the contemplation of the invisible from here,

> not only of all created things
> under the moon, but of those also
> which, intellectual, lucid, are Stars . . .

Perhaps it could be argued that Ortega y Gasset's thought frees us from worshiping such stars, that is, frees us from the net of metaphysics; ideas are not in any mental heaven: we have invented them with our thoughts. They are not the traces of universal order nor the image of cosmic harmony: they are uncertain lights which guide us on in darkness, signals we make to one another, bridges to cross to the other shore. But this is precisely what I miss in his work: there is no other shore, no other side. The *ratiovitalism* is a solipsism, a cul-de-sac. There is a point at which the Western and Eastern tradition, Plotinus and Nāgārjuna, Chuang-tzu and Schopenhauer, meet: the final end, the supreme good, is contemplation. Ortega y Gasset taught us that to think is to live and that thought separated from living soon ceases to be thought and becomes an idol. He was right, but he cut away the other half of life and thought. Living is also, and above all, to glimpse the other shore, to suspect that there is order, number, and proportion in all that is and that, as Edmund Spenser said, movement itself is an allegory of repose:

> That time when no more Change shall be,
> But stedfast rest of all things firmly stayd
> Upon the pillours of Eternity.
> —"Mutability Cantos"

Because of this, his reflections on history, politics, understanding, ideas, beliefs, love, are a knowledge—not a wisdom.

This essay—written without notes and confiding in my memory—is not an examination of Ortega y Gasset's ideas but of the impression they have left on me. Like so many other Latin Americans of my age, I had passionate recourse to his books during my adolescence and early adulthood. Those readings marked and shaped me. He guided my first steps, and to him I owe some of my first intellectual delights. To read him in those days was almost a physical pleasure, like swimming or walking in a wood. Then I drew hack from him. I got to know other countries and I explored other worlds. At the end of the war I settled in Paris. In those days they held in Geneva some international conferences which achieved a certain notoriety. They consisted of a series of six public lectures, given by six European figures and followed, in each case, by discussions in small groups. In 1951 I was invited to participate in these discussions. I accepted: one of the six lecturers was Ortega y Gasset. On the day of his lecture I listened to him emotionally. Also angrily: beside me some provincial French and Swiss professors were making fun of his accent when he spoke in French. On leaving, they wanted to belittle him: I don't know why they were offended. The discussion next day began badly due to the malevolence of these same professors, though, fortunately, a generous and intelligent intervention by Merleau-Ponty put matters straight. I paid little attention to those petty disputes: I wanted to get near Ortega y Gasset and talk to him. At last I managed to do so and the next day I visited him in the Hôtel du Rhone. I saw him there twice. He met me in the bar: a large room with rustic wooden furnishings and a huge window looking out on the impetuous river. A strange sensation: one could see the raging and frothing water falling from a high floodgate, but, because of the thickness of the windowpanes, one could not hear it. I remembered the line from Baudelaire: *Tout pour l'oeil, rien pour les oreilles.*

Despite his love for the German world and its mists, Ortega y Gasset was, in physical and spiritual terms, a man of the Mediterranean. Not wolf nor pine: bull and olive. A vague similarity—stature, manners, coloring, eyes—with Picasso. He could have said with more authority

than Rubén Darío: "here, beside the Roman sea / I speak my truth . . . "
I was surprised by the flickering of his bird-of-prey look, I am not sure
whether eagle- or hawk-like. I realized that, like tinder, he was easily
fired, though the blaze did not last long. Enthusiasm and melancholy,
according to Aristotle the contradictory extremes of the intellectual temperament. He struck me as proud without being disdainful, which is the
best kind of pride. Also open and able to take an interest in his fellow
creature. He greeted me openly, invited me to take a seat, and asked the
waiter to serve us whiskeys. In answer to his questions, I told him I lived
in Paris and that I wrote poems. He shook his head reprovingly and rep-
rehended me: dearly Latin Americans were incorrigible. Then he spoke
with grace, openness, and intelligence (why did he never, in his writing,
use the familiar tone?) of his age and of his looks (those of a bullfighter
who has cut off his pigtail), of Argentinean women (nearer to Juno
than to Pallas), of the United States (something might yet sprout there,
though it is an excessively horizontal society), of Alfonso Reyes and his
little Asiatic eyes (he knew little about Mexico and that seemed to him
enough), of the death of Europe and its resurrection, of the bankruptcy
of literature, again of age (he said something which would have shaken
Plotinus: thinking is an erection and I still think), and of much else.

The conversation tended, at times, toward exposition; then, toward
narrative: anecdotes and happenings. Ideas and examples: a master. I
sensed that his love of ideas extended to his auditors; he watched me to
see if I had understood him. Before him I existed not as an echo; rather,
as a confirmation. I understood that all his writings were an extension
of the spoken word and that this is the essential difference between the
philosopher and the poet. The poem is a verbal object, and though it is
made of signs (words), its ultimate reality unfolds beyond those signs: it
is the presentation of a form; the discourse of the philosopher uses forms
and signs, it is an invitation to realize ourselves (virtue, authenticity, stoic
calmness, what have you). I left him with my brain boiling.

I saw him again the next afternoon. Roberto Vernengo, a bright
young Argentinean who was his guide in Switzerland and who was well
acquainted with German and French philosophy, was with him. We
went for a walk in the city. Roberto left us, and Ortega and I walked

for a while, returning to his hotel along the bank of the river. Now one could hear the roar of the water falling into the lake. The wind began to blow. He told me that the only activity possible in the modern world was thought ("Literature is dead, it's a store that's closed down, though they still haven't found this out in Paris") and that, to think, one needed to know Greek or, at least, German. He halted for a moment and interrupted his monologue, took me by the arm, and, with an intense look which still moves me, he said: "Learn German and start thinking. Forget the rest." I promised to obey him and accompanied him to the door of his hotel. The next day I took the train back to Paris.

I did not learn German. Nor did I forget "the rest." In this I did follow him, however: he always taught that it is not necessary to think, in itself, that all thought is thought toward or about "the rest." That "rest," whatever name we give it, is our circumstance. "The rest," for me, is history; that which is beyond history is called poetry. We are living an Ending, but ending is no less fascinating and worthy than beginning. Endings and beginnings resemble each other: at the outset, poetry and thought were united; then an act of rational violence divided them; today they tend, almost at random, to come together again. And his third piece of advice: "start thinking"? His books, when I was a young man, made me think. From then on I have tried to be faithful to that first lesson. I'm not too sure that I think now as I did at that time; but I do know that without his thought I could not, today, think at all.

Mexico, October 1980

LUIS BUÑUEL:
THREE PERSPECTIVES

I. BUÑUEL THE POET

The release of *L'Age d'or* and *Un chien andalou* signals the first considered irruption of poetry into the art of cinematography. The marriage of the film image to the poetic image, creating a new reality, inevitably appeared scandalous and subversive—as indeed it was. The subversive nature of Buñuel's early films resides in the fact that, hardly touched by the hand of poetry, the insubstantial conventions (social, moral, or artistic) of which our reality is made fall away. And from those ruins rises a new truth, that of man and his desire. Buñuel shows us that a man with his hands tied can, by simply shutting his eyes, make the world jump. Those films are something more than a fierce attack on so-called reality; they are the revelation of another reality which contemporary civilization has humiliated. The man in *L'Age d'or* slumbers in each of us and waits only for a signal to awake: the signal of love. This film is one of the few attempts in modern art to reveal the terrible face of love at liberty.

A little later, Buñuel screened *Land Without Bread*, a documentary which of its genre is also a masterpiece. In this film Buñuel the poet withdraws; he is silent so that reality can speak for itself. If the subject of Buñuel's surrealist films is the struggle of man against a reality which smothers and mutilates him, the subject of *Land Without Bread* is the brutalizing victory of that same reality. Thus this documentary is the necessary complement to his earlier creations. It explains and justifies them. By different routes, Buñuel pursues his bloody battle with reality. Or rather, against it. His realism, like that of the best Spanish tradition—Goya, Quevedo, the picaresque novel, Valle-Inclán, Picasso—consists of a pitiless hand-to-hand combat with reality. Tackling it, he flays it. This is why his art bears no relation at all to the more or less tendentious, sentimental, or aesthetic descriptions of the writing that is commonly called realism. On the contrary, all his work tends to stimulate the release of something secret and precious, terrible and pure, hidden by our reality itself. Making use of dream and poetry or using the medium of film narrative, Buñuel the poet descends to the very depths of man, to his most radical and unexpressed intimacy.

After a silence of many years, Buñuel screens a new film: *Los Olvidados.* If one compares this film with those he made with Salvador Dali, what is surprising above all is the rigor with which Buñuel takes his first intuitions to their extreme limits. On the one hand, *Los Olvidados* represents a moment of artistic maturity; on the other, of greater and more total rage: the gate of dreams seems sealed forever; the only gate remaining open is the gate of blood. Without betraying the great experience of his youth, but conscious of how times have changed, that reality which he denounced in his earlier works has grown even more dense— Buñuel constructs a film in which the action is precise as a mechanism, hallucinatory as a dream, implacable as the silent encroachment of lava flow. The argument of *Los Olvidados*—delinquent childhood—has been extracted from penal archives. Its characters are our contemporaries and are of an age with our own children. But *Los Olvidados* is something more than a realist film. Dream, desire, horror, delirium, chance, the nocturnal part of life, also play their part. And the gravity of the reality it shows us is atrocious in such a way that in the end it appears impossible to us, unbearable. And it is: reality is *unbearable;* and that is why, because he cannot bear it, man kills and dies, loves and creates.

The strictest artistic economy governs *Los Olvidados.* Corresponding to this greater condensation is a more intense explosion. That is why it is a film without "stars"; that is why the "musical background" is so discreet and does not set out to usurp what music owes to the eyes in films; and finally, that is why it disdains local color. Turning its back on the temptation of the impressive Mexican landscape, the scenario is reduced to the sordid and insignificant desolation, but always implacable, of an urban setting. The physical and human space in which the drama unfolds could hardly be more closed: the life and death of some children delivered up to their own fate, between the four walls of abandonment. The city, with all that this word entails of human solidarity, is alien and strange. What we call civilization is for them nothing but a wall, a great No which closes the way. Those children are Mexicans, but they could be from some other country, could live in any suburb of another great city. In a sense they do not live in Mexico, or anywhere: they are the forgotten, the inhabitants of those wastelands which each modern city breeds on its outskirts. A world closed on itself, where all acts are reflexive and each step returns us to our point of departure. No one can get out of there, or out of himself, except by way of the long street of death. Fate, which opens doors in other worlds, here closes them.

In *Los Olvidados* the continuous presence of the hazard has a special meaning, which forbids us from confusing it with mere chance. The hazard which governs the action of the protagonists is presented as a necessity which, nonetheless, *could have been avoided.* (Why not give it its true name, then, as in tragedy: *destiny?*) The old fate is at work again, but deprived of its supernatural attributes: now we face a social and psychological fate. Or, to use the magical word of our time, the new intellectual fetish: an historical fate. It is not enough, however, for society, history, or circumstances to prove hostile to the protagonists; for the catastrophe to come about, it is necessary for those determinants to coincide with human will. Pedro struggles against chance, against his bad luck or his bad shadow, embodied in the Jaibo; when, cornered, he accepts and faces it, he changes fate into destiny. He dies, but he makes his death his own. The collision between human consciousness and external fate constitutes the essence of the tragic act. Buñuel has rediscovered this fundamental ambiguity: without human complicity, destiny is not fulfilled and tragedy is impossible. Fate wears the mask of liberty; chance, that of destiny.

Los Olvidados is not a documentary film. Nor is it a thesis, propagandistic, or moralizing film. Though no sermonizing blurs his admirable objectivity, it would be slanderous to suggest that this is an art film, in which all that counts are artistic values. Far from realism (social, psychological, and edifying) and from aestheticism, Buñuel's film finds its place in the tradition of a passionate and ferocious art, contained and raving, which claims as antecedents Goya and Posada, the graphic artists who have perhaps taken black humor furthest. Cold lava, volcanic ice. Despite the universality of his subject, the absence of local color, and the extreme bareness of his construction, *Los Olvidados* has an emphasis which there is no other word for but *racial* (in the sense in which fighting bulls have *casta*). The misery and abandonment can be met with anywhere in the world, but the bloodied passion with which they are described belongs to great Spanish art. We have already come across that half-witted blind man in the Spanish picaresque tradition. Those women, those drunks, those cretins, those murderers, those innocents, we have come across in Quevedo and Galdós, we have glimpsed them in Cervantes, Velázquez and Murillo have depicted them. Those sticks—the walking sticks of the blind—are the same which tap all down the history of Spanish theater. And the children, the forgotten ones, their mythology, their passive rebellion, their suicidal loyalty, their sweetness which flashes out, their tenderness full of exquisite ferocity, their impudent affirmation of themselves in and for death, their endless search for communion—even through crime—are not and cannot be anything but Mexican. Thus, in the crucial scene in the film—the "libation" scene—the subject of the mother is resolved in the common supper, the sacred feast. Perhaps unintentionally, Buñuel finds in the dream of his protagonists the archetypal images of the Mexican people: Coatlicue [Aztec goddess of death and fertility] and sacrifice. The subject of the mother, a Mexican obsession, is inexorably linked to the theme of fraternity, of friendship unto death. Both constitute the secret foundation of this film. The world of *Los Olvidados* is peopled by orphans, by loners who seek communion and who do not balk at blood to find it. The quest for the "other," for our likeness, is the other side of the search for the mother. Or the acceptance of her definitive absence: the knowledge that we are alone. Pedro, the Jaibo, and his companions thus reveal to us the ultimate nature of man, which perhaps consists in a permanent and constant state of orphandom.

Witness to our age, the moral value of *Los Olvidados* bears no relation at all to propaganda. Art, when it is free, is witness, conscience. Buñuel's work proves what creative talent and artistic conscience can do when nothing but their own liberty constrains or drives them.

Cannes, 4 April 1951

II. BUÑUEL'S PHILOSOPHICAL CINEMA

Some years ago I wrote about Buñuel. This is what I said:

> Though all the arts, even the most abstract, have as their ultimate
> and general end to express and re-create man and his conflicts,
> each of them has particular means and techniques of enchant-
> ment and thus constitutes its own domain. Music is one thing,
> poetry another, cinema something else again. But sometimes an
> artist manages to transcend the limits of his art; then we engage
> a work which finds points of reference outside its world. Some
> of the films of Luis *Buñuel—L'Age d'or, Los Olvidados*—while
> they remain films, take us toward other boundaries of the spirit:
> some of Goya's engravings, a poem by Quevedo or Péret, a pas-
> sage from Sade, an absurd character from Valle-Inclán, a page
> of Gómez de la Serna . . . These films can be enjoyed and judged
> as film and at the same time as something which belongs to the
> wider and freer world of those works, precious among all others,
> which have as their object not only to reveal human reality to us
> but also to show us a way to transcend it. Despite the obstacles
> which the real world sets in the way of similar projects, Buñuel's
> attempt develops under the double arch of beauty and rebellion.
>
> In *Nazarin*, with a style that flees from all complacency
> and rejects all suspect lyricism, Buñuel tells us the story of a
> quixotic priest, whose concept of Christianity soon sets him
> at odds with the Church, society, and the police. Nazarin
> belongs, like many of Galdós's characters, to the great tradition
> of Spanish madmen. Their madness consists of taking Chris-
> tianity seriously and of trying to live in accordance with the
> Gospels. The man who refuses to admit to himself that what
> we call reality is reality and not just an atrocious caricature of
> the true reality, is mad. Like Don Quixote, who discerned his
> Dulcinea in a peasant girl, Nazarin perceives in the monstrous
> sketches of Andra the whore and Ujo the hunchback the help-

less image of fallen men; and in the erotic delirium of Beatriz, an hysteric, he perceives the disfigured face of divine love. In the course of the film—in which scenes in the best and most terrible Buñuel manner, now with more concentrated and therefore more explosive rage, abound—we witness the *cure* of the madman: that is, his torture. Everyone rejects him: the powerful and self-satisfied because they consider him a nuisance and, in the end, dangerous; the victims and the persecuted because they need another, more effective type of consolation. He is pursued not only by the powers that be, but by social equivoque. If he begs for alms, he is an unproductive person; if he seeks work, he breaks the solidarity of the salaried. Even the sentiments of the women who pursue him, reembodiments of Mary Magdalen, turn out ambiguous in the end. In the jail where his good works have landed him, he receives the final revelation: his "goodness," quite as much as the "evil" of one of his companions in punishment, a murderer and church-robber, are equally useless in a world which worships efficiency as the highest value.

Faithful to the tradition of the Spanish madman, from Cervantes to Galdós, Buñuel's film tells the story of a disillusionment. For Don Quixote, illusion was the chivalric spirit; for Nazarin it is Christianity. But there is something more. As the image of Christ fades in Nazarin's consciousness, another begins to emerge: that of man. Buñuel makes us witness, by means of a series of episodes that are exemplary in the good sense of the word, a double process: the disappearance of the illusion of divinity and the discovery of the reality of man. The supernatural gives place to the marvelous: To human nature and its powers. This revelation is embodied in two unforgettable moments: when Nazarin offers *otherworldly consolations* to the dying lover and she replies, gripped by the image of her beloved, with a phrase that is genuinely frightening: *no to heaven, yes to Juan;* and at the end, when Nazarin rejects the alms of a poor woman, only to accept them after a moment of doubt—no longer as a gift but as a token of comradeship. Nazarin the loner has ceased to be alone: he has lost God but he has found men.

This little text appeared in a handout that accompanied the showing of *Nazarin* at the Cannes Film Festival. It was feared, rightly as it proved, that confusion would arise over the meaning of the film, since it is not only a criticism of social reality but also of the Christian religion. The risk of confusion, which all works of art run, was greater in this instance because of the nature of the novel which inspired Buñuel. Galdós's theme is the old opposition between the Christianity of the Gospel and its ecclesiastical and historical distortions. The hero of the book is a rebellious and enlightened priest, a true Protestant: he abandons the Church but stays with God. Buñuel's film sets out to show the opposite: the disappearance of the figure of Christ from the consciousness of a sincere and pure believer. In the scene of the dying girl, which is a transposition of Sade's "Dialogue Between a Priest and a Dying Man," the woman affirms the precious, irrecoverable value of earthly love: if there is a heaven, it is here and now, in the moment of the carnal embrace, not in a timeless, bodiless beyond. In the prison scene, the sacrilegious bandit appears no less absurd a man than the enlightened priest. The crimes of the former are as illusory as the holiness of the latter: if there is no God, there is no sacrilege or holiness either.

Nazarin is not Buñuel's best film, but it is typical of the duality that governs his work. On the one hand, ferocity and lyricism, a world of dream and of blood which immediately calls to mind two other great Spaniards: Quevedo and Goya. On the other, the concentration of a style not at all baroque in character which leads him to a kind of exasperated sobriety. The straight line, not the surrealist arabesque. Rational rigor: each of his films, from *L' Age d' or* to *Viridiana*, is unfolded as a *demonstration*. The most violent and free imagination at the service of a syllogism honed sharp as a knife, irrefutable as a rock: Buñuel's logic is the implacable reason of the Marquis de Sade. This name clarifies the relationship between Buñuel and surrealism: without that movement he would have been a poet and a rebel anyway; thanks to it, he sharpened his weapons. Surrealism, which revealed Sade's thought to him, was not for Buñuel a school of rapture but of reason: his poetry, while it remained poetry, became criticism. In the closed cloister of criticism, rapture spread its wings and clawed its own breast with its nails. Bullring surrealism, but also critical surrealism: the bullfight as philosophical demonstration.

In a primary text of modern letters, *De la Litterature Considerée comme une Tauromachine* (*Of Literature Considered as an Art of Bull-fighting*), Michel Leiris points out that his fascination with bullfighting depends on the fusion between risk and style: the *diestro* (skilled matador)—the Spanish word is exact—should face the bull's charge without losing composure. True: good manners are indispensable for dying and for killing, at least if you believe, as I do, that these two biological acts are at the same time rites, ceremonies. In bullfighting, danger achieves the dignity of form, and form the veracity of death. The bullfighter locks himself into a form which opens out on the danger of dying. It is what in Spanish we call *temple* (temper): musical intrepidity and fine tuning, hardness and flexibility. The bullfight, like photography, is an exposure, and the style of Buñuel, by matched artistic and philosophical choice, is that of exposure. To expose is to expose oneself, risk oneself. It is also to externalize, to show and to demonstrate: to reveal. Buñuel's stories are an exposure: they reveal human realities as they submit them, as if they were photographic plates, to the light of criticism. Buñuel's bullfight is a philosophical discourse, and his films are the modern equivalent to Sade's philosophical novel But Sade was an original philosopher and a middling artist: he did not realize that art, which loves rhythm and litany, excludes repetition and reiteration. Buñuel is an artist, and his films are subject not to poetic but philosophical reproach.

The reasoning which governs all Sade's work can be reduced to this idea: man is his instincts, and the true name of what we call God is fear and mutilated desire. Our morality is a codification of aggression and humiliation; reason itself is nothing but an instinct which knows itself to be instinct and which is afraid of being so. Sade did not set himself the task of proving that God does not exist: he took this for granted. He wanted to demonstrate what human relations would be like in an effectively atheist society. This is the essence of his originality and the unique character of his attempt. The archetype of a republic of truly free men is the Society of the Friends of Crime; of the true philosopher, the ascetic libertine who has managed to achieve impassiveness and who ignores laughter and tears alike. Sade's logic is total and circular: he destroys God but he does not respect man. His system can give rise to many criticisms, but not to that of incoherence. His negation is universal: if he affirms anything it is the right to destroy and be destroyed. Buñuel's criticism has a limit: man. All our crimes are the crimes of a phantom: God. Buñuel's theme is not man's guilt, but God's. This idea, present in all his films, is more explicit and direct in *L'Age d'or* and in *Viridiana,* which are for me, with *Los Olvidados,* his fullest and most perfect creations. If Buñuel's work is a criticism of the illusion of God, that distorting glass which will not let us see man as he is, what are men *really* like and what sense will the words love and fraternity have in a *really* atheist society?

Sade's answer does not satisfy Buñuel, of course. Nor do I believe that, at this time of day, he rests content with the descriptions which offer us philosophical or political utopias. Apart from the fact that these prophecies cannot be verified, at any event not yet, it is clear that they do not correspond to what we know about man, his history and his nature. To believe in an atheist society governed by natural harmony—a dream we have all had—would be today like repeating Pascal's wager, only in the opposite sense. More than a paradox, it would be an act of despair: It would command our admiration, not our assent. I do not know what answer Buñuel could give to these questions. Surrealism, which denied so many things, was motivated by a gale of generosity and faith. Among its ancestors are counted not only Sade and Lautréamont but also Fourier and Rousseau. And perhaps it is the last of these, at least for André Breton, who is the true origin of the movement: exaltation of passion, unlimited confidence in the natural powers of man. I do not know if Buñuel is closer to Sade or to Rousseau; it is more likely that both conduct an argument within him. Whatever his beliefs on this score, it is the case that in his films neither Sade's nor Rousseau's answer appears. Reticence, timidity, or disdain, his silence is troubling. It is troubling not only because it is the silence of one of the great artists of our time, but also because it is the silence of all the art of this first half-century. After Sade, as far as I know, no one has dared to discover an atheist society.

Something is lacking in the work of our contemporaries: not God, but man without God.

—Delhi, 1965

III. CANNES, 1951:
LOS OLVIDADOS

I must have been about seventeen when I first heard of Luis Buñuel. I was a student at the National Preparatory School and I had just discovered, in the display cases of the Porrua and Robredo bookstores, near San Ildefonso, the books and magazines of the new literature. In one of these publications—*La gaceta literaria (The Literary Gazette)*, which Ernesto Jiménez Caballero published in Madrid—I read an article on Buñuel and Dalí. This article was illustrated by both of them, with reproductions of Dalí's paintings and stills from their two films: *Un chien andalou* and *L'Age d'or*. The stills excited me more deeply than the pictures by the Catalan painter: in the film images, the mixture of everyday reality and madness was more effective and explosive than in the mannerist illusionism of Dalí. A few years later, in the summer of 1937 in Paris, I met Buñuel face to face.

One morning, at the door of the Spanish consulate, where I had gone with Pablo Neruda to pick up a visa, we bumped into him. Pablo stopped him and introduced us. It was a fleeting encounter. That same year I managed at last to see the two famous films, with the smell of cordite in the air: *Un Chien Andalou* and *L'Age d'or*. For me, the second film was, in the strict sense of the word, a revelation: the sudden appearance of a truth hidden and buried, but alive. I discovered that the age of gold is in each of us and that it has the face of passion.

Many years later, in 1951, again in Paris, I saw Luis Buñuel again at the house of some friends: Gaston and Betty Bouthoul. During that period I saw him quite often; he came to my house, and finally one day he called to entrust me with a mission: I was to present his film *Los Olvidados* at that year's Cannes Festival. I accepted enthusiastically, without hesitation. I had seen the film at a private showing with André Breton and other friends. A strange detail: the night of the showing, at the other end of the little projection room, Aragon, Sadoul, and others were present. When I saw them I thought for a moment that a pitched battle would ensue, as in the days of their youth. I exchanged glances with Elisa Breton, who showed signs of nervousness; but all and sundry sat down silently and a few minutes later the showing began. I think it was the first time Aragon and Breton had seen each other since their rift, twenty years before. The film moved me: it was animated by the same violent imagination and for the same implacable reason as *L'Age d'or*, but Buñuel, through using a very strict form, had managed a greater concentration. As we left, Breton praised the film, though he regretted that the director had conceded too much, at certain points, to the realist logic of the story at the expense of the poetry or, as he said, of the marvelous. For my part, I thought that *Los Olvidados* showed the way not to overcome superrealism—can anything be overcome in art and literature?—but to unravel it; I mean that Buñuel had found an exit from the superrealist aesthetic by inserting, in the traditional form of the narrative, the irrational images which spring up out of the dark side of man. (In those years I set myself a similar task in the more restricted domain of lyric poetry.) And here perhaps it is not out of place to say that in the best works of Buñuel a rare faculty is revealed, a faculty which could be called *synthetic imagination*, that is, totality and concentration.

As soon as I got to Cannes I met with the other Mexican delegate. He was a producer and exhibitor of Polish origin who lived in Paris. He said he was aware of my nomination as Mexican delegate to the festival and he pointed out that our country had sent another film to the festival In fact, Buñuel was participating in the festival in his own right, invited by the French organizers. The Mexican delegate also told me that he had seen *Los Olvidados* in Paris, and it seemed to him, despite its artistic merits, an esoteric film, aestheticist and at times incomprehensible. In his judgment, it had no chance whatsoever of winning any prize. He added that various Mexican high functionaries, as well as numerous intellectuals and journalists, were against the showing at Cannes of a film that denigrated Mexico. This last point was unfortunately true, and Buñuel has referred to the subject in his memoirs (*My Last Sigh*), though discreetly, without naming his critics. I will follow his example, but not without stressing that, in this attitude of theirs, the two evils which at that time our progressive intellectuals suffered from came together: nationalism and socialist realism.

The skepticism of my colleague in the Mexican delegation was made up for by the enthusiasm and goodwill that various friends, all admirers of Buñuel, showed, among them the legendary Langlois, director of the Cinématheque de Paris, and two young superrealists, Kyrou and Benayoun, who put out an avant-garde magazine, *L'Age du cinéma*. We visited many notable artists who lived in the Côte d'Azur, inviting them to the event at which the film was to be shown. Almost all of them accepted. One of those most keen to show himself in favor of Buñuel and of free art was, to my surprise, the painter Chagall. On the other hand, Picasso proved evasive and reticent; in the end, he didn't show up. I recalled his hardly friendly attitude to Apollinaire in the matter of the Phoenician statuettes. Most generous of all was the poet Jacques Prévert. He lived in Vence, a few kilometers from Cannes. Langlois and I went to see him, we told him our worries, and a few days later he sent us a poem in praise of Buñuel which we hurried into print. I believe it caused a certain stir among the critics and journalists attending the festival.

I wrote a little essay as a kind of introduction. Since we had no money we mimeographed it. On the day of the showing I handed it out to all comers at the door of the theater. A few days later a Paris newspaper printed it. Buñuel's film immediately occasioned many articles, commentaries, and discussions. *Le Monde* praised it to the skies, but *L'Humanité* called it "a negative film." Those were the years of socialist realism, and the *positive message* was exalted as the central value of works of art. I remember the furious argument I had one night shortly after the showing with Georges Sadoul. He told me Buñuel had *deserted* the true realism and that he was paddling, though talentedly, in the sewage of bourgeois pessimism. I replied that his use of the word *desert* revealed that his idea of art was worthy of a sergeant and that with the theory of socialist realism the intention was to conceal the null Soviet social reality . . . The rest is known: *Los Olvidados* did not get the grand prix, but with that film begins Buñuel's second and great creative period.

—Mexico, 1983

JORGE GUILLÉN

Jorge Guillén is a Spaniard from Castile, which doesn't mean he's more Spanish than the Spaniards of other regions but that he is Spanish in a different way. He is no purist: Guillén is a European Spaniard and belongs to an historical moment in which Spanish culture was opening out to the thought and art of Europe. But unlike Ortega, who enlivened and inspired that group, Guillén was closer to France than to Germany. He pursued his university studies in Paris, where he was married first and where he taught. He also gave courses at Oxford. He returned to Spain and promptly became a leading figure of a generation which Gerardo Diego introduced in 1925 in a celebrated anthology. It was a generation parallel to the one that in Mexico gathered around the magazine *Contemporáneos*. The Civil War scattered the Spanish poets. Guillén lived for years in the United States. For much of his life he has been a university professor. He has lived for long stretches in Italy, where he married for the second time. A whole European. Also a complete Spanish-American: he knows our continent and has friends in all our countries.

His work is extensive and almost entirely in verse. Three books: *Cántico (Canticle)*, *Clamor (Tumult)*, and *Homenaje (Homage)*. The subtitles are illuminating: *Cántico: Fe de vida (Faith in Life)*affirmation of being and affirmation of what is. This book has had very great influence on our language. *Clamor: Tiempo de historia (The Time of History)—the* poet in the corridors—errors and horrors—of contemporary history. *Homenaje: Reunión de vidas (Joining of Lives)—the* poet not among men or confronting them but with them. And above all with women: Guillén is a poet for whom woman exists. I am sure he would agree if he heard me say that woman is the highest form of being. *Reunión de vidas*, with poets living as well as dead: in that book Guillén converses with his masters, his antecedents in the poetic art, and his contemporaries and successors. When he began writing he was thought a severe poet; now we realize that he has also been an extremely fecund poet: in 1973 he published a new book, simply called Y *otros poemas (And Other Poems)*.

Guillén belongs to a group of writers who knew they were part of a tradition that transcends linguistic frontiers. All of them felt that they were not only German, French, Italian, or Spanish but European. The European consciousness, a victim of nationalisms, is progressively attenuated until it almost vanishes in the nineteenth century. Its rebirth, at the beginnings of this century, is something Europe had not experienced since the eighteenth century. Examples of this sensibility include Rilke, Valéry Larbaud, Ungaretti, Eliot. Here I should mention two Latin Americans: Alfonso Reyes and Jorge Luis Borges. It is instructive to note that an of them wrote in their native language and in French—except Borges, who has written in English. In those years Paris was still the center, if not of the world, at least of art and literature . . . In that Paris of the first third of the century Guillén spent decisive formative years. The Paris of Huidobro had been one of revolt in art and poetry: Picasso, Reverdy, Tzara, Arp, the beginnings of surrealism. Guillén is nearer to the *Nouvelle Revue Française* and, above all, to *Commerce*, the great poetry magazine edited by Paul Valéry, Leon Paul Fargue, and Valéry Larbaud—the great Larbaud, friend of Gómez de la Serna, Reyes, Güiraides.

Because of his classical bent Guillén suggests a Mediterranean Eliot. But literary essays and critical writing do not occupy the same place in Guillén's work as they do in Eliot's. And there is something else which radically distinguishes him from Eliot: in his work there is scarcely a trace of Christianity. His subject is sensual and intellectual: the world touched by the senses and the mind. Profoundly Mediterranean poetry, Guillén is very near to Valéry. He was his friend, experienced his influence, and his translation of "Le cimetière marine" is a masterpiece. All the same, the similarities between Valéry and Guillén do not cancel out the deep differences. Valéry is a spirit of prodigious insight, one of the truly luminous minds of this century. He is a great writer endowed with two qualities which in others appear opposed: Intellectual rigor and sensuality. But these admirable and unique gifts are as if lost in a kind of vacancy: Unsupported, they lack world. The I, the consciousness, has swallowed the world. This evaporation of reality, is it the price the skeptic must pay if he wants to make sense to himself? I doubt it. Hume was no less a skeptic, and yet his work has an architecture which Valéry's lacks.

Valéry's powers of deconstruction were greater than his powers of construction. His *Cahiers* are an imposing ruin. Valéry was a most powerful spiritual lever which lacked a pivot point. Guillén's critical and analytical powers are not as great as Valéry's, but his spiritual lever did not lack a pivot.

For Guillén reality is what we touch and see: faith in the senses is the poet's true faith. This provides him common ground with certain painters. Not the realists but rather an artist like Juan Gris, in whom the rigor of abstraction is fused with a fidelity to the physical object. In Guillén, good Mediterranean that he is, sensuality is dominant, and this draws him toward another great painter, Matisse. These names, it seems to me, trace Guillén's spiritual profile: his lucidity calls Valéry to mind; his almost ascetic rigor before the object allies him with Juan Gris; the line which swerves like a feminine river evokes Matisse. But the light which illuminates his poetry is that of the Castilian plains, the light which shines down to us from Fray Luis Ponce de León and his Horatian odes.

Guillén returned to Spain in 1924. He was thirty years old. He had not yet published a book. He was a late developer, unlike Lorca and Alberti. The panorama of Spanish poetry in those days was extremely rich. Never since the seventeenth century had Spain had so many excellent poets. That was the best period of Juan Ramón Jiménez. It was also the period of his influence on the young writers. Juan Ramón was writing a simple, inspired poetry in the traditional vein of the Spanish lyric: songs, romances, *coplas,* and other popular forms. Short poems, almost exclamations; fresh poems, sudden fountains. Poetry of popular rhythms and yet aristocratic, refined, and as is clear to us today, a boneless poetry, without architecture, excessively subjective. Though the young poets followed Juan Ramón, their images came from creationism and ultraism. Huidobro's system of metaphor had stirred the poets of Latin America and Spain a few years earlier. A strong but very Spanish amalgam of traditionalism and avant-garde: Alberti composed madrigals to the train ticket and Salinas songs to the radiator.

There was much talk in those years of "pure poetry." Juan Ramón defined it as the simple, the plain and refined: a word reduced to the essential. In fact, Juan Ramón was not defining "pure poetry" so much as his own poetry. Guillén was returning from France, where the notion of "pure poetry" was also in the ascendant. The French conception was more rigorous. Abbé Bremond had defined "pure poetry" with a nondefinition: it was the undefinable, what is beyond sound and sense, something which was confused with prayer and ecstasy. Though for Valéry poetry was neither gibberish nor prayer, his definitions too were, in their apparent simplicity, enigmatic: poetry was all that which could not be said in prose. But what can't be said in prose? In a letter to a friend Guillén defines his position in brief. It is typical of Guillén to formulate his poetic in a letter to a friend: Huidobro had launched various manifestos, and others of us have written essays and even books. It is worth quoting part of his letter, well known though it is:

> Bremond has been and remains useful. He represents the popular apologetic, like a poet-catechist for Sunday morning. And his lecture is a sermon. But how far all this mysticism is, with its metaphysical and ineffable phantom, from pure poetry, according to Poe, to Valéry and the young poets of there and here! Bremond speaks of poetry in the poet, of a *poetic state*, and that's already a bad sign. No, no. There is no poetry but that achieved in the poem and there is no way to set against the poem an *ineffable state* which is corrupted when it is carried out . . . Pure poetry is mathematics and chemistry—nothing more—in the good sense of that expression suggested by Valéry and which some young mathematicians and chemists have made their own, understanding it in a different sense, but always within that initial, fundamental direction. Valéry himself repeated it to me, once, one morning in the rue de Villejust. Pure poetry is all that remains in the poem after all that is not poetry has been eliminated. *Pure* is the same as *simple* in chemical terms. . . . Since I call *pure, simple*, I come down resolutely on the side of composed, complex poetry, the poem with poetry and other human things. In sum, quite a pure poetry, *ma non troppo*, if one takes as the unit of comparison the *simple* element in its greatest inhuman and superhuman theoretical rigor.

Guillén denied that there were "poetic states": poetry is in the poem, is a verbal deed. This attitude radically separated him not only from Bremond but, at the other extreme, from the surrealists, who attributed more importance to the poetic experience than to the act of writing poems. Guillén was aware that, whatever else, a purely poetic poetry would be quite boring. And something more serious: it was linguistically impossible since language is by nature impure. A "pure poetry" would be one in which language had ceased to be language. The idea of "pure poetry" was very much of its period. Years before, physics had tried to isolate the ultimate components of matter. For their part, the cubist painters reduced objects to a series of relations on a plane. Following the example of the physicists and painters, as Jakobson has more than once recalled, the linguists had attempted to discover the ultimate elements of language, the signifying particles. This intellectual orientation was powerfully manifest in the work of Edmund Husserl, the phenomenologist. The philosophers of this persuasion, too, attempted to reduce things to their essences, and thus regional ontologies of the chair, the pencil, the claw, the hand were made. Unfortunately, these ontologies almost always ended in expressions such as these: The chair is the chair, poetry is poetry (or: all that is not prose). Phenomenology issues, I'm afraid, in tautologies. But tautology is, perhaps, the only metaphysical affirmation which men can reach. The most we can say about being is that it is.

MOST CRITICS HAVE INSISTED on the ontological character of "Mas alla," the opening poem of *Cantico:* affirming what is and affirming being. I have always looked a little distrustfully at philosophical explanations of poetry. Still, in this instance, interpretation can serve us as a point of departure for a fuller understanding of the poem, so long as we do not forget even for a moment that "Mas ana" is not a philosophical treatise but a poem. The ideas of the poem interest and arouse us not because they are true but because Guillén has made them poetically true. The axis on which "Mas alla" turns, and more generally, the axis of all the poetry in *Cántico,* is an affirmation which appears at the beginning and end of the poem: *quiero ser* (I want to be), Two-edged phrase: I want being and I want to be. This double and universal wanting is already present in Plato: all beings want to be because the supreme good is being. That is why Saint Augustine thought that evil was nothing but the absence of being.

Generally speaking, also since Plato, being is identified with essence. What is the being of the chair, table, star? Its essence, its idea. Ultimate realities, essential realities, are ideas: intellectual forms we can contemplate, whether in the starry sky or in the space, at once ideal and subject to the senses, of the geometric bodies. But Guillén's poem does not affirm being as essence or as idea but as passing: being is blood and time, eternity suspended. An eternity which is manifest in dates, places, and circumstances: today, Monday, in this room, in the morning. Is this a form of materialism? No, the ultimate reality is neither material nor ideal: it is a wanting, a relationship, an interchange. We have before us a paradoxical realism since it supports itself by affirming the instant as eternity.

Guillén's realism looks like relativism. It is established on flux, that is, on time. When the poem begins, huge time surrounds the sleeper. Later, made energy, it manifests itself in things. That energy moves things and changes them. The world is relation because it is time which is movement which is passing which is change. Movement of one thing toward another and change of one thing into another. Here Guillén's universalizing strategy comes into play: being—an absolute—becomes relative, becomes particular and is manifest in this and that; this and that are relative, are time, are instants, but each instant is all time, each instant is a totality. The now becomes forever, a forever that is happening now and is happening for ever. Here is wherever, and wherever is the center of the universe. First movement: being is not an essence or an idea: it is a passing, an energy crystallized in a here and now. Second movement: here is central, the point toward which all points converge; and the now is an always which is an instant, a suspended eternity. Man is the agent of this transmutation. Or rather: man's desire to be is. The desire is his and his alone: at the same time, it is the desire of all creatures and all things. It is a universal wanting. What is more, the plural universe is a desire to be in unison.

Man is the point of intersection of this plural universe of desire, and that is why each man is central. But man is central not because he is the creation of the demiurge. Man is not king of creation nor the favorite son of the creator. Man is the point of intersection between chance and necessity. I use deliberately the title of the book by the biologist

Jacques *Monod*—*Chance and Necessity*—because there is a curious coincidence between Guillén's poetic thought and contemporary biology. For Guillén, man's being is at the same time the expression of universal totality—his body follows its circuit well, as those of the stars do—and the result of a chance collision of forces and energies: atoms, cells, acids. Another biologist, François Jacob, says that cells have no function but to reproduce, copy, and duplicate themselves. We might say that they are in love with themselves, like Narcissus and like Luzbel. Sometimes, when they copy themselves, by a well-understood principle of physics, changes occur. These are mutants. These mutants pass through the strainer of natural selection; some vanish, and others, as they grow strong, perpetuate themselves until they give rise to new species. But the cells of Jacob and Monod are a desire to be which only wants to be, while Guillén's will to be is, like that of all men, a desire to be which contemplates itself, reflects itself, and, above all, speaks. It is an accord which does not recognize itself as such. Man rescues the instant when he speaks it, names it. The present endures not only and exclusively because, like the cells, it repeats itself, but because it sees itself through the moment. In that momentary apparition, consciousness accedes to a kind of vertiginous eternity—and names it. An eternity which lasts as long as it takes the poet to say it and us to hear it. It is enough.

Man—that universal desire of being and that desire of universal being—is a moment of change, one of the forms in which energy is manifest. That moment and that form are transitory, circumstantial: here and now. That moment will disappear, that form will be scattered. Nonetheless, that moment includes all moments, is all moments; that form binds itself with all forms and is in every part. How do we know this? We know it without knowing it. We feel it when we live certain experiences. For example, when we wake up. Except that really to wake up we must take account of the fact that the world in which we wake up is a world which wakes up with us. Without eyes and soul man could not know that each minute is on the crest of time and at the center of space. But eyes and soul are not enough: the world is incomprehensible, the ultimate reality is invisible, untouchable. No matter: we have language. By means of the words we get dose to things, we call them *evidences, prodigies, riddles, transcendencies*. Language is a dike against nameless chaos. The world of relations which is the universe is a verbal world: we wander among things which are names. We ourselves are names. Landscapes of names which time unceasingly destroys. Wasted names which we have to invent anew each century, each generation, every morning when we wake up. Poetry is the process by which man names the world and names himself. That is why man is the legend of reality. And I would add, the legend of himself.

Guillén's here and now resemble the instant which dissolves all instants. It is the instant of lovers and also that of mystics, especially Eastern ones, with which Guillén is perhaps not acquainted, and whom he would probably disapprove of if he knew them. That instant annuls the contradiction between this and that, past and future, negation and affirmation. It is not the union, the marriage of contraries, but their scattering. On this vision of the other aspect of being—the blank aspect: vacancy—it is not easy to erect a metaphysic. But it is possible to build a wisdom and above all a poetics. It is an experience which we have all lived and which some have thought. Poets are those who, whatever their beliefs, language, and age, manage to express it.

—In *Mediciones*, 1979

TWO NOTES ON JOSÉ REVUELTAS: CHRISTIANITY AND REVOLUTION

FIRST NOTE

When the armed struggle ceased and what has come to be called "the constructive phase of the Mexican Revolution" began, two different forms of artistic expression, the novel and painting, avidly addressed themselves to the recent past. The consequences of this engagement have been the "Mexican school of painting" and the "Novel of the Revolution." Over the last twenty years the novel has served to express the authors' nostalgias, hopes, and disillusions with the revolution, rather than any more literary undertakings. Technically poor, these works are more picturesque than descriptive, more in the nature of genre writing than realism . . . The novelists of the revolution, and among them the great myopic talent of Mariano Azuela, blinded by the frenzy of gunpowder or by that other frenzy of the corrupt generals' diamonds, have reduced their theme to that: many deaths, many crimes and lies. And a superficial stage set of burned villages, maddening jungles, and godless deserts. In this way they have mutilated fictional reality—the only reality that matters to the true novelist—by reducing it to a pure chronicle or a framed portrayal of customs. All the "Novels of the Revolution" have been narratives and chronicles, even those of Mariano Azuela. (Valéry Larbaud declared that Martín Luis Guzmàn reminded him of Tacitus: a strange way to praise a novelist!)

The next generation has hardly attempted the novel. Made up as it is by a group of literati, poets, and essayists, it has shown a degree of repugnance, if not disdain, for the realities which surround it. The novel has been the Cinderella of these writers, who rally under the banner of curiosity and evasion. After them, there have been isolated attempts: those of the most recent group of Mexican writers (Juan de la Cabada, Efrén Hernández, Rubén Salazar Mallén, Andrés Henestrosa, Rafael Solana, Francisco Tario). Almost all of them evince a marked preference for that hard and strict genre, the short story. Just as in painting the generation of "muralists" has been succeeded by a group of young artists which a patronizing North American critic dubbed the "little masters," so these new Mexican prose writers, successors to the "Novelists of the Revolution," have excelled above all in the writing of short stories and narratives. One of Juan de la Cabada's books, *Paséo de mentiras* (*Passage of Lies*), brings together in a few pages some stories and a novella which make him, up to now, the most interesting and enigmatic of all; one novel, *Camino de perfección* (*Road of Perfection*), and particularly some bitter and harsh stories, lead one to believe that Rubén Salazar Mallén also has the necessary talent to give Mexico a real novel.

The most ambitious and impassioned—and the youngest, too—is José Revueltas (twenty-seven years old, affiliated from the age of fourteen with the Communist Party; his political ideas have given him a chance to get to know the insides of the country's jails several times, in the time of President Rodríguez). José Revueltas has published a first novel, *El luto humano* (*Human Sorrow*), which has received an award in a national competition. Before that he had written some mysterious, stammering stories; a short novel, *El quebranto*,* and a narrative, *Los muros de agua* (*The Walls of Water*), in which he tells of the life of a penal colony in the Pacific. (He was imprisoned there for two years, before he reached the age of twenty.) Revueltas's novel has aroused both the most ardent praise and the sourest criticism. A Marxist critic has charged him with pessimism, but other enthusiasts have been quick to cite Dostoevski.

El luto humano tells a dramatic story: a group of peasants goes on strike at an "irrigation system" established by the Mexican Revolutionary government. The strike and the consequent drought cause the

---

* It was never published in full, except for the first chapter (*Taller* 2, April 1939), because Revueltas lost the manuscript.

government plan to fail and the exodus begins. Only three families insist on staying on in that deserted place. One day the river, dry until that time, swells and breaks its banks and a flood isolates the characters of the novel on a rooftop. Alcohol, hunger, and jealousy finish them off. The novel opens when the river begins to swell and ends just as the buzzards settle down to devour the dying. All these events take place in a period of a few days. But the novel scarcely alludes to what the peasants actually do to escape the flood; Revueltas prefers to tell us what they think, what they remember, what they feel. Often he displaces his characters; in their place he expounds his own doubts, his faith and his despair, his opinions about death or about Mexican religiosity. The action is interrupted each time a character, before dying, summarizes his life . . . A constant religious concern invades the work: Mexicans, pious by nature, and lovers of blood, have been deprived of their religion, without the Catholic faith having been enough to satisfy their hard thirst for eternity. Adam, a murderer, who believes himself to be the embodiment of Fate, and Natividad, a murdered leader, symbolize, in very religious terms, the past and future of Mexico. Between them move the rancorous present-day Mexicans, and their taciturn women represent the earth, thirsty for water and blood, a baptism that combines, together with agricultural fertility rites, ancient Aztec and Christian rites. In the closing pages the author tries to convince himself—more than the reader—that by a better use of natural resources and a better distribution of wealth, this religiosity without hope, this blind love of death, will vanish from the Mexican soul. The novel is clearly contaminated with sociology, religion, and ancient and modern Mexican history. There is some contamination in the language, which is at times brilliant, at times strangely turgid.

These faults damn the work, but not its author. Because, oddly, the reader feels himself infected with the same fascination to which the novelist is prey. Revueltas feels a kind of religious revulsion, of love composed of horror and repulsion, for Mexico. True, Revueltas has not written a novel, but, all the same, he has cast light into himself. Seduced as much by the myths of Mexico as by its realities, he has made himself a part of that drama which he attempts to depict. Endowed with talent, imaginative force, quite uncommon vigor and sensibility—and devoured by a haste which does not let him, it would seem, linger over his faults—José Revueltas is now ready to write a novel. In this attempt he frees himself of all his phantoms, all his doubts and opinions. As is the case with much Mexican painting, which reveals a great vigor that often remains outside the picture, beyond the frame, Revueltas has brought together all his great modeling and prophetic power, but without managing to apply it to his object: the novel. In short, for what am I reproaching Revueltas? I reproach him—I now realize—for his youth, since all those defects, that lack of soberness in the language, that desire to say it all at once, that lack of concentration and that reluctance to trim the useless wings of words, ideas, and situations, that absence of discipline—within and without—these are nothing but the faults of youth. In any event, Revueltas is the first writer among us who has tried to create a deep work, remote from genre writing, superficiality, and the cut-price psychology which dominate today. Perhaps nothing will remain of this work of his but its spirit: isn't this enough for a young man who is just starting, and starting us, on the task of creating for ourselves an imaginative world, strange and disturbingly personal?

—*Sur*, July 1943

SECOND NOTE

When I reread the preceding note, which Luis Mario Schneider dug out of an old issue of *Sur*, I immediately felt the need to clarify, correct, and extend it. It is one beginner's criticism of another beginner; what is more, it is far too cutting and categorical. My excuse is that those faults are frequent among the young. I end by reproaching Revueltas for his youth, and that censure is perfectly applicable to the opinion I held at that time. Youth does not justify other errors. For instance, in the first paragraph I condemn the novelists of the Mexican Revolution. That was a silliness: among them there are two excellent writers, Martín Luis Guzmán and Mariano Azuela. Both were masters of their art. Martín Luis Guzmán's prose, bright as that of a Roman historian, has a kind of classical transparence: its subject is terrible, but he traces it with a calm, firm rhythm. Azuela was not "a great myopic talent"; nor was he dull: he was a lucid writer, in control of his resources, and he explored many roads which others have traveled since. But when I wrote my note on *El luto humano* (1943), the novel of the revolution had turned itself from a movement into a school: the invention was now a recipe. In this sense I was not wrong: the appearance of *El luto humano*, published a few years before *Al filo del agua* by Augustín Yañez (1947), was a break and a beginning. Despite its imperfections, Revueltas's novel set something in motion which is not yet exhausted.

My analysis of *El luto humano* is too brisk. I point out with excessive severity the narrator's unskillful devices and the frequency with which his voice displaces that of his characters. Those defects are due, at least in part, to the difficulty and novelty of what Revueltas was setting out to say and what he managed to say more felicitously years later. The young novelist wanted to use the new techniques of the North American novel (the Faulkner of *The Wild Palms* is constantly present) to write a chronicle that was at once epic and symbolic, about an episode which seemed to him to possess the quality of a revolutionary exemplum. The purpose was contradictory: Faulkner's realism (perhaps all realism) implies a pessimistic view of man and of his earthly destiny; in its turn, Revueltas's epic chronicle is undermined by religious symbolism, for lack of a better expression. The peasants fight for land and water, but the novelist continually suggests that that fight alludes to another, one not entirely of this world. Though my note stresses the religiosity of Revueltas, it does not describe its paradoxical character: a vision of Christianity *within* his Marxist atheism. Revueltas lived his Marxism as a Christian, and that is why he lived it, in Unamuno's sense, as agony, doubt, and negation.

In speaking of the religiosity of the Mexican people, I mention "rancor," an inexact word. I attribute it to the great catastrophe of the Conquest, which deprived the Indians not only of their world but of their otherworld: that of their gods and mythologies. Still, when with the key of baptism it unlocked the gates of heaven and hell for them, Catholicism paradoxically gave them the possibility of coming to terms with their old religion. Perhaps Revueltas thought that, "on a higher historical plain," revolutionary Marxism would perform in the face of Christianity the same function that Christianity performed in the face of the pre-Columbian religions. This idea would explain the importance of the Christian symbolism in the novel. Moreover, he was always fascinated by popular beliefs and myths. A friend told me how once, half in jest, half seriously, it occurred to Revueltas to celebrate a marriage rite not before the altar of the Virgin of Guadalupe but before the goddess Coatlicue in the Museum of Anthropology. I remember too that on the night of the 1971 Corpus Christi massacre, when a number of friends were gathered at Carlos Fuentes's house and we discussed what we might do, Revueltas approached me and with an undefinable smile on his face whispered in my ear: "Let's all go dance before the Holy Lord of Chalma!" A phrase reveals a man: "Atheism," André Breton once told me, "is an act of faith." The *witticisms* of Revueltas were oblique confessions.

At the end of my note I point to the real significance of *El luto humano:* "Revueltas has not written a novel, but . . . he has cast light into himself." Today I would say: that work was a stage in his pilgrimage, a real Way of the Cross, toward the light. And this is the source of the central question, which Revueltas faced bravely from his very short novel, *El quebranto,* and which he never stopped asking himself: What light, the light *here,* or *there?* Perhaps here is there, perhaps revolutions are nothing but the road that here travels toward there. Revueltas's action seems to be secretly inspired by this idea. He was a militant revolutionary, novelist, and author of philosophical and political essays. As a militant he was a dissident who criticized with identical passion capitalism and bureaucratic "socialism;" the same duality is evident in his novels, stories, and essays. Thus, on the one hand, there is a remarkable continuity between his life and his work: it is impossible to separate the novelist from the militant and the militant from the author of texts of philosophical, aesthetic, and political criticism; on the other hand, that unity contains a fracture, an excision. Revueltas was in a continual dialogue—or more precisely, a permanent dispute—with his philosophical, aesthetic, and political ideas. His criticism of Communist orthodoxy was self-criticism at the same time. His case is not unique, of course; on the contrary, it is more and more common: the dissidence of Marxist intellectuals is one expression, perhaps the central one, of the universal crisis of that doctrine. But there is something that sets Revueltas's doubts and criticisms apart from the others: the tone, the religious passion. And there is something more: the questions which Revueltas time and again asked himself make no sense and cannot be answered except within a religious frame of reference. Not that of just any religion but specifically that of Christianity.

For Westerners the opposition between atheism and religion cannot be resolved. This has not been the case with other civilizations: in its strictest and purest form, Buddhism is atheist. And yet that atheism does not root out the divine: like all beings, without excepting men or the Buddha himself, the gods are bubbles, reflections of emptiness. Buddhism is a radical critique of reality and the human condition: the true reality, *sunyata*, is an undefinable state in which being and nonbeing, the real and the unreal, cease to be at odds and, in coming together, annul themselves. Thus history is nothing but shadow play, illusion—like everything else. This is also why Buddhist religious observance is essentially contemplative. By contrast, for Christianity the incarnation of Jesus and his sacrifice are deeds that are at once supernatural and historical. Not only does divine revelation unfold in history, but history is the testing ground for Christians: souls triumph and are lost here, in this world. The Marxist Revueltas takes on the Christian heritage with all its consequences: the weight of human history. The nexus between Christianity and Marxism is history; both are doctrines which identify with the historical process. The condition in which Marxism is possible is the same as that for Christianity: action on this world. And the rivalry between Marxism and Christianity is manifest here on earth: to fulfill himself and his mission, revolutionary man has to evict God from history. The first revolutionary act is the critique of Heaven. The relation between Marxism and Christianity implies, at the same time, a bond and a breach. Buddhism—in general terms, all Eastern thought—ignores or disdains history. At the same time, immersed in an atmosphere of the divine, surrounded by gods, it does not acknowledge the notion of a unique creator God. Oriental atheism is not really atheistic; in a strict sense, only Jews, Christians, and Muslims can be atheists: they are believers in a single creator God. Bloch very rightly said: "Only a true Christian can be a good atheist; only a true atheist can be a good Christian."

The Christian Marxism of Revueltas can only be understood from the double perspective I have just sketched. In the first place, the idea of history conceived as a process endowed with meaning and direction; secondly, irreducible atheism. Now, between history and atheism a further opposition opens out: if God disappears, history ceases to mean. Christian atheism is tragic because, as Nietzsche saw it, it is a negation of meaning. For Dostoevski, if there is no God, everything is permissible, everything is possible; but if everything is possible, nothing is: the infinity of possibilities annuls them and resolves them in impossibility. In the same way: the absence of God makes everything thinkable; but everything equals nothing: everything and nothing are not thinkable. Atheism sets us face to face with the unthinkable and the impossible; that is why it is terrifying and, literally, unbearable. Also, that is why we have installed other deities in God's vacant niche: Reason, Progress. These principles come down to earth, become incarnate and turn into the secret activators of history. They are our Christs: the nation, the proletariat, the race. In Revueltas's novel, the old man is called Adam, like our father; and the new man, the collective Christ, is called Nativity. The history of the Son of Man begins with the Nativity and culminates with the Sacrifice; the Revolution obeys the same logic. That logic is rational, "scientific": historical materialism; and it is supernatural: transcendence. The "scientific" is explicit; the supernatural, implicit. Divine transcendence disappears, but, surreptitiously, by means of revolutionary action it continues to function. As Bloch also said, revolution is "to transcend without transcendence."

The hostility between Marxism and Christianity never entirely disappears but it is attenuated if the terms change places. For Christianity we men are sons of Adam, the child of God. In the beginning is God, who is not only the giver of meaning but the creator of life. God is before history and after it: he is the beginning and the end. For a Christian Marxist like Bloch or Revueltas, God cannot be before; in fact, God does not exist: the original, primordial reality is man or, better said, human society. But historical man is hardly man at all; to realize himself, truly to be man, he must pass through the trials of history, must triumph over it and transform its fatal course into liberty. Revolution makes men of men—and more than men: man's future is to be God. Christianity was the humanizing of God; revolution promises divinity to man. Abrupt change of places: God is not before but after, not the creator of men but their creature. Bloch alters the Biblical phrase and says *I am what I will be* (Ernst Bloch, *L'athéisme dans le christianisme,* Gallimard, 1978).

Revueltas never formulated his ideas with Bloch's clarity, but the *temper* of his writings and his life corresponds to this agonizing and contradictory vision of Marxism and Christianity. Of course, he reached these attitudes independently and by his own route. It was not philosophy that guided him but his personal experience. In the first place, the religion of his childhood; then his interest in Mexican common life, all of it impregnated with religiosity; and finally, his philosophical and poetic temperament. This last was decisive: Revueltas asked himself philosophical questions which Marxism—as among others Kolakowski and Bloch himself have recognized—cannot answer except with scientist commonplaces. In fact, those questions have only metaphysical and religious answers. Metaphysics, after Hume and Kant, is forbidden to us moderns. Thus Revueltas resorts intuitively and with passion, in a movement back to the earliest elements in his being, to the religious answers, mingled with the millenarian ideas and hopes of the revolutionary movement. Though philosophy enthralled him, he was above all a creative artist. His religious temperament drew him to communism, which he saw as the way of sacrifice and communion; that same temperament, inseparable from the love of truth and the good, led him at the end of his life to a criticism of bureaucratic "socialism" and Marxist clericalism.

Marxism has turned into an ideology and today functions as a pseudoreligion. The transformation of a philosophy into an ideology and of this into a religion is not a new phenomenon: the same thing happened with Neoplatonism and Gnosticism. Nor is the transformation of a religion into a political power and of a priesthood into a clerical bureaucracy anything new: Roman Catholicism has known these perversions. The historical peculiarity of communism is in the fact that it is not really a religion but an ideology that works as though it were a science, the Science; thus, it is not a church but a party which does not resemble other parties so much as the militant orders and brotherhoods of the Catholics and Muslims. Communist parties begin as little sects but as soon as they grow, they turn into closed churches. (I use the plural because in the Communist movement schisms and divisions proliferate.) Each church believes that it possesses universal truth; this pretension would not be perilous were it not for the fact that the bureaucracies which govern these groups are motivated by an equally universal desire to dominate and proselytize. Each member of each church is a missionary and each missionary a potential inquisitor. Revueltas's religiousness was far removed from these ideological fanaticisms; his true spiritual affinities are to be found on the other side, near the primitive Christians, the fourth-century Gnostics, and the Protestant rebels and revolutionaries of the Reformation. Within the Catholic Church he would have been as much a heretic as he was within the Communist orthodoxy. His Marxism was not a system but a passion, not a faith but a doubting and, to use Bloch's terminology, a hope.

It was no less difficult for Revueltas to live with himself than it was for him to live with his Communist comrades. For years he tried to be a disciplined militant, and each attempt ended in a breach and expulsion. He used the Hegelian dialectic to postpone the definitive breach; like so many others, he told himself that evil is a snare of history so that it might the better fulfill itself, that denial is a moment in the process which inevitably turns into affirmation, that the revolutionary tyrants are tyrants in order to protect liberty, and that—as the Spanish theologians of the seventeenth century and in the twentieth century Prosecutor Vishinsky and the Bolsheviks tried in 1936 and 1938 have brilliantly proven—the guilty are innocent and the innocent guilty. These are the riddles of divine will or of historical necessity. The justification of evil began with Plato; in his retractions and recantations, Revueltas did nothing more than pursue a two-thousand-year-old tradition. As the Neoplatonist Proclus said, matter itself "is good, despite being infinite, obscure and formless." (For the ancients infinity was an imperfection since it lacked form.) But the resources of dialectics are exhausted while the evil expands without ceasing. In the end Revueltas had to confront the reality of bolshevism and his own reality. He did not resolve this conflict—who has ever managed to do that?—but he had the courage to formulate it and think it through. He loyally lived out his inner contradiction: his atheist Christianity, his agonized Marxism. Many praise the courage with which he suffered prisons and hardships on account of his ideas. It's true, but it must be borne in mind, too, that Revueltas practiced another kind of heroism, no less difficult and austere: intellectual heroism.

His work is uneven. Some pages seem to be rough drafts rather than definitive texts; others are remarkable and entitle him to a unique and separate place in Mexican literature: *Los dias terrenales, Los errores, El apando,* and, above all, the stories of *Dios en la tierra* and *Dormir en tierra,* many of them admirable. But the literary excellence of these works, considerable though it is, does not altogether explain his attractiveness. In our world everything is relative, good and evil, pleasure and pain. Though the majority are content, a few rebel and, possessed by a god or by a devil, demand *everything*. They thirst and hunger for the absolute. Don't ask me to define it: the absolute is by definition undefinable. Revueltas suffered from that hunger and that thirst; to satisfy them he was writer and he was revolutionary. If I look among modern Mexicans for a kindred spirit, I have to go to the opposite ideological camp and to an earlier generation: to José Vasconcelos. Like Revueltas, he had a passionate nature but was unable to subject his passion to discipline; he was a writer of impulses and prophecies, copious and careless, sometimes dull and other times luminous. For both, political action and metaphysical adventure, historical polemic and meditation, were interconnected. They united the active life with the contemplative or, more accurately, the speculative life: in their works there is not really disinterested contemplation—what I take to be the highest wisdom—but meditation, reflection, and, in his best moments, spiritual flight. The work of Vasconcelos is larger and richer than that of Revueltas, but no deeper or more intense. But the point is, they belong to the same psychic family. They are the opposite of Reyes, who made an absolute of harmony; and of Gorostiza, who adored perfection with so exclusive a love that he preferred to be silent rather than write something less than perfect.

Despite their spiritual resemblance, Vasconcelos and Revueltas took very different roads. Nourished on Plotinus and believing in his mission as a crowned philosopher, Vasconcelos felt he had been sent down from on high: that is why he was an educator; Revueltas believed in the rebel apostles and saw himself as an emissary of the lower world: that is why he was a revolutionary. The spiritualist Vasconcelos never doubted: the devil—that spirit of denial and patron of philosophers—did not tempt him: the world tempted him (power) and the flesh (women). Vasconcelos confessed that he had desired his neighbor's wife and that he had fornicated with her, but he never admitted that he had made a mistake. The only sins which the materialist Revueltas confessed to were sins of the spirit: doubts, denials, errors, pious lies. In the end he repented and undertook the criticism of his ideas and of the dogmas in which he had believed. Vasconcelos did not repent; he exalted Christian humility the better to cover his foes with invectives; Revueltas, in the name of Marxist philosophy, undertook an examination of his conscience which Saint Augustine and Pascal would have appreciated and which impresses me on two counts: for the scrupulous honesty with which he performed it and for the subtlety and depth of his analysis. Vasconcelos ended up in the embrace of Catholic clericalism; Revueltas broke with the Marxist clerisy. Which of the two was the true Christian?

—Mexico D.F., 12 April 1979

LUIS CERNUDA:
THE EDIFYING WORD

I.

In 1961 the *Mercure de France* devoted an issue to Pierre Reverdy, who had recently died. Luis Cernuda wrote a few pages valuable not so much for what they say about Reverdy as for what they reveal, obliquely, about Cernuda himself: how he identifies poetic conscience with ethical purity, his taste for the essential word, which, not always justly, he set against what he called the sumptuousness of the Spanish and French traditions. But I recall that article not to stress the affinities between the French and the Spanish poet—though the influence of Reverdy on Cernuda would be worth pursuing—but because what Cernuda wrote three years ago on the destiny of dead poets seems today to have been thought and said about his own death: "What country suffers its poets with pleasure? Its living poets, I mean, since there is no country which doesn't adore its dead poets." Spain is no exception. Nothing is more natural than that the literary journals of the Iberian peninsula should publish homages to the poet: "Since Cernuda has died, long live Cernuda"; nothing is more natural, again, than that poets and critics, all together, cover with the same gray sediment of praises the oeuvre of a spirit which with admirable and inflexible obstinacy never stopped affirming his dissidence. When the poet is buried, we can discourse without risk about his work and make it say what it seems to us it ought to have said: where he wrote separation, we will read union: God where he said devil; homeland, not inhospitable land; soul, not body. And if "interpretation" is impossible, we will erase the forbidden words: rage, pleasure, nausea, boy, nightmare, solitude . . . I do not want to suggest that all those who praise him try to whitewash what was black, nor that they do this entirely in bad faith. It's not a deliberate lie but a pious substitution. Perhaps without being aware, moved by a sincere desire to justify their admiration for a work which their conscience reproves, they transform a particular and unique truth—sometimes unbearable and repellent, like all that is truly fascinating—into a general and inoffensive truth, acceptable to all. Much of what has been written recently on Cernuda could have been written about any other poet. There have even been those who affirm that death has returned him to his native land ("When the dog is dead, rabies are at an end"). One critic, who claims he knows Cernuda's work well and admires it, does not hesitate to write: "The poet had a tragic fault: the inability to recognize any other kind of love but romantic love; thus conjugal love, paternal and filial love, were all closed doors for Cernuda." Another critic is of the view that the poet "has found a world in which reality and desire are in harmony." Has that writer asked himself what that paradise would be like, and what its angels and divinities would be?

Cernuda's work is an exploration of himself; a proud affirmation, in the last account not without the humility of its irreducible difference. He said it himself: "I have only tried, like every man, to find my truth, my own, which will not be better or worse than that of others, only different." To serve his memory, it is useless to build him monuments which, like all monuments, conceal the dead, but rather it is necessary to go deeply into that different truth and set it against our own. Only then will his truth, because it is distinct and irreconcilable, come near to our own truth, which is neither better nor worse than his, but our own. The work of Cernuda is a road toward our own selves. That is what gives it its moral value. Because, despite being an excellent poet—or, more accurately, *because* he was one—Cernuda is one of the very few moralists Spain has given us, in the sense in which Nietzsche is the great moralist of modern Europe and, as he said, "its first psychologist." The poetry of Cernuda is a criticism of our values and beliefs; in it destruction and creation are inseparable, since what it affirms implies the dissolution of what society regards as just, sacred, or immutable. Like Pessoa's, his work is a subversion, and his spiritual fecundity resides in the fact that he puts to the test the systems of collective morality, both those established on the authority of tradition and those which social reformers propose to us. His hostility to Christianity is no less intense than the repugnance he feels for political utopias. I am not suggesting that one has to agree doors of hell have shut, and for the poet not even the resource of Aden or Ethiopia is left: wandering the five continents, he always lives in the same room, talks to the same people, and his exile is everybody's. Cernuda did not know this—he was too intent upon himself, too abstracted in his uniqueness—but his work is one of the most impressive personal testimonies to this truly unique situation of modern man: we are condemned to a promiscuous solitude and our prison is as large as the planet itself. There is no exit or entrance. We move from the same to the same. Seville, Madrid, Toulouse, Glasgow, London, New York, Mexico City, San Francisco: was Cernuda really in those cities? Where are those places in fact?

All the ages of man appear in *La realidad y el deseo*. All, except infancy, which is evoked only as a lost world whose secret has been forgotten. (What poet will give us, not the vision or the nostalgia of childhood, but childhood itself, who will have the courage and the genius to talk as children do?) Cernuda's book of poems could be divided into four parts: adolescence, the years of apprenticeship, in which he surprises us with his exquisite mastery; youth, the great moment when he discovers passion and discovers himself, a period to which we owe his most beautiful blasphemies and his best love poems—love of love; maturity, which begins as a contemplation of earthly powers and ends in a meditation on human works; and the final period, already at the last boundary of old age, his gaze more precise and reflexive, his voice more real and bitter. Different moments of a single word. In each period there are admirable poems, but I prefer the poetry of his youth ("Los placeres prohibidos," "Un rio un amor," "Donde habite el olvido," "Invocaciones") not because the poet is entirely in possession of himself in them but precisely because he is not: a moment in which guessing has yet to become certitude, certitude formula. His early poems seem to me to be an exercise whose perfection does not exclude affectation, a certain manneredness from which he never entirely freed himself. His mature books evince a plaster classicism, that is, a neoclassicism: there are too many gods and gardens; there is a tendency to confuse eloquence with diction, and it is indeed odd that Cernuda, constant critic of that inclination of ours toward the "noble tone," did not perceive it in himself. Finally, in his last poems reflection, explication, and even impertinences take up too much space and displace the list would be endless.) Thus Cernuda is antagonistic to Spain for two reasons: because of his polemical Spanishness and because of his modernity. As to the first, he belongs to the family of the Spanish heterodox; as to the second, his work is a slow reconquering of the European heritage, a search for that central current from which Spain set itself apart a long time ago. It is not a matter of influences—though like any poet he has suffered many, most of them beneficial—but of an exploration of himself, not now in a psychological sense but of his history.

Cernuda discovers the modern spirit by way of surrealism. He has often said how seductive Reverdy's poetry was for his sensibility—Reverdy, master of the surrealists and his own. In Reverdy he admires the "poetic asceticism"—equivalent, he claims, to Braque's—which makes him build a poem with the minimum of verbal material; but more than the economy of his means he admires his *reticence*. That word is one of the keys to Cernuda's style. Seldom have bolder thought and more violent passion made use of more chaste expressions. Reverdy was not the only Frenchman to overwhelm him. In a letter dated 1929 written from Madrid, he asks a friend in Seville to return various books to him *(Les pas perdus* of André Breton, *Le libertinage* and *Le paysan de Paris* of Louis Aragon) and adds: "Azorín, Valle-Inclán, Baroja: what does all that stupid, inhumane, rotten Spanish literature matter to me?" Let purists not be too scandalized. In those same years Breton and Aragon found that French literature was equally inhumane and stupid. We have lost that lovely unbuttonedness; how much harder it is now to be insolent, unjustly just, than in the 1920s.

What does Cernuda owe to the surrealists? The bridge between the French avant-garde and Spanish-language poetry was, of course, Vicente Huidobro. After the Chilean poet, contacts increased and Cernuda was neither the first nor the only one to have felt the fascination of surrealism. It would not be difficult to point out in his poetry and even in his prose the traces of certain surrealists, such as Eluard, Crevel, and, though he is a writer at the opposite pole from him, the dazzling Louis Aragon (in his early manner). But unlike Neruda, Lorca, or Villaurrutia, for Cernuda surrealism was something more than a lesson in style, more than a poetic or a school of verbal and imagistic associations: It was an attempt to embody poetry in life, a subversion which embraced language quite as much as institutions. A morality and a passion. Cernuda was the first and almost the only one who understood and made his own the true meaning of surrealism as a movement of liberation—not of verse but of consciousness: the last great spiritual shaking-out of the West. To the psychic commotion of surrealism must be added the revelation of André Gide. Thanks to the French moralist, Cernuda accepts himself; from that time on his homosexuality was not to be a sickness or a sin but a destiny freely accepted and lived. If Gide reconciles Cernuda with himself, surrealism will serve him to set his psychic and vital rebellion within a vaster, more total subversion. The "forbidden pleasures" open a bridge between this world of "codes and rats" and the underground world of dream and inspiration: they are earthly life in all its taciturn splendor ("marble members," "iron flowers," "earthly planets") and they are also the highest spiritual life ("exalted solitude," "memorable freedoms"). The fruit these harsh liberties offer us is one of mystery, whose "taste no bitterness corrupts." Poetry turns active; the dream and the word cast down the "anonymous statues;" in the great "hour of vengeance, its brilliance can destroy your world." Later Cernuda abandoned surrealist mannerisms and tics, but his essential vision, though his aesthetic was different, remained that of his youth.

Surrealism is a tradition. With that critical instinct which distinguishes great poets, Cernuda traces the current back: Mallarmé, Baudelaire, Nerval. Though he kept faith with these poets, he did not stop at them. He went to the source, to the origin of modern Western poetry: to German romanticism. One of his themes is that of the poet confronting a world hostile or indifferent to men. Present in his earliest poems, from "Invocaciones" on, it develops with an increasingly somber intensity. The figure of Hölderlin and those of his descendants are his model; soon those images are transformed into another, entrancing and terrible: that of the devil. Not a Christian devil, repulsive and terrifying, but a pagan one, almost a boy. It is his double. Its presence is to be a constant in his work, though it changes with the years and each time its words sound more bitter and hopeless. In the image of the double, always the untouchable reflection, Cernuda seeks himself but he also seeks the world: he wants to know that he exists and that others exist. The others: a race of men different from men.

Beside the devil, the companionship of dead poets. Reading Hölderlin and Jean Paul and Novalis, Blake and Coleridge, is something more than discovery: a recognition. Cernuda goes back to his own. Those great names are living persons, invisible but dependable intercessors. He talks with them as if he talked with himself. They are his true family and his secret gods. His work is written thinking of them: they are something more than a model, an example, or an inspiration: they are a gaze that judges him. He has to be worthy of them. And the only way to be worthy is to affirm his truth, to be himself. The moral theme reappears. But it will not be Gide, with his psychological morality, but Goethe who will guide him in this new phase. He does not seek a justification but an equilibrium; what the young Nietzsche called "health," the lost secret of Greek paganism: the heroic pessimism which created tragedy and comedy. Often he spoke of Greece, of its poets and philosophers, of its myths, and, above all, of its vision of beauty: Something which is neither physical nor corporeal and which is perhaps only a musical chord, a measure. In *Ocnos*, when he speaks of "beautiful knowledge"—because he knows beauty or because all knowledge is beauty?—he says that beauty is measure. And thus, by a road which leads from surrealist rebellion to German and English romanticism and from there to the great Western myths, Luis Cernuda recovers his double heritage as a poet and as a Spaniard: the European tradition, the sense and savor of the Mediterranean noon. What began as a polemical and unbounded passion ends in a recognition of measure. A measure, it is true, in which other things— also of the West—do not fit. Among them, two of the greatest: Christianity and woman. "Otherness" in its most absolute manifestations: the other world and the other half of this one. Nonetheless, Cernuda makes a virtue of necessity and creates a universe in which two essential elements are not lacking, one peculiar to Christianity, the other to woman: Introspection and the mystery of love.

I have not spoken of another influence which was of the first importance both on his poetry and on his criticism, especially after *Las nubes* (1940): Modern English poetry. In his youth he loved Keats and later on felt himself drawn toward Blake, but these names, especially the latter, belong to what could be called his demonic or subversive half: They nourished his moral rebelliousness. His interest in Wordsworth, Browning, Yeats, and Eliot is different in kind: he seeks in them not so much a metaphysic as an aesthetic conscience. The mystery of literary creation and the theme of the ultimate significance of poetry—its relations with truth, with history, and with society—always concern him. In the reflections of the English poets he found—formulated in a way different from or similar to his own—answers to these questions. One evidence of this interest is the book he devoted to the poetic thought of the English lyric poets. I believe I am right in thinking that T. S. Eliot was the living writer who exerted the most profound influence on the mature Cernuda. I repeat: an aesthetic, not a moral or metaphysical influence: the reading of Eliot did not have the liberating effects that his discovery of Gide had done. The English poet makes him see the poetic tradition with new eyes, and many of his studies of Spanish poets are composed with that precision and objectivity, not without eccentricity, which are among the charms and perils of Eliot's critical style. But the example of this poet can be seen not only in Cernuda's critical opinions but also in his creative work. His encounter with Eliot coincides with the change in his aesthetic; having assimilated the experience of surrealism, he does not bother to seek new forms but rather to express himself. Not a norm but a measure, something which neither the French moderns nor the German romantics could give him. Eliot had felt a similar necessity, and after *The Waste Land* his poetry is poured out into increasingly traditional molds. I could not say whether this attitude of return, in Cernuda and in Eliot, benefited or harmed their poetry; in one sense, it impoverished them, since surprise and invention, the wings of the poetry, disappear to some extent from their mature work; in another sense, perhaps without that change they would have become mute or impoverished in a sterile search, as happens with great creators such as Pound and cummings. And it is commonplace that nothing is more tedious than the professional innovator. In a word, Eliot's poetry and criticism helped Cernuda to moderate the romantic he always was.

Cernuda had a predilection, from the first, for the long poem. For modern taste poetry is, above all, verbal concentration, and therefore the long poem faces an almost insuperable problem: to bring together extension and concentration, development and intensity, unity and variety, without making the work a collection of fragments and without recourse to the vulgar expedient of amplification, either. *Un coup de des,* maximum verbal concentration in a little over two hundred lines, some of them a single word in length, is an example, to my mind the highest example, of what I want to say. It is not the short poem but the long one that requires the use of scissors; the poet should exercise remorselessly his gift of elimination if he wants to write something that isn't prolix, dispersed, or diffuse. Reticence, the art of saying the unsaid, is the secret of the brief poem; in the long poem silences do not work suggestively, do not speak, but are like the divisions and subdivisions of musical space. More than a form of writing, they are a form of architecture. Mallarmé had already compared *Un coup de des* to a partita, and Eliot had called one of his great compositions *Four Quartets.* Cernuda thought it was the best poem Eliot had written, and we often discussed his reasons for this preference, since I was drawn to *The Waste Land*—which, of course, ought also to be regarded as a musical construction.

Though our poet did not learn the art of the long poem from Eliot—he had written them before reading Eliot, and some of them are among the most perfect poems he made—the English writer's ideas clarified his own and partly modified his conceptions. But ideas are one thing, the temperaments of each another. It would be useless to seek in his work the principles of *harmony, counterpoint,* or *polyphony* which inspire Eliot and St.-John Perse; and nothing could be more remote from the "simultaneity" of Pound or Apollinaire than the linear development, like that of vocal music, of Cernuda's poems. The melody is lyrical, and Cernuda is only, and outstandingly, a lyric poet. Thus the form most congenial to his nature was the monologue. He wrote monologues throughout his life, and it could even be said that his work is a long monologue. English poetry showed him how monody can turn back on itself, unfold and question itself: it taught him that monologue is always dialogue. In one of his studies, he alludes to the lesson of Robert Browning; I would add that of Pound, who was the first to exploit the monologue of Browning. (Compare, for instance, the use of questions in "Near Périgord" and in the long late poems of Cernuda.) And here I think I ought to say something on a subject which troubled him and about which he wrote pages of great insight: the relations between spoken language and the poem.

Cernuda points out that the first writer to proclaim the poet's right to employ "the language really used by men" was Wordsworth. Though it isn't altogether correct to say that this precedent is the origin of the so-called prosaicism of contemporary poetry, it is as well to distinguish between this idea of Wordsworth's and Herder's, who saw in poetry "the song of the people." Popular language, if indeed it exists and is not just an invention of German romanticism, is a survival from feudal times. It is a form of nostalgia to cultivate it. Jiménez and Antonio Machado always confused "popular language" with spoken language, and that is why they identify the latter with traditional song. Jiménez thought that "popular art" was simply the traditional imitation of aristocratic art; Machado believed that the true aristocracy resided in the people and that folklore was the most refined art. However different these points of view appear to us, both reveal a nostalgic view of the past. The language of our time is different: It is the language spoken in the great city, and all modern poetry, from Baudelaire on, has made that language the point of departure for a new lyricism. As a reaction against the aesthetic of the exquisite and singular which the Latin American poets had made fashionable, the simplicity of the so-called popular Spanish poetry is no less artificial than the complications of the symbolists. Influenced by Jiménez, the poets of Cernuda's generation made of ballad and of song their favorite genre. Cernuda never succumbed to the affectation of the popular (an affectation to which we owe, all the same, some of the most seductive poems of our modern lyricism) and tried to write as one speaks; or rather: he set himself as the raw material of poetic transmutation not the language of books but of conversation. He did not always succeed. Often his verse is prosaic, in the sense in which *written* prose is prosaic, not living speech: something more considered and constructed than said. Because of the words he uses, almost all of them Correct, and because of an overfastidious syntax, Cernuda sometimes "talks like a book" rather than "writes as one speaks." What is miraculous is that that writing should suddenly condense into scintillating expressions.

In Campoamor Cernuda perceived an antecedent of poetic prosaicism; if he had been, it would be a regrettable antecedent. One shouldn't confuse philosophical table-talk with poetry. The truth is that the only modern Spanish poet who has used *naturally* the spoken language is the forgotten José Moreno Villa. (The only one and the first one, *Jacinta la pelirroja,* was published in 1929.) In fact, the first to use the poetic possibilities of prosaic language were, strange as it may seem, the Latin American modernists: Darío and, most of all, Leopoldo Lugones. In Campoamor's poems, the end-of-century rhetoric decays into expressions which are pseudophilosophical commonplaces and thus constitutes an example of what Breton calls the "descending image." The symbolists set the colloquial idiom face to face with the artistic to produce a dash within the poem, as one can see in *Augurios* by Rubén Darío, or else they make the urban speech the raw material of the poem. This latter procedure is that of the Lugones of the *Lunario sentimental.* Toward 1915, the Mexican poet López Velarde learned the lesson of the Argentinean poet and managed to fuse the literary and spoken language together. It would be tedious to mention all the Latin American poets who, after López Velarde, make prosaidsm a poetic language; six names will suffice: Borges, Vallejo, Pellicer, Novo, Lezama Lima, Sabines . . . Strangest of all, this comes not from English poetry but from the master of Eliot and Pound: the symbolist Jules Laforgue. The author of the *Complaintes,* not Wordsworth, is the source of this trend, both among the English and among the Latin Americans.

Often it is said of Cernuda, and more generally of the poets of his generation, that they "close" a period of Spanish poetry. I confess that I do not know what this means. For something to "close"—if it is not a definitive ending—it is necessary for something or someone to open another period. The Spanish poets themselves, beyond odious comparison, do not seem to me to have initiated a movement; I would even say that, as far as the matter of language and vision is concerned—and that is what counts in poetry—they come over as singularly timid. This is not a reproach: the second romantic generation was no less important than the first and it gave us a central name: that of Baudelaire. Novelty is not the sole poetic criterion. In Spain there has been a change of tone, not a break with the past. That change is natural, but it shouldn't be confused with a new era. Cernuda neither closes nor opens an era. His poetry, unmistakable and distinct, forms part of a universal tendency which in the Spanish language begins, a little behind time, at the end of the last century and which is still not over. Within that historical period his generation, in Latin America and in Spain, occupies a central place. And one of the poets central to that generation is—Luis Cernuda. He did not create a common language or style, as Rubén Darío and Juan Ramón Jiménez did in their day or, more recently, Vicente Huidobro, Pablo Neruda, and Federico García Lorca. Perhaps on this rests his value and his future influence: Cernuda as a poet is a loner for loners.

In a tradition which has used and abused but seldom reflected on words, Cernuda represents the conscience of the language. A similar example is that of Jorge Guillén, except that while for him poetry lives—to use the jargon of the philosophers—at the realm of being, Cernuda's is temporal: human existence is his domain. In both poets, more than *reflection*, we find poetic meditation. Reflection is an extreme and total process: the word turns upon itself and denies itself a meaning in the world, to denote only its own meaning and thus to annul itself. We owe to poetic reflection some of the cardinal texts of modern Western poetry, poems in which our history is at once assumed and consumed: negation of itself and of traditional meanings, an attempt to establish another meaning. Spaniards have seldom felt distrust before the word, seldom experienced that dizziness which consists of seeing language as the *sign of nothingness*. For Cernuda meditation—almost in the medical sense: to watch—consists of leaning on another mystery: that of our own passing. Life, not language. Between living and thinking, the word is not an abyss but a bridge. Meditation: Mediation. The word expresses the distance between what I am and what I am being; at the same time, it is the only way of transcending that distance. By means of the word my life is arrested without pausing and sees itself seeing itself; by means of it I catch up with myself and pass myself by, and contemplate myself and turn into someone *else—another myself* who taunts my misery and in whose taunt my entire redemption is summarized.

The tension between a life ignorant of itself and conscience of self is resolved in the transparent word. Not in an impossible beyond, but here, in the instant of the poem, reality and desire reach an accord. And that embrace is so intense that it not only evokes the image of love but also that of death: in the breast of the poet, "just like a lute, death, death only, can make sound the promised melody." Few modern poets, in any language, give us this chilling sense of knowing ourselves to be before a man who *really speaks*, effectively possessed by the fatality and the lucidity of passion. If it were possible to define in a phrase the place Cernuda occupies in modern Spanish-language poetry, I would say he is the poet who speaks not for all, but for each one of us who make up the all. And he wounds us in the core of that part of each of us "which is not called glory, fortune, or ambition" but *the truth of ourselves*. For Cernuda the object of poetry was to know himself, but, with the same intensity, it was an attempt to create his own proper image. Poetic biography, *La realidad y el deseo* is something more, too: it is the history of a spirit which, in its self-recognition, transfigures itself.

III.

It is now customary to say that Cernuda is a love poet. That is true, and from this theme all the others spring: solitude, boredom, exaltation of the natural world, contemplation of the works of men . . . But one must begin by stressing something he never concealed: his love was homosexual and he did not know or speak of any other. There is no possible doubt: with admirable courage, if one considers the Spanish public and literary establishment, he wrote *boy* where others prefer to use more ambiguous nouns. "The truth of myself," he said in a poem he wrote in his youth, "is the truth of my actual love." His sincerity is not a taste for scandal nor a challenge to society (his challenge is elsewhere): it is an intellectual and moral point of honor. Moreover, one runs the risk of missing the point of his work if one omits or attenuates his homosexuality, not because his poetry can be reduced to that passion—that would be as wrong as to ignore it—but because it is the point of departure of his poetic creation. His erotic preferences do not explain his poetry, but without them his work would be different. His "different truth" sets him apart from the world at large; and that same truth, in a second movement, leads him on to discover a further truth, his and all of ours.

Gide gave him the courage to give things their proper names; the second book of his surrealist period is called *Los placers prohibidos*

(*Forbidden Pleasures*). He does not call them, as one might have expected, *perverse* pleasures. If one needs pluck to publish this kind of book in the 1930s in Spain, one needs still greater lucidity of mind to resist the temptation of adopting the role of ostracized rebel. The rebellion is ambiguous; those who affirm their "wickedness" consecrate the divine or social authority that condemns them; the condemnation includes them, negatively, in the order which they violate. Cernuda does not feel himself to be wicked: He feels excluded. And he doesn't lament this: he gives back blow for blow. The difference between him and a writer like Genet is revealing. Genet's challenge to the social world is more symbolic than real, and thus to make his gesture dangerous he has had to go further: eulogy of theft and treason, cult of criminals. Confronted by a society in which the honor of husbands still resides between the legs of women and in which "machismo" is a widespread disease, Cernuda's frankness exposed him to all sorts of actual risks, physical and moral. On the other hand, Genet is marked by Christianity—a negative Christianity; the sign of original sin is his homosexuality, or, more precisely, through it and in it is revealed the original stain: all of his deeds and works are the challenge and homage that nothingness raises against being. In Cernuda the sense of guilt hardly appears, and against Christian values he sets up others, his own, which seem to him the only true ones. It would be hard to find, in the Spanish language, a less Christian writer. Genet ends in the negation of negation: the black men who are white who are black who are white in his play. It is what Nietzsche called "incomplete nihilism," which does not transcend itself nor take itself for granted and is content to put up with itself. A Christianity without Christ. Cernuda's subversiveness is simpler, more radical, more sane.

To recognize one's homosexuality is to accept that one is different from others. But who are the others? The others are the world at large—and the world belongs to the others. In that world with the same fury heterosexual lovers, the revolutionary, the black, the proletarian, the expropriated bourgeois, the lone poet, the half-wit, the eccentric, and the saint are pursued. The others pursue everyone and no one. They are everyone and no one. Public health is the collective illness sanctified by force. Are the others real? A faceless majority or an all-powerful minority, they are a gaggle of ghosts. My body is real: is sin real? Prisons are real: are laws real as well? Between man and what he touches there is a zone of unreality: evil. The world is built on a negation, and institutions—religion, family, property, state, fatherland—are ferocious embodiments of that universal negation. To destroy this unreal world so that at last the true reality might emerge . . . Any young person—not only a homosexual poet—can (and should) reflect on this. Cernuda accepts that he is different; modern thought, especially surrealism, shows him that we are all different. Homosexuality becomes synonymous with liberty; instinct is not a blind impulse: it is criticism transformed into deed. Everything, the body itself, acquires a *moral coloring*. In these years (1930) he becomes a Communist. A fleeting commitment, since in this matter as in so many others the Trojans are as stupid as the Greeks. The affirmation of his own truth makes him recognize the truth of others: "because of my pain I understand that others suffer greatly," he was to say years later. Though he shares our common destiny, he does not propose a panacea to us. He is a poet, not a reformer. He offers us his "true truth," that love which is the only liberty that exalts him, the only liberty worth dying for.

The true truth, his and everyone else's, is called desire. In a tradition which, with very few exceptions—they can be counted on the fingers, from *La celestina* and *La lozana andaluza* to Rubén Darío, Valle-Inclán, and García Lorca—identifies "pleasure" with "agreeable sensation, spiritual contentment, or diversion," Cernuda's poetry violently affirms the primacy of eroticism. That violence grows calmer with the years, but pleasure continues to occupy a central place in his work, beside its opposite-complement: solitude. They are the pair which govern his world, that "landscape of brooding ash" which desire peoples with radiant bodies, beautiful and glowing savages. From Baudelaire to Breton, the destiny of the word *desire* is confused with that of poetry. Its meaning is not psychological. Changing and still the same, it is energy, time's will to become embodied, vital hunger or anguish of death: it has no name and all names. What or who desires what we desire? Though it takes on the form of fate, it is not fulfilled without our liberty and in it one can read all our free will. We know nothing of desire, except that it crystallizes into images and that those images do not cease to trouble us until they become realities. We hardly touch them, and they disappear. Or is it we who disappear? Imagination is desire in motion. It is the imminent, what summons up the Apparition; and it is the distance which erases it. With a certain laziness one tends to see in Cernuda's poems mere variations on an old commonplace: Reality in the end destroys desire, our life is a continual oscillation between privation and satiety. It seems to me that they say something else as well, something more true and terrible: if desire is real, reality is unreal. Desire makes the imaginary real, it makes reality unreal. The whole being of man is the theater of this continual metamorphosis; in his body and soul desire and reality interpenetrate and change, join and divide. Desire peoples the world with images and unpeoples reality at the same time. Nothing satisfies it because it turns living beings into ghosts. It feeds on shadows, or better said, our human reality, our substance, time and blood, nourish its shadows.

There is a point of intersection between desire and reality: love. Desire is vaster than love, but love-desire is the most powerful of desires. Only in that desiring of one being among all others does desire expand to its fullest extent. Who knows love wants nothing else. Love reveals reality to desire: That desired image is something more than a body which vanishes: it is a soul, a conscience. The erotic object turns into the beloved person. By means of love, desire at last touches reality: the other exists. This revelation is almost always painful because the existence of the other presents itself to us simultaneously as a body which is penetrable and a consciousness which is not. Love is the revelation of an alien liberty, and nothing is harder than to acknowledge the liberty of others, above all that of a person who is loved and desired. On this rests the contradiction of love: desire aspires to consummate itself by the destruction of the desired object; love discovers that that object is indestructible . . . and nothing can be put in its place. What is left is desire without love or love without desire. The first dooms us to solitude: those interchangeable bodies are unreal; the second is inhumane: can what is not desired be loved?

Cernuda was very aware of this genuinely tragic condition of love, of all love. In the poems of his youth the violence of his passion blindly collides with the unexpected existence of an irremediably alien conscience, and that discovery fills him with rage and shame. (Later, in a prose text, he alludes to the "egoism" of youthful loves.) In the books of his maturity the theme of Western love and mystical poetry—"the beloved transformed into the lover"—appears frequently. But union, the ultimate end of love, can be achieved only if it is realized that the other is a different and free being: if our love, instead of trying to abolish that difference, turns into the space in which it can unfold. Amorous union is not identity (if it were we would be more than men) but a state of perpetual mobility like play or, like music, of perpetual recapitulation. Cernuda always affirmed his different truth: did he see and acknowledge the truth of others? His work provides a double answer. Like almost all human beings—at least, like all those who really love, and there are not that many of them—in the moment of passion he is alternatively worshiper and adversary of his beloved; later, in the hour of reflection, he understands bitterly that if they did not love him as he wanted it was perhaps because he did not himself know how to love entirely disinterestedly. To love we ought to overcome ourselves, suppress the conflict between desire and love—without suppressing either one or the other. Difficult union between contemplative and active love. Not without struggles and vacillations did Cernuda aspire to this, the highest union; and that aspiration indicates the meaning of the evolution of his poetry: the violence of desire that never ceases to be desire tends to develop into the contemplation of a loved person. When I write that down, I am troubled by a doubt: can one speak of a loved person in Cernuda's case? I am thinking not only of the temper of homosexual love—with its underlying narcissism and its dependence on the world of childhood, which makes it capricious, tyrannical, and vulnerable to the illness of jealousy—but also of the disturbing insistence of the poet on considering love as an almost impersonal, fated thing.

In one poem from *Como quien espera el alba* (1947) he says: "Love and not the beloved is eternal." Fifteen or twenty years earlier he had said the same thing, with greater exasperation: "It is not love that dies, but we ourselves." In both instances he affirms the primacy of love over lovers, but in the poem of his youth he stresses man's death and love's immortality. The difference in tone shows the meaning of his spiritual evolution: in the second text love is no longer immortal but eternal and the "we" becomes "the beloved." The poet does not participate: he sees. He moves from active to contemplative love. What is remarkable is that this change does not alter the central vision: it is not men who realize themselves in love but love which makes use of men to realize itself. The idea of the human being as a "plaything of passion" is a constant theme in his poetry. Exaltation of love and a debasement of men. Our little value derives from our mortal condition: we are changed and we do not resist the changes of passion; we aspire to eternity and one instant of love destroys us. Deprived of its spiritual sustenance—the *soul* which Platonists and Christians gave him—the creature is not a person but a momentary condensation of inhuman powers: youth, beauty, and other magnetic forms in which time and energy manifest themselves. The creature is an apparition and there is nothing behind it. Cernuda seldom uses the words *soul* or *conscience* in speaking of his lovers; nor does he even allude to their particular physical characteristics, or to those attributes which, as the vulgar expression has it, give people "personality." In his world the face, mirror of the soul, does not reign, but the body. What this word means for the Spanish poet will not be understood unless it is stressed that in the human body he perceives the code of the universe. A young body is a solar system, a nucleus of physical and psychic irradiations. The body is the source of energy, a fountain of "psychic matter" or manna, a substance neither spiritual nor physical, a force which, according to primitive men, moves the world. When we love a body we do not adore a person but an embodiment of that cosmic force. Cernuda's love poetry goes from idolatry to veneration, from sadism to masochism; he suffers and delights with that will to preserve and to destroy the thing we love, in which consists the conflict between desire and love—but he ignores the otherness. It is a contemplation of *that which is loved,* not of the lover. Thus in the conscience of the other person he sees nothing but his own questioning face. That was his "true truth, the truth of himself." There is another truth; each time we love we lose ourselves: we are other, love does not realize the I myself: it opens up a possibility for the I to change and develop. In love it is not the I that is fulfilled but the person: the desire to be other. The desire to be.

If loving is desire, no law which is not the law of desire can subject it. For Cernuda love is a break with the social order and a joining with the natural world. And it is a break not only because his love differs from that of most but because all love shatters human laws. Homosexuality is not exceptional; the really exceptional thing is love. Cernuda's passion—and also his rage, his blasphemies and sarcasms—spring from a common root: from its origin Western poetry has never ceased to proclaim that the passion of love, the highest experience of our civilization, is a transgression, a social crime. The words of Melibea, the moment before she hurled herself from the tower, words of the fall and perdition but equally of blame for her father: all lovers can repeat them. Even in a society like that of the Hindus, which has not made love the chief passion, when the god Krishna puts on flesh and makes himself a man, he falls in love; and his loves are adulteries. It must be repeated again and again: love, all love, is immoral. Let us imagine a society different from ours and all those that history has known, a society in which the most complete erotic liberty prevailed, whether the infernal world of Sade or the paradisal world that modern sexologists propose to us: there love would be an even greater scandal than it is here among us. Natural passion, revelation of being in the person loved, bridge between this world and the next, contemplation of life or death: love opens the doors to a state which escapes the laws of common sense and current morality. No, Cernuda did not defend the right of homosexuals to live their life (that's a problem for social legislation) but he exalted as man's supreme experience the experience of love. A passion which takes on this or that form, always different and, nonetheless, always the same. Unique love for a unique person—though it is subject to change, disease, betrayal, and death. This was the only eternity he desired and the only truth he believed to be dependable. Not the truth of man: the truth of love.

In a world scoured by the criticism of reason and the wind of passion, so-called values become a scattering of ashes. What survives? Cernuda returns to ancient nature and discovers in it not God but the divinity herself, the mother of gods and myths. The power of love does not proceed from men, weak beings, but from the energy which moves all things. Nature is neither matter nor spirit for Cernuda: it is movement and form, it is appearance and it is invisible breath, word and silence. It is a language and more: a music. Its changes have no finality: it ignores morality, progress, and history; it is enough for it that it is, as is the case with God.

And like God it cannot go beyond itself because it has no limits and all its transcendence is endlessly to contemplate and reflect itself, nature is a ceaseless changing of appearances and an always remaining the same as itself. An endless interplay, which means nothing and in which we can find no salvation or damnation at all. To watch it play with us, to play with it, to fall with and into it—that is our destiny. In this vision of the world there is more than a trace of *The Joyful Wisdom* and, above all, of the pessimism of Leopardi. World without creator though breathed over by a poetic breath, something I do not know whether or not to call religious atheism. True, at times God appears: he is the being with whom Cernuda talks when he talks with no one and who vanishes silently as a momentary cloud. He might be called an embodiment of nothing—and it returns to nothing. And yet veneration, in the sense of respect for the holy and divine, which skies and mountains, a tree, a bird, the sea, always the sea, inspire in him, are constant features from his first to his last book. He is a poet of love but also of the natural world. Its mystery fascinated him. He proceeds from a fusion with the elements to a contemplation of them, a development parallel to that of his love poetry. Sometimes his landscapes are arrested time and in them light thinks as it does in some of Turner's paintings; others are built up with the geometry of Poussin, a painter he was among the first to rediscover. Faced with nature, man does not cut a very good figure either: youth and beauty do not save him from his insignificance. Cernuda does not see in our unworthiness a trace of the fall, still less some proof of future salvation. The nothingness of man is without remission. He is a bubble of being.

Cernuda's negation resolves itself into an exaltation of realities and values which our world degrades. His destruction is creation, or better said, the resurrection of occult powers. Faced with traditional religion and morality and the substitutes which industrial society offers us, he affirms the contradictory pair desire-love; faced with the promiscuous solitude of cities, solitary nature. What is man's place? He is too weak to resist the tension between love and desire; nor is he a tree, cloud, or river. Between nature and passion, both inhuman, there is our consciousness. Our misery consists in our being time; a time which runs out. This lack is wealth: because we are finite time we are memory, understanding, will.

Man remembers, knows, and works: he penetrates into the past, present, and future. In his hands time is a malleable substance; in converting it into the raw material of his deeds, thoughts, and works, man avenges himself on time.

There are three ways into time in Cernuda's poetry. The first is what is called an *accord*, the sudden discovery (by means of a landscape, a body, or music) of that paradox which is to *see* time hesitate without ceasing to flow: "timeless instant . . . fullness which, repeated through a lifetime, is always the same . . . what most resembles it is that getting inward by means of another body at the moment of ecstasy." Everyone, children and lovers, we have all felt something like this; what distinguishes the poet from others is the frequency and, most of all, the consciousness of those states and the need to express them. Another road, different from that of fusion with the instant, is that of contemplation. We look at any reality—a dump of trees, the shadow which brims a room at nightfall, a pile of rocks beside the road—we look without taking note, until slowly what we see reveals itself as the never seen and, at the same time, as the always seen: "looking, looking . . . nature likes to conceal itself and one must surprise it watching for long periods, passionately . . . looking and word make the poet." Do we look or do things look at us? And what we see, are they things or is it time which condenses itself into an appearance and then dissolves? In this experience distance intervenes; man does not become fused with externality, but his look creates between it and his conscience a space, propitious for revelation. What Pierre Schneider calls mediation. The third way is the vision of human works and of the work itself. After *Las nubes* it is one of his central themes and it is expressed mainly in two ways: the double (characters from myth, poetry, and history) and meditation on works of art. This is how he gains access to historical, human time.

In a note which precedes the selection of his poems in the *Antología* of Gerardo Diego (1930), Cernuda says that the only life which seems to him worth living is that of mythological or poetic beings, like the *Hyperion* of Hölderlin. This should not be taken as a challenge or an uncharacteristic statement; he always thought that daily reality suffers from unreality and that the true reality is that of imagination. What makes daily life unreal is the deceptive character of communication between people. Human communication is a fraud or, at least, an involuntary lie. In the world of the imagination things and beings are more of a piece and complete; the word does not conceal but reveals. In "Dístico español," one of his last poems, the real reality of Spain turns for him into an "obstinate nightmare: it is the land of the dead and in it everything is born dead"; he challenges that Spain with another, imaginary but more real, inhabited by "heroes loved in an heroic world," neither closed nor grudging but "tolerant of contrary loyalty, in accordance with the generous tradition of Cervantes." The Spain of Galdós's novels shows him that daily life is dramatic and that in the darkest existence "the paradox of being alive" is latent. Among those novel characters it is not strange that he should recognize himself in Salvador Monsalud, the "Frenchified" revolutionary and the fantastic lover, who never surrenders to the unreasonable mess that we call reality. And what young Latin American has not longed to be Salvador Monsalud: to fall in love with Genara and Adriana; to fight against the "ultras" and also against the "charlatan who deceives the people with his silvery spittle," to feel torn between horror and pity for the brother mad and in love with the same woman, the somnambulant Carlist guerrilla, the fratricide Carlos Garrote; who has not wished in the end to find *Soledad*, that reality more real and strong than all the passions?

Who does the poet address when he talks to a hero of myth or of literature? Each of us has in us a secret interlocutor. He is our double and something more: our contradictor, our confidante, our judge and only friend. The man who cannot talk alone to himself will be unable to talk truly with others. When he addresses myth creatures, Cernuda speaks for his own benefit, but in this way he talks to us. It is a dialogue which aims obliquely to elicit our response. The moment of reading is a now in which, as in a mirror, the dialogue between the poet and his imaginary visitor is reflected in the dialogue between the reader and the poet. The reader sees himself in Cernuda who sees himself in a phantom. Each seeks his own reality, his truth, in the imaginary character. Besides figures from myth and poetry, there are historical persons: Góngora, Larra, Tiberius. Rebels, marginalized beings, exiled by the stupidity of their contemporaries or by the fatal course of their own passions, are also masks, personae. Cernuda does not hide behind them; on the contrary, by means of them he recognizes and goes deeper into himself. The old literary device ceases to be that when it is changed into an exercise in introspection. In the poem dedicated to Ludwig of Bavaria, another of his last works, the king is alone in the theater and listens to the music "fused with the myth as he contemplates it: the melody helps him *to know himself, to fall in love with what he himself is.*" In speaking of the king, Cernuda writes of but not for himself; he invites us to contemplate his myth and to repeat his gesture: self-knowledge through the alien object.

Faced with the Escorial palace, or a Titian canvas or Mozart's music, he perceives a truth vaster than his own, though it is not contradictory or excluding. In works of art time makes use of men to fulfill itself. But it is time made solid, humanized: an epoch. Fusion with the moment or contemplation of ephemerality are experiences in and of time, but in a certain sense outside history; the vision which a work of art provides is an experience of historical time. On the one hand, the work is what is commonly called an expression of history, dated time; on the other, it is an archetype of what a man can do with his time: turn it into stone, music, or language, transmute it in form, and infuse it with meaning. Open it out to the understanding of others: return it to the present. The vision of the work implies dialogue, recognition of a truth distinct from ours and which, nonetheless, directly concerns us. The work of art is a presence from the past made continually present. However incomplete and poor our experience, we repeat the creator's gesture and we go through the process in the opposite direction to the artist's; we move from a contemplation of the work to an understanding of its occasion: a situation, a concrete time. Dialogue with works of art consists not only of hearing what they say but of re-creating, reliving them as presences: to awaken their present. It is a creative repetition. In Cernuda's case the experience serves him, moreover, to understand his mission as a poet better. The initial rupture with the social order is followed by participation in history—but without betraying the rebellious stance which, in substance, remained the same until his death. Thus the creations of others bring him to a consciousness of his task: history is not only time lived and died but time which is transmuted into work and deed.

In contemplating this or that creation, Cernuda perceives that fusion between the individual will of the artist and the will, almost always unconscious, of his time and world. He discovers that he writes not only to tell the "truth about himself," his true truth is also that of his language and his people. The poet gives a voice "to the mute mouths of his own kind" and thus frees them. The "others" have become "his own." But to state that truth it is not a matter of repeating the commonplaces of the pulpit, the public tribunal, the council of ministers, or the radio. The truth of all is not at variance with the conscience of the solitary nor is it less subversive than individual truth. This truth, which cannot be confused with majority or minority opinions, is concealed, and it is the poet's job to reveal it, free it. The cycle opened in the poems of his youth closes: negation of the world which we call real and affirmation that the reality that is real is the one that desire and creative imagination reveal; exaltation of natural powers and recognition of man's task on earth: to create works, to make life out of dead time, to give meaning to blind transience; rejection of a false tradition and discovery of a history which has not ended yet and into which his life and his work are woven as if in new accord. At the end of his days, Cernuda is unsure whether to credit the reality of his work or the unreality of his life. His book was his real life and was constructed hour by hour, as one might raise a building. He built with living time and his word was *scandalstone*. He has left us a body of work which is in every sense *edifying*.

—Delhi, 24 May 1964